Project Portfolio Management Strategies for Effective Organizational Operations

Luca Romano
PMI Central Italy Chapter - CUOA Business School, Italy

PMI CENTRAL ITALY CHAPTER

IGI GLOBAL
DISSEMINATOR OF KNOWLEDGE

www.igi-global.com

A volume in the Advances in IT Personnel and Project Management (AITPPM) Book Series

Published in the United States of America by
IGI Global
Business Science Reference (an imprint of IGI Global)
701 E. Chocolate Avenue
Hershey PA, USA 17033
Tel: 717-533-8845
Fax: 717-533-8661
E-mail: cust@igi-global.com
Web site: http://www.igi-global.com

Library of Congress Cataloging-in-Publication Data

Names: Romano, Luca, 1967- editor.
Title: Project portfolio management strategies for effective organizational operations / Luca Romano, editor.
Description: Hershey, PA : Business Science Reference, [2017]
Identifiers: LCCN 2016055208| ISBN 9781522521518 (hardcover) | ISBN 9781522521525 (ebook)
Subjects: LCSH: Project management. | Strategic planning.
Classification: LCC HD69.P75 P76247 2017 | DDC 658.4/012--dc23 LC record available at https://lccn.loc.gov/2016055208

This book is published in the IGI Global book series Advances in IT Personnel and Project Management (AITPPM) (ISSN: 2331-768X; eISSN: 2331-7698)

British Cataloguing in Publication Data
A Cataloguing in Publication record for this book is available from the British Library.

Advances in IT Personnel and Project Management (AITPPM) Book Series

Sanjay Misra
Covenant University, OTA, Nigeria
Ricardo Colomo-Palacios
Østfold University College, Norway

ISSN:2331-768X
EISSN:2331-7698

Mission

Technology has become an integral part of organizations in every sector, contributing to the way in which large enterprises, small businesses, government agencies, and non-profit organizations operate. In the midst of this revolution, it is essential that these organizations have a thorough knowledge of how to implement and manage IT projects as well as an understanding of how to attract and supervise the employees associated with these projects.

The **Advances in IT Personnel and Project Management (AITPPM)** book series aims to provide current research on all facets of IT Project Management including factors to consider when managing and working with IT personnel. Books within the AITPPM book series will provide managers, IT professionals, business leaders, and upper-level students with the latest trends, applications, methodologies, and literature available in this field.

Coverage

- IT Entrepreneurship
- Project Management Software
- Project Sponsorship
- Outsourcing of IT Projects
- Requirements Management
- Cost-Effective Methods for Project Management
- IT Personnel Management
- Project Planning
- IT Strategy
- Measuring Project Success

IGI Global is currently accepting manuscripts for publication within this series. To submit a proposal for a volume in this series, please contact our Acquisition Editors at Acquisitions@igi-global.com or visit: http://www.igi-global.com/publish/.

The Advances in IT Personnel and Project Management (AITPPM) Book Series (ISSN 2331-768X) is published by IGI Global, 701 E. Chocolate Avenue, Hershey, PA 17033-1240, USA, www.igi-global.com. This series is composed of titles available for purchase individually; each title is edited to be contextually exclusive from any other title within the series. For pricing and ordering information please visit http://www.igi-global.com/book-series/advances-personnel-project-management/77666. Postmaster: Send all address changes to above address.

Titles in this Series

For a list of additional titles in this series, please visit: www.igi-global.com

Handbook of Research on Leveraging Risk and Uncertainties for Effective Project Management
Yuri Raydugin (Risk Services & Solutions Inc., Canada)
Business Science Reference • copyright 2017 • 504pp • H/C (ISBN: 9781522517900) • US $275.00 (our price)

Managing Project Risks for Competitive Advantage in Changing Business Environments
Constanta-Nicoleta Bodea (Bucharest University of Economic Studies, Centre for Industrial and Services Economics, Romania) Augustin Purnus (Technical University of Civil Engineering Bucharest, Romania) Martina Huemann (WU-Vienna University of Economics & Business, Austria) and Miklós Hajdu (Budapest University of Technology and Economics, Hungary)
Business Science Reference • copyright 2016 • 348pp • H/C (ISBN: 9781522503354) • US $210.00 (our price)

Strategic Integration of Social Media into Project Management Practice
Gilbert Silvius (LOI University of Applied Sciences, The Netherlands & University of Johannesburg, South Africa)
Business Science Reference • copyright 2016 • 343pp • H/C (ISBN: 9781466698673) • US $210.00 (our price)

Strategic Management and Leadership for Systems Development in Virtual Spaces
Christian Graham (University of Maine, USA)
Business Science Reference • copyright 2016 • 389pp • H/C (ISBN: 9781466696884) • US $210.00 (our price)

Modern Techniques for Successful IT Project Management
Shang Gao (Zhongnan University of Economics and Law, China) and Lazar Rusu (Stockholm University, Sweden)
Business Science Reference • copyright 2015 • 374pp • H/C (ISBN: 9781466674738) • US $225.00 (our price)

Handbook of Research on Effective Project Management through the Integration of Knowledge and Innovation
George Leal Jamil (Informações em Rede, Brazil) Sérgio Maravilhas Lopes (CETAC.MEDIA - Porto and Aveiro Universities, Portugal) Armando Malheiro da Silva (Porto University, Portugal) and Fernanda Ribeiro (Porto University, Portugal)
Business Science Reference • copyright 2015 • 602pp • H/C (ISBN: 9781466675360) • US $285.00 (our price)

Handbook of Research on Technology Project Management, Planning, and Operations
Terry T. Kidd (Texas A&M University, USA)
Information Science Reference • copyright 2009 • 610pp • H/C (ISBN: 9781605664002) • US $265.00 (our price)

Managing Very Large IT Projects in Businesses and Organizations
Matthew Guah (Erasmus University Rotterdam, The Netherlands)
Information Science Reference • copyright 2009 • 358pp • H/C (ISBN: 9781599045467) • US $165.00 (our price)

IGI GLOBAL
DISSEMINATOR OF KNOWLEDGE
www.igi-global.com

701 E. Chocolate Ave., Hershey, PA 17033
Order online at www.igi-global.com or call 717-533-8845 x100
To place a standing order for titles released in this series, contact: cust@igi-global.com
Mon-Fri 8:00 am - 5:00 pm (est) or fax 24 hours a day 717-533-8661

Editorial Advisory Board

Table of Contents

Detailed Table of Contents

Project Portfolio Management (PPM) is an "old-new" emerging discipline. More and more organizations are discovering PPM as an "alternative" to Strategic Planning. In reality the two disciplines should walk along, obtaining from this coexistence mutual benefits. Strategic Planning is often too far from reality and fails due to this distance. Project Management is too much down-to-earth, being focused on delivering, sometimes without knowing the real rational behind what is produced. PPM is a smart and wise connection between these too distant worlds (it has to be highlighted that also the people involved in the two disciplines are very dissimilar). PPM is a step into the future keeping a tight connection with the near past and with the ongoing activities performed by the organization. PPM supports organizations' need to shape their future. It is a complex process, taking time and resources, but the returns are worth the effort.

This chapter describes and clarifies the boundaries between strategic management and project/program portfolio management (PPPM) processes, and identifies who holds primary responsibilities for key elements of these inter-related sets of management processes. The main issues considered include: The differences between strategic project management and operational project management. The elements in the strategic project management practices and processes that should be considered to be within the responsibility of 'project management.' The role of a typical PMO in relation to 1) strategic management processes, and 2) both the strategic and operational project management processes. The importance of identifying the differences between transformative and commercial projects and programs and also between the major categories of projects and programs within enterprises. The origins of the two basic types of projects within project-driven compared to project-dependent enterprises.

The strategy of any organisation and strategic planning are related to Portfolio Management. This chapter is focused on the relationship between the Organization's strategy and portfolio management. The purpose of this chapter is to explain the importance of strategic planning and its relationship with portfolio management. The focus of this chapter is to explain first the main elements of the organization's strategy based on the research from different authors and researchers plus the author's experience, then to explain the relationship between strategic planning and the portfolio management process, following with the explanation of the portfolio management context elements, defining the concepts of the mission, vision and objectives. The use of a case study tries to add value and achieve a better understanding of all the concepts explained in this chapter.

This chapter deals with something which is widely spoken about, and very little know: Strategic Management. Following an evidence based approach, the author objective is to explain why Strategic Management is a scale invariant process that allows who uses it to identify possible and plausible solutions to complex issues. Some of the basics and analyticals of strategic management, such as strategic planning, SWOT analysis, Scenarios, are going to be described in detail. Detailed considerations will be presented on the issue of time and timing, a fundamental parameter that is too often neglected or taken as granted. The importance of strategic management to allow organisations to learn, change and evolve will be described. Some considerations on the importance of using the proper representation of the organisation's structure will be presented.

This chapter will discuss how to more effectively implement the enterprise portfolio management system (EPMS). In order to be successful in delivering an EPMS that will benefit the organization, the implementation team must understand that they going to make a significant change to how the organization operates, and that any significant change such as this can expect to encounter resistance. Effective implementation requires an understanding of the organization's current problems and priorities, the creation and implementation of the system that will resolve those problems, and preparations to overcome resistance through effective Organizational Change Management (OCM). The implementers must truly be convinced that this effort is going to make a difference to the larger organization and that their dedication and change leadership will make it successful. This chapter will help the implementing team see the benefits of enterprise portfolio management, help them convince others of those benefits, and become the leader in implementing the EPMS.

Portfolio management methodology is usually linked with the concept of "portfolio cycle" (often 1 year of activities). This means that organizations experience, once a year, a time in which ongoing activities are analyzed and their status reported; new initiatives are collected, assessed, prioritized and selected in competition with ongoing components. Being the aim of portfolio management to select the best set of components supporting the organization in achieving the strategic objectives, strategy should drive the preparation of the "next portfolio cycle". It may be the case that the strategy is not clear, not ready to be used, not stable. Adaptive Portfolio Management requires to move away from the collect-assess-prioritize-select-implement-control-review approach (all these actions are performed during each and every "portfolio cycle") towards a more flexible model where organizations manage these important activities "continuously".

Project portfolios produce value through the coordinated execution of the projects and programs within the portfolio. The performance of the portfolio is evaluated by the generated business value and potential future opportunities it creates. This same performance measure is not applied to the projects within the portfolio. Projects are evaluated based on an operational measure of project efficiency that considers performance of project scope, budget, and schedule. Inconsistencies between portfolio and project performance decrease the value offered by each project and the overall value of the portfolio. In this study, a framework and solution are presented that expand the measures of project success to include criteria that better align with the goals of the project portfolio. The enhanced project success measures include project efficiency, customer impact, team impact, organizational success, and future preparation. The solution is applied to the project management process to demonstrate potential integration into project management practices.

Demand Management is the process an organization puts in place to internally collect new ideas, projects and needs during the creation of a Portfolio (from now on PTF). This collection is done internally but should also consider the external market situation and the general Strategy of the Organization. Demand contains two main actions: initiatives Collection and Assessment (following the Strategic Objectives definition) and preceding the start of the Portfolio budgeting, prioritization and selection phases. What is possible to do to better manage Demand and maximize the value added to Portfolio Management? The first opportunity is that Demand can represent a connection with the business and the entire Organization. A second opportunity is that a continuous Demand Management approach can simplify the portfolio collection, prioritization and selection. For Demand Management to be a real opportunity in Portfolio Management should be organized and planned respecting the interpretation of the matter and the maturity of the Organisation and should be also treated as a specific matter.

Foreword

Would you tell me, please, which way I ought to go from here?
That depends a good deal on where you want to get to.
I don't much care where –
Then it doesn't matter which way you go.
— Lewis Carroll, Alice in Wonderland

This is an important book. It addresses a difficult topic, and it undertakes to inform us of critical skills that will take us into a new direction. This is always a challenge, as going in a new direction requires an appreciation that the destination has advantage, benefit, and value.

We live in a world of projects. Projects are undertaken in order to provide a benefit to a larger organization. It would seem like a simple concept. Yet, there are increasing questions about the value of projects in relation to organizational success and strategy. In point, there is a vital chain that links organization success through projects, programs and portfolio.

The potential disconnect between a project outcome and organizational strategy are many. At the starting point, projects are often charged as a process for the delivery of a product or service. In the drive for completion, there can be a tendency to ignore strategic imperatives that may be considered the domain of executives in the C-suite. The context of a project is framed within pressures of financial realities, schedule drivers and performance requirements. Such an environment focuses energy toward the operational and day to day concerns. In addition, there has been the critical mistake of considering and developing project managers as lesser than executive leaders, the latter who determine strategy, vision, and value.

Portfolio Management is a method for aligning projects toward the strategic goals of the organization. This is a simple statement for a complex endeavor. Anything that must accommodate organizational strategy and execution of projects are easier to say than to do. Nonetheless, it would be a significant accomplishment to ensure that all projects and programs are aligned under an organizational strategy and that the management and leadership of projects require strategic alignment. If the authors of this book contribute simply to the acceptance that projects demand competence in this domain, it would make a great contribution.

In reality, the authors of 'Project Portfolio Management Strategies for Effective Organizational Operations,' have much higher aims. The intent of this book is to improve competence and capability in portfolio management, and the knowledge is organized with a practitioner in mind. This serves as a significant contribution to a field that has far too long been comfortable as a discipline that executes and delivers, without responsibility for strategic organizational benefit. This contribution represents a mindset of change that may appear subtle, but represent dramatically different thinking for how projects are conceived and why project managers matter.

The mindset of change is represented by the chapters of the book. Time is taken to consider strategy, and the relationship to projects, enterprise and portfolio. The reader is presented with current tools and techniques that enhance strategic thought. There is encouragement of a learning based approach, essential and often neglected, that aligns with the modern reality of accelerated learning and the knowledge organization. Strategies for preparing and implementing the portfolio management approach is covered and offer understanding and experience for those working within an organization. This includes a chapter that takes on the challenge of optimizing portfolio value through comprehensive metrics.

The authors have also considered one of the great faults and criticisms of previous strategic management efforts – the inability to manage change and the need for adaptive response. Adaptive portfolio management offers the view that there is essential need for a flexible model where organizations can respond quickly, continuously and in adaptive response. This is critical in the volatile environment where change is constant and there is a need for the project professional to understand and management change.

Organizations, leaders and practitioners are looking for ways to ensure direction, purpose, and allocation of resources. Portfolio management promotes a way of thinking, planning, and collaborating that optimizes project benefit through integration with strategic intent. This book offers an integrated method, incorporating examples, for an organization to understand how to make portfolio project management successful. It offers valuable insight in the path to take for a reader who cares about a final destination of project success and benefit realization for the larger organization.

Edward J. Hoffman
Knowledge Engagement LLC, USA

Edward J. Hoffman *is CEO, Knowledge Engagement, LLC. Knowledge Engagement is engaged in research, education, and consulting services at a strategic organizational level. He directly supports the Project Management Institute as a Strategic Advisor with a focus on integrated systems for talent management, knowledge engagement and learning strategies. Dr. Hoffman retired from NASA as a senior executive after thirty-three years. He was appointed the first NASA Chief Knowledge Officer in 2011 and held responsibility for system-wide strategy, integration and deployment of knowledge services.*

Preface

Ignoranti quem portum petat, nullus suus ventus est
- Seneca

This is not the first book on the Project Portfolio Management and will not be the last. The matter has been treated and discussed for some time, but is still evolving. Project Portfolio Management is an issue at the border between two worlds, the world of strategic planning and the projects implementation world. Often these two worlds are far apart and do not speak, the first always looking at the organizations' external environment, and to the future, the second focused on the careful production of results and the completion of the tasks of which it is responsible. But in the end it is a matter of fact that there is nothing more inefficient and ineffective than an organization that does not carefully manage the vital link between strategy and actions.

The title of the book (Project Portfolio Management Strategies for Effective Organizational Operations) is indicative of the approach at the base of what presented: the use of Project Portfolio Management strategies to make effective business operations. Business operations will be effective only if (in addition of being well organized and carried out) it will also be in line with the strategic objectives of the organization and pursue the defined strategic trajectory. The main objective of Project Portfolio Management is to ensure that these strategic goals, resulting from the Vision and Mission, are understood, shared and efficiently implemented.

To give the reader an overview of the subject matter I will quote the authors of this book.

Strategic Planning is part of Strategic Management and can be defined as an organizational planning and decision process of defining the strategy and allocating appropriate resources to pursue the strategy (A. Aparo von Flüe).

A project portfolio consists of the programs and projects supporting a given higher-level strategy to define more than one portfolio on a strategic basis in large organizations to reflect product line, geographic or technological divisions of the organization, industry or market. In general, a project portfolio is a group of several "delivery" or "commercial" projects that are related to a well-defined major strategic objective (R.D. Archibald).

The goal of long term growth requires a balanced Project Portfolio (J. Gumz).

The success of the project portfolio is dependent upon the success of the projects within the portfolio. If the projects are unable to deliver the results, the portfolio will not achieve its goals. In other words, the collection of projects must be successful in order for the portfolio to be successful. In Project Portfolio Management both the project, and the overall portfolio must be measured and evaluated in order to determine success. The ability of the project to improve business success and better prepare the organization for the future match the goals of a project portfolio. (B. Olson).

Project Portfolio Management is a process, but people make the process work; values are the principle guiding their actions as they perform their work. The Project Portfolio Management human resources can help executives to better understand the organization's capability and how it can contribute to accomplish the organization's strategy. Professionals participating the Project Portfolio Management need to play an active role as participants in the strategic planning process rather than being reactive (A. Bucero).

With an understandable, top-down view of their entire project portfolio, executives and managers can more readily understand where dollars are being spent and which projects continue to be worthwhile (F. Parth).

The organizational urge for using and applying new tools, methods and techniques for increasing their competitiveness is tremendous. The market competitive pressing, the reduction of error margins and the need to do things perfectly at the first shot are creating an increasing demand for solutions that can resolve those problems, achieving the best performance possible with the minimum risk and cost. There is no consensus about the type of method or technique that automatically improves any organization, despite of their own problems or status, restrictions and competitive advantages, strengths and weaknesses. Nevertheless, project management tries to see the organization as a whole, and systematically challenge the difficulties encountered with new re-thinking processes in order to increase the organizational performance (A. Amaral).

The main driver for a company to decide to implement portfolio management is to move from a tactical approach, in which the same, routine work is pursued as desired by clients, to a strategic view in which the company's programs, projects, and operational work is the portfolio, and all work then is prioritized for greater effectiveness. Nevertheless, as professionals in the field can confirm, portfolio does this breakthrough but this does not mean it is flawless. If the main reasons that drive companies to set up a project portfolio are to forge the link between project selection and business strategy and to yield the right balance of project and investments, it is evident that these are the fields in which companies expect the major added value in terms of portfolio effectiveness (G. Levin - N. Pitotti).

Project Portfolio Management discipline states that there is the need of an integrated vision of the set of projects that an organization puts in place. According to the writers an integrated analysis in key value creation should be performed. This combines two key areas of "survival" and "growth" for an organization: sustainability analysis and organizational design (L. Aiello - M. Gatti).

The contemporary competitive environment, with its widespread lack of information, misleading signs and difficulties in forecasting future scenarios, makes the investments in the acquisition and management of projects always riskier. Consequently, one of the objectives of a manager is the assessment of risk across project portfolio. Companies must learn to manage innovation strategically to achieve a competitive advantage through a well-balanced portfolio (F. Nonino).

The methodology and the implementation of project portfolio management aims to implement a powerful and consistent link between the objectives and actions.

In almost all of the chapters of this book, this problem is at least enunciated. In many chapters the authors have tried to give answers and ideas that we hope will help organizations to improve the way they manage the implementation of its strategic objectives.

The book is of course also directed to those who want to keep abreast of the latest research and thinking in the field of Strategic Management, Portfolio Management, Program Management and Project Management. The authors come from different backgrounds and heterogeneous environments, this mix between multiple background is one of the main values of the book that wants to be a collector of experiences and research on the subject.

Many of the chapters open up new fronts of study and reflections, assuming and proposing further researches on various issues. Our goal was in fact also to stimulate research. The authors do not believe to have access to the "truth" having all the answers.

Authors also invite readers to be curious and do not settle for what is already available, trying and testing new methods to enable organizations to be more efficient and effective.

OVERVIEW OF THE BOOK

What follows is a chapter-by-chapter overview of the contents of this book.

Chapter 1

Project Portfolio Management (PPM) is an "old-new" emerging discipline. More and more organizations are discovering PPM as an "alternative" to Strategic Planning. In reality the two disciplines should walk along, obtaining from this coexistence mutual benefits. Strategic Planning is often too far from reality and fails due to this distance. Project Management is too much down-to-earth, being focused on delivering, sometimes without knowing the real rational behind what is produced. This chapter explains that PPM is a smart and wise connection between these too distant worlds (it has to be highlighted that also the people involved in the two disciplines are very dissimilar). PPM is a step into the future keeping a tight connection with the near past and with the ongoing activities performed by the organization. PPM supports organizations' need to shape their future. It is a complex process, taking time and resources, but the returns are worth the effort.

Chapter 2

This chapter describes and clarifies the boundaries between strategic management and project/program portfolio management (PPPM) processes, and identifies who holds primary responsibilities for key elements of these inter-related sets of management processes. The main issues considered include: The differences between strategic project management and operational project management. The elements in the strategic project management practices and processes that should be considered to be within the responsibility of 'project management.' The role of a typical PMO in relation to 1) strategic management processes, and 2) both the strategic and operational project management processes. The importance of identifying the differences between transformative and commercial projects and programs and also between the major categories of projects and programs within enterprises. The origins of the two basic types of projects within project-driven compared to project-dependent enterprises.

Chapter 3

The strategy of any organization and strategic planning are related to Portfolio Management. This chapter is focused on the relationship between the Organization's strategy and portfolio management. The purpose of this chapter is to explain the importance of strategic planning and its relationship with portfolio management. The focus of this chapter is to explain first the main elements of the organization's strategy based on the research from different authors and researchers plus the author's experience, then to explain the relationship between strategic planning and the portfolio management process, following with the explanation of the portfolio management context elements, defining the concepts of the mission, vision and objectives. The use of a case study tries to add value and achieve a better understanding of all the concepts explained in this chapter.

Chapter 4

This chapter deals with something which is widely spoken about, and very little know: Strategic Management. Following an evidence based approach, the author objective is to explain why Strategic Management is a scale invariant process that allows who uses it to identify possible and plausible solutions to complex issues. Some of the basics and analytics of strategic management, such as strategic planning, SWOT analysis, Scenarios, are going to be described in detail. Detailed considerations will be presented on the issue of time and timing, a fundamental parameter that is too often neglected or taken as granted. The importance of strategic management to allow organizations to learn, change and evolve will be described. Some considerations on the importance of using the proper representation of the organization's structure will be presented.

Chapter 5

This chapter will discuss how to more effectively implement the enterprise portfolio management system (EPMS). In order to be successful in delivering an EPMS that will benefit the organization, the implementation team must understand that they going to make a significant change to how the organization operates, and that any significant change such as this can expect to encounter resistance. Effective implementation requires an understanding of the organization's current problems and priorities, the creation and implementation of the system that will resolve those problems, and preparations to overcome resistance through effective Organizational Change Management (OCM). The implementers must truly be convinced that this effort is going to make a difference to the larger organization and that their dedication and change leadership will make it successful. This chapter will help the implementing team see the benefits of enterprise portfolio management, help them convince others of those benefits, and become the leader in implementing the EPMS.

Chapter 6

Portfolio management methodology is usually linked with the concept of "portfolio cycle" (often 1 year of activities). This means that organizations experience, once a year, a time in which ongoing activities are analyzed and their status reported; new initiatives are collected, assessed, prioritized and selected in competition with ongoing components. Being the aim of portfolio management to select the best set of components supporting the organization in achieving the strategic objectives, strategy should drive the preparation of the "next portfolio cycle". It may be the case that the strategy is not clear, not ready to be used, not stable. This chapter is focused on the concept of Adaptive Portfolio Management and the need to move away from the collect-assess-prioritize-select-implement-control-review approach (all these actions are performed during each and every "portfolio cycle") towards a more flexible model where organizations manage these important activities "continuously".

Chapter 7

Project portfolios produce value through the coordinated execution of the projects and programs within the portfolio. The performance of the portfolio is evaluated by the generated business value and potential future opportunities it creates. This same performance measure is not applied to the projects within the portfolio. Projects are evaluated based on an operational measure of project efficiency that considers performance of project scope, budget, and schedule. Inconsistencies between portfolio and project performance decrease the value offered by each project and the overall value of the portfolio. In this chapter, a framework and solution are presented that expand the measures of project success to include criteria that better align with the goals of the project portfolio. The enhanced project success measures include project efficiency, customer impact, team impact, organizational success, and future preparation. The solution is applied to the project management process to demonstrate potential integration into project management practices.

Chapter 8

Demand Management is the process an organization puts in place to internally collect new ideas, projects and needs during the creation of a Portfolio. This collection is done internally but should also consider the external market situation and the general Strategy of the Organization. Demand contains two main actions: initiatives Collection and Assessment (following the Strategic Objectives definition) and preceding the start of the Portfolio budgeting, prioritization and selection phases. In this chapter one questions is analyzed. What is possible to do to better manage Demand and maximize the value added to Portfolio Management? The first opportunity is that Demand can represent a connection with the business and the entire Organization. A second opportunity is that a continuous Demand Management approach can simplify the portfolio collection, prioritization and selection. For Demand Management to be a real opportunity in Portfolio Management should be organized and planned respecting the interpretation of the matter and the maturity of the Organization and should be also treated as a specific matter.

Chapter 9

The project management area uses several techniques and tools to identify, select, monitor and manage the projects portfolio of the organizations. However, these techniques still present problems and difficulties which, sometimes, inhibit their use. Project Portfolio Management (PPM) is considered a problem of considerable difficulty and complexity, which requires its constant monitoring by the organization, according to the strategic guidelines chosen. Thus, this chapter presents an innovative approach for selecting the portfolio of projects by using DEA, and the development of a set of generic indicators, to support the decision makers in considering multiple projects. Each decision maker can use all or some of the indicators proposed, thus each one's knowledge, sensitivity and intuition are taken into account, namely for indicators such as risk perception, level of innovation, market clock speed, project's complexity.

Chapter 10

Extracting and consolidating knowledge from past projects can help managers in selecting projects with the correct level of riskiness, while market analysis gives directions for reaching the objective of a balanced project portfolio. To this extent, the chapter discusses strategic importance of project selection and the role of risks and uncertainties in project portfolio management and presents different some fundamental and innovative frameworks and project selection methodologies for balancing risks. Finally, the chapter proposes a model containing an innovative methodology, based on artificial neural networks, to help managers in balancing project portfolio and assessing projects during the selection phase on the basis of risks, uncertainties and critical success factors.

Chapter 11

Developing a portfolio management system that can effectively and efficiently select and prioritize the projects that best support strategic goals, this is only the start of portfolio management. To ensure that the enterprise portfolio management system (EPMS) can continue to operate and grow as the organizational environment changes and the strategic goals change, the EPMS must be implemented within the organizational structure that ensures it will remain relevant in the future. This chapter discuss two architectures to the administrative housing of the EPMS, within a PMO or as a separate stand-alone organization. Both have their advantages and disadvantages. In either case, once the EPMS is implemented it must be controlled and managed as any other group within the larger organization. This requires a structure, roles and responsibilities, personnel and IT resources, an annual budget, and all the other administrative functions required to manage a department. As the maturity level of the EPMS evolves the growth must be managed to continue to support the organization.

Chapter 12

The chapter is an overview on organizational models for project management, identifying the characteristics of a possible reference model that joins to the necessity of portfolio management. The approach to portfolio management requires attention to the integrated management of projects; this is why the organizational structure matrix "differentiated" could be a useful reference point. This chapter proposes, therefore, a reworking of the organizational structure design criteria considering both the Value Chain of

Porter is the matrix structure "differentiated". Ultimately, the contribution configures the characteristics of the organizational model for portfolio in relation to the type of project - internal/process, external/product mix - in order to improve the performance of internal projects whose objectives are not always explicit. The basic idea of this work is to apply the concept of Porter's value chain not only functions but also the portfolio of projects that the company has.

Chapter 13

Ideally, the portfolio is at the highest level of an organization as it shows the organization's truest intent, direction, and priorities. But, portfolios can exist at various levels such as business units, departments, divisions, and even at the program level. At the program level, the program manager can be considered a mini portfolio manager. The objective is at any time to ensure the portfolio represents a view of its selected components and reflects the organizational strategy and objectives regardless if the programs or projects have interdependencies, as the portfolio represents all the work under way in the organization. This means portfolio management includes all the activities to identify and align organizational priorities, determine governance and performance frameworks, measure the value/benefit of what is being done, make investment decisions, foster communication, and manage resource allocation. This chapter illustrates the various interrelations between program and portfolio management to show how programs can support portfolio in delivering business value.

Chapter 14

The falling price of crude oil has caused the price of diesel and gasoline to drop, workers to be laid off, and competitors to consider merging. It has also provided a real-world view of companies applying project portfolio management as projects have been delayed, put on hold indefinitely, or closed down completely. Energy companies have shelved $400bn of spending on new oil and gas projects since the price collapse, delaying millions of barrels a day in future output from the Gulf of Mexico, Africa, Kazakhstan, and other areas. The price of crude oil, which traded above $100 since 2011 has dropped over 50% since September 2014 due to a lack of global demand plus continued production by Saudi Arabia and others. This chapter will look at strategies and tactics used by companies including Chevron, Royal Dutch Shell, and Total SA in reviewing and rebalancing their project portfolios. These approaches have application to other industry sectors.

Luca Romano
PMI Central Italy Chapter – CUOA Business School, Italy

Acknowledgment

I dedicate this book to my father. Wherever you are Dad, I know you are proud of your son.

I thank all the authors who not only wrote chapters but have also proactively participated in this journey.

Thank you Lucia Aiello, António Amaral, Russell Dean Archibald, Madalena Araújo, Andrea Aparo von Flüe, Alfonso Bucero, Francesco Saverio Colasuonno, Mauro Gatti, Roberta Grimaldi, Joy Gumz, Ginger Levin, Fabio Nonino, Brandon Olson, Frank Parth and, last but not least, Nicole Pitotti.

I also thank some colleagues and friends that were instrumental in feeding my inspiration, pushing me to "dream big" and start this book: Andrea Aparo von Flüe, Sergio Gerosa, Francesco Mastrandrea, and Ugo Stocco.

Finally, my warmest thanks to my lovely wife Patrizia and my son Matteo for their support and for the time they allowed me to dedicate to this challenging endeavor.

Chapter 1
Portfolio Management as a Step into the Future

Luca Romano
PMI Central Italy Chapter – CUOA Business School, Italy

ABSTRACT

Project Portfolio Management (PPM) is an "old-new" emerging discipline. More and more organizations are discovering PPM as an "alternative" to Strategic Planning. In reality the two disciplines should walk along, obtaining from this coexistence mutual benefits. Strategic Planning is often too far from reality and fails due to this distance. Project Management is too much down-to-earth, being focused on delivering, sometimes without knowing the real rational behind what is produced. PPM is a smart and wise connection between these too distant worlds (it has to be highlighted that also the people involved in the two disciplines are very dissimilar). PPM is a step into the future keeping a tight connection with the near past and with the ongoing activities performed by the organization. PPM supports organizations' need to shape their future. It is a complex process, taking time and resources, but the returns are worth the effort.

INTRODUCTION

Strategic Management

To introduce Project Portfolio Management (PPM) it is imperative to talk about Strategic Management.

The key objective of a company is to achieve a strategic advantage against competitors in the referential market. When an organization does not have competitors (example: the Public Sector) the final strategic objective is to satisfy its stakeholders and final clients (shareholders). As stated by Johnson, Scholes, and Whittington (2008), strategy can be defined as *the direction and scope of an organization over the long-term: which achieves advantage for the organization through its configuration of resources within a challenging environment, to meet the needs of markets and to fulfil stakeholder expectations.*

DOI: 10.4018/978-1-5225-2151-8.ch001

Strategy is also described as the direction and scope of an organization over the long term, in order to get an advantage in a changing environment through its configuration of resources and competences, with the aim of fulfilling stakeholder expectations (Pinto, 2007).

An organization's strategy has to be multi-level:

- A Top-level strategy referring to the overall scope of the organization (at this level company will be concerned about the shareholders expectations and should consider geographical issues.
- A Middle level strategy about the different businesses within the corporate and how these businesses will compete within their markets (price, innovation, etc.).
- A Bottom level strategy at the operational level of the organization. Here companies are concerned on how the organization delivers effectively (the corporate and business level strategies) in terms of resources, processes and people.

Therefore, a strategy must be broken down into strategic goals and these goals have to be assigned to different structures located in several levels within the Organization. These objectives should be Specific, Measurable, Achievable, Relevant and Time-based (SMART). These goals will move the organization in the "strategic direction" considered optimal. This is what is usually called "strategy in action": the organization actions are aligned with the pre-defined strategic trajectory. Strategic goals when reached produce changes in the organization. Programs and Projects produce changes too.

According to The Standard for Program Management (PMI, 2013c): *programs and projects deliver benefits by enhancing current capabilities or developing new capabilities that support the sponsoring organization's strategic goals and objectives.*

Referring to Figure 1, *organizational strategy is a result of the strategic planning cycle, where the vision and mission are translated into a strategic plan within the boundaries of the organizational values.*

Figure 1. Portfolio and strategic planning
Source: Adapted from the Program Management Standard, Third Edition, Project Management Institute, PMI®.

Organizations build a strategy to define how their vision will be achieved. The strategic plan is subdivided into a set of organizational initiatives that are influenced in part by market dynamics, customer and partner requests, shareholders, government regulations and competitor plans and actions. These initiatives may be grouped into portfolios (of Programs, Projects or other work) *to be executed during a predetermined period* (PMI, 2013c).

The goal of linking portfolio management to the organizational strategy is to establish a balanced, operational plan that will help the organization achieve its goals and to balance the use of resources to maximize value in executing programs, projects, and other operational activities (PMI, 2013c).

Project Portfolio Management

Project Portfolio Management is a discipline that can be described as follows (PMI, 2013b):

1. *A portfolio is a component collection of programs, projects, or operations managed as a group to achieve strategic objectives. The portfolio components may not necessarily be interdependent or have related objectives. The portfolio components are quantifiable, that is, they can be measured, ranked, and prioritized.*
2. *A portfolio exists to achieve one or more organizational strategies and objectives and may consist of a set of past, current, and planned or future portfolio components. Portfolios and programs have the potential to be longer term with new projects rotating into the portfolios or programs, unlike projects that have a defined beginning and end.*
3. *At any given moment, a portfolio represents a view of its selected portfolio components and reflects the organizational strategy and objectives.*
4. *If a portfolio is not aligned to its organizational strategy, the organization should reasonably question why the work is being undertaken. Therefore, a portfolio should be a representation of an organization's intent, direction, and progress.*

Basically, Portfolio Management Methodology aims to connect strategy with actions.

This methodology exploits the organization's strategy to create a set of criteria and a mathematical model to evaluate company potential initiatives on the basis of their alignment with the mentioned strategy and the expected benefits to be produced. This analysis, done after the definition of the strategy and before the implementation of the initiatives (that the strategy should put in place), helps the organization to focus on the right projects, investing time and money in what:

- Is aligned with strategic objectives;
- Has a potential to generate value;
- Has an acceptable probability of success;
- Is feasible (timeline, resources, technology, etc..) within the chosen portfolio;

while terminating project and activities no longer useful to achieve strategic objectives.

If it is true that theoretically Portfolio Management never ends as it must be constantly renewed and never fully releases a "final deliverable" that completes the activities, it is also true that a Portfolio has a lifecycle that evolves year after year following a never ending spiral.

In this lifecycle some topic moments are clearly recognizable, and they are not necessarily in sequence:

1. **Strategy Definition:**
    a. Organization's Strategy definition (part of strategic planning).
    b. Organization's Strategic objectives definition and breakdown (part of strategic planning).
2. **Portfolio Authorization:**
    a. Internal collection of ideas, new initiatives, needs, ongoing projects and activities. This phase could be or not directly connected with the Strategic Planning process. In a perfect world all the ideas, initiatives, needs, projects, activities would arise from the Strategy defined and the screening and selection activity would only select the best ones. In the real world these initiatives would arise from the several functions of the Company and could be not aligned with the actual Strategy and need to be verified in their alignment.
    b. Ideas, initiatives, needs, ongoing projects and activities Assessment and Selection.
    c. Portfolio balance, Authorization and Release.
3. **Components Realization:**
    a. Programs, projects, operations development and control (part of program/project management and managing operations).
    b. Portfolio Governance and Communication.
    c. Portfolio Reporting.
4. **Review:**
    a. Strategic objectives achievement verification through Portfolio components completion.
    b. Company strategy & objectives review and update (part of strategic planning).
    c. Portfolio review and update as output of the Components completion and the Strategy review and update.

Implementing a PPM system within any company creates a stress for the organization as PPM is something that permeates the whole structure vertically and horizontally. It implies the need to change culture, processes, habits, training programs and roles.

The organizational expected impacts of the Project Portfolio Management key statements are listed in the following Table 1

PPM is real change for any company, it should be introduced and used when there is a good level of project management culture as for to succeed it needs wide support and top management sponsorship.

PPM implementation should be designed, planned, sponsored, communicated, progressively implemented, monitored & controlled, tailored and supported. This could take many years and could be one of the key transformations for a company.

In the following paragraphs the author will expose some of the key aspects of Portfolio Management implementation, and share some ideas and solutions to help organizations using PPM to define and shape their future.

Background

Even though the real need for a Project Portfolio Management (PPM) theory is quite brand new as it can be collocated at the beginning of the new millennium, the first notions and rudiments about this matter appeared in early 1950s, when one of the first studies in this field was published by Harry Markowitz (Markowitz, 1992). Markowitz is widely recognized as the father of the Modern Portfolio Theory, an approach to financial portfolio which aims at identifying a set of investments resulting in the best ROI

Table 1. Changes driven by a Project Portfolio Management (PPM) System

Project Portfolio Management	Impacts on
A portfolio is a component collection of programs, projects, or operations managed as a group to achieve strategic objectives.	The fact that an Organization could be accustomed to manage projects separately and departments could not be used to share information.
A Strategy is the direction and scope of an organisation over the long term, which achieves advantage in a changing environment through its configuration of resources and competences with the aim of fulfilling stakeholder expectations.	The fact that often the strategic direction is not clear and not fully shared among Departments. A PPM needs a defined, communicated and measurable strategy to refer to as without this "glue" connecting the several projects it's impossible to manage the Portfolio as a whole.
The portfolio components are quantifiable, that is, they can be measured, ranked, and prioritized.	Components (Projects, Programs and Operations activities) needs to be well defined and described in a way they can be analysed and measured. This means that the yearly process to collect and assess the new projects becomes more complex and time consuming. Complexity is often used to dispute PPM.
A portfolio exists to achieve one or more organizational strategies.	This means that a Portfolio should be managed as a unique system, means that the strategy will be achieved in a collaborated way. The Organization will need to understand that there is a chain of benefits produced by the several projects that needs to be considered in a unitary way.
PPM includes interrelated organizational processes by which an organization evaluates, selects, prioritizes, and allocates its limited internal resources to best accomplish organizational strategies.	This means an Organization needs to create a centralized system to manage the PPM. This centralization assure a unique management that helps to have the right level of control over the situation.

according to different levels of risk. The theory was conceived to be applied to the financial industry, but then it was widely used in different sectors. In 1981 Warren McFarlan, professor at the Harvard Business School, elaborated a modern theory for IT projects in the belief that just like the MPT for financial investments, a similar risk-based theory for IT projects was needed. Not only was he right, but it was just the beginning. Nowadays, in Modern Project Management, PPM is used for the composition of project portfolios in IT but also in such diverse fields as construction (Vergara & Boyer, 1977).

In 1992 Wheelwright and Clark went quite close to the commonly shared concept of Project Portfolio Management, describing a process called Aggregate Project Plan (APP) which was still a Project Management concept, but provided managers with a categorized set of projects to be balanced according to short and long term, resources and time. The link between project portfolio and business strategy, that is the truest expression of the PPM theory, became crystal clear by the end of the millennium, when Dye and Pennypacker (Dye & Pennypacker, 1999) defined Project Portfolio Management as the art and science of applying a set of knowledge, skills, tools and techniques to a collection of projects, in order to meet or exceed the needs and expectations of an organization's investment strategy. Projects are essential to the survival and growth of organization. Failure in the management of projects in an organization will impair the ability of the organization to reach its objectives in an effective and efficient manner (Cleland, 1999). With the introduction of PPM, though, the significance of managing a single project with the aim of a short-term success started to seem less meaningful. Projects deserve to be deeply analyzed and integrated together to avoid the risk of just managing multiple projects, which is rather different from managing a Project Portfolio.

In 1999 in his article entitled "Project Portfolio Management: A Song Without Words?" Harvey Lavine assess that the traditional Project Management concept has evolved into something he calls Enterprise Project Management, whose fundamental characteristic was that of reflecting the importance of consolidating and integrating all of the firms' projects for universal access and evaluation. A further evolution has driven companies towards a shift from traditional project-centric objectives to higher-level operational objectives (Lavine, 1999). In 2005 Lavine has referred to Project Portfolio Management as a recognized set of practices that may be considered the biggest leap in project management technology since the development of Program Evaluation and Review Technique and Critical Path Method in the late 1950s.

Nowadays, most of the literature on Strategic Project Management emphasizes the importance of aligning projects with corporate strategy. As a matter of fact, according to an overview of Project Portfolio Management Organizations using projects as ways to develop corporate strategies the implementation of strategy proves to be the most complex phase. Companies and professionals working in the field know that a project portfolio is an assortment of projects managed collectively to achieve the benefits of the portfolio and to realize the overall strategy of the organization (Petro & Gardiner, 2015). This assortment does not necessarily have to encompass projects of a similar nature; but it is their strategic direction and objectives that gets them into the portfolio and keeps them inside the portfolio. To get into portfolio, projects must undergo a selection phase.

Selecting the right projects is crucial for the success of project-based business models (Müller et al., 2008). Available project alternatives usually far exceed the number of projects that can be executed with an organization's limited resources at any given time, and choosing the right projects in a particular context is seldom easy (Engwall & Jerbrant, 2003). Therefore, selection and prioritizations prove to be critical phases in the Project Portfolio Management process.

The typical activities in PPM's scope are the gathering of possible projects, their prioritization and selection according to available resources, and the evaluation of running projects concerning their continuing fit with the portfolio (Petro & Gardiner, 2015). These activities usually involve particular optimization algorithms or management techniques that make use of specific project selection criteria (Doerner et al., 2006). Nevertheless, companies have considerable leeway in the development of their selection criteria, and different measures as well as the wide variety of industries, project types, and strategy choices make inter-organizational standardization impractical (Krumm & Rolle, 1992). Therefore, from the very beginning, PPM was recognized as having its major concern in defining the value of a set of projects; as a result of this, the main issue dealt with in the first literature was project portfolio selection and the tools available to evaluate end then prioritize project proposals.

On this subject, back in 1964, Baker and Pound elaborated a survey about the evaluation and selection of R&D projects. They found that the use of numeric models, namely Payback Period (PBP) and Average Annual Rate of Return was pretty frequent and increased indeed in the following years. The theoretical foundations of Cost/benefits analysis dates back to half of 19th century, but actually its practical consistency emerged with the work of Kaldor and Hicks in 1943. The key passage of CBA lies in the use of financial methodologies like Net Present Value (NPV) and Internal Rate of Return (IRR) to make homogeneous time comparison between different values.

A second assessment made a decade later supported that formal models were still the most used, namely profitability ones. Baker and Freeland (1975) operated a distinction between benefits measurement techniques, relating with the evaluation on single projects on economic or noneconomic basis, and project selection/resources allocation techniques, dealing with portfolio development. Nevertheless, they also reported about the arising necessity for models using multiple criteria in the decision-making process. The focal point was on the need to quantify what was not easily quantifiable with strictly numerical models used exclusively. Moreover, subjectivities coming across the decision process were hard to translate into objective numerical models, along with the interrelations between projects which, if properly analyzed, may cause unsatisfactory results or either more productive ones.

Multiple-criteria analysis became of particular interest in the 1970s, but actually drew inspiration from Benjamin Franklin from late 18th century, who used to evaluate selected criteria with weighted scores in its everyday life decision process. The need for selection models which could take into account more than one criterion originates from the necessity to evaluate and compare more than one criterion. As a result of this, there is no longer just one optimal solutions derived by the evaluation of alternatives against one criterion, but there is a set of solutions generated by a trade-off between the different criteria. In the 1970s professor Thomas L. Saaty developed the Analytic Hierarchy Process (AHP), a multi-criteria decision model which helps in identifying the best solution in terms of the one that better suits the various criteria derived by the breaking down of the problem into a number of factors.

The strategic feature of project selection was first identified by Suresh and Meredith (1986), who categorized the models into three different groups, economic, strategic and analytic. The economic approach includes the classical CBA methods, ROI, NPV, PBP, IRR, while the strategic approach deals with business goal and competitive advantage, comprising therefore comparative models like Pairwise Comparison (AHP, Q-Sort) and weighted scoring models.

Obviously, as computer science unfold, the use of selection models became much more popular. Thanks to the advent of automation systems, at the beginning of the millennium software and web applications for Project Portfolio Management were used to manipulate data in a sophisticated, but fast way. Decision-making softwares, frequently based on MCDA, are decision support tools that help management in the Selection and Prioritization phase, but they are not decision makers. That is why Project Portfolio needs to be managed. It is portfolio manager's responsibility deciding which set of projects makes best fit for the portfolio (Lycett et al., 2004). The perfect balance of such a project pool reflects the technological capabilities and the investment needs that are tuned into the organization's resources and processes (Archer and Ghasemzadeh, 2007). Sure, the difficulty in maintaining this balance stems from the wide range of possible project combinations which form a portfolio under organizational, structural and other constraints (Petro & Gardiner, 2015).

As McFarlan underlines, in order to build a good Project Portfolio, a set of good projects is not enough: *twenty good projects may not make a good portfolio if, for example, seven of the twenty all impact a single department of an organization (Lagace, 2003)*

Therefore, in order to be effective, PPM is carried out by the application of carefully designed set of processes with the intention to achieve the overall growth and success of the organization (Levine, 2005).

Several authors have addressed the issue of alignment of projects with business objectives from the perspective of managerial leadership, change management, project management or a combination of some of these, generating strategic alignment models, such as the model of Box and Platts (2005), based on a set of operational management techniques called Business Process Management. Morris and Pinto (2007) also addressed the alignment of projects to corporate strategy from a business process perspective.

Martinsuo and Lehtonen (2007) linked portfolio success with the average success of projects within the organization. The success of those projects are measured against long-term and short-term success factors. Interestingly, their research revealed that single project management success is not sufficient to measure PPM effectiveness since a project evaluation is usually carried out apart from the portfolio (Petro & Gardiner, 2015). An earlier set of scorecard-type measures comprised four dimensions for measuring and defining portfolio success:

1. The average success of projects, including customer satisfaction (Shenhar et al., 2001);
2. The ability to understand the market in relation to the available technical capabilities within the organization;
3. The organization's ability to enforce strategic alignment for all its projects, and
4. The ability to balance the portfolio expenditure.

On the other hand, portfolio failures have variously been attributed to poor strategic management (Matheson & Matheson, 1998), lack of involvement from business leaders (Kebdall & Rollins 2003), and the wrong team skill set in designing and managing the portfolio (Jeffery & Leliveld, 2003). The lack of portfolio management leads to poor control and coordination between projects, conflicting objectives, un-met deadlines, resistance to change, and most importantly lack of benefit realization (Payne, 1995). McGrath and Macmillan (2000) added to this list: loss of revenue, non-efficient use of resources, loss of strategic alignment, and an unbalanced set of projects within the portfolio.

THE PORTFOLIO MANAGEMENT PROCESS

To simplify the explanation of the Project Portfolio Management process it is possible to try to examine it in one single representation.

Organizations basically need to:

- Define the objectives and related strategy the for the next years.
- Select a list of ongoing or new Portfolio Components (programs, projects, activities) to achieve these objectives.
- Implement the Portfolio Components.
- Control the components' performance alone and as a group.
- Review the components' planning and the objectives/strategy.
- Verify the realization of the expected benefits to eventually redefine the objectives and strategies for the next year/planning cycle

For the author there are nine areas that have to be studied separately, but are intimately connected:

1. Vision, Mission, Objectives and Strategy definition.
2. Demand management.
3. Budgeting.
4. Prioritization and selection.
5. Portfolio governance and communication.
6. Portfolio implementation.
7. Portfolio reporting.
8. Strategy and portfolio review.
9. Benefits realization.

Figure 2 shows the relationships between them (Romano L., Grimaldi R., Colasuonno F.S., 2016). Let's now go through a description of the 9 Areas (Romano L., Grimaldi R., Colasuonno F.S., 2016).

Figure 2. The relationships between the 9 PPM areas

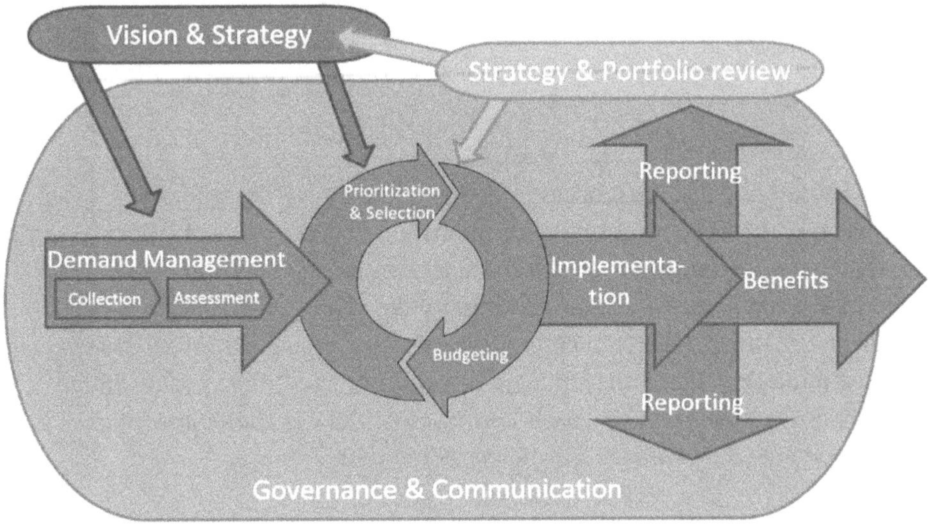

Vision and Strategy Definition

An organization needs a strategic vision to describe the future that this organization wants to create. The strategic vision should be an inspiration for the people interacting with this organization. Based on this vision in mid and short-term there is a need to define a mission that can be broken down into several objectives. Objectives are more manageable than a "vision," as they are conceptually smaller and more measurable, and are used to transfer the vision into results. Strategic objectives must be, quantifiable, measurable, and timed. The executive performance of an organization can be measured by the level of achievement of the strategic objectives.

It is out of the scope of this chapter to analyze how an organization should formulate the right vision-mission-objective-strategy to succeed; this matter is vast and depends on several factors. What discussed here is how to use a set of strategic objectives that are already defined. From this chapter's point-of-view, the analysis will not focus on the capability of the strategic objectives to produce a competitive advantage for the organization, but on the fact that the organization is correctly pursuing the defined objectives with its actions.

Demand Management

Demand represents the set of activities of Collection and Assessment (following the Strategy definition) necessary to start the overall portfolio budgeting, prioritization and selection.

Collection is the process an organization puts in place to collect ideas, projects, needs, etc. This collection will support the portfolio definition, as it will produce a list of programs/projects/actions to assess, prioritize, and select. Collection is focused on Old Initiatives not previously selected (OL), Ongoing Components (OC) and New Initiatives (NI).

Assessment creates what is usually called Business Case (BC). The BC contains at least information about needs, objectives, deadlines, budget, requirements and expected benefits. The structure and the depth of the BC depends on the level of maturity of the organization. BC must be coherent primarily with the prioritization and selection process. BC are, instead, frequently used only to obtain funding approval. This is not sufficient.

Budgeting

Budgeting could be described as the process to define and approve the amount of resources available/ needed for the management of the portfolio of components. This process could be more or less complex depending on the kind of organization analyzed. Budgeting must be done at Portfolio level and should be decomposed into several clusters/baskets to simplify the selection.

Any component will utilize budget to be implemented and organizations should choose to invest in what will produce a future value in the strategic direction defined. Financial techniques, such as Net Present Value, Break Even Analysis, Payback Period, Cost/Benefit Ratio, and Internal Rate of Return (IRR) will help an organization with such decisions (Pinto, 2007).

Prioritization and Selection

Prioritize and select means to rank the components on their alignment with the strategic direction and then select the best set of components that are feasible for the budget available at the level of risk accepted (Romano, 2013a). There could be several sets of components. A set more aligned with the strategy, but riskier; another less aligned, but less risky and with a lower cost. If it is possible to choose to be less aligned or more or less risky, an organization cannot choose a component's set that is not feasible or that is over budget.

Methodologically, prioritization starts from the output of the assessment. Assessment should provide all the information to implement the prioritization. The prioritization is usually done using a model containing measures based on: strategic alignment, risks, human resources, technical feasibility, marketing, etc. Based on this information, components are ranked top-down on the base of the score gained on the measures or on a balanced mix of measures. This ranking could be "all against all" or could be structured in several clusters/baskets where components with similar characteristics compete against each other. The decision on how to create these clusters/baskets is very important, as it limits the competition and, for the author, is a strategic decision by itself.

The clusters/baskets could be based on: organizational area; new/old initiatives; compulsorily; advancement in a component's life cycle; prevalent strategic objective; kind of activity (run, grow, transform, mandatory); or interconnections between components and programs. The total budget available could be previously assigned to clusters/baskets or assigned after the prioritization on the base of the value added contained in the clusters/baskets.

The selection process is necessarily iterative as the perfect portfolio of components rarely exists and there is always the need of balancing and negotiation.

Based on the budget available (that could be expanded with more funding), and the delivering capacity of the organization (that could be expanded with partnerships or external vendors), top management will authorize the portfolio for the coming period.

Portfolio Governance and Communication

Portfolio governance means to define roles, responsibilities, and accountabilities. It also means defining the communication and reporting process. The Portfolio governance process is supposed to manage all the activities supporting the construction of the connection between strategy and actions.

Implementing an office within the organization to supervise the "whole picture" could be a good idea, as concentrating all the rings of the chain in one structure increases the probability of maintaining a tight connection between strategy and actions. Clearly, supervising does not mean the responsibility or the accountability of all the activities. These activities will be realized from the numerous actors, but there is the need for an orchestra conductor that is responsible for the entire process.

Governance also means defining the rules, setting up a steering committee, and clarifying who has the power to decide and who has to participate in making decisions (other governance roles generally are: demand managers, project owners, top management, portfolio managers, and portfolio management office).

Portfolio Implementation

Portfolio implementation is related to the realization of the components selected and authorized. This activity is strictly related to project management and operations management. In this area, the focus is on "doing things right." Project managers, program managers, and managers are doing their day-to-day job.

From this chapter's point-of-view, it is important to consider how managers will manage during the implementation lifecycle, the expected changes from the original route defined at the beginning for the authorized components. This is because the route declared in the BC, in scope definition, and in the project management plan is the expected alignment of the component with the organization's strategy. From that route comes an expected output/outcome/benefit that will implement the strategy.

Often, managers implement components on which they have not been involved since the beginning, when these components are assessed, budgeted, connected with strategy, and selected. Their ability in "strategy-aligned decision making" during the route is limited from the fact that, often, they are treated as mere executors. And mere executors are rarely able to make right decisions.

Portfolio Reporting

Portfolio reporting means not only to report the status of single projects/program/operations, but also the status of the whole portfolio and, moreover, the status of achievement of the strategic objectives. In this interconnection, the bottom-up reporting activity usually done acquires an extreme importance for the organization.

Information like the deviation of planned versus actual duration of components, milestones missed, or resource availability, acquire a huge importance from a portfolio point-of-view. As program managers manage interdependencies between projects with common objectives, portfolio managers must manage and solve interdependency problems among heterogeneous components.

The reporting process should be uniform, continuous, and centralized. It should gather data from the process used to control projects/programs/operations, adding aggregate data for a portfolio point-of-view. Portfolio reporting and adjustment should be done constantly.

Strategy and Portfolio Review

At a certain state of progress, strategy and portfolio review means to answer some important questions, such as:

- Is the actual portfolio sufficiently supporting the strategic objectives?
- Are there new initiatives more aligned with the strategy and could replace ongoing ones?
- Is the strategy still correct in the actual market conditions?

Instead of driving the portfolio with small corrections, the organization has to verify whether the portfolio and/or strategy are still adequate. This process is very complex and its application should be considered with caution. A more frequent strategy and portfolio review improves an organization's flexibility to market changes, but in contrast, increases management complexity and divergences. For instance, some components cannot be terminated for several reasons (technical, political, legal, relational, etc.), new initiatives to include could use budget from a different clusters/baskets and finally, to change an outcome of a component to better support a changed strategy could be impossible.

Benefits Realization

Benefits realization is the verification of the real value for the organization realized by the components. This benefit could be, or not be, aligned with the strategic direction.

A key point in benefits realization is: how and when will the organization measure it? Who will measure it? How is it possible to insulate the positive effects produced by the component output from other beneficial effects?

The earlier the benefits are produced from an output (deliverable)/outcome (change produced), the better. This could happen during, immediately after, or far after the lifespan of a project, a component and the whole portfolio (Figure 3). For sure, benefits management must start before an activity is initiated and continue after it has been delivered.

Figure 3. Value/benefits realization

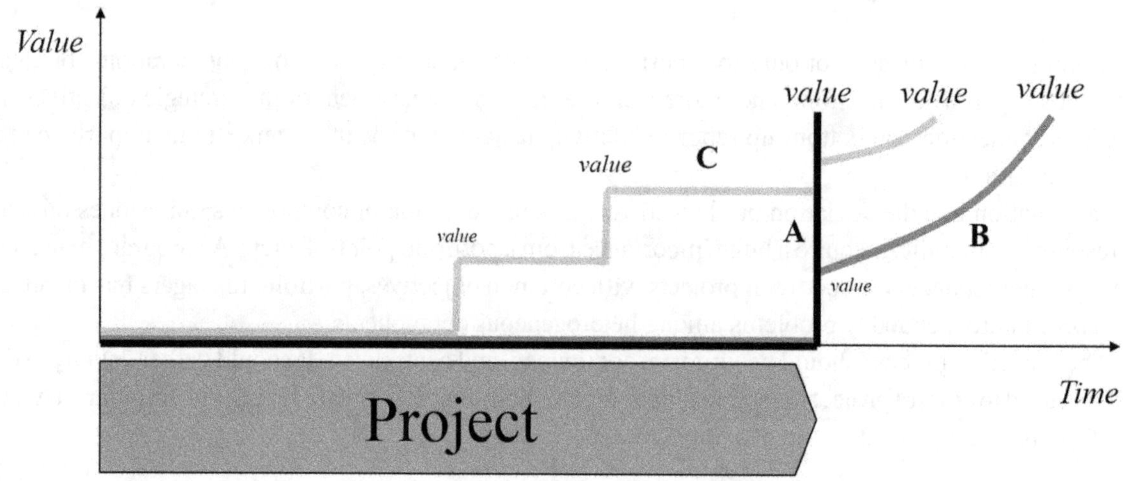

Often, benefits are declared, but not managed. In this, the use of programs can help. Years-long programs with multiple projects can be used as a "spaceship" transporting many projects and benefits. The program manager is primarily responsible for benefits realization and having a long engagement will provide time and commitment to define, realize, and measure the benefits assigned and strategy connected.

CHALLENGES AND ISSUES IN PROJECT PORTFOLIO MANAGEMENT

There are many challenges and issues in PPM, many will be addressed by the other chapters in this book, the author wants to focalize the attention on 3 challenges:

1. Relationship between Strategy and Actions.
2. The need of a sound prioritization and selection process.
3. A Project Portfolio Management System evolution.

Relationship between Strategy and Actions

As already written, as stated by Johnson, Scholes, and Whittington (2008), strategy can be defined as *the direction and scope of an organization over the long term: which achieves advantage for the organization through its configuration of resources within a challenging environment, to meet the needs of markets and to fulfill stakeholder expectations.* The author would modify this phrase saying: Strategy is the direction and scope of an organization over the long-term: "which appears to be able to produce" an advantage for the organization.

The author already referred to what the Project Management Institute (PMI) states in *The Standard for Portfolio Management* – Third Edition about portfolio management: *a portfolio is a component collection of programs, projects, or operations managed as a group to achieve strategic objectives (…) at any given moment, a portfolio represents a view of its selected portfolio components and reflects the organizational strategy and objectives* (PMI, 2013b, pg 3).

In the mind of the author of this chapter, there is always a link that connects strategy with the actions performed in most organizations. If there is a connection, it does not mean that:

- The official strategy (called from now on "conscious strategy") will produce a real advantage.
- The outputs produced from the actions (and the final advantages or disadvantages arising from what is done) are aligned with the direction of the official strategy (these final effects will be called "unconscious strategy").

In any case, organizations "do things," even if they do not have a declared and/or internally shared strategy, and even when they do not have a strategy at all. In this second case, their strategy is declared from what they do.

Big and structured companies have a well-defined process to identify their corporate strategy and then break it down into smaller ones for business units, operations etc. These companies have a strategic planning process in place.

Frequently, this is not what happens in smaller companies where this process is often not structured and sometimes not present at all. In these situations, the company strategic direction is more a "feeling" that flows top-down through the structure, sometimes mentioned during conventions, other times written in brochures, or discussed among employees during coffee breaks.

In this kind of scenario most of the people and most of the projects are managed on a day-to-day strategic approach, where mid-managers base their decisions on two approaches:

1. Keep on doing what done in the last 6-to-12 months.
2. Try to understand the company strategy and try to realize it.

If you have the opportunity to look at the portfolios of these organizations, this comes out very clearly as they have:

- Many former projects still in place and with resources still assigned.
- Some projects alive but stopped somewhere.
- Ready-to-start new projects based on the new strategic objectives.
- New ideas (good and bad) not linked to any strategy.

This kind of project portfolios are often affected from a strong multitasking syndrome as well. Referring to Dr. Eliyahu M. Goldratt "Theory of Constraints" (TOC) (Goldratt, 1997), in this kind of situation:

- Most projects are late.
- Most strategic objectives are missed or not aimed at all.
- Resources are multi-utilized and overbooked.

The link between the actual board strategy direction and what happens in these organizations could be very weak as these portfolios are a mix of many strategies (declared, hidden, deduced, unreal) coming from many "business as usual" years.

Quoting Benko and McFarlan: *if you want to find out where your company is going to be three to five years from now, don't look at your stated strategy. Instead, look at your Project Portfolio. That's where you're making your investments, and it's those investments that determine your firm's direction.* (Benko and McFarlan, 2003).

Starting from this point, every organization has a strategy and a connection, the question is: are the actions performed producing any utility? Let us go back to the concept of conscious and unconscious strategy (Romano, 2015).

A conscious strategy defines, in advance, what the organization assumes will be the right direction and scope to gain an advantage in the future. This assumption can be right or wrong, and the actions performed by the organization must be aligned with the strategic direction to verify it.

An unconscious strategy is the sum of the actions performed, and can be right or wrong in the creation of an advantage in the future.

Simplifying, the strategy can be (or partially be) right or wrong; the actions can be (or partially be) aligned or not aligned.

So, there is a mix of: conscious, unconscious, right, wrong, aligned, and not aligned.

Looking at Table 2, it is possible to say that moving from row A to B means implementing a formal strategic planning process. Moving from column 2 to 3 means implementing a formal portfolio process.

Table 2. Conscious and unconscious strategy and alignment to actions

			1	2	3
				Actions Not Aligned	**Actions Aligned**
A	**C**	Unconscious strategy	Right	*Not applicable*	Future value No strategy definition No portfolio
	D	Unconscious strategy	Wrong	*Not applicable*	No future value No strategy definition No portfolio
B	**E**	Conscious strategy	Right	(go to row C or D) Good strategy definition Poor portfolio	Future value Good strategy definition Good portfolio
	F	Conscious strategy	Wrong	(go to row C or D) Poor strategy definition Poor portfolio	No future value Poor strategy definition Good portfolio

The gray area represents situations in the middle that are very common.

Column 1 is out of the scope of this chapter, as it refers to the ability of an organization to predict the future and act accordingly.

The best situation is in E3, where a conscious right strategy is followed by the right actions/initiatives creating the expected benefits. The second best is in C3, as a future value is more important than processes and procedures (even if there is a lot of work to do to stabilize this situation: not being structured, the success achieved could be not replicable).

D3 is the worst situation because in the absence of a strategic planning process the organization is moving in the wrong direction.

This reflection shows that the approach that can be followed by an organization in the implementation of its strategy is neither straight, nor simple. The level of maturity in several fields is also a constraint in PPM and must be taken into consideration when an improvement path is designed.

The Need of a Sound Prioritization and Selection Process

Prioritize and select means to rank the components on their alignment with the strategic direction and then select the set of components that are feasible for the budget available at the level of risk accepted (Romano, 2013a).

Organizations must develop a model that effectively screens alternatives. The final objective is to create something capable of picking potential "winners" from the large set of possible choices. To follow the strategic direction only initiatives that have high potential toward the strategic direction should be selected.

Here are five important issues that managers should consider when evaluating Portfolio projects screening models (Souder, 1983):

1. **Realism:** An effective model must reflect organizational objectives, including firm's strategic goals and mission. Criteria must also be reasonable in light of such constraints on resources as money and personnel. Finally, the model must take into account risks, performance, cost, and time.

2. **Capability:** A model should be flexible enough to respond to changes in the conditions under which projects are carried out (long-term versus short-term projects, projects of different technologies or capabilities, projects with different commercial objectives). It should be robust enough to accommodate new criteria and constraints, suggesting that the screening model must allow the company to use it as widely as possible in order to cover the greatest possible range of project types.
3. **Flexibility:** The model should be easily modified if trial applications require changes. It must, for example, allow for adjustments due to changes in exchange rates, tax, and so forth.
4. **Ease of Use:** A model must be simple enough to be used by people in all areas of the organization, both those in specific project roles and those in related functional positions. Further, the screening model that is applied, the choices made for project selection, and the reasons for those choices should be clear and easily understood by organizational members.
5. **Cost:** The screening model should be cost effective. A selection approach that is expensive to use in terms of either time or money is likely to have the worst possible effect: causing organizational members to avoid using it because of the excessive cost of employing the screening model. The cost of obtaining selection information and generating optimal results should be low enough to encourage use of the models rather than diminish their applicability.

With these criteria in mind, let's consider some of the more common project-selection techniques.

Checklist Model

It is the simplest way to do project screening. This method creates a list of criteria that pertain to organization's choice of projects, and then applying them to different possible projects. If the organization's strategy is focused on producing fast low cost products, it is possible to say that low-cost projects that can be brought to the marketplace within one year will be favoured. There could be literally dozens of relevant criteria. Thus, checklists may best be used in a consensus-group setting, as a method for initiating conversation, stimulating discussion and the exchange of opinions, highlighting the group's priorities. The flaws in such a model include the subjective nature of such ratings as high, medium, or low. Such terms are inexact and subject to misinterpretation or misunderstanding. (Pinto, 2007).

Simplified Scoring Model

In the simplified scoring model, each criterion is ranked according to its relative importance. Organization's choice of projects will thus reflect the desire to maximize the impact of certain criteria on the final decision. In order to score the simplified checklist, is possible to assign a specific weight to each criteria. What there is the need to do, is to assign importance weights to each criterion, assign score values to each of them in terms of its rating (High= 3, Medium =2, Low= 1), multiply importance weights by scores to arrive at a weighted score for each criterion, add the weighted scores to arrive at an overall project score as the final score for each project becomes the sum of all its weighted criteria.

Analytical Hierarchy Process

The Analytic Hierarchical Process (AHP) technique was elaborated by Thomas L. Saaty at the Wharton School of the University of Pennsylvania at the end of 1970. The major benefit of AHP is that it provides the decision makers with a ranking of projects derived by paired comparisons against quantitative, but also qualitative criteria. AHP is a comparative approach, therefore it is easy to understand and use until the number of projects to compare remains sound (Saaty, 1980).

Profile Models

Profile models allow managers to plot risk/return options for various alternatives and then select the project that maximizes return while staying within a certain range of minimum acceptable risk. "Risk," for many, is a subjective assessment. All projects will be assigned some risk factor value and be plotted relative to the maximum risk that the firm is willing to assume. The profile model makes use of a concept most widely associated with financial management and investment analysis-the "efficient frontier". One advantage of the profile model is that it offers another alternative to compare project alternatives, this time in terms of the risk/return trade-off (Pinto, 2007).

The prioritization and selection process is a key moment in PPM as from this process organizations must acquire the best set of components to pursue their strategic objectives. As many other processes, this should be shaped around the level of maturity of the performing organization.

A Project Portfolio Management System Evolution

A PPM system cannot be implemented in few months and the sponsorship from Top Management is necessary but not sufficient to have a successful Portfolio Management System.

Based on the experience of the author, organizations can follow several paths in the development of a PPM and these paths despite their differences could drive to a successful implementation.

There are many aspects to consider when an Organization wants to start a PPM, in the following list are itemized the ones the author considers important for the objectives of this chapter:

1. The Change produced by a PPM.
2. The Sponsorship available.
3. The Extent of the PPM implementation.
4. The Processes to write/change.
5. The Software supporting the implementation.
6. The initiatives Prioritization and Selection model.
7. The External Connections to the PPM system.
8. The level of Completeness of the PPM system.

Any of these areas could be measured by some indicators.

For example, the Software used (5) could be "handmade" based on MS Office or with the purchase of a well-structured and somehow more professional PPM software.

For the scope of this paragraph it is possible to define these relevant indicators:

1. **Change:**
    a. PPM as a single stand-alone project.
    b. PPM as part of a bigger change Program.
    c. PPM driven Change Program.

2. **Sponsorship:**
   a. No sponsorship from Top Management.
   b. Sponsorship from Top Management.
3. **Extent:**
   a. PPM for a single Department/Area.
   b. PPM for the whole Organization.
4. **Processes:**
   a. Processes based on common sense.
   b. Processes formalized.
   c. PPM centralized office.
5. **Software:**
   a. PPM based on MS Office.
   b. PPM Software purchased.
   c. PPM Software utilized.
6. **Prioritization and Selection Model:**
   a. Prioritization and selection done subjectively.
   b. Prioritization and selection done with objective rules.
   c. Prioritization and selection based on strategic alignment.
7. **External Connections:**
   a. PPM culture and training disseminated.
   b. PPM and budgeting connected.
   c. PPM, PM, PMO connected.
   d. Strategy and Portfolio reviews during the year.
8. **Completeness:**
   a. Risk management in PPM.
   b. Resource allocation and balancing in PPM.
   c. Budget estimate in PPM.
   d. Projects interdependency in PPM.

These are many indicators, but more could be defined describing the level of maturity of the PPM system in an organization. Some are more complex than others. Some cannot be "switched on" too early or before others. In author's experience, there are some preferred paths followed by organizations. Some are counterintuitive. Gaining the right level of sponsorship is not always a prerequisite for a successful PPM system implementation (Romano, 2016).

In the following part of this paragraph two paths followed by real organizations will be presented, showing positive and negative aspects.

No Initial Sponsorship

It has been observed (International Insurance Company) an evolution of a PPM system starting from a situation described in Table 3. The relative case study showed that there was an evolution per year. In other scenarios the same evolution can be achieved in a shorter period of time. Bold indicators show an improvement or a change done from an evolution to another.

Table 3. No initial sponsorship evolution scenario

Area	Indicators		
	First Evolution	**Second Evolution**	**Third Evolution**
Change.	1.1.PPM as a single stand-alone project.	1.1.PPM as a single stand-alone project.	1.1.PPM as a single stand-alone project.
Sponsorship.	2.1.No sponsorship from Top Management.	**2.2.Sponsorship from Top Management.**	2.2.Sponsorship from Top Management.
Extent.	3.1.PPM for a single Department/ Area.	**3.2.PPM for the whole Organization.**	3.2.PPM for the whole Organization.
Processes.	4.1.Processes based on common sense.	4.1.Processes based on common sense.	**4.2.Processes formalized.** **4.3.PPM centralized office.**
Software.	5.1.PPM based on MS Office.	5.1.PPM based on MS Office.	5.1.PPM based on MS Office.
Prioritization & Selection.	6.3.Prioritization and selection based on strategic alignment.	6.3.Prioritization and selection based on strategic alignment.	6.3.Prioritization and selection based on strategic alignment.
External connections.	None.	None.	None.
Completeness.	8.3.Budget estimate in PPM.	8.3.Budget estimate in PPM.	**8.1.Risk management in PPM.** 8.3.Budget estimate in PPM. **8.4.Projects interdependency in PPM.**

As it is possible to notice, this is a scenario where top management sponsorship was gained on the way. The PPM project implementation started in a single department and was stand-alone and never used to create a wide change in the company. There was no use of a PPM software and the processes were formalized late in the life of the PPM system. The PPM was simple as its completeness was improved (but not all the areas were fully improved) after three years. On the contrary the prioritization model was immediately and professionally connected with the strategic objectives. Nevertheless, it was a successful implementation, creating an improvement in the governance of the company, creating new job opportunities. Later in the chapter this case study will be deeper analyzed.

Over Structured Toward Simplicity

The second scenario is completely different, presenting how a big public company evolved from an over-structured, formal and somehow unmanageable situation to a simpler one where PPM represented a change driver to pass through complexity.

In this scenario there was an already structured situation with a PPM software purchased but improperly utilized. PPM was one of the key activities of a well Top Management sponsored change program. A centralized PPM office was created. Nevertheless, the first implementation of the PPM system was within a single department (IT) with simple and subjective Portfolio components Prioritization & Selection model. As it is clear from the representation in Table 4, there was a huge improvement in the PPM system in the third evolution (but not all the areas were fully improved), maybe concentrating too much the added features to the PPM system.

This set of Areas and relevant Indicators can support organizations to analyze and shape their evolution toward a PPM implementation using past experience to anticipate problems and avoid pitfalls.

Table 4. Over structure toward simplicity evolution scenario

Area	Indicators		
	First Evolution	Second Evolution	Third Evolution
Change.	1.2. PPM as part of a bigger change Program.	1.2. PPM as part of a bigger change Program.	1.2. PPM as part of a bigger change Program.
Sponsorship.	2.2.Sponsorship from Top Management.	2.2. Sponsorship from Top Management.	2.2. Sponsorship from Top Management.
Extent.	3.1. PPM for a single Department/ Area.	**3.2. PPM for the whole Organization.**	3.2. PPM for the whole Organization.
Processes.	4.1. Processes based on common sense. 4.3. PPM centralized office.	**4.2. Processes formalized.** 4.3.PPM centralized office.	4.2. Processes formalized. 4.3. PPM centralized office.
Software.	5.1. PPM based on MS Office. 5.2. PPM Software purchased.	5.1.PPM based on MS Office. 5.2. PPM Software purchased. **5.3. PPM Software utilized.**	5.1. PPM based on MS Office. 5.2. PPM Software purchased. 5.3. PPM Software utilized.
Prioritization & Selection.	6.1. Prioritization and selection done subjectively.	6.1. Prioritization and selection done subjectively. **6.2. Prioritization and selection done with objective rules.**	6.2. Prioritization and selection done with objective rules. **6.3. Prioritization and selection based on strategic alignment.**
External connections.	None.	7.2. PPM and budgeting connected. 7.4. Strategy and Portfolio reviews during the year.	**7.1. PPM culture and training disseminated.** 7.2. PPM and budgeting connected. **7.3. PPM, PM, PMO connected.** 7.4. Strategy and Portfolio reviews during the year.
Completeness.	8.3.Budget estimate in PPM.	8.3.Budget estimate in PPM.	**8.1. Risk management in PPM.** 8.3. Budget estimate in PPM. **8.4. Projects interdependency in PPM.**

SOLUTIONS AND RECOMMENDATIONS

The main objective of the book is to provide the reader solutions and recommendations related to the PPM field, in this chapter the author wants to focus on three suggestions:

- PPM bottom-up implementation tactic as a possible first step in strategic planning.
- Evolve Analytic Hierarchical Process prioritization and selection method with Balanced Scorecards and Benefits Models.
- PPM system evolution implementation paths.

PPM Bottom-Up Implementation Tactic as a Possible First Step in Strategic Planning

One solution in the implementation of a Project Portfolio Management system when there is lack of initial sponsorship from Top Management is the one proposed by the author in the International Journal of Information Communication Technologies and Human Development Volume 8, Issue 3, July-September-2016 and here contextualized.

The application of PPM needs a strategy to refer to. How is it possible to proceed without a strategy?

This study wants to show how and why it is possible to use PPM to drive a formalized Strategic Planning and this way start an incremental loop toward a structured process that will improve the linkage between Strategy and projects implementation (Romano, 2016).

The case studies the author is referring to are four: a International Insurance Company, a web Bank, a traditional Bank, a Government Regional Office.

All of the case studies developed a PPM system starting from a department within the organization without an initial involvement of Top Management in the process. Their common starting point was that there was no sponsorship from the top. All case studies involved Top Management after the first "pilot" implementation period and this way of approaching affected their future path defining the strategy and managing projects. (Romano, 2016).

What to do when Strategic direction in not declared, or not known, as Top Management is not involved?

The approach followed was to use ongoing and new declared initiatives (more tangible than a not clear and not declared Strategy) to describe the strategic direction using PPM methodology to involve and convince not initially committed Top Management. It worked every time.

As written in the cited article:

In all our case studies the department requesting a PPM system for a better project portfolio management wasn't a direct extension of the Managing Director or the Board of Directors. The understanding of the Corporate Strategy was usually low.

During the initial phases of a PPM implementation process, we usually ask an evidence of the Corporate Strategy and only in one case we received a structured document. Nevertheless, this document was a very high level document and it was not sufficiently shared within the organization.

At this point the problem we always face is that it is impossible to screen and rank a list of old and new components without a set of selection criteria that reflects the strategy.

We have always solved this problem with a "pilot phase".

As the sponsorship of the PPM project was not high enough to involve in the process the right individuals, we have always defined a set of selection criteria with the people involved in the PPM implementation using their understanding of the strategy (supposed strategic direction).

The method we always followed to set-up the selection model was the application of the Analytic Hierarchy Process (AHP) and Pairwise Comparison (Romano, 2016).

Basically these steps were followed (Romano, 2016):

1. Break down the strategy perceived into interrelated elements, hierarchically ordered (Strategy Tree).
2. Establish the priority among the Alternatives/Projects using AHP and Pairwise Comparison. The weights were assigned on the basis of importance, preference and likelihood.
3. Produce a ranking of the Alternatives/Projects on the base of the produced benefits aligned with the strategy.
4. Evaluate the Alternatives/Projects on their likelihood to success (Risk analysis), Costs and Feasibility. After Benefits evaluation, is crucial to consider the projects under the other three fundamental axis.
5. Use a model to find the set of components with the highest sum of benefits score (also called priority) respecting defined constraints of budget, risk, feasibility.
6. Develop reports to support the implementation decision

As written in the cited article: *at the end of the "pilot" PPM project, results are usually presented to the Top Management. A hundred per cent of the times the Board of Directors asked the application of the process to the entire organization. As first step in the following "full PPM implementation", we went through the step 1 (Strategy Tree) with Top Management and in that activity we finally had the right people deciding the right criteria to breakdown the corporate strategy. PPM selection when well-structured and supported is relatively easy to apply and allows the change of some parameters, being immediately able to analyze the impact of these changes to the originally selected portfolio scenario. This is something Top Managers like very much.* (Romano, 2016)

It can be said that it is possible to proceed in PPM implementation without a good sponsorship and without a formal strategy to refer to.

Even when the PPM process is started bottom-up, the output is so valuable that the first implementation "moves" organizations toward the correct process and this involved the right people to participate and to "formalize" the Corporate Strategy in implementation objectives.

It can be summarized why this is possible (Romano, 2016):

1. The method is both simple and solid.
2. The reports produced are very professional and show the organization from a new point of view.
3. When the prioritization and selection model is flexible lets the Managers to "play" with hypothesis with an immediate feedback.
4. The first pilot implementation is fast and results are far better than expectations.

Why PPM Could Be a First Step in the Creation of a Formalized Strategic Planning Process within an Organization

After the selection of a Portfolio of components, the implementation phase begins. Selected components should be planned (or re-planned if ongoing) in detail and then realized producing deliverables, outcomes and benefits. This starts the implementation, monitor & controlling loop of activities. During the implementation phase, components and portfolio status reports are realized. Detailed reports show how single components are going, if they are meeting their objectives and if they are on track (time, cost, quality).

Moreover, Portfolio reports show whether the entire Portfolio is moving to the right direction and how much the holistic view of the Portfolio is still compliant with the organization's strategy. This second point of view is new to organizations without a strategic planning process in place, where initiatives are evaluated singularly and not as a whole (Romano, 2016). This analysis should assess and measure not only the outputs produced by the components, but also the real benefits realized and their alignment with the strategic direction (Romano, 2013b).

The Board of Directors during the implementation phase is usually very busy and are interested only in status reports. Especially during the first implementation year, after the strong interest produced by the PPM selection phase, companies are back on business as usual. But there will be a Team who will be assigned the responsibility to follow the PPM that knows that there will be the need to re-apply the process for the next coming year and to do this, there will be the need of a clear strategy defined from the Top (Romano, 2016).

This is the sparkle created by the PPM that will force a better strategic planning from the Top Management. Aware of the results and pushed from the bottom, companies have developed, communicated and broken down clearer strategies in the years following a first PPM implementation.

Instead of remaining in the Managing Director's mind, strategic objectives have been discussed and defined as they will be used to assess and select the components. This improves the way strategies are worked out. In fact intangible concepts are difficultly transformed into actions. (Romano, 2016)

Corporate Strategy – Business Unit Strategy – Strategy in action – Strategy implementation is the right process to develop a Strategic Planning and a PPM system letting the organization to grow (Romano, 2016).

Evolve Analytic Hierarchical Process Prioritization and Selection Method with Balanced Scorecards and Benefits Models

One of the common way to prioritize and select the initiatives of a portfolio is the already mentioned Analytic Hierarchical Process.

The major benefit of the Analytic Hierarchical Process (AHP) technique is that it provides the decision makers with a ranking of projects derived by paired comparisons against quantitative but also qualitative criteria. AHP is a comparative approach, therefore it is easy to understand and use until the number of projects to compare remains sound.

Simplifying, there are 3 steps in the AHP (Romano, 2013a):

1. Breaking down the decision problem into interrelated elements, hierarchically ordered. The three major levels are the general objectives or goals, criteria and alternatives. The number of levels depends on the complexity of the decision, meaning that more complex decisions may demand sub-criteria, allowing more specificity to the process. Usually, a top-down approach is followed in order to simplify the braking down of the criteria.
2. AHP uses Pairwise Comparison to establish the priority among the alternatives. Pairwise Comparison is crucial for the AHP model. The weights are assigned on the basis of importance, preference, and likelihood. The ratio given by the evaluation of a couple of alternatives in terms of their importance, preference, and likelihood represents the relationship between them. As a matter of fact, it allows comparing factors that are not objective figures like numbers, but subjective judgments. The fundamental scale created by Saaty helps in assigning a numeric value from 1 to 9 to qualitative judgments. The result of this comparison is the degree of importance of each element, which

can be used to build a matrix, one for each alternative in respect of each criterion or sub-criteria, and one to evaluate the importance of each criterion relative to general objective.

3. Sensitivity analysis is also performed in order to understand to what extent does a change in scores affect the entire process. Being AHP dependent on assigned weighted scores, a variation in this phase may vary the ranking. "What-if" scenarios can be useful for managers to have a picture of what would happen if different weights are assigned.

Simplifying the AHP steps are:

1. Breakdown your decision / objective / strategy in criteria and sub-criteria.
2. Assess the importance of each criterion relative to the general objective.
3. Evaluate each alternative in respect of each criterion and general objective.
4. Establish the priority among the alternatives.

This is the technique that can be applied as a support of any kind of decision.

How can an organization apply AHP to Portfolio Management? These are the steps to follow (Romano, 2013b):

1. Gather and study the information available about the Company and the market to have a clear understanding of the business.
2. Gather and study internal documents about the future Strategic Direction.
3. Meet and interview executives to get their opinions and ideas about the future development of the company.
4. Organize meetings with the executives (sometimes called *Strategic Portfolio Committee*):
    a. In the first part of the first meeting the company strategy must be broken down into AHP criteria and every criterion into sub-criteria. This process will continue till an agreement is found within the participants. These criteria and sub-criteria must be able to be used as indicators to assess the alternatives in their ability to fulfill the strategic objectives.
    b. In the second part of the first meeting the criteria and the sub-criteria must be weighted on the basis of importance, preference and likelihood. This process is done using a method called *Pairwise* (Saaty, 1999). One of the major strengths of AHP is the use of Pairwise Comparison to derive accurate ratio scale priorities, instead of using traditional approaches of 'assigning' weights. This process compares the relative importance, performance or likelihood of two elements with respect to another element in the level above. A judgment is made as to which is more important and by how much. There are three modes for Pairwise Comparison: numerical, verbal, and graphical. As usual this process will continue till an agreement is found within the participants.
    c. In the next days the result of the work done is distributed to participants and everyone can analyze and change what decided together.
    d. After an adequate amount of time another meeting is organized to stabilize and define the final criteria / sub-criteria matrix that will be used to assess the initiatives. Criteria and sub-criteria could be grouped (clusters/baskets) and used only to assess the initiatives belonging to each group.

5. Prepare "a template" to evaluate every initiative (ongoing or new) on the criteria / sub-criteria defined. This evaluation happen following these steps:
   a. Demand: the Departments / Functions / Business Units will collect their action plans for the next year (or any future period of time the Portfolio is referred to). This means also to re-analyze the actual ongoing and to design new proposals.
   b. New initiatives: every proponent (the sponsor of the proposal) must fill the template that usually has 2 parts. One part contains the description of the initiative (Business Case): the objectives, budget, scheduling, team, etc.. The other part is the evaluation template where for every sub-criterion the proponent assigns a score on the basis of how much the initiative fulfill the sub-criterion. Within this template a separate section based on the same methodology to evaluate the level of risk could be created.
   c. Ongoing initiatives: the original assessment should be updated and revised, in particular whether the original criterion were modified.
   d. After negotiations and reviews a final set of assessed initiatives is sent to the Strategic Portfolio Committee.
6. During the Portfolio Selection & Adjustment the Strategic Portfolio Committee has to select the final portfolio analysing the several portfolio scenarios available using some criteria:
   a. Analyze and compare the benefits theoretically generated from the scenario selected and showed in the sum of the scores they received in the evaluation template.
   b. Analyze, assess and define the level of risk of the scenarios.
   c. Calculate the investment needed for the scenarios.
   d. Analyze and assess the feasibility (resources availability, scheduling, capabilities, etc..) of the scenarios.
   e. Take care of the mandatory projects that must be included in any scenario.
   f. Consider the balance between ongoing components to be completed and new initiatives.
   g. Consider the Departments / Functions / Business Units level of contribution in the chosen scenario as all the organizational structure should be represented.
7. Formally release and communicate the approved portfolio and start the implementation activities.

In 2013 the author tried to implement an evolution in an AHP-PPM system. The original model was evolved using Balanced Scorecard (BSC).

BSC could represent for the Organization an opportunity to improve their poor Strategic Planning. Furthermore, the original AHP-PPM system suffered a sort of "isolation" from the pre-existing processes and tools as it was managed as a stand-alone system.

Studying BSC was clear that there were many point of contact with an AHP-PPM system (especially during the selection phase) and in some way AHP-PPM covers areas left uncovered from the BSC.

Balanced Scorecard (BSC) is a performance measurement framework that adds strategic non-financial performance measures to traditional financial metrics to give managers and executives a more 'balanced' view of organizational performance (Kaplan & Norton, 1996).

Kaplan and Norton describe the innovation of the balanced scorecard as follows:

The balanced scorecard retains traditional financial measures. But financial measures tell the story of past events, an adequate story for industrial age companies for which investments in long-term capabilities and customer relationships were not critical for success. These financial measures are inadequate, however, for guiding and evaluating the journey that information age companies must make to create future value through investment in customers, suppliers, employees, processes, technology, and innovation.

The BSC presents managers with four different perspectives from which to choose measures. It complements traditional financial indicators with measures of performance for customers, internal processes, and innovation and improvement activities.

Quoting again Kaplan & Norton (Kaplan & Norton, 1996):

The objectives and the measures for the Balanced Scorecard are more than just a somewhat ad hoc collection of financial and nonfinancial performance measures; they are derived from a top-down process driven by the mission and strategy of the business unit. The Balanced Scorecard should translate a business unit's mission and strategy into tangible objectives and measures. The measures represent a balance between external measures for shareholders and customers, and internal measures of critical business processes, innovation, and learning and growth.

The measures are balanced between:

- *The outcome measures.*
- *The results from past efforts.*
- *The measures that drive future performance.*

And the scorecard is balanced between:

- *Objective, easily quantified outcome measures.*
- *Subjective, somewhat judgmental, performance drivers of the outcome measures.*

BSC wants to translate an organization's vision into a set of performance indicators distributed among the famous four perspectives:

1. Financial.
2. Customer.
3. Internal Business Processes.
4. Learning and Growth.

The four perspectives of the scorecard permit a balance between shorthand long-term objectives, between outcomes desired and the performance drivers of those outcomes, and between hard objectives measures and softer, more subjective measures.

1. Financials

The BSC retains the financial perspective since financial measures are valuable in summarizing the readily measurable economic consequences of actions already taken. Financial performance measures indicate whether a company's strategy, implementation, and execution are contributing to bottom-line improvement. Financial objectives typically relate to profitability-measured, for example, by operating income, return-on-capital employed or economic value-added.

2. Customers

In the customer perspective of the BSC, managers identify the customer and market segments in which the business unit will compete and the measures of the business unit's performance in these targeted segments. This perspective typically includes customer satisfaction, customer retention, new customer acquisition, customer profitability, market and account share in targeted segments.

3. Internal Business Processes

This perspective focuses on the internal business results that lead to financial success and satisfied customers. To meet organizational objectives and customers' expectations, organizations must identify the key business processes at which they must excel. Key processes are monitored to ensure that outcomes will be satisfactory. Traditional approaches attempt to monitor and improve existing business processes. The scorecard approach will usually identify entirely new processes at which an organization must excel to meet customer and financial objectives.

4. Learning and Growth

This perspective looks at:

- The ability of employees.
- The quality of information systems.
- The effects of organizational procedures.

in supporting accomplishment of organizational goals.

Processes will only succeed if adequately skilled and motivated employees, supplied with accurate and timely information, are driving them. The financial, customer, and internal-business-process objectives on the Balanced Scorecard will reveal large gaps between the existing capabilities of people, systems, and procedures and what will be required to achieve breakthrough performance achieving through investments in re-skilling employees, enhancing information technology and systems, and aligning organizational procedures and routines.

Every perspective has 4 columns (Table 5). In the first column the chosen objectives are described.

Referring to what written from Kaplan & Norton (Kaplan & Norton, 1996):

Table 5. The four columns of the Balanced Scorecards

Objectives	Measures	Targets	Initiatives

- **Objectives:** They are the short- and long-term tangible strategic objectives derived from an organization's vision and strategy. Some organizations attempt to decompose the high-level strategic objectives of the business unit scorecard into specific objectives at the operational level. For example, an on-time delivery (OTD) objective on the business unit scorecard can be translated into an objective to reduce setup times at a specific machine, or to a local goal for rapid transfer of orders from one process to the next.
- **Measures:** In formulating customer objectives for the scorecard it will become clear that each executive had a different definition as to what (for example) "superior service to targeted customers" represents and who were the targeted customers. The process of developing operational measures for the scorecard brought consensus among the executives. The measures are financial and nonfinancial and are balanced between the "***outcome measures*** (lag indicators)" the final results from past efforts: Return on equity, Customer retention, New product revenue, etc. - and the "***performance drivers*** (lead indicators)" that drive future performance: Satisfaction Survey, Product Development Cycle, Revenue Mix, etc. ... Citing Kaplan & Norton "*even 20 to 25 measures across the four perspectives, could communicate and help implement a single strategy (...)*". So rather than view the multiple measures as requiring complex trade-offs, the strategic linkages enabled the scorecard measures to be tied together in a series of cause-and-effect relationships. Collectively, these relationships described the strategic trajectory".
- **Targets:** The targets refer to the scorecard measures that, if achieved, will transform the organization. The targets should represent a discontinuity in business unit performance: doubling the return on invested capital in the next year, or a 150% increase in sales during the next five years, etc. .
- **Initiatives:** They are the actions an organization puts in place in the attempt to successfully transform themselves in the future, these initiatives must be aligned with what stated in the BSC.

The steps to implement BSC defined by Kaplan & Norton can be summarized as described in Table 6 (Kaplan & Norton, 1996).

As should be evident reading the BSC methodology, the similarities between what stated from Kaplan & Norton and the idea of AHP-PPM system are numerous.

In Table 7 there is a summarization done by the author of the connections between the two methodologies.

On the basis of these connections it is possible to say that:

1. An approved BSC is a perfect input for the AHP-PPM initiatives evaluation template where Objectives and Measures can be translated into criteria and sub criteria.
2. The AHP-PPM Pairwise methodology, used to assess relative importance of criteria could support the balancing activity within the BSC.
3. The implementation (Action plan) step defined by Kaplan & Norton in the BSC could be easily covered from AHP-PPM methodology.
4. The Measures and Targets defined in the BSC in connection with the AHP-PPM reporting and controlling system are ideal to monitor that the organization is following the original Strategic Direction.
5. The periodic reviews aiming to keep the BSC aligned with the strategic direction and the AHP-PPM controlling and reporting system can converge in a single process.

Table 6. BSC implementation steps

1. Preparation	***2. Interviews: First Round***
The organization must first define the business unit for which a top level scorecard is appropriate. In general, a scorecard is appropriate for a business unit that has its own customers, distribution channels, production facilities, and financial performance measures.	*Each senior manager in the business unit—typically between 6 and 12 executives— receives background material on the balanced scorecard as well as internal documents that describe the company's vision, mission, and strategy. The balanced scorecard facilitator conducts interviews with the senior managers to obtain their input on the company's strategic objectives and tentative proposals for balanced scorecard measures.*
3. Executive Workshop: First Round	***4. Interviews: Second Round***
The top management team is brought together with the facilitator to undergo the process of developing the scorecard. During the workshop, the group debates the proposed mission and strategy statements until a consensus is reached. The group then defines the key success factors: "If I succeed with my vision and strategy, how will my performance differ for shareholders; for customers; for internal business processes; for my ability to innovate, grow, and improve?" After defining the key success factors, the group formulates a preliminary balanced scorecard containing operational measures for the strategic objectives.	*The facilitator reviews, consolidates, and documents the output from the executive workshop and interviews each senior executive about the tentative balanced scorecard.*
5. Executive Workshop: Second Round	***6. Executive Workshop: Third Round***
A second workshop, involving the senior management team, their direct subordinates, and a larger number of middle managers, debates the organization's vision, strategy statements, and the tentative scorecard. At the end of the workshop, participants are asked to formulate stretch objectives for each of the proposed measures, including targeted rates of improvement.	*The senior executive team meets to come to a final consensus on the vision, objectives, and measurements developed in the first two workshops; to develop stretch targets for each measure on the scorecard; and to identify preliminary action programs to achieve the targets. The team must agree on an implementation program, including communicating the scorecard to employees, integrating the scorecard into a management philosophy, and developing an information system to support the scorecard.*
7. Implementation	***8. Periodic Reviews***
A newly formed team develops an implementation plan for the scorecard, including linking the measures to databases and information systems, communicating the balanced scorecard throughout the organization, and encouraging and facilitating the development of second-level metrics for decentralized units.	*Each quarter or month, a blue book of information on the balanced scorecard measures is prepared for both top management review and discussion with managers of decentralized divisions and departments. The balanced scorecard metrics are revisited annually as part of the strategic planning, goal setting, and resource allocation processes.*

Source: Kaplan & Norton, 1996

Table 7. Similarities between BSC and an AHP based portfolio management system

BSC	**AHP-PPM**
BCS aims to translate a business unit's mission and strategy into tangible objectives and measures.	To implement the AHP-PPM system there's the need to breakdown the Strategic Direction into criteria and sub-criteria.
The scorecard is balanced between: objective, easily quantified outcome measures and subjective, somewhat judgmental, performance drivers of the outcome measures.	AHP allows comparing factors that are not only objective figures like numbers, but subjective judgments.
BSC wants to create a balanced set of Objectives-Measures, on this set there's the need to find a common understanding and agreement.	AHP-PPM aims to weight the several criteria on the basis of their importance, performance or likelihood for the participants, a choice and a judgement is made, an agreement must be found.
BSC is focused on translating mission and strategy into tangible objectives and measures; from there, initiatives must be defined.	AHP-PPM is focused on assessing how much initiatives are aligned with the Strategic direction.

6. An actual project portfolio could be assessed in a "BSC way". This means to verify whether your Portfolio is balanced between the four BSC perspectives.
7. The components contained in an actual portfolio could be assessed in their linkage with the Strategic Objectives declared from a Company inserting them as initiatives in a BSC and analysing the resulting cause-and-effect relationships map.

An overview on an implementation of this idea could give the reader more indications. The case study refers to a banking and insurance multinational company. This organization started from the 10 Strategic Objectives declared for 2013:

1. Maintain profitability MOTOR Business Unit (BU).
2. Increase profitability NON MOTOR BU.
3. Increase Revenues MOTOR and NON MOTOR BU.
4. Increase Revenues LIFE Business Unit.
5. Reduce General expenses.
6. Increase processes efficiency.
7. Complete Project "ALPHA".
8. Decrease number of complaints.
9. Improve Managerial culture.
10. Improve Brand awareness.

The organization worked on the Strategic objectives listed above with a BSC point of view and first assigned these objectives to the four perspectives (Table 8).

Then was analysed how many initiatives (Projects) of the approved portfolio were possible to allocate to each perspective/objective how shown in Table 9.

Observations:

- The situation does not look so balanced between perspectives.
- The objectives were heterogeneous and some looked sub-objectives of others.
- Mapping the initiatives on the strategic objectives was not easy at all as there was not a clear link between them → their objectives → the strategy, despite the fact there was a PPM system in place.

Table 8. Case study strategic objectives mapped with BSC

Financial	Customers	Internal Business Processes	Learning and Growth
1. Maintain profitability MOTOR BU.	8. Decrease the number of complaints.	6. Increase processes efficiency.	9. Improve Managerial culture.
2. Increase profitability NON MOTOR BU.	10. Brand awareness.	7. Complete Project ALPHA.	
3. Increase Revenue MOTOR and NON MOTOR BU.			
4. Develop LIFE BU.			
5. General Expenses reduction.			

Table 9. An application of BSC approach to an existing portfolio

Objectives	Measures	Targets	Initiatives	
Financial				
1. Maintain profitability MOTOR BU.	Comb. Ratio (*Claims costs / Premiums*): 94%.	2013	7	28
2. Increase profitability NON MOTOR BU.	Comb. Ratio (*Claims costs / Premiums*): 96%.	2013	2	
3. Increase Revenue MOTOR and NON MOTOR BU.	53 Mln Euros / + 4%.	2013	10	
4. Develop LIFE BU.	Agency Channel + 10%. Banks Channel +100%.	2013	1	
5. Reduce General Expenses.	5% per year.	2013	8	
Customers				
8. Decrease number of complaints.	From 4.800 to 2.500 per year.	2013	3	7
10. Improve Brand awareness.	Aided Awareness 24%.	2013	4	
Internal Business Processes				
6. Increase processes efficiency.	Improve project BETA with 2 more structures.	2013	21	24
7. Complete Project ALPHA.	Complete roll-out.	30 June 2013	3	
Learning and Growth				
9. Improve managerial culture.	Feedback meetings for +60% employees. 13.000 training hours same budget 2012.	2013	1	

To further analyse the declared objectives and support the implementation of a consistent BSC-AHP system was decided to use an idea from G. J. Rankins (G.J. Rankins, 2006). Strategic mapping and Benefits models were then mixed together.

Benefits models create a cause-effects diagram to map the alignment of the projects with the strategic objectives. Benefits model analysis also assures that each strategic objective will be adequately served by projects.

Starting from the original idea, benefits models use a cause-effect chain that was used in this this way:

DRIVER → OBJECTIVE → BENEFIT ← OUCOME ← OUTPUT ← INITIATIVE

As stated by Rankins: *"Benefits are defined as the quantifiable and measurable improvement resulting from an outcome (..) Dependencies between benefits will influence the sequencing and prioritisation of projects and benefit realisation activities (..) A Benefit Model covering the entire set of benefits should be created in order to understand the interrelationships between benefits and the various projects in the program's portfolio".*

In the presented case study, the cause-effect sequence was modified to make the model applicable to the specific situation and one of the results (based on a sub-set of the Strategic objectives) is shown in Figure 4.

Figure 4. The original simplified "under construction" benefits map in the case study

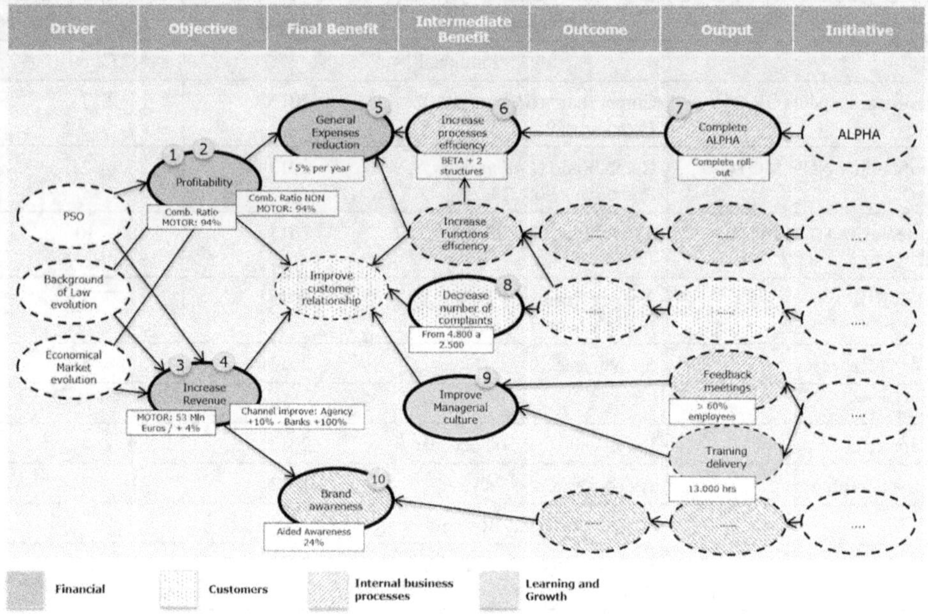

Where numbers are the ID of the objectives and the colours are the BSC perspectives. The dotted ovals show items inserted to build the map and not originally considered in the Strategical statement. This application is useful as mapping causes and effects shows, for example:

- When objectives and benefits are not sufficiently served by initiatives.
- When it is not defined the expected outcome (change).
- When a connection between objectives and benefits is missed.
- When there is a break-down somewhere in the conceptual flow.

To design such cause-effect diagram there is the need to deeply analyse the motivations behind any of the Objectives and to add more information and more detail than what written in a company brochure. This process is very valuable.

Key remarks are:

- Even if the process should move from left to right from the objectives to the initiatives the process works conversely to validate and map the alignment of an existing portfolio with the strategic objectives.
- Doing such a mapping for the entire set of objectives and initiatives is complex and very time consuming but surely less expensive than pursuing initiatives not aligned with the strategic direction.
- This map connected with the BSC is valuable during the Portfolio setup and during the Portfolio monitoring as if any BSC Objective will have Measures and Targets, the initiatives aiming to achieve these objectives will need to have and meet measures and targets consistent with the objectives they will contribute to accomplish.

How to use what analysed and detailed with the Benefit Map in a BSC-AHP portfolio selection model is very straightforward.

Basically the four BSC perspectives can be translated in the AHP criteria and the objectives into the AHP sub-criteria. In some cases, depending on the level of breakdown, BSC objectives can be translated into AHP criteria & sub-criteria as between the four perspectives objectives could be linked by cause-effect connections.

For example, without considering the un-balancing of the original strategy formulation, the 10 objectives were translated into an AHP criteria/sub-criteria tree like in Figure 5 (where level 2 are the criteria and level 3 are the sub-criteria).

Next step should be to assess the importance of each criterion relative to the general objective. This AHP process applied to a BSC structure will force executives to re-analyse objectives as "improve managerial culture" could be considered less important than "increase profitability NON MOTOR BU".

Organizations can then use the BSC sub-criteria to evaluate the initiatives in their potential to (in the example):

- Maintain profitability in the MOTOR BU.
- Decrease the number of complaints.
- Complete Project ALPHA.
- Etc.

The question will be: "*how much this initiative will: decrease the number of complaints?*"

The final output will be an evaluation template as described earlier based on the BSC.

BSC provides AHP-PPM system with another important input: Measures.

Measures could be used as a reference in the activity of assigning a score (during Screening) on the basis of how much the initiatives (actual and proposed) respect the sub-criterion.

Figure 5. An AHP criteria/sub-criteria tree based on a BSC structure

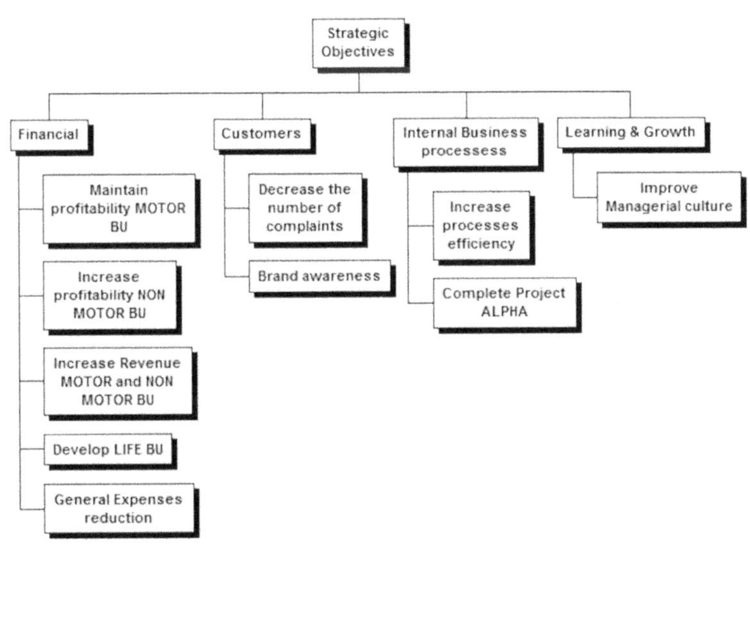

The aggregated Measures to assess the projected success of the selected portfolio are then in the "measures" and "targets" columns of the BSC.

On the basis of what written so far it is possible, in Table 10, to summarize a process that connects strategy with actions using BSC in connection with an AHP-PPM system.

This to create a single Management System from Strategy definition to projects selection, implementation and control.

PPM System Evolution Implementation Paths

Based on what presented in the previous paragraph "A Project Portfolio Management System evolution" in author's mind there is a better way to both shape the evolution of a PPM system, and using the Areas and the relevant Indicators listed below in Table 11.

Surely, every path must be shaped around the organizations, their past history, maturity and ability to manage organizational change. In some case a fourth evolution is needed, in very few cases two are sufficient. In any case this is just a starting point.

FUTURE RESEARCH DIRECTIONS

Future and emerging trends in Portfolio Management could be summarized in the following set of issues:

- Definition of the roles and the relationship between Project Managers and Portfolio Management and generalizing how organizational structures fit with Project Portfolio Management.
- Connections and synergies between the budgeting and control system and Portfolio Management.

Table 10. Steps in applying BSC in connection with AHP in a PPM system

Activity	Output
Design the BSC following the Kaplan & Norton steps 1 to 6.	Draft Balanced Scorecard.
Transform the BSC into an AHP criteria/sub-criteria tree and eventually review the BSC to be compliant with such a use.	• Final Balanced Scorecard. • AHP criteria/sub-criteria Tree.
Assess the importance of each criterion relative to the general objective following the AHP methodology and applying Pairwise.	AHP criteria/sub-criteria weighted tree.
Develop a draft Benefit Model based on the BSC and the AHP Tree.	Draft Benefit Model (without enablers).
Prepare a template to evaluate every initiative (ongoing and new) on the criteria / sub-criteria defined.	• AHP initiatives evaluation template. • Demand (ongoing and new).
Assess every initiative on the evaluation template and collect final set of assessed initiatives.	Final set of evaluation templates.
Execute Portfolio Selection & Adjustment activities developing Benefits Models for top 3 portfolio scenarios.	• Top 3 portfolio scenarios. • Final Benefits Models.
Balance, chose, release and communicate the approved portfolio.	Approved project portfolio.
Set-up a Project Portfolio reporting and controlling system connected with BSC objectives, measures and targets.	BSC / AHP-PPM reporting and controlling system.

Table 11. Optimal suggested PPM evolution scenario

Area	Indicators		
	First Evolution	**Second Evolution**	**Third Evolution**
Change.	1.1. PPM as a single stand-alone project.	1.3. PPM driven Change Program.	1.3. PPM driven Change Program.
Sponsorship.	2.2. Sponsorship from Top Management.	2.2. Sponsorship from Top Management.	2.2. Sponsorship from Top Management.
Extent.	3.1. PPM for a single Department/ Area.	3.2. PPM for the whole Organization.	3.2. PPM for the whole Organization.
Processes.	4.1. Processes based on common sense. 4.2.Processes formalized.	4.2. Processes formalized. 4.3.PPM centralized office.	4.2. Processes formalized. 4.3. PPM centralized office.
Software.	5.1. PPM based on MS Office.	5.1. PPM based on MS Office. 5.2. PPM Software purchased.	5.3. PPM Software utilized.
Prioritization & Selection.	6.3. Prioritization and selection based on strategic alignment.	6.3. Prioritization and selection based on strategic alignment.	6.3. Prioritization and selection based on strategic alignment.
External connections.	7.2. PPM and budgeting connected.	7.1. PPM culture and training disseminated. 7.2. PPM and budgeting connected.	7.1. PPM culture and training disseminated. 7.2. PPM and budgeting connected. 7.3. PPM, PM, PMO connected. 7.4. Strategy and Portfolio reviews during the year.
Completeness.	8.3. Budget estimate in PPM.	8.1. Risk management in PPM. 8.3. Budget estimate in PPM. 8.4. Projects interdependency in PPM.	8.1. Risk management in PPM. 8.2. Resource allocation and balancing in PPM. 8.3. Budget estimate in PPM. 8.4. Projects interdependency in PPM.

- A wide research verifying the paths followed by organizations in implementing their Project Portfolio Management Systems.

CONCLUSION

Project Portfolio Management is a wide discipline full of interconnections with other matters. PPM supports the connection between Strategy and actions and is a great opportunity for organizations to improve their Strategic Management process simplifying the complexity associate to the existence of too many heterogeneous processes and not coordinated roles. Following chapters are focused on giving an overview on many key aspects of Project Portfolio Management. With PPM organizations will be able to better shape their future and accept changes with the right level of flexibility.

REFERENCES

Archer, N., & Ghasemzadeh, F. (2007). Project portfolio selection and management. In P. W. G. Morris & J. K. Pinto (Eds.), *The Wiley Guide to Project Program & Portfolio Management* (pp. 94–112). Hoboken, NJ: John Wiley & Sons. doi:10.1002/9780470172391.ch11

Baker, N. R., & Freeland, J. (1975). Recent advances in R&D benefit measurement and project selection methods. *Management Science, 21*(10), 1164–1175. doi:10.1287/mnsc.21.10.1164

Baker, N. R., & Pound, W. H. (1964). R and D project selection: Where we stand. *IEEE Transactions on Engineering Management, Volume, EM-11*(4), 124–134. doi:10.1109/TEM.1964.6446420

Benko, C., & McFarlan, F. W. (2003). *Connecting the dots*. Boston: Harvard Business School Press.

Box, S., & Platts, K. (2005). Business process management: Establishing and maintaining project alignment. *Business Process Management Journal, 11*(4), 370–387. doi:10.1108/14637150510609408

Cleland, D. I. (1999). The Strategic Context Of Projects. In *Project Portfolio Management: Selecting ad Prioritizing Projects for Competitive Advantage*. Centre for Business Practices.

Cooper, R. G., Edgett, S. J., & Kleinschmidt, E. J. (2002). Portfolio management: fundamental to new product success. In P. Belliveau, A. Griffin, & S. Somermeyer (Eds.), *The PDMA Toolbook for new product development*. Hoboken, NJ: John Wiley & Sons.

Doerner, K., Gutjahr, W., Hartl, R., Strauss, C., & Stummer, C. (2006). Pareto ant colony optimization with ILP preprocessing in multiobjective project portfolio selection. *European Journal of Operational Research, 171*(3), 830–841. doi:10.1016/j.ejor.2004.09.009

Dye, L. D., & Pennypacker, J. S. (1999). *Project Portfolio Management: Selecting ad Prioritizing Projects for Competitive Advantage*. Centre for Business Practices.

Engwall, M., & Jerbrant, A. (2003). The resource allocation syndrome: The prime challenge of multi-project management? *International Journal of Project Management, 21*(6), 403–409. doi:10.1016/S0263-7863(02)00113-8

Goldratt, E. M. (1997). *Critical Chain*. Great Barrington, MA: North River Press.

Kaplan, R. S., & Norton, D. P. (1996). *The Balanced Scorecard – translating strategy into action*. Harvard Business School Press.

Krumm, F. V., & Rolle, C. F. (1992). Management and application of decision and risk analysis in Du Pont. *Interfaces, 22*(6), 84–93. doi:10.1287/inte.22.6.84

Lagace, M. (2003). *Putting the Project Puzzle Together*. Harvard Business School Working Knowledge. Available at http://hbswk.hbs.edu/item/3389.htm

Leliveld, I., & Jeffery, M. (2003). *IT portfolio management challenges and best practices*. Kellogg School of Management.

Levine, H. (2005). *Project Portfolio Management: A Practical Guide to Selecting Projects, Managing Portfolios, and Maximizing Benefits*. Jossey Bass.

Lycett, M., Rassau, A., & Danson, J. (2004). Programme management: A critical review. *International Journal of Project Management*, *22*(4), 289–299. doi:10.1016/j.ijproman.2003.06.001

Markowitz, H. M. (1992, March). Portfolio Selection. *The Journal of Finance*, *7*(1), 77–91.

Martinsuo, M., & Lehtonen, P. (2007). Role of single-project management in achieving portfolio management efficiency. *International Journal of Project Management*, *25*(1), 56–65. doi:10.1016/j.ijproman.2006.04.002

McFarlan, F. W. (1981). Portfolio Approach to Information Systems. Boston. *Harvard Business Review*, *59*(5), 142–150.

McGrath, G. R., & Macmillan, I. C. (2000). Assessing technology projects using real options reasoning. *Research-Technology Management*, *43*(4), 35–49.

Meredith, J. R., & Suresh, N. C. (1986). Justification Techniques for Advanced Manufacturing Technologies. *International Journal of Production Research*, *24*(5), 1043–1057. doi:10.1080/00207548608919787

Morris, P., & Pinto, J. K. (2007). *The Wiley guide to project, program, and portfolio management*. Hoboken, NJ: Wiley & Sons.

Payne, H. (1995). Management of multiple simultaneous projects: A state-of-the-art review. *International Journal of Project Management*, *13*(3), 163–168. doi:10.1016/0263-7863(94)00019-9

Petro, Y., & Gardiner, P. (2015). An investigation of the influence of organizational design on project portfolio success, effectiveness and business efficiency for project-based organizations. *International Journal of Project Management*, *33*(8), 1717–1729. doi:10.1016/j.ijproman.2015.08.004

Pinto, J. K. (2007). *Project management: Achieving competitive advantage* (3rd ed.). Upper Saddle River, NJ: Prentice Hall.

Project Management Institute (PMI). (2013). *The standard for portfolio management* (3rd ed.). Newtown Square, PA.

Rankins, G. J. (2006) Aligning Projects to Strategy using Balanced Scorecards and Benefits Models. *Proceedings 3rd International Conference on Project Management*.

Romano, L. (2013a). *Rise and Fall of Project Portfolio Management: Triumph and Collapse: A Case Study*. Paper presented at the 2013 PMI Global Congress, Istanbul. Turkey.

Romano, L. (2013b). *How to evolve a Project Portfolio using Balanced Scorecards: a case study*. Paper presented at the 2013 PMI Global Congress, New Orleans, LA.

Romano, L. (2014). *Corporate Strategy for PMs. Why strategic alignment and awareness is so important*. Paper presented at the 2014 PMI Global Congress, Dubai. UAE.

Romano, L. (2015). *Vision-Strategy-Objectives-Projects-Outputs & return. Do we need an ultimate management model?* Paper presented at the 2015 PMI Global Congress, Orlando, FL.

Romano L. (2016). Corporate Strategy from the Bottom: Project Portfolio Management Can Help Clarify Your Strategy. *International Journal of Information Communication Technologies and Human Development, 8*(4), 34-50.

Romano, L., Grimaldi, R., & Colasuonno, F. S. (2016). *Demand management as a critical success factor in Portfolio Management*. Paper presented at the 2016 PMI Global Congress, Barcelona. Spain.

Saaty, T. L. (1980). *The Analytic Hierarchy Process*. New York: McGraw-Hill.

Saaty, T. L. (1999). *Decision Making for Leaders: The Analytic Hierarchy Process for Decisions in a Complex World*. Pittsburgh, PA: RWS Publications.

Shenhar, A. J., Dvir, D., Levy, O., & Maltz, A. C. (2001). Project Success: A Multidimensional Strategic Concept. *Long Range Planning, 34*(6), 699–725. doi:10.1016/S0024-6301(01)00097-8

Vergara, A. J., & Boyer, L. T. (1977). Portfolio theory: Applications in construction. *Journal of the Construction Division, 103*(1), 23–38.

Wheelwright, S. C., & Clark, K. B. (1992). Creating project plans to focus product development. *Harvard Business Review, 70*(2), 70–82. PMID:10117370

KEY TERMS AND DEFINITIONS

Analytic Hierarchy Process: The Analytic Hierarchical Process (AHP) technique was elaborated by Thomas Saaty in Pennsylvania at the end of 1970. The major benefit of AHP is that it provides the decision makers with a ranking of projects derived by paired comparisons against quantitative but also qualitative criteria.

Benefit: Quantifiable and measurable improvement resulting from an outcome.

Project: A temporary systems or work systems that are constituted by teams within or across organizations to accomplish particular tasks under time constraints.

Project Management: Project management is the application of knowledge, skills and techniques to execute projects effectively and efficiently. It is a strategic competency for organizations, enabling them to tie project results to business goals — and thus, better compete in their markets.

Project Portfolio Management: centralized management of processes, methods, and technologies used by project managers and project management offices (PMOs) to analyze and collectively manage current or proposed projects based on numerous key characteristics.

Project Screening: Project Screening is an assessment of projects to select those which are not suitable for further consideration. Project screening includes completing a preliminary examination of the project opportunity to obtain an idea of whether the more time-consuming and costly effort for further business case development is reasonable.

Project Selection: Project Selection usually refers to choosing the best choice from various proposals based on some key indicators

Strategic Tree: A diagram used in strategic decision making, valuation or probability calculations.

Strategy: It is a high-level plan to achieve one or more goals under conditions of uncertainty.

Chapter 2
Inter-Relationships between an Enterprise's Strategic Management Process and Its Program/Project Portfolio Management Process

Russell Dean Archibald
Archibald Associates LLC, USA

ABSTRACT

This chapter describes and clarifies the boundaries between strategic management and project/program portfolio management (PPPM) processes, and identifies who holds primary responsibilities for key elements of these inter-related sets of management processes. The main issues considered include: The differences between strategic project management and operational project management. The elements in the strategic project management practices and processes that should be considered to be within the responsibility of 'project management.' The role of a typical PMO in relation to 1) strategic management processes, and 2) both the strategic and operational project management processes. The importance of identifying the differences between transformative and commercial projects and programs and also between the major categories of projects and programs within enterprises. The origins of the two basic types of projects within project-driven compared to project-dependent enterprises.

INTRODUCTION

In order to survive and prosper, all business, industrial, governmental, and non-governmental organizations must evolve and grow in response to economic, political, technological, and environmental changes. In order for the growth of any organization to be managed strategically and effectively, rather than reactively, the organization's strategic managers must design and implement a practical, coherent strategic growth management process. Since projects and programs are the primary vehicles that all enterprises use for

DOI: 10.4018/978-1-5225-2151-8.ch002

their growth and survival, these vehicles must be managed within appropriate portfolios to achieve the greatest results in the shortest time and with the least expenditure of scarce resources. This Chapter describes these two fundamental management processes and explains their interconnections.

1. Part 1, The Strategic Growth Management Processes Within an Enterprise, presents and discusses a proven five phase strategic growth management process and briefly describes the responsibilities of the strategic managers and planners involved in this important process.
2. Part 2, Project/Program Portfolio Management (PPPM), presents and discusses a typical 12 step process for defining and managing a portfolio of projects, shows how this process is related to the five phase strategic growth management process, and discusses the division of the responsibilities for the two processes. It also discusses the various ways to identify project and program portfolios from the strategic management perspective.
3. Part 3, Project and Program Types and Categories, describes the need for properly identifying the various possible types of projects, programs, and their portfolios from the project management perspective, and describes the important differences between transformative and commercial projects and programs. Because creating new projects is the key to success in strategic growth management,
4. Part 4, The Origins of Projects and Programs, describes the various origins of projects for project-driven versus project-dependent organizations, and for transformative versus commercial projects and programs.
5. Summary and Conclusion, summarizes the Chapter and presents the major conclusions that can be drawn from the information presented.

MAIN FOCUS OF THE CHAPTER

Part 1: The Strategic Growth Management Processes within an Enterprise

Strategic Planning is a comprehensive process for determining what a business should become and how it can best achieve that goal. It appraises the full potential of a business and explicitly links the business's objectives to the actions and resources required to achieve them. Strategic Planning offers a systematic process to ask and answer the most critical questions confronting a management team, especially large, irrevocable resource commitment decisions (Bain & Company, 2015).

Senior line managers in the organization are the creators of the growth strategies and the "owners" of the projects that will carry them out, with a designated project sponsor with executive responsibility for each project, and a project manager as the focal point of integrated responsibility and accountability for planning and executing each one. Strategic management sets the future course of the organization and selects the projects to be added to the project portfolios. Project management plans, authorizes and executes the specific efforts that implement the growth strategies. The managers of these projects are acting for and representing the project owners, and receive their direction through the project sponsor (Archibald 2003, p 15).

Building on strategic, long-range planning and related management processes developed over the past decades, well-managed enterprises today utilize *integrated strategic growth management processes* to define, approve and control their current and future growth plans and the related actions that are required to achieve their agreed strategic objectives. These "growth plans and related actions" mainly consist of portfolios of programs and projects.

Figure 1 illustrates a widely used five-phase strategic growth management process that has been applied across a number of industries, business sectors, and governmental and non-governmental agencies in several countries. The integrated processes summarized in Figure 1 incorporate and use the fundamentals of several strategic planning approaches, including, for example, *competitive strategies, business environment assessment, industry structure analysis* (Porter, 2008); *portfolio analysis* using the *Boston Consulting Group's Box* (BCG, 2008); plus a number of others. This five phase process is used by firms across the economic spectrum, though it was developed to offer working managers who are responsible for their own strategic planning a simple-to-follow process that moves their planning initiative from concept fully through implementation.

This Growth Management Process for Strategic Management provides a powerful roadmap for the strategic management team to follow in the required sequence to produce the desired growth and survival of any enterprise.

Phase 1: Describe the Relevant Environment - Develops the information necessary to have in hand in order to draw the required conclusions that will lead to committing to the future direction for the organization. The crossroad issues, which are those key issues that will determine which direction (size, markets, geography, products, technologies, and other dimensions) that the enterprise will take in the coming years, must be identified, documented, and agreed. The planning process to be used must also be agreed and the information that is needed must be identified and collected. The business environment of the enterprise must be documented.

Figure 1. The Growth Management Process for Strategic Management™
Source: GMC, 2012, copyright 2012 by Growth Management Center, Inc., www.agendas.net. Used with permission.

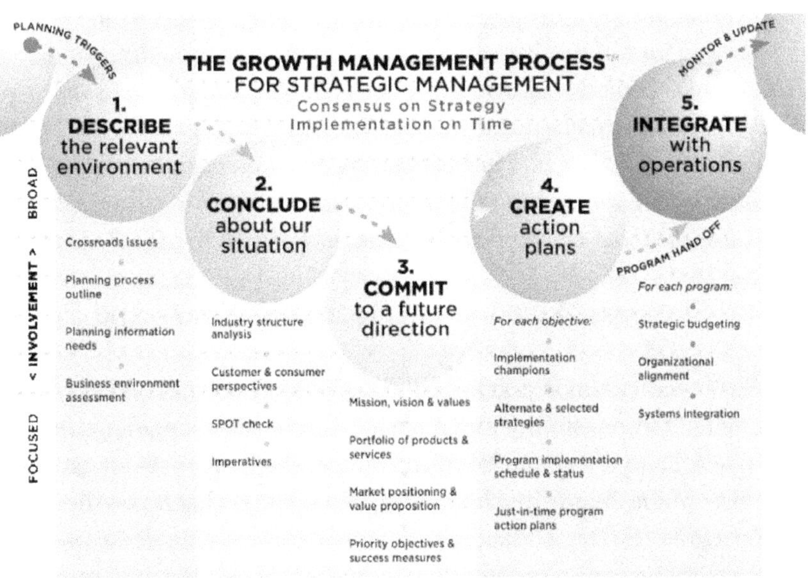

Phase 2: Conclude About Our Situation - Provides the important conclusions that will be used during Phase 3. These include an accurate structural analysis of the industry in which the enterprise is operating, sound perspectives of the enterprise's customers and consumers, SPOT (Strengths, Problems, Opportunities, and Threats) evaluations, and the applicable key imperatives (those facts, situations, and goals that cannot be changed or ignored.)

Phase 3: Commit to a Future Direction - Documents the strategic goals and objectives of the enterprise. Only after the results of the first two phases are available is it possible to document the mission, vision and values of the enterprise. In this phase the agreed portfolios of products and services for the future are defined. The strategic priority objectives are documented related to market positioning and the enterprise's value proposition, and the means of measuring success in achieving these objectives are defined and agreed. It should be noted that some strategic planning processes start with a statement of the company's mission, but experience has shown that only after Phases 1 and 2 of the process in Figure 1 are completed can valid statements of the Mission and Vision for the organization be prepared or revised and accepted.

Phase 4: Create Action Plans - Develops for each alternative strategic objective the possible programs and projects that can be envisioned and selects the best of these to be integrated with ongoing operations within the limits of available resources.

Phase 5: Integrate with Operations - Develops integrated budgets and schedules, assigns responsibilities, and initiates the work needed to plan, execute and control the selected programs and projects in coordination with the ongoing operations of the enterprise.

Phases 4 and 5 overlap and must be integrated with the project, program, and portfolio management (PPPM) concepts and methods within the enterprise. As stated by Robert Eskridge, the principal developer of this Growth Management Process:

The CREATE phase is the timing interface between strategic decisions (Priority Objectives in the COMMIT phase) and "handing off" programs which have already been scheduled, vetted and resourced, to those who will guide their implementation. The interface between decisions and implementation is the unique role of Project Management in strategic planning. For mid-market businesses, which are typically not large enough to have a formal project management function or formally-trained project managers, it is the SIMPLICITY of the project management approach which guarantees that strategic objectives will be implemented. In our experience, when more complex project management approaches are thrust upon mid-market business executives, the project management element dies of its own complexity and weight. Breaking the objective down into stages, and sequencing those stages is the value added by project management, even without PM software or trained PM's (Eskridge R, 2016).

Responsibilities for Strategic Management Decisions, Plans, and Processes

In the 1980s and 1990s it was common practice for a senior staff person, typically with a title like Vice President - Planning, to hold responsibility for preparing a company's long range or strategic plan for the coming one to three years. This person would typically interview various senior executives to obtain their views of what the future of the enterprise should be, then collect what he or she felt was the pertinent information, and prepare the "Strategic Plan." Such plans were often elaborate projections to which the key senior executives of the company were not necessarily committed, and were rarely fully implemented.

Today the senior executives who are responsible for execution of strategic management decisions at corporate and major operating division levels of an organization are also held responsible for creating the integrated strategic growth plans that incorporate these strategic decisions. These strategy managers include the chief executive officer/CEO and other senior corporate level executives, directors and managers of subsidiary business units, functional area managers within a subsidiary business unit, and directors or managers of major operating departments, product line and geographic units.

At the Board of Directors level the strategic roles are to:

- See that strategic management tasks and processes (see Figure 1) are performed adequately.
- Review important strategic moves and officially approve strategic plans.
- Ensure that strategic proposals are adequately analyzed and superior to alternatives.
- Evaluate the caliber of top management's strategy-making and implementing skills (Thompson & Strickland, 2003. Slides 49 and 53).

The Role of Strategic Planners

The "C Level" executives in most large organizations today hold direct strategic responsibilities for the portions of an enterprise for which they are responsible. However, in many organizations one or more people are identified as "Strategic Planners," who may report to the CEO or the CIO.

The role of strategic planners includes these important responsibilities:

- Collect information needed by the strategy managers.
- Conduct background analyses as needed.
- Establish and administer an annual strategy review cycle.
- Coordinate the review and approval of strategic plans.
- Assist all managers to focus on strategic issues (Thompson & Strickland, 2003. Slides 49 and 53).

Planners should not make strategic decisions or do strategic thinking for strategic managers, because:

1. Planners usually know less about the situation, placing them in a weaker position than line managers to devise workable action plans; and
2. This practice separates responsibility and accountability for strategy-making from implementing.

This is a major flaw in strategic management within many organizations. It allows managers to hand off decisions to planners and avoid doing their own strategic thinking, and the result is that implementers have little or no "buy in" or commitment to someone else's strategies.

In the following Part 2 the relationships and interfaces between the strategic and the PPPM processes are discussed in more detail.

Part 2: Project/Program Portfolio Management (PPPM) (Archibald, 2015)

As enterprises mature in the project management discipline they recognize that programs and projects, like all investments, must be managed on a portfolio basis. Multi-project or program management is a step in the right direction, but more formalized project portfolio management goes beyond traditional program management. The key differences between portfolio and multiple project management are shown in Table 1.

Types of Project/Program Portfolios from a Strategic Perspective

Within a small enterprise there may be only one overall corporate project/program portfolio, but in large organizations it generally makes more sense to define more than one portfolio on a strategic basis to reflect product line, geographic or technological divisions of the organization. In these larger organizations portfolios are defined and identified in several ways. In general, a project portfolio is a group of several "delivery" or "commercial" projects that are related to a well-defined major strategic objective, as illustrated below in Figure 2. Strategic transformative projects and programs, discussed later in paragraph 3.1, may be managed either within a portfolio or as stand-alone efforts, depending on their size and complexities.

Portfolios can be named to indicate the nature of the strategic objectives they are meant to achieve. Generic examples include:

- **Value-Creating:** New or improved product, service, or market.
- **Operational Process Improvement:** Projects that make the organization more efficient and satisfy some fundamental functional work.
- **Compliance:** "Must-do" projects required to maintain regulatory compliance (Combe & Githens, 1999).

Alternatively, portfolios can be identified to indicate their innovative purpose. According to Harvard Professor Clayton M. Christensen (Christensen, 2012):*executives and investors might finance three types of innovations with their capital*, and he goes on to identify these three portfolio types:

1. Empowering innovations that create jobs, because they require more and more people who can build, distribute, sell and service these products. Empowering investments also use capital – to expand capacity and to finance receivables and inventory.
2. Sustaining innovations that replace old products with new models.... They keep our economy vibrant — and, in dollars, they account for the most innovation. But they have a neutral effect on economic activity and on capital.
3. Efficiency innovations that reduce the cost of making and distributing existing products and services.... Taken together in an industry, such innovations almost always reduce the net number of jobs,

Table 1. High-level comparison of project portfolio management and multiple project management

	Project Portfolio Management	Multiple Project Management
Purpose	Project selection and prioritization	Resource allocation
Focus	Strategic	Tactical
Planning Emphasis	Long & medium-term (annual/quarterly)	Short-term (day-to-day)
Responsibility	Executive/senior management	Project/resource managers

Source: Dye & Pennypacker, 2000

> because they streamline processes. But they also preserve many of the remaining jobs — because without them entire companies and industries would disappear in competition against companies abroad that have innovated more efficiently.

An objective is a statement of where we want to go and a strategy describes how we are going to get there. A strategic growth plan for a large organization will contain several strategic objectives. Often it is difficult to relate these strategic objectives to the ongoing operations of the enterprise. It can be beneficial to define more specific operational strategies that will achieve the strategic objective. For example, the strategic objective may be to enter a new international market with existing products or services. Operationally this can be achieved either by 1) acquiring or partnering with an existing company, or 2) establishing a new venture there. Depending on which of these is chosen, the projects or programs to achieve the strategic objective will be very different. This hierarchy of objectives, strategies, programs and projects is illustrated in Figure 2.

Others have defined other types of project portfolios that reflect the specific organizational and industrial environments that are involved, as shown in these references: Pellegrinelli (1997), Dye and Pennypacker (1999), United Kingdom Government, Best *Management Portfolio: Management of Portfolios (2002), PMI The Standard for Portfolio Management, 3rd ed.(2013b).* Further discussion of project, program, and portfolio categorization from the project management perspective is presented below in Part 3.

In whatever manner an enterprise defines their commercial, innovative, and transformative project portfolios they must establish an effective process for managing these portfolios.

Figure 2. Schematic of strategies, projects, a program and a project portfolio
Source: Archibald 2003, p 13.

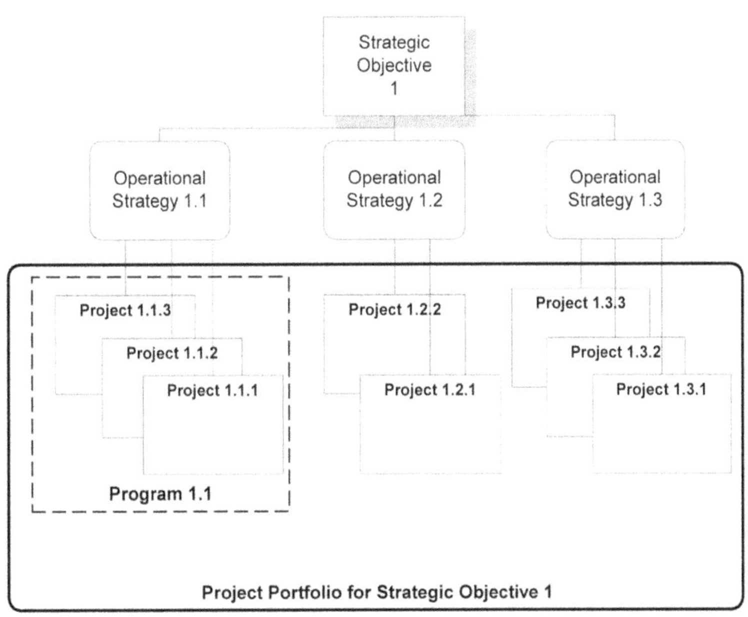

Strategic Project Management: The Project/Program Portfolio Management (PPPM) Process

A typical project/program portfolio management process consists of the following 12 steps (not always in this identical sequence) that are related as shown here to Phases 4 and 5 in the Strategic Management Process in Figure 1:

Strategic Process "Phase 4. Create Action Plans" includes these six PPPM steps:

1. Define and re-define as needed the project portfolios required.
2. Define the project types and categories (see Part 3 below) that exist within each portfolio based on established criteria.
3. Identify and group all current and proposed projects (see paragraph3.5 below) within their appropriate categories, programs, and portfolios.
4. Validate all projects within each portfolio with the organization's strategic objectives.
5. Prioritize projects within programs and portfolios.
6. Establish and maintain a key resources data bank showing limitations over time.

Strategic Process "Phase 5. Integrate with Operations" includes PPPM Steps 7 to 12:

7. Allocate available resources to programs and projects within each portfolio.
8. Develop and approve each project portfolio master schedule.
9. Compare financial needs for current and proposed projects with availability within each portfolio.
10. Decide how to respond to shortfalls in money or other key resources and approve the list of currently funded and new projects and their priorities within each portfolio.
11. Define, plan, schedule. authorize, and manage each program and project and its risks using the organization's established project management/PM processes and supporting systems and tools for each project's category, size and risks. This step comprises the entire practice of what has traditionally been thought of as "project management."
12. Periodically repeat these 11 steps to reprioritize, reallocate resources to, and reschedule all programs and projects as required within each portfolio.

In organizations that are mature in their PPPM capabilities a *Project Portfolio Steering Group* or *Portfolio Governance Committee* is responsible for this portfolio management process and for making the decisions that are involved in its effective use, with support for all twelve steps from the appropriate Project Management Office/PMO, but most specifically for Steps 6, 8 and 11. This PPPM process is actually the *strategic project/program management process* for the organization, and application of this process is the responsibility of the strategy managers (discussed earlier in paragraph 1.1) of the enterprise. Step 11 can be considered to be the *operational project/program management process* that is the direct responsibility of one or more PMOs within the enterprise.

Managing the Strategic Project/Program Portfolio Management Processes

As discussed earlier, executives and senior managers – the 'strategy managers' of the organization – hold responsibility for managing the overall Project/Program Portfolio Management process, and for making the important strategic decisions resulting from application of this process. For each project portfolio there usually will be a Project Portfolio Steering Group comprised of the responsible strategy managers from within the affected parts of the organization. The appropriate PMO will usually have broad responsibilities relating to the on-going, operational project management (Step 11) of all active projects and programs within the active portfolios. The PMO typically will also provide significant project manager and staff support relating to the current status of all active projects and programs, or 'portfolio components,' such as earned value to date of each project, plus their risk management status, etc., that will be vital inputs to the periodic review (Step 12) of the PPPM process.

The PMO will usually provide the preliminary master project schedules for new projects being considered for selection and authorization. However, the resulting decisions – selecting new projects, changing project priorities, re-allocating resources, project cancellation or major changes in project scope, etc. – reach into the strategic and line authority of senior executives. This is especially true when a portfolio contains one or more "transformative" projects or programs (discussed later in Part 3). Many PMOs presently lack the expertise needed to objectively apply the strategic analyses that are required to properly advise these senior executives on these important strategic decisions. Granted, this expertise can be developed within a PMO, but only time will tell if the project management discipline will be allowed to, in effect, take over the strategic decision-making for much or all of an organization, or whether the existing strategic discipline will gain the needed expertise to fully exploit the power of project management methods in strategic management of the enterprise. The discipline of strategic planning and management is presently rather highly developed, as can be seen at www.sps.org.uk/ or www.strategyplus.org/ plus other related web sites.

Project/Program Portfolios are primarily useful at the strategic level to determine if the proper 'balanced portfolios' have been achieved regarding the expenditure of money and other scarce resources to reach the strategic objectives of the enterprise. It is unlikely that project portfolios will often be managed in the same manner as a multi-project program is supposed to be, unless the portfolio consists entirely of 'commercial' or 'delivery' projects (see Part 3 below). Because of the strategic nature of project portfolios, in most situations the use of a 'plural executive' is recommended, such as a Project/Program Portfolio Steering Group (Archibald 2003, pp 177-179) or a PPPM Governance Council (Levine 2005, p 58) to make on-going major decisions regarding projects and programs within a specific portfolio.

Operational Project Management

Operational project management includes application of all the knowledge areas and processes described in the PMI PMBOK Guide (PMI 2013a), including the specific practices, systems and methods to be used for defining, work authorization, planning, and controlling projects and multi-project programs. These operational PM responsibilities include, for each project and program within each portfolio and for each defined project type and category:

- Select and assign project and program managers.
- Design/select/apply the best project life-cycle models for each project type and category.
- Select and implement the specific project planning, scheduling, executing, and controlling methods and software tools to be used.

The actual selection and approval for execution of transformative projects and programs (see paragraph 3.1 and Part 4 below) is within the scope of strategic project management. Carrying out the detailed project definition, planning, scheduling, work authorization, reporting, and controlling methods and systems is within the scope of operational project management.

Project Portfolio Management Information System Applications

One of the greatest remaining challenges today for enterprises wanting to achieve the full benefits of effective project portfolio management is to adapt and implement a truly integrated and fully capable information system that provides the needed project/program/portfolio planning, scheduling, estimating, accounting, evaluating, reporting, and risk management information that is efficiently integrated with the corporate accounting and resource management information systems.

Some of the most widely used project portfolio management information systems include:

- Advanced Management Solutions: Realtime Enterprise.
- CA Technologies.
- Compuware Changepoint.
- Dekker, Ltd: Dekker Trakker.
- Deltek Integrated Program Management.
- HP Project and Portfolio Management Center.
- IBM Rational Software.
- Microsoft: MS Project and Project Server.
- Oracle Primavera P6 Enterprise Project Portfolio Management.
- Planview Enterprise Portfolio Management.
- SAP Portfolio and Project Management.
- Safran North America: Project Management Toolkit.
- Spider Project.

Details related to each of these information systems can be found by searching these names online.

The Need for One Integrated System Within an Enterprise

In larger organizations project management capability frequently develops independently in various parts or divisions of the enterprise over the years, creating islands of expertise, knowledge, and experience. Often these islands are using different project and program management information systems that have been developed internally or licensed from different providers. This creates a difficult integration problem when top management decides that a project portfolio management system is now required for the total corporation. While it is technically possible in many cases to tie several different systems together at some level, the best solution in the long term is to select one system that has all the capabilities needed both in the present situation and within the foreseeable future of the organization.It is useful to point out that Milrood (Milrood, 2011) says:

- Vision of a single software platform for PPM will not be achieved during the next three years.
- The high number of small success projects are promoting the adoption of agile and flexible tools.

- Companies are moving to faster, more iterative and lighter approaches that are results, not process driven.

The difficulty of integrating information from several project management information systems used within different parts of an organization has led to the development of systems like the Safran Project Management Toolkit, listed above. This Toolkit and its related software applications enable the effective, current integration of information from a number of separate project management systems to provide the current, integrated resource and schedule information needed to manage portfolios effectively at the total enterprise level.

This problem is especially acute within project-driven companies when several major customers demand that the company use a specific project management system to conform to the system that customer is using internally.The lack of full system integration results in faulty decisions caused by conflicting, inaccurate, and out-of-date information, and it also results in un-needed expense and high error rates caused by multiple entries of information into the various separate systems.The selection and implementation of one enterprise project portfolio information system in itself is a complex transformational project that requires the use of sound project management practices. The responsibility for such a project is usually given to a high-level Project Management Office(PMO).

Part 3: Project and Program Types and Categories

This Part3 continues the earlier discussion of defining project and program portfolios that was presented in paragraph 2.1, with further discussion of the differences between basic types of projects and programs and presentation of a methodology for systematically categorizing projects and programs for consideration when defining project and program portfolios, especially those that are intended to achieve the enterprise's strategic objectives.

Transformative vs. Commercial Projects (Archibald, 2015, pp. 15-16.)

It is necessary and useful to recognize the differences between:

- Major, strategic transformative projects and programs that are intended to change or transform the enterprise significantly and thereby achieve its strategic vision, mission and objectives.
- Routine "delivery", "commercial", "deployment", "process, service, product improvement", or "compliance" projects that generate income and profit, reduce cost, otherwise improve the services or products provided to the enterprise's customers or constituents, or comply with laws and regulations, within the enterprise's established strategic vision and objectives, without creating significant changes within the enterprise itself.

Pfeiffer (Pfeiffer, 2004) describes a useful approach to differentiating between what he calls "deployment" and "development" projects. Table 2 shows his comparison of these two project types.

In addition to these two types of projects and programs, there are two basic types of organizations that rely on project management for their continued success:

Project-Driven Organizations that:

Table 2. Basic differences of project types

Basic Differences of Project Types	
Deployment [Delivery] Project	**Development [Transformative] Project**
Civil construction. Installation of a system.	Development of new products. Organization of social change.
Advance measured by products. "Final Product" relatively clear.	Advance aimed at reducing uncertainties, measured by indicators.
Life Cycle generally cascade.	Various life cycles possible.
Leadership style based on command and control.	Leadership style focused on learning.
Highly structured information system.	Less formal communication system.
Task oriented organization of Human Resources.	Human Resources need to adapt and evolve in order to respond to changes.
Progress relatively linear.	Processes very dynamic.

Source: Pfeiffer, 2004, p 5.

- Rely on "delivery" projects for normal revenue.
- Are usually mature in the management of these "delivery" projects.
- May be less mature in management of transformative programs and project.

Project-Dependent Organizations that:

- Derive most of their revenues from selling products or services and not from selling projects.
- Are often not very mature in the management of their project management capabilities.
- Rely on projects and project management for expansion or development of new products or processes.
- Often employ Project-Driven organizations for specific needs, especially for parts of their transformative projects and programs.

Examples of *project-driven* enterprises include architect/engineer/constructor, general contractor, and specialty contractor firms; software development firms who sell their products or services on a contract basis; telecommunications systems suppliers; consultants and other professional services firms; and other organizations that bid for work on a project-by-project basis. Growth strategies in such organizations are reflected in the type, size, location and nature of the projects selected for bidding, as well as the choices made in how the required resources will be provided (in-house or out-sourced) to carry out the projects, if and when a contract is awarded or the project is otherwise approved for execution.

The second class of organizations—those that are *project-dependent* for growth— includes all others that provide goods and services as their mainstream business. Projects within these organizations are primarily internally sponsored and funded. Examples include manufacturing (consumer products, pharmaceuticals, engineered products, etc.), banking, transportation, communications, governmental agencies, computer hardware and software developers and suppliers, universities and other institutions, among others. These organizations depend on projects to support their primary lines of business, but projects are not their principle offering to the marketplace. Many of these sponsors of internally funded projects are important buyers of projects from project-driven organizations.

It is important when defining project and program portfolios for strategic planning purposes to recognize whether your organization is project-driven or project-dependent, and also to recognize whether specific projects and programs are considered to be "commercial" or "delivery" in nature or "transformative." Transformative projects and programs will almost always require full application of the best available project management methods and the most experienced program managers. These programs are discussed in the following section.

Transformative Programs

While the traditional definition of a program as *consisting of a group of related projects* (PMI 2013b, p. 552) is still widely used in many industries and governmental agencies, in recent years most authorities observe that program management has evolved in many organizations to encompass a broader range of activities with broader objectives.

Thiry (Thiry, 2010. p.16) defines program management as *The governance and harmonized management of a number of projects and other actions to achieve stated business benefits and create value for the stakeholders.* It is better to differentiate this from the traditional definition of a program by using Thiry's definition to refer to strategic transformative programs. The "other actions" in his definition are typically ongoing operations within the enterprise, and the broader objectives "to achieve stated business benefits and create value for the stakeholders" are predominantly strategic in nature.

This new definition shows us that a strategic transformative program is truly an enterprise within the parent enterprise, whereas a typical commercial project, with its limited scope, time, and well-defined objectives and deliverables, is just that: a project. There can of course be large, major projects (in addition to strategic programs) that are truly strategic and transformational in nature. Several commercial projects do not usually make a strategic program, in this latest understanding of what an enterprise-changing program is.

All Significant Innovations Are Achieved through Projects/ Programs (Archibald 2015, pp 3-4.)

When the reader is persuaded that the above statement is valid then it is obvious that all executives in every kind of human enterprise need to know the characteristics of projects and how best to govern and manage projects, programs, and their portfolios. Achieving strategic objectives will invariably require significant innovations within the enterprise.

Some notable characteristics of innovation are:

- The starting point for innovation is the generation of creative ideas. Innovation is the process of taking those ideas to market or to usefulness.
- Innovation concerns the search for and the discovery, experimentation, development, imitation and adoption of new products and services, new processes and new organizational arrangements.
- Innovation is the conversion of knowledge and ideas into a benefit, which may be for commercial use or for the public good; the benefit may be new or improved products, processes or services.
- Innovation is the process that transforms ideas into commercial value.
- Innovation = Invention + Exploitation.

A project is the best – perhaps only – method of achieving innovation.

Structured, well-managed innovation depends on application of sound project management principles and practices, as illustrated in Figure 3.

The alternative of simply throwing an idea on the table at a staff meeting and seeing if anyone will start making it happen will not get the job done. Innovation begins in every case with an idea generated by an individual, or sometimes by a small group of people collaborating to solve a problem, develop a new product or service, or create and satisfy a customer need. Transforming that idea into the reality of something new – a new or improved process, service, or product, or even a new enterprise – is rarely if ever the result of one person's effort, even though one person will lead the effort as the project manager.

This transformation requires a structured approach to:

1. Bring together all the skills and other resources needed in a structured team and
2. To define the resulting project in terms of its objectives, scope, cost and other resources, together with its schedule for completion. This is project management at the basic level.

Defining Project, Program, and Portfolio Categories from the Project Management Perspective

In addition to defining project/program portfolios from a strategic perspective, as discussed above in Part 2, consideration must be given to the type and category of the specific projects and programs that a portfolio contains, as well as the sources of funding that will pay for the projects and programs. This section presents useful information regarding how best to define and identify portfolios from the project management perspective.

Practical experience over many decades in managing the several types and many categories of projects has led to:

Figure 3. Every innovation is a project
Source: Archibald, 2013.

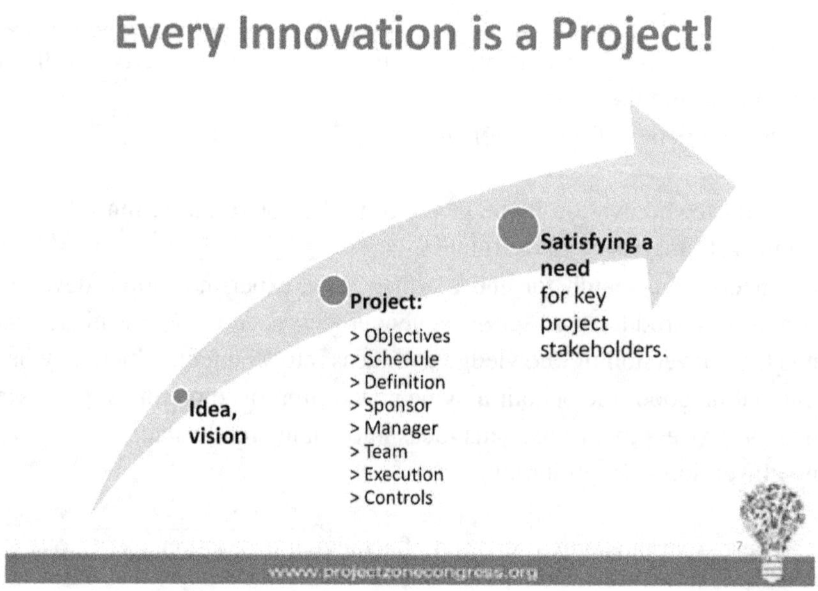

- Recognition, definition and understanding of the project management principles and practices that are common to all (or at least many) projects in all types of human endeavors and organizations, as documented in the several PM bodies of knowledge and the PM literature in general; and also
- Recognition that the diversity inherent within the many existing and potential projects demands that projects be segregated in several ways for several purposes to continue to improve the ways in which both the buyers (owners) and sellers (contractors or developers) of projects:
    1. Strategically select and prioritize their projects.
    2. Operationally plan and execute their projects individually, within programs, and within project portfolios.
    3. Educate and train the managers and specialists involved in projects and PM; and
    4. Develop and manage the careers of managers and specialists involved in projects.

For example, for strategic purposes projects are often categorized by market share and strategic intent or in the other ways that have been discussed in Part 1 of this Chapter, but for operational purposes they are often grouped in twelve project categories based on the end results of each project, and identifying the most appropriate project life cycle model used for each category, as shown in Table 3.

Another example of the need for systematic project categorization relates to whether predictive or adaptive project life cycle models will be used for a particular project category, and which of the many models within each of the project types is best for a specific project: Agile, SCRUM or Extreme Programming/XP are often used for IT projects, but not for capital facilities design and construction or for very many other categories of projects.

Part 4: The Origins of Project and Programs (Archibald 2015, pp 20-21)

One of the most challenging aspects of strategic project/program management is the creation of new transformative and innovative projects and programs that will achieve the strategic growth objectives that have been established within an enterprise's strategic growth plan. Where do these projects and programs originate? This Part 4 explores and discusses this question.

Systemic vs. Incremental Innovation

Systemic innovation differs from incremental innovation that can be accomplished within a single company context or within a discrete project context. Prieto (Prieto, 2011) states that:

Systemic innovation is that form of innovation that requires multiple specialist firms to change their process in a coordinated fashion.

Examples of systemic innovation in the engineering and construction industry include:

- *Integrated supply chain management.*
- *Prefabrication of building systems.*
- *3D CAD virtual design and construction tools.*
- *Building Information Models (BIM).*
- *Project Finance Initiatives (PFI) and Public Private Partnerships (PPP).*

Table 3. Project categories/sub-categories with each category having similar project life cycle phases and project management process

Project Categories with Similar Life Cycle Project Management Models/Processes	Examples
• Aerospace/Defense Projects o Defense systems o Space o Military operations	• New weapon system; major system upgrade. • Satellite development/launch; space station modification. • Task force invasion.
• Business & Organization Change Projects o Acquisition/Merger o Management process o Improvement o New business venture o Organization re-structuring o Legal proceeding	• Acquire and integrate competing company. • Major improvement in project management. • Form and launch new company. • Consolidate divisions and downsize company. • Major litigation case.
• Communication Systems Projects o Network communications systems o Switching communications systems	• Microwave communications network. • 4th generation wireless communication system.
• Event Projects International events National events	• 2012 Summer Olympic Games; 2014 World Cup Match. • 2013 U. S. Super Bowl; 2016 U. S. Political Conventions.
• Facilities Projects o Facility decommissioning o Facility demolition o Facility maintenance and modification o Facility design-procurement-construction ▪ Civil ▪ Energy ▪ Environmental ▪ High-rise ▪ Industrial ▪ Commercial ▪ Residential ▪ Ships	• Closure of nuclear power station. • Demolition of high rise building. • Process plant maintenance turnaround. • Conversion of plant for new products/markets. • Dam; highway interchange. • Power generation plant; pipeline. • Chemical waste cleanup. • 40 story office building. • New manufacturing plant. • Shopping center; office building. • New housing sub-division. • New tanker, container, or passenger ship.
Information Systems (Software) Projects	New project management information system(Information system hardware is in the product development category).
• International Development Projects: o Agriculture/rural development o Education o Health o Nutrition o Population o Small-scale enterprise o Infrastructure: energy (oil, gas, coal, power generation and distribution), industrial, telecommunications, transportation, urbanization, water supply and sewage, irrigation)	People and process intensive projects in developing countries funded by The World Bank, regional development banks, US AID, UNIDO, other UN, and government agencies; and Capital/civil works intensive projects—often somewhat different from *5. Facility Projects* as they may include, as part of the project, creating an organizational entity to operate and maintain the facility, and international lending agencies impose their project life cycle and reporting requirements.
• Media & Entertainment Projects o Motion picture o TV segment o Live play or music event	• New motion picture. • New TV episode. • New opera premiere.
• Product and Service Development Projects o Information tech. Hardware o Industrial product/process o Consumer product/process o Pharmaceutical product/process o Service (financial, other)	• New desk-top computer. • New earth-moving machine. • New automobile, new food product. • New cholesterol-lowering drug. • New life insurance/annuity offering.
• Research and Development Projects o Environmental o Industrial o Economic development o Medical o Scientific	• Measure changes in the ozone layer. • How to reduce pollutant emission. • Determine best crop for sub-Sahara Africa. • Test new breast cancer treatment. • Determine if life exists on Mars.
Healthcare Projects	Major surgical procedure.
Other Categories?	Disaster recovery, other…

Source: Archibald, 2013, pp. 30-32

- *Modularization.*

Many of these are characteristic of successful large programs.

These important systemic innovations often require transformative programs within an individual enterprise for it to survive and prosper in the new industry environment.

Prieto refers to systemic innovation in the largest industry in the world, the engineering construction industry. In the USA this industry accounts for 9% of the GDP. Systemic innovation is also required in large, multinational companies as well as large governmental agencies. In smaller organizations systemic innovation can also produce useful results, but it is more likely that incremental innovation is more frequently used in most situations.

Innovation obviously depends on creative ideas. This discussion does not explore the sources of new ideas, but rather focuses on how to transform those ideas into desirable benefits. As Michael Ray and Rochelle Myers state in the introduction to their 1989 book Creativity in Business:

One of the main problems in U. S. business today is that there are too many ideas, not too few. Dozens of solutions appear and disappear in chaotic piles of data, crowds of expert opinion, and a jumble of contradictory statistics and reports on every aspect of every issue. The pressure of limited time is increased by indecision and, beneath it all, the nagging suspicion that others will find your efforts insufficient and the results poor.

The Project Incubation/Feasibility Phase (Archibald et al, 2012)

In the various PMI and IPMA standards for project and program management the project life cycle typically begins with a "Project Starting Phase." However, there is very little in the project management literature concerning where and how projects actually originate. In almost every case the standard "Project Starting Phase" must begin with a reasonable understanding of what the principle objectives, scope, desired schedule, and order of magnitude cost of the project are expected to be, including:

- What the project will create (new product, facility, service, information system, organization, other principle deliverables).
- What business benefits will be produced for the organization that will pay for the project, as will be detailed in the Business Case that is produced during the traditional Project Starting Phase.
- Verification that the project is aligned with the strategic plans and objectives of the sponsoring organization.
- A reasonable idea of the overall scope of the project together with its expected time schedule and cost, and whether the needed money and other key resources can reasonably be expected to be available, as will be verified and detailed in the Project Charter that is produced during the Project Starting Phase.
- Preliminary or conditional approvals that the project will require from governmental authorities or other agencies (environmental, economic, health, others) as well as any intellectual property and physical rights of access that are needed for the project to succeed.

- Overall economic, technological, political, social, and physical feasibility of the project, including the level and acceptability of the various risks that are involved.

A project will not normally be authorized to enter the Project Starting Phase until sufficient information, as listed above, is available and its feasibility has been established. The basic question here is:"Where does this initial 'embryonic knowledge and understanding' about the potential project come from?" This information will be accumulated through a process of "information buffering" over a period of time prior to authorizing any project to enter the current standard Project Starting Phase, and this occurs in every case during the usually undefined but always present Project Incubation/Feasibility Phase. We "buffer" and store in an appropriate manner the information about the embryo project, its scope, results and feasibility, and the cognitive constraints that exist within the project team members. This information buffering is similar to downloading a movie on your television set: the movie (or the project) cannot begin until sufficient data and knowledge has been obtained and compiled locally.

Origins of Two Project Types within Project-Driven and Project-Dependent Organizations

The origins of transformative and commercial projects and programs are rather different within each of the two type of organizations that have been identified. Table 4 summarizes the origins of:

1. Innovative, transformative projects and programs and
2. Commercial or delivery projects within project-drive and project dependent organizations.

It is worth noting that many transformational projects or programs include the purchase of delivery projects from outside suppliers that are actually project-driven companies or agencies. This depends on the internal decision whether to "buy" or to "make" the products or results for selected portions (sub-projects) of the transformational project or program.

CONCLUSION

Two Well-Integrated Management Processes Are Required. In order for the growth of any enterprise to be managed strategically and effectively, rather than reactively, the strategic managers within the enterprise must design and implement a practical, coherent strategic growth management process. Since projects and programs are the primary vehicles that all enterprises use for their growth and survival, these vehicles must be managed within appropriate portfolios to achieve the greatest results in the shortest time and with the least expenditure of scarce resources. Every organization therefore must have an established strategic growth management process that is integrated with its strategic project/program portfolio management/PPPM process.

Examples of These Two Management Processes Were Presented. A five phase Strategic Growth Management Process and a typical twelve step Project/Program Portfolio Management Process were presented, and the relationships between and responsibilities for these processes were discussed.

Strategic Versus Operational Project Management. The strategic PPPM process is the responsibility of the strategy managers of the organization with substantial support from the corporate and subordinate

Table 4. Origins of two project types within project-driven and project-dependent organizations

Project Type → Organization Type	Type 1: Commercial or Delivery Projects	Type 2: Development or Transformative Projects and Programs
Project-Driven Organizations	• Marketing or Business Development Department develops four project portfolios: o Customer relationship, o Network relationship, o Delivery, and o Offering portfolios (Tikkanen et al 2007). o They evaluate requests for proposals/RFPs from customers that result from usually long-lasting relationships and extensive marketing efforts, or develop proposals initiated internally. • Project proposals that comply with well-established strategic goals and are within the known capabilities of the organization are prepared and approved prior to submittal to the customers. • Project Starting Phase is not initiated until a proposal is negotiated and a contract is signed by both parties. • A full-time Project Manager is usually appointed only during the Project Starting Phase. • Project management functions must be applied in proposal preparation but frequently they are not.	Statements below for Project-Dependent Organizations also apply here to Project-Driven Organizations.
Project-Dependent Organizations	Few if any commercial/delivery projects exist in project-dependent organizations. If so the above comments apply.	• Ideas for transformative projects/programs for major organizational change; acquisitions; mergers; or new markets, products, processes or services come from strategic managers, marketing - business development, R&D, past customers, consultants, or individuals. • Development of the idea into project objectives, scope, et al occurs over a period of time prior to the project entering the Starting Phase. Often this requires the assistance of a PMO. • Only when the 'embryonic understanding' of the potential project has been approved does the project enter the Project Starting Phase.

Source: Archibald 2015, pp 20-21.

PMOs. The operational project management process includes the methods, systems, tools and procedures that are described in the several project management bodies of knowledge; these are the responsibility of the corporate and subordinate PMOs.

Definition of Project/Program Portfolios Must Include both Strategic and Project Management Considerations. These two perspectives must be considered when defining project/program portfolios within a specific enterprise. Examples for each perspective were presented and discussed.

Transformative Versus Commercial Projects and Programs. The differences between transformative and commercial project and programs were presented and discussed. Project/program portfolios that include transformative projects or programs must be managed by the appropriate strategy managers of the organization. Portfolios that include only commercial or delivery projects and programs may be managed by the appropriate PMO without daily direction from the organization's strategy managers.

One Integrated PPPM Information System is Required Within One Enterprise. One of the greatest remaining challenges today in achieving excellence in PPPM is to adopt and fully implement a truly integrated PPPM information system for a given enterprise. Several examples of these were identified.

Two Basic Types of Enterprises Are Project-Driven and Project-Dependent. These enterprise types were defined and reasons for differentiating between them were presented.

Origins of Transformative Versus Commercial Projects and Programs. The origins of transformative projects/programs are different from the origins of commercial or delivery projects/programs, depending on whether the organization is project-driven or project-dependent. These different origins were identified and discussed.

Innovation is Required to Create Transformative Programs to Achieve Every Enterprise's Growth Strategies. Therefore, excellent project/program portfolio management processes are required to successfully manage the future of every enterprise.

The Future Balance Will Change Between the Strategic Management and the Project Management Disciplines. In some areas of industry and government the discipline of project management, as exemplified by the Corporate PMO movement, will take on more and more responsibility for strategic growth management of an enterprise in the coming years. This trend will become more evident in those industries dominated by the need for innovation and the continued rapid technological advances in digital information and communication systems.

REFERENCES

Archibald, R., Di Filippo, I., & Di Filippo, D. (2012). The Six Phase Comprehensive Project Life Cycle Model Includes the Project Incubation-Feasibility Phase and the Post-Project Evaluation Phase. *PM World Journal, 1*(5). Available at http://pmworldjournal.net/?article=the-six-phase-comprehensive-project-life-cycle-model-including-the-project-incubationfeasibility-phase-and-the-post-project-evaluation-phase-2

Archibald, R. D. (2003). Managing High-Technology Programs and Projects (3rd ed.). Hoboken, NJ: John Wiley & Sons. Retrieved from www.russarchibald.com

Archibald, R. D. (2008). *The Interfaces Between Strategic Management of an Enterprise and Project Portfolio Management Within the Enterprise*. 22nd IPMA World Congress, Milan, Italy. Retrieved from http://russarchibald.com/recent-papers-presentations/strategic-enterprise/

Archibald, R. D. (2013). *Leading and Managing Innovation.* Paper presented at the 2013 PMI Frankfurt Project Zone Germany Congress. Retrieved from http://russarchibald.com/recent-papers-presentations/innovation-projec-manage/innovation-pmifc/

Archibald, R. D. (2013). *A Global System for Categorizing Projects*. The International Project Management Association/IPMA's Project Perspectives 2013. Retrieved from http://www.ipma.world/assets/re-perspectives_2013.pdf

Archibald, R. D., & Archibald, S. C. (2015). *Leading and Managing Innovation - What Every Executive Team Must Know about Project, Program, and Portfolio Management*. Boca Raton, FL: CRC Press, Taylor & Francis Group. Retrieved fromhttp://leadingandmanaginginnovation.com/

Bain & Company. (2015). *Strategic Planning*. Retrieved 17 August, 2016, from http://www.bain.com/publications/articles/management-tools-strategic-planning.aspx

BCG. (2008). Retrieved 17 August, 2016, fromhttp://tutor2u.net/business/strategy/bcg_box.htm

Christensen, C. M. (2012, November 3). A Capitalist's Dilemma, Whoever Wins on Tuesday. *The New York Times*.

Combe, M. W., & Githens, G. D. (1999). Managing Popcorn Priorities: How Portfolios and Programs Align Projects with Strategies. *Proceedings of the PMI 1999 Seminars & Symposium.*Newtown, CT: Project Management Institute.

Dye, L. D., & Pennypacker, J. (2000). Project Portfolio and Managing Multiple Projects: Two Sides of the same Coin? *Proceedings. of the 2000 PMI Seminars & Symposium.*

Dye, L. D., & Pennypacker, J. S. (Eds.). (1999). *Project Portfolio Management – Selecting and Prioritizing Projects for Competitive Advantage*. West Chester, PA: PM Solutions' Center for Business Practices.

GMC, Inc. (2012). *The Growth Management Process for Strategic Management*. Truckee, CA: Growth Management Center, Inc. Retrieved from http://www.agendas.net/

IPMA Individual Competence Baseline 4th Version (ICB4). (2015). Retrieved from http://products.ipma.world/product/icb/

Levine, H. A. (2005). *Project Portfolio Management*. San Francisco, CA: Jossey-Bass.

Milrood, B. (2011). Why Should Anyone Be Led by a Project Manager. Garter special briefing for ENI University. *Project Manager 2014*. Retrieved from http://www.slideshare.net/msproject/garter-project-manager-2014

Pellegrinelli, S. (1997). Programme management: Organising project based change. *International Journal of Project Management*, *15*(3), 141–149. doi:10.1016/S0263-7863(96)00063-4

Pfeiffer, P. (2004, October). Environmental Project Management in Brazilian Municipalities. Experiences of a Brazil-Germany Technical Cooperation Project. *PMI GovSig Magazine*, 10.

Porter, M. (2008). Retrieved 17 August, 2016, from http://en.wikipedia.org/wiki/Michael_Porter

Prieto, B. (2011). Systemic Innovation and the Role of Program Management as an Enabler in the Engineering & Construction Industry. *PM World Today, 13*(8).

Project Management Institute. (2013a). A guide to the project management body of knowledge (PMBOK® guide) (5th ed.). Newtown Square, PA: Author.

Project Management Institute. (2013b). The standard for portfolio management (3rd ed.). Newtown Square, PA: Author.

Ray, M., & Myers, R. (1989). *Creativity in Business*. Broadway Books.

Strategic Management. (2008). Retrieved from http://en.wikipedia.org/wiki/Strategic_management

Thiry, M. (2010). *Program Management*. Farnham, UK: Gower.

Thompson, A. A., & Strickland, A. J. III. (2003). *Strategic Management: Concepts and Cases*. McGraw-Hill.

Tikkanen, H., Kujala, J., & Artto, K. (2007). The marketing strategy of a project-based firm: The Four Portfolios Framework. *Industrial Marketing Management*, *36*(2), 194–205. doi:10.1016/j.indmarman.2006.03.006

United Kingdom Government. (n.d.). *Best Management Portfolio*. Available at: http://webarchive.nationalarchives.gov.uk/20110822131357/http:/www.cabinetoffice.gov.uk/resource-library/best-management-practice-bmp-portfolio

KEY TERMS AND DEFINITIONS

Commercial or Delivery Projects: Generate income and profit, reduce cost, otherwise improve the services or products provided to an enterprise's customers or constituents, or comply with laws and regulations, within the enterprise's established strategic vision and objectives, without creating significant changes within the enterprise itself.

Operational Project Management: Application of all the knowledge areas and processes described in the PMI PMBOK Guide (PMI 2013a), including the specific practices, systems and methods to be used for defining, work authorization, planning, and controlling projects and multi-project programs.

PMO Responsibilities: Responsibilities assigned to the Project/Program Management Office.

Project Categories: Systematic identification of the nature of specific projects.

Project-Dependent: Organizations or enterprises that depend on projects a) for new products, markets and services, b) compliance with regulations, and c) expansion of production or distribution facilities. These enterprises produce most of their revenue from the sale of products and services.

Project-Driven: Organizations or enterprises that primarily produce their revenue or deliver their services through planning and execution of commercial/delivery projects.

Project Origins: The sources of projects; how projects are conceived.

Project/Program Portfolio: Collections of projects or programs that are desired to be managed on a well-coordinated basis that usually depend upon common resources.

Strategic Plan: How an enterprise will achieve its strategic goals and objectives.

Strategic Project Management: Selection, authorization, and approval for execution of both transformative and commercial/delivery projects and programs to achieve the enterprise's approved strategic goals and objectives.

Transformative Projects and Programs: Produce significant changes within the enterprise regarding its products, services, markets, and how it carries out its business.

Chapter 3
Linking Organization's Strategy and Strategic Planning with Portfolio Management

Alfonso Bucero
Bucero, Spain

ABSTRACT

The strategy of any organisation and strategic planning are related to Portfolio Management. This chapter is focused on the relationship between the Organization's strategy and portfolio management. The purpose of this chapter is to explain the importance of strategic planning and its relationship with portfolio management. The focus of this chapter is to explain first the main elements of the organization's strategy based on the research from different authors and researchers plus the author's experience, then to explain the relationship between strategic planning and the portfolio management process, following with the explanation of the portfolio management context elements, defining the concepts of the mission, vision and objectives. The use of a case study tries to add value and achieve a better understanding of all the concepts explained in this chapter.

INTRODUCTION

Most of companies exist to achieve results and to produce some benefits. Every firm tries to satisfy some market or customer needs, but on the other hand, their motivations and "bottom line" are certainly different. For example, the author, a project and portfolio management practitioner, created his own consulting company fourteen years ago. If anybody were asking the author why did he create his organization, his answer would be "because he wanted to help organizations to develop a positive attitude to manage their projects, programs and portfolios adding some value to his customers and stakeholders". That's the author's approach as an example.

Looking at competitors in the project management consulting's field, every company has a different strategy and approach. However, it never has been found the perfect organization, which always assured excellent results over the years. Perhaps one of the reasons is the constant change in our environment,

DOI: 10.4018/978-1-5225-2151-8.ch003

that is inevitable. Using a metaphor, the plants in a garden change depending on the weather, insects, and amount of raining and so on. Plants survive being adapted to the change conditions, and because somebody takes care of them. Then, in a similar way, organizations need to be able to adapt to the changing conditions if they want to succeed in long term; and their managers need to spend some time to help on that adoption to the changing environment. Organization's objectives generate some pressure among managers and employees in organizations, taking into account that most of the organizations want to achieve benefits as soon as possible.

One of the main concerns from executives is to achieve better results from the projects they are managing in their organizations and better collaboration from other departments or business units affected by those projects. In the author experience, some projects are unlinked to the strategy, and usually when you ask to different executives in the organization, most of them are not aware of the total number of projects they have. Therefore, a common sentence heard in many meetings, workshops and conferences is "*we are managing too many projects*". Organizations need to select projects linked to the organizational strategy because that would help to solve such problems and, it is a good starting point to put together the appropriate elements that may create a better environment for project success.

This chapter covers a series of steps for linking organization's strategy and strategic planning with portfolio management. These steps constitute a process that may applied to any endeavor. Included throughout are suggestions for action as well as guidelines to navigate many pitfalls along the path. Process tools help illustrate ways to prioritize projects. The lessons learned are from consulting with many firms over a long time and from personal experiences in applying the lessons within several multinational companies worldwide. Managers in organizations are more and more concerned about getting better results from the projects under way in their organizations and getting better cross-organizational cooperation. Project managers on projects are looking for help when setting project goals. When project managers understand organizational strategy, they have a guide for action. It definitely helps them to define the goals of the project. On the other hand, the author found project managers in organizations who did not know their organization's strategy. The lack of communication among project managers and managers is unfortunately very common in organizations.

BACKGROUND

Organizations implement only 63% of their strategies' potential value according to Mankins and Steele. On the other hand, 66% of corporate strategy is never implemented (Mankins and Steele, 2005). The major focus on strategy research has been on their formulation (Grundy, 1998; Morris & Jamieson, 2005). But according to Hrebiniak (Hrebiniak, 2013), it is more difficult to make strategy work than to make strategy. Then, organizations have some room for improvement in terms of linking their strategy with their project portfolio.

Understanding the strategy may also be a motivational factor for project managers. A necessary question at the beginning of a project is, "why the organization is doing this project?" Understanding how their project is a part of a total system to achieve these types of goals will help motivate project managers. The project manager needs to ask his or her sponsor that question. More clear links to strategy helps develop cooperation among projects and people. In the author experience projects, generally speaking, do not usually have dedicated resources; they need to share them with other projects and with other departments or business units. To use effectively the organization resource pool, project managers must be aware of the existence of other projects, of what resources they require, about what the project priorities are, and how all the projects contribute to achieve the organization's strategy.

Working as a project manager, the author felt alone several times. I mean that he felt lack of support from his management team. Project managers need to know that they are not alone when managing projects in organizations; that means that others require resources too. They will be more cooperative with other projects when they see the needs of their project in the light of the needs of the entire organization.

Current literature highlights the importance of project portfolio management in evaluating, prioritizing, and selecting projects in line with strategy (e.g. Archer & Ghasemzadeh, 2004; Cooper et al., 2001; Englund & Graham, 1999). It is pre-eminent in choosing the "right projects" and therefore an important part of strategic management in organizations (Morris & Jamieson, 2005).

Müller et al. (2008) shows the positive relation between strategy conform portfolio selection and project portfolio performance. A few other studies found project prioritization as part of the portfolio management process to be a key success factor (e.g. Cooper et al., 1999; Elonen & Artto, 2003; Fricke et al., 2000).

Project Portfolio Management is a process, but people make the process work; values are the principle guiding their actions as they perform their work. More specifically, values define standards that govern the actions of the organization and behaviors of individuals working in the organization. Individuals within the organization will conduct themselves in a manner that is consistent with their own values, which may be in conflict with those of the organization. This is especially true in organizations with a disparate workforce comprising personnel from various parts of the world. What might be acceptable in one part of the world may not be in another.

Based on the previous cited research, there are still many companies that do not link their strategy with their portfolio of projects and they need to know how to do it.

KEY ISSUES IN STRATEGY AND PORTFOLIO ALIGNMENT

Lack of Teamwork

Cooperation across an organization requires that executives work together, as a team, sharing a systemic approach to projects (Graham & Englund, 2000). That means they look at projects as a set of interrelated activities in order to achieve a common goal. The common goal is to achieve the overall strategy of the organization. Usually all projects draw from one resource pool, so they are interrelated as they share the same resources. Thus, the system of projects is itself a project, with the smaller projects being the activities that lead to the larger project goal.

In the author's experience working with executives in organizations, there's was a lack of executive teamwork throughout the organization. If executives not model desired behaviors, there is little hope that the rest of the organization can do it for them because they should lead by example. That lack of executives' cooperation is usually reflected in the behavior of project teams, and there is little chance that project managers alone resolve the problems that arise. The author suggests to use the sentence:

I need you, I want you and I respect you

between project managers and executives to generate much more interaction among those key roles in any project (executive sponsor and project manager).

The committee concept is one mechanism that the author used in "CG (Spanish Savings Bank) to establish a strategic direction for projects spanning organizational boundaries, to solve strategic issues. As a result, that committee typically involved executives coming from different business units in the Bank, allowed to talk, discuss and vote in order to facilitate that committee to make good decisions early and manage those decisions daily. Usually its role is to set directions, manage multiple projects or a set of projects, and aid in cross-organizational issue resolution.

The mechanism used in "CG" is an example of linking organizational strategy with the projects to be executed and how to make a decision about which projects to run. First of all, that committee identified how to define a project selection criteria, then each criterion was scored according its importance, the third step was an expert's evaluation and finally they calculated the final score and results.

In a committee, the scoring mechanism chosen was a project assessment process based on some criteria, where the experts qualified all items to be reviewed. For instance, let's assume there are only four projects but the organization can only can deal with one of them; the result of the selection process would be applying an objective method to choose the most beneficial. The first step is to define objective criteria. Usually those criteria were taken from the organization's strategic objectives taking into account the vision, mission and strategic objectives. The basic thing here is that all criteria need to be aligned with the organizational strategy. CG established some objective criteria to be applied to the new requested projects. For this case the criteria were as follows (Table 1).

Not all criteria have the same importance for the organization. People involved in decision making need to consider to give a weight to each criterion between a determined range. The scoring in the example the range will be from 1 to 5 where 1 is the less important and 5 the most important. At the meeting of the committee, the participants defined the importance of each criteria and then independently every one gave a numeric value to each criterion. Results were consolidated and calculated using a statistical formula (Table 2).

The next step consists on evaluating each project regarding the criteria. To do that an evaluation format was designed to record all project data in each criterion. The scoring range may vary. However, for this case a score from 1 to 10 was used. Table 3 shows an example of one of the formats. It is important that all scores are done having the right level of knowledge about all the projects. Several people must be involved doing the evaluation individually.

Table 1. Criteria definition

Criteria	Description
Return of investment.	This item is better scored as quickest the project recovers the investment.
Degree of alignment with the organizational strategy.	This item is better scored when its results contribute more to the strategic objectives.
Easy to make.	This item is better scored as less research is required for the project.
Provider's dependency.	Higher score based on the provider's dependency.
Probability of a request for more projects from the same customer.	This item is better scored as higher is the possibility of continue working on for the customer on new projects.

Table 2. Weighted criteria calculation

Criteria	CUELLO, S	ORTEGA, S	RUEDA, E	QUINTERO, A	Scoring
Return of investment.	5	5	5	5	5
Degree of alignment with the organizational strategy.	4	2	3	3	3
Easy to make.	2	2	4	3	3
Provider's dependency.	-2	-3	-5	-2	-3
Probability of a request for more projects from the same customer.	3	3	3	3	3

Table 3. Evaluation register

Project Assessment Sheet Organization: Organization xyz Project name: Project XYZ Assessor name: Silvio Cuello Evaluation date: 10/Sep/2009 Note: Each item will be assessed using a score from 1 to 10 where 1 is low related to the criteria and 10 is totally associated to the criteria.		
Criteria	**Evaluation**	**Notes**
Return of investment.	1	Long term Return of Investment (ROI)
Degree of alignment with the organizational strategy.	9	It is almost achieving 80% of strategic objectives.
Easy to make.	1	It needs to do a lot of research work.
Provider's dependency.	1	No provider dependent
Probability of a request for more projects from the same customer.	10	This new product may generate more new clients.

To calculate results, all values from all criteria and projects need to be added up from all evaluations multiplied by the weight (Table 2) and ordered as you can see at Table 4.

The project with the highest score will have resources assignment priority. In this case, project D was scored 357 points obtaining the best score.

This is a subjective process as it depends on the thoughts of the people involved, but having several assessors with a high organizational knowledge there is a high probability that resources destined to new project development will be well focused and aligned to the organizational strategy.

Table 4. Consolidated results

Criteria	Project A	Project B	Project C	Proyect D
DP	-12	-48	-78	-39
FF	12	39	42	105
GA	108	72	39	81
MP	120	75	93	60
RI	20	55	120	150
Total general	248	193	216	357

Strategic Planning and Project Portfolio Management Processes

Where your organization does want to be in two or three years from now?

The basics of the strategic plan are to achieve an organizational state in which everyone shares a common vision for the future, understands what is essential to achieve that vision, and is motivated to contribute to the organization's success. Some big organizations, do strategic planning at corporate level.

Then, based on the corporate plan, each group or division in the organization's hierarchy performs its own strategic planning process, albeit at a more tactical level appropriate for the subset of the corporate goals it supports. Ideally these plans will roll up to form an integrated whole and roll down to goals and objectives at the lower level, and the initiatives undertaken to achieve them, all supporting the corporate strategy.

The author found many approaches to strategic planning but suggests the often-used sequence of defining or sharpening the organization's vision, mission and goals and then making an assessment about the readiness of the organization to achieve its goals. The author suggests to run the readiness assessment first. How to develop such assessment will be discussed later in this chapter.

So, the organization needs to identify the goals, identify the gaps regarding the ability to achieve their goals and then define the objectives needed to achieve each goal (Figure 1).

Usually mature organizations just review their existing strategic plan. On the other hand, new organizations need to do strategic planning as the first time. People are involved on strategic planning, so they need to:

- Know very well their strategic planning process.
- Understand very well the content of the strategic plan and how relevant it is to the Project Portfolio Management process.
- View strategic planning for the organization as a key part of the Project Portfolio management process.

Figure 1. The four steps in the strategic phase of project portfolio management

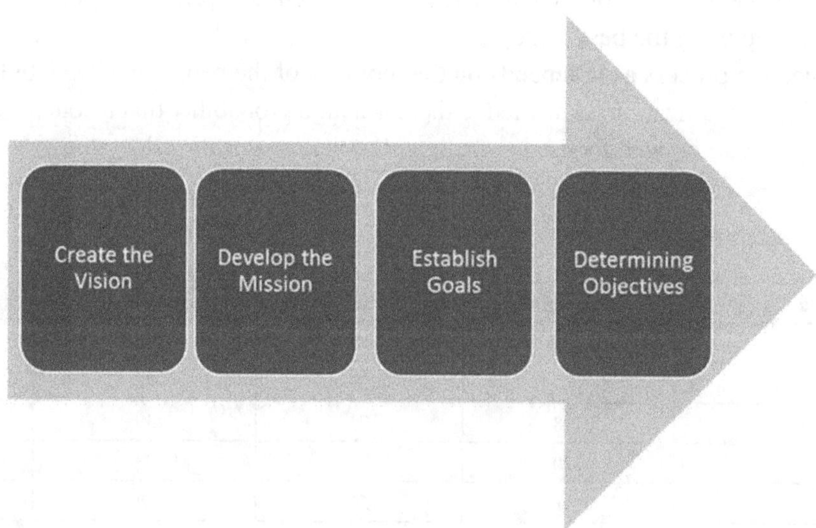

Create a Vision

The Vision establishes why the organization or firm exists – its reason for being. In most cases, the vision of the organization was defined previously such as with established businesses, government agencies, and military organizations. In other cases, the vision and values may not be established, communicated, or fully understood by the organization. Having a clear understanding of why the organization exists, the environment in which it operates, and how it wants to conduct its activities is fundamental to effective strategic planning and increases the likelihood of developing a mission, goals, and objectives that are relevant, valid, and achievable. However, in many organizations managers do not spend enough time on that. Even in organizations with well-defined missions and values, strategic planning gives them an opportunity to re-evaluate them to discover the changes that may be required (Figure 2).

Develop the Mission

Deciding where to go is usually not easy to be determined. For organizations contemplating their mission, determining where they want to be in the future and what they want to achieve can be difficult because of uncertainty regarding the future. If we knew exactly what would happen over the next three to five years, it would be easy to develop a mission that is appropriate and achievable.

Figure 2. Organizational context of portfolio management
Source: Adapted from the Portfolio Management Standard, Third Edition, Project Management Institute, PMI®.

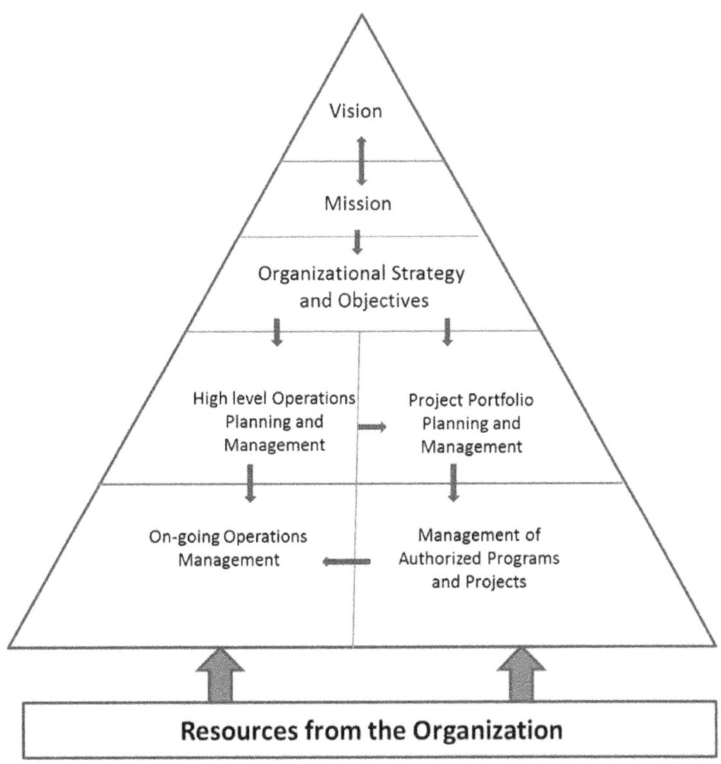

Unfortunately, organizations and most senior managers do not have psychic abilities. Instead, organizations describe where they are, and state where they would like to be, or what they want to have achieved, at some point in the future. They develop this statement about the future based on known information regarding the past and present and what is assumed about the future.

Establish Goals

Goals enable organizations to set high aspirations without actually defining the measurable objectives and initiatives that will support them. Depending on the organization and its processes, procedures, and leadership, some organizations may refer to goal setting by some other terminology such as issues and scenarios. However, as a goal-based approach is common, author uses the establishment of goals to describe this step of strategic planning. Goals are the means to achieve the mission and are statements of the broad achievements necessary for the mission to be realized. Goals state what is to be achieved over a longer term, perhaps three to five years, while the objectives that support them define specific targets toward achievement of the goal over a shorter timeframe, perhaps one to two years.

Determining Objectives

Objectives represent the next level of detail in the strategic plan's hierarchical structure and provide performance targets to be accomplished to meet the parent goal. Conceptually, attainment of the objectives will lead to meeting the goal that eventually and collectively leads to achieving the mission. While there is no prescribed number of objectives required for each goal, it is not uncommon to establish approximately five objectives for a single goal; perhaps more if needed. While the strategic plan often covers a rolling-wave five-year period, objectives are normally specified for completion over a one – to two-year period and can be updated during periodic review of the strategic plan.

SOLUTIONS AND RECOMMENDATIONS

Improve Teamwork

A Committee exercises leadership by articulating a vision, discussing it with the project managers, asking them their concerns about and needs for implementing the strategy, listening carefully to them and showing them respect so they become engaged in the process. In that way, executives and project managers develop the joint vision that is so necessary for implementation of strategy.

According to Englund and Bucero (Englund, Bucero, 2014) the process for selecting projects needs to be formalized. Most such processes involve a management committee taking over the process of project selection. This committee develops criteria for project selection such that all projects selected contribute to the achievement of organizational strategy. The committee also develops an estimate of the resources available for projects so that the number of projects selected is within the means of the organization to complete by the time they are needed. This committee starts by applying their criteria to the current situation, thus decreasing the current number of projects, which is not an easy task.

After project selection, the executive committee sets priorities for the scheduling of projects. That is, instead of attempting to do three projects at once, for example, projects are scheduled in series such that a lower priority project is not begun until the higher priority project is completed. Doing projects in series helps to speed project completion and thus contribute to eliminating project backlog.

Next, the executive committee appoints a project sponsor. This is important, because no difficult project ever succeeds in a hierarchical organization unless there is someone at the top who really wants the project results. The project sponsor then works with the project manager and departmental managers to ensure proper project staffing. Proper staffing means that people working on projects are working on only one at a time. It also means that core team members are committed to the project from the beginning to the end and that departmental managers ensure such team members participation for the project duration.

Finally, the executive committee ensures that a competent project manager is appointed. This means that the person appointed will no longer be selected based solely on technical knowledge but rather based on training and ability to manage projects in the business organization. In addition, the executive committee ensures that all project members are trained in project management techniques in order to maximize their performance in project settings. Working on projects is much different than working in departments, and project performance increases when people are trained in these differences.

Professionals participating in the PPM (Project Portfolio Management) need to play an active role as participants in the strategic planning process rather than being reactive. The PPM human resources can help executives to better understand the organization's capability and how it can contribute to accomplish the organization's strategy. To be effective, portfolio and project management personnel needs to understand their organization's strategic planning process and know what information to provide, and when. In some organizations, executives developing the strategic plan may not fully appreciate how the portfolio and project capabilities relate to the strategic plan, mainly because nobody explained it to them; the leaders in portfolio management needs to spend some time to educate executives in such cases.

The author suggests that PPM personnel should be involved in the organization's strategic planning process; however, the level of involvement can vary greatly depending on the organization's existing strategic planning process, its policies, and procedures. The degree to which involve PPM personnel throughout the organization has to be established. An effective process requires an organizational environment where information is freely exchanged and communicated both vertically and horizontally.

In silos organizations where information is firewalled by departments, divisions, or functional areas, the PPM process can be effective within these limits, but PPM may be less effective on an enterprise-wide basis (as indeed may be the case with all processes, not just PPM). It is very common that personnel performing projects are not sufficiently informed about why the project is being undertaken, that is, how the project is expected to contribute to strategic objectives. The managers responsible for portfolio and project management must communicate these expected contributions to those working on the projects and hold them accountable for recognizing how changes in the project scope, cost, and schedule may impact these expected contributions. A clear and concise strategic plan is the prime mechanism for defining and communicating organizational goals and objectives throughout the organization, at all hierarchical levels.

Corporate Appraisal and Strategy Definition

In order to find the gaps between an organization's current state and its vision so that goals can be derived, the organization needs to evaluate its current state. This process is also known as corporate appraisal, position audit, or assessing the present position. The organizational evaluation process can be conducted at the beginning of strategic planning, concurrently with other activities, or even after the mission, goals, and objectives have been developed, at least in preliminary form. It is not our intent to specify one approach or another for conducting the organizational assessment as that will depend on a myriad of factors. Rather, it is more important for project portfolio managers to understand the activities being performed, the reasons they are being performed and the impact on portfolio management.

Having a good selection of a portfolio of projects aligned with strategic objectives is contingent on a clear understanding of the organization's strategic plan and its objectives. The contribution of candidate projects to achieve the objectives needs to be determined. Several steps need to be considered as follows:

1. Define a proper vision.
2. Correct the Mission statement.
3. Properly establish goals.
4. Properly establish objectives.

Define a Proper Vision

Why is it necessary to re-evaluate the vision during strategic planning?

There are many reasons:

- **Mergers and Acquisitions:** Changes in the operating environment of the organization's generates frequently mergers and acquisitions; as they do, the new organization needs to consider the impact on future business activities – customers to be served or products to be produced. In some cases, strategic alliances are formed between organizations that may affect the vision of both organizations and the portfolio of projects they undertake as part of the alliance.
- **Governmental Reorganizations:** Changes in Government agencies generated by political changes (political elections, for example). New professionals could undertake a management position in the organization, so the organization's vision needs to be evaluated.
- **Changes in an Organization Operating Environment:** When people, processes or infrastructure (environment) change in the organization's environment there's the need to review the organization's vision.

Then is highly recommended to evaluate the vision periodically asking questions to the main organization stakeholders. This needs to be an executive's reminder in the benefit of the organization.

The Correct Mission Statement

While having, a strategic vision does not automatically guarantee success, the later steps of creating goals and objectives are dependent on having something to achieve (the mission). Mission can be viewed as another tool to increase the chances of success, especially if all is clear, coherent, easily communicated, consistent, and flexible.

Flexibility might seem a strange characteristic as the mission eventually requires a defined direction supported by specific goals. However, the strategy must be flexible to accommodate uncertainty and change in the operating environment, which may require revising or redefining the mission, the anchor point to determining goals. In an uncertain environment, strict adherence to a static strategic plan is a prescription for disaster. Flexibility doesn't mean abandoning the vision/mission, it is simply recognizing the need to tune the vision/mission continuously to an ever-changing business environment.

Properly Set Goals

To establish goals, the mission must be scrutinized to determine gaps between the organization's current state and where it wants to be in the future. Goals may be internal or external. For instance, an internal goal could be: to improve an organizational capability or measure such as improving employee retention.

An external goal may be to improve customer service. All areas of the organization are fair game for goal setting and include technology, capabilities, personnel, training, processes, projects, customers, competitors, resources and so forth. The important point to consider in developing goals is to determine what is required to close the gap between the organization's current states and where it wants to be in the future. Just as a mission must be achievable and relevant to the vision, goals need also be achievable and relevant to the mission. When defining each goal, strategic planners must also determine how they will know the degree for which the goal is achieved.

Properly Establish Objectives

The methods for establishing objectives are many, but a common technique used to define objectives precisely is the SMART technique (Jackson, Susan E., Aparna Joshi, and Niclas L. Erhardt):

- **S**pecific.
- **M**easurable.
- **A**ttainable (or achievable).
- **R**elevant (or realistic).
- **T**ime – Bounded.

Each objective should be specific and easy to understand. This reduces ambiguities and increases common understanding. Ideally, being specific would result in a number such as "200" versus the less specific "a lot" that can be interpreted differently. In other words, objectives should be measurable. Some would argue that if an objective is not quantifiable it is wrong. Albert Einstein would disagree as has been noted. As we mentioned previously, subjective measures can be as effective as quantitative measures if using the appropriate technique and obtaining measurements from the right people. Objectives must be achievable; unattainable objectives could be demoralizing because the responsible will expect to fail from the beginning as they believe that the objective cannot be achieved, at least not in the available timeframe.

Objectives need to be relevant by directly supporting the goal in a meaningful way. Finally, objectives must have a target timeframe. For a strategic plan covering a specific period, such as five years, one objective might specify an annual performance target, for example, revenue for the next fiscal year. Another may span the life of the five-year strategic plan, perhaps the net present value of the profits for the next five years. Goals are usually a longer-term (three to five years), while the objectives supporting the goal usually define shorter-term performance targets (one to two years) to achieve the goals. Although the manner or method used by the organization to derive objectives may differ, portfolio managers must clearly understand the objectives as well as how they contribute to meeting the goals. This is because project portfolios are selected as the combination of projects that best support the objectives, and, through them, the goals.

Strategic Plan Definition

While the organization wants to develop the right strategic plan to ensure future success, the plan needs to be constructed in a way that can be communicated effectively and interpreted uniformly throughout the organization, especially if the organization is distributed across many geographies and cultures.

Before moving to prepare a strategic plan, the organization need to do an organizational assessment that begins by using a method to analyze the strengths and weaknesses of the organization. This process uses the strengths, weaknesses, opportunities, and threats (SWOT) analysis technique because it is one of the most popular and recognized methods, it is not necessarily the best method for every organization. Organizations undertake the assessment process in a variety of ways; organizational assessment depends on many factors, including leadership, size of the organization, familiarity and experience with strategic planning, and internal processes and procedures to name a few. Nevertheless it is typical for all organizations to employ a variety of personnel within the organization to help develop the SWOT list. One should not confuse the output of the SWOT process, a simple list of items categorized under the labels of strengths, opportunities and threats, with the real final result. Additional analysis must be conducted to better understand the output of SWOT in terms of its meaning for the organization.

It is important to use the right people when performing the SWOT analysis to ensure a feedback that is useful and in context. In some organizations the involvement of low level managers to assess opportunities and threats might be inappropriate because they lack of information regarding the external business environment or the strategy in general. The key point is to use those, within the organization, who are best positioned to provide accurate information in the right context.

Portfolio management personnel should be aware of the techniques as well as their advantages and disadvantages, and understand the types of PPM information that might be beneficial to effectively contribute to organizational assessment. In this particular technique, Strengths and Weaknesses are internal to the organization while Opportunities and Threats are often, but not always, external. As the portfolio management experts within the organization, PPM personnel are in a unique position to provide valuable insight and contribute to this process. Separately from the organizational strategic planning process, portfolio managers should consider performing their own assessment to assess the capabilities and limitations of the organization's PPM process.

The strategic plan must contain a focused message to prevent any ambiguities or misunderstandings. What follows is an example of the content of a Strategic Plan.

Section 1: Executive Summary

The Executive Summary of your strategic plan should be completed last, and this section merely summarizes each of the other sections of your plan. The Executive Summary is important since it will help other key constituents, such as employees, advisors, and investors, quickly understand and support your plan.

Section 2: Business Description

An elevator pitch is a brief description of your business. Your elevator pitch is included in your strategic plan since it's key to your business' success, and often should be updated annually. Here's why it's important: if your employees can't clearly and concisely articulate your business to others, you inevitably miss out on sales and other opportunities.

Section 3: Company Mission Statement

Your company mission statement explains what your business is trying to achieve. While it may seem unimportant, it's not. You see, for internal decision-making, your mission statement guides employees to make the right decisions; decisions that are in line with helping the company achieve its mission. For external parties, such as investors, partners, and customers, your mission can inspire them to take the actions you want.

Section 4: SWOT

The reason to include a SWOT analysis (analysis of your Strengths, Weaknesses, Opportunities and Threats) in your Strategic Plan is to help in determine the best opportunities to pursue to achieve your growth goals. It also helps to identify which strengths you must develop in the near future to improve your company.

Section 5: Goals

Setting and achieving goals is the hallmark of successful companies and is a critical element of your strategic plan. The key is to first identify your 5 year or long-term goals. Next, identify your one-year goals; that is, what you must achieve in the next year for it to be successful and to put your company on the right trajectory achieving your 5 year goals.

Then work backwards two more times to determine your goals for the next quarter and the next month. Ideally you update your strategic plan monthly to modify this section.

Section 6: Key Performance Indicators (KPIs)

Great businesses understand their metrics and KPIs. By tracking your KPIs, you know exactly how your business is performing and can adjust as needed.

For example, a basic KPI such as "Total Sales" is critical to be managed if the company is performing well. "Underlying" KPIs are equally important. For example, if sales are affected by 1) number of visitors to your website, 2) number of visitors who complete a contact form, 3) number of proposals you issue to these leads, and 4) the proposal closing ratio, then each of these KPIs should be tracked. Then, if for instance, the number of visitors to your website decreased, you would know and fix this immediately, rather than waiting until sales plummet later. So, it's critical to identify the KPIs you will track in your business and list them in this section of your strategic plan.

Section 7: Target Customers

In this section of your strategic plan, you will identify the requests and the needs of each of your target customer groups. This is important in focusing your marketing efforts and getting a higher return on investment on your advertising expenditures. This is because the more you can "speak" directly to your target customer requests and needs in your marketing, the better you will attract them.

Section 8: Industry Analysis

Your industry analysis doesn't have to be a comprehensive report on what's going on in your market. However, you should conduct an analysis to ensure the market size is growing (if not, you might want to diversify), and to help identifying new opportunities for growth.

Section 9: Competitive Analysis & Advantage

Similarly, to your industry analysis, your competitive analysis doesn't have to be a thorough report listing every detail about every competitor. Rather, in addition to defining who your key competitors are, you should list their strengths & weaknesses. Most importantly, use this analysis to determine your current competitive advantages and ways to develop additional advantages.

Section 10: Marketing Plan

In addition to your strategic plan, the author recommends to develop a comprehensive marketing plan describing how you will attract prospects, convert them to paying customers and maximize your lifetime customer value.

The Strategic Plan Completion

As soon as we have an approved strategic plan, the process of transitioning from the strategic phase to the screening phase can begin. This process requires considerable coordination and interaction by PPM with senior executives as well as with the organization's operations to determine the combination of projects that will best contribute to achieving the objectives. After developing the strategic plan, many organizations do not take a formal step to prioritize the defined objectives. Specifying the relative importance of the objectives with respect to the goal is a prerequisite for effective portfolio selection; we have elected to identify it as a fifth major step in strategic planning. Those who participate in evaluating the relative priorities of the objectives are generally the same people who played key roles in the development of the strategic plan. Part of determining the anticipated contribution of a project that is a candidate for portfolio selection is the relative importance (in terms of achieving the goal) of the objectives that it supports. Thus, before the relative anticipated contribution of a project can be determined, the objectives hierarchy needs to be prioritized. Prioritizing objectives provides valuable insight to the organization when trade-offs such as allocation of constrained resources have to be made. The author has deliberately included this step, because the objectives are not equally important. It is more likely that some objectives will contribute more to accomplishing the goal than others. After prioritizing objectives, the portfolio management process can progress to screening and selecting the combination of projects that maximizes benefit to the organization.

The ultimate portfolio decisions and approval are the responsibility of executive management. Typically, multiple goals are defined in the strategic plan, each supported by multiple objectives. The author has chosen to use only one of the goals from the fictitious organization's (BUCERO Business School) strategic plan to illustrate the concept without overly complicating the material. The tools and techniques used are suited to support as many goals and objectives as identified in the strategic plan and can be used to support as many levels of strategic plans and portfolios as required by the organization.

To provide an example, the author will use a fictitious organization, the Bucero Business School (BBS), based on a real academic institution's strategic plan.

BBS Business School Background and Strategic Plan

Founded in 2002, the BBS has become one of the leading business schools in Europe. With its business success, and the subsequent rise in business school prestige. BBS has experienced a 15% increase in year-to-year applications. However, its outdated campus infrastructure and facilities are not adequate to support these enrollment increases and thus threaten the university's ability to continue to deliver the necessary degree of academic quality. As a result, the university's Board of Directors has authorized the development of the BBS Campus Renewal Program. Approved in 2016, this plan intends to revitalize the university's campus infrastructure and facilities to meet its vision, mission and strategic objectives. The plan will be governed by the university Board of Directors and execute under the guidance of the University Facilities team.

BBS Vision

The BBS vision is to become the leading business school by 2018 by "attracting and retaining faculty with a passion for teaching, experience in working with organizations worldwide, and the insights gained from their research by increasing student applications by 25% per year while growing the student population by 15%; thus, becoming increasingly selective; and by providing the best facilities for living, working, and learning on campus".

The vision of the Campus Renewal Program is to deliver the optimal infrastructure and facilities during the next three years to support the vision of BBS.

BBS Mission

The mission of BBS is to educate leaders who will shape the practice of business across the country and around the world, teaching them how to put into action both the knowledge and the analytical skills that they receive.

The mission of the Business School facilities team is to plan, build, operate, and maintain the physical infrastructure of the University to provide students, faculty, staff, and guests with a safe, clean, and secure environment in which to live, work. Learn and succeed.

The purpose of the Campus Renewal Program is to modernize and revitalize the educational, residential, athletic, and recreational infrastructure in a manner that best supports BBS's mission, goals and objectives.

BBS Goal

At BBS, research, teaching, learning, and campus community interaction occur with synergy and integration. This environment fosters innovation, critical thought, academic exploration, and creativity. BBS serves the nation and the world by advancing education across a range of business disciplines.

We have discussed the vision and mission of the university and the vision and mission of the Campus Revitalization Program separately. Henceforth, our discussion is confined to the Campus revitalization program that draws its goals and objectives from a single BBS strategic plan goal that was refined during the strategic planning session conducted by the president and academic officers and approved by the Board of Trustees. That goal is:

Campus facilities and surroundings will contribute to shared learning, collaborative research, and a sense of community by providing an environment that is conducive to dynamic interchange and that enhances the quality of life on campus.

BBS Objectives

The facilities objectives are divided into the following five major areas of focus or categories:

- Academic land use and facilities.
- Services and Administration Facilities.
- Intercollegiate Athletics Facilities.
- Recreation Services Facilities.
- Residential and Conference Facilities.

The objectives and sub-objectives for each of these are described in some detail. They will become the basis for Analytic Hierarchy Process (AHP) decision model to support the selection and management of the portfolio of facilities projects nominated or underway as part of the Campus Revitalization program.

BBS Objectives and Sub-Objectives

1. Academic Land Use and Facilities Objectives and sub-objective. Meet the academic needs identified in the space needs analysis conducted by the University Facilities under the updated guidelines of the State Commission on Higher Education.
    a. Provide high quality facilities to meet institutional needs by renovating or replacing obsolete facilities
    b. Use technology to improve learning, teaching and research
        i. Facilitate interactive, participative, and project-based learning
        ii. Provide distance learning technology capability
    c. Accommodate a project enrollment growth of 10% per year through academic year 2017-2018 for both undergraduate and graduate populations
    d. Address needs of nontraditional and community audiences
        i. Enhance evening class facilities
        ii. Provide concert, presentation, and conference facilities
    e. Use campus buildings for continuing and distance education
2. Services and Administration Facilities objectives and sub-objectives
3. Restructure existing delivery system facilities to meet current and future demands for convenient and efficient service.
    a. Improve existing and add new facilities for administrative and student services staff.
        i. Centralize front office high touch student transaction services such as registration and financial aid
        ii. Relocate back-office administrative services to perimeter locations

   b. Provide food, health, and other student and employee services efficiently and in a customer-oriented manner.
   c. Improve services, transportation, and communication systems linking various parts of the campus.
4. Intercollegiate Athletics Facilities objectives and sub-objectives. Help student-athletes succeed in both venues and advance the institution's winning spirit and drive.
   a. Improve facilities for intercollegiate competition to be comparable to others in the prestigious Big Kahuna conference
   b. Enable compliance with federal Title IX requirements by ensuring facilities for women's sports teams
   c. Improve athletic support facilities (restrooms, concessions, media support facilities, and food service areas) and ingress-egress in the stadium complex
5. Recreation Facilities objectives and sub-objectives. Help students, faculty, and others achieve a healthy mind/body balance by providing quality recreation programs and facilities.
   a. Upgrade existing outdoor facilities to accommodate increased demand
   b. Improve student support facilities and recreation center
6. Residential and Conference Facilities objectives and sub-objectives. Create a living and learning environment outside of the classroom and provide affordable housing for students.
   a. Provide student, staff, and faculty housing and related facilities to meet the diverse needs of single and family populations
      i. Provide affordable students housing for at least the current percentage of students (30%) living on a campus as enrollment grows
      ii. Provide residence facility lounges, meeting spaces, and wireless high speed network access
      iii. Modernize dining service facilities: Meet dining service capacity goals and Support a community experience in the dining facilities
      iv. Provide family housing with childcare facilities
   b. Provide conference, lodging, and specialized dining facilities
      v. Establish sufficient conference facilities to accommodate meeting, lodging, and dining facilities for year-round conferences
      vi. Provide seasonal conference facilities with sufficient lodging and dining

The strategic plan completion is a must before establishing the components for your portfolio.

Then the objectives and sub-objectives would be components of the project portfolio of the Bucero Business School (BBS).

Strategic Planning and Project Portfolio Management

The output of the organization's strategic planning efforts, and of the first four steps in the PPM strategic phase, is a strategic plan that clearly articulates the organization's vision, mission, goals, and objectives. Preferably project portfolio managers have been invited to participate in this process. While the differences in styles and approaches for developing, and communicating the organization's strategic plan are many, project portfolio managers need to understand the strategic plan and apply its intent to the PPM process by ensuring that the projects selected will best support the achievement of organizational goals and objectives. Ultimately, the purpose of the organization's PPM capability is to contribute to the organization's success. That is not possible if the strategic plan, vision, goals, and objectives are not clearly understood by those who help to select and manage the portfolios.

Although the strategic planning process is performed by the organization's executive-level management, portfolio management needs the results of strategic planning as an integral input to the PPM process. The better that responsible driving portfolio management understand the organization's strategic planning process and the goals and objectives defined by it, the better equipped they are to design, develop, and implement a flexible and responsive PPM process that can select the optimal portfolio and react quickly to future strategic changes. As more organizations embrace PPM, more involvement will be sought from those who can perform it.

CONCLUSION

- As more organizations move forward a collaborative environment in conducting their strategic planning, active participation by Project/Program/Portfolio standards will enhance not only the substance and quality of the strategic plan, but also provide a better understanding of what the organization is trying to achieve to those responsible for its success.
- Linking organization's strategy and strategic planning with portfolio management is a need for organizational success.
- Cooperation across an organization requires that executives work together as a team looking at projects as a set of interrelated activities in order to achieve a common goal. The common goal is to achieve the overall strategy of the organization.
- Professionals participating in the PPM (Project Portfolio Management) need to play an active role as participants in the strategic planning process rather than being reactive.
- Having a clear understanding of why the organization exists, the environment in which it operates, and how it wants to conduct its activities is fundamental to effective strategic planning and increases the likelihood of developing a vision, goals, and objectives that are relevant, valid, and achievable.

REFERENCES

Archer & Ghasemzadeh. (2004). *Project Portfolio Selection and Management.* San Francisco, CA: Wiley & Sons.

Cooper, . (1999). Multilevel design of performance measurement systems: Enhancing strategic dialogue throughout the organization. *Management Accounting Research, 10*(3), 233–261. doi:10.1006/mare.1998.0098

Elonen, S., & Artto, K. A. (2003). Problems in managing internal development projects in multi-project environments. *International Journal of Project Management, 21*(6), 395–402. doi:10.1016/S0263-7863(02)00097-2

Englund, R., Randall, L., & Bucero, A. (2012). *The complete project manager: Integrating people, organizational, and technical skills.* New York: Management Concepts Inc.

Graham, M., & Englund, R. (1999). Creating an Environment for Project Success. San Francisco, CA: Jossey Bass Editors.

Grundy, T. (1998, February). Strategy implementation and project management. *International Journal of Project Management, 16*(1), 43–50. doi:10.1016/S0263-7863(97)00016-1

Hrebiniak, L G. (2013). *Making Strategy Work: Leading Effective Execution and Change.* Upper Saddle River, NJ: FT Press.

Jackson, S. E., Joshi, A., & Erhardt, N. L. (2003). Recent research on team and organizational diversity: SWOT analysis and implications. *Journal of Management, 29*(6), 801–830. doi:10.1016/S0149-2063(03)00080-1

Mankins, M. C., & Steele, R. (2005). Turning great strategy into great performance. *Harvard Business Review, 83*(7), 65–72. PMID:16028817

Morris, P., & Jamieson, A. (2005). Moving from corporate strategy to project strategy. *Project Management Journal, 36*(4), 5–18.

Müller, R., Martinsuo, M., & Blomquist, T. (2008). Project portfolio control and portfolio management performance in different contexts. *Project Management Journal, 39*(3), 28–42. doi:10.1002/pmj.20053

KEY TERMS AND DEFINITIONS

Criterion: Something that is used as a reason for making a judgment or decision. Some criterion need to be used to establish a portfolio of projects.

Committee Concept: It is one mechanism that the author used in "CG (Spanish Savings Bank) to establish a strategic direction for projects spanning organizational boundaries, to solve strategic issues.

Project Prioritization: A well-defined project prioritization is very important for those organizations which have a clear strategy in place.

Project Screening: Project Screening is an assessment of project applications to select those which are not suitable for further consideration. Project screening includes completing a preliminary examination of the project opportunity (project application) to obtain an idea of whether the more time-consuming and costly effort for further business case development is reasonable.

Project Selection: Project selection is the first important part of project portfolio management. The responsibility is with the leadership team of the organization. Typically, they establish a steering committee that overlooks the process of selecting projects.

Rolling Wave Planning: is the process of project planning in waves as the project proceeds and later details become clearer. Work to be done in the near term is based on high level assumptions; also, high level milestones are set. As the project progresses, the risks, assumptions, and milestones originally identified become more defined and reliable.

Strategic Planning: Strategic planning is an organization's process of defining its strategy, or direction, and making decisions on allocating its resources to pursue this strategy.

Teamwork: The process of working collaboratively with a group of people in order to achieve a goal. Executive teamwork is a must in portfolio management.

Chapter 4
Are You Pondering What I Am Pondering?
Eccentric Consideration on Strategic Management

Andrea Aparo von Flüe
Sapienza University of Rome, Italy

ABSTRACT

This chapter deals with something which is widely spoken about, and very little know: Strategic Management. Following an evidence based approach, the author objective is to explain why Strategic Management is a scale invariant process that allows who uses it to identify possible and plausible solutions to complex issues. Some of the basics and analyticals of strategic management, such as strategic planning, SWOT analysis, Scenarios, are going to be described in detail. Detailed considerations will be presented on the issue of time and timing, a fundamental parameter that is too often neglected or taken as granted. The importance of strategic management to allow organisations to learn, change and evolve will be described. Some considerations on the importance of using the proper representation of the organisation's structure will be presented.

INTRODUCTION

It could be that the first Strategic Planner, in the sense that he was the first to write a book about it, was General Sun Tzu. His historicity is uncertain, but his lifetime is dated around 544-496 BC. Since that time, Strategy has been a major *techné,* in Greek art, in both the military, and the business world. As it happens quite often when a topic becomes popular, many people start to talk about it, sharing the denomination of the words, but not their contents. The author attempts to reframe the Strategic Management issue, in order to make it fit for today fast changing, complex, globalised eco-systems. To do so, he starts giving acceptable definitions of the strategic vocabulary words. Then he analyses some of the elements that are standard tools in the strategic analysis field, highlighting some of the problems that their use may generate. In the final part of the chapter, possible solutions are presented and discussed.

DOI: 10.4018/978-1-5225-2151-8.ch004

The approach that the author presents is not a canonical one. The readers will find the definitions, attributes and characteristics of key elements like Vision, Mission, Objectives and Strategy rather different from what, presumably, they have experience of. The following considerations are the result of thirty-plus years of professional experiences working for major international companies being in charge of technology intelligence and strategic planning, of what has been learned being an entrepreneur, and many years of sharing all this with my wonderful university students.

The author considers himself neither an academician having the final word, nor a consultant selling the final solution, but just an amateur story teller, and the narrative does not want to be antagonistic to other stories, other interpretations. It is just one of the many stories that can be told.

The author does not want to come up with a recipe to be followed in order to prepare a palatable strategic analysis. His effort is to have the readers think about the presented issues and problems, and make a personal effort to come up with possible solutions, combining their experiences, knowledge, abilities, and curiosity.

BACKGROUND

Strategic Management in the recent years has been strong on analysis, but weak on results. Its toolbox has been packed with dozen new paradigms, approaches, rationales, beliefs. Great deal of attention has been given to shareholder value, and finance drives planning in many companies. Strategic management has problems. If one prefers it has a big problem made of a set of sub-problems. In this essay these components will be defined and analysed. Let us start with the problems, then the authors shall describe the elements than, properly combined, may bring solutions, eventually.

KEY ISSUES IN STRATEGIC MANAGEMENT

Issue #1: Definitions

Words, a pretty dangerous tool, are used taking as granted that who is uttering them, and who is listening to them, share both denomination and contents of these words. Too often this is not the case. On the contrary, almost always the denomination is shared, but the contents are not. Whenever words are used, definitions have to be shared. It has not to be "the" definition, pure and perfect, but it is of utmost importance to agree and share "a" meaningful definition.

Therefore, let us define "Strategic" and "Management", and to do so it is strongly recommended to start with the words' etymology.

Strategic is the attribute deriving for the word Strategy. Strategy comes from Greek στρατηγία stratēgia, "art of troop leader; office of general, command", which derives from the word Strategos, στρατηγό, meaning "army leader".

In classical terms, a strategy describes how the ends (goals) will be achieved by the means (resources). Strategy is a high level plan to achieve one or more goals under conditions of uncertainty and of limited resources that have to be mobilized in an optimal way to execute actions targeted to attaining predetermined, measurable goals. From the 18th century, when the word was translated into Western vernacular languages, until the 20th century, the word "strategy" came to denote *a comprehensive way to try to pursue political ends, including the threat or actual use of force, in a dialectic of wills (Strategy, n.d.)* in a military conflict, in which both adversaries interact.

Therefore, Strategy has a military origin, it deals with war, with resources, with goals. What is the goal of a war? Not the destruction of the enemy. Not at all. Let us take the case of Alexander III of Macedon, aka Alexander the Great, famous Strategos Autokrator, commander-in-chief with full power. He created one of the largest empires of the ancient world, stretching from Greece to north-western India. He would never have been able to achieve this goal if he had destroyed the enemy. In order to advance, to sustain his growth in a continuous way, he needed the enemy resources to feed his army, to support the population of the country he conquered. His goal, the final goal of every war, is to win, to get possession and control of the enemy land, resources, and people, minimizing the loss of wealth.

To apply the concept of Strategy to civil organizations one has to understand the difference in goals among a military organization and a civil one. To do so let us find the answer to a very simple question: What is the ultimate *raison d'être* of a civil organization? Nowadays, the trivial answer in our highly industrialized countries is: Profit. Totally wrong.

The strategic objective of whatever organization is to create wealth over time, in a continuous and sustainable way. If this creation is done in a virtuous way, one of its statistical metrics is profit. It is the same relationship which exists in meteorology between weather and climate. Weather is something that is measured daily every 6 hours, worldwide, with a standardised set of instruments and relative metrics: temperature, pressure, wind speed and directions, humidity, precipitations, solar radiation. If these measurements are elaborated over a period of time of at least thirty years, then one can speak of climate. There is no instrument that can measure climate: it is a statistically derived dimension. Same applies to profit. If wealth is created continuously over a sufficient long period of time, then profit is a dimension which described the long term dynamics of the organization. Do not do it properly and you will find yourself facing cases like the Enron one….

Let us go back to strategy, an activity that require planning –it has to be mentioned that one of the fathers of strategic management, Henry Mintzberg (1978), from McGill University, defines strategy as *a pattern in a stream of decisions* to contrast with the view of strategy as planning.

Strategy requires an appropriate thinking. Some scholars have a more "religious" approach: Dr. Vladimir Kvint (2010) defines strategy as *a system of finding, formulating, and developing a doctrine that will ensure long-term success if followed faithfully*. It is quite hard to accept that decisions that may be vital for an organization are taken because of a more or less implicit faith.

In any case strategy deals always with the future.

A final definition, by C. Ebert of VCS-Vector Consulting Services (Vector Consulting Services, n.d.), of Strategy: a long-term plan of action designed to achieve an objective, most often "winning", while considering complex situations, given one's environment, strengths and weaknesses. Success needs strategic planning and strategy implementation. Strategy thus is more than a plan. It is a consistent goal-oriented behaviour.

It answers three questions:

1. What will we do?
2. For whom do we do it?
3. How can we avoid or beat competition?

Management

Now it is the turn of the word "management". There are almost as many definitions as scholars. Irwin, Terry and Rue (Irwin, Terry, & Rue, 1982) have defined management as: *A process or form of work which involves the guidance and direction of a group of people to the aims or objectives of the organization.*

Stoner (1982) however, means the term as: *The process of planning, organizing, leading and controlling the effort of organizations members and of using all other organizational resources to achieve stated organizational goals.*

Johnson and Stinson (Johnson & Stinson, 1978) frame the concept in a few words: *Management is the process of working with and through other people to accomplish organizational goals.*

Koontz, O'Donnell and Weihrich (Koontz, O'Donell, & Weihrich, 1990) definition sounds rather utopian: *management is the establishment of an environment for group effort in such a way that individuals will contribute to group objectives with the least amount of such inputs as money, time, effort, discomfort and materials.*

Ernest Dale (1973) proposes a definition which sounds like a summary of other definitions: *The process by which a manager of an organization uses resources efficiently to achieve the general objectives at minimum cost and with maximum profit.*

These definitions have some elements in common, and there are features emerging, some of them rather trivial:

- Management is a process.
- Resources have to be used efficiently.
- Things get done.
- Management deals with people, their abilities, skills, and capabilities.

Carlos C. Lorenzana (1993), in his book Management: Theory and Practice, summarizes many different honourable scholarly definitions defining management as: *The process by which a manager of an organization efficiently utilizes resources to achieve its overall goals at minimum costs and maximum profit.* Honourable for sure, but to the author it seems that he did not get the point right speaking about profit…

Let us see now what the Online Etymology Dictionary (n.d.) reads for the word "manage": *1560s, probably from Italian maneggiare "to handle", especially "to control a horse"; ultimately from Latin noun manus "hand" (see manual (adj.). Influenced by French manège "horsemanship" (earliest English sense was of handling horses), which also was from Italian. Extended to other objects or business from 1570s. Slang sense of "get by" first recorded 1650s. Related: Managed; managing. Managed economy was used by 1933.*

Management has to do with handling.

For the Merriam-Webster Dictionary, a manége is:

1. A school for teaching horsemanship and for training horses;
2. The art of horsemanship or of training horses;
3. The movements or paces of a trained horse.

In French "*manége*" is a riding academy, a riding arena, an exercise rectangle.

In Italian "*maneggio*" has the same meaning as in French, but it is the verb "*maneggiare*", which is of our interest because it is tightly related to "*manipolare*", which translates in English with the verb "to manipulate".

Going back to the Merriam-Webster Dictionary, one finds out that the definitions of "manipulate" are:

1: to treat or operate with or as if with the hands or by mechanical means especially in a skilful manner; 2a:to manage or utilize skilfully; 2b: to control or play upon by artful, unfair, or insidious means especially to one's own advantage; 3: to change by artful or unfair means so as to serve one's purpose.

One's purpose or the purpose of the organization to which one belongs, possibly in an executive position.

Obviously, it is much more elegant to say that someone is a Manager, instead of saying the he/she is a Manipulator. But in essence a Manager is a Manipulator. We shall be back on this issue.

This definition game con be concluded asserting that Strategic Management is the key business process within an organization providing the right environment to both define, plan, agree, evaluate, implement its strategy, and because of their involvement in the process, to energize its people.

It consists of five sub-processes:

1. Strategic direction (e.g., vision, mission, values and goals).
2. Operational direction (e.g., resources, people, policies).
3. Strategy evaluation (e.g., SWOT, positioning, markets).
4. Strategy planning (e.g., competition, new entrants, new rules).
5. Strategy implementation (e.g., RD&E, products).

Strategic Planning therefore is part of Strategic Management and can be defined as an organizational planning and decision process of defining the strategy and allocating appropriate resources to pursue the strategy.

A key facilitator in strategy planning is to determine what to do and what not to do, as well as how to best cope with external constraints and risks.

Risk

What is risk? Once more the author is joggling with a word that everybody uses, and almost always with the wrong acceptation.

Quoting Simon and Garfunkel (1964)… Webster Dictionary, my old friend, I've come to talk with you again…: *"Risk": possibility of loss or injury: peril; 2: someone or something that creates or suggests a hazard, 3a: the chance of loss or the perils to the subject matter of an insurance contract; also: the degree of probability of such loss; b: a person or thing that is a specified hazard to an insurer; c: an insurance hazard from a specified cause or source <war risk>; 4: the chance that an investment (as a stock or commodity) will lose value.*

None of these definition is acceptable. Risk in Strategic Management has a different meaning.

Little help comes from the Etymology Dictionary: *"risk (n.) 1660s, risque, from French risque (16c.), from Italian risco, riscio (modern rischio), from riscare "run into danger," of uncertain origin. The Englished spelling first recorded 1728. Spanish riesgo and German Risiko are Italian loan-words.*

With run (v.) from 1660s. Risk aversion is recorded from 1942; risk factor from 1906; risk management from 1963; risk taker from 1892".

Indeed, risk has to do with the possibility of running into danger. The primary danger in business management is not just losing something of value, but also gaining something unexpectedly.

This time we check what Wikipedia (Risk, n.d.) has to say: ... *risk results from a given action or inaction, foreseen or unforeseen. Risk can be defined as the intentional interaction with, and uncertainty is a potential, unpredictable, and uncontrollable outcome; risk is a consequence of action taken in spite of uncertainty....*

The risk of an action, or decision, is function of the outcome. How can risk be measured? There are many formal methods.

The probability of an event is estimated by using the frequency of past similar events. Obviously, rare events' risks are difficult to estimate, but it is often the case that the rarer the event, the more severe the consequences.

Risk is measured as the expected value of an undesirable outcome. This combines the probabilities of various possible events and some assessment of the corresponding harm into a single value. The associated formula for calculating risk is then:

R = (probability of the accident occurring) × (expected loss in case of the accident).

For example, if performing activity X has a probability of 0.01 of suffering an accident of A, with a loss of 1000, then total risk is a loss of 10, the product of 0.01 and 1000.

Situations are sometimes more complex than the simple binary possibility case. In a situation with several possible accidents, total risk is the sum of the risks for each different accident, provided that the outcomes are comparable:

$R=\sum_{\text{For all accidents}}$ (probability of the accident occurring) × (expected loss in case of the accident).

For example, if performing activity X has a probability of 0.01 of suffering an accident of A, with a loss of 1000, and a probability of 0.000001 of suffering an accident of type B, with a loss of 2,000,000, then total loss expectancy is 12, which is equal to a loss of 10 from an accident of type A and 2 from an accident of type B.

Plan

A plan is a shared sequence of actions, having an unchangeable defined end time, that have to be undertaken to achieve a measurable goal.

Whenever an action deadline is not respected, either because the goal has been achieved too early, or too late, the plan has to be redesigned for scratch. Changes to previously defined plans are not allowed.

The time horizon of the plan defines the kind of plan. Fiscal year long plan is called a budget. 36 Months plans are typically strategic plans. From 60 months it is a Long View Plan, also known as scenario.

All right, we shall use these concepts later on.

Issue #2: Time

Strategy can be a plan, or it can be considered "a pattern in a stream of decisions", or it can have some more exotic and diversified definitions, as we have just seen. What is always present in all these different definition is time. Always present, and too often its importance is underestimated. What is time. How would you define time? If you are a physicist you consider it an immanent dimension, something which is always present; a non-spatial continuum that is measured in terms of events which succeed one another from past through present to future. No event, no flow of events, then no past, no present, no future. There is a past, a present and a future if there are observable phenomena that do show measurable changes: a tree, a person, a rock, the universe. Time is the measured or measurable period during which an action, process, or condition exists or continues.

Time is the thing that is measured as seconds, minutes, hours, days, years, etc. And seconds, minutes, hours a day are always the same. 24 hours a day, 60 minutes an hour, 60 seconds a minute (Strategy, n.d.). Why then so many scholars do say that things have changed, that strategic management is increasing difficult because time has accelerated? Well, they say something wrong, very wrong. Shall be back on this in the next chapter.

Issue #3: People

"Get the right idea, find the right people, and success will smile at you…": popular wisdom. Too bad that it is plainly wrong wisdom. It should read "Get the right people, find the right idea, and success will smile at you…". Ideas are easy to find, pretty inexpensive, at least in the first stages of development, very often rather fascinating.

Finding the right people is a totally different story. It takes time, it is expensive, and it is a very scarce resource.

A strategy is always a plan for transformations, changes, learnings, improvements. It is a course of action. If one decides to go for a cruise on a sailing boat, it is easy to decide the final destination, who shall be the person in charge, i.e. the skipper, the Master and Commander. What is not easy at all is to decide who is going to be part of the crew. And who is not going to be part of it. Hire and promote people with talents, not skills. They should be razor-sharp, obstreperous. They have to be managed in a way that allows them to initiate and demand learning. Yes and No are not acceptable answers: they want to know, learn, be part of the definition of values and priorities. Seek people who seek varied experiences. Encourage people to think, not to obey.

Once the right crew is on board, no need to define the optimal waypoints' sequence for the planned course, because if the final destination –the objective- is known to everyone, and shared by everyone, it shall be reached, no matter what.

The objective defines the strategy. A strategy is never realised the way it was intended. It is always a mistake to talk about "a" strategy. One should always think in terms of "strategies". Realised strategy equals Intended strategy minus Unrealised strategy plus Emergent strategy (Figure 1). More or less what happens on board once you left the harbour.

In his book "Good to Great" Jim Collins (2001) uses a different metaphor: *Look, I don't really know where we should take this bus. But I know this much: If we get the right people on the bus, the right people in the right seats, and the wrong people off the bus, then we'll figure out how to take it someplace great.*

Figure 1. Intended vs. realized strategies

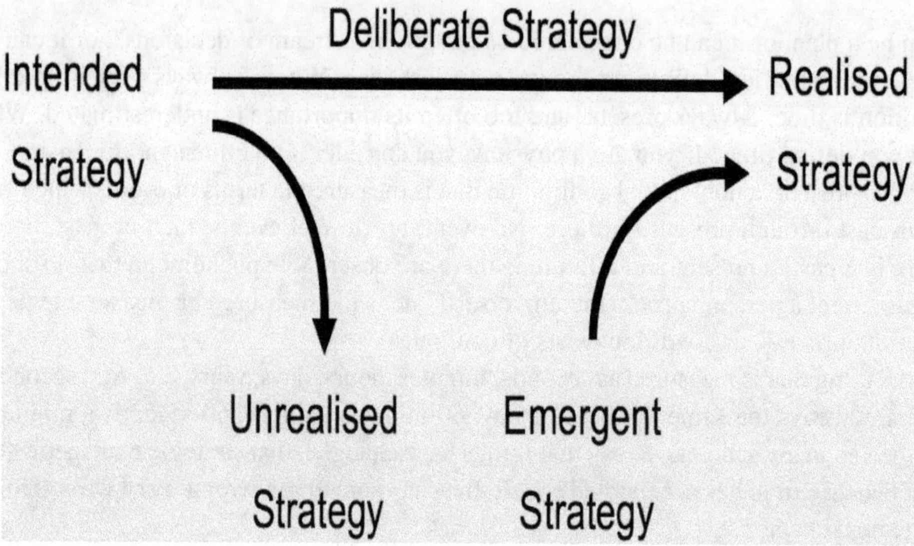

Always begin with "who", rather than "what". Things to change pretty fast. The ecosystem can be modified rather suddenly. People do not. People must learn in order to change, and learning is not a fast process. People are the most rigid, high inertia component in whatever organisation.

Issue #4: Structure

No one is allowed to talk about strategy if he/she has not read carefully the seminal book by Alfred D. Chandler "Strategy and Structure" (1962) . His central thesis is that structure follows strategy. Whenever there is a major change in corporate strategy, consequence of a drastic change in the long-term goals and objective/s of an organization, driven by market changes, new products, players, and technologies, there must be a change in the structure. Structure is defined as the architecture, i.e. the set of processes, relationships and communication channels of the organization through which strategy is administered. Changes in an organization's strategy always involve administrative changes which, in turn, require a new or refashioned structure for the successful implementation of the new strategy.

To graphically represent a structure, organigrams have to be used.

Definition of "Organigram": etymology: Organization + Gram; a graphical representation of the structure of an organization, showing groups and departments and their interconnections and inter-responsibilities.

The organigram is also often called "organizational chart". It is a diagram showing the structure of an organization and the relationship and relative ranks of its parts and positions/jobs.

According to Wikipedia, the first organizational charts of American business was created by Daniel McCallum around 1854.

The first organigrams were not so easy to read as can be seen in the 1917 organizational chart of The Tabulating Machine Co. which later on became IBM (Figure 2).

Figure 2. The Tabulating Machine Co. organigram, 1917

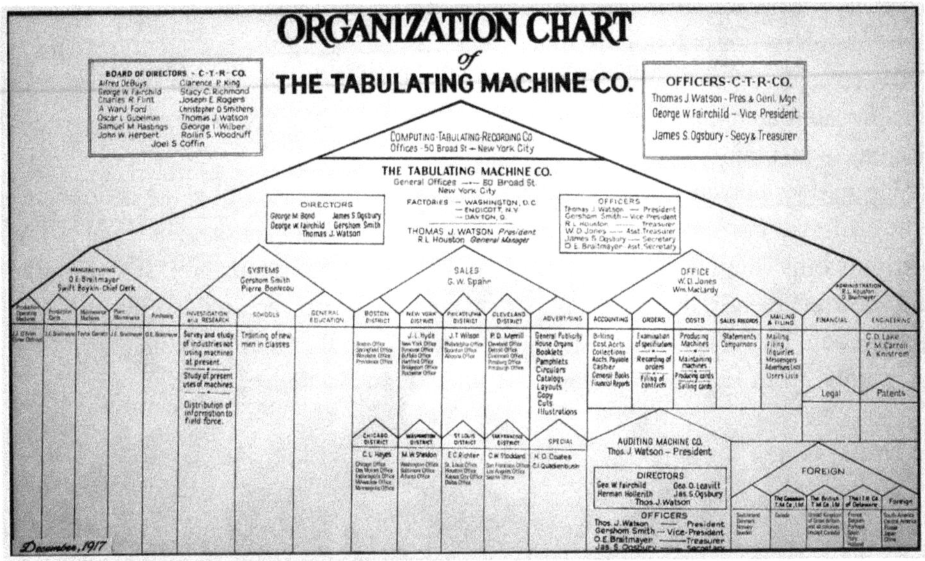

Interesting to notice that in the old time, organizational charts represented the company structure, enabling the visualisation of the complete organisation, whilst nowadays they represent the power structure of the president/chairman of the company, the relations between managers to sub-workers, directors to managing directors, chief executive officer to various departments, and so forth (Figure 3).

The different types of organization charts include:

- Hierarchical.
- Matrix.
- Flat (also known as Horizontal).

Figure 3. Power structure representation: organigram

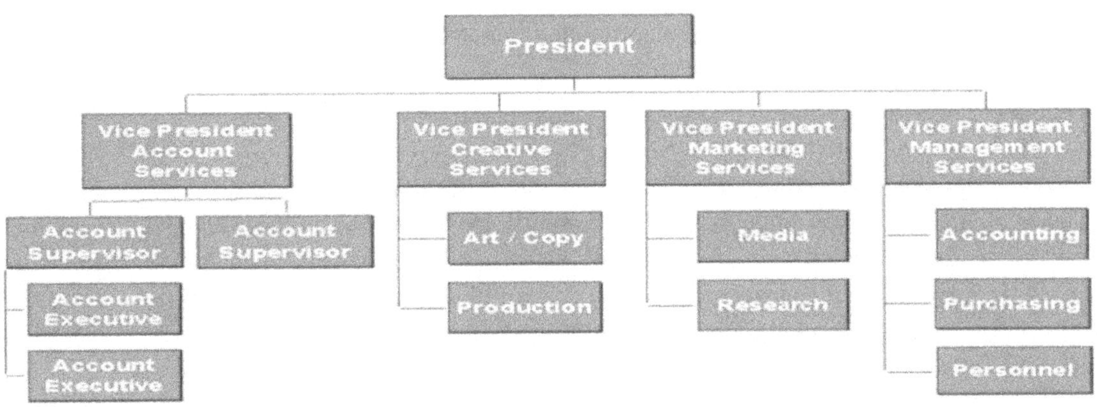

The accepted form for making organization charts is purely hierarchical. Start with the principal official, department or function first, and then add the others, obviously below, in the order of their rank.

What is the use of a representation like that? When is an organigram taken out from the high security safe of the HR Executive Senior Vice President? Usually it happens in two occasions. Preparing the Annual report because an updated organigram has to be printed, or when something went badly wrong and someone has to be blamed for.

An organigram does not say how the organization creates wealth, where the added value, perceived as such by the customer basis as value proposition, is generated. It is not an evidence of the set of functions and activities that define the competitive position of the organization. It does not help analyst to understand how efficiently the company is managed. No portfolio analysis compares organigrams. Something else could be a much better representation and a rather helpful tool. The author is referring to the Organigraphs. Wait for the next chapters and the reader will see…

Issue #5: Matrixes

It started many years ago. Legend says it was 1970 when Bruce. D. Henderson created the Growth-Share matrix. At that time major corporations were humongous after more than two decades of continuous, double digit growth. Some of them where totally integrated: from ore mines to steel plants, to automotive assembly lines, consumer financial services, insurance and so on so forth. In those years, the Italian Fiat Group, owned by the Agnelli family, was present in all of the economic sectors listed in the Italian National Economy Input-Output matrix.

Then things started to slow down. It became necessary to start selecting the businesses in which to stay, those that had to be dismissed, and the ones that needed more thinking and data to decide either to keep them, to invest or to sell them, cashing in.

It was in those years that Portfolio management evolved from being an academic exercise to a very important management tool.

The BCG (Boston Consulting Group)-matrix is an analytical tool used in particular in strategic management and in portfolio analysis to analyse the activities of an organization, the business units of a corporation in order to design and manage a balanced portfolio (Figure 4).

The BCG is a nice matrix, small in size, just 2 by 2, and very quantitative. It is the graphic representation of a well done SWOT analysis which is another two by two matrix.

The Market Growth dimension refers to the Opportunities and Threats elements of the SWOT analysis because it relates to components external to the company, not under its direct control. The Strengths and Weaknesses always refer to companies' internal dimensions, and are reflected into the capacity of the company to influence its market share.

Too bad that after the Growth-Share matrix, year after year, new ones have been proposed, always increasing the size of the matrix. The McKinsey one, also known as the Industry Attractiveness-Business Position Matrix, aka GE matrix, is a three by three one (Figure 5).

The Market Life Cycle-Competitive Strength matrix by Arthur D. Little is four by four (Figure 6).

What is really interesting to notice is that all matrixes being proposed by major consulting companies show regions where the answer to the selection problem sound pretty naïf, or obvious: "Question Mark", "Up or Out", "Caution"; "Be aware"… . Nobody ever wrote the honest answer: "No idea what you should do".

Figure 4. Boston Consulting Group growth-share matrix

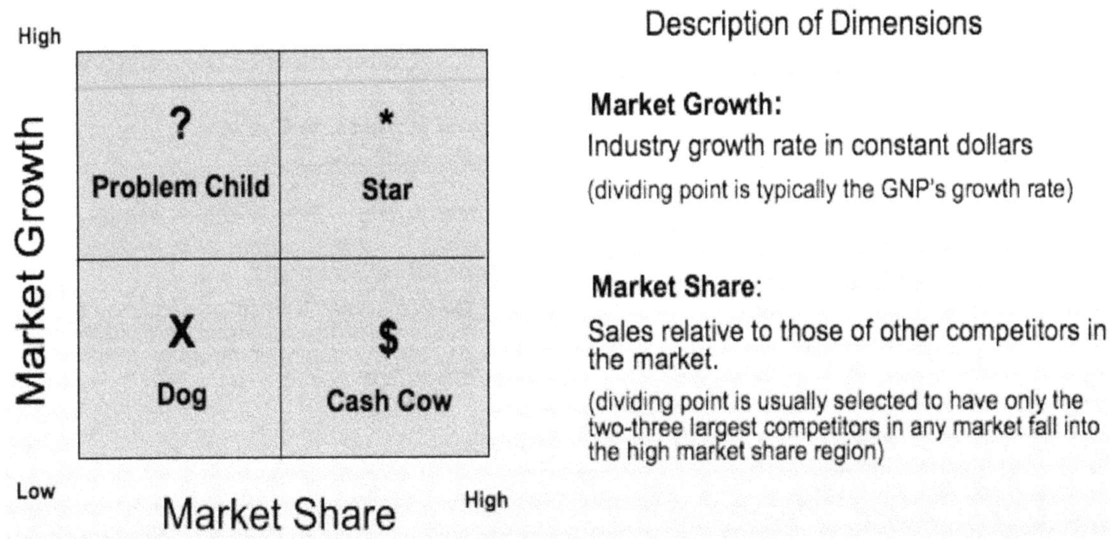

Figure 5. McKinsey & Co. industry attractiveness-business position matrix

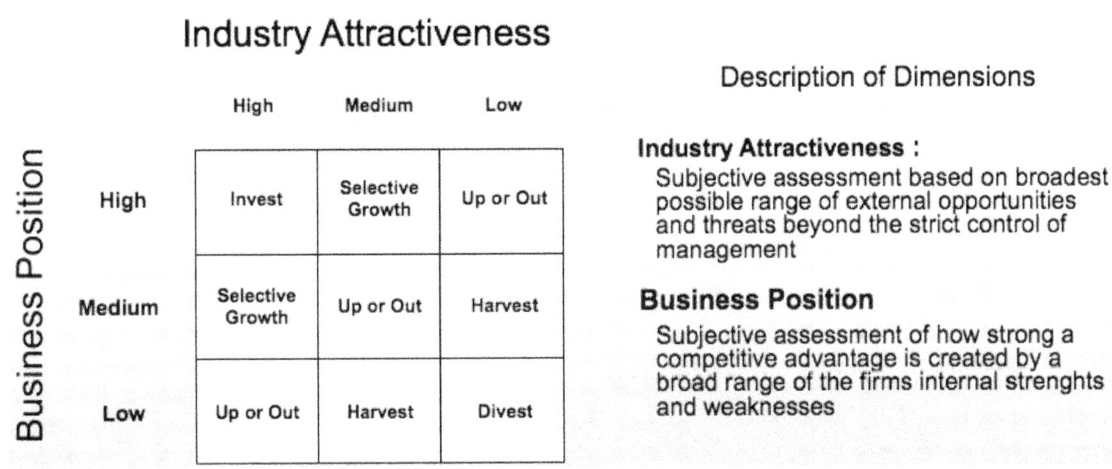

Just to give an example of how perverse the matrixes approach has become, give a look to the five by four Technology Matrix (Figure 7). It is not clear what kind of decision making process can make a good use of it. Positioning products or processes in a matrix does not always help to find an acceptable solution to a portfolio management issue.

Issue #6: SWOT

SWOT analysis has just been mentioned, and it is worth looking at this basic tool more in detail. SWOT, is an acronym for Strengths, Weaknesses, Opportunities, and Threats. It is a method that evaluates four elements always present in whatever project or venture. A SWOT analysis can be performed if, and only

Figure 6. Arthur D. Little market life cycle-competitive strength matrix

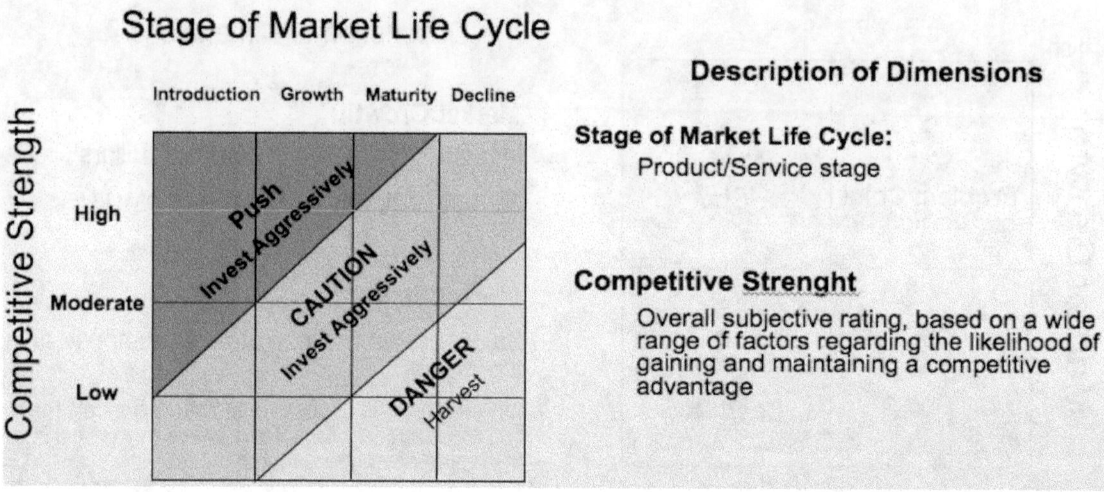

Figure 7. Finmeccanica technology matrix

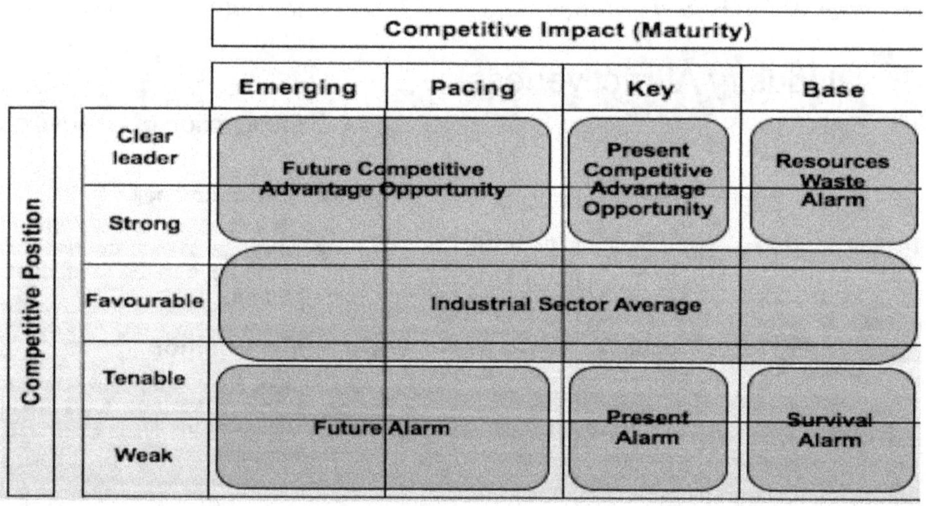

if one or more objectives have been identified. Every and each objective requires its "private", dedicated SWOT analysis. Once the objective has been defined, and no objective can be defined if it has not a metrics, then the SWOT analysis helps identifying the internal and external factors that are favourable and unfavourable to achieve that objective (Figure 8).

The origins of the SWOT analysis remain obscure. Some people say it was born at Harvard, others say MIT or at the Stanford Research Institute (SRI).

In any case, SWOT is here to stay and it is an analysis that has to be developed as a collaborative with a variety of contributions coming from all interested stakeholders. A SWOT analysis being the effort of a couple of rather expensive "experts" is just a waste of time.

Figure 8. SWOT components

Inside
(Strengths, Weaknesses)

- Resources
- Financial health
- Employees and business competencies
- Physical assets and technology
- Research and Development
- Organizational Culture

Outside
(Opportunities, Threats)

- Markets and Customers
- Position in Product Lifecycles
- Competitors
- Trends (technology, users, etc.)

It goes without saying, that SWOT analysis can also be used in perverse ways, such as defending *a priori* decided objectives. This misuse leads to limitations on brainstorming possibilities and "real" identification of barriers and opportunities.

The four SWOT dimensions are defined as follows (SWOT analysis, n.d.):

- **Strengths:** Characteristics of the business or project that give it an advantage over others.
- **Weaknesses:** Characteristics that place the business or project at a disadvantage relative to others.
- **Opportunities:** Elements in the environment that the business or project could exploit to its advantage.
- **Threats:** Elements in the environment that could cause trouble for the business or project.

Identification and measurement of SWOTs elements can inform whether the objective is attainable. If the objective is not attainable, a different objective has to be selected repeating the process.

But SWOT analysis, if done in a more updated version, can be very helpful to understand your own position. We shall see this issue and the method in a short while.

Issue #7: PEST and PESTEL

Two acronyms to be known: PEST stands for Politics, Economy, Society and Technology; PESTLE stands for the same as above with two added dimensions: Law and Environment. Both are frameworks to be used in scanning the external environment, i.e. to identify the Opportunity-Threats factors of the SWOT analysis. There other variations of these basic two which take into account ethics, demography, intercultural, ecological, regulatory factors.

It has to be stressed that the first three factors in PEST are independent ones, whilst Technology has always to be dependent from one of the three or a combination of them.

STRATEGIC PLANNING PROPOSED SOLUTIONS AND RECOMMENDATIONS

The author has described the elements that do define the space-problem of Strategic Management today. It is just a list, but it is needed to analyse and discuss the possible solution to the fore listed problems. It has to be clear that the problem is not in the words, element or methodology being used, but in the combination of these factors that can define a complex solution made by a number of components.

Solution Component #1: The Basic Six Elements for Learning and Change

Strategy is a plan to achieve an organisation's objective or objectives in order to create wealth over time in a sustainable way. Therefore, one cannot talk about strategy if the objective/s has/have not been defined. In order to define the objective/s, the mission must be made explicit. To make the mission explicit a vision must be declared. All these elements, plus two that have not yet been introduced, are key for every process of continuous growth, which creates wealth sustainable over time.

In all there are six elements, six bricks that have to be piled one over the other in the right order (Figure 9). It has not to be a perfect alignment, but it must be sufficiently well done for the pile of bricks to stay up.

Vision is at the top of the pile; brick number 2 is the Mission; brick number three is the set of Objectives, at least one element must be in the set; brick number four the set of strategies relative to the Objectives; brick number five are the Actions relative to the Strategies; brick number six is the set of Goals defined by the set of Actions.

Figure 9. The change and learning bricks' pile

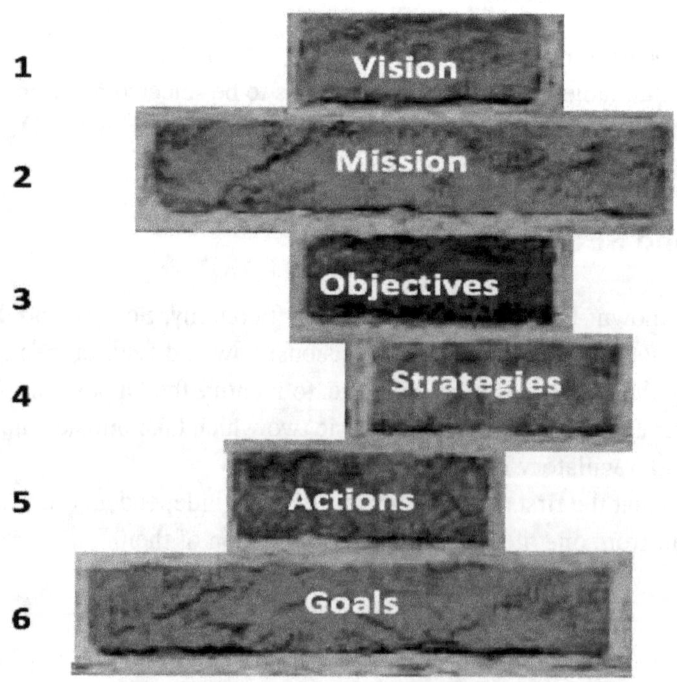

Each of these bricks, of these elements is associated to a question. Answering the question one can identify the elements' contents.

Vision is linked to the question "for Who" and "for What" does the organisation, the company exist. What is the essence of its being in existence? What is its motivation. Vision is a philosophical primitive. It is the one and only element that does not have a metrics. It is a final assertion, a not appealable verdict. It is the general framework of whatever has to do with the organisation/company. Vision implies the acknowledgment of the ecosystem at large to which all elements belong. Please notice that the above listed six elements have a fractal geometry, therefore they are scale invariant. The same elements and question can be asked at the personal level: "for what and for who am I doing what I am doing, shall I do what I will do". The vision is the starting point of all processes that deal with change and learning.

Once the "For Who" and "For What" questions have been answered then, and only then, the mission issue can be addressed answering to a very simple, but of utmost importance question: "Who". Given my vision, who have I to be, what abilities, competences, experience, talents, shall I have to realise my vision. Mission has to do with identity, with the perception that the people have of themselves, as individuals and as part of an organisation, a community. Too often this point is totally misunderstood. Take the Vision and Mission statement of major companies and one will find that they are wrong.

A couple of examples.

General Electric's Mission and Vision

General Electric Company's (GE) mission is to usher in the next industrial era and to "build, move, power, and cure the world." Its vision is to focus on businesses that connect to its core competencies and is a market leader in (Stephans, n.d.).

Too bad that both statements are formally wrong. First comes the vision, then the mission. Moreover, the vision statement addresses and answer the question "for what", totally forgetting the "for who" one. The mission does not answer the question "Who": who are the people with whom the company will materialise its vision. As it will be shown in a while, it is not a mission statement, but the description of either an objective, or a goal.

Ford Motor Company's Vision Statement is "*people working together as a lean, global enterprise for automotive leadership.*" (Thompson, 2015) The company also explains, "*Automotive leadership is measured by the satisfaction of our customers, employees, investors, dealers, suppliers and communities.*"

Thus, Ford's vision statement has the following major points:

- Global leadership.
- Emphasis on stakeholders.
- Lean business.

In this case, the vision statement is almost correct. What is wrong is the order of the list of major points. It should be:

- Emphasis on stakeholders (for who).
- Global leadership (for what).
- Lean business (for what).

Ford Motor Company's Mission Statement is *One Team. One Plan. One Goal.* Ford explains that the expanded form of its mission statement is as follows:

- **One Team:** People working together as a lean, global enterprise for automotive leadership, as measured by: Customer, Employee, Dealer, Investor, Supplier, Union/Council, and Community Satisfaction.
- **One Plan:** Aggressively restructure to operate profitably at the current demand and changing model mix; Accelerate development of new products our customers want and value; Finance our plan and improve our balance sheet; Work together effectively as one team.
- **One Goal:** An exciting viable Ford delivering profitable growth for all.

The mission statement would have been much more correct if Ford would have declared that the statement was "One team". In this case it would have been centred on people.

The other two elements of the mission statement are, again, either objectives or goals.

Interesting the case of Oerlikon.

- **Vision:** Oerlikon creates innovative industrial solutions for a better life.
- **Mission:** Oerlikon strives to be your most reliable business partner worldwide; We increase value through high-quality innovative industrial solutions, continuously; We engage highly qualified professionals; Our commitment is your success.

The vision statement is correct at the fifty per cent, because it answers one of the two basic questions, the "for what" one. Not clear "for who" it does what it does. The other question is answered in the first assertion of the mission statement, i.e. *Oerlikon strives to be your most reliable business partner worldwide.*

Of the other three parts of the mission statement only the third one deals with the mission, reading: *We engage highly qualified professionals.* The other two assertions are again, objectives or goals.

Therefore, a nice Oerlikon Vision would have been: "Oerlikon creates innovative industrial solutions for a better life, striving to be your most reliable business partner worldwide". Does it sound convincing?

The mission statement?

"We engage highly qualified professionals". Concise, direct, effective.

The author strongly recommends to do this exercise every possible time. Take the Vision and Mission statement and check them.

Once it is clear who is who, on what kind of people the company can count on, then, and only then, the objectives can be defined. It is not a simple task. It requires creativity, a multidisciplinary approach, willingness to take risks, inspiration, passion. An objective is a specific result that a person or system aims to achieve within a time frame and with available resources. A starting time and a closing time are required. To achieve an objective to early or to late is always a dangerous mistake. Once these time are fixed, they cannot be changed. If one changes them, then also the objective has to be changed. There is a specific time for specific objectives. The objective has to be specific and measurable. Objectives deal with permissions. If the permission is not granted, by the company decision makers, by oneself, no objective can exist. Permission are intimately linked with believes. If one does not believe to be able to do something, the permission to do this something will never be granted. It happens too many times that companies find themselves at the edge of chaos only because they do not believe in their capacity, they will not grant themselves the permission to act.

Objectives answer the questions "Why?"

Only if the objective is properly defined can the strategy to achieve that goal be defined. Hence, strategy exists as a function of the objective. Always.

Strategy answers the question "How?", "When? and "Where?". How will the available resources, material and immaterial, be deployed when in a set of actions to take place where in order to reach the goals defined by the objectives. The set of actions is also known as "Tactics". Strategy identifies the opportunities and external constraints that have to be taken into account, to which one has to react or be proactive.

The author strongly recommends a careful reading of the Johnson & Johnson "Our Credo"., available at the URL https://www.jnj.com/about-jnj/jnj-credo. Robert Wood Johnson, former chairman of the company from 19332 to 1963, crafted "Our Credo" in 1943, and it is much more than a moral compass to be social responsible. It is the narrative, continuously updated and revised, consequence of having almost perfectly aligned the six bricks that have been already described, and it is a recipe for business success.

To consolidate the ideas that have been presented, an example can be of great help.

Let us take the case of President George W. Bush and the Iraq war and consider this important page of modern history as if it is a "business case".

First element to consider is the vision. Vision answers, in the framework and logics proposed by the author, to the questions: For Who and For What does the Organisation exist?

The first proposed vision was not very convincing: "Axis of Evil": war against terrorism. Not very inspiring. Did not answer the questions "For Who" and for "What".

The second one could have been convincing: "Grave and Growing danger to the US", because Saddam Hussein had "weapons of mass destruction". Too bad that this assertion was quite exaggerated and manipulated, not backed-up field evidence.

At last, the third Vision ended up being the winning one: "Liberty". Simple, clear concept. Everybody can agree with it. Many metaphors can be sketched on its basis. Very effective from a marketing point of view to create consensus. International consensus. More than 30 nations became part of the "coalition of thc willing". Thc Iraq war was a World War, but few noticed it.

Then comes the Mission, i.e. finding an answer for the question "Who?".

The author asks permission to underline the fact that very many honourable colleagues have a complete different interpretation of what mission is all about. They consider mission the objectives meta-level, i.e. the general description of what the organisation is supposed to achieve, from which objectives should be extracted. As declared in the introduction, it is not an issue about who is right and who is wrong. What matters is the internal coherence of the various, different interpretations. If it is present, then whatever description is acceptable.

Let us answer to the proposed question. Who do I have in my organisation, what are their competences, abilities, experiences, relationships? In the Iraq war case under analysis, there are four Who: Army, Navy, Air Force, Marines.

Thank to these four Who, the design of plausible objectives can be put together. If the Marine Corps would not have been available, it would have been a total nonsense to set as an objective the conquest of the harbour of Bassora by night by sea. No Air Force no dominance and control of the air space. No Army? Impossible to take possession of the bridges on the Euphrates river.

Once the Objectives are clearly defined, then it is a matter of designing the strategy that, making the optimal use of available resources, allows the Coalition of the Willing to reach the planned goals thorough a sequence of well executed actions.

Solution Component #2: Understand Your Position

Would you tell me, please, which way I ought to go from here?

That depends a good deal on where you want to get to, said the Cat.

I don't much care where– said Alice.

Then it doesn't matter which way you go, said the Cat" (Carroll & Tenniel, 1965).

The Cheshire cat is right. If one does not care where to go, it does not matter which way to go. It also true that the sure way not to get lost, is not knowing where to go". But even if one knows where to go, this is of little help if it is not clear where one is, from where one starts his/her journey. Same is true for organisations and companies.

One has to know and understand his/her position.

SWOT analysis is a good tool to obtain this result, but it is not sufficient. It is a good thing to appreciate internal capabilities, expressed as Strengths and Weaknesses, and external Opportunities and Threats, but these elements make sense if one put them in relation with the competitors SWOT analysis. In other words, multiple SWOT have to be made: one on ourselves, and one for each of our competitors (Figure 10). But even this is not sufficient.

Figure 10. Multiple SWOT analysis

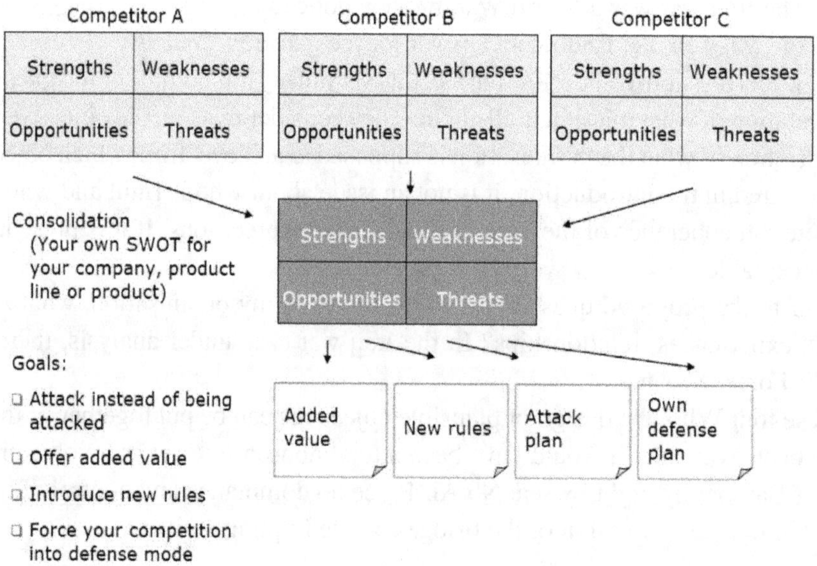

The complementors (Brandenburger & Malebuff, 1996) SWOT analysis has also to be performed. To explain what a complementor is, we have to go back to the given definition of company, or organisation at large: An organisation exists to create wealth in a continuous and growing way over time. Therefore, a competitor, is somebody who shall do whatever he/she can to reduce our wealth over time. A complementor is the exact opposite: it is somebody wo shall do everything he/she can to increase our wealth over time. In game theory, a competitor plays with us, in the best case, a zero-sum game: he/she does not increase his/her wealth and we are reducing ours. His/her objective is to push us into a negative sum game: he/she increases her/his wealth and we have ours proportionally reduced.

The complementor does whatever he/she can to have us playing a positive sum game: we increase our wealth, he/she increases her wealth, in a virtuous, continuously growing spiral. To make an example, it is the kind of relationship between Intel and Microsoft. The more powerful the chip, the more refined the operating system, and the more refined the operating system, them more applications will be available, increasing the market base and the number of potential customers. The more the customers, the higher the sales, the higher the money available to develop a new chip, more powerful, supporting a better operating system, on which more applications can run, making happy a wider customer base, which will buy more computers, more chips, more revenues, more money for R&D for new chips, and on and on…

If the goals of the competitors SWOT analysis are to be pro-active instead of reactive, to increase the added value embedded in ones' products and services, being market leader and rules maker, the goals of the complementors analysis is to create new patterns, to share risks, to define non-linear value added network in place of the classical, linear, value added chain.

It is very important, to understand the basic difference between linear phenomena and non-linear ones, between chain based dynamics, and network ones. Please refer to Figure 11.

Let us consider a classical Cartesian coordinate system where the x-axis is time, and the y-axis is whatever function of time: i.e. revenues or employees or market share, always as a function of time.

Conventional wisdom says that the ideal growth path to follow is the one indicated with letter a.

Figure 11. Linear and nonlinear phenomena

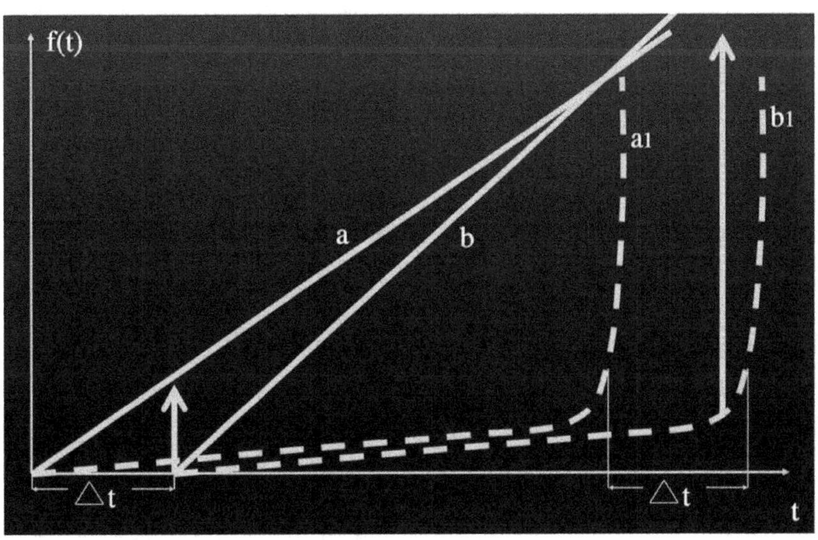

Nice, clean, linear. Let us assume that this is the revenues' curve of company A which, at a given time t_0 starts to sell an innovative sneaker. Mister A does everything right and the revenues grow.

Lady B, owner of company B is not an innovator like mister A, she is much less risk prone. She understands that Mr a has a nice product, and she starts to analyse his performances. She does a nice SWOT competitor/complementors comparative analysis and she understands that she has to jump into this new market. Given the fact that she starts with a time delay Δt, she finds herself in a better situation that the one that Mr A effaced at the beginning of him selling the new product. Now customers now the product, it is easier to understand their neds, the value proposition to make, the narrative supporting the product. She performs as well as Mr A, but because of the afore listed advantages, after a while, according to curve b, she will eventually surpass Mr A, even if he continues to do everything right.

Curve a and b are purely theoretical ones because in real life, nothing, ever, obeys to a linear dynamic. Linearity is an approximation of non-linearity, introduced because it is much easier to joggle with in mathematical terms. Linear equations are easy to integrate, and whenever there is a model made of linear equation function of time, easy forecasting is possible. Real life is non-linear. Going back to Mr A and lady B, a different story can be told. Mr A takes his risks and introduces a new, innovative sneaker on the market. He does everything correct and he follows curve a_1. The growth curve a_1 shows an initial, painful, slow growth. Mr A does not panic, he sticks with his new product, continues to invest on it. Pioneer customers buy the sneaker, people start to see them around, youngsters consider them very cool, they start to share comments and experience on the social networks and- bang- almost overnight the demand explodes. Mr A was expecting it, because he knows that network based dynamics are always exponential. He had enough sneakers in stock to fulfil the exploding demand. Great success. He is on Time magazine front page. In the meantime, Lady B is standing by, studying, analysing, waiting. After the same time delay Δt of the already told linear story, she puts herself in action, tracing curve b_1. She does her best, same great performance of Mister A, but whatever she does she will never beat, or even join Mr A. She will never make it; does not matter how much money she will pour her the new product. She will end filing for Chapter 13 because the relative gap between her revenues and Mr A ones will never close down as it did in story 1. The fact of the matter is that when Mr A changes his curve gradient from almost flat to almost vertical, his relative power will be such that whatever lady B does, he will crunch her. The differential, represented in Figure 11 by the grey up-arrows, in story 1 gets smaller and smaller over time, in story 2, once Mr A is after the elbow of the J curve, it goes to infinity and beyond. Whatever B moves, A will checkmate. Game over.

Moral of the stories: no dynamic is linear, no strategy can be linear, no portfolio management can be linear. If someone shows you nice linear curves, it is because he/she is either cheating, or he/she gives to much thrust to consultants and excel graphs.

Solution Component #3: Strategic Management Is a Never-Ending Cycle, Defined by All Company's Members

Q.: When shall a strategic management cycle start?

A.: Never, because it never stops from the day one of the coming in existence of whatever organization, and no organization can start it existence if it does not have a strategy.

Strategic management is a continuous process, which starts when the Vision has been defined and communicated, and the Mission is understood, i.e. the right men are the right place and everybody knows for who and for what the organisation/company exists. If a gap shows up because of a misalignment of the intended strategy with the executed one, then it is time to sit again at the strategy drowning board in order to find out why that gap has opened, It has to be noticed that gaps can be either positive, or negative. A positive gap is a situation in which the results are much better than expected, generating problems. An example. A car manufacturer introduces on the market a new model, and it had planned that the basic version of the car would account for 70 per cent of sales, whilst the top of the range, 25 per cent more expensive, and with higher margins, would fill the 30 per cent of manufacturing capacity left.

Customers not always behave as expected, and 70 the car manufacturer find out that the 70 per cent of them want to buy the luxury version. Too bad that all suppliers' contracts were signed based on the planned 70-economic/30-luxury mix. The result is a catastrophe. Not only the contracts have to be discussed again, not only there are lots of basic versions' cars piling up, unsold, not only customers are badly upset because the waiting time is too long, but many of them, once the need for a new car has been triggered, to fulfil it buy a competitors' car.

Even if the word strategy, as has been seen, derives from the word *Strategos*, the Master and Commander in Chief in ancient Greece cities-state, it is not a one-man task. Neither is it a team work. It is an organization wide effort. Everybody in the company has to be involved. At every level. One should talk of Total Strategy Planning, meaning that the totality of the company has to be involved with the strategic management effort. As already said, it is a continuous process. Every time a gap shows up, every time the distance between intended strategy and realised strategy broadens up, every time either the objective time or the strategy deployment time, or the actions timetable is not respected, every time there is an evolution or change in the company's vision, then the planning process has to be started again. It has not to be a rearrangement, a fine tuning of a previous process: it has to start from scratch.

The formal strategic planning for a large, multiple business units' company, is represented in Figure 12. Obviously, the more the organisation is small and simple, the faster the planning process, but it will always require twelve steps, following a path which goes up and down the organisation.

Figure 12. Formal strategic planning process

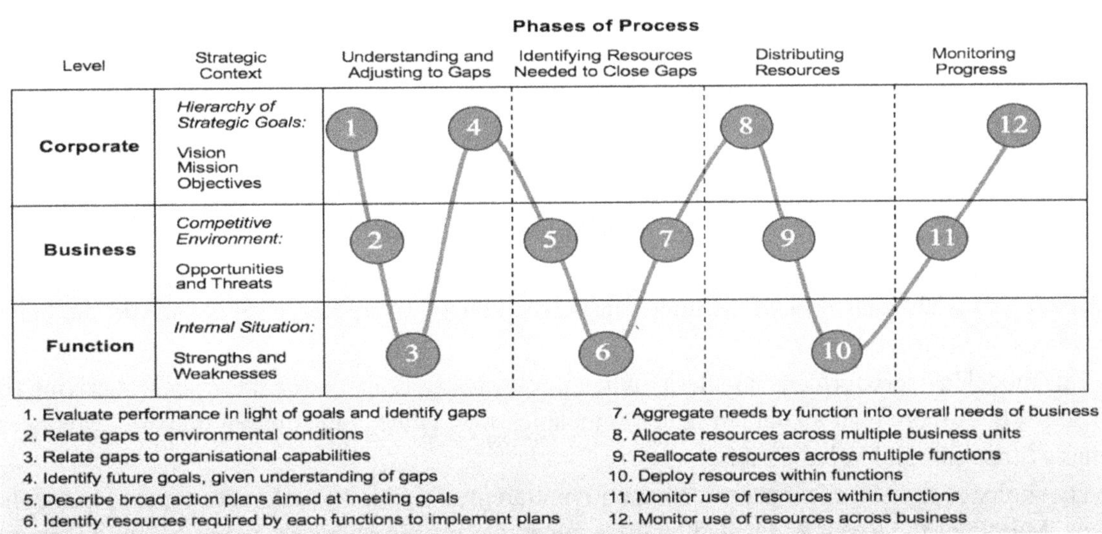

The process starts at the corporate level. The Board of Directors responsibilities are to check and confirm, or change, the Vision; verify the Mission; define the Objectives and fix the strategies' hierarchy.

First thing to do is, periodically, is to evaluate the recorded performances in light of goals and identify gaps. Quoting Confucius: "Study the past if you would define the future".

If a gap is identified, then the Business level comes into play and the various Business Units (BUs) are asked to relate the gap to the environmental, external conditions (step 2), and in turn, the various BUs' functions are asked to do the same looking at the internal dimensions, at the organisational capabilities (step 3).

The collected information, data and knowledge, are send to the Corporate Level where (step 4) they are used to understand gap's causes and consequences, and to identify future strategy, actions and goals.

These elements are transmitted to the Business Units and they are asked to describe their broad individual action plan aimed at reaching the proposed goals (step 5). On the basis of the sketched action plans, the functions level identifies which are the resources required to implement the submitted action plans (step 6). The needs expressed by the functions are aggregated into overall needs of the business units (step 7) and then communicated to the Corporate level. The available resources are then allocated at the different Business Units and they take care of reallocating them across the multiple functions (step 8). The functions, once they receive the resources, display them in operations (step 10).

The last two steps are usually considered the least exciting ones, but they are absolutely critical. The success of whatever plan follows the 25 to 75 rule: the last two steps (step 11 and step 12) are responsible for the 75 per cent of the final success. For sure, the design and building of a strategy is much more fun that its monitoring and control. But the devil is in the execution. The best people should be responsible of it. It is not a routine work, it's the company leaders' work. Only well monitored and controlled activities can produce a track record allowing weak signals to be detected, gaps to be seen just when they open up, minimising wastes and risks.

The periodic curve shown in Figure 12, swinging up and down in the organisation's structure, involves everybody. The amplitude is function of the company size. The frequency is a function of the market/products life cycle. The shorter the life, the higher the frequency. Strategic planning revisions can be done on a weekly basis if one works in the high fashion business, or on a ten years basis if the company manufactures commercial airplanes… and never forget that moving fast does not imply moving in the right direction

Solution Component #4: Competitive Analysis

The author has touched in the previous solution component #3 the issue of competitors and complementors, and their role in positive, zero and negative sum games. It is worth to talk about it in greater detail, because it deeply affects the competitive position analysis. To tell the truth, it heavily influences the analysts "Weltanschaung".

The most widely known model for representing the competitive positioning is the Michael Porter's five forces one (Figure 13).

This model had an enormous popularity when it was presented. It made a lot of sense, deriving from a field study of more than a hundred major companies worldwide, and is based on two key concepts: Generic Strategies and Value Chain.

The choice of one of the four generic competitive strategies - Overall Cost Leadership, Differentiation, Focus, Middle of the Road- is dictated by the competitive position which is the result of the interplay of the five forces.

Figure 13. Michael Porter's five forces model

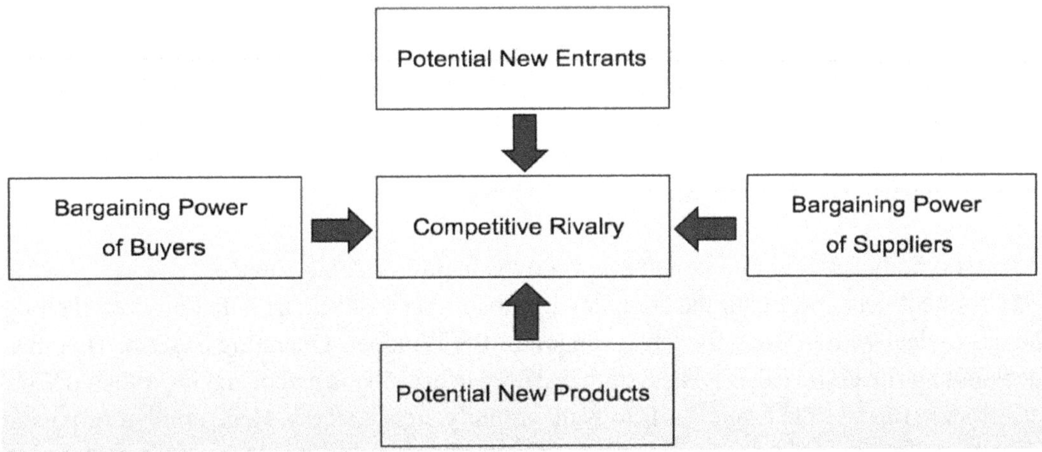

There are two main problems with this model. The first one is that it is applicable if the ecosystem is almost static, things change very slowly, and it is possible to consider the interplay between the five independent forces as linear and independent. This is no more the case. That world has evaporated.

Moreover, the competitive position is the result of the pressures generated by the five forces. Pressure is the ratio between a force and a surface: the larger the surface, the lower the pressure, the force being equal. Therefore, the larger the company, the better it is, because the pressure will be lower. Too bad that the larger it is, the longer its reaction time becomes, and it gets into the dinosaur syndrome: the animal is deadly wounded, but it does not know it because its nervous system is so slow and large that before its brain gets alerted, it is already dead.

The second problem is that it is based on value chains. As it has been already shown, nowadays there are value networks. A total different story. To apply today Porter's model is very, very dangerous.

A.M. Brandenburger and B. J. Malebuff (op. cit.1966)"Co-opetion" model is much more interesting and is a tool that can be used with success, but handling it with due care (Figure 14).

Figure 14. Co-opetition value network

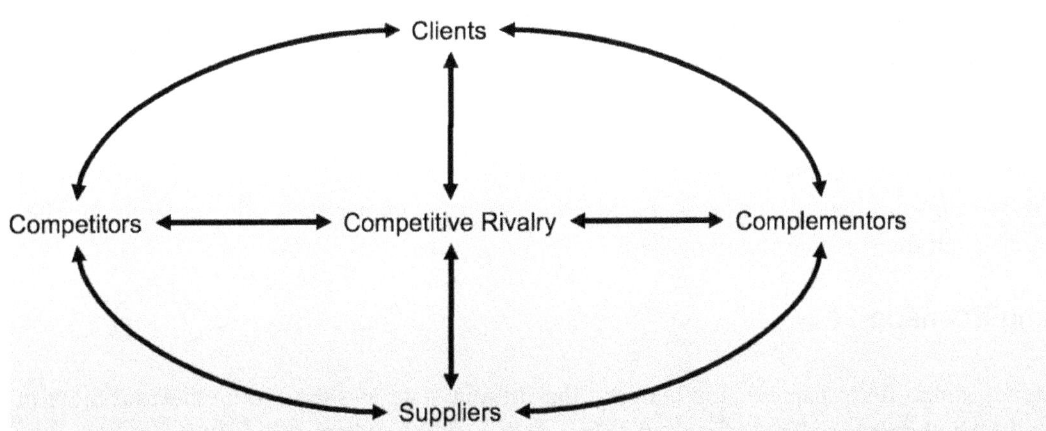

No chains, no forces, no pressures, no generic strategies in this case, only continuous non-linear dynamics, game theory at its best, and a lot of jazz.

Because of the interplays and the fact that it is a system in a non-equilibrium state, whatever tiny disequilibrium can induce major changes. Roles can change, relationships can change all the time.

Let us assume that the company is, once more, Intel. Its complementor is Microsoft. To be noticed that the opposite is also true. Microsoft sees Intel as its complementor. This is always the case: complementor and company have a relationship of mutual interest.

Case #1: Everybody is doing its job, and everybody is happy. Nothing happens.

Case #2: A client gets upset with the company Microsoft because she/he is fed up with the bugs she/he has to deal with in using the latest version of the Windows Operating System. Then the client decides to write his own operating system. He does it, organising and managing a shared Web based effort and after a while Linux starts to walk around. Great success. Huge number of people, well of servers, start to use it. So many that Intel offers Mr. Torvalds, this is the name of the gentleman behind Linux, to design and manufacture a Linux dedicated microprocessor. At this point Intel plays the complementor to Microsoft in the Windows ecosystem, but is a competitor to it in the Linux one. Nothing is static any longer. A Client can become a competitor, a complementor can become a supplier and the supplier can become a complement. All possible combinations are possible. Welcome non-linear complexity.

Solution Component #5: Scenario Planning

It has been said at the very beginning that strategic management is a *teché*, i.e. art. This may explain the title of Peter Schwartz's (1991) book "The Art of the Long View: Planning for the future in an Uncertain World", considered the seminal publication on scenario planning.

The author knows that at this point the readers are expecting to get an acceptable definition of what Scenario Planning is about. No reason why expectation should be disappointed.

Scenario planning is a strategic planning method used to look beyond the time scale of strategic planning. It is quite normal to look 20 or more years in the future. A scenario is a plausible story based on a sequence of possible events. It is not a quantitative method. To tell the truth a scenario is a set of plausible stories. The analysis starts from a very simple question: what if….? What if in 30 years' time cold fusion is commercially available? What if climate change has no anthropic cause and is a consequence of natural phenomena? What if we shall live 200 years, on average, healthy, strong and efficient?

Combining known facts about the future, with the three key driving forces –Politics, Economy and Society- narratives of the future can be build. Again there is no such thing as a "true" or "false" scenario. It is only a story, a fiction.

There are many different processes that can be followed to build a scenario. The author proposes three of them. Some elements are present in all three proposed approaches, other are unique. The author will describe all three of them, step by step.

Building Scenario 1

It starts focusing on the gap existing between the Present state and the Future Desired State in order to identify the elements of discontinuity that have to be generated in order to fill the gap (Figure 15).

Figure 15. Building scenario #1

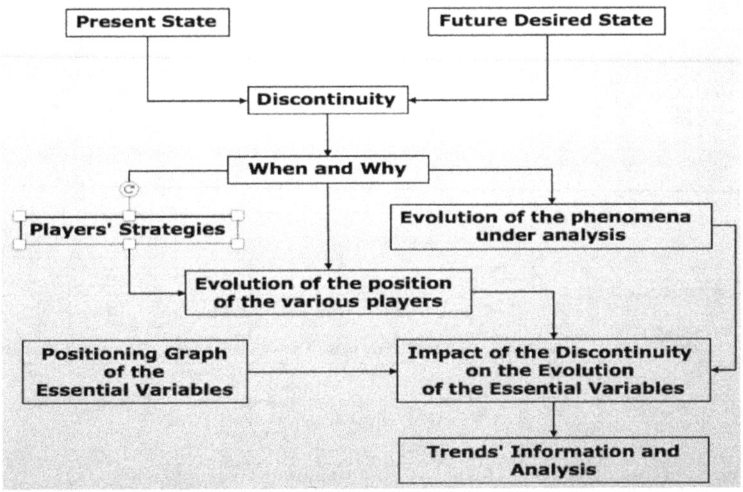

When the elements of discontinuity have been identified, then the question "When and Why" they will show up has to addressed and answered.

The answers allow the definition of the players' strategies and the evolution of the positioning of the different players on the common playground being described in terms of its components: Politics, Economy and Society. The When and Why answers allow also the understanding of the possible evolution of the phenomena that have been identified analysing the gap between Present State and Future State.

Combining the elements feeding the evolution on the phenomena under analysis, together with the evolution of the positioning of the various players and the interplay of the Essential Variables, the impact of the discontinuity on the evolution of these essential variables emerges in term of trends.

The last step is the analysis of these trends in order to put together their narrative. Does not matter which process is followed to build a scenario. There are always three possible outcomes: a positive, a neutral and a negative story; an optimistic, a neutral and a pessimistic narrative. Three and no more than three. One is dangerous because the risk that the listener ends up thinking that it is a "true story" is always present. The better the story, the higher the probability. There is no true or false, it is pure phantasy. Two are dangerous because they can ignite religious wars between "believers". Three is the perfect number to feed dialogues ad discussions.

The second approach is much more analytical that the first one, mainly qualitative. It is a combination of processes typical of the long term planning and of methods used I strategic planning. This explains why it may be possible to elaborate forecasts, not just "what if "stories.

As shown in Figure 16 the process starts combining the on-going phenomena affecting the organisation performing the Scenario Analysis with the analysis of its ecosystem. In essence it is just a normal SWOT analysis with the added value of the input coming from the Structural Analysis of the organisation. This allows the identification of the problem-space, i.e. the space in which the problem/s has/have to be found, and the set of variables that optimise its description. The next step is the configuration of an advanced SWOT matrix, where one of the dimensions are the external variables, whilst the other one are the internal dependent factors. In mathematical terms, this step defines the functions and their dependent variables. The ex-post analysis and the present state analysis have the objective of describing

Figure 16. Building scenario #2

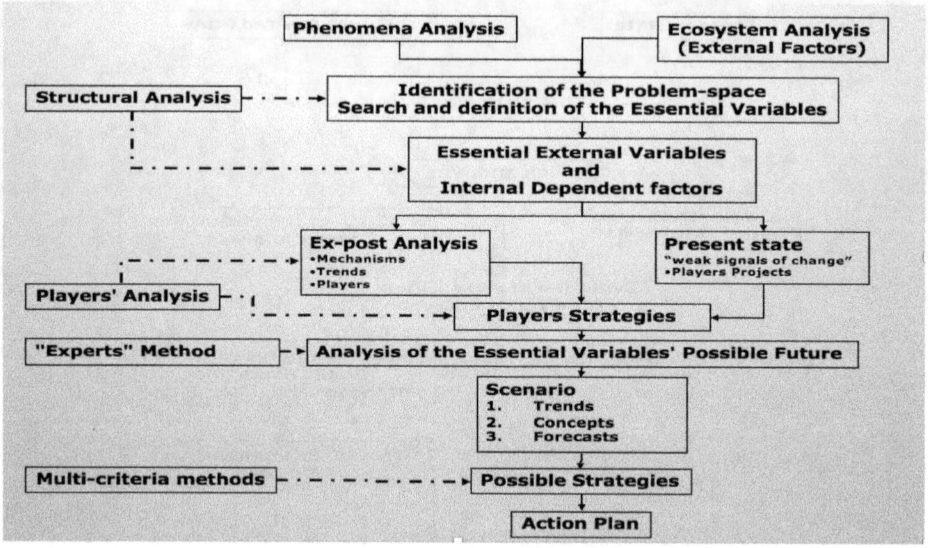

the players' strategies, based on their analysis in order to understand who is who, where he is, what he does and with which timing: competitors, complementors, customers, suppliers.

At this stage, the scenario builders find them self almost at lost because of the very high number of possible alternatives. A selection is needed and the Experts method is a very effective tool. A presentation of the strategies set will be made to a variegated group external experts and they will make motivated choices, based on their best knowledge.

As a result of this selection it is possible to analyses the possible future of the essential variables and a scenario can be sketched. Because of the high volume of analytical data being available, and because of having defined a set time based functions and variables, forecasts can be made, at least for a well pondered subset of essential variables. Applying multi-criteria methods to the obtained results, possible strategies can be formulated and relative action plans deployed.

The last scenario building process is, apparently, the more elegant and simple of the three being presented. The reason why it is apparently simple lies in the fact that it is the most difficult to use because its main variable is the one, as explained before that has zero elasticity: time.

Two are the time based analysis that have to be performed: diachronic and synchronous. Knowing that it may bother the reader, proper definitions are mandatory.

According to the Merriam -Webster Dictionary Diachronic is defined as: *": of, relating to, or dealing with phenomena (as of language or culture) as they occur or change over a period of time"*.

Same source, definition of Synchronous: *"1: happening, existing, or arising at precisely the same time; 2: recurring or operating at exactly the same periods"*.

The process of this third scenario building method (Figure 17) is analogous to the one that is used to shoot a movie. A story board is prepared, showing the sequence of actions, scenes, actors involved. Then the shooting begins, transferring the story board discrete scenes into chunks of exposed film. At the end of the shooting, the editing starts, the chunks are cut and pasted and at the end the movie is ready.

Figure 17. Building scenario #3

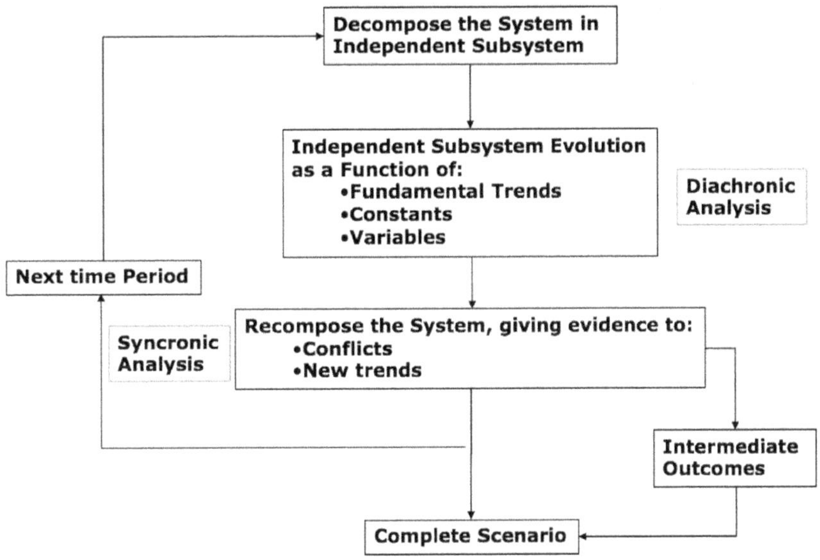

The first thing to do decide is which time lapse has to be used and freeze it. Then the Grand System has to be decomposed into a set of independent sub-system. Having done that, the sub-systems are analysed one at a time, always using the identical time lapse. The results are then assembled, recomposing the Grand System, which is not the same as before because it has aged of the time lapse that has been used. New trends are highlighted, conflicts emerge. Then another time lapse is added, and the process starts again. The iteration continues until the desired time horizon has been reached. For each time lapse, intermediate results can be extracted. When the scenario builders decide that enough is enough, they perform a synchronous analysis, adding up all the recorded time based results, they do the proper editing and the scenario, the movie showing the future, is ready. Easy to describe, very hard to do. The analysts must be very knowledgeable of the problem-space they are dealing with, very neutral, very smart. The risk is ending up not with a with a critical mass of data triggering a result, but with a critical mess.

Solution Component #6: Time

Yes, indeed, time, together with "people" are elements both of the problem pace, and of the solution space. time "is" the most important dimension to be taken into account in planning. it does not matter if it is strategic, marketing, product, portfolio, whatever planning… No time, no planning. It is the only dimension that does not have elasticity, none at all, zero. It is not renewable; one cannot stock it. The only thing that it is possible to do is to fix the Time Zero when the process shall start and the End Time. For every and each project there is only one Time Zero and one End Time. They cannot be changed. If one of them changes, then the project changes, its mission, objectives, strategies, goals. Everything. The two time-tics are interlinked. If one changes, also the other must change according to the other one. If the process is late, it is never possible to fix the problem just moving the End Time down the timeline. If one stretches the closing time, pushing it forward, then the contents of the stretched planning process loose whatever meaning. Whenever the time changes in a planning process, the process has to be redesigned from scratch.

The life-time of the process is function of the process itself. The economic-financial planning known as budget, must have the same life-time of the fiscal year. Strategic planning usually does not go beyond 36 months' time. Long Term/Scenario Planning does not start before 36 months.

Solution Component #7: Organigraphs

The last paragraph of Problem #4 "Structure" underlines the fact that organigrams does not say how the organization creates wealth, what generates the customers' value proposition. In order to do that, "Organigraphs" (Harvard, 2014), created by Mintzberg and Van der Heyden (1999) are needed.

They are not just pictures of a company structure; they are also maps, showing the organisation's territory, what the company is, its Vision: why it exists, for who.

Organigraphs contain two conventional components: set and chain.

A set (Figure 18) is made of items, quite often loosely connected one to the other as a collection, a group, or a portfolio. Many professional service firms operate as sets, usually sharing common resources—facilities, funds, overall management.

Organizations exist for purposes of connection, usually shown by the second component: chains, so embedded in business management culture that strategies are described in terms of value chains –remember Porter - and logistics in terms of supply chains. Chains, by geometry, are linear, standardized, reliable, comfortable (Figure 19).

Figure 18. Set

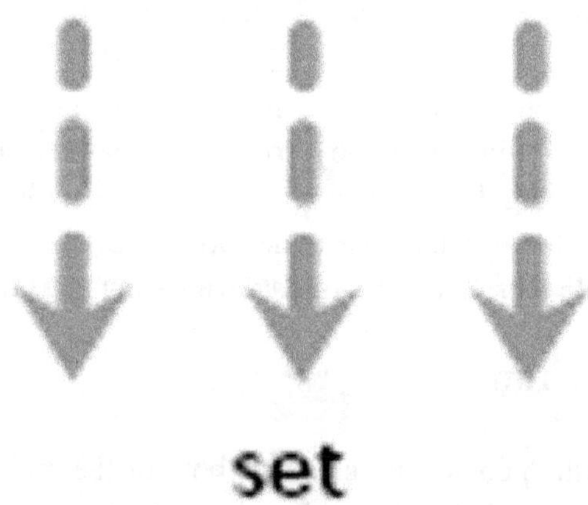

Figure 19. Chain

Remember the difference between linear curves and exponential ones? Linear is artificial; non-linear is the real life. Chains cannot clarify and systematize the complex processes that constitute business today. Hubs and Web, the two less conventional components of the organigraphs, suggested by Mintzberg and Van der Heyden, can.

A hub is a coordinating centre (Figure 20).

It is any physical or operational point at which people, things, or information move. A manager can be a hub. Just think of a football coach. And so can a core competence. In fact, in many instances chains may also be considered hubs.

Oftentimes connections are more complicated than that and webs describe this reality (Figure 21).

Webs, as we have come to see, are nets with no centre; they allow open-ended communication and continuous movement of people and ideas.

Figure 20. Hub

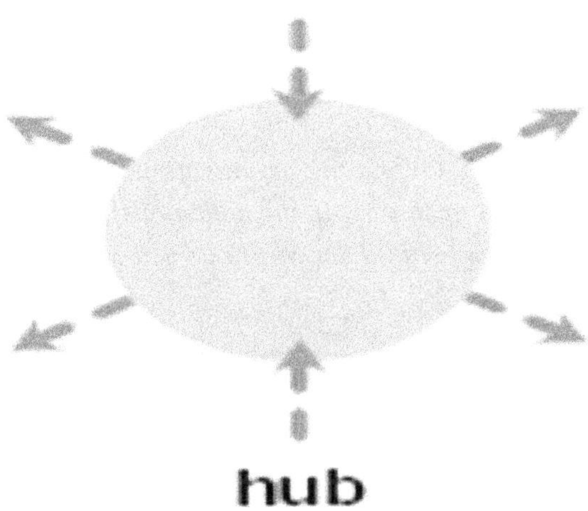

Figure 21. Web

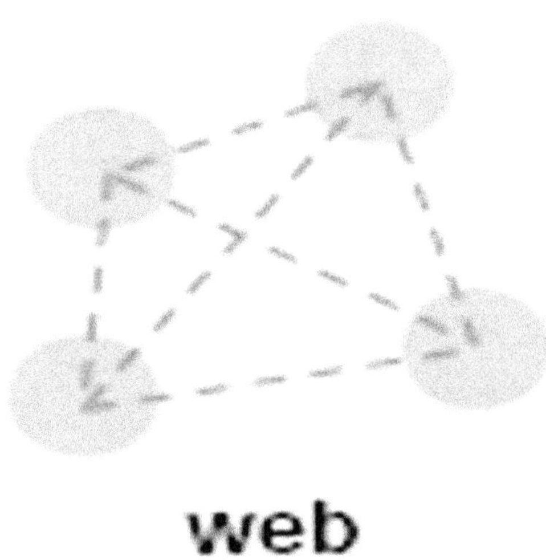

Any complex project can be seen as a web. The same is true for every portfolio that has to be managed.

These four elements -set, chain, hub and web- expand both how organizations are viewed, and our thinking about strategy.

When an organigraph is drawn using sets, chains, hubs, and webs, and other shapes conveying meaning, as funnels, suggesting a chain in which a transformation takes place, present in the organigraph of a newspaper presented in Figure 22, interesting things happen.

Unlike the organisational chart with its hierarchical rules of arrangement, an organigraph requires the creation of a customised picture of the organisation to be drawn. Organigraphs have to do with relationships and processes. Imagination, creativity, open-mind are required. Pretty rare abilities.

The author quotes here the explanation that Mintzberg and Van der Hayden give in their essay to show how an organigraph works.

...let's look at the exhibit "Organigraph of a Newspaper". A newspaper brings in a variety of materials from society—news, photographs, and the like. Employees at the newspaper screen the material, transform it, and assemble it into a single document. The document then goes to a plant for reproduction, and the copies are distributed back to society, indeed to many of the same people responsible for the inputs, such as letters to the editor and classified ads.

The newspaper organigraph shows that while the organization's overall flow is a chain, other forms coexist within it. The reporters' relationships with the community, for example, can be seen as a web: the stock-in-trade of many reporters is to build networks of sources. And the whole newspaper might be

Figure 22. Organigraph of a newspaper

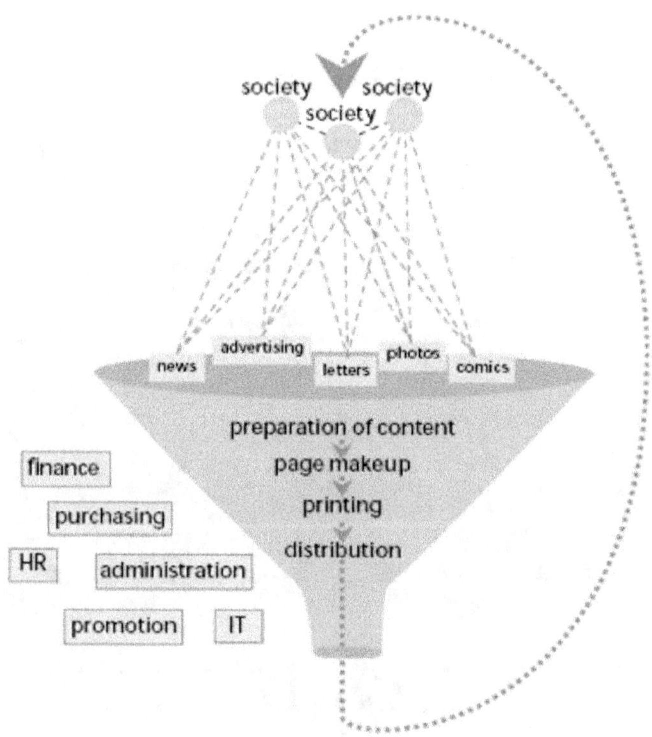

considered a hub, upon which all sorts of inputs converge—classified and other advertisements, letters to the editor, article ideas, and so on—to be dispersed back into society. Because they are not integral to the main linear flow of the organization, various support and administrative functions, such as purchasing and finance, are shown around the hub, not within it.

What a different picture than the traditional org chart! For a comparison, see the exhibit "Newspaper Org Chart." (Figure 23).

Those little stacked boxes imply an organization consisting of independent agents. The picture doesn't even show advertisers, and it suggests that the human resources department is somehow in the thick of the company's operating processes. The organigraph, in contrast, shows that advertisers are both sources of content (as part of the web) and customers and puts HR's role in perspective. It also draws attention to the scope of the business, suggesting which activities ought to be retained inside the core of the company and which might be candidates for outsourcing, such as printing and distribution.

RECOMMENDATIONS

It is now time to offer a possible, quite innovative approach to strategic management and planning. A sort of check list that allows the design of a plausible strategy. Please notice that this approach is scale invariant, it is an object showing a fractal geometry. It can be used to design a personal strategy, an organisation's or company's one, or a National strategy. No short cuts, please. All steps have to be covered. In the right order. Is like putting a jigsaw puzzle together. To get the full image, all pieces must be available. No missing parts.

Here comes the checklist:

Figure 23. Newspaper organigram

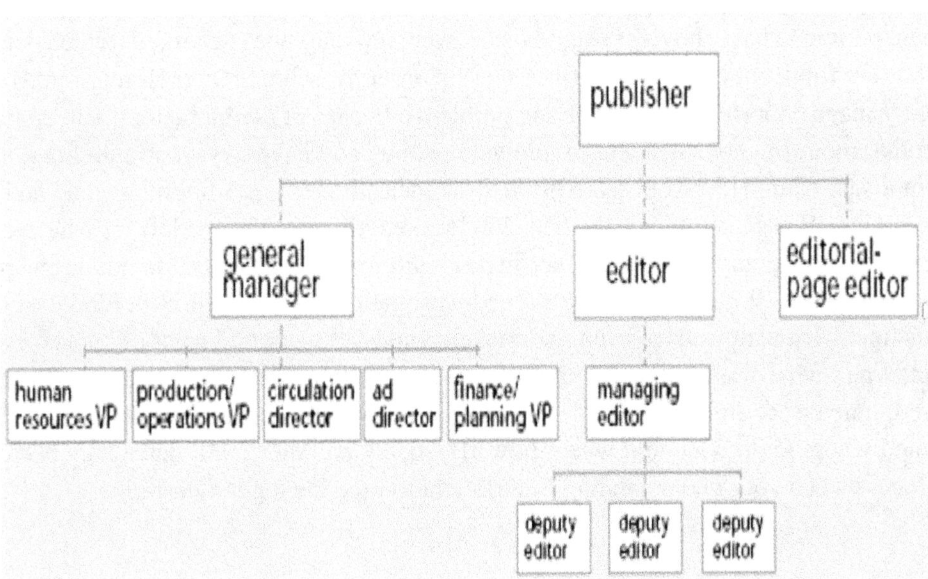

1. Vision, Mission and Objectives.
2. Right people on board.
3. Gap analysis.
4. Time frame.
5. Organigraph.
6. PEST and or PESTEL.
7. SWOT analysis (simple and complex).
8. Positioning matrixes.
9. Long Term/Scenario planning.
10. Story Telling.
11. Execution, Monitoring and Control.

Step 1: First thing to do is to be sure that the Vision is clear to everybody, that its ethics is shared and so are values and characteristics linked to the ethical values. It takes time, a lot of time to get it right and it has a capital importance. It has been discussed why management is synonymous of manipulation. Managers manipulate resources, both material and human. To maximise the probability that this manipulation is done in order to achieve the best possible result in terms of wealth creation and growth in the best interest of all shareholders and stakeholders, a shared ethic is needed. The more a company is ethically sound, the more its culture is honourable and powerful. A Honourable culture is based on vision and its related ethical values ad characteristics and gives agility, focus, and attracts the talents (Bell & Harari, 2001). The vision generates trust, faith. If the reader finds the time, the author strongly recommends to watch the cartoon "Aladdin" (1992), by the Walt Disney Animation Studios. There is a full moon night scene, a glittering river is flowing in the background and Aladdin is standing on a flying carpet, on the wrong side of a balcony on which stands Jasmine. The two are flirting, and Aladdin is inviting her for a little romantic tour on his flying carpet. Jasmine is quite dubious, not sure what to do. But then Aladdin asks her the question, the one to which the only possible answers are Yes or No. He asks her: "Do you have faith in me?". Jasmine does not answer, she stretches her arm, he takes her hand and… well, the author wish not to ruin the suspense. Trust and faith make impossible things happen.

Step 2: Then, be sure to have the right people on board, the wrong ones debarked (which does not mean that they are fired, but placed in the right spot) in order to assign them their mission. Have the best people manage opportunities, not solving problems. In case of doubt, better not to embark. Do not forget that money is not sufficient to motivate people, and keep always in mind that it is so easy to demotivate them. Have your team discuss the ideas, issues and solution as long and as fiercely as the timing allows it. But once the decision is taken, there is no time left for whatever revision.

Step 3: Perform the gap analysis. It does not matter who made it happen. It is not an investigation to find who to blame. It is more a Crime Scene Investigation kind of approach. Find the crime scene, its timeline, what actions have been undertaken, what did work and what did not work, what was expected and what was not expected. Do not waste time to find the villain. Look for intended, realised, unrealised, emergent and deliberated strategies. Understand which resources have been allocated where to do what and when; how effectively and efficiently have they been used; stop the process when your understanding is sufficient to produce a good narrative.

Step 4: Define the time horizon of the next planning cycle having it fitted with the life cycle of your main products/services. Once defined, freeze it. It becomes untouchable. If you change it, everything has to be pondered from the very beginning. Nothing, ever, should be taken for granted.

Step 5: Take out of the safe in the office of the Vice President for Human Resources the company organigram, and make an attempt to sketch your company organigraph. Forget the internal hierarchy, forget the cause-effect relationships. Ask yourselves how your customers see you, how do they think that you create value for them. Find out who are the hubs and the web architects in your company. It is not difficult; you have just to follow the information flows. The points in which the flow is higher are the hubs. The nodes where the information increases its value because of knowledge being added are the webs. The organigraph making is a process managed by asking and carefully listening to the answers. The organigraph will bring evidence to decide which functions and activities have to be internal, which can be bought from the outside, and which can be outsourced. It is not plan cosmetics, it's a critical representation which feeds the Strengths and Weaknesses analysis.

Step 6: To know where to go, it helps a lot to know from where one starts. PEST and PESTEL analysis is an activity that should be continuous, a daily monitoring of the external environment in order to minimize whatever kind of surprises. A set of folders that are adjourned continuously. The political, economic and social environments are those where changes, evolutions, and revolutions occur. Technology is a secondary dimension. It has never been the case that technology has triggered a major political, economic or social change.

Step 7: Among all the tools that are available for strategic analysis, SWOT is the like of a Swiss army knife. The more one uses it, the better the results, and it is really amazing how much understanding can come out of a well done SWOT analysis. Once more, it is a never ending activity. Whenever something changes, either internally or externally, their possible effects have to be studied, the impacts and consequences analysed, and the strategic team has must reconvene around the drawing table. The analysis should always be simple, i.e. looking internally to the organization to which one belongs, and complex, which means applying the same kind of analytical process to the first three competitors, and to the first three complementors. It is of utmost importance to know how our value can be reduced by whom, and it is important to know who are our allies. Whatever organization has boundaries. They can be fuzzy, but nevertheless they exist. The complex SWOT analysis highlights them.

Step 8: Positioning matrix are instrumental to make sense of big data sets. PEST, PESTEL, SWOT analysis generate huge amount of data. Matrixes help to map those data, always keeping in mind that a map is never, ever, the territory. It is an approximation, a tool to reduce the risk of getting lost. The infamous KISS acronym applies also in this case. There are two interpretations for what KISS stands for: Keep It simple and Stupid, but also Keep It simple, Stupid! Two are the author's recommendations. The first one is to keep the number of matrix dimensions as low as possible: two by two is much better that three by three. The second one is to never forget that every single element placed in a matrix has an internal complexity that has to be taken into account. At this point a risk evaluation has to be performed. It is impossible to have a case in which risk is equal to zero. By definition it cannot be zero. One has to evaluate the probability of obtaining the positive outcome and the consequences of it. Usually this evaluation is done looking at the negative outcome and at its impacts. It is much more difficult and challenging to think positively than negatively. And remember there is no difference between an optimist and a pessimist. An optimist is just a very well informed pessimist.

Step 9: The Strategic Plan is ready. Its deliverables have to be the following:

1. Vision
2. Mission
3. Objectives
4. Strategies and relative Strategic goals
5. Position evaluation (e.g. SWOT, Market forces)
6. Needs: Customers and Markets being addressed
7. Actions: What, When, Who
8. Resource Allocation (who shall do what)
9. Contingency Plans
10. Business Plan Deliverables:
11. Company Analysis
    a. Industry Analysis
    b. Customer/Market Analysis
    c. Competitive Analysis
    d. R&D plan (e.g. roadmaps, objectives, resources)
    e. Market plan (e.g. segments, channels, tests, launch dates)
    f. Operations plan (e.g. pilots, manufacturing, service)
    g. Management team (roles and responsibilities)
    h. Financial Plan (e.g. cash flow, funding)

All the collected information, knowledge, items, phenomena, everything that has been elaborated and collected in the process of defining the strategic plan has to be used to draft, in parallel to the strategic plan, the Long Term Scenario. If the strategic plan has to be reconsidered every time something changes internally or externally, the Long term Planning, or Scenario Planning, can be reviewed, say, once a year. When the team is working on closing the annual budget, it should also revise the company's scenario. Strategic plans have a time horizon, on average, between 24 and 36 months. Multiply these value by a factor from the twenty, and the future is yours.

Remember that long term planning is not an extrapolation of existing trends. One has to look for discontinuities, for non-linear dynamics, for plausible sequences of events, not probable ones. There is no modelling behind a scenario, no forecasting whatever, just good guessing, crackpot thinking, rationality.

Step 10: It is so nice to do the analytical work. It is also quite entertaining doing the formulation of the strategy. Much less exciting is its implementation (Figure 24).

Too bad that the success of a strategy lies into its implementation. Five per cent of the effort goes into the two first activities. The real work, the hard one, is implementing the strategy, which means assigning to the right people the strategic leadership, building the action programs, defining the goals' metrics, and the sequence and timing of the monitoring and control activities.

The best way to put this implementation process in place is to build a story that can be told to the organisation's members. All of them. At all levels. All the on-board crew must be informed about the journey's objectives, strategy, actions and goals. A story than should, must be discussed, consensus has to be generated. If someone does not like the narrative, no need to keep him/her on board. Again, this does not mean that firing is the option. Firing should never be an option. It has always a negative connotation, and the responsibilities are always shared. Not being on board does not imply not being on the team. Support roles have the same prestige that operational ones.

Figure 24. The strategy planning process

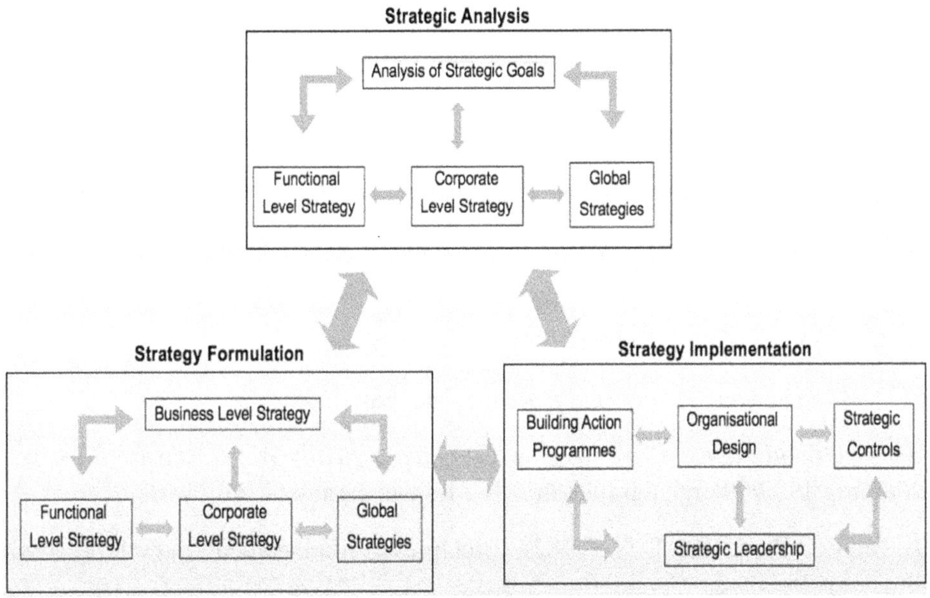

Step 11: The last box in the proposed check list is Execution, Monitoring and Control. It is the day by day activity that allows thing to happen. It requires attention, stamina, being mono-maniac, obsessed, and somehow paranoid. Take Intel's Andy Groove autobiography, and read the title: "Only Paranoid Survive". He was not joking when he chose it, but very, very serious. Execution, monitoring and control are key for success. Always. Whatever you do.

CONCLUSION

Strategy planning, strategic management exist not in the domain of science, but of technology. It is an art, and as it is the case for all arts, experience play a fundamental role. The responsibility of these activities cannot be assigned to a junior. Seniority is very important.

It must be clear to everybody, stakeholders and shareholders, that there is only one Strategos in whatever organization. The one and only one commander in chief, is the CEO. He/she makes the strategic decisions. All others, at different levels with different roles and responsibilities are sherpas. They are instrumental to make the conquest of the company's Mount Everest possible. Everyone in the company is a Sherpa, and all of them should have the proper check list to work with. Continuously.

The proposed check list is just that: a proposal. Every single organisation should design its own personal, cherished check list, improving it, year by year. Because management, being a company, being an entrepreneur, personal happiness is a never ending story of learning, change, growth, failures, successes, and fun.

REFERENCES

Bell, C. R., & Harari, O. (2001). *Beep Beep! Competing in the Age of the Road Runner*. New York, NY: Warner Books, Inc.

Brandenburger, A. M., & Malebuff, B. J. (1996). *Co.opetition*. Doubleday.

Carroll, L., & Tenniel, J. (1965). 6. In *Alice's adventures in Wonderland*. London: Macmillan.

Chandler, A. D. Jr. (1962). *Strategy and Structure: Chapters in the History of the Industrial Enterprise*. Cambridge, MA: The MIT Press.

Collins, J. (2001). *Good to Great*. HarperCollins Publishers Inc.

Dale E. (1973). *Management: Theory and Practice*. McGraw-Hill.

Harvard. (2014). *Organigraphs: Drawing How Companies Really Work*. Retrieved January 29, 2016, from https://hbr.org/1999/09/organigraphs-drawing-how-companies-really-work

Irwin, R. D., Terry, G.R., & Rue, L.W. (1982). Principles of Management. Dow Jones-Irwin.

Johnson, T. W., & Stinson, J. E. (1978). *Management Today and Tomorrow*. Addison-Wesley Educational Publishers Inc.

Koontz, H., O'Donnell, C., & Weihrich, H. (1990). *Essentials of Management. McGraw-Hill Education.*

Kvint, V. (2005). *Business and Strategic Management*. St. Petersburg, Russia: St. Petersburg University of Humanities and Social Sciences' Publishing House.

Lorenzana, C. C. (1993). *Management Theory and Practice*. Manila, Philippines: RexBook Store.

Mintzber, H., & Van der Heyden, L. (1999, September-October). Organigraphs: Drawing How Companies Really Work. *Harvard Business Review*.

Mintzberg, H. (1978, May). Patterns in Strategy Formation. *Management Science. INFORMS*, *24*(9), 934–948.

Online Etymology Dictionary. (n.d.). Retrieved June 29, 2016, from http://www.etymonline.com/

Risk. (n.d.). Retrieved May 29, 2016, from https://en.wikipedia.org/wiki/Risk

Schwartz, P. (1991). *The Art of the Long View*. Doubleday.

Simon and Garfunkel. (1964). *Sounds of silence* [CD]. Nashville, TN: CBS.

Stephans, J. (n.d.). *Market Realist*. Retrieved February 9, 2016, from http://marketrealist.com/

Stoner, J. A. F. (1982). *Management*. Madison, WI: Prentice-Hall.

Strategy. (n.d.). Retrieved August 29, 2016, from https://en.wikipedia.org/wiki/Strategy

SWOT Analysis. (n.d.). Retrieved April 29, 2016, from https://en.wikipedia.org/wiki/SWOT_analysis

Thompson, A. (2015). *Ford Motor Company's Vision Statement, Mission Statement - Panmore Institute.* Retrieved February 29, 2016, from http://panmore.com/ford-motor-company-vision-statement-mission-statement

Vector Consulting Services. (n.d.). Retrieved June 29, 2016, from https://consulting.vector.com/

KEY TERMS AND DEFINITIONS

Action: The accomplishment of a thing over a period of time, in stages.

Analysis: A careful study of something, in particular a system, to learn about its parts, what they do, and how they are related to each other; an explanation of the nature and meaning of something.

Chain: A series of decisions, activities, actions, results that are connected to each other in a line and used for obtaining a certain result; a series or group of things or people that are connected to each other in a linear way. Chains, by geometry, are linear, standardized, reliable, comfortable.

Competitor: Someone who is trying to do whatever he/she can do to reduce someone else wealth or wealth creation's ability; someone who plays a negative sum game.

Complementor: Someone who is trying to do whatever he/she can do to increase someone else wealth or wealth creation's ability; someone who plays a positive sum game.

Customer: Someone who buys goods or services from a business; someone who acknowledges the added value in a product/service and is willing to ay a price for it.

Ethics: An area of study that deals with ideas about what is good and bad behavior; a branch of philosophy dealing with what is morally right or wrong; a set of beliefs, characteristics and values.

Goal: Something measurable that you are trying to do or achieve.

Hub: A coordinating system; the fixed central part or place of a system, around which other parts are revolving.

Management: The act or skill of controlling and making decisions; the act or process of deciding how to allocate whatever resource.

Measure: The act or process used to measure things using a standard of measurement.

Metrics: A standard of measurement; an explanation of the nature and meaning of something.

Mission: A task or job that someone is given to do: there can be no mission if there are not the people to whom the mission is assigned.

Objective: Based on facts rather than feelings or opinions; not influenced by feelings; existing outside of the mind; existing in the real world; element that allows the continuous, sustainable, growth of a complex system.

Organigram: A graphical representation of the structure of an organization, showing groups and departments, their interconnections and inter-responsibilities, and relative ranks of its parts and positions/jobs.

Organigraph: Graphical representation of the internal territory of an organisation.

PEST: Acronym for Political, Economic, Social and Technological Analysis.

PESTLE: Acronym for Political, Economic, Social, Technological, Legal and Environmental Analysis.

Planning: The act or process of making a plan to achieve or do something. A plan is a set of actions that have been thought of as a way to do or achieve something; something that a person intends to do; a detailed agreement for telephone service, medical care, insurance, etc.

Positioning Matrix: Something (such as a situation or a set of conditions) in which something else develops or forms.

Scenario: A description of what could possibly happen; a written description of a play, movie, opera, etc.

Set: A number of items, quite often loosely connected one to the other as a collection, a group, or a portfolio.

Strategy: Pattern in a stream of decisions taken to optimise the allocation of available resources, according to a plan, in order to achieve the organisation's objectives.

Supplier: Someone who takes an active role in your value proposition creation.

SWOT: Acronym for Strengths, Weaknesses, Opportunity, Threats.

Tactic: An action or method that is planned and used to achieve a particular goal; tactics: the activity or skill of organizing and moving soldiers and equipment in a military battle.

Vision: The ability to see: sight or eyesight; something that you imagine; a picture that you see in your mind; something that you see or dream especially as part of a religious or supernatural experience.

Web: A non-regular, geometric, entity connecting nodes and hubs in a space, showing specialized functions along its connecting branches.

Chapter 5
Preparing the Organization for Portfolio Management:
Overcoming Resistance and Obstacles

Frank R. Parth
Project Auditors LLC, USA

ABSTRACT

This chapter will discuss how to more effectively implement the enterprise portfolio management system (EPMS). In order to be successful in delivering an EPMS that will benefit the organization, the implementation team must understand that they going to make a significant change to how the organization operates, and that any significant change such as this can expect to encounter resistance. Effective implementation requires an understanding of the organization's current problems and priorities, the creation and implementation of the system that will resolve those problems, and preparations to overcome resistance through effective Organizational Change Management (OCM). The implementers must truly be convinced that this effort is going to make a difference to the larger organization and that their dedication and change leadership will make it successful. This chapter will help the implementing team see the benefits of enterprise portfolio management, help them convince others of those benefits, and become the leader in implementing the EPMS.

INTRODUCTION

There are many benefits to an effective portfolio management process as have been shown in the literature. However, the lifespan of a portfolio management process is short. They are either bureaucratic, they do not satisfy management's expectations, or employees and managers won't accept the new processes. Understanding of these typical problems allows the project team to overcome them with proper implementation.

Companies that handle numerous projects simultaneously require a more formal and structured management approach for project portfolios. Enterprise-level project portfolio management has become a

DOI: 10.4018/978-1-5225-2151-8.ch005

key competence to implement strategies and remain competitive (Diedrich & Lehtonen, 2005; Killen et al, 2008; Martinsuo & Lehtonen, 2007).

To be successful in delivering a solution that will benefit the overall organization, the implementing team must understand that they going to make a significant change to how the organization operates, and any change can expect to encounter resistance. Effective implementation requires an understanding of the organization's current problems and priorities, how to create and implement the system that will resolve those problems, and be prepared to overcome resistance.

The implementation of an Enterprise Portfolio Management System (EPMS) is a complex endeavor comparable to implementing an Enterprise Resource Planning (ERP) system or a Client Relationship Management (CRM) system. All of these projects have high failure rates due to the complexities of making changes to how the organization operates. The primary difficulties lie not in the software or the data itself, but in the fact that the process of implementation changes how management and employees do their work on a day by day basis. Process changes are being imposed on people who generally see no need to change.

The specific details of the implementation depends on the organization to a large extent (Petro & Gardiner 2015). The organization's structure, its culture, the internal political environment, whether it is national-level or trans-national all play a part in how and effective EPMS will be implemented (see Patankul 2015).

This chapter will examine the primary causes of failure and how to overcome them. The chapter looks at the decision-making process and environment that upper management faces, challenges to organizations in today's environment that lead management to implement EPMS, understanding management's goals and expectations, overcoming resistance through effective organizational change management (OCM), and convincing both management and employees of the benefits of an effective EPMS.

For the sake of clarity, let us define some terminology because it is not consistent across industries. Both programs and portfolios include multiple projects. Often when we talk about a program we call it a project. What are the distinctions? Using the definitions published by the Project Management Institute we can define each exactly as:

- **Project:** A project consists of a unique set of processes consisting of coordinated and controlled activities with start and end dates, performed to achieve project objectives.
- **Program:** A group of related projects managed in a coordinated way so as to obtain benefits not available by managing them individually. Programs may include related work outside of the scope of the discrete projects within the program.
- **Portfolio:** A collection of projects or programs and other work that are grouped together to facilitate effective management of that work to achieve strategic business objectives. The projects or programs of the portfolio may not be independent and not directly related to each other.

A project is a specific effort to produce a deliverable, whether a new product, a service, a business process, or any other beneficial output. A program is so large and complex that it includes multiple projects to produce the outcome, such as a construction program, an engineering program, new aircraft development, and so on.

A portfolio is a collection of both projects and programs. A large portfolio, such as an enterprise-wide portfolio, may include lower-level portfolios within it.

One way to view the difference between a project and a portfolio is that if a project within a program fails, the entire program fails. If a project within a portfolio fails, it doesn't affect the other projects within the portfolio.

BACKGROUND

Decision-Making

Cook (2007) and others have pointed out that there are many reasons why organizations choose the wrong projects – capturing the wrong information; decision-making bias; not knowing what metrics to use; not focusing on their capabilities of successfully competing a project; not taking a strategic viewpoint in selecting project; sub-optimizing the portfolio for political reasons, and others.

The goal of an enterprise-level portfolio management system (EPMS) is to facilitate executive decision-making. The EPMS provides management decision-makers the information they need, and only the information they need, to decide which projects to select to support strategic objectives. One of the difficulties in designing the system is to understand what information management needs and setting up the filters to support the project selection decisions.

A properly designed system takes into account its own limitations, primarily the inability of an algorithm-based system to make perfect selections on which projects should be prioritized and funded. Corporate strategy changes, technologies change, the economic environment changes. The human brain is much better adapted to filtering all the parameters of a changing environment than any software based system and so the EPMS should be designed to support decision-making, not to replace it.

The EPMS should be designed to accept inputs from anyone in the organization without filtering on which projects could be done. The built-in algorithms will filter the inputs based on criteria determined by upper management and then present a list of possible projects with recommended priorities taking into account resource and budget constraints. Management will have the opportunity to select the best projects based on the information. They are not constrained with blindly following the list presented, but have the option of selecting projects that rank closely together in the prioritized list.

Because decisions are heavily influenced by how the information is presented to us, a better approach is to have a gatekeeper in charge of collecting the data and presenting it in a complete and unbiased format to the decision makers. This is what a well-designed portfolio management system does.

At the "working" levels of the organization it seems obvious which projects should be done – the projects that provide the greatest benefits. The unstated assumption here is that the projects selected should have the greatest benefits to "our" part of the organization. The lower in the hierarchy the more narrow the viewpoint and the shorter the time outlook.

The decision on the best project is not so obvious as you go higher in the organization. The upper management team and the executive level have multiple groups and divisions they are responsible for, if not the entire organization. They must decide which parts of the organization to allocate the money to for the projects, money that will not be spent on other parts of the organization. Priorities in multiple parts of the organization must be balanced against each other based on assumptions about the future. Not just the near-term future, but how to position the organization five years from now. Unlike Warren Buffett, who once famously said *"My idea of a group decision is to look in a mirror"* as referenced in

Buffett and Clark (2006) these decisions require the focused and committed agreement among multiple high-level stakeholders.

The decision environment takes into account not only the organization, it's resources and it's strategic goals but also the external environment. Every organization, whether government, privately owned, publically owned, or non-profit exists in the overall environment and is heavily influenced by that environment. The environment consists not only of the economic environment and physical environment, but for privately-owned and publicly-owned organizations also the competitive environment. What competitors are doing now has a direct influence on what we will be doing in the future.

Predicting the future environment requires developing skills and capabilities that may not pay off immediately. For the long term, projects should be selected not just for their short-term financial benefits but to allow future new markets and knowledge growth. These often go un-selected because their ROI is unpredictable, but they will build the capabilities for the company's future growth and profitability according to work done by Maniak et al. (2014).

Providing accurate and reliable information for decision-making provides a defense against short-term projects that may not be the best route to the future growth of the organization. These "exploration" projects are potentially the most beneficial ones because the products they produce will be the organization's future. Sony changed the whole music world with the Sony Walkman in 1979, Apple changed it again with the iPod in 2001. In between the two Sony built on it's original Walkman, but the only major change was to create a CD-based portable player. There were no other substantial, ground-breaking changes. When the iPod was released it completely overtook Sony's bread and butter income stream in portable music players.

Kodak invented the first digital camera in 1975. But their income stream was from selling film and shot down any project that threatened that income. IBM invented the first really usable PC, but was unable to get any priority on it because the decision makers viewed the company as a mainframe company and wanted nothing to threaten that. These are the kinds of decisions that can either make or break a company in a changing external environment. Part of the job of the EPMS is to make the best case for these exploration projects so show the future benefits are greater than the high risks involved in doing them.

Organizational Challenges

An organization of any type is a living entity. It grows and expands when environmental conditions are right, it contracts, often painfully, when conditions are poor. All parts of the organization work together, more or less efficiently, towards the goals of the organization. The environmental conditions for a small not-for-profit are vastly different than they are for an international, for-profit organization or for a government organization. But they all respond to their environment.

In an organization, nothing is done in isolation. All company activities are done in an environment created by all the other company activities as well as by the organization's competitors and outside environment. Whether a project gets approved and funded, or not, depends on how that project benefits the organization *in comparison to* the other projects being considered. When the external environment changes, there is a cascading flow of changes internal to the organization.

This internal environment includes the culture of the organization, its financial capabilities, its geographic location(s), the legal and regulatory framework it operates in, how well established its internal processes are, its technology infrastructure, internal competitiveness between and among the divisions, and all other internal influences. Some organizations, such as General Motors, before its bankruptcy, are intensely competitive internally to the point of becoming dysfunctional.

Other organizations are internally highly cooperative, and some organizations are so big that they are internally competitive, such as Hewlett-Packard before it's last reorganization in 2010, that they do not even realize that divisions are competing with each other because of poor internal communications among upper management.

Internal Process Development, Growth, and Deterioration

It would be reassuring to believe that organizations are well-planned entities that are focused on their long-term goals, have well-designed internal processes, and provide a highly-rewarding experience for their employees as well as many benefits to their external stakeholders, this is not the reality of life today and probably has never been the reality.

Most organizations are poorly planned to start with and deteriorate from there. They start out small and develop internal processes that are sufficient to help them operate in their existing environment. The emphasis is on survival and growth and not on efficiency. The rapid growth, and even more rapid death, of most dot-coms in the late 1990s is a good example as is the downfall of much of the financial industry in the late 2000's.

As organizations grow their internal processes expand in size until it becomes obvious that the processes no longer work. Processes are created as needed and rarely documented. At some stage of growth the organization is large enough that this ad hoc management style no longer works and professional management is brought in. Processes are re-designed, maybe documented or maybe not, and for awhile the organization continues its growth in a more planned fashion.

As growth continues these re-designed processes are also overcome and become less efficient. But at this point they are rarely redesigned and the inefficiencies are lived with until it becomes obvious to upper management that there are serious internal problems (usually employees saw these problems long before management does). Further, in today's business environment a lot of growth occurs through mergers and acquisitions (M&As). When two companies merge their existing processes are rarely merged effectively and the resulting entity becomes less efficient as employees struggle to figure out how to do their jobs. The recent merger of United Airlines and Continental Airlines made good sense from a high-level management financial analysis, but resulted in massive disruption of the combined entity's operations and a great deal of customer unhappiness. United Airlines dropped from near the top of customer quality rankings to the bottom less than a year after the merger began.

IMPACTS OF EXTERNAL CHANGES

The parts of the organization that are impacted the greatest by changes are the layers at which much of the project management work is done. In today's rapidly changing, internationally-competitive environment management is under a lot of pressure to reduce costs and to become more profitable. The normal approach is to reduce headcount, either by laying off staff, by attrition, or by outsourcing to the current low-cost provider somewhere else in the world. The result of this approach is to put more work on fewer employees.

This means that a very typical project environment involves both the project manager and the team working on several projects instead of being focused on one. Everyone is multi-tasking, with well-researched and documented reductions in productivity as quoted by Santosus (2003). When an employee is working on five different things, they cannot be as effective or as efficient as when they are concentrating on just one or two.

While project managers don't like to deal with constraints, the reality is that project management exists within the physical, cultural, and economic environment of every company. The PM's ability to manage projects is constrained by many factors outside project management itself. These limitations extend to the EPMS and, in fact, are major inputs to the filtering criteria used to analyze and approve projects.

In the IT department the situation is even worse, the staff there not only works on projects, they are usually working on daily operations at the same time: bug fixes, application upgrades and implementations, system maintenance, security patches, etc. All of which distract them from project work. Research on multi-tasking shows that doing multiple things at the same time is equivalent to an IQ drop of 10-15 points, the same IQ drop as smoking a joint of marijuana.

In addition to the reduced productivity, more mistakes are made leading to more work having to be checked and redone. Rework, which is always unplanned, has ripple effects because it takes people away from what the planned work was, further impacting projects in work. There is a large body of research on the negative impacts of multitasking as quoted in Bannister and Remenyi (2009)

Challenges Created by a Changing Environment

For these and for other reasons managing a project in the typical organization is highly challenging. Management is often using a central pool of personnel that are working on multiple projects. "Teams" often do operational work outside of projects. Management's typical response to this situation is sometimes derogatorily referred to as "Peanut Butter Resource Management" – just spread the people around over more and more work.

Too many factors that impact projects are outside the project manager's control. Worse, in many organizations there is no common agreement of what a project manager should be doing. Functional managers do things the way they've always done them and consider the project managers to be schedule keepers.

Strong inter-dependencies among multiple projects compounds the problems. These dependencies can be created by sharing personnel, equipment, facilities or by competing for limited funding. A problem on one project quickly spreads to others. Scheduling uncertainty on one project means we don't know exactly when tasks will happen. When one task on that project runs late, there's an impact on other projects that need those resources. This makes scheduling projects in a multi-project environment very challenging and is a major source of projects running late. It is also a strong driver to implement an EPMS and to install an enterprise-capable project management tool.

Creating accurate schedules is subject to a wide variety of influences as shown in Figure 1.

All of which lead to uncertainty in the schedule. In a multi-project environment where resources are shared, as we've just seen there is an additional, and very strong, cascading effect from other projects that are scheduled to use the same resources as we are. In the manufacturing industry there is a well-known constraint called Little's Law. It says that cycle time equals the work in progress divided by the throughput: CT = WIP/TP.

Figure 1. Influences on schedule uncertainty

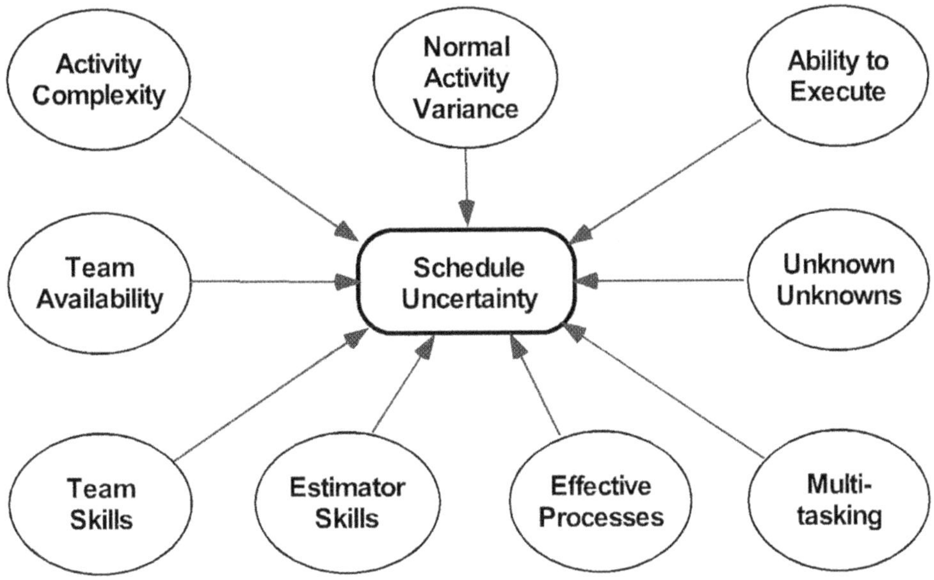

Benefits of an EPMS to a Changing Environment

In order to improve how quickly projects get done, the organization needs to reduce the number of projects in work.

We can view a multi-project environment as a complex system. There are interdependencies among the various components of the system as shown by the example of shared resources above. The field of systems analysis teaches that one characteristic of a complex system is that responses are non-linear. The same input can produce different outputs depending on other influences on the system. A response to a particular demand for a resource is not a repeatable event, it is dependent on the time in which the demand is made. A project manager might offer the resource to another project next week but can't offer it today because she needs that resource. Same request, different response.

Other typical impacts commonly experienced are that adding resources to one project usually means removing them from other planned work, often another project. Increasing overtime means lowering productivity. Adding more projects reduces the ability to finish any of them on schedule. These are common situations that are often not taken into account before a change is made to the portfolio.

Because there's a time delay between making a change and seeing the effects, complex systems are inherently unstable. A danger by management is to try and over-manage the full collection of projects. You cannot manage ten separate projects the same way you manage a single project. In this environment flexibility is more important than rigid adherence to plans. Why spend weeks planning out a project schedule in detail when there's a 90% chance the schedule will be impacted by other things?

Another area that is impacted by adding more projects to the portfolio without analysis is quality. The more overworked people are, the lower the resulting quality in the project, in the product, and in the decision-making process. Quality in a physical product can be measured and there are many quality systems that can be used. Quality in processes and in decision-making is much more difficult to quantify and to measure. Mistakes are made more often but they are rarely traced back to the fact that people are seriously overworked, tired, and making bad decisions.

In a complex environment there are many of these impacts and inter-dependencies that are not knowable in advance. No one in the organization understands the entire set of projects in work or their interdependencies. A functional manager that needs a resource from a project may not realize that obtaining that resource impacts not just one project, but several projects that had scheduled that resource.

This is where an EPMS can be most beneficial. A common solution is to use a Program Management Office (PMO) to provide the infrastructure within which the EPM system can exist. The PMO provides a central location for all information related to projects in work. It presents the information in a way that allows management to understand what's going on in all projects.

In order to overcome the objections that will be raised by the managers and division heads that don't want an EPMS because it reduces their control, the person implementing the new system must understand all of these constraints, problems, dependencies, and impacts and prepare to counter the arguments that will be raised.

PREPARING THE ORGANIZATION FOR PORTFOLIO MANAGEMENT

Identifying the Decision Makers

An EPMS should only be implemented for the long-term benefits of the organization. It has few benefits in the short term, and in fact the implementation process will be disruptive and confusing to many people in the organization unless they are properly prepared. Until management and employees get comfortable with the EPMS and familiar with its processes productivity is actually likely to temporarily decrease.

Long-term growth and improvement is the province of upper management. Ultimately the results belong to executive level under the overall guidance of the board of directors. Under various levels of presidents, executive vice-presidents, senior vice-presidents, and just plain vice-presidents comes the lower level of directors and under them multiple layers of managers. Further down we have supervisors in those organizations that have a large level of working-level employees.

The higher up the management level the more they are charged with the long term improvement to the organization. These are the people who have to:

1. Buy into the benefits of enterprise-wide portfolio management,
2. Approve the funding and the resources for it, and
3. Who will be members of the Governance Committee and the lower-level Steering Committees who will make the decisions on which projects to approve and to fund.

In a large organization there are likely to be separate companies, divisions, and groups. Their relationship to the top of the organization will vary from completely autonomous, to semi-autonomous, to completely controlled by the central organization. At each level there are responsibilities commensurate with that level.

At the top level of every large organization we have an executive Governance Counsel or something equivalent. They, or a committee similar to them, will make the highest-level decisions on where the organization's money will be put in the next year's expenditures. Below them, depending on how large the organization is, we have Steering Committees that make the same decisions for individual business units, divisions, or groups.

A very simple organization chart for an international company might look something like the chart shown in Figure 2.

Not all international companies are organized around geographic regions. Some are organized around product lines as illustrated in Figure 3.

Either way, enterprises organize in the way that makes sense to them. The exact organizational structure is important because it has an impact on how the EPMS is designed. Depending on the level of the organization that is doing portfolio management, an EPMS that is designed for one division or

Figure 2. Simple organization chart for international company

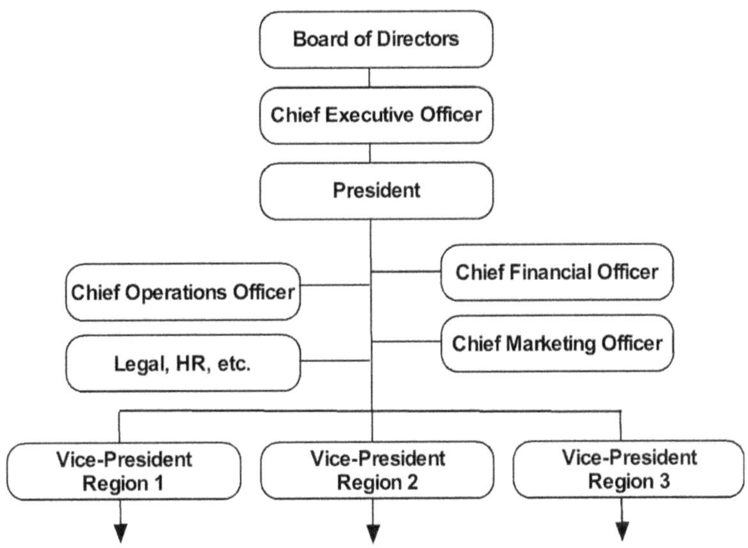

Figure 3. Product-oriented organization

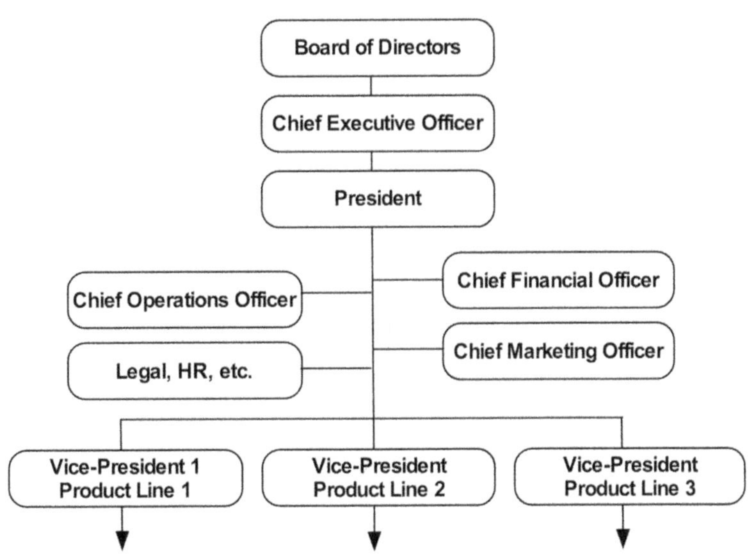

business unit of a medium-size consumer products company would have a very different structure than one designed for an international corporation that sells products world-wide.

With all these people who should make the decisions on which projects to fund? The primary criterion for who should be on the committee is that group of executives or managers who have budgetary control over that part of the organization. The ultimate responsibility for allocating the annual budget of the organization belongs to the executive level. As the budget is detailed down into different parts of the organization there will be lower-level governance committees that make the decisions appropriate to that level.

If internal coordination and communications is good then the various levels have a good understanding of the strategic goals of the organization, how their area supports those goals, and make rational decisions without regard to anything else except the most effective way to achieve those goals.

There are various categories of the total budget that are dependent on the strategic goals of the organization. The specific categories will depend on the level of the organization that is making the project decisions. For example, at the division or group level there will generally be a specific budget for IT projects. How this money is allocated will depend on what the IT goals are. (In a perfect world IT goals are obtained from the business and reflect how IT can best support the business goals.)

The above discussion is a very simplistic description of the governance structure in most organizations and it ignores one of the critical aspects of selecting projects – dealing with the internal politics.

While it is true that everyone in a management role cares about the long-term growth of the organization, in the short term they care more about advancing their own small part of the organization, and in fact they get rewarded and promoted for doing so. Their emphasis is on their group (whatever the size) growing and advancing. In turn this will lead to more responsibilities and greater advancement for themselves.

Why is this important? Because this structure often pits one manager or one group against another in competition for financial resources and projects. While most managers would acknowledge that all parts of the organization are important, each manager also feels that his or her part of the organization is more critical to the overall organization than other groups.

From this inherent situation will come most of the resistance to implementing the EPMS and most of the difficulty in managing it. By taking away the ability of managers to make individual decisions on which projects to fund the EPMS will take away some of their power and authority. Unless managers are sold on the benefits of the EPMS to themselves individually, they see no benefits to it, only downsides.

In this hierarchy from the bottom of the organization to the very top, where does portfolio management fit in? Looking from strategy, to portfolio, to program, to project, and finally to operations we can compare the focus of each of these, the alignment, the stakeholders, and the indicators as Abdollahyan (2012) has done and shown in Table 1.

Abdollahyan's use of the term buzzword may be understood as alignment.

This matrix shows how portfolio management fits into the overall framework of implementing strategy within the organization so that the day-to-day operations of the company support the long-term goals.

Goals and Expectations

The goal here is not just to deliver an EPMS. The goal is to deliver the information that management needs to decide on the best projects to put money and resources in. The tool is to develop an EPMS that does that, to deliver an EPMS that satisfies what management needs and that the participants will want

Table 1. Differences among strategy, portfolio, program project, and operations

	Strategy	Portfolio	Program	Project	Operations
Focus	Mission, vision, and objectives	Strategy delivery	Outcomes, "benefits"	Outputs, "deliverables"	Sustained business
Buzzword	Strategy	Strategic alignment	Benefits realization	Product and capability delivery	Business-as-usual
Stakeholder	Owners, shareholders, market	C-level and middle management	Sponsors, beneficiaries, and other stakeholders	Sponsors, clients, users, and other stakeholders	Management, clients, users, and other stakeholders
Indicators	Enterprise value indicators	Portfolio value indicators	Benefits and project performance indicators	Project performance indicators	Operational excellence indicators

to use. Does the last sentence sound like two different goals? They're not. They are in fact the same goal, but inexperienced project managers may lose sight of the distinction. The goal is to not just deliver technology and a new business process, the goal is to deliver a way for the entire organization to become more efficient and more effective by improving how projects are selected and prioritized. The EPMS will make a significant improvement in how the organization works. How much of an improvement? A white paper on effective portfolio management systems written for IDC by Perry and Hatcher (2008) shows that for the companies surveyed:

- Number of projects managed increased 35%.
- Cost per project was reduced 37%.
- Redundant projects dropped 78%.
- IT staff productivity increased by 14%.
- Project failure rate dropped 59%.
- The total annual benefit per 100 users is $83,500.
- Payback occurred in 7.4 months.
- Return on investment was $5.57 for every $1 spent on portfolio management.

PMI's 2012 Pulse of the Profession (PMI 2012) research showed the drivers for portfolio management are as shown in Figure 4.

These are the items that senior management is most interested in. Determining goals and expectations is the process of gathering the business needs for the EPM system. What is it that management expects from it? Why did they decide to do it? Are their expectations realistic? Did someone read a one-page article in a management journal on the benefits of portfolio management and decide this is what we need?

Determining management's expectations, both stated and unstated, is a major part of starting the effort. This part of the project is too often either forgotten entirely or done poorly. Too many non-project managers think that spending time determining in detail what they need, determining the requirements, doesn't seem like "real work" – it is not planning the schedule, it is not coding, it is not meeting with vendors, it is not testing. But long experience in project management emphasizes that everything else the team does and the success of the project will depend on how thoroughly the team understands what the decision-makers need, want, and expect. Literally everything else on the project is based on that.

Figure 4. Drivers of portfolio management

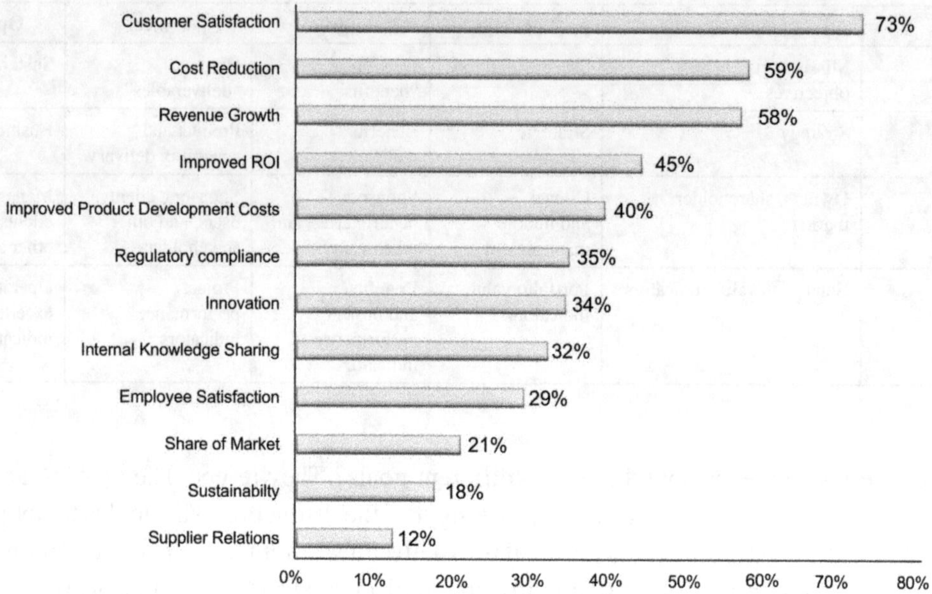

How do we measure whether we've been successful or not? The EPMS itself will use financial criteria as part of the decision criteria for approving a project, and the most common financial filter is Return on Investment (ROI). ROI measures the financial returns from the money the company is spending on the project. It is a straightforward and very simple calculation.

Every financial filter has limitations. A more sophisticated EPMS will compare ROI, Internal Rate of Return (IRR), and Net Present Value (NPV) to select the projects that provide the greatest benefits.

But not all projects are susceptible to purely financial filters. Think about the traditional public works project – a new highway, a dam, or a bridge. How do you calculate the financial return on those? For these types of projects, the Benefit/Cost Analysis is typically used. While fruitful, the BCA is subject to a lot of assumptions and is highly inaccurate. Research by Flyvbjerg (2009), for example, has shown that public works such as roads has a typical cost overrun of 20% and an overestimate of the benefits of almost 10%.

For projects such as the EPMS itself, sometimes a better calculations is Return on Expectations (ROE). This should answer the question whether the EPMS delivered what was expected.

Pepsi Cola is a well-known world-wide organization. They have a product strategy, a marketing strategy, an advertising strategy, an environmental strategy, and other strategies. And these are not only for the overall corporate organization, these also exist for each company in the Pepsi family. There are multiple drinks, "convenience" foods, cereals, cookies, and other product companies within the family, all having their own strategic goals and plans that are subsidiary to the top-level organization's. So strategic goals really means the specific long-term goals at the level of the organization you're developing the EPMS for. Despite these disparate goals, for many years Pepsi had a single strategic goal *"Beat Coke"*. Virtually all investment decisions were made with that single goal in mind.

Sometimes the long-term goals can be very tactical instead of strategic. For example, look a the car industry during the recent economic downturns. Instead of planning for 5-7 years of growth and advancement, the major US car manufacturers were planning for survival and cost savings. As documented by Lassa (2009) General Motors was looking at:

- Cut its North American nameplate lineup from 48 down to 36 by 2012. Hummer, Saab, and Saturn will account for most of those cuts.
- Reduce workforce by 47,000 globally, including 10,000 white collar (3,400 U.S. white collar).
- Close 14 North American factories by 2012, five more than in the December 2 plan.
- Reduce U.S. dealers from 6,200 currently to 4,700 in 2012 and 4,100 in 2014.
- Seek to convert bondholder debt and funding to autoworkers' retirement health care funds into GM stock.

Each one of these efforts is a project, a big one, and will consume a lot of time, effort, and resources. You can very easily build an EPMS at the corporate level of GM just to handle these types of projects.

OVERCOMING RESISTANCE AND OBSTACLES IN IMPLEMENTING PORTFOLIO MANAGEMENT

Organizational Change Management (OCM)

In implementing the EPMS the most difficult part is obtaining acceptance for it from the rest of the organization. By acceptance we mean more than just acknowledging that it exists, we mean a willingness to use it because they see the benefits of it and it is user friendly. By comparison everything else in the effort is straightforward and relatively easy.

It easy to design and install an EPMS, it is far more difficult to implement it so that people will use it effectively and efficiently. This is no different than implementing any other significant process change in an organization such as Enterprise Resource Planning (ERP) implementations. The failure rate for ERP packages is extremely high. Poor implementations have literally driven companies into bankruptcy. According to work published by Lancaster (1995) For business process re-engineering projects only 20 – 30% of them are successful. We could cite many examples of business process improvement (BPI) initiatives that never deliver the benefits expected.

There will be a loss of productivity until employees adapt to the new processes. As shown by Dochtermann, et al. in Figure 5 (Dochtermann 2011) there is a drop in productivity until the organization recovers, but it is a much worse drop and longer recovery without effective OCM processes in place.

Where does the loss come from? Table 2 shows the differences in how employees spend their time during normal work routines and after a major change ((Dochtermann, 2011).

The problem is not with poor technology, the software works very well. Nor with poor business process design. The answer is that many processes in an organization interact with people, and getting people to change how they do their job is the most difficult of all project management efforts.

People don't mind changing, they change all the time, but they hate having change forced on them. A survey of Fortune 500 executives by Schiemann (1992) said that the primary reason changes fail was because of internal resistance. In a similar survey conducted by Deloitte Consulting at about the same time, 80% of the CIOs surveyed said that resistance was the main reason why IT projects failed.

Figure 5. Loss of productivity with and without OCM

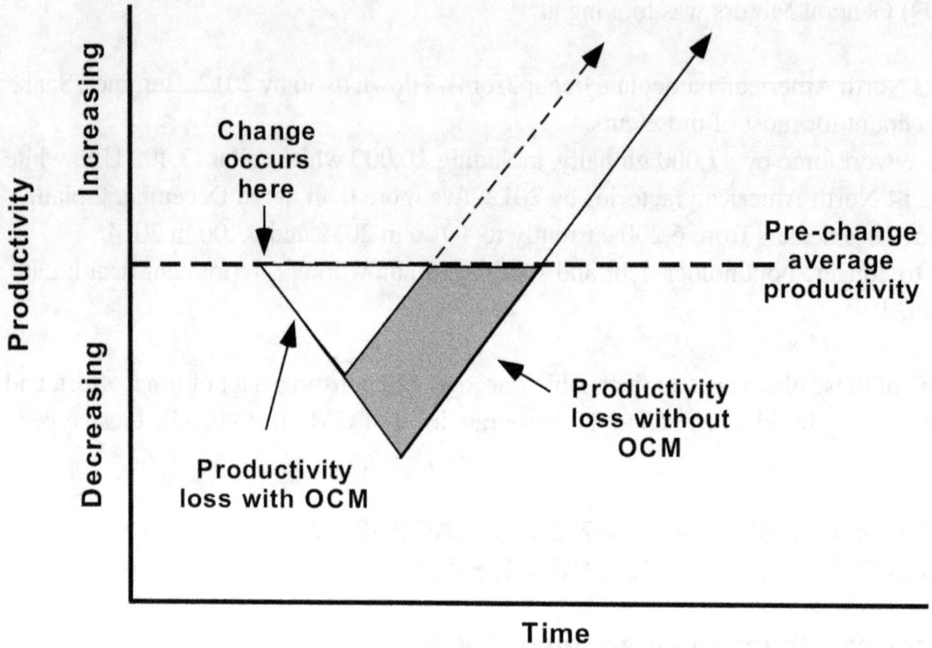

Table 2. Allocation of employee time

Time Allocation	
Normal	**Transition**
Personal 21%	Personal 21%
Social/Gossip 19%	Social/Gossip 40%
Productive Work 60%	Productive Work 16%
	Retraining 23%

Before the organization can being the effort to implement the EPMS it must understand the comfort level internally to accept it. Just because upper management wants something doesn't mean lower level managers do or the employees do. The organization must answer six questions:

1. What is the history of implementing significant changes? How successful have we been in the past?
2. Does the organizational culture support changes and taking risks?
3. Do people trust each other from different departments and work effectively together?
4. Can people handle more change?
5. Can both management and employees be convinced the change will benefit them?
6. How disruptive will this change be? (Because it will be disruptive until everyone accepts it.)

Efforts at this stage should be directed towards understanding how accepting the stakeholders will be in receiving and using the EPMS.

Resistance and Why It's Important

What is resistance? For the purposes here resistance is any behavior in an organization that slows or stops change. There is nobody in the organization that has the title of "resistor" and who is just waiting to ruin the EPMS implementation. People don't resist just to resist, they resist because they see the change as detrimental to everything they've worked for in the organization. They don't see what they're doing as impeding progress, they see it as survival.

Too often management takes a simple-minded approach and tries to get employees supportive of this major change by putting up motivational posters or by printing a slogan on a coffee cup, but experience shows it doesn't work that way. Managers who think that motivational posters actually work are insulting the intelligence of the employees. There is an old saying in change management that in any significant organizational change 20% of the people impacted will be supportive of the change, 20% will not change no matter what you do, and the middle 60% can be swayed if you implement the change correctly shown in Figure 6.

The people who are most willing to change are either new to the organization, are very accepting of change, or see the problems with how things are done now. The people who will never change have often been there the longest, see no reason for anyone to change how they work, or simply dislike change. The project manager for the EPMS implementation should be aiming to convince that middle 60%. If the EPMS is implemented correctly, those employees can become supportive. If you have a failure early in the implementation process, those same employees will move into the "I'll never change" camp.

Categories and Types of Resistance

Ignoring, for a moment, the people who just dislike all changes, there are three different categories of resistance: rational resistance, emotional resistance, and personal resistance. Each category requires a

Figure 6. Supportive, subversive, and persuadable percentages

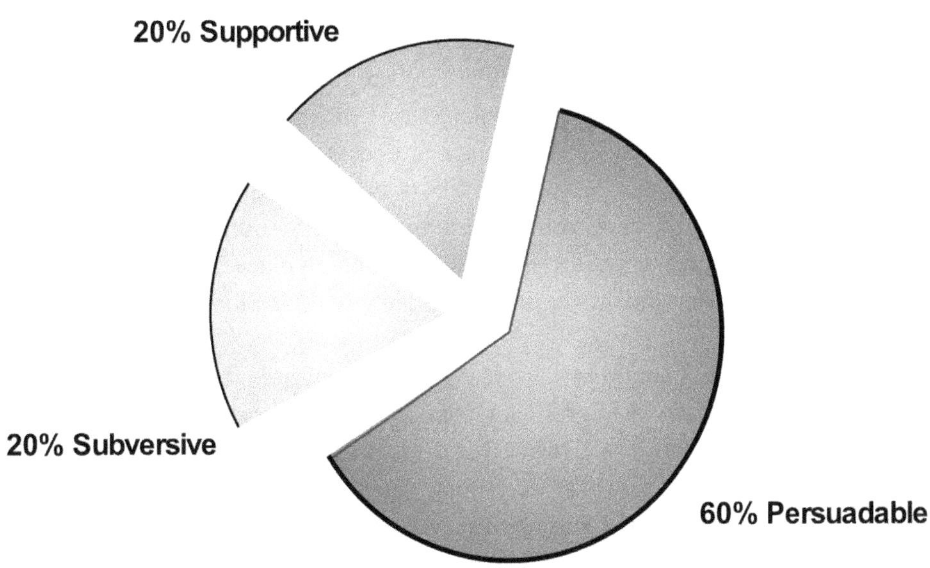

different approach. The project manager in charge of the EPMS implementation needs to spend some time very early in the project to determine which resistance is being faced, or which combination of resistance is being faced.

Rational resistance occurs because people honestly believe that the EPMS will not be the right approach. They have looked at the same problems the EPMS is trying to solve and have determined there's a better solution. This is the easiest type of resistance to deal with because it is defined by facts and logical arguments. Solid ROI calculations and logical arguments are more likely to overcome rational resistance. Unfortunately, too many managers think that *all* resistance is rational resistance when in reality most of it is not.

While the processes involved in providing a prioritized list of possible projects is very rational and data-driven, the reality of decision making is that most people, even top-level managers, make decisions at a sub-conscious level, even an emotional level according to both Harvard Business School (2016) and Kahneman, D. (2012).

Emotional resistance is what happens when people are concerned that this implementation is going to reduce their power, take staff away from them, change their working relationships, get them laid off, or do something else detrimental to their jobs. Once management starts talking about making changes to work processes, people immediately start worrying about their jobs. This is called the FUD factor – Fear, Uncertainty, and Doubt. A lot of efforts of Organizational Change Management are designed to overcome the FUD factor by recognizing it, dealing with it, and reassuring people that their current jobs are safe or that they will be retrained for their new jobs. Any really major change effort in an organization needs to spend a significant amount of effort in this area to be successful.

This type of resistance will be exhibited even by upper managers in an organization if they feel their power or authority will be affected by the change. The author led a series of business process improvement (BPI) projects for a large electrical utility, and ran into significant resistance from the business unit leads. While they all agreed that the organization needed to significantly improve it's business processes, it was all the other business processes that needed to be changed, not the ones that each manager owned. As soon as it was apparent that the BPI effort would remove processes they controlled, they immediately began to demonstrate all the signs of covert resistance – not showing up for meetings, not reviewing or signing documents, making changes immediately before deadlines, and so on.

One of the major sources of resistance to EPMS will come from the existing project managers within the organization. While we would hope to think that they are fully behind any improvements to project management, the reality is that existing project managers are the ones who are most impacted by implementing an EPMS. Currently they are free to manage projects their own way and to report progress in the ways that make their projects look best. The EPMS reduces their ability to look good by instituting a set of progress metrics that apply consistently to all projects. Undoubtedly some projects that looked good before will look much worse when the new metrics are put in place. Project managers will lose the ability to paint a rosy picture and gloss over problems. They will also lose some freedom in managing projects the way they want.

Parth (2002) describes the situation at Toyota's USA headquarters during the implementation of a PMO for the IT department. There was significant resistance from the project managers (all contractors) who saw their ability to manage projects in ways that were most comfortable for them being taken away. They also resisted the standard metrics that were imposed on all projects, allowing Toyota for the first time to compare the multiple projects according to a consistent set of criteria. As part of the OCM effort, a monthly status meeting for all project managers was held where they could be presented the current status of the PMO implementation, ask questions, and present summaries of their own projects. After several months this status meeting took on the culture of a therapy session where the project managers could compare notes and sympathize with each other.

Existing project managers will be a major source of resistance within the organization and they must be given special attention and their inputs considered carefully in the design and implementation process. Fortunately, they will also receive a great benefit from the new system. Research has shown that the organizations that take EPM seriously do fewer projects, so the workload of the PMs can be reduced and they can concentrate on doing a better quality job on fewer projects (if management decides that they can lay off project managers and keep a heavy workload on them, the EPM implementation has failed before it is done. This is not a viable option).

Personal resistance is resistance to the people working on the EPMS implementation or to the department or group they represent. The project team should never take it personally. The source of this category of resistance is based on history with the project manager or with his or her department/division/group. In a large, mature organization this is unfortunately not as rare as one would hope.

Many, perhaps most, of today's organizational leaders have Master's in Business Administration (MBA) degrees or the international equivalents. They are taught an analyze/think/change process in making changes to an organization. Information about a problem is collected and analyzed, logical solutions are presented in documents and PowerPoint presentations, and people will change based on the hard facts presented. This is a very rational approach.

Assumptions of this rational approach include:

- Managers have "perfect information".
- Objectives are known and agreed to.
- Managers are rational, systematic, and logical.
- Managers work in the best interests of their organizations.
- Ethical decisions do not arise in the decision-making process.
- The problem is clear and unambiguous.
- The alternatives and their consequences are known or predictable.
- Time and resources are not a consideration.
- The decisions will be implemented willingly and supported by all stakeholders.

The problem with this approach is simply that it doesn't work most of the time. People, at all levels of the organization, only behave rationally when it is to their best interest to do so. The rest of the time they behave in a manner that protects and expands what they have. If they think implementing an EPMS is going to have a negative impact on them, they will immediately, and subconsciously, be suspicious of it and start to resist it. Whether the resistance is Emotional or Personal Resistance, reacting with a rational argument will be completely ineffective. When someone is worried about losing their job after the change, giving them more data about how good the change will be for the organization is a waste of time. The project team must deal with them at the level they're reacting from. Distributing a monthly newsletter about the project will not communicate what they need to hear.

Not all types of resistance-motivated behavior are the same. There is active resistance (actively working against you) and passive resistance (slow responses to e-mails, not showing up for meetings, etc.). There is also overt resistance where people tell you straight out they are not going to support the project, and there is covert resistance where they just are not going to cooperate with you, but they won't tell you that. Table 3 summarizes these four types:

Table 3. Types of resistance behavior

Overt	This is more difficult to deal with. Someone or some group is resisting the implementation, but it's hard to pin them down. They always have an excuse for not reading a document, not showing up for meetings, etc.	This is the easiest type of resistance to deal with. It is obvious and the person or group behaving this way is known. They're usually very straightforward about saying they're not happy with the change.
Covert	This is the most difficult situation to deal with. The sense is that progress is not being made the way it should be, but for no known reason. People are outwardly supportive, but are criticizing the effort behind the team's back or working quietly on opposing efforts	This is more difficult to deal with. There is obvious resistance, but the reasons for it and the source are unknown.
	Passive	**Active**

Example of Resistance

In 2014 and 2015 the author worked with the Saline Water Conversion Corporation (SWCC) in Riyadh, Saudi Arabia. SWCC develops and manages some of the largest desalination projects in the world, but consistently failed to deliver these complex, multi-billion dollar projects on schedule or within budgets. The author was called in when one plant grew from a planned US $1.6 billion to $6.4 billion with no end to the growth in site. Over the course of two years the author led a small team and:

- Developed solid project management processes.
- Created, along with the HR department, a career path in project management identifying the skills, training, and experience needed for managing different size projects.
- Developed an enterprise-wide program management office system with a PMO in each of the Kingdom's two field offices (Jeddah and Dammam) and an over-arching PMO at headquarters in Riyadh.
- Identified the requirements for personnel needed to do the work without the significant overtime, burnout, and turnover SWCC was experiencing.
- Provided a tools assessment for the engineers to work with the contractors and consultants on-line instead of massive amounts of engineering drawings which filled up entire conference rooms with rolls of paper.
- Worked with procurement and with the legal department on improvements to the procurement and contracting process.
- Developed a schedule to implement the changes over a 5-year period of time so the existing organization did not experience significant disruption.
- Marketed the entire effort to the engineering staff and to each level of management up to the highest level in the organization, the Governor's Office.

The effort was carefully planned and developed specifically to support the organization. Yet engineering management did not see any need to change. The way they had learned to do things 30 years ago still resulted in high-quality desalination plants, and they did not see a need to change the organization. The resistance was overt, but not strong enough to convince engineering management to change, but also not strong enough that the effort was stopped.

What finally led them to start adopting the changes was not created internally. In January 2015 the king of Saudi Arabia died, and a new king, King Salman, was appointed to replace him. King Salman had a much more modern background and education than any previous leader and started making improvements to how the Kingdom was governed. One small change was that SWCC would have to become profitable in the future instead of continually over-spending their budgets. The need to become profitable got the attention of SWCC management and they began to take these new processes much more seriously. (See Parth, 2015).

Steps in OCM

In the literature on OCM there is a great deal of emphasis on getting the active involvement of the people who are going to end up living with the change. They *must* be involved from the earliest stages to the final implementation and operations. They have to buy into the change, not just intellectually but emotionally as well. People truly must believe that the change is to their benefit. All motivational posters and all the great talks by management on the benefits to the organization will not convince people that the change is going to help them in their day to day jobs and their relationships with the people they interact with. As soon as management starts talking about change the FUD factor comes into play as mentioned earlier.

In classic OCM theory there are four stages of involvement that are required:

1. **Understanding:** Stakeholders understand the nature of the problem.
2. **Acceptance:** Stakeholders understand the need for a solution.
3. **Participation:** Stakeholders participate in finding or defining the solution.
4. **Ownership:** Stakeholders take ownerships of the solution.

Understanding

At the initial level, the employees must understand the nature of the problem. This is where memos and presentations can be used. The emphasis of the early communications is to obtain understanding of the problem. This is whcrc thc implcmentation team communicates that EPMS can solve the problems that are being seen and what the benefits of the EPMS are. It is critical to make a compelling case for the EPMS at this stage because if the stakeholders are not completely convinced of the need for it, everything else after this point will be far more difficult. In Hammer and Champy's classic book *Re-engineering the Corporation* they talk about the "burning platform" (Hammer and Champy. 1998).

In James Collins book *Good to Great*, organizations that create a culture where people understand the business challenges seldom need to worry about getting alignment, motivation, or even managing change. (Collins 2001) While there is more to success than just making a case, when people do "get it" less time is wasted getting ready for each new initiative.

Acceptance

Once all of the stakeholders understand what the issues are and the benefits of EPM, have the stakeholders meet in teams to define the challenges that they are currently facing by not having EPM: wasted efforts on duplicate projects, low-benefit projects being approved while high-benefit projects suffer from lack of resources, conflict, and so on.

During this stage have the teams outline an EPM solution that would work within the culture of the organization. Also have them define the challenges that would be seen in implementing the EPM solution. Encourage different viewpoints but create a very clear vision and start developing the tactical approach to the implementation.

A significant number of stakeholders are going to be the project managers currently in the organization. It is important that they accept the new EPMS because it provides them greater benefits than the pain they're suffering now with the problems of changing priorities, having a heavy workload, and having their resources taken away by higher priority projects.

Participation

The next stage of OCM is to have the stakeholders actively participate in defining the solution. The implementation team can provide the outline of the EPM approach but they must be involved in the details of how it works on a day-by-day basis. People are much more likely to be supportive if they have an input to the design. An additional benefit is that a team of expensive outside consultants is not required to design and implement the new system. Internally-developed solutions are much more agreeable and acceptable.

Ownership

The final stage is to get key stakeholders to own the solution by getting them involved in the design and implementation. They act as Subject Matter Experts (SMEs) and will guide the implementation in a way that gets the greatest percentage of that middle 60% to be supportive.

One of the significant, long-term benefits of getting the direct involvement of the stakeholders is that they now understand the system and can utilize it effectively. Michael Robin suggests *"In today's knowledge-intensive global economy, performance is [hard to predict] and standardized behavior may not breed success."* ... *"One of the clearest impacts on organizational productivity from experience-based learning can be seen in higher levels of employee retention, which ultimately results in a greater transfer of knowledge into informed action. While retention levels for traditional learning from lectures or reading are typically just 3 to 5 percent, retention levels with experience-based learning have been known to reach 80 to 90 percent."* (Robin 2000).

The ADKAR model for individual change management was developed by the research company Prosci (http://www.prosci.com) with input from more than 1000 organizations from 59 countries. This model describes five required building blocks for change to be realized successfully on an individual level. The building blocks of the ADKAR Model include:

- **Awareness:** of why the change is needed.
- **Desire:** to support and participate in the change.
- **Knowledge:** of how to change.
- **Ability:** to implement new skills and behaviors.
- **Reinforcement:** to sustain the change.

There has been a significant amount of research in the field of how and why people respond to change, see McFarland (2012). The research has not come from consulting organizations, but from the field of neurology in their studies of what causes human behavior. One field of investigation has developed the SCARF model of how people react to change from the SCARF website http://www.scarf360.com/index.shtml.

There are other views of commitment, such as the Patterson-Conner Commitment Curve (Patterson 1982) but they are variations on the existing views rather than radically different views.

Selling the Benefits of EPM

There are many direct and indirect benefits to EPM. There are also some downsides to implementing it. Fortunately the downsides are temporary while the benefits are long term. Which benefits should be emphasized when EPM is communicated to management will depend on what is most important to them: long-term financial savings? A higher project success rate? Fewer duplicated projects? Making better management decisions faster? Increased profitability? Less stress on the employees? All of these are potential benefits of EPM.

Of the many research articles on EPM, the results are consistent. According to Cooper et al. (2003) if an organization does portfolio management well it can expect to significantly improve the business as shown in Figure 7.

PMI has done extensive research on the benefits of portfolio management. Their 2012 report Pulse of the Profession, shows that organizations that always do portfolio management have a significantly higher project success rate than the average.

Personalizing the Benefits for Stakeholders

The discussion on OCR emphasized that benefits should be personal to the person being communicated with, some of the possible benefits of a strong EPMS that have been shown include:

Figure 7. Benefits of portfolio management comparing best vs. worst companies

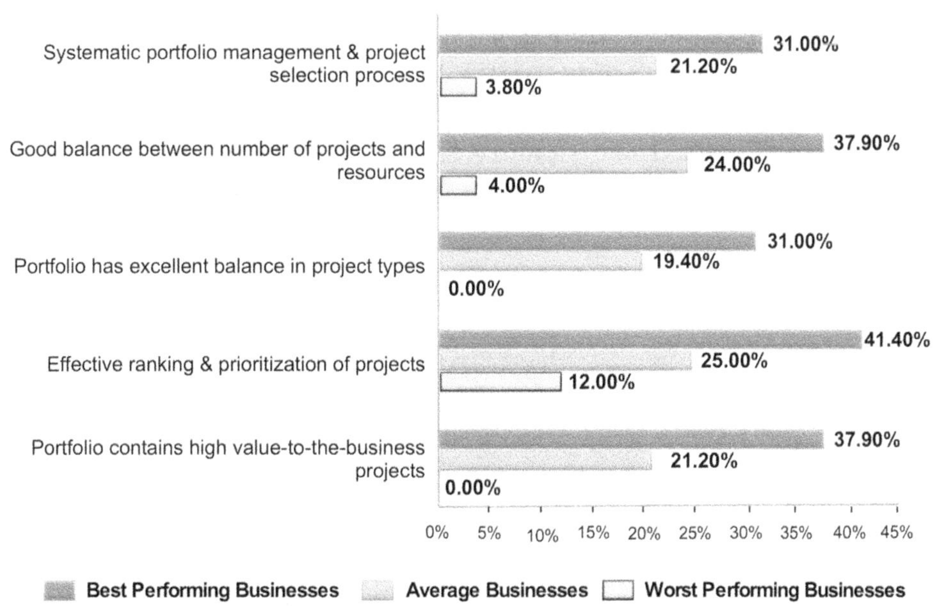

- Closer alignment of the organizations strategies and long-term plans with the money spent.
- Decreased Time to Market (Rizzuto 2005).
- Maximize value of project investments while minimizing risk.
- Increased profitability by reducing waste and improving efficiencies.
- Improve communication and alignment between managers and executives.
- Allow planners to schedule resources more efficiently.
- Reduce the number of redundant projects and make it easier to kill projects.
- Closer alignment of groups/divisions/business units with the overall enterprise.
    - With an understandable, top-down view of their entire project portfolio, executives and managers can more readily understand where dollars are being spent and which projects continue to be worthwhile. Whatever EPMS tool is selected, it will provide a more consistent and accurate view of where the project money is being spent.
- Better governance.
- EPM helps managers monitor project progress in real time and measure each project to the same metrics.
    - Cost reductions and productivity increases.
- EPM helps managers identify redundant projects, inter-project dependencies, and poorly-allocated resources.
- Business-based decision making.
- Executives can make decisions based not only on projected costs and risks, but also on expected returns in relation to other initiatives. Business managers can make decisions faster and with more confidence.
- Improved productivity for individual employees.
- By better selection of projects and less wasted time on poor projects, the system will provide each employee less multi-tasking and overtime, making everyone's job a lot easier and less stressful.

When coordinating with upper management numbers are good. Their emphasis is on measuring the performance of the company and increasing it. What numbers? Generally what benefits will they get for their investment of time and money in EPM. PMI and PMSolutions annually do surveys of portfolio management and PMOs. For 2012 PMI (PMI 2012) showed the following benefits in Table 4.

Joint research published by Project Perfect and META Group (Urusov, 2005) shows that organizations that evaluate information technology projects by what their business impacts are and what their potential business values will be implement projects that result in 25 percent more improvement to the

Table 4. Benefits increase of portfolio management

	Highly Effective at Portfolio Management	Minimally Effective at Portfolio Management	% Increase
Average Percentage of Projects			
Completed on time	68%	50%	36%
Completed on budget	64%	54%	19%
Met original goals and business intent	77%	65%	18%
Met/Exceeded forecasted ROI	62%	48%	29%

bottom line. The Commonwealth Bank in Australia does about 300 projects annually at a cost of AU $500M - $1B. If they saved even 5% of their project costs by implementing EPM that's a savings of AU $25 – 50 million. These are the sort of numbers that get management's attention and need to be emphasized during presentations to upper management.

This is the area where "out of the box" portfolio solutions largely fail. They have a limited set of numbers that can be adjusted by management, but the adjustable fields fail to take into account the uniqueness of the organization and the potentially wide variety of considerations management needs to take into account when selecting projects to invest in.

While a rational, numbers-based approach works for upper management, lower level managers will require convincing in other areas than financial. They will be interested in how this new major system will make their jobs easier and help them expand their areas. Project managers, for example, will be able to concentrate on actually managing their projects and not on data gathering and analysis.

Many of the benefits of an effective EMPS will be non-financial benefits to individual projects. Hiner (2012) listed some of these (with selected quotes):

Number 1: Strategic value.

This is one that an EPMS system is designed to provide.

Number 2: Future deferment.

...If you're considering a proposal and see that it offers the organization a variety of options to choose from down the road, the benefits can be significant. ... Business environments change all the time, which often makes long-term planning inefficient.

Number 3: Building goodwill.

...Sometimes, a proposal or an initiative delivers fantastic value to your organization's partners, employees, or the community. ...

Number 4: Driving best practices.

Projects that don't have immediate ROI but lead the company to adopt best practices are valuable in three respects:

1. Best practices should lead to improved quality or efficiencies.
2. Adoption of best practices reaffirms the organization s position as an industry leader…
3. It often makes the organization more competitive, …

Number 5: Creating capacity.

...Examples include freeing up of physical office space, creation of available production capacity, or freeing up somebody's time. All of these are great benefits, but sometimes they get misinterpreted or overlooked.

How to Sell an EPMS

In this paper we have mentioned supporting the strategic goals of the organization, but do the employees know what those goals are? Sometimes the goals described in the Vision and Mission statements that are commonly published in the organization's annual SEC filing of their annual report (for publically held companies) or in some other high-level document. But any large organization can have multiple strategies. In executive-speak Petit & Hobbs (2012) show how we best can communicate three goals of portfolio management:

Goal 1: Value maximization: To allocate resources so as to maximize the value of the portfolio in terms of some business objectives such as profitability. ... The values of projects to the business are determined, and projects are ranked according to this value until there are no more resources.

Goal 2: Balance: To achieve a desired balance of projects in terms of a number of parameters: long-term projects vs. short-term ones; high-risk vs. sure bets; and across various markets, technologies, and project types.

Goal 3: Strategic direction: To ensure that the final portfolio of projects reflects the business' strategy, that the breakdown of spending across projects, areas, markets, etc., mirrors the business' strategy, and that all projects are on strategy.

The typical EPMS implementation starts with upper management (the C-level, VPs, senior directors, etc) learning that there are benefits to it. They will authorize a study to see what the benefits can be to the organization. Once these benefits have been defined and upper management agrees, what usually happens is that the implementation project is approved.

But experience tells us that just because upper management agrees that something needs to be done doesn't mean that all the employees will support it. A solid EPMS impacts the ability of several lower levels of management (directors, senior managers, managers, including project managers) to decide where to spend their annual budget. It also impacts the freedom of project managers to manage projects the way they want to. They will be required to spend more time on keeping the more detail levels of the project schedule updated than they did before and gives them less time to do true management. This is where the last section's discussion of Organizational Change Management becomes so important. Those are the principles that must be utilized when working with these people to understand their concerns and to get their inputs to design a system that will benefit them.

These two groups of stakeholders will look at the proposed EPMS project and immediately decide what the impact is to them, often even before any presentations or briefings have been given. In both cases the short-term impact is not highly positive and there is likely to be resistance from both groups. Middle management won't like the fact that they are not free to select their pet projects and project managers won't like the constraints on their freedom to manage projects.

For both groups, the specific benefits need to be identified and sold to them on a very personal basis. How does it benefit them doing their job on a daily basis. This is truly a sales job –the lead manager on the EPMS implementation needs to:

1. Propose the idea and tell them that it's important to upper management because of the long-term benefits to the organization.
2. Listen carefully to their concerns and be honest about understanding the impacts to them.
3. State what the benefits are to them. This will require meeting with them to understand how an EPMS can most benefit them. That is, get their inputs as described in the last section.
4. Get them involved in designing and implementing the EPMS. This gives them a much greater understanding of the system and how it can benefit them. People will "buy into" something they have helped create much more readily than something that is imposed on them.

The best salespeople have a deep understanding of both the product they're selling and the people they're selling to. The "customers" here are professional managers and skilled technical people. They are very intelligent and have usually spent many years both in education and in experience to get where they are. They expect to be dealt with seriously and to have their concerns listened to. They are being sold a process that is going to impact their work life.

The approach to getting the highest percentage of support for the EPMS implementation is to use what the goals and expectations are that were gathered during the initial interviews. During this effort the project lead determined the fundamental problems that the organization was trying to address by implementing an EPM system and can target those expectations in selling the benefits throughout the organization.

Some departments in the company learned how to justify their efforts many years ago. Marketing departments know it is critically important to show the expected financial benefits of a marketing project before it gets approved. The fact that often these numbers are not achieved does not slow them down. IT departments, by contrast, are still learning how to build a solid business case to justify their investments. (The noted high failure rate of IT projects does not help their cases).

Research done by Cooper et al. (2001) in the area of new product development helps underline some reasons for doing portfolio management. As shown in Figure 8, the primary reason to do portfolio management is to maintain a competitive position, following closely by making best use of scarce resources.

Guaranteed returns on an investment such as EPMS is not a necessity in building justification for a project. Upper management has learned through experience that nothing is certain. Decisions are made based on the best information available at the time. It is incumbent on the EMPS lead to provide upper management accurate information on the costs and benefits of the EPMS effort in order to get them to approve it.

One very important consideration to keep in mind is that in any organization, especially a mature, established one, there will be internal politics. We reward the members of that organization for doing a good job in the area that they're in by promoting them. This establishes a personal emphasis on expanding and improving the area the manager works in. Good managers strongly believe that their areas are highly important and will fight to grow them. But in portfolio management the emphasis is on the overall organization, not on any one individual area. This means that each manager has to compromise their area for the higher-level benefits, in contrast to what's been important to their career growth up until now.

Portfolio management will be viewed as threatening by some of the organization's managers. It not only takes away their ability to select pet projects and requires them to compromise, it also establishes a more detailed level of accountability than many are used to. Prior to now they were rarely called to task if a project wasn't successful. But now each project is rationally selected based on its contribution

Figure 8. Primary reasons to implement a portfolio selection process
1 is not a major reason and 5 is a critical reason.

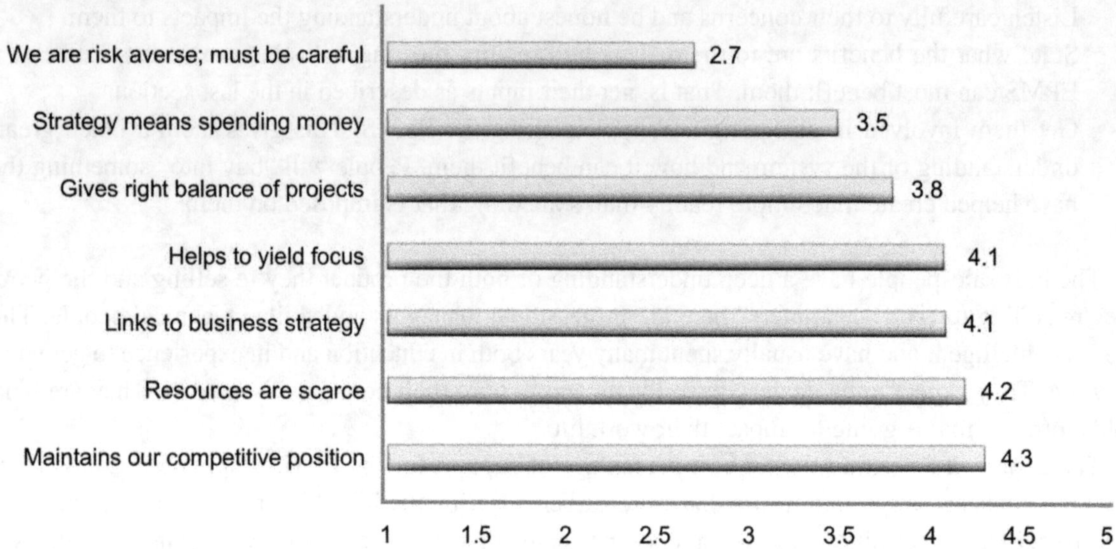

to strategic goals (balanced with its risk) and the manager is called to account if those promised benefits are not met.

Now that we have determined what the organization is looking for, identified those who are supportive and those who are critical, just how does the EPMS team go about the details of actually selling the benefits of EPMS? It is critical to identify who will be supportive of the project and who will be subversive.

We start by identifying all of the stakeholders that are:

- Involved either directly with the project.
- Whose interests will be affected by the project, both positively and negatively, and
- Who will be affected by the end product of the project, either positively or negatively (if this is a large group of end users, then categorize them as well as you can).

Identify the stakeholders by name, by the part of the organization they are in, their role in that part of the organization, their active role in the project (if any), how they will be affected (good or bad) by the project, their ability to influence the project, what support the EPMS team needs from them, and if their support is not what we need, how can we get it.

The level they will be affected by the project can be numbered from 1-10, 1 being a low level of impact and 10 being a very high level of impact. The level of impact should not be a guess by you, it needs to come from them. Let them tell you how they think they will be impacted by the project.

In a similar fashion, the level of support can also be numbered from 1-10, with 1 being a low level of support and 10 being a high level.

Their ability to influence the project is a critical item. If they are negatively impacted by the project AND their ability to influence it is high, this will cause problems for the team because the team will be fighting them during the entire implementation effort. If they are negatively impacted BUT their ability to influence it is very low, the team's action plan should be to keep them informed of the project but prioritize efforts into other areas. Influence can be direct influence over the EPMS implementation schedule, budget, and resources. Indirect influence is their ability to influence the people who do have direct influence over the project.

Managers at all levels deal with so much information that the more efficiently they can grasp the benefits the quicker you will receive acceptance and buy-in. Multiple articles and books in how to present information point out that graphics is a much more effective way to communicate ideas than text is. A simple graphic such as Figure 9 will convey a lot of positive information.

Overcoming Political Dangers

According to the survey published by PMI in their 2012 Pulse of the Profession quoted earlier, 67% of organizations surveyed have a Portfolio Management Office, and an additional 7% are considering one. Most of these PMOs are performing portfolio management, so the value of doing portfolio management is widely recognized by top management.

However, just because the executive level recognizes the value does not mean that this appreciation filters down through the rest of the management layers. Most projects are still selected based on what is best for the individual managers, not for the organization as a whole. Decision makers often try to go around the process to get their pet projects selected.

Commitment across all levels of the organization are crucial to success of the effort. Part of the implementation team's job is to determine if the organization is just "going through the motions" to make the Board of Directors happy or are they really trying to improve. Do managers really not see the benefits or have they just not have bought into it because they don't see the benefits. This is done much more effectively by an internal team rather than hiring outside consultants to perform the implementation.

Middle and upper managers below the executive level have enough autonomy to run their area in a way that makes most sense to them. Anything that poses a threat to that autonomy, such as taking away their ability to pick their own projects, will be resisted. Part of the implementation work is to understand that this will happen and be prepared for it with a strong OCM effort and sufficient communications.

Figure 9. Cost savings as a result of implementing portfolio management

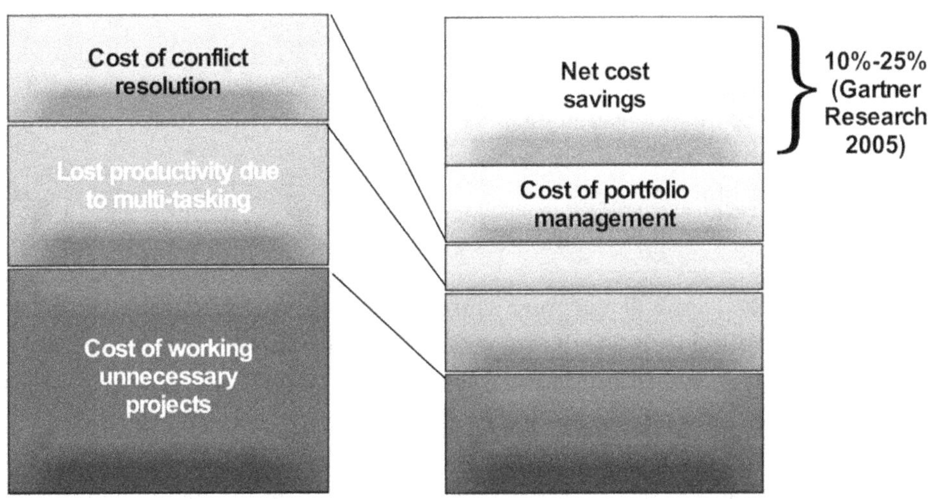

The Business Case

After you've done all the work to research the benefits of an EPMS, interviewed the decision-makers on what they want out of it, de-conflicted their needs, researched ways to properly prepare the organization for the coming changes, and done all the prep work, the project team still must get formal approval to design, develop, and implement it.

The business case is the written justification that convinces upper management that this project should be done. It is to show the benefits of the EPMS. It provides the benefits of the project to the organization, the costs of the project, and the risks associated with it. A major part of the business case is the financial justifications discussed earlier. The business case is used to "sell" the project to the decision-makers.

At the top of the organization their primary interests lie in moving the entire organization towards its strategic goals. They need numbers that show the benefits, and the more the numbers can be justified the more convincing the argument will be.

During periods of economic growth executives are more willing to spend money to grow the company. There's a feeling of "we can do even more" and a desire to get bigger. During periods of economic downturn it would seem rational that the executives would be more willing to authorize work that reduces costs or to improve productivity. Unfortunately the opposite is usually what happens. They become more reluctant to spend money no matter how good the long-term payoff is and so the justification needs to be even better. Hint: Get someone from the marketing department to help gather the information needed here and to help write it. Marketing people are, as a rule, better at communicating these areas than technical people are. They've been doing it a lot longer.

There are many different templates for business cases. Exactly what goes into the document depends on the type of project and in what management wants to see. A business template for an IT project would be very different than that from a pharmaceutical development project or for a new factory. Most organizations that do projects have their own internal templates for a business case document. The organizations we find that have the most detailed business case templates are government organizations. This is because of the heavy oversight of most government projects and the probability of an audit if the project runs into trouble. So there is strong emphasis placed on justifying the project.

In general, the most important parts of the business case, the part that "sells" the EPMS project, would include the following:

- What is the business need or what problem does it solve?
- What is the proposed solution?
- How does the project fit into the strategic plan?
- What is the cost of the project?
- What are the benefits of the project?
- What are the risks inherent in the project?

Experienced project managers will recognize a lot of these sections. They are commonly documented in the project charter. The differences are the emphasis on the business so we include some competitive analysis and ROI calculations. Sometimes the business case is appended to the project charter. Oftentimes the business case substitutes for the project charter. If you already have a business case, there is very little that needs to be added to it to make it a proper project charter. If you develop a separate project charter, at the very least attach the success criteria and the financial justification from the business case.

Executive Summary

This is a short summarization of the rest of the document. It emphasizes the benefits, costs, and risks. Most of the executives will read the summary, make a decision, and browse the rest of the document to reinforce their decision. This should be the last section written but it must be the best written. The project is highly likely to be approved or rejected on how well the executive summary sells it.

Current Situation

Why is the organization doing this? What's the problem, the pain, that's causing them to develop an EPMS? Or what's the benefit of doing so? If there's no real problem, why should management approve this major effort?

This section must be written so that the decision-makers see the problems that not having an EPMS causes. The more you can convince people there are significant problems the EPMS can solve, the more likely you are to get it approved. If the project team can put financial numbers around the items showing how much productivity is lost or how much money is wasted they will significantly improve the chances of getting approved.

Product Overview

Here's where the team describes what the EPMS will look like, and how it will operate, once it's implemented and integrated into the overall organization.

High-Level Objectives

High-level objectives for the EPMS should be the solution to the problems described in the section on the current situation and they should be quantifiable to the extent possible. For example:

- Increase productivity of the IT department by 10% by killing duplicate projects.
- Reduce time-to-profit for new product development by 6 months.
- Select more projects that support strategic rather than departmental objectives.
- And so on.

Remember the goal – to implement a system that will significantly improve how the organizations selects projects and moves towards its strategic goals. The more that goal can be made specific and measurable the better the chances of getting the project approved.

Competitive Position

Executives are always worried about what the competition are doing. Are they getting ready to release a new product? Are they gaining market share? Are they more efficient than our organization?

Developing a new product or a new service that will increase market share or save internal costs is highly thought of by executive decision-makers. They are always looking to get ahead of their competition, or to stay ahead if they're already out in front. A properly designed and implemented EPMS will improve the chances of selecting highly profitable projects, getting them to market quicker, and reducing internal waste. That's what should be emphasized in the business case. Apple Computer is widely recognized for having a very strict new product development approach. They actively cut out projects that do not meet increasingly strict profitability and/or market-share criteria. They are also famously secret about their product development approaches.

Impacts

This section describes the impacts to the on-going work in the organization. What are the impacts to operations? What are the impacts to existing projects? How many people will be pulled away from their normal daily work, and for how long?

Here's where the business case must phrase things very carefully. There will be impacts, especially in the short term. The implementation will need to have people working on the project who are doing other work and will need to be pulled off it. It will likely disrupt other projects in work.

Once the EMPS is implemented, it will look first at the existing projects in the organization and identify any overlapping projects, duplicate projects, and projects that need to be killed. Once project managers and team members hear this is going to happen, they will either stop working on projects that, in their minds, are likely to be cancelled or they will protest vigorously to protect their projects. So there will be impacts to doing the EMPS, but it must be emphasized in the business case that the negative impacts are short-term and that the organization will be much better off in the long term.

Potential Risks

Every project has risks. This one is no exception. What is a risk? A risk is anything that can happen in the future that will impact the success of the project.

In this section of the business case the project lead captures the risks that are known at this point. Have a tight schedule? That's a risk. Don't have dedicated resources to implement the EMPS? That's a risk.

Assumptions

An assumption is anything that is expected to be true for planning purposes. If the lead thinks there will be enough dedicated resources to do the work, that is an assumption. If he or she thinks this project will have interference from managers in other departments, that's an assumption. If the project is planned out expecting that software and hardware prices will not change in the future, that's an assumption.

The entire plan – schedule, budget, deliverables, is based on assumptions. The more of these assumptions that can be defined and documented, the better the planning processes will be. Determine what assumptions are being made to understand better the weak points in the plans.

One statement that is always true in planning projects – any assumption becomes a risk if it turns out not to be true. There's an inverse relationship between risks and assumptions. If there was an assumption that the team would have a highly skilled data base analyst (DBA) to design the data base, and later find out there is none available, now there is a risk.

Alternatives

A section of alternative solutions to the stated problems is a common one in the business case. What other ways are there to solve the problems stated in the Current Situation? Are there simpler solutions? Is there something less costly or less disruptive that we can do instead? Because management has been thinking so much about the portfolio management solution that they have become focused on it, the lead should obtain inputs from other people who are less tied to a single solution.

Of course, one solution is always to do nothing. This is the default solution. If upper management isn't feeling enough pain from the problems or if they have not convinced them of the benefits of this project, this is the solution they will often pick – to do nothing.

Financial Costs and Benefits

This is the crux of the business case. Here is where the financial justification of the EMPS are documented. The emphasis of this part of the business case will be hard numbers, the more detailed the numbers the better.

For most projects it is easier to identify the costs than it is the benefits. It is reasonably straightforward to estimate the size of the project, the resources that will be needed, and any expected expenditures and come up with reasonable rough numbers for the costs.

It is much harder to come up with valid numbers for the benefits. There are always a lot of loose assumptions in defining the benefits of a project. Do we expect an increase in market share because of what this project will provide? How much? 5% market share increase? 10%? 2%? Do we expect to increase the productivity of the IT department by implementing an EPMS? If so, how much? A 2% increase in productivity for 250 people is a significant improvement. But where did the financial analyst come up with that 2% number? It will be an assumption at this point unless there are detailed and reasonable calculations to support it.

When doing the cost/benefit calculations, the team can calculate either the specific costs of the EPMS implementation project, or calculate the total costs of ownership (TCO). These are different calculations and the benefit calculations depend on which of these two are used.

The implementation costs would include the cost of the team members developing and implementing the system, any software or hardware purchased, and the costs associated with ancillary personnel such as internal user groups or business analysts that will be involved part-time with the effort. Implementation costs are calculated up to the point when the system becomes operational.

Total Costs of Ownership include any on-going licensing and maintenance fees for software and hardware and the operating costs once the EPMS is in use. Future software maintenance costs should not be ignored. For some databases, such as Oracle, these costs can be 22% per year of the original purchase costs – a significant amount. Typically these life-cycle costs would be calculated out for a period of 3 to 5 years. The organization's financial department will help with this calculation.

Almost always for an EPMS the TCO should be the emphasis. This is because the greatest benefits come in the future. If the business case just calculates the cost of the EMPS implementation itself it will not have the opportunity to show the benefits.

One consideration for management is to identify whose pocket the operational costs of the portfolio come out of. That is, who is the organization is going to pay for it. If the EPMS is part of the PMO, the operational budget should be put into the PMO's budget. For people who work in other departments but are part of how the EPMS operates, some percentage of their cost should come of out the EPMS budget.

CONCLUSION

In this chapter we have developed an effective process for implementing an enterprise portfolio management system to overcome well-known causes of failure. The chapter discusses the decision-making process that upper management utilizes to determine which projects to fund and how to identify who those decision-makers are and how to influence them. By understanding the decision-making process in an organization the project management implementation team can identify the specific goals and expectations that will be designed into the system to ensure that management gets the information they require to select the optimum projects based on criteria they identified. An "out-of-the-box" software solution will not usually prove successful for most organizations because it cannot be flexible enough to take into account the organization's unique characteristics and still be commercially viable to appeal to a broad category of organizations..

The chapter summarizes some of the challenges that are faced both by organizations and by project managers in identifying and developing successful projects to achieve strategic goals. As an example of a successful portfolio system we provided a case study of an organization that has developed a highly effective system and implemented it over a series of years.

Because much of the root cause of failure lies in the internal resistance of the organization's personnel the chapter covers appropriate material in the field of organizational change management and how to overcome it. Finally, the chapter provides ideas on how to "sell" the concept of portfolio management to both the executive decision-makers and the employees to make it more acceptable to the organization.

REFERENCES

Abdollahyan, F. (2012). *Management of Value as PPM Strategy*. Paper presented at the 2012 PMI EMEA Congress, Marseille, France.

Bannister, F., & Remenyi, D. (2009). Multitasking: The Uncertain Impact of Technology on Knowledge Workers and Managers. *The Electronic Journal Information Systems Evaluation*, *12*(1), 1–12.

Buffett, M., & Clark, D. (2006). *The Tao of Warren Buffett*. New York: Scriber.

Collins, J. (2001). *Good to Great*. New York: HarperCollins.

Cook, D. (2007). *The 5 Reasons Organizations choose the Wrong Projects*. Paper presented at the 2007 Project Management – Setting the Standard conference by the Australian Institute of Project Management National Conference, Hobart, Tasmania.

Cooper, R.G., Edgett, S.J., & Kleinschmidt, E.J. (2001). New Product Development: Results of an Industry Practices Study. *R&D Management Magazine*, *31*(4).

Cooper, R. G., Edgett, S. J., & Kleinschmidt, E. J. (2003). *Best Practices in Product Innovation: What Distinguishes Top Performers*. Product Development Institute. Retrieved from www.prod-dev.com

Cooper, R. G., Edgett, S. J., & Kleinschmidt, E. J. (2005). Benchmarking Best NPD Practices. *Research-Technology Management*, *47*(1), 31–43.

Diedrich, P., & Lehtonen, P. (2005). Successful management of strategic intentions through multiple projects – reflections from empirical study. *IJPM*, *23*(5), 386–391.

Dochtermann, D., Jesus-Olhausen, A. L., & Cermak, T. (2011). *Introduction to a Project Portfolio Management Maturity Model*. Paper presented at the 2011 PMI North American Congress.

Flyvbjerg, B. (2009). Survival of the Unfittest. *Oxford Review of Economic Policy*, *25*(3), 344–367. doi:10.1093/oxrep/grp024

Hammer, M., & Champy, J. (1998). *Re-engineering the Corporation*. New York: HarperCollins.

Harvard Business School On-line Forum. (n.d.). *Why Don't Managers Think Deeply?* Accessed March 02, 2016 from http://hbswk.hbs.edu/item/5952.html

Hiner, J. (2012). *Look beyond the dollar signs to validate your projects*. Retrieved Nov, 2012 from http://blogs.techrepublic.com.com/hiner/?p=2773&tag=nl.e053

Kahneman, D. (2012). *Thinking, Fast and Slow*. New York: Farrar, Straus and Giroux.

Lancaster, H. (1995, January 17). Reengineering Authors Reconsider Reengineering: An interview with Michael Hammer and James Champy. *Wall Street Journal*.

Lassa, T. (2009, March). GM's Survival Strategy: Divisions, Nameplates to Disappear. *Motor Trend Magazine*.

Maniak, R., Midler, C., Lenfle, S., & Le Pellec-Dairon, M. (2014). Value Management for Exploration Projects. *Project Management Journal*, *45*(Sept/Oct), 55–66. doi:10.1002/pmj.21436

Martinsuo, M., & Lehtonen, P. (2007). Role of single-project management in achieving portfolio management efficiency. *IJPM*, *25*(1), 56–64.

McFarland, W. (2012). *This is Your Brain on Organizational Change*. Retrieved April, 2016 from https://hbr.org/2012/10/this-is-your-brain-on-organizational-change

Parth, F. R. (2002). *PMO Development at Toyota Financial Services*. Paper presented at ProMac 2002 International Conference on Project Management, Singapore.

Parth, F. R. (2015). *Project Control Through an Effective PMO - A Case Study*. Paper presented to the UAE chapter of AACE, Abu Dhabi, UAE.

Patankul, P. (2015). Key attributes of effectiveness in managing project portfolio. *International Journal of Project Management*, *33*(5), 1084–1097. doi:10.1016/j.ijproman.2015.01.004

Patterson, R. W., & Conner, D. (Eds.). (1982, April). Building Commitment to Organizational Change. *Training and Development Journal*, 18-30.

Perry, R., & Hatcher, E. (2008). *How Project and Portfolio Management Solutions Are Delivering Value to Organizations*. White paper published by IDC Sept. 2008.

Petit, Y., & Hobbs, B. (2012). *Project Portfolios in Dynamic Environments*. Newtown Square, PA: Project Management Institute Publications.

Petro, Y., & Gardiner, P. (2015). An investigation of the influence of organizational design on project portfolio success, effectiveness and business efficiency for project-based organizations. *International Journal of Project Management, 33*(8), 1717–1729. doi:10.1016/j.ijproman.2015.08.004

PMI. (2012). *2012 Pulse of the Profession – Project Portfolio Management: Driving Success from the Top Down*. Project Management Institute.

Rizzuto, J. (2005). *Trading Places*. Retrieved March 15, 2015 from http://www.projectsatwork.com/article.cfm?ID=226042

Robin, M. (2000, March). Learning By Doing. *Knowledge Management*.

Santosus, M. (2003, September 15). Why More is Less. *CIO Magazine*.

Schiemann, W. (1992, April). Why Change Fails. *Across the Board*.

Urusov, D. (2005). *IT Portfolio Management Model*. White paper published June 2005. Retrieved January 2006 from www.projectperfect.com.au

KEY TERMS AND DEFINITIONS

Benefits Management: Designing the project, in this chapter the EPMS implementation, to provide benefits as quickly as possible and incrementally increase them during the roll-out of the EPMS.

EPMS: Enterprise Portfolio Management System. The organization-wide portfolio management system including tools, processes, and resources. Distinguished from a lower-level portfolio management system.

OCM: Organizational Change Management. An approach to introducing major change in an organization by preparing each stakeholder in advance and during the change process itself. The goal is to mitigate any resistance to the changes.

Project: A project consists of a unique set of processes consisting of coordinated and controlled activities with start and end dates, performed to achieve project objectives. (ISO 21500)

Program: A group of related projects managed as a single group in order to obtain control not available by managing the projects in isolation.

Portfolio: The collection of all projects within an organization. They may be managed individually or managed collectively.

PMO: Portfolio Management Office or Program Management Office. When a PMO is used to manage a program it is the Program Management Office. When a PMO is used to manage the portfolio of projects it is the Portfolio Management Office.

Resistance: Behavior of the members of an organization that slows down or stops changes.

Steering Committee: The high-level group of executives that has overall responsibility and oversight of the portfolio.

Chapter 6
Adaptive Portfolio Management

Luca Romano
PMI Central Italy Chapter – CUOA Business School, Italy

ABSTRACT

Portfolio management methodology is usually linked with the concept of "portfolio cycle" (often 1 year of activities). This means that organizations experience, once a year, a time in which ongoing activities are analyzed and their status reported; new initiatives are collected, assessed, prioritized and selected in competition with ongoing components. Being the aim of portfolio management to select the best set of components supporting the organization in achieving the strategic objectives, strategy should drive the preparation of the "next portfolio cycle". It may be the case that the strategy is not clear, not ready to be used, not stable. Adaptive Portfolio Management requires to move away from the collect-assess-prioritize-select-implement-control-review approach (all these actions are performed during each and every "portfolio cycle") towards a more flexible model where organizations manage these important activities "continuously".

INTRODUCTION

The early days of Strategic Thinking can be traced back to the famous *Art of War* by Sun Tzu, unanimously considered to be the first treatise on strategy. Written presumably around 500 BC, it is still used today by political representatives, business leaders and thinkers as a source of inspiration. The same can be said, for the book *On War* published in 1832 by Carl von Clausewitz, Major General in the German Prussian army. Interestingly, among the various insights and principles that can be applied to the business world, both of them speak about how to react to changes or, much better, how to be prepared to face them.

The Art of War teaches us *to rely not on the likelihood of the enemy's not coming, but on our own readiness to receive him; not on the chance of his not attacking, but rather on the fact that we have made our position unassailable (Sheetz-Runkle, 2014).* Von Clausewitz firmly believe in the need of *a philosophy of strategy that contains the seeds of its constant rejuvenation—a way to chart strategy in an unstable environment (Pietersen, 2016).*

As a matter of fact, and as it will be discussed in this chapter, organizations needs strategy for the same reasons that drive the armies' need for military strategies: to give direction and purpose, to organize

DOI: 10.4018/978-1-5225-2151-8.ch006

resources in the most effective way and to coordinate the decisions made by different individuals (Grant & Jordan, 2015): these are the fundamentals of strategic management.

Strategic management is such a broad concept that numerous definitions have been given. It can be defined as *the art and science of formulating, implementing, and evaluating cross-functional decisions that enable an organization to achieve its objectives* (David, 2011). In other words, strategic management refers to the comprehensive collection of activities and processes that organizations put in place to coordinate and align resources and actions with vision, mission and objectives. The formulation of these three basic concept is the first stage of the strategic management process. The vision expresses management's ambitions expressing the rational "for what and for who" the organization exists. A mission statement is a description of the actual intentions of the organization and usually is less general and more linked to the current situation. An objective (short or long term) is a measurable and quantifiable management commitment to achieve several results. The strategy expresses "how" the organization wants to achieve the strategic objectives. The sequence Vision + mission + objectives + strategy is generally called strategic planning (Thompson, Strickland, Gamble, 2009).

The road to get to this definition starts in the strategy heydays of the second half of the 20th century, when the concept of corporate planning was developed in response to the increasing difficulty the organizations faced in coordinating decisions and maintain control over firms that were growing in size and complexity. This *long-term planning* (usually with the typical time horizon of five years) sets objectives strategies and goals, forecasting economic trends and guides the organization's expenditures allocation. However, again due to the turbulent external environment, firms had difficult time in forecasting in detail a five-year span.

As a result, the emphasis given to strategy planning shifted to strategy making through what will be named strategic management, which involves the analysis of both the internal and the external environment, with the aim of optimizing resources in relation to the organizational objectives providing the organization with a framework for anticipating and facing change, in order to develop abilities to cope with uncertainties (Bracker, 1980).

At the present time, to make long lasting effective strategies is even more difficult than years ago in the recent past, maybe so difficult that it should not be attempted at all. Strategic agility, organizational flexibility and resilience are key not only to survive, but also to get competitive advantage (Aurik, Jonk, Fabel, 2014)

Doz and Kosonen (2008) say that *most companies die not because they do the wrong things, but because they keep doing the what used to be the right things for too long.*

The focus given to strategy in the literature of the 20th century covers mostly the concept of how to make a strategy, rather than how to make it work, (Meskendahl, 2010) which is definitely more difficult (Hrebiniak, 2006). This is where project portfolio management practices definitely have a say.

Project Portfolio Management (PPM) manages the identification, assessment, prioritization and selection of the set of components (projects, programs and operations activities) that appear to implement strategy in the best way. To stay in the military vocabulary, Shenhar et al. (2001) point out that projects, and even more project portfolios, are *powerful strategic weapons* as they turn out to be central building block in implementing the intended strategy of an organization.

Project Portfolio Management methodology is usually linked with the concept of "portfolio cycle" (often 1 year of activities). This means that organizations experience, once a year, a time in which ongoing activities are analyzed and their status reported; new initiatives are collected, assessed, prioritized and selected in competition with ongoing components.

These PPM activities are very complex, time consuming and have to be performed with a waterfall approach as there is a deadline to respect, and the new "portfolio cycle" (with the selected components) cannot be authorized and started before the completion of the process. Being the aim of portfolio management to select the best set of components supporting the organization in achieving the strategic objectives, strategy should drive the preparation of the "next portfolio cycle".

It may be the case that the strategy is not clear, not ready to be used, not stable. The selection in these situations is incomplete and organizations are forced to choose without having the needed information.

After several years of real life application of portfolio management methodology there is the need to make a step forward in how organizations manage their portfolios and (for organizations with the right level of maturity in this matter) there could be a more effective way to manage this process.

Adaptive Portfolio Management requires to move away from the collect-assess-prioritize-select-implement-control-review approach (all these actions are performed during each and every "portfolio cycle") towards a more flexible model where organizations manage these important activities "continuously".

This chapter will present some ideas and some suggestions, analyzing how, when and where it is possible to be adaptive.

A FLEXIBLE APPROACH IN MANAGING A PROJECT PORTFOLIO

An Historical Example of Flexibility

The author some years ago had an inspiration on flexibility in the implementation of a vision/mission from a book about Napoleon, the French Emperor (Vincenti, 1985). In particular, the author was inspired by what happened before the Battle of Austerlitz.

Between the end of 1804 and autumn 1805 Napoleon has been debated for a serious purely military problem: to start or not to start the invasion of England to aggressively defend France?

He assembles in the fields of Boulogne over 200,000 men while yards were working feverishly to build flat-bottomed boats judged the most suitable to cross the Channel carrying the troops.

Napoleon visiting the camp and the port of Boulogne stares at the opposite side of the Channel, the land where he has become public enemy number one. Although they never set foot on British soil, Napoleon's troops received careful and invaluable training for any possible military operation. Boredom among the troops occasionally set in, but Napoleon paid many visits, and conducted lavish parades, in order to boost morale. Napoleon multiplies the inspections, visits and parades at the Boulogne camp, but does not decide to start the invasion, also listening to the voices of war coming from the continent, beginning with King Gustav IV of Sweden who dreams of an anti-Napoleon crusade. A few days later, with a typical sudden change of his strategic genius, he decided to suspend the invasion.

He orders to that which will be christened "La Grande Armée" to leave the French coast to point instead to the north and to the east.

The goal is no longer the English coast, but the heart of Germany. In fact, a coalition against France was formed by the UK, England, Austria, Sweden, the King of Naples and Russia.

At the beginning of the new campaign French soldiers received two pairs of shoes: for the purpose of victory they were more important than their weapons. The speed of movement was in fact an essential condition in the Napoleonic strategies, because from speed depend decisive factors as the surprise effect, the strategic surrounding, and the timely concentration on the battlefield.

All the soldiers of the time were great walkers, capable of an average distance of 20-30 km in a normal 8-hour day, increasing it to 40-60 km in conditions of necessity. The great masses of men, however, had to proceed in long columns so that the march of the first man could end up before the beginning of the last row, making complex maneuvers of large concentrations of troops virtually impossible. A French organizational revolution, institutionalized by Napoleon just before the war, partially solved the problem, by articulating "La Grande Armée" in the Army Corps, balanced infantry forces, cavalry, artillery and services led by experienced officers, independent, but able to coordinate with each other in their wide-ranging movements.

This organizational revolution creating independent armed bodies allowed agile movements to large concentrations of troops, inconceivable before, and impossible for the other armies of the time.

So the corps of the Grande Armée, despite rain and snow, moved to a stunning average of 40 kilometers a day along parallel paths behind the Austrian concentration in Ulm, reaching the Danube on October the 7th.

The high level of training, and the perfect organization of the Grande Armée, had allowed Napoleon to achieve the greatest "Manoeuvre sur les derrieres (behind)" he had ever conceived: while from the front his cavalry drew the attention of the Austrians, the majority of the troops came to their shoulders, surrounding them.

After 15 days Napoleon enters his tent dictating to secretaries the 7th bulletin of "La Grande Armée": "In fifteen days we changed our objectives and made a new campaign: what we planned is concluded. This coalition, who so ostentatiously and imprudence had gathered around our borders, is annihilated".

There are several key aspects and lessons learned that can be drawn from this historical tale. Here is a list:

- It is better to change objectives, strategy and tactics if this will produce an advantage for the Organization.
- If you don't change quickly you will lose an opportunity.
- Often it is worth to change your objectives/strategy even if you have spent a lot of time/money on the previous one if it is no longer correct.
- If Top Management wants to be adaptive, all the structure must be able to be adaptive.
- The way an Organization is structured can be an advantage or a disadvantage. Organizations that wants to be adaptive have to reach the right level of maturity.
- Employees must be trained to be adaptive, and ready to apply the changes.
- Technical aspects and facilities are important to create an adaptive environment.
- Being adaptive is a competitive advantage.
- Organizations cannot be a hundred per cent adaptive.

A Waterfall Approach

Project Portfolio Management is a discipline that can be described as a component collection of programs, projects, or operations managed as a group to achieve strategic objectives. At any given moment, a portfolio represents a view of its selected components and reflects the organizational objectives and strategy. If a portfolio is not aligned to its organizational strategy, the organization should reasonably question why the work is being undertaken. Therefore, a portfolio should be a representation of an organization's intent, direction, and progress (PMI, 2013b).

This means that the actions performed by the organization should always aim for the achievement of the strategic objectives: if Napoleon wants to go to Austerlitz, the troops cannot go to England.

Organizations are complex systems and are not fighting a war. This is good news, but it also means that the level of discipline is nowhere near as in army corps. Moreover, Portfolio decisions involve so many people and critical aspects that are in most cases are done once a year (with some timid reviews during the approved portfolio life-cycle).

The author has observed that in Project Portfolio Management, organizations have the inclination to stabilize the process to avoid uncontrolled complexity. This is a good thing, but over-stabilization limits adaptability. After the first years of implementation of a PPM system, organizations tend to start to shield the decisions taken during the assessment and selection phase at the expense of an adaptive management system. Projects must be completed the way initially defined, budgets are stable and changes are hard to be accepted. Sometimes changes (for instance new mandatory projects) are pushed from top management into the set of actual components claiming not to change anything. Early PPM Organizations develop a sort of an infallibility syndrome as is it simpler to say that what originally decided must be done, than accept "errors" and rehear the Portfolio. Asking a PM to meet the original budget assigned, even if a change of scope is needed due to a change in the context, is an example.

This is due to the fact that a new PPM system creates a great stress to the organization as new and unknown complexity is added to preexisting way of doing things. The decrease of discretionary power produced by a PPM shouldn't also be underrated. PPM is complex and pervasive, involving so many political aspects that stability is preferred to agility. To move forward in the direction of the correct level of adaptiveness, organizations need to increase their level of maturity in PPM. Meanwhile they prefer to stabilize the system as a cure against confusion and discretionary decisions. In these instances portfolio reviews are very complex, and the attitude to stop what already financed is very low.

This conservative approach goes hand-in-hand with the fact that production lines, project managers, resources managers, and so on, want to know their planned level of engagement to organize work and define budget (broken down into several baskets and assigned).

All these aspects push toward a waterfall way of managing the portfolio.

1. Before the Start of the Next Portfolio Cycle:
    a. **Define the Strategic Objectives:** Objectives are used to translate the vision into results. They are more manageable than a "vision," being conceptually smaller and more easily measurable. Strategic objectives must be, at the very least, quantifiable, measurable, and timed.
    b. **Collect the Initiatives:** It is the process an organization puts in place to collect ideas, projects, needs, etc. Collection is focused on Old Initiatives not previously selected, Ongoing Components and New Initiatives.
    c. **Assess the Initiatives:** Assessment creates what is usually called a business case (BC). The BC contains at least information about needs, objectives, requirements and expected benefits, cost-benefits and financial analysis, deadlines, budget, risks, operational impacts, constraints.
    d. **Prioritize the Initiatives:** To prioritize the initiatives means to rank the components on the basis of their alignment with the strategic direction. Prioritization starts from the output of the assessment.

   e. **Select the Initiatives that Will Become Components of the Portfolio:** Select the initiatives means to choose the best set of components to achieve the strategic objectives that are feasible for the budget available at the level of risk accepted. This is the selection that will be financed. Usually, though, organizations maintain a budget reserve to increase portfolio flexibility.
2. During the Portfolio Cycle
   a. **Detailed Planning before the Implementation:** The detailed planning is the activity performed, usually from the project manager, to bottom-up plan the program/project selected. This activity is referable to the preparation of the Project Management Plan as indicated by PMI. (PMI, 2013a).
   b. **Implement the Components:** Portfolio implementation is the realization of the components selected and authorized. This activity is strictly related to project management and operations management. Project managers, program managers, and managers are doing their day-by-day job.
   c. **Control and Report the Implementation and the Portfolio:** Portfolio controlling and reporting means not only to report the status of single projects/program/operations, but also the status of the whole portfolio and, moreover, the status of achievement of the strategic objectives.
   d. **Review Components, Portfolio, and Eventually the Strategy:** At a certain state of progress, strategy and portfolio reviews are means to answer some important questions, such as: is the actual portfolio sufficiently supporting our strategy? Are there New initiatives more aligned with our strategy that could replace ongoing ones? Is our strategy still correct in the actual market conditions?
   e. **Benefits Realization Control:** Benefits realization control is the measure of the real value realized by the components for the organization. This benefit could be, or not be, aligned with the strategic direction.

In a perfect world, what has been stated during the assessment of the Initiatives c) and their Selection e) is correct and will remain correct, therefore also the strategic objectives will not change. Theoretically this is what the perfect PPM would produce. In the real world, though, the choices made were the best choices possible in a specific period of time and context. The problem is that reality doesn't care about our plans and changes around us. Managers know that the only thing to do is to adapt, but still during the portfolio life-cycle the more the control of the implementation h) and the reviews j) show that there is a gap to cover with some changes, the more the level of panic will rise.

Back to Napoleon's tale, if we decided to attack England why are we turning back and march toward Austerlitz?

Why There Is the Need to Change Ongoing Portfolios

Which are the main causes of a change in an ongoing Portfolio? The causes for a need of change in an approved ongoing Portfolio are several, and have different nature and impact. Here is a collection of possible ones:

1. The strategic objectives are no longer appropriate.
2. The initiatives collection was incomplete.

3. There are new initiatives that were not predictable during the collection.
4. The initiatives assessment was not precise and because of this the detailed planning done after the selection is different than the assessment done before the selection.
5. The prioritization was not correct.
6. The selection was not correct.
7. The implementation of the components does not follow what planned.
8. The plan to implement the components must be changed as it will not produce the expected results.
9. The benefits produced by the portfolio are not as expected and not aligned with the strategic objectives.

Of course, the items listed above do not cover all the possible causes of change, but, by considering them as the main or most common situations, it is possible to go in depth inside their root cause to understand where do they come from, why they do happen and which are the possible solutions to put in place to cope with them. All these findings are reported in Table 1.

Figure 1 shows in a matrix the 9 main causes presented. A further analysis of these possible causes of change and how to possibly avoid them will be discussed in details in the following lines.

Table 1. Main causes to change an on-going portfolio

Cause	Why It Happens	What to Do	And Also..	Level of Impact on the Existing Portfolio
The strategic objectives are no longer appropriate.	The analysis of the market and the need of final clients were wrong or the context has changed.	Re-align the strategic objectives to reality to gain a real advantage for the organization and the shareholders.	Re-align Portfolio components to the new strategic objectives Change, re-prioritize and select the correct set of initiatives to achieve the new strategic objectives.	The highest - depends on the gap between old and new objectives.
The initiatives collection was incomplete.	The collection was not properly performed due to a wrong mapping of the organization or a wrong process. Not all the areas are represented, blind spots emerged.	Collect missing ongoing and new initiatives to complete collection previously done.	Perform an assessment of what collected and relaunch the prioritization and selection phase. Define e new Portfolio, basically.	High – depends on the impact of what originally missed.
There are new initiatives that were not predictable during the collection.	New needs, new regulatory, new requests, new technologies, new ideas.	Assess the new initiatives.	Verify on the base of the status of the portfolio the opportunity to insert new components.	High.
The initiatives assessment was not precise and so the detailed planning done *after* the selection is different (+ or -) than the assessment done *before* the selection.	Due to the limited time available and the uncertainty of the future real implementation, the assessment could have been done too quickly, top down and not involving the right people.	Negotiate and accept the new assessment analyzing the impact produced on the portfolio approved .	Modify the portfolio balance on the base of the detailed assessment trying to sacrifice the less is possible.	Medium.
The prioritization was not correct.	The model utilized was not able to represent the priorities of the Organization.	Manually balance the portfolio and improve the model utilized.		Low.

continued on next page

Table 1. Continued

Cause	Why It Happens	What to Do	And Also..	Level of Impact on the Existing Portfolio
The selection was not correct.	The selection model utilized was not able to select the best set of initiatives to achieve the strategic objectives.	Correct the selection model and select correctly (possible delays in the Portfolio approval).		Medium.
The implementation of the components do not respect what planned.	The projects are not on scope – on time – on budget due to normal causes of skidding.	Assess the status of the whole portfolio and verify gaps. Do an estimation to complete analysis and rebalance the entire portfolio.	Consider if the situation aids new initiatives insertion or suggests ongoing components exclusions.	Medium.
The plan (one or many) to implement the components must be changed as it will not produce the expected results.	The scope of the projects was not clear or it was misunderstood. The plan is not correct as it generates insufficient / incomplete results.	Formalize the changes in the original project plan to be able to achieve the expected results, analyzing the impact on the whole Portfolio.	Consider if the situation aids new initiatives insertion or suggests ongoing components exclusions.	Medium.
The benefits produced by the portfolio are not the expected and not aligned with the strategic objectives.	Outputs and results could not produce the expected benefits and not serve the strategic objectives.	Reconsider the benefits produced by the future components and the ongoing components themselves to align the portfolio direction with the achievement of the Strategic objectives.	Consider actions to support the outputs already produced in their ability to produce strategically aligned tangible benefits.	Medium on the actual portfolio cycle, as it could be solved in the next. Nevertheless, it could be high for the Organization.

Figure 1. Portfolio change causes mapping

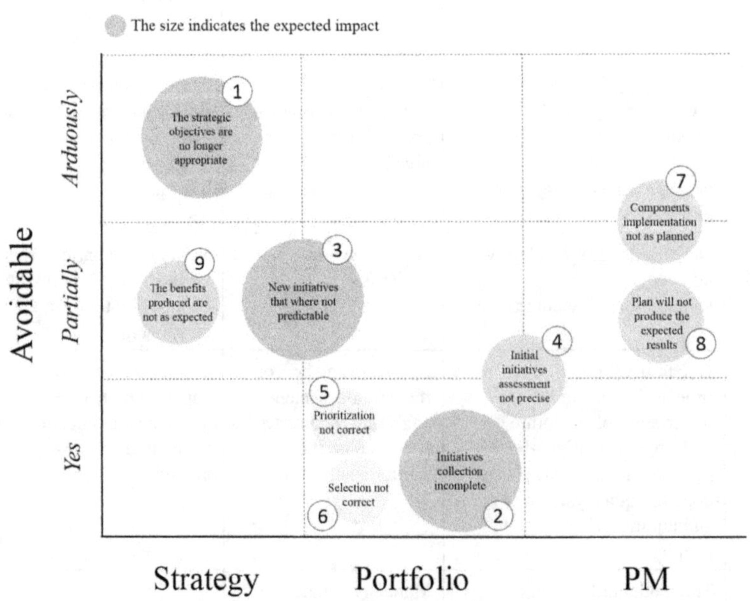

To avoid those situations, first of all, it is important to distinguish the causes, namely number 2-6-5, that relates to the level of portfolio management maturity in the Organization. If this is the root, then they can be almost "proactively" avoidable with the definition and application of correct processes and good tools, and sure they will decrease in time, taking advantage of the learning curve. Either way the impact on the Portfolio (PTF) of cause 2 could be high.

The central horizontal row is unevenly populated.

Cause Number 1: The strategic objectives are no longer appropriate – is due to a change in the environment where the organization operates. It is very hard to prevent this from happening, the environment is clearly unstable by nature. Moreover, control over the context by organizations is generally limited. This is the main and most important cause of a portfolio change as this kind of change *must* be applied. Therefore, its impact on the portfolio could be very high.

Cause Number 3: New initiatives that were not predictable – could be proactively estimated with forecasting activities, but cannot be completely avoided. This cause is also related to the kind of business the organization is involved-in as more stable environments show less causes of this kind. The impact on the Portfolio of this kind of cause could be high.

Cause Number 4: Assessment of the initiatives not precise – is half in the Portfolio and half in the Project Management area because this inaccuracy is highlighted by the difference between the initial estimate done before the selection, and the estimate done during the detailed planning after the selection being part of the Planning Phase in managing projects (PMI, 2013a). The impact depends on the ability of the resources in charge for the initial initiatives assessment to understand the scope of the future project and assess it properly. Time is limited and the precision is influenced by the maturity in this kind of estimating and the level of innovation of the initiative analyzed. Performing this activity, organizations with a longer experience in PPM take also advantage from the learning curve.

Cause Number 7: Components implementation not as planned – is in the project management area and depends on the normal and expected imprecision of planning compared to reality. To stay in the military field, the Prussian Army Field Marshall Helmuth Karl Bernhard Graf von Moltke said that *no plan of operations extends with any certainty beyond the first contact with the main hostile force*. And also Napoleon was used to say: *I have never had a plan of operations*. This cause is partially or arduously manageable due to the normal unpredictability of the future.

Cause Number 8: Components plan will not produce the expected results – is again in the project management area, but it is due to a not sufficient initial definition of scope and requirements of the project. As a result, the plan is wrong because what had to be achieved was not clear. Of course, the level of innovation introduced by the project may influence this cause. The mitigation could come with a better project management process and with the use of more experienced PMs.

Cause Number 9: The benefits produced are not as expected – is revealed by measures collected after the completion of the implemented activities. If the projects are finished while the portfolio cycle is still ongoing, this evidence can be considered as a cause of change in the Portfolio. It is in the strategy area because the benefits achievement serves the strategic objectives.

The probability to face these nine main causes depend on several characteristics of the organizations summarized in Table 2.

Table 2. Characteristics increasing the probability of a change in an ongoing Portfolio

Characteristics	More Probable PTF Change Causes
High external environment instability.	• New strategic objectives (1). • New initiatives not predictable (3). • Benefits not aligned with strategic objectives (9).
Organization's size and complexity.	• Incomplete initiatives collection (2). • New initiatives not predictable (3). • Not correct prioritization (5). • Not correct selection (6).
Cutting edge products/services based on innovative technologies.	• Do a not precise initial initiatives estimate (4). • Implement initiatives not respecting plans (7). • Do not produce the expected results (8). • Benefits not aligned with strategic objectives (9).
Low maturity in Strategic Planning.	• New strategic objectives (1). • New initiatives not predictable (3). • Not correct prioritization (5). • Not correct selection (6).
Low maturity in Project/Program.	• Do a not precise initial initiatives estimate (4). • Implement initiatives not respecting plans (7). • Do not produce the expected results (8).
Low maturity in Portfolio.	• Incomplete initiatives collection (2). • Not precise initial initiatives estimate (4). • Not correct prioritization (5). • Not correct selection (6). • Benefits not aligned with the strategic objectives (9).

Due to a change in the market, organizations performing in fast-unstable environments have a higher probability to have new or changed strategic objectives (1). Such an external environment may give birth to unpredictable new initiatives (3) and also to changes in the environment itself which may cause, as a consequence, changes in the strategic objectives and therefore misalignment between benefits and strategy (9).

Big and complex organizations have a higher probability to do an incomplete initiatives collection (2) because of both their complexity and the high number of stakeholders involved. Moreover, complexity in the internal environment can bring new, not predictable, initiatives (3). The great number of stakeholders and interest involved can mislead the process of prioritization (5) and selection (6).

Organizations with business in cutting edge products/services based on innovative technologies, for which is very difficult to precisely define a scope, are more likely to do a not precise initial initiatives estimate (4). More often than not, unstable scope leads to projects which are late and out of budget (7) since their plans are based on requirements not perfectly definable. In addition, innovation is not always predictable and organizations in this field may gain results different than expected (8). As results are unpredictable, also the benefits are unsure and therefore, innovative organizations may have benefits not aligned with the strategic objectives (9).

On the other hand, the case of organizations having low maturity in their strategic or management capabilities is quite different.

Organizations with a low maturity in Strategic Planning have a higher probability to come across new strategic objectives (1) not because of changes coming from the outside, but due to a wrong strategic planning consequence of wrong strategic objectives. If the strategic forecast is uncomplete or wrong, new not predictable initiatives (3) may arise. If the definition of the strategic priorities is not correct, prioritization (5) and selection (6) are misled.

Organizations with a low maturity in Project/Program Management have a higher probability to make a not precise initial initiatives estimate (4), therefore implementing initiatives not respecting the plans (7) due to poor PMs, and inexperience in estimating, planning and forecasting. At the same time, unexperienced organizations are very likely not to produce the expected results (8) due to the fact that the initial scope of the projects was not clear or misunderstood, and the process and experience in doing scope definition is low.

Organizations with a low maturity in Portfolio Management have a higher probability to do an uncomplete initiatives collection (2) and not correct prioritization (5) and selection (6) because of inexperience and poor demand processes. Also in this case, poor role definitions, scheduling or processes may determine unprecise initial initiatives estimate (4). A not correct portfolio/strategy control & review process may lead organizations to have benefits not aligned with the strategic objectives (9).

Referring to Table 3, columns c-d-e refers to characteristics that could be avoided with maturity, training and experience. It is where most of the effort should be dedicated being the payback granted. "Troops training" and good processes are a key requirement to be able to "leave the French coast to point instead to the north, to Austerlitz".

Columns a and b refers to organization's structural characteristics and could be impossible to be avoided or mitigated in the short term.

Column f depends on the external environment and most of the time is out of the factors that can be controlled by the organization.

Apart from grey columns, organizations could not be able to do much to decrease the probability of a change in their ongoing portfolio. Organizations producing cutting edge products for unstable markets must be ready to adapt.

In any case nobody is immune to change and must be prepared to it.

Resist to change is more difficult than to accept it.

AN ADAPTIVE APPROACH TO PROJECT PORTFOLIO MANAGEMENT

Adapt or Adaptive

We know that an organization cannot be a one hundred per cent adaptive. Being fully adaptive means to be unstable/uncertain and this instability has a price. How much, where and when to be adaptive must be well considered. A cost/opportunity analysis is needed.

In biology, an adaptation, also called an adaptive trait, is a trait with a current functional role in the life of an organism that is maintained and evolved by means of natural selection. Adaptation refers to both the current state of being adapted and to the dynamic evolutionary process that leads to the adaptation. (Wikipedia, 2016).

In our PPM context, being "adapted" means to be able to shape the right set of initiatives achieving the right strategic objectives to be successful in the actual environment. Being "adaptive" means to be quickly able to change what is routinely done to adapt activities and deliverables to an alteration of the status-

Table 3. Summary table of relationships between change causes and organization's characteristics

Main Causes to Change an Ongoing Portfolio		Area	Avoidable (Worst Option)	Characteristics					
				a	b	c	d	e	f
				High Organization's Size and Complexity.	Cutting Edge Products/ Services Based on Innovative Technologies	Low Maturity in Strategic Planning.	Low Maturity in Project /Program.	Low Maturity in Portfolio.	High External Environment Instability.
1	The strategic objectives are no longer appropriate.	Strategy	Arduously			X			X
2	The initiatives collection was incomplete.	Portfolio	Almost	X				X	
3	There are new initiatives that were not predictable during the collection.	Portfolio	Partially	X		X			X
4	The initiatives assessment was not precise and because of this the detailed planning done after the selection is different than the assessment done before the selection.	Portfolio	Partially		X		X	X	
5	The prioritization was not correct.	Portfolio	Almost	X		X		X	
6	The selection was not correct.	Portfolio	Almost	X		X		X	
7	The implementation of the components do not follows what planned.	Project Manag.	Arduously		X		X		
8	The plan to implement the components must be changed as will not produce the expected results.	Project Manag.	Partially		X		X		
9	The benefits produced by the portfolio are not as expected and not aligned with the strategic objectives.	Strategy	Partially		X			X	X

quo that originally justified the decisions, and subsequently the actions. The more these modifications are big and impacting, the more the need to be adaptive to maintain or improve the strategic advantage.

The fact that there will be a modification in the environment justifying an adaptation is sure. Where, when and at which level the needed change will appear could be predictable or unpredictable, as deeply analyzed in the previous paragraph.

In any case, adaptive organizations have an advantage on non-adaptive ones even if there is always a cost in being more adaptive.

Adaptive Portfolio Conceptualization

It is the author's opinion that Adaptive Portfolio should be achieved using adaptation layers, as shown in Figure 2. Objectives/Programs/Projects/Activities placed at the bottom (calm area) are considered more stable and not continuously challenged in their alignment with the strategic mission.

On the contrary, at the top (windy area) one shall find the Objectives/Programs/Projects/Activities that, due to their nature, must be continuously monitored as their presence in the portfolio is neither stable, nor granted.

The portfolio should be also decomposed creating baskets with "similar" content. This decomposition simplifies portfolio components management and increases adaptiveness. Decomposition, improving parallelism, increases mobility, autonomy and delegation. This is applicable when the organizations' maturity is adequate as adaptiveness increases global complexity.

These concepts will be clarified in the following pages.

Some considerations before the description of an Adaptive Portfolio:

- There are several level of change and subsequent adaptation in Project Portfolio Management. Project Task level, Project phase level, Project level, Program level, Portfolio level, Strategic objective level, Mission level, Vision level (Figure 3). The more the change moves from the bottom (change a task) to the top (change the mission) the more is complex to be adaptive as a higher level of change will impact all the lower connected levels.
- Adaptive Portfolio is mostly needed when systems are closed (limited budget, resources, production capacity…).
- The first step in becoming adaptive is to be available to change organization's objectives and strategy. Top Management must be available to change its plans and also to stop ongoing initiatives.
- A good status reporting system is a prerequisite for being adaptive. You cannot effectively change your objectives if you "don't know where are your troops".
- Adaptiveness is positively correlated to the maturity of the organization in Strategic Planning, Project/Program management and Portfolio management (Table n.3).

Figure 2. Adaptation layers

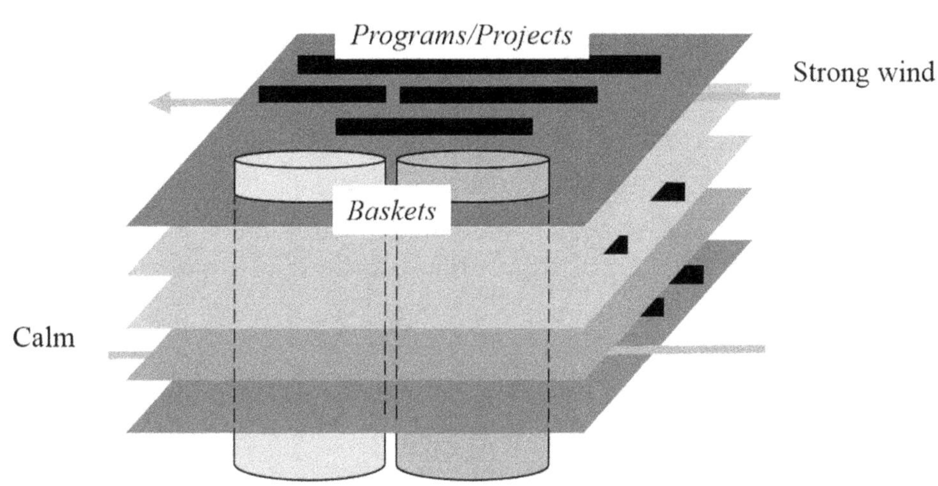

- Adaptiveness is clearly more required when the organization's characteristics are such to increase the probability for a change in an ongoing Portfolio. This is mostly true for big and complex organizations when they have cutting edge products/services based on innovative technologies, and when the external environment is unstable.
- An organization must be adaptive in delivering. "Adapting for adapting" is useless. Continuous change without delivering a tangible value is impracticable.

Figure 4 summarizes the steps to set-up an Adaptive Portfolio environment.

The first dimension is related to the minimization of changes to the ongoing portfolio due to immaturity or errors. In Napoleon's words, "train the troops". Just like a commander doesn't want to lose the battle because of unexperienced soldiers, organizations clearly do not want these changes. This dimension is connected with what stated in Table 3 about the characteristics of the organization.

The best application of Adaptive portfolio is in fact ineffective (as merely focused on fixing problems) if, for instance, due to poor project management, projects are not properly managed and, because of this, affected by delays or scope creep.

There are some characteristics (related to Portfolio Management) the organizations can work-on to improve their ability to have a PTF not affected by errors (Table 4).

This improvement effort is a prerequisite to create a better manageable situation where to apply Adaptive Portfolio, minimizing the changes induced by inefficiencies.

Surely there are other characteristics of organizations (technical expertise, testing, auditing, quality, etc..) that should be improved to minimize errors, but these are outside the scope of this chapter.

The second dimension in Adaptive Portfolio aims at organizing the Portfolio to be adaptive. To do this there are two main activities an organization should perform.

First, analyze and categorize the Strategic objectives to be used in an Adaptive Portfolio environment.

This means to define the strategic objectives *stability* and *priority*.

Figure 3. Levels of adaptation in organizations

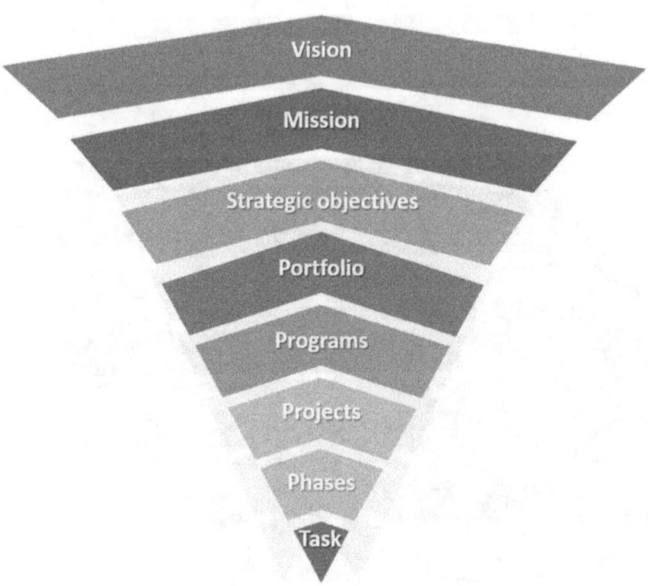

Figure 4. Steps in the set-up of an adaptive portfolio environment

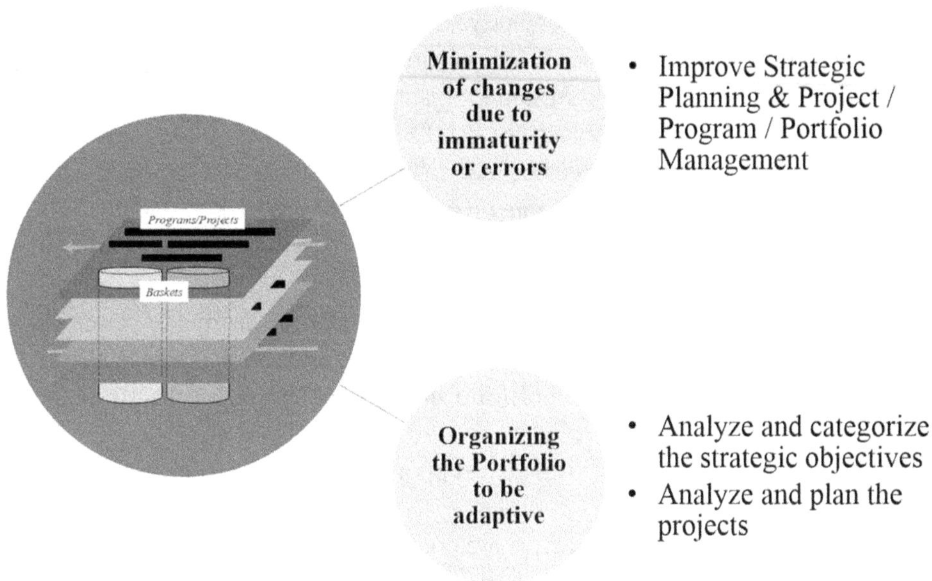

Table 4. Minimizing PTF changes due to errors (refers to previous Tables 2 and 3)

Improving	Minimizes Mainly PTF Change Causes	… That Will However Be Influenced by the Following Characteristics
Strategic Planning: Training, maturity, external support, skilled resources, market experience, right processes, …	New strategic objectives (1).	High external environment instability.
	New initiatives not predictable (3).	• High organization's size and complexity. • High external environment instability.
	Not correct prioritization (5).	High organization's size and complexity.
	Not correct selection (6).	High organization's size and complexity.
Project/Program Management: Training, maturity, skilled resources, external support, PM certification, right processes, PMO, ….	Do a not precise initial initiatives estimate (4).	Products / services very innovative or based on innovative technologies.
	Implement initiatives not respecting plans (7).	Products / services very innovative or based on innovative technologies.
	Do not produce the expected results (8).	• High external environment instability. • Products / services very innovative or based on innovative technologies.
Portfolio Management: Maturity, training, external support, skilled resources, portfolio committee, right processes connected with Strategy and PM, …	Incomplete initiatives collection (2).	High organization's size and complexity.
	Not precise initial initiatives estimate (4).	Products / services very innovative or based on innovative technologies.
	Not correct prioritization (5).	High organization's size and complexity.
	Not correct selection (6).	High organization's size and complexity.
	Benefits not aligned with the strategic objectives (9).	• High external environment instability. • Products / services very innovative or based on innovative technologies.

Stability should be assessed by the organization considering the probability of a modification (cancelling or a change in the measures) in the objective during the period of its validity.

Some objectives will be stable because the organizations have decided or are forced to pursue them (i.e.: key objectives impacting the whole mission, objectives intimately connected with the past story and/or the culture of the Organization, objectives - and serving projects - close to the conclusion, mandatory projects, etc..). Some objectives are supposed to be more stable than other due to their nature, to the past trends or due to the portion of the strategic mission they are supporting.

Stable objectives will be pursued and the connected projects will be finished. Only unexpected exceptional situations will change this.

Priority is generally defined using weighted quali-quantitative measures to prioritize strategic objectives. This prioritization can be done for the whole set of objectives or inside baskets of comparable objectives. Decomposing and ranking the portfolio in this way simplifies the strategic planning and improves adaptiveness.

Prioritizing the strategic objectives will give a support to future decisions within the same layer of stability.

Stability and priority of a strategic objective are connected, but not directly related (Table 5).

Which and how many objectives to consider stable, is a strategic decision. Organizations cannot be a hundred per cent adaptive or a hundred per cent stable.

The number of stability layers could vary. As a starting point, it is possible to group objectives at least in two categories: stable and unstable.

Second, analyze and properly plan the projects to be implemented in an Adaptive Portfolio:

1. Decomposing projects into small self-consistent value-added chunks.
2. Analyzing and verifying their predictability.

Self-consistent value-added chunks planning. All Projects should be broken down into smaller deliverables for a better management and control. Tools like the Work Breakdown Structure support the Project Manager in Planning and Control activities (PMI, 2013a). The concept of breaking-down to simplify is widely used in Project, Program and Portfolio Management methodologies.

In Adaptive Portfolio, the idea is to analyze the possibility to break-down projects into smaller self-consistent value-added chunks, as shown in Figure 5. A self-consistent project chunk is a group of activities producing an output within the project that will produce a self-consistent tangible value for the organization even if the project will be stopped after its delivery. For an easy application refer to a training program of 30 x 2 classroom days directed to 3 Departments. Even if the program will be stopped after the completion of the first 10 x 2 classroom days delivered only to the first Department there will be a tangible value for the organization anyway. Stopping a project transferring resources to another project due to a unexpected change without producing a value and therefore wasting the investment already done

Table 5. Examples of stability and priority in strategic objectives

Unstable	Increase revenues from a definite set of clients	Expand overseas
Stable	External communication improvement	Improve employees skills on BA
	High Priority	**Low Priority**

is always possible, but this is surely not optimal and usually creates disappointment and is never well accepted. Self-consistent project chunks also address this psychological and team management problem.

To support adaptiveness, projects should be planned (when possible) to produce "value-added intermediate outputs" (VAL) after small-medium-big chunks of activities (these chunks are surely similar to deliverables even if a "standard deliverable" could not be able to produce a self-consistent value). In this way, even if the project will be stopped, the organization has gained an advantage from the chunks already completed anyway. If a chunk of activities producing a VAL is started, the organization gets to a "point of no return" (PNR), meaning that it is "forced" to finish it otherwise it will be a waste money or an indefinitely postponement of the delivery. PNR gives stability to PMs and Teams even in an Adaptive Portfolio environment. The projected date of completion of the self-consistent value-added chunks will be called "chunk milestone" (CM). With a wide application of this tool there will be the possibility to create a Portfolio value-added chunks milestones map to have a holistic understanding of the status of each project and the actions that can be taken at the least loss of value. Chunk milestones map will represent a reference for adaptation (Figure 6). This map should be constantly updated on the results of the projects status reporting.

In Figure 6, after the approval of the portfolio, there will be a number of Programs/Projects under implementation to serve the strategic objectives during the portfolio life-cycle. The chunks milestone map will show where and when it will be possible to stop a project if there's the need of a change after a review of the Portfolio. Later in this chapter it will be clear which rules to apply performing this activity.

Analyze and verify portfolio projects predictability. This is a common project/program management problem. As stated from PMI, *complexity is a characteristic of a program or project or its environment that is difficult to manage due to human behavior, system behavior and ambiguity* (PMI, 2014). The more the requirements and the activities to perform are clear the more the project is predictable (less probability to autonomously delay and/or change scope). Moreover, if it is clear "what I want", the requirements of the final output are well defined and when it is easy to state "how I will do it" as the knowledge in the specific implementation area is available, the project is stable and predictable. There could be projects with clear requirements (I know what I want) and not clear implementation processes

Figure 5. Self-consistent value-added chunks

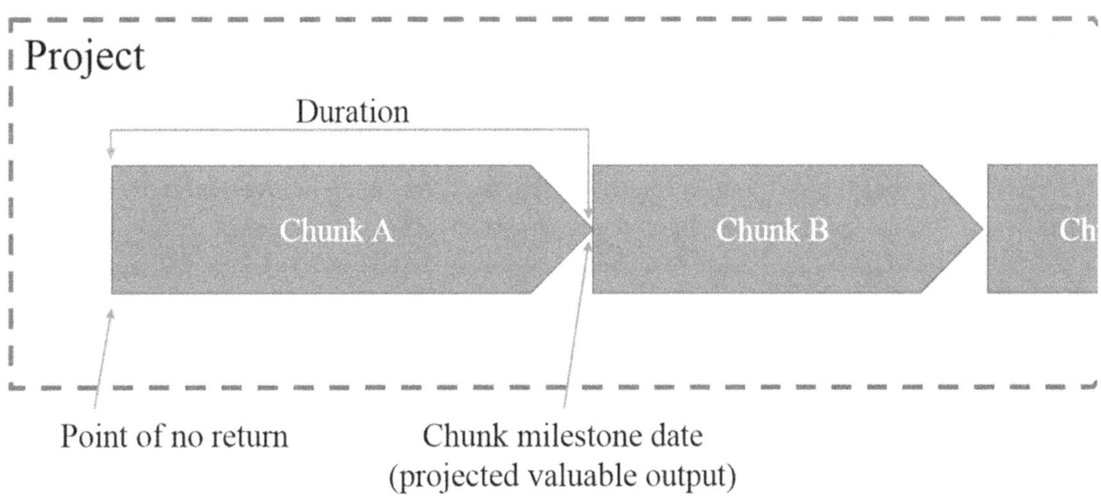

Figure 6. Portfolio self-consistent value-added chunks milestones map

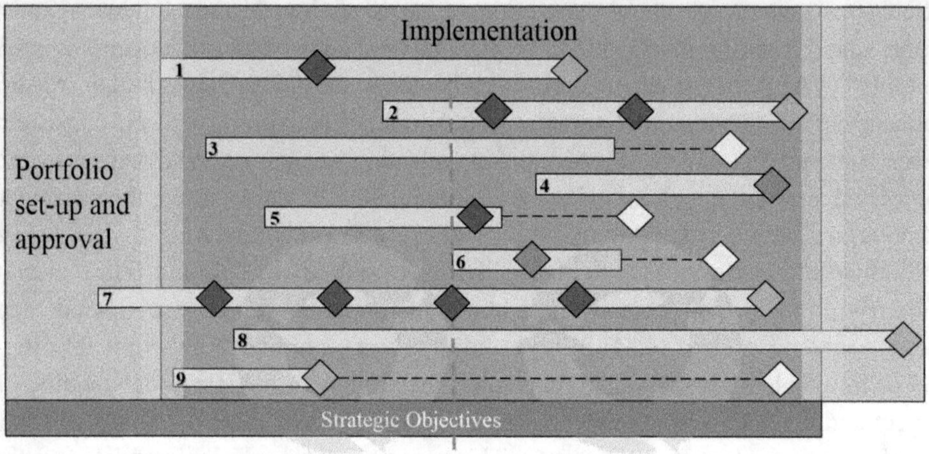

(I don't know how to do it) and on the contrary projects with available knowledge in the implementation area, but not clear requirements.

Merging All Together

For a Portfolio to be organized to be adaptive the outputs of the two main activities presented so far (analyze and categorize the Strategic objectives - analyze and properly plan the projects) must be mixed together creating the adaptation layers (Figure 7).

Where strategic objectives Stability and Priority are connected with Unpredictability of projects creating 8 conceptual areas with fantasy names assigned by the author.

For example, high priority unstable strategic objectives could be in the "Fire" or "Tornado" area depending on the level of unpredictability of the projects that support the objective. Low priority stable strategic objectives will be in the "Rocks" or "Apples" area always depending the level of unpredictability of the projects, and so on.

A map of the Portfolio done in this way not only supports adaptiveness but also gives valuable information for tactic decisions that will be further investigated in the following pages.

Adaptive Portfolio Implementation

There's the need of some predetermined rules to utilize the layers mapping presented in Figure 7. Being adaptive in PPM means to react to the changes proactively trying to maximize the balance between value production and flexibility. In case of a change necessity in the Portfolio there will be the need for an action. What follows could be considered adaptive "rules of engagement":

1. Strategic Objectives priority is the first input for change decisions.
2. At the same level of priority, stable strategic objectives should be favored.
3. PTF changes are done primarily trying to take advantage of chunks planning.

Figure 7. Adaptation areas layers

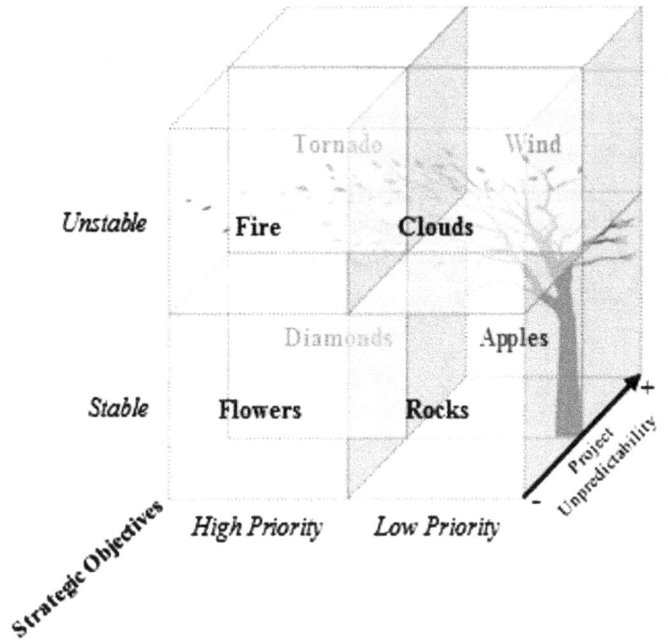

Figure 8 contains two examples to clarify the adaptive approach in portfolio change decision making.

Case A: A predictable project 1 supporting a high priority unstable objective, during the portfolio review emphasizes the need for more budget or production capacity due to the change in the unstable objective served. Using the upcoming valuable milestone of project 2 (supporting a lower priority objective), there will be the possibility to stop project 2 and transfer budget or capacity to project 1.

Case B: An unpredictable project 9 supporting a high priority stable objective, during the portfolio review shows the need for more budget or production capacity due to a change in the project caused by not clear initial requirements. If no other solutions are available, it would be possible to stop unpredictable project 5 supporting a less stable strategic objective, and close to a valuable milestone, and transfer budget or capacity to project 9.

These suggestions as general adapting rules. Organizations need to define their own rules of engagement.

Transfer resources from a project to another to apply a change is simple when resources are interchangeable (like money), but could become impossible and useless when there is availability of resources not needed or the competences required are unavailable or inaccessible.

Moreover, an Adaptive Portfolio should centralize the overall control, but also decentralize tactical decisions to increase overall flexibility.

What follows are some suggested tools to increase interchange, effectiveness and delegation in tactical decision making in an Adaptive Portfolio environment.

Figure 8. Adaptive portfolio rules of engagement application

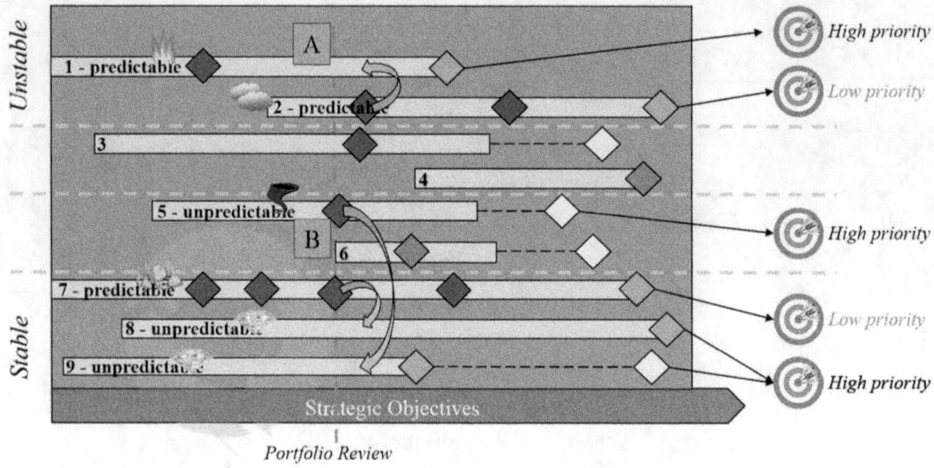

1. **Programs:** The Project Management Institute (PMI) defines program as *"A group of related projects, subprograms, and program activities that are managed in a coordinated way to obtain benefits not available from managing them individually"* (PMI, 2013c). Also Thiry defines program management as *the governance and harmonized management of a number of projects and other actions to achieve stated business benefits and create value for the stakeholders* (Thiry, 2010).

Organizations that want to manage Adaptive portfolios should encourage the utilization of Programs within their portfolios. Programs are flexible by definition being focused on achieving final Objectives/Benefits, according to which projects are often changed/moved within the program. The Program Manager will have the responsibility to produce benefits and will have a budget (and often a budget reserve) to be used autonomously for that scope. Being often longer than one year, programs can be placed outside the prioritization/selection portfolio activities to simplify them. Therefore they can be somehow independent from the portfolio-cycle. The application of chunks planning within the Program creates a self-consistent adaptive environment (Figure 9). Programs are one application of the Napoleon's idea to divide troops into smaller self-consistent and independent groups.

2. **Budget Baskets and Reserves:** The way budget is assigned to Programs/Projects should be compatible with what stated before. At least there could be the opportunity to evolve from a concept of "project budget and/or capacity" to an assignment of a bigger budget not only to Programs, but also to set of projects grouped on the base of organization's defined classes (Figure 10). This scenario

Figure 9. Program management in adaptive portfolio

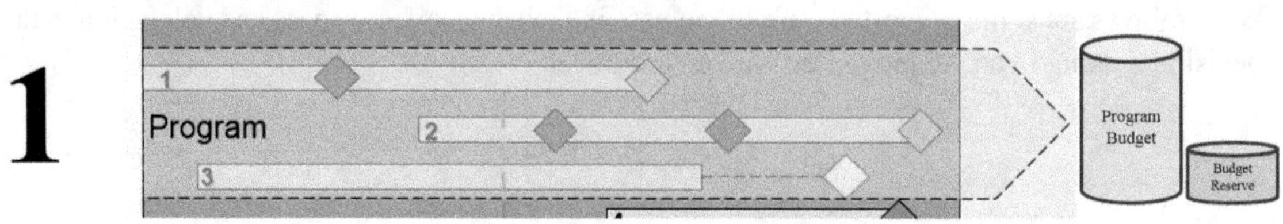

differs from Program Management. Several projects could be not "related" to each other, and not supporting the same strategic objectives. The assignment of responsibilities and roles should then follow this direction. Also reserves should be assigned following the approach presented so far. Reserves increase autonomy and adaptiveness even if they lock resources limiting the number of program/project the organization will implement. Nevertheless, also reserves could be managed adaptively with a shared approach between several baskets and a clear assignment process based on priority.

3. **Homogeneous Capacity/Competence Baskets and Reserves:** The projects broken down into self-consistent value-added chunks could also be grouped (even virtually) into self-adaptive homogeneous projects sets (same resources pool, same technology, same clients, similar output, data rate, etc..) to highlight the opportunity to support each other in case of a change at the end of the delivery of the self-consistent value-added chunk (Figure 11). This kind of grouping should be done in parallel with the previous two as the kind of support (resources typology, technology, …) a project may need, could not be available in the same program or cannot be acquired using money. In this situation the support should be searched elsewhere. Also the creation of a sort of internal trading exchange environment (and mentality) where projects support each other is a step in this direction. These homogeneous capacity baskets could be also useful in portfolio selection as the predetermined availability of the resources in a determined competence (for example J2EE programming) can be used as a constrain in the selection model.
4. **Responsibility Assignment Using Adaptation Layers:** Adaptation layers could be also a useful support to resources assignment as objectives instability, priority and projects unpredictability are evidences that should influence organizations in the selection of the Project Manager and his/her Team (Figure 12). Strategic Objectives instability and projects unpredictability suggest the utilization of skilled resources with a good attitude to change. Stability and predictability suggest the utilization of well-organized resources and stable teams.

Figure 10. Budget baskets and reserves in adaptive portfolio

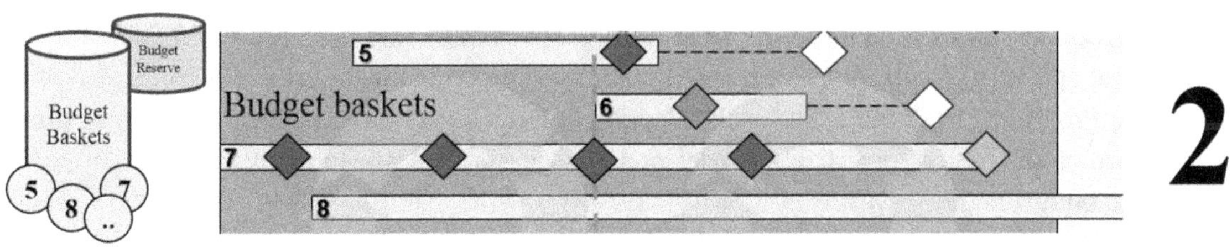

Figure 11. Homogeneous capacity baskets and reserves in adaptive portfolio

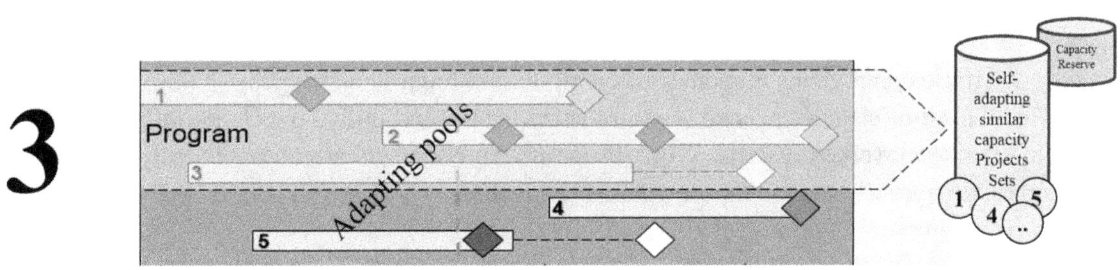

Figure 12. Resource assignment using adaptation layers

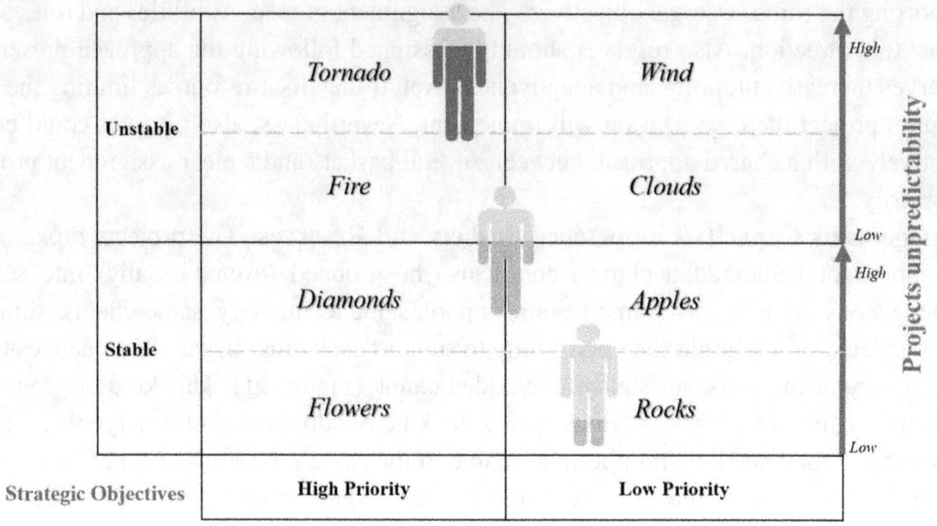

Adaptive Portfolio Roadmap and Governance

To complete the paragraph (as a consequence of what deeply discussed so far) are below listed some high-level steps to follow (they are not in a mandatory sequence) in the implementation of an Adaptive Portfolio:

1. Collect, plan and analyze strategic objectives stability.
2. Produce a priority based ranking of strategic objectives as a reference for future decisions.
3. Assign strategic objectives to stability layers (stable to unstable).
4. Collect new initiatives and on-going portfolio components. Assess, prioritize and select the new portfolio components based on their support to strategic objectives. Authorize the Portfolio that represents the strategy to pursue the strategic objectives in the next portfolio cycle (and beyond).
5. Analyze and verify portfolio projects predictability (unpredictable to predictable).
6. Create Programs, Budget Baskets, self-adaptive homogeneous projects sets, other set of projects grouped on the base of organization's defined classes (for centralized management).
7. Assign budget and reserves.
8. Formalize the assignment of Programs/Projects to strategic objectives and stability layers.
9. Plan projects creating self-consistent value-added chunks.
10. Create a Portfolio chunk milestones map using defined chunk milestones.
11. Define regular adaptiveness reviews to analyze:
    a. Strategic objectives stability and requested changes.
    b. Portfolio components implementation report and requested changes.
12. Define the set of changes needed (and prioritize them), and utilize the chunk milestones map to define the adaptiveness actions. When Programs and sub-sets are autonomously able to apply changes, do not escalate, but report what has been done.

The governance and control of the Adaptive Portfolio should be also done following some indications.

- Project and Program management skills are very important, therefore Managers responsible should be selected also considering their attitude to change. To be able to properly react when needed, these resource must be early involved throughout the clarification of the strategic objectives served by the Projects/Programs they will manage.
- Reporting and control tools should be very efficient and effective as the ability to react to changes depends on the availability of the right information. Delays, blind areas and inefficiency decrease adaptiveness.
- An Adaptive Portfolio Committee should be created to continuously manage the adaptation layers. This committee should constantly verify what has been done, what will be done in the next chunks and which are the actual new requests (from the market, from the clients, from other departments, from technology, etc..) and decide how to proceed giving immediate feedback to "on field troops" up to the next check-point.
- There should be an activity of "continuous demand management" (L. Romano, R. Grimaldi, F.S. Colasuonno. 2016) feeding the adaptation layers with information about new requests, new needs, new technological improvements.
- Adaptive portfolio approach works when bottlenecks are limited. The application in the implementation of the projects (and the single chunks) of Lean methodologies and Agile approaches will favor (but not assure) flexibility.

FUTURE RESEARCH DIRECTIONS

As discussed, Adaptive portfolio management is something that depends on a number of factors. The level of maturity in the disciplines of Project/Program/Portfolio is one of them, being a key point to effectively apply Adaptive Portfolio. Things that look complex the first time become simple because of the learning curve. In addition, also the kind of project itself may have a say: the fact that an organization implements projects to sell products to final clients or directly sells the projects or does project for the internal usage of the final output, changes the way to be adaptive. Budget and resource availability in general is another aspect that can influence the application of adaptation layers, which may vary if the budget available is fixed or can be increased or depending on the possibility to expand the engaged resources (increasing the production throughput). All of these factors lie in the field of research, as Adaptive Portfolio Management is an area where further investigation is ongoing. As a matter of fact, the application of adaptation layers to day-to-day activities (operations), for instance the speed of the external market and its relationship with the level of competitiveness, will change the need and the application of Adaptive Portfolio Management: an area that needs to be further investigated. Finally, Adaptive Portfolio Management combination with Lean methodology and Agile mentality is under investigation.

CONCLUSION

Adaptive Portfolio Management is more than an idea. It is a necessity. All Portfolios should be flexible and able to bow to the needs of the organizations. A one hundred per cent flexibility is not possible as organizations need stability and stability require roles clearness and resources certainty. Adaptive Portfolio Management aims to define adaptation layers based on the level of flexibility. It also does an extensive usage of the concept of decomposition as breaking down portfolios, strategic objectives, programs, projects, budget assignments and capacity pools, increases flexibility. Adaptive Portfolio Management is for top-notch organizations where the experience and maturity in Strategic Planning and Project/Program/Portfolio Management is high. Organizations have in fact to consider that building and running an Adaptive Portfolio means to acquire a competitive advantage increasing the management complexity.

REFERENCES

Aurik, J. C., Fabel, M., & Jonk, G. J. (2015). *The future of strategy: A transformative approach to strategy for a world that won't stand still*. New York: McGraw-Hill Education.

Bracker, J. (1980). The Historical Development of the Strategic Management Concept. *Academy of Management Review*, *5*(2), 219–224.

David, F. R. (2011). *Strategic management: Concept & cases* (13th ed.). Upper Saddle River, NJ: Prentice Hall.

Doz, Y. L., & Kosonen, M. (2008). *Fast strategy: How strategic agility will help you stay ahead of the game*. Harlow, UK: Pearson/Longman.

Grant, R. M., & Jordan, J. (2015). *Foundations of strategy* (2nd ed.). Hoboken, NJ: Wiley and Sons.

Hrebiniak, L. G. (2006). Obstacles to effective strategy implementation. *Organizational Dynamics*, *35*(1), 12–31. doi:10.1016/j.orgdyn.2005.12.001

Meskendahl, S. (2010). The influence of business strategy on project portfolio management and its success. A conceptual framework. *International Journal of Project Management*, *28*(8), 807–817. doi:10.1016/j.ijproman.2010.06.007

Pietersen, W. (2016). *Von Clausewitz on War: Six Lessons for the Modern Strategist.* Retrieved October 16, 2016 from http://www.gsb.columbia.edu

Project Management Institute (PMI). (2013a). A guide to the project management body of knowledge (PMBOK® guide) (5th ed.). Newtown Square, PA.

Project Management Institute (PMI). (2013b). *The standard for portfolio management* (3rd ed.). Newtown Square, PA: PMI.

Project Management Institute (PMI). (2014). Navigating complexity. A practical guide. Newtown Square, PA: PMI.

Romano, L., Grimaldi, R., & Colasuonno, F. S. (2016, May). *Demand management as a critical success factor in Portfolio Management.* Paper presented at the 2016 PMI Global Congress, Barcelona, Spain.

Sheetz-Runkle, B. (2014). *The Art of War for Small Business: Defeat the Competition and Dominate the Market with the Masterful Strategies of Sun Tzu.* New York: AMACOM, American Management Association.

Shenhar, A. J., Dvir, D., Levy, O., & Maltz, A. C. (2001). Project success: A multidimensional strategic concept. *Long Range Planning, 34*(6), 699–725. doi:10.1016/S0024-6301(01)00097-8

Thiry, M. (2010). *Program Management.* Farnham, UK: Gower.

Thompson, A. A., Strickland, A. J., & Gamble, J. E. (2009). *Strategia Aziendale.* Milano: McGraw-Hill.

Vincenti, L. (1985). *La Vita Di Napoleone Bonaparte.* Milano: Alberto Peruzzo Editore.

Wikipedia. (2016). *Definition of Adaptation.* Retrieved 27 July, 2016, from https://en.wikipedia.org/wiki/Adaptation

KEY TERMS AND DEFINITIONS

Component: A selected initiative that will be implemented in the actual Project Portfolio of an Organization.

Initiative: An idea, a project, a program, a group of activities that are proposed to be included in a Portfolio.

Program: A group of related projects, subprograms, and program activities that are managed in a coordinated way to obtain benefits not available from managing them individually.

Scope Creep: In project management refers to uncontrolled changes or continuous growth in a project's scope. This can occur when the scope of a project is not properly defined, documented, or controlled. It is generally considered harmful.

Self-Consistent Value-Added Chunk: A group of activities within a project producing an output that will produce a self-consistent tangible value for the organization even if the project will be stopped after this specific delivery.

Chapter 7
Optimizing Portfolio Value through Comprehensive Project Metrics

Brandon Olson
The College of St. Scholastica, USA

ABSTRACT

Project portfolios produce value through the coordinated execution of the projects and programs within the portfolio. The performance of the portfolio is evaluated by the generated business value and potential future opportunities it creates. This same performance measure is not applied to the projects within the portfolio. Projects are evaluated based on an operational measure of project efficiency that considers performance of project scope, budget, and schedule. Inconsistencies between portfolio and project performance decrease the value offered by each project and the overall value of the portfolio. In this study, a framework and solution are presented that expand the measures of project success to include criteria that better align with the goals of the project portfolio. The enhanced project success measures include project efficiency, customer impact, team impact, organizational success, and future preparation. The solution is applied to the project management process to demonstrate potential integration into project management practices.

INTRODUCTION

The premise of project portfolio management (PPM) is that organizations operate with a finite set of resources and these resources must be carefully applied and managed. The purpose of PPM is to identify, select, and prioritize projects in order to realize the highest value for the organization (Rad & Levin, 2008). The priority used in selecting projects not only focuses on the benefits offered to the organization but also the contributions the project outcomes make toward the organization's goals. In an effort to increase the portfolio's contributions toward the organizational goals the PPM project prioritization uses business value and strategic alignment as key drivers in selecting projects for the portfolio.

DOI: 10.4018/978-1-5225-2151-8.ch007

Much of the effort in establishing PPM practices rely on top-down governance and value measures at the strategic level. While there is undoubtable benefit to investing effort at the strategic level, more work should be made in establishing PPM practices at the individual project level. The success of the project portfolio is dependent upon the success of the projects within the portfolio. If the projects are unable to deliver the results, the portfolio will not achieve its goals. In other words, the collection of projects must be successful in order for the portfolio to be successful. In PPM both the project and the overall portfolio must be measured and evaluated in order to determine success. However, there are inconsistencies between project success evaluations and the evaluation of portfolio success.

The evaluation of projects has historically been carried out through the iron triangle of schedule, cost, and performance of scope (Kloppenborg, Tesch, & Manolis, 2014). The continued primary focus on the iron triangle is especially true of inexperienced Project Managers (Müller & Turner, 2007). This operational perspective of project success can be misleading. For instance, a project is considered successful if the entire scope is delivered on-time and within budget. However, if the organization is unable to realize the desired benefits from the project outcomes, the success of the project is misleading. The operational perspective of success is especially misleading in the context of PPM where the portfolio relies on the value and alignment of the project outcomes. The budgetary and schedule success of the individual projects do not directly contribute to the portfolio success as much as the effectiveness of the project deliverables in creating organizational value.

Recognizing the gap between the historical operational mindset of project success measures and the usefulness of the project deliverables, changes have been made in expanding the definition of project success. Jugdev and Müller (2005) argued that project success must consider both the operational measures as well as measures of strategic effectiveness. Davis (2014, 2016) proposed project success measures in terms of the perspectives from senior management, the project core team, and project recipients.

A shift has occurred in acknowledging the need for a greater definition of project success. Many forms of project success measures exist that move beyond the operational perspectives. A framework of project success criteria has emerged that is based upon four categories: efficiency, customer impact, business success, and future preparation (Kloppenborg, Manolic, & Tesch, 2009; Malach-Pines, Dvir, & Sadeh, 2009; Pinto, 2004; Shenhar & Dvir, 2007). These additional forms of project success measures, particularly business success and future preparation, better align with the PPM goals of organizational value.

The ability of the project to improve business success and better prepare the organization for the future match the goals of a project portfolio. Increased success and improved future preparation is the business value resulting from the project. While the business value is mostly concerned with financial performance measures, it should be acknowledged that non-financial benefits such as ecological, societal, and learning benefits may also be realized from a project and should be considered in evaluating a project's success (Martinsuo & Killen, 2014). In order to improve the performance of a project portfolio, the projects and programs within the portfolio must consider the business success and future preparation contributions the project or program makes to the portfolio.

In addition to better aligning and supporting the project portfolio, managing the benefits the project contributes to the organization also increases the success of each individual project. Benefits management (BM) is the method of guiding and controlling projects, and the corresponding organizational change, in a manner that optimizes the benefits offered to the organization (Ward & Daniel, 2006). Application of BM also increases the success of the project; especially when paired with project management practices (Badewi, 2015).

There exists a need to connect the goals of the project portfolio to the projects within the portfolio. This need cannot be satisfied through the project's operational goals of the iron triangle but must include strategic measures. A more comprehensive project evaluation model is needed to better evaluate the true success of the project and its contribution to the portfolio success and organizational value. The project success measures should include efficiency, customer impact, business success, and future preparation attributes. Additionally, any model of evaluating project success must include a means to connect the goals of the portfolio to the goals of the programs and projects within the portfolio.

The purpose of the chapter is to demonstrate the need to connect projects and programs with the project portfolio and to present a framework to ensure this connection is established at the beginning of the project and is applied throughout the entire project lifecycle. This framework includes a set of project success measures and goals that not only address the operational perspectives but also incorporate meaningful strategic perspectives. Using this framework, a project can be better assessed for its inclusion within a given portfolio, monitored and communicated during its execution to ensure project and portfolio goals are met, and evaluated at the end of the project to determine the true strategic and operational success of the project.

The need to connect the individual projects and programs with the overall portfolio goes beyond simply providing metrics that are meaningful to each. Project artifacts such as the project charter and project reporting must incorporate the common metrics to support portfolio alignment. Additionally, project processes and organizational processes must be modified to ensure common and meaningful project metrics are sufficiently communicated and interpreted by the organization. The proposed framework will not only provide enhanced project and portfolio metrics but will also include a methodology for integrating these metrics into the project management practice. The common metrics and enhanced project management practices are needed to improve the organization's ability to align the goals of the individual projects with the portfolio. This alignment supports the optimization of the portfolio's strategic benefits and provides greater transparency for project selection and evaluation processes.

BACKGROUND

Prior to evaluating PPM practices and metrics at the project level, the project hierarchy must first be discussed in order to establish the relationship between projects, programs, and portfolios. This relationship is central to the discussion of PPM practices and success metrics at the project level. As part of the project hierarchy discussion a deeper understanding of the project portfolio and the project portfolio governance structure is needed to establish the processes and connections between projects and portfolios. In addition to the project hierarchy, a discussion of the PPM constructs of business value and strategic alignment must also take place to provide an understanding of the value and alignment attributes used in portfolio success measures. The project hierarchy, project portfolio, project portfolio governance structure, business value, and strategic alignment are the components used to design a project-level PPM solution and are first introduced in order to support a subsequent articulation of a proposed solution.

Project Hierarchy

The project hierarchy consists of portfolios, programs, and projects. In a simplified hierarchy, a portfolio consists of programs and each program consists of projects. Figure 1 illustrates a sample portfolio hierarchy. However, a portfolio can also be made up of subportfolios, programs, and projects and a program may include subprograms and projects. Each element in project hierarchy represents an organizational investment with planned outcomes intended to benefit the organization and each is structured in a way to be managed and evaluated. While this commonality exists across all elements of the hierarchy, each element has a separate, but connected, purpose.

The portfolio consists of a set of programs and projects. Portfolio management is applied to the suite of programs and projects to ensure the relationships between all programs and projects within the portfolio are defined and resources are allocated according to a defined priority (PMI, 2008a). Each program within a portfolio consists of a set of related projects that are centrally controlled to ensure the interdependencies between projects are coordinated and the overall goals of the related projects are achieved (PMI, 2008b). A project within a program or a project without a related program is a temporary effort associated with a defined start and end that is carried out to achieve a specific and unique goal (PMI, 2013a). Unlike portfolios and programs, a project exists only over a specific period of time whereas portfolios and programs can exist longer or indefinitely as projects and programs are moved in and out of the portfolio or program structure.

Each of the three elements within the hierarchy have a common purpose of creating a structure to manage and coordinate activities to achieve the defined goals. Although commonality exists across layers of the hierarchy, each level of the hierarchy has a different scope and objective. Projects have a scope of a specific change objective and success is measured by the acceptance of the deliverables and the time and resources required to provide the deliverables (PMI, 2013a). A program's scope is larger but is still evaluated based upon acceptance of the set of project deliverables within the program. The portfolio is more distinct with an organizational scope and evaluated based upon the value created for the organization and its alignment with the organization's strategies.

Figure 1. Sample portfolio hierarchy

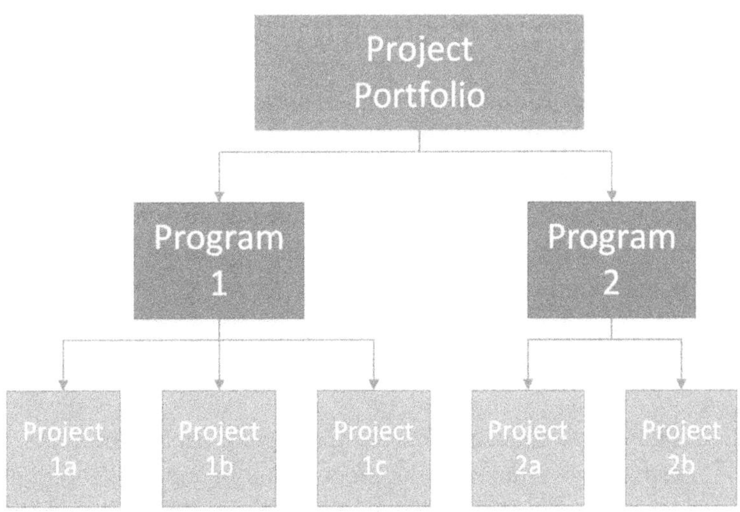

Project Portfolio

Similar to a financial portfolio containing a collection of financial investment assets, the project portfolio consists of a set of project investments. Both financial and project portfolios have a goal to provide the greatest benefits to the portfolio stakeholders. While the financial portfolio fulfills its purpose through financial gains, the project portfolio fulfills its purpose through the benefits delivered to the organization as a result of the project output. The financial portfolio and the project portfolio are designed and managed to achieve the greatest gains or benefits. This is accomplished by selecting the investments that are forecasted to result in the highest level of gains. Financial and project portfolios are also monitored to find new opportunities and ensure the anticipated gains take place. The portfolio serves as the managing structure for the investment. An organization may elect to manage all investments as part of a single portfolio or may elect to design multiple portfolios where each portfolio specializes in a specific topic, specific business area, or a specific investment strategy.

Due to constraints on resources, organizations are unable to invest time and financial and human capital in every project opportunity. As a result, the organization must carefully choose which projects and programs to invest in. As a project portfolio is constructed, projects are selected from a larger pool of projects. This selection takes place with the understanding that not all projects can be selected. The process used to select projects for the portfolio applies criteria beyond simply highest priority. The project selection often uses some form optimization method (Delvin, 2005) to maximize the value of the suite of projects within the portfolio. This often results in a more complex selection process than simply taking the top projects from a prioritized list. As a result, the collection of projects selected in the portfolio will offer the greatest benefits to the organization with the resources available.

Once the projects and programs are selected for the portfolio, a continued monitoring and evaluation must take place. The portfolio must continue to be monitored to ensure it produces the targeted benefits and these benefits continue to support the organization's needs. Projects and programs which cannot achieve the desired benefits or which benefits no longer align with the organization's needs may be closed and removed from the portfolio. Underperforming and outdated projects are removed from the project portfolio so that the resources may be applied to projects that offer improved benefits or better alignment with the organization's goals. Additionally, as projects are completed, resources dedicated to these projects become available creating opportunities for new projects to be added to the portfolio. As projects are removed or as projects complete, the portfolio lifecycle is repeated by selecting new projects or programs while continuing to monitor the projects and programs that remain in the portfolio.

Through project selection and portfolio monitoring, a constant cycle exists in the portfolio and requires management of the portfolio throughout its life. The cycling of projects into and out of the portfolio results in a portfolio existing as a long-term entity rather than a fixed time effort indicative of programs and projects. Using concepts like business value and strategic alignment, the cycle of selection and monitoring continually evaluates the portfolio to ensure the organization is able to extract the greatest benefits from the project and program investments.

Portfolio Governance

The project portfolio requires governance to ensure the organization maximizes the benefits offered through the portfolio. Portfolio governance is the process that includes selecting and funding projects for the portfolio, monitoring and controlling the execution of the portfolio, communicating the portfolio

Figure 2. Sample portfolio governance structure

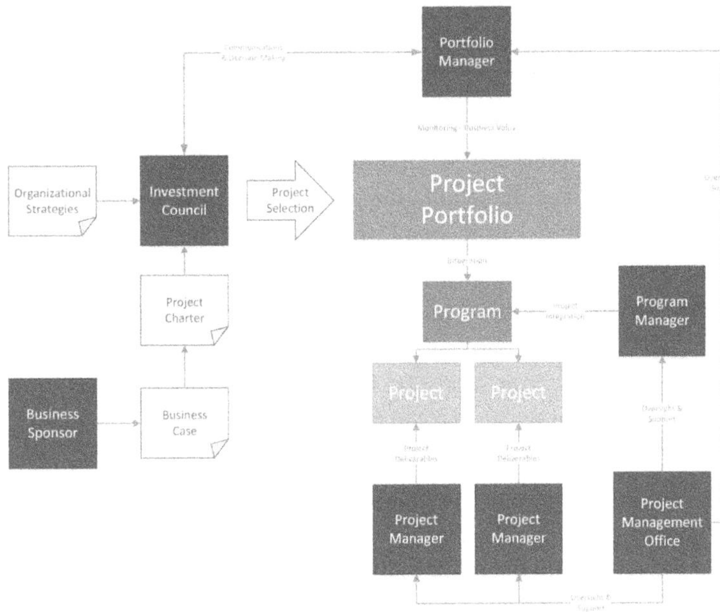

decisions, and aligning the portfolio with the strategic goals of the organization (PMI, 2013a). Managing the project portfolio requires the application of several different roles, responsibilities, accountabilities, and approval levels. A governance structure includes roles for an Investment Council, Business Sponsor, Portfolio Manager, Program Manager, Project Manager, and Project Management Office (Devlin, 2005). Each role serves a different purpose, but together the roles provide the governance structure needed to effectively guide the project portfolio to achieve the desired results. Also, while not explicitly described, there is an inherent reporting relationship between the defined roles that is partially structured by the project hierarchy. Figure 2 illustrates a sample governance structure of the portfolio roles.

The organization's executive team initially forms the *Investment Council* as the organization's strategies are developed. Using these strategies, the portfolio-level Investment Council selects the projects and programs for the portfolio. In addition to members of the organization's executive team, the council may also include leaders from specific business units if the portfolio is focused on a specific unit within the organization. The council may also consist of stakeholders and project sponsors from across the organization that have a vested interest in the outcomes of the portfolio.

The Investment Council provides oversight over the portfolio and also participates in selecting the programs and projects to include in the portfolio. The council is a leadership team that represents the group of individuals most connected with the organization's strategies and is in a positon to align these strategic goals with the anticipated outcomes of the projects and programs. The success of the Investment Council is based upon the performance of the portfolio as evaluated by the organization's executive board.

Each project or program to be evaluated for inclusion in the project portfolio should have a leader from the organization serving as the *Business Sponsor*. The Business Sponsor is the individual advocate for the proposed project and is commonly responsible for funding the project and will assume responsibility for the outcomes delivered from the project or program. This role is responsible for developing a business case for the project. The business case justification is communicated through a project charter (Whitten

& Bentley, 2006) that provides the anticipated benefits as well as the estimated resource investments. The Investment Council considers the justification outlined in the project charter to make a determination of the project's inclusion in the portfolio.

Although project selection, financial evaluation, and alignment decisions are addressed by the Investment Council, the *Portfolio Manager* role exists to oversee the portfolio for the organization. This role is responsible for monitoring, controlling, and communicating the status of the portfolio and working with the Investment Council on decisions regarding changes to the portfolio. The Portfolio Manager serves as a communications hub between the individual projects and programs and the Investment Council. The Portfolio Manager also coordinates integration of the programs and projects within the portfolio and works with the Business Sponsors to ensure the portfolio delivers the anticipated business value.

Programs within the portfolio are governed by a *Program Manager*. This individual is responsible for the delivery of a set of integrated projects that make up the program. The Program Manager is responsible for these projects and reports to the Portfolio Manager. Through this reporting relationship, the Program Manager oversees the high level execution of the individual projects within the portfolio. This monitoring commonly focuses on the integration between projects and resource allocation of the projects within the program.

The next role within the portfolio governance structure is the *Project Manager*. The Project Manager is responsible for the most granular level of the portfolio; the individual project. This role is responsible for the planning and delivery of the project outcomes. The Project Manager ensures the entire scope of the project is delivered and the project is completed on time and within the allocated budget. The Project Manager also must ensure the project deliverables meet the expectations of the Business Sponsor and other project stakeholders. If the project is a part of a program, the Project Manager typically reports through the Program Manager.

The portfolio governance structure also includes a *Project Management Office* (PMO). Although this entity may exist as a Portfolio Management Office or a Program Management Office, a simplification is made here and this entity will be referred to as the Project Management Office. The PMO provides education, support, and oversight over the portfolio, program, and project management practices in the organization. This entity may exist within a specific operational unit of the organization, for a specific project or program, or across the entire organization (PMI, 2013b). The PMO provides support for standards development and improvement, project and program delivery, portfolio management, talent management, reporting and performance management, organizational change management, administrative and tool support, knowledge management, and strategic planning (PMI, 2013b). The organization's project, program, and portfolio capabilities are developed through the PMO in an effort to continually improve project, program, and portfolio success.

In applying Devlin's (2005) governance structure, the portfolio is guided by input from the organization's executive team and controlled by the Portfolio Manager, Program Managers, and Project Managers. The governance structure relies on careful coordination across roles but provides oversight from several different perspectives. The Project Manager provides oversight of the project-level outcomes while the Program Manager ensures the integrated set of projects are delivered in a coordinated manner and the entire set of projects achieve the desired results. The Portfolio Manager oversees all programs and projects within the portfolio to ensure coordinated delivery but, perhaps more importantly, that the portfolio achieves its strategic goals.

Business Value

Value is a common term in the vernacular of PPM. The value, or business value, is used as a metric to prioritize and evaluate projects and programs within the portfolio where the goal is to maximize the value realized from the project portfolio. The value is maximized by selecting the suite of projects that provide the highest value to the organization. Although other factors are considered in project selection for the portfolio, business value is commonly included in the selection criteria.

While the business value metric is a common form of evaluation, the definition of value is not commonly defined across organizations. The definition of value is partially dependent upon the organization's focus, strategy, and project objectives (Levine, 2005) but can be simplified as the long-term capabilities of the organization to produce cash or to provide beneficial public services (Serra & Kunc, 2015). For-profit organizations seek to optimize the value of the portfolio by selecting and implementing the collection of projects that maximize the net profit for the organization. These projects typically either provide opportunities for additional revenue or reduction of expenses. Non-profit organizations look at value in terms of the scope, scale, and quantity of services they can provide through projects that result in either increased funding or decreased expenses.

Strategic Alignment

Another common term associated with PPM is strategic alignment. This term is often used to complement business value as a means to evaluate and prioritize projects within the portfolio. Strategic alignment refers to the extent an effort supports the organization's long-term goals. In the context of PPM, the project portfolio is shaped to include projects which produce outcomes that best advance the long-term goals of the organization.

While business value indicates the benefits to the organization, the strategic alignment indicates the degree these benefits support the long-term goals of the organization. A project considered for a portfolio may produce significant business value to the organization but this business value may not necessarily advance the organization toward its long-term goals. As a result, both the business value and strategic alignment are often included in the evaluation of projects within a portfolio.

It should be noted that organizations may have different strategies and, therefore, evaluate the strategic alignment of a project differently. Alignment may be dependent upon the type of business or its current environment (Kumar, Ajjan, & Niu, 2008). For instance, if an organization is pursuing a low-cost market, cost reduction projects may provide better strategic alignment than product innovation projects. In selecting projects for the portfolio and evaluating their performance within the portfolio, the current long-term goals of the organizations must be considered. These goals may change and, as a result, a project evaluated as highly aligned may no longer be considered aligned if the organization's goals shift. For this reason, alignment is more than a single determination but is rather continually considered as project performance is monitored within the portfolio.

PROJECT METRICS

Projects represent investments and a need for change. An organization invests time and human and financial capital into projects with the intent to achieve some form of change that offers benefits to the organization. Due to these investments and expectations of the project outcomes, both the projects and the project portfolios have an expectation to be successful. However, success in project management is inconsistent with success in portfolio management. Project management focuses on the operational success of the project while portfolio management is more concerned with the organizational benefits.

The differences in determining success at the project and portfolio levels result in challenges in optimizing the benefits of each project and the portfolio as a whole. Additionally, divergence in project metrics also result in project team members and project stakeholders motivated by goals that do not necessarily result in increased performance of the organization.

Success determination and the metrics used to make this evaluation must be revised. Projects should no longer rely only on operational goals to determine success but must also consider the goals aligned with supporting the project portfolio. This means that projects managers and project management methodologies must incorporate organizational benefit considerations. Organizational benefits must be a key factor in determining project success and must drive the decisions and behaviors of project stakeholders.

Before a solution for improved project evaluation is proposed, issues of operational success and the corresponding stakeholder behaviors are discussed. Additionally, the elements required to architect an enhanced project success methodology are introduced. These elements include new project metrics, benefits management, and project conceptualization and communications.

Operational Success

Projects have historically been guided by operational measures and the success of these projects evaluated by fulfillment of these measures. The iron triangle of schedule, cost, and performance to scope is commonly used as the key driver for managing projects (Kloppenborg, Tesch, & Manolis, 2014). Projects are guided by the goals of delivering the entire scope of the project within the allocated budget and targeted completion date. The targets of scope, budget, and schedule represent the project's efficiency (Pinto, 2004) and are measures of the project's operational success.

If the project was able to deliver the entire scope within the budget and schedule expectations, the project was a success. This success measure evaluates the factors associated with the project's operations. The operational success measure does not evaluate the contributions the project makes to the organization but rather evaluates the project's success in operating as expected. As Jugdev and Müller (2005) argued, project success must evaluate both the operational effectiveness as well as the strategic performance.

Operational project success measures do not evaluate the change benefits resulting from the completed project. In fact, these operational measures do not guarantee improved strategic performance. For instance, a project may deliver the entire scope within the budget and schedule expectations but the organization may not be able to apply the outcomes to achieve the desired benefits or the outcomes may not significantly contribute to the long-term organizational goals. Outcomes from a successful project may not produce value for the organization. When the project does not provide value, the success of the project should be questioned. A project should not be considered a success when the outcomes fail to achieve the desired value.

Project Metrics and Team Behaviors

Projects guided by the scope, schedule and budget goals are managed to optimize performance against these goals. In this form of project management, success is evaluated by comparing the planned scope, schedule, and costs against the actual scope, schedule, and costs at the end of the project (deCarvalho, Patah, & Bido, 2015). This means that measures, decisions, and actions are focused on achieving these operational goals. The operational goals of the project therefore influence the project stakeholder's behaviors and drive the project processes.

Projects driven by operational goals may make decisions that are counter to the goals of PPM. Due to the drive toward achieving operational success, project teams and project stakeholders may make decisions or take actions that improve project operational performance but do not improve the benefits or strategic alignment of the project outcomes. For instance, a project team may decide to forgo an opportunity to enhance the project deliverables in order to ensure the budget and schedule expectations are met when these enhanced deliverables would have dramatically increased the value of the project to the organization. In this case, it may have been more advantageous for the team to expand the scope and increase the budget and schedule in order to enhance the deliverables and increase the value of the project to the organization.

Another behavior of the operational metrics that is detrimental to PPM success is the organizational change management. As project outcomes are produced, acceptance of the outcomes by the organization may be challenging. The operational goals of the project do not address the organization's acceptance and application of the deliverables; the project is evaluated on its ability to produce the deliverable and not to ensure the deliverables are adopted. The project output may meet the organization's expectations but the value goals cannot be achieved if the organization is unable to adopt or apply the project output.

Expanded Success Metrics

Project operational metrics do not support, and at times are counter to, the strategic goals of PPM. While the operational metrics encourage performance against the project's operational goals, it does not necessarily improve the value the projects offer to the organization. The operational metrics of scope, budget, and schedule are recognized as an assessment of the project's efficiency or the how well the project was managed (Pinto, 2004). The efficiency of the project does not determine the effect the project outcomes had on the organization.

Rather than simply considering project efficiency as a means to evaluate project success, a common expanded framework of the measures for project success has been proposed (Kloppenborg, Tesch, & Manolis, 2014; Malach-Pines, Dvir & Sadeh, 2009; Pinto, 2004; Shenhar & Dvir, 2007; Shenhar & Levy, 1997). In this framework, the dimensions of project success were expanded to include the impact to the customer, contributions to business success, and preparation for the future. Additionally, impact on the team (Shenhar & Dvir, 2007) has also been included in this enhanced project success framework. Together these five dimensions (see Figure 3) represent a more complete evaluation of a project's success.

The *project efficiency* dimension is the evaluation of the project's ability to achieve the operational goals. This is a measure of the portion of the project scope delivered, the difference between the planned and actual budget, and the difference between the planned and actual schedule. These operational measures demonstrate the capabilities of the project team to plan and execute the project. While this success dimension is a common method of evaluating project success, it represents only the organization's minimum expectation of the project (Pinto, 2004). Organizations must expect more than efficient projects; they need impactful results. Additional dimensions are needed to evaluate the impact of the project on the stakeholders.

Figure 3. The five dimensions of project success

One of the primary stakeholders in the project is the customer and, therefore, the project's impact on the customer should be included when determining the project's success. The *impact to the customer* dimension is used to evaluate the effectiveness of the project outcomes in meeting the customer's technical specifications, addressing business needs, providing a high level of satisfaction, and ensuring the outcomes were adopted. This dimension provides the customer's perspective on the project success and targets the immediate impact on the project's customers. The customer dimension is available for measure shortly after the project is completed. Once the outcomes are adopted and the customer has a chance to react to the new change, customer impact data can be collected to evaluate this success dimension.

Completed projects not only offer outcomes to the customers but can also provide a positive influence on the project team members. The *impact on the team* dimension evaluates the benefits offered to the project team and tolls the project had on the team. The influence of the project on the team may include the level of satisfaction the team experienced, the overall morale of the team, the new skills acquired as a result of the project, and the extent of team member turnover. This dimension provides the team's perspective of the project and represents the continued development and retention of project team members. The indirect benefit of this dimension is the increased knowledge and skills gained by the team members that is available as contributions to future organizational efforts. The team dimension measures can be determined shortly after the project has been completed and the project team has a chance to reflect on the project experience and data gathered.

In addition to the contributions to the customers and project team members, the project must also demonstrate benefits to the organization. The *organizational success* dimension evaluates the benefits realized by the organization as a result of the completed project. These benefits may be in the form of reduced expenses, increased revenue, or expanded services or products. The benefits may also come in the form of indirect financial benefits such as new organizational learning opportunities, increased customer satisfaction, or compliance with regulatory requirements. The results of the organizational success dimension will not be immediately detected and must be evaluated after the project has been completed and the outcomes have been adopted and in place for a period of time.

The final success dimension is also a perspective of the organization but focuses on potential rather than current benefits. The *preparation for the future* dimension is used to evaluate the potential opportunities the project created for the organization. These opportunities may come in the form of new products or services, new markets, new or improved technologies, and new competencies or capabilities. The preparation for the future dimension represents the extent the project created potential growth for the organization. While this growth has yet to be realized, the potential can be evaluated and attributed to the project outcomes. Measures for this dimension cannot be captured until late after the project has been completed.

Each of these dimensions provide a unique perspective on the project success but, unfortunately, each dimension is only relevant at a point in time. The entire five dimensions cannot be measured directly upon completion of the project but are measured as the influences of the project outcomes are experienced by the project team, customers, and the organization. Figure 4 is a diagram outlining the importance of each project success dimension, over time, upon completion of the project.

The operational, or efficiency, measure is not sufficient to truly evaluate the entire success of a project. The five dimensions of project success represent an enhanced framework to evaluate the success of a project through the perspectives of the project stakeholders. Applying this expanded suite of metrics allow the project team and the organization to better understand and evaluate the impact the project had on the organization.

Figure 4. The time dependent dimensions of project success
Source: Adopted from Shenhar & Dvir, 2007.

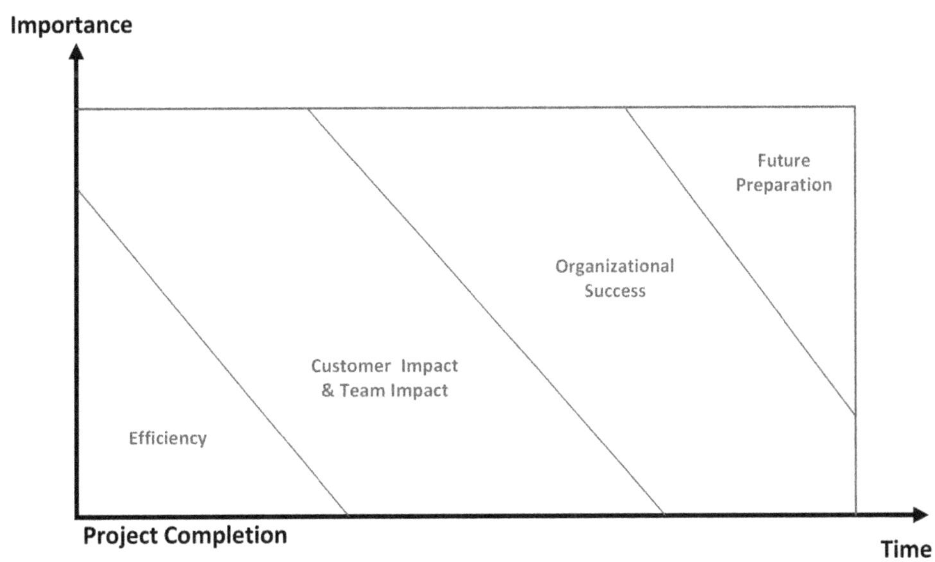

Benefits Realization Management

The expanded success metrics demonstrate that projects can be evaluated beyond their operational efficiency. These additional metrics evaluate the benefits that result from executing the project and the project's outcomes. However, despite an accepted framework for enhanced project metrics (Kloppenborg, Tesch, & Manolis, 2014; Malach-Pines, Dvir & Sadeh, 2009; Pinto, 2004; Shenhar & Dvir, 2007; Shenhar & Levy, 1997) and a clear connection between projects and business strategies, organizations continue to evaluate projects by efficiency. Resistance to evaluating projects by the delivered benefits is partially due to the difficulty of measuring project benefits (Zwikeal & Smyrk, 2012) and the inconvenience of measuring benefits long after the project has been completed (Yu, Flett, & Bowers, 2005). Benefits realization management (BRM), also referred to as benefits management, has been proposed as a solution to be applied to projects to clarify the value and strategic relevance of the project (Serra & Kunc, 2015) and to guide the delivery of planned benefits.

Benefits realization management is a method of controlling and guiding projects that is applied to increase the organization's ability to achieve the maximum gains from projects and resulting changes (Ward & Daniel, 2006). This method addresses the gap between business strategy planning and applying projects to execute these strategies. When paired with effective project management practices, BRM increases the overall success of projects in achieving the planned benefits (Badewi, 2015; Serra & Kunc, 2014). This is accomplished by establishing a relationship between the outputs resulting from the project with the outcomes leading to the benefits from the project.

A governance framework was established (Badwei, 2015) to demonstrate the relationship of project management with benefits management. In this framework project management is paired with benefits management during the project lifecyle. The framework identifies the Project Manager governing the project initiation, planning, execution, controlling, closing of the project and delivering the project output and the benefits owner. The framework also assigns benefits management to a benefits owner who is responsible for realizing the benefits of the project by identifying the potential benefits, planning for the benefits, building a business case for the project, implementing the benefits, and auditing the actual benefits gained from the project. The benefits manager in this framework is the same role as the Business Sponsor in the project governance structure.

Benefits management is initiated well before the project begins, is carried out during the project execution, and continues after the project ends. In addition to a longer duration, benefits management also has a broader scope than implementing the project output. Benefits management requires guiding the organization through the changes needed to take advantage of the project outcomes and realize the intended benefits. It also requires a coordinated effort with the project team to ensure the maximum benefits are achieved from the project output.

Project Conceptualization

Enhancing project metrics to include strategic goals requires a reconceptualization of projects and the types of information communicated by the project team to the project stakeholders. Projects must be viewed as strategic efforts and associated with targeted business value. This business value must be clear to the project team and stakeholders so that decisions can be made that optimize the value offered through the project output.

Linking the project to specific strategic goals enables the project team and stakeholders to better understand all goals associated with the project. This association also supports decisions regarding changes to the project variables of scope, schedule, and budget. For instance, if a change order is received, the cost and schedule implications of the requested change can be weighed against the additional business value generated from the change. The increase in business value may be used to justify a decision to accept or decline the change request. This allows the organization to evaluate project changes in the context of organizational value rather than through the lens of functionality or other operational variables.

In addition to better defining the true success of a project, enhancing the project measures to include strategic evaluation also supports evaluation of project changes. Projects represent strategic initiatives and are investments by the organization that are associated with the delivery of increased value to the organization. Traditional project management practices do not account for these strategic measures. These measures must be embedded in the project process from project initiation to project closing.

SOLUTIONS AND RECOMMENDATIONS

In order to advance the application of enhanced project measures, all measures must be embedded in the project management processes. The solution outlined in this section applies the project success dimensions noted in the literature to current project management practices to demonstrate how these strategic measures can be incorporated into the project management methodology. The proposed framework associates the entire portfolio governance structure with the project success dimensions. The purpose of this framework is to evolve project conceptualization from an operations-centered endeavor in order to realize the strategic importance the project plays in the organization and to expand project evaluation to consider all five dimensions of success.

Project Success Evaluation Framework

Although traditional project success evaluations have focused on the operational measure of project efficiency, additional measures exist that can be used to better assess the true success of the project. The proposed framework applies five dimensions of project success as a means to provide enhanced project evaluation. The five dimensions are as follows:

1. **Project Efficiency (PE):** The ability of the project team to deliver the entire scope within the allocated budget and schedule expectations.
2. **Customer Impact (CI):** The extent that the customer needs were met and the project output adopted.
3. **Team Impact (TI):** The growth and strain the team experienced as a result of executing the project.
4. **Organizational Success (OS):** The direct and indirect benefits the organization gained as a result of executing the project and adopting the project output.
5. **Future Preparation (FP):** The new long-term opportunities made available to the organization as a result of executing the project and adopting the project output.

In addition to the five dimensions of project success, it must be recognized that success is not an evaluation of a single role in the project or only an evaluation of the project team. Many project stakeholders contribute to the success of the project and the proposed framework recognizes five different roles that participate in the success dimensions. The five roles are as follows:

1. **Project Manager (PM):** The individual responsible for initiating, planning, executing, monitoring, and closing the individual project.
2. **Project Management Office (PMO):** The project organization supporting and governing projects in the organization or within the business unit.
3. **Business Sponsor (BS):** The business leader who is the owner of the project deliverables and is often responsible for funding and justifying the project.
4. **Project Portfolio Manager (PPM):** The individual who monitors the project portfolio and communicates between the individual projects, Business Sponsors, and the Investment Council.
5. **Investment Council (IC):** The executive level group who determine the mix of projects in the portfolio, assess alignment with strategic priorities, and consult with the PPM on portfolio management decisions.

It should be noted that, in the case of this framework, projects and programs are not differentiated. The Program Manager assumes the role of the Project Manager for the purposes of the framework. Although a hierarchy exists between the Project Manager and the Program Manager, the evaluation measures are similar enough at each level so as to remove the duplication by associating both levels as a single role of Project Manager.

The project success evaluation framework, illustrated in Figure 5, associates the portfolio management roles with the dimensions of project success. In this framework, each success dimension is represented by a circle and associated with a single portfolio governance role. Each portfolio governance role is represented by a square. Arrows are used to indicate the flow of information from the creator to the recipient for each success measure.

Figure 5. The project success evaluation framework associating portfolio governance roles with the dimensions of project success

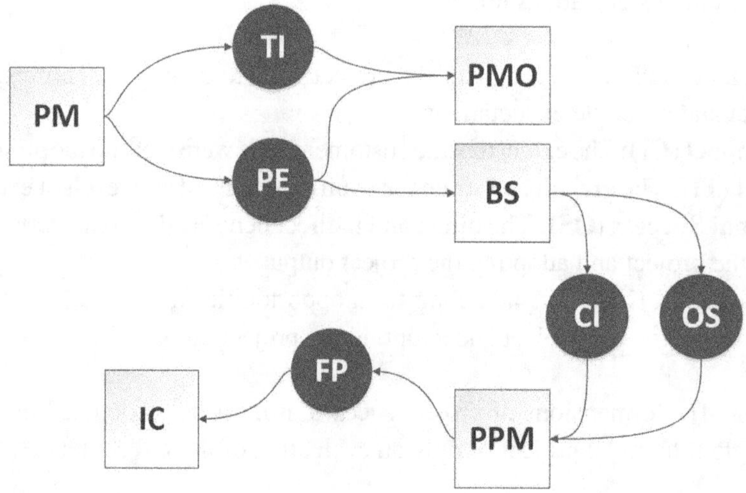

In the project success evaluation framework, the Project Manager interacts with the PMO and Business Sponsor to determine both the project efficiency as well as the team impact. The original operational measure of project efficiency (PE) is monitored and reported by the Project Manager and the measure shared with the Business Sponsor and the PMO. The Project Manager also collects data, monitors, and reports team impact measures. Collected data and the team impact evaluation measures are then shared with the PMO.

Although the Business Sponsor works with the Project Manager to determine the project efficiency, this role also interacts with the Project Portfolio Manager to evaluate the project's client impact and organizational success measures. These two measures as well as the reported project efficiency values are communicated to the Project Portfolio Manager.

The final project success evaluation measure is the future preparation measure. The Project Portfolio Manager considers the client impact and organizational success results along with the organization's strategies. These three evaluations enable the Project Portfolio Manager, in collaboration with the Investment Council, to identify the extent new opportunities were created from the project and the potential value of these opportunities for the organization.

The framework itself simply illustrates that project success is a determinate of several factors and each role in the project portfolio governance structure contributes to both determining project efficiency and contributions to the organization. Although the framework is useful to make the case for multidimensional success evaluation and the diverse contributions to success evaluation, it must be applied to the project management processes to provide proper context.

Project success evaluation does not take place only after the project is complete. As observed in Figure 4, project success evaluation continues to take place long after the project has been completed. However, what is not visible in this diagram are all the activities required to evaluate project success. From identifying success targets, to collecting data, to reporting measures, to archiving results for future application, success evaluation and the actions to increase success take place throughout the project as well as before the project begins and after the project completes.

The proceeding sections contain descriptions of the success evaluation activities that take place during each project phase. These phases follow the structure of the project management process groups as defined in the Project Management Body of Knowledge (PMI, 2013a). These process groups are initiation, planning, execution, monitoring and controlling, and closing. During each of these phases project success evaluation takes place. A part of this evaluation is the application of benefits management to project management as described by Badewi (2015). The activities for each phase include not only data collection and reporting of success measures but also the types of actions that may be taken to respond to the success evaluations along the way.

Application to Project Initiation

Project success evaluation is predicated on some type of definition of success. A project can only be determined successful if it achieves a defined goal. In the Project Initiation phase, the criteria for determining the project success is defined. In traditional project management practices, this phase is where the baseline scope, budget, and schedule targets are established. These targets are defined in the project charter. Establishing these goals as the project is defined allows the organization to assess the merits of a proposed project and, if approved, provides guidance for the project team on the expectations for the project. Project success evaluation traditionally begins in the Project Initiation phase and the proposed solution recognizes this importance and applies this phase to establish criteria for all five project success dimensions. All project success criteria can be centrally articulated in the project charter and should include the following success targets:

1. **Customer Impact:** Anticipated direct and indirect benefits the project will provide the customer.
2. **Organizational Success:** Estimated business value created as a result of the proposed project.
3. **Future Preparation:** Alignment rating of project with organizational strategies to generate new opportunities.
4. **Project Efficiency:** Scope, budget, and schedule performance targets for the project.
5. **Team Impact:** Expected skills and expertise to be developed by the project team as a result of the proposed project and how the organization will benefit from these acquired skills.

Placement of the full success criteria in this document ensures visibility to all project stakeholders and ensures the project is initially assessed for placement into the portfolio based upon the established success criteria.

As a potential project is conceived, the Business Sponsor establishes many of the project success criteria when the project charter is developed. The initial concept of the project is linked to some form of change and this change is associated with benefits to the Business Sponsor's business unit. The Business Sponsor must form a clear vision of what this change looks like and the benefits the change will provide to the business unit. A form of quantifiable value should be forecasted but some qualitative values, such as customer satisfaction or organizational learning, can be included in the criteria to address all forms of value. The anticipated change and resulting benefits should be included in the project charter. The anticipated project deliverables and the planned business process impacts are associated with the customer impact success criteria. Additionally, the forecasted value of the change should also be calculated and then associated with the organizational success criteria. Using the project vision and anticipated changes and business value, the Business Sponsor consults with the Project Portfolio Manager or a members of the Investment Council to determine the alignment of the proposed project with the organization's strategies and to identify new opportunities the change will provide the organization.

The customer impact and organizational success criteria are established with this initial project visioning. The future preparation success criterion is established as a result of the Investment Council or Project Portfolio Manager consultation. All three of these criteria must be clearly documented in the project charter.

Now that the vision of the completed change is established and the customer impact and organizational success criteria documented, the Business Sponsor moves on to develop the criteria for the project efficiency. If a Project Manager is assigned to the project at this point, the project efficiency criteria will be determined as a collaborative effort to ensure both stakeholders agree to and own this criterion. Regardless of the assignment of a Project Manager, the PMO should be engaged to support determination of project efficiency targets based on actuals of past projects with similar domain and scope. Using the project vision articulated earlier by the Business Sponsor, the Business Sponsor and the Project Manager determine the project deliverables and a high level plan for producing these deliverables. Using this plan the Business Sponsor and Project Manager develop cost and schedule estimates for executing the plan. These estimates, along with an articulated project scope of what is to be delivered, form the project efficiency success criterion. This criterion is then documented in the project charter.

In addition to the project efficiency criterion, creation of the high level delivery plan also results in identification of potential skills and expertise that will be developed by the project team. The new competencies of the project team can be applied to benefit other efforts in the organization. The value of these skills and application to organizational needs emerge as the delivery plan is analyzed. The competencies and their relative value to the organization are identified and quantified by the Project Manager and Business Sponsor with support by the PMO and documented in the project charter.

Through the vision of the Business Sponsor and collaboration of the Business Sponsor, Project Manager, Project Portfolio Manager, PMO, and members of the Investment Council, an initial set of project success criteria is established in the project charter. The project charter documents the baseline criteria for customer impact, team impact, organizational success, project efficiency, and future preparation. Although changes to the project vision and plans will occur over the life of the project, the project charter provides the success criteria for the initial visioning of the project.

Once the project charter is complete and the customer impact, team impact, organizational success, project efficiency, and future preparation success criteria established, the project may be submitted to the Investment Council for review. The established and clearly articulated success criteria provide the means for the Investment Council to assess the project for value and alignment, as well as other factors, to determine placement of the project in the organization's current project portfolio. If all projects across the organization standardize on the project charter content and include the initial five success criteria the Investment Council may be able to uniformly compare project potential for all projects and make determinations based on the established success targets.

Application to Project Planning

Projects approved by the Investment Council for inclusion in the project portfolio may continue through the Project Initiation phase and move on to the Project Planning phase. During the planning phase a more detailed plan for creating the project output is developed. As the plans are created, opportunities are encountered to increase the project success. The following success factors may be further improved during the Project Planning phase:

1. Customer Impact.
2. Organizational Success.
3. Future Potential.

These three success criteria must be considered when developing the project plan. Opportunities for additional value in these three areas should also be assessed and incorporated into the project planning.

As the details of the project plan emerge, the Project Manager should begin to assess the influence the project activities and timeline will have on the project team. This assessment should consider new opportunities for the team to obtain valuable skills, the opportunities for building relationships with new areas of the organization, and other potential benefits the project offers to the development of the project team members.

In addition to the benefits offered to the project team members, the Project Manager must also consider the challenges the project will place on the project team. These challenges may include the stress associated with a tight project schedule, difficulties of working with challenging stakeholders, frustrations working with unproven or unstable technologies or tools, and any other undesirable experiences the project team may face. The Project Manager should collaborate with the PMO for assistance in making this assessment and to determine the best method to document and communicate the results of the assessment. This team impact assessment refines the baseline criteria established in the project charter during the Project Initiation phase for the team impact project success criterion.

Application to Project Execution

Using the detailed project plans, the project team begins executing the project according to the plans. As the deliverables are generated, each deliverable should be assessed in its ability to achieve the anticipated customer impact, organizational success, and future potential criteria. Deliverables unable to meet the anticipated targets for these areas should either be reworked or the forecasted value updated and communicated to the Business Sponsor. In many cases, the Business Sponsor will determine if the exiting deliverable is acceptable or should be returned to the team for rework. In addition to the quality assessment of the project deliverables in contributing to the client impact, organizational success, and future potential goals, the project will encounter changes to the initial project vision and corresponding project plans.

Changes to the initial project vision and plans should be centralized through a change request process. In this process individual changes to the initial project vision and plans are defined and submitted for evaluation and approval. Using the larger definition of project success, these changes should not only be evaluated in terms of impact to the baseline project efficiency goals but must also include the other success goals as well. In addition to describing the changes to the project deliverable, the change request should assess the influence the change will have on all five project success dimensions. Addressing all five dimensions allows the Business Sponsor to better understand the true benefits of the proposed change. This understanding provides an improved determination of the anticipated costs against the entire set of forecasted benefits that result from the adopted change. The set of project success criteria are applied to provide an improved form of assessment for the change orders and allows for a consistent, objective, and more complete evaluation of the requested change.

As project changes are approved, the project plans and success criteria must be updated to integrate the changes. This means the schedule, scope, and budget may increase but it also means the anticipated team impact, client impact, organizational success, and future potential may also change. The project stakeholders must recognize the impact of the change requests to the project success criteria and the Project Portfolio Manager must consider these changes when evaluating the status of the project in the portfolio.

Application to Project Monitoring and Controlling

While the project is executed, the Project Manager continues to monitor the project for performance against not only the project efficiency criteria but also the team impact, client impact, organizational success, and future preparation criteria. As gaps between the planned and observed success evaluations are identified, these gaps are communicated and plans are made to address these gaps or revise the forecasted success measures. The current state of the success measures must also be shared with the Business Sponsor and Project Portfolio Manager so the project status in the portfolio can be properly assessed.

The Project Manager and Business Sponsor must also evaluate the project and scan the business for new opportunities to extract additional value from the project. As new opportunities for value are identified, potential change requests may be developed or the project plan modified slightly to allow the deliverables to provide these new benefits. These new opportunities may arise with potential enhancements to currently planned deliverables or may involve development of new deliverables.

Application to Project Closing

During the first four phases of the project, all dimensions of the project success criteria were defined and monitored. These benefit management and project performance activities ensured the potential benefits were both identified and maximized. Along the way, performance against the forecasted success measures were used to assess the project in terms of its ability to meet the organization's expectations and is priority in the project portfolio. If the project proved unable to deliver the anticipated performance measures or its output became out of alignment with the organization's strategies, the project may have been paused or stopped and removed from the project portfolio.

Immediately upon completion of the project and full delivery of the project output, the project is closed. In addition to the closing processes for the project, an assessment of the project performance takes place. The final project scope, budget, and schedule values are compared to the planned scope, budget and schedule. The gap between these two measures are used to evaluate the project performance. This operational evaluation should apply the current planned performance criteria rather than the baseline criteria established in the project charter since the project most likely encountered changes and no longer fits the initial vision and plans articulated in the project charter. Assessment of the project efficiency success is captured and reported to both the Business Sponsor and the PMO. The Business Sponsor communicates the results to the Project Portfolio Manager so the project status in the portfolio may be updated. Additionally, the Project Manager reports the results to the PMO for evaluation of changes to project process standards and for inclusion in historical values for future project estimations.

Shortly after the project is completed and the project closed, the team impact success criteria may be evaluated. The PMO or Project Manager of the team uses some form of data gather techniques to determine the influence the project had on the project team members and other stakeholders. The results can be summarized and compared to the planned impact to determine the level of success of team development for this team impact success measure. This evaluation is most likely a qualitative evaluation but can be reported as a quantitative value of the difference between planned and actual impact to the project team. The results should be reported to the PMO for tracking and application to the skills and competencies inventory.

The client impact success measure can also be assessed shortly after the project is completed. The Business Sponsor should evaluate the true impact the project made on the business processes and the effectiveness of the changes to the organization resulting directly or indirectly from the project. These changes can be observed directly or can be captured through other forms of data collection. The measured changes are compared to the planned changes to determine the extent the project was successful in making a positive impact on the customer. These results should be shared with the Project Portfolio Manager to support evaluation of the future potential success measure.

As time passes after the project closed, an additional project success measure can be evaluated. The organizational success measure can be assessed once the project has been completed and changes have been in place for a period of time. Time is required to pass before this measure is collected and evaluated since the true benefits of the change cannot be realized immediately after the project. Successes in the form of increased revenue from enhanced or new products or decreased expenses due to process improvements take time to realize. Sufficient time must be given for these changes to take place and the results to be observed. Once the results can be observed these results are captured and evaluated against the planned success benefits of the project. This comparison will indicate if the investment in the project provided the expected level of return. These results are determined by the Business Sponsor and communicated to the Project Portfolio Manager to support an updated performance evaluation of the portfolio and to contribute to the evaluation of the future potential success measure.

The final project success measure cannot be taken until a substantial amount of time passes after the project is completed. The future preparation project success measure can be evaluated once the changes have been in place and benefits realized. Although initial future potential can be identified during the project delivery and during the customer impact and organizational success evaluations, these initial future potential measures are only preliminary and cannot capture all opportunities that are available due to the project. As the changes resulting from the project are in place, a new understanding of the organization's current state is made. This new understanding can then be evaluated for the new opportunities the organization has available that were not available prior to the project. This growth potential is then compared to the planned future opportunities to determine the project's final measure of success.

Although the enhanced project success measures require additional time and are more complex than the operational project efficiency measure, the results provide an improved evaluation of the project's impact and allow the organization to better understand how projects contribute to future growth. Additionally, the organization can study these results to determine the types of projects that provide the greatest benefit.

The proposed framework and solution extend the current operational project efficiency measure. The additional measures were identified in the literature as providing the ability to assess the actual impact of the project on the organization and organizational benefits resulting from the project. This framework was then applied to the project management process groups (PMI, 2013a) to articulate how the project success evaluation may be incorporated into the project environment. The results of this solution provide a more robust and rigorous evaluation of project success and align the view of project success at the Project Manager level with the view of success of the Project Portfolio Manager.

FUTURE RESEARCH DIRECTIONS

The proposed framework and solution is a first step in introducing change to project success evaluation. The proposed model requires further evaluation and validation. Future research studies can be initiated to determine the fit of this model to actual project management and portfolio management practices. The model should be evaluated by project and portfolio management practitioners to determine relevance and to solicit refinements or additions to the solution. Future studies should also be conducted to determine the effectiveness of the model in preventing, or reducing, the funding of projects that are not able to deliver the anticipated benefits to the organization. Additionally, since the model calls for significant collaboration between the Business Sponsor, Project Manager, and Project Portfolio Manager, studies should be conducted to determine the effect the increased collaboration has on the organization.

CONCLUSION

It is widely accepted that the project success evaluations of scope, schedule, and budget are not effective in determining the return on investment for the organization. An enhanced set of project success measures have been proposed over time but these measures have failed to become readily adopted in project management and portfolio management practices. The proposed framework and corresponding solution demonstrates how these enhanced measures of project success fit within the project portfolio governance structure and how the measures can be applied to current project management practices. Adoption of this solution requires significant changes to the project management and portfolio management processes but results in a better understanding of the value the project provides to the organization. These changes also enable the organization to better determine those projects that will provide the greatest benefit and ensure these benefits are realized as the projects are executed.

REFERENCES

Badewi, A. (2015). The impact of project management (PM) and benefits management (BM) practices on project success: Towards developing a project benefits governance framework. *International Journal of Project Management*. doi:.10.1016/j.iproman.2015.05.005

Davis, K. (2014). Different stakeholder groups and their perceptions of project success. *International Journal of Project Management*, *32*(2), 189–201. doi:10.1016/j.ijproman.2013.02.006

Davis, K. (2016). A method to measure success dimensions relating to individual stakeholder groups. *International Journal of Project Management*, *34*(3), 480–493. doi:10.1016/j.ijproman.2015.12.009

deCarvalho, M. M., Patah, L. A., & Bido, D. (2015). Project management and its effects on project success: Cross-country and cross-industry comparisons. *International Journal of Project Management*, *33*(7), 1509–1522. doi:10.1016/j.ijproman.2015.04.004

Delvin, J. (2005). Using the analytic hierarchy process to improve enterprise project portfolio management. In H. A. Lavine (Ed.), *Project portfolio management: A practical guide to selecting projects, managing portfolios, and maximizing benefits*. San Francisco, CA: Jossey-Bass.

Jugdev, K., & Müller, R. (2005). A retrospective look at our evolving understanding of project success. *Project Management Journal*, *36*(4), 19–31.

Kloppenborg, T. J., Manolic, C., & Tesch, D. (2009). Successful sponsor behaviors during project initiation: An empirical investigation. *Journal of Managerial Issues*, *20*(1), 140–159.

Kloppenborg, T. J., Tesch, D., & Manolis, C. (2014). Project success and executive sponsor behaviors: Empirical life cycle stage investigations. *Project Management Journal*, *45*(1), 9–20. doi:10.1002/pmj.21396

Kumar, R., Ajjan, H., & Niu, Y. (2008). Information technology portfolio management: Literature review, framework, and research issues. *Information Resources Management Journal*, *21*(3), 64–87. doi:10.4018/irmj.2008070104

Levine, H. A. (2005). *Project portfolio management: A practical guide to selecting projects, managing portfolios, and maximizing benefits*. San Francisco, CA: Jossey-Bass.

Malach-Pines, A., Dvir, D., & Sadeh, A. (2009). Project Manager-project (PM-P) fit and project success. *International Journal of Operations & Production Management, 29*(3), 268–291. doi:10.1108/01443570910938998

Martinsuo, M., & Killen, C. P. (2014). Value management in project portfolios: Identifying and assessing strategic value. *Project Management Journal, 45*(2), 56–70. doi:10.1002/pmj.21452

Müller, R., & Turner, R. (2007). The influence of Project Managers on project success criteria and project success by type of project. *European Management Journal, 24*(4), 1346–1357.

Pinto, J. K. (2004). The elements of project success. In D. I. Cleland (Ed.), *Field guide to project management* (pp. 14–27). Hoboken, NJ: Wiley & Sons. doi:10.1002/9780470172346.ch2

Project Management Institute. (2008). *The standard for portfolio management* (2nd ed.). Newtown Square, PA: Author.

Project Management Institute. (2013a). *A guide to the project management body of knowledge* (5th ed.). Newtown Square, PA: Author.

Project Management Institute. (2013b). *PMI's pulse of the profession: PMO frameworks*. Retrieved from http://www.pmi.org/~/media/PDF/Publications/PMI_Pulse_PMO-Frameworks.ashx

Rad, P., & Levin, G. (2008). What is project portfolio management? *AACE International Transactions*, TC31-TC34.

Serra, C. M., & Kunc, M. (2015). Benefits realization management and its influence on project success and the execution of business strategies. *International Journal of Project Management, 33*(1), 53–66. doi:10.1016/j.ijproman.2014.03.011

Shenhar, A., & Dvir, D. (2007). *Reinventing project management*. Boston, MA: Harvard Business School Press.

Shenhar, A., & Levy, O. (1997). Mapping the dimensions of project success. *Project Management Journal, 28*(2), 5.

Ward, J., & Daniel, E. (2006). *Benefits management: Delivering value from IS & IT investments*. England: Wiley.

Witten, J., & Bentley, L. (2006). *Systems analysis and design methods* (7th ed.). Boston, MA: McGraw Hill.

Yu, A. G., Flett, P. D., & Bowers, J. A. (2005). Developing a value-centered proposal for assessing project success. *International Journal of Project Management, 23*(6), 428–436. doi:10.1016/j.ijproman.2005.01.008

Zwikael, O., & Smyrk, J. (2012). A general framework for gauging performance of initiative to enhance organizational value. *British Journal of Management, 23*(1), S6–S22. doi:10.1111/j.1467-8551.2012.00823.x

KEY TERMS AND DEFINITIONS

Business Sponsor: A leader in the organization designated as the owner or recipient of the project deliverables who is often responsible for securing funding and defining the business case for the project.

Customer Impact: The influence of the project on the customer associated with the adopted changes and resulting benefits of these changes.

Future Preparation: New opportunities created as a result of the project which prepare the organization for long-term success.

Investment Council: A group of senior leaders responsible for ensuring an optimized value is generated from the organization's investments in the project portfolio.

Organizational Success: A measure of the direct and indirect benefits achieved through the adoption of the project deliverables.

Project Governance: The management framework created to establish decision making, roles, responsibilities, and accountabilities within the portfolio, program, and project management.

Project Efficiency: A project execution measure of the ability to achieve the scope, schedule, and budget goals.

Strategic Alignment: The extent an objective supports the long-term goals of the organization.

Team Impact: The influence the project had on developing the project team and the strain the project placed on the team.

Chapter 8
Demand Management as a Success Factor in Project Portfolio Management

Luca Romano
PMI Central Italy Chapter – CUOA Business School, Italy

Roberta Grimaldi
INAIL, Italy

Francesco Saverio Colasuonno
INAIL, Italy

ABSTRACT

Demand Management is the process an organization puts in place to internally collect new ideas, projects and needs during the creation of a Portfolio (from now on PTF). This collection is done internally but should also consider the external market situation and the general Strategy of the Organization. Demand contains two main actions: initiatives Collection and Assessment (following the Strategic Objectives definition) and preceding the start of the Portfolio budgeting, prioritization and selection phases. What is possible to do to better manage Demand and maximize the value added to Portfolio Management? The first opportunity is that Demand can represent a connection with the business and the entire Organization. A second opportunity is that a continuous Demand Management approach can simplify the portfolio collection, prioritization and selection. For Demand Management to be a real opportunity in Portfolio Management should be organized and planned respecting the interpretation of the matter and the maturity of the Organisation and should be also treated as a specific matter.

DOI: 10.4018/978-1-5225-2151-8.ch008

INTRODUCTION

Demand Management (from now on DM) is the process an organization puts in place to internally collect new ideas, projects and needs during the creation of a Portfolio (from now on PTF). This collection is done internally but should also consider the external market situation and the general Strategy of the Organization. Demand is successful when the final output is useful to prioritize and select a valuable strategic aligned portfolio. The more the process is able to capture the real strategic commitment of the Organization and merge it with the past ongoing activities the more Demand is a success factor in building the correct portfolio and support planning and project management. There are many aspects of this process to take into consideration and this chapter aims to address the many questions about this activity: who should manage the Demand? How could Demand take into consideration the Strategic Direction without frustrating bottom-up new ideas/projects proposal? How the attention on old and new components should be balanced? How should Demand be managed to be aligned with the specific characteristics and requirements of Organizations?

Background

Demand Management is usually included inside Project Portfolio Management (PPM) activities. In several international Project Portfolio Management standards, the words "Demand Management" are not used and this set of activities is not debated. In the real world Organizations are struggling with this phase as it is very complex and involves many stakeholders.

Traditionally, Demand Management is thought of a topic in supply chain management, composed of operational and strategic sub-processes that focus on determining sales forecasting, synchronize it with the production capacity of the company and the chain, incorporate the company strategy, and map customer needs (Croxton et al., 2008). Often, Demand management is linked with marketing processes as it is the key interface between the production activities of a company, and planning and market control systems, encompassing several activities including forecasting, processing customer orders, establishing delivery dates (Vollmann et al., 2004). It includes marketing and its coordination between the agents in the Supply Chain (internal and external) and Demand Planning (Mentzer & Moon, 2005).

The same purpose of meeting customers' need is somehow reported also in the ICT field, where, in order to manage planning, production and delivery, just like in any other properly managed business, the organization has to balance orders for its products and services (i.e., Demand) with the ability to produce them in terms of resource and scheduling constraints (i.e., Supply) (Gentle, 2007).

ITIL V3 framework 2007 Edition used to refer to Demand management as an aspect of the Capacity management process in the Service Strategy book. The 2011 Edition, instead, clarifies differences between the two processes and recognized to Demand management the dignity to be defined as a standalone process within the service strategy stage, aimed to understand, anticipate and influence customer demand for services. In this way, Demand management works in accordance with capacity management to ensure that the service provider has sufficient capacity to meet the required demand (Cannon, 2011).

According to ITIL (2011), the purpose of IT service strategy is to define how the service provider will enable and how the organization will achieve business outcomes. Therefore, ITIL demonstrates that Demand management is associated with a number of other processes, like strategy management, service portfolio management, financial management, business relationship, and capacity management. This means that demand can actually come from different sources, not only related to supply chain.

Operational Demand management, comes directly from IT and addresses internally driven activities aimed at the management of key IT assets that are the basis for the enterprise's ability to conduct core operations. Tactical Demand is referred to day to day activities and consists of everyday requests from other departments, usually referred to by IT execs as "keeping the lights on." Strategic Demand, is the demand for new projects that provide innovation and enable new business products and services. Typically, strategic demand accounts 20% of the IT budget but enables the most relevant opportunities for business growth. (Symons, 2006).

Best practice for managing strategic demand and the tight link between the strategic plan and project initiatives is done via Project Portfolio Management (PPM). Project portfolio management provides processes for evaluate, prioritize and monitoring projects.

Bashab and Piot (2007) defined IT Demand management as *a metaproject* that determines which of the IT projects should be commissioned and then executed by calculating their financial value and prioritizing the project proposals taking into account the value but also other factors, first of all the IT department capacity.

But, even if the general rule is to avoid the risk to produce too little of what is required, too much of what is not required, or deliver late, or have problems with product quality or customer satisfaction (Gentle, 2007), Demand management activities change depending on the kind of business the Organization operates in. Some examples follow.

For an IT Organization that works only for "internal clients" Demand Management is a key activity as from the Demand IT gathers all the information about the next year activities. In this case the collection is generally only inside the same Organization.

For an Organization producing products for the mass market Demand Management can be both internal and external. Internal for improvements requested from the various Departments (IT, Processes, Organization, R&D) and external for the production of new or reengineered products that will meet the new or evolved needs and explicit requests of the final clients. The ratio between internal/external depends on the kind of products/services produced.

A construction company (and also a consulting company) basically sells projects to final clients. In this kind of business Demand Management is a peculiar process as the Portfolio depends on the direct engagements received from the clients (or the tenders won), in this scenario Demand is more oriented to the selection of the right tenders to participate reflecting the defined strategic direction in the "construction field", than to select the projects to include in the Portfolio. Here the limit is the production capacity (and also the ability of the organization to manage such capacity) called sometimes throughput (Goldratt, 1997).

HOW TO PROPERLY MANAGE DEMAND IN A PROJECT PORTFOLIO

Demand Management in the Portfolio Management Process

As already stated DM is often not exhaustively covered in portfolio management publications. It is frequently taken for granted that the activities related to this phase of the PTF process will be undertaken properly. Maybe there are so many complex things to do that DM is a "B-phase" in Portfolio. In reality in authors experience this phase was really time consuming, complex, politically tricky to manage and mission critical. It is not just a collection and deserves attention.

To simplify the explication of the Project Portfolio Management process the next figure tries to represent it in one single macro-process.

The full Portfolio Management process (Figure 1): defines the strategy and the objectives of the next years; selects a list of Components (programs, projects, activities) to achieve these objectives; implements them; controls Component's performance alone and as a group; reviews the Component's planning and reviews the strategy/objectives; and finally verifies the realization of the expected benefits to eventually redefine the strategy and the next year's targets.

Refer to Chapter 1 in this book for a description of the 9 areas, for the focus of this chapter let's zoom the Demand Management area (Romano, Grimaldi, Colasuonno, 2016).

Demand contains two main actions:

1. Initiatives Collection and Assessment (following the Strategic Objectives definition) and
2. Preceding the start of the Portfolio budgeting, prioritization and selection phases.

The initiatives Collection is the process an organization puts in place to collect new ideas, projects, needs. This collection will support the final portfolio definition as it will produce the full list of programs/projects/actions that will be assessed, prioritized, and selected to define the approved Portfolio and start (or continue, as it will be clearer later) the implementation. The Collection is focused on three main items: Old Initiatives not previously selected (OL), Ongoing Components already included in the Portfolio (OC), New Initiatives (NI) (Figure 2).

For the sake of clarity, the difference between an Initiative and a Component is that the Initiatives are all the Project/Programs/Activities that could be inserted in a Portfolio. Initiatives become Components when selected and authorized to be part of an approved starting Portfolio. Usually once a year (for one-year life cycle portfolios) all the Components (considered on-going as under implementation) become Initiatives again as concur to the new Portfolio cycle selection.

Figure 1. The relationships between the 9 PPM areas

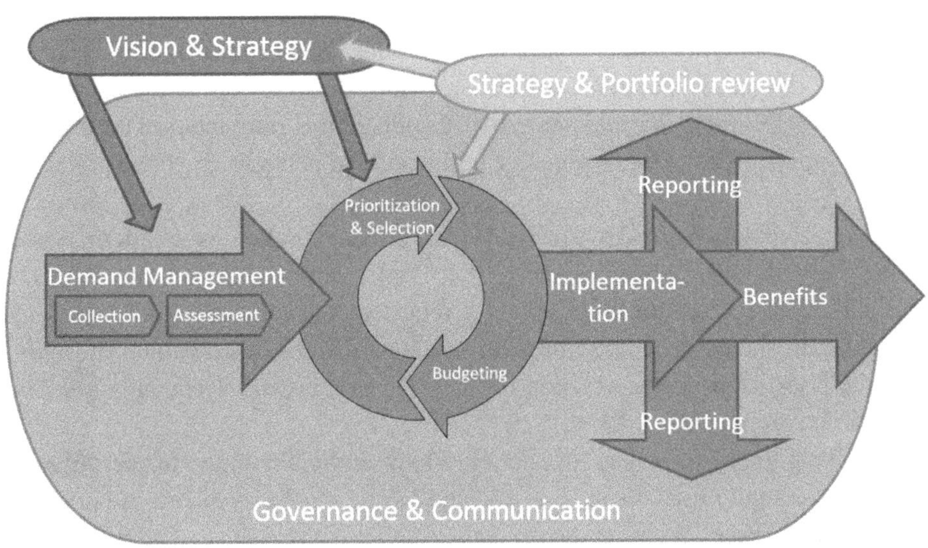

Figure 2. PTF collection

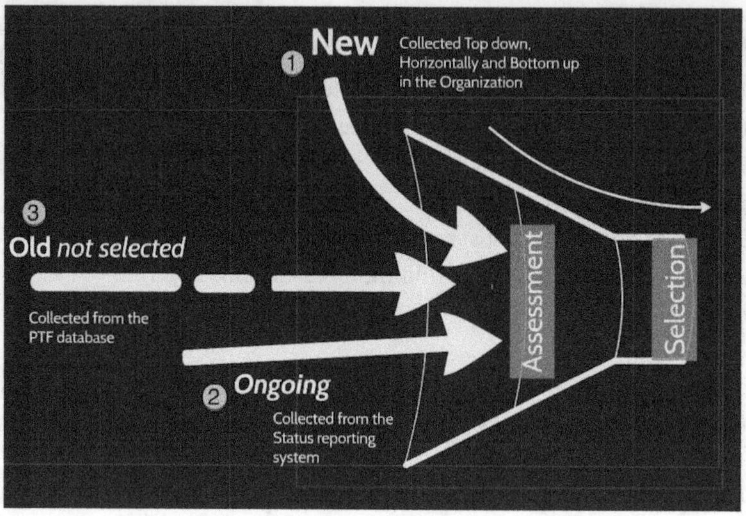

Based on this all the activities the organization is doing at the time of the definition of the new portfolio can be considered Ongoing Components. OC are then, for example, projects started in the previous portfolio and not yet completed due to a planning that was longer than the duration of the portfolio or due to delays. Ongoing Components represent the past strategic direction, but most of the time, are still actual and there is a convenience to complete them. Nevertheless, Ongoing Components are usually subjected to the prioritization and selection process. Information and status reporting about Ongoing Components will be available from the project management system already in place or (if the process considers operations routinely activities not part of a project) from the management system.

The process to collect New initiatives differs from organization to organization but basically moves Top-down, Horizontally and Bottom-up. In Top down collection will be considered what emerges from the strategic planning. Strategic objectives could have been broken down into implementation initiatives that should be included in the Portfolio. Horizontal collection is focused on acquiring implementation needs coming from the several structures of an Organization that could not be raised from the strategic planning. These needs could be driven by the strategic objectives or not. Bottom-up collection could be contained into Horizontal when organizational structures collect needs and ideas of new initiatives internally with their employees. When the horizontal collection is only focused on managers of Functions, with bottom-up collection Organizations could decide to perform an "open collection" from the employees.

The second main action performed by Demand Management is called **Assessment.** Assessment aims to generate what is usually called a business case (BC). The BC contains at least information about needs, strategic justification, objectives, deadlines, budget, requirements and expected benefits. The structure and the depth of the BC should depend on the level of maturity of the organization. BC must be coherent primarily with the prioritization and selection process. BC are, instead, frequently used only to obtain funding approval. This is not sufficient.

The BC has to be a living document that not only lives at the beginning of the Initiative, but when the Initiative is approved and implemented, is updated during her lifecycle and is part of the reporting and re-prioritization processes.

Another common problem with the BC is its depth and complexity. As the BC is generally prepared for all the Initiatives (even for those that will not be selected), there must be a cost-opportunity analysis at the base of its structuring. About the content (among other information), the BC should be structured in a way that the Initiatives will be also analyzed for the level of expected future contribution to the achievement of the strategic objectives.

The Demand Management Key Activities

As already stated DM is the process an organization puts in place to internally collect new ideas, projects and needs during the creation of a Portfolio. This collection is done internally but should also consider the external market situation and the general Strategy of the Organization. Theoretically, all the new proposals should emerge in alignment with the strategic direction defined. Often DM is also a critical evaluation of the on-going activities within the Portfolio Components. DM is successful when the final output is useful to prioritize and select a valuable strategic aligned portfolio. The more the process is able to capture the real strategic commitment of the Organization and merge it with the past ongoing activities the more Demand is a success factor in building the correct portfolio. At the end of all the analysis, the real strategy of an Organization is what the Organization does and not what written in official brochures.

From what stated so far it is clear that the Demand cannot be considered as a mere harvesting activity. There is (before DM) a strategy that gives the direction and (after DM) a selection model that should select the best beneficial set of Components aligned with the strategic objectives.

Authors point of view is that organizations should approach DM with a proactive style trying to address strategy while collecting new ideas and not "just ask" and then verify the alignment of what collected with the strategic direction.

This also means that in case of the existence of a "Demand Management Responsible", this person should be part of the Top Management as a proactive representative of the strategic direction during the collection and assessment.

It is probably better to concentrate under the same responsibility the collection and assessment of New and On-going Components (Romano, Grimaldi, Colasuonno, 2016).

In the following paragraphs will be deeper investigated the 4 DM actions already introduced:

- New Initiatives collection.
- Ongoing Components collection.
- New Initiatives assessment.
- Ongoing Components assessment.

The *Collection of new initiatives* could be then related to:

1. New initiatives directly defined and suggested from top management as fundamental implementation of the strategic objectives. These kind of "new activities" are the best way to implement the strategic objectives as there is a clear strategical reason to proceed in that direction.
2. New needs coming from the Organization (directions, divisions, offices, employees, etc..). These kind of initiatives are important as represent the voice of the structure and show what is considered important sometimes despite the strategy declared.

3. Formal new requests from a Department to another (for example Finance to IT). These requests could be eventually not aligned with the strategy but very important for the requestor and challenging for the executor.
4. Old initiatives not selected in the previous Portfolio selection process and still valuable.

The presentation of New Initiatives must be stimulated.

Organizations shouldn't take for granted that all the needs will be officially presented during the formal Demand process. Missing some important new needs will produce a future request of change in the approved Portfolio and despite all the formalities behind the official portfolio set of Components approval, if the missed request is important it will be "forced" into the actual set of Components overbalancing the Portfolio.

The process to collect New initiatives is complex and time consuming and differs from organization to organization and as already briefly stated can move (Figure 3):

- Top-down.
- Horizontally.
- Bottom-up.

In Top down collection Organizations have to consider what emerges from the strategic planning. If an organization uses the Kaplan and Norton Balanced Scorecards (BSC) for example, every strategic objective will be represented from one or more initiatives to be implemented in the following years. These initiatives will be controlled through the measures defined in the BSC (Robert S. Kaplan and David P Norton, 1996).

Figure 3. PTF collection directions

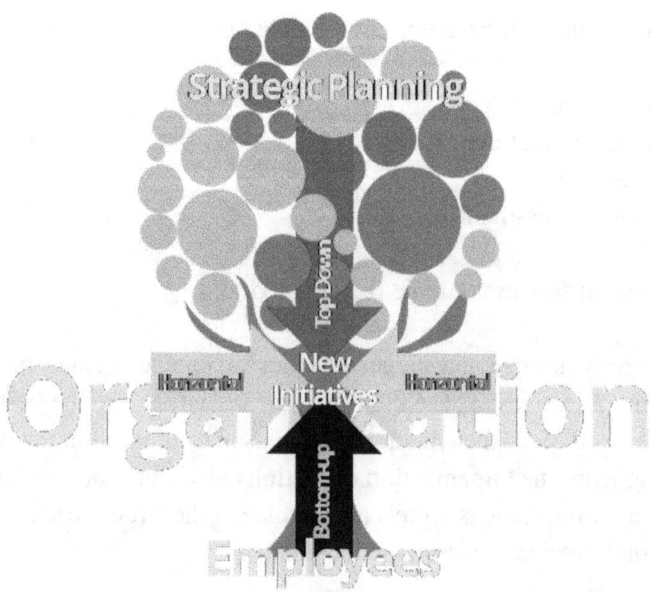

Here is where strategic planning and portfolio management merge into a single point. During a hypothetical "first year" of an Organization the Strategy drives the actions and in the following periods there will be an update of the original Strategy and/or of the actions performed. A strategic planning could be built on a three-year base and during the initial strategy direction definition several initiatives (Programs, Projects, Operations) could be defined from Top Management. Some will be immediately executed and become Portfolio Components in the first year and some other spread in the following years. Every year there will be some of the original strategic initiatives completed, some still on-going and some new that should be inserted in the next portfolio cycle.

Within the Strategic planning set of defined actions there will be yearly the need of choosing the best group of initiatives for the portfolio cycle coming reshaping the multiyear planning.

Horizontal collection is focused on acquiring implementation needs coming from the several structures of an Organization that could not be raised from the strategic planning. These needs could be driven by the actual strategy or not. Most of the organizations show a disconnection between what written in top management documents and what really done. The more the organization is old, complex and bureaucrat the more this could happen.

Horizontal collection is time consuming and complex as there are many stakeholders to involve in the process. In this kind of activity Demand Management is central. No one else will perform effectively and efficiently this collection without a Demand structure. A key aspect in DM role during this activity is the routing of the requests collected toward the known strategic objectives. Demand will sit side by side with requestors and proactively anticipate and negotiate any slide away from the strategic direction. This will also manage and define in advance their expectations.

Bottom-up collection could be contained into horizontal (when organizational structures collect needs and ideas of new initiatives internally with their employees). When the horizontal collection is focused only on managers of Functions, Organizations could decide to perform an "open collection" from the employees. DM is then a change agent and works to generate consensus through personal involvement.

The Collection of ongoing Components. Some Components will last more than one year and there will always be ongoing programs/projects or activities to be considered in the new portfolio cycle.

This collection is a result of Program and Project status reporting. To plan the future is essential to know the actual status and the estimate at completion of Ongoing Components.

It is also important to consider the Project Portfolio management timetable.

DM will necessarily happen before the end of the actual cycle of approved portfolio of Components. This will mean that there will be the need to perform an assessment of the ongoing activities some months before the authorization of the new portfolio.

This collection has to be handled with care as some ongoing Components:

- Will be finished and will not be considered for the coming new Portfolio cycle (and this will be highlighted from the status reporting system).
- Will probably finish before the next portfolio cycle, but in case of a delay should be inserted at least in the Prioritization & Selection or (if close to completion) directly in the new portfolio and financed.
- Will surely continue in the next portfolio cycle and will be continued anyway or inserted once again in the Prioritization & Selection process.

As a starting point, talking about **Assessment** within a portfolio management environment means to acquire all the info required to finally select the right set of Components for the strategic objectives defined. This means to understand what kind of benefits Components are supposed to produce and if these benefits are aligned with the strategic objectives.

There is also the need to know:

- How much this will cost.
- When it will start.
- How long it will take.
- How risky it will be.
- If these activities are feasible from our organization
- If there are other Components doing the same kind of job.
- …

The thoroughness of this assessment will influence the prioritization and the selection, but as already stated, the time available to perform this activity is limited by the usual portfolio timeline.

Organizations must define standard processes and templates for this phase as standardization helps in finishing on time and speed-up the learning curve (it has been observed that a good level of quality vs time is achieved only after some years of application). The information about the initiative that are essential to implement a correct prioritization & selection process are at least:

- Objectives, macro requirements and success factors.
- Strategic alignment.
- Scheduling.
- Budget and source of funding.
- Level of risk.
- Impacts on the organization (technical, resources, organization).
- Prerequisites.

Stakeholders to involve are many and their number could vary. Final output should be contained in a single database as this data will be used many times now on till the end of the implementation over and over every year for future portfolios.

This information will be used to prioritize the Initiatives on their alignment with the strategic direction and then select the set of Components that are feasible for the budget available at the level of risk accepted maximizing the expected strategic benefits (Romano, 2013).

Assessment is different for New initiatives and Ongoing components ones.

New initiatives assessment must be performed from scratch and the level of detail should be properly balanced considering the time available and the thoroughness of the analysis. This last advice is always a big problem as the collection/assessment of New initiatives usually happen 2-3 months before the launch of the new portfolio and the time available is an issue.

New Initiatives are pre-assessed (Business Case) to create a knowledge base. After the selection the initiatives approved are further investigated (post-selection) and planned as they will be started in the coming portfolio cycle.

Based on this method this pre-selection assessment will be done for all the Initiatives even if some of them will not be included. This is a key point as a cost benefits analysis must be done.

Is a matter of fact that a higher effort/cost with a more detailed pre-selection assessment and more time spent for the whole set of new initiatives (some of which will not be selected) will produce the beneficial effect of having a better knowledge base for the prioritization and the selection phase. Also the post-selection detailed planning will be simplified. But increase thoroughness of this pre-selection assessment could delay the final authorization of the Portfolio, mostly when the level of maturity of the Organization is not aligned with the defined complexity of the Business Case.

It has been observed that it takes time for Organizations to select the correct level of detail of the pre-selection new initiatives "template" that for the level of maturity can be completed on the time available to release the Portfolio. As presented in Figure 4 an increase in the level of maturity of an Organization enables more accurate and detailed on-time pre-selection assessments. It must be also taken into consideration that, as shown from the dotted curve representing the value added to Portfolio from a more detailed assessment, due to the intrinsic inaccuracy of any forecast this curve has an asymptotic trend that (after a certain level) makes unworthy more precision.

This means that there is a moment to stabilize the pre-assessment template at a level of detail that for the single organization balances thoroughness, requested effort and time available.

Ongoing Components assessment is generally easier as they were already assessed before their original selection. It becomes complex when organizations don't have a good project status reporting system. Ongoing Components assessment should be primarily focused:

Figure 4. Organization's maturity and pre-selection initiatives assessment

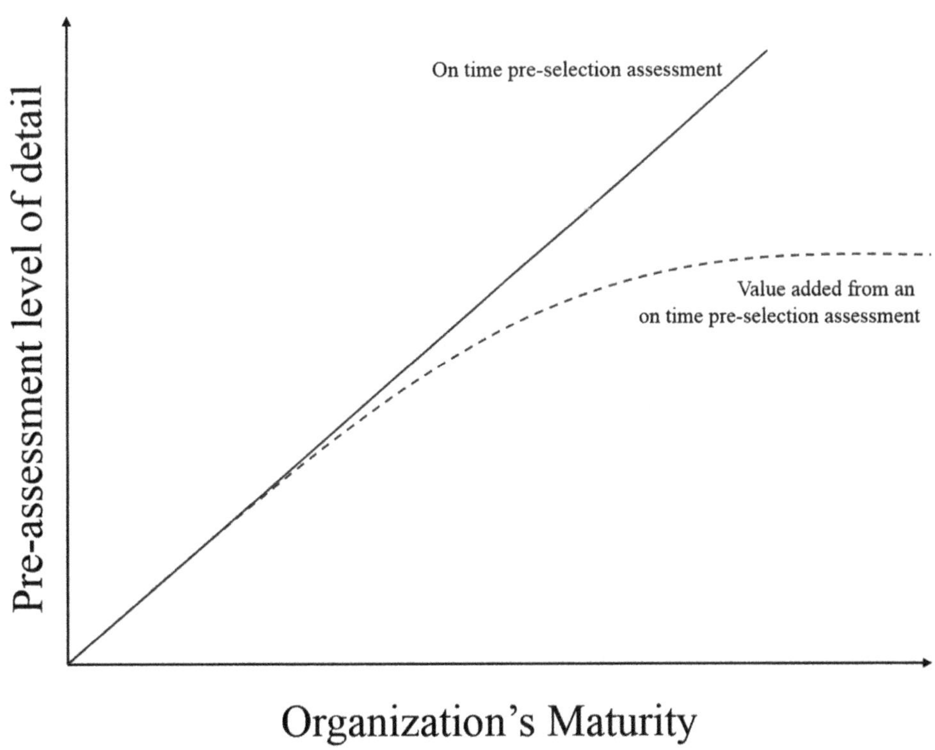

- On the status of the implementation (time, cost, risk, issue).
- On the estimate to complete (time and costs).
- On the alignment with the actual strategic direction.

What collected should be comparable with what acquired from the assessment of New initiatives even though Ongoing Components, as already started, should be prioritized differently.

The key point for on-going Components assessment is the analysis of the relationship between the results already produced *vs* the actual alignment with the strategic objectives.

Simplifying a strategic aligned ongoing Component should be prior and included in the next Portfolio. Only the existence of a more prior ongoing component justifies an exclusion when funds are not sufficient. Additionally, the use of Programs where ongoing projects are managed within the bigger set simplifies Portfolio Management, as long the Program is alive and aligned with the Organization's Mission and Objectives the selection is at least internal and is a Program Management activity.

During the *Prioritization & Selection there will be a competition between initiatives* as some will be excluded on the base of some parameters. Has been observed that depending on the approach of the Organizations performing PPM, this competition can be Full, Partial or Null.

In an "Full competition" Ongoing Components will be considered in the prioritization & selection and compete with New. This is an "all against all" competition. In this case it is very important that the tools and the indicators used to assess Ongoing Components are comparable with the ones used for New.

In "Null competition" there's the need to finish Ongoing Components anyway. In this case the Assessment is a mere status reporting and re-planning. Only New initiatives will compete each other.

In any case Ongoing Components must be status reported and re-planned as they will consume budget, resources, etc.. diminishing the availabilities for the New ones.

In "Partial competition" it is possible to find situations in the middle.

For instance, to grant that past investments will be properly considered during the prioritization and the selection:

- Components very close to completion can be marked and automatically selected.
- Components "seniority" can be considered in prioritization models favoring already started initiatives.
- Multiyear programs can be considered as a whole and automatically selected as directly connected with multiyear strategic planning.

Usually this activity involves Project/Program Managers and Sponsors. DM is responsible for organizing the collection of the information and for the quality and thoroughness of the data collected. In doing this is very important that Organizations create a tight link with the Planning and Control department when available.

DEMAND MANAGEMENT AS A SUPPORT FOR PORTFOLIO MANAGEMENT

The Right Focus for Demand Management

What is possible to do to better manage Demand and maximize the value added to Portfolio Management?

Organizations cannot:

- Only keep on doing the Ongoing Components not completed.
- Implement only New initiatives.
- Exclusively ask top management which are the initiatives the Organization should perform in the next PTF cycle.
- Do only what Organization's internal clients are asking.

Simplifying Organizations:

- Cannot simply keep on doing what done in past OR stop all the Ongoing Components not finished and do only New initiatives.
- Must include what requested from the Organization (broadly speaking) as we cannot only focus on what defined as strategic from top management.

In Portfolio Management the discussion about the balance between New, Old and Ongoing Components in a selected set of components within a portfolio is very interesting. A portfolio with a higher percentage of ongoing components confirmed is more conservative and less innovative? Is this kind of portfolio more stable and demonstrates that the decisions taken in the past were correct?

Theoretically the sole situation without problems is the first year of a new organization.

Top management defines the Mission, break it down into objectives and objectives into project/actions. These would be the Components of a "first year" portfolio.

From the second year on, there will be the need to balance ongoing not finished with new. Some Components will be completed and ready to produce benefits, but some other (somehow more complex) will need more time to be finished and will need to be financed in the next portfolio. New needs will arise during the first implementation year, strategic objectives could change and the Organization will need to update what done and what to do.

Another interesting debate is about the typology of the Initiatives.

The authors disagree with the fact that there are Strategic activities *relating to the gaining of overall or long-term advantage* (Online Oxford Dictionaries, 2016) and non-strategic activities. Everything is done in an Organization is strategic as affects the final results and the final success. There could be initiatives clearly and directly related to specific actual strategic objectives, but all the activities performed during a portfolio cycle are "strategy in action" (Romano, 2014) as at least were selected in the past and are still part of our portfolio of Components.

What is important to understand is if the organization is doing something not aligned with the strategic objectives and not "serving" them. We should disinvest in such initiatives.

A classification that is surely accept by the authors is between Projects/Programs and Operations (PMI, 2013). Where Projects/Programs produce something new and Operations produce value from what already available.

Moreover, authors found useful to classify Projects/Programs in 4 categories: Transform, Grow, Run and Regulatory (Bell, 2012). Where:

- Transform means doing something completely new to our Organization (new market/sector or new business models or new channels).

- Grow means to improve something already existing (evolve, improve or differentiate a product/market).
- Run means to support or improve what the Organization does that is not directly producing revenues or not directly related to final clients.
- Regulatory means to implement something due to a new law or an obligation.

Summarizing it is possible to say that producing products day-to-day in a factory is Operation, implementing a Quality System project is Run, make a new release of a SW product is Grow and opening the first office in Taiwan is Transform. All these activities are strategic as they concur to the success or the failure of the organization (Figure 5).

A Portfolio should be divided (and generally this classification is useful to assign the budget as well) into initiatives that will produce a change in the status-quo (Projects and Programs) and initiatives that will produce a value from what we already have (Operations). The change produced could be radical (Transform), an improvement (Grow), supportive (Run) or mandatory (Regulatory).

Opportunities in Demand Management

Managing Demand Management "professionally" and not only as a step in Portfolio Management assigning formal and long-lasting responsibilities to these duties creates a series of opportunities to Project Portfolio Management.

The first opportunity is that Demand can represent a Connection with the business and with the entire Organization.

The focus of Demand management is to transfer the wishes and the needs of the key stakeholders to the implementation activities. There are several stakeholders involved during the collection performed by Demand Management, these stakeholders represent the business but also the several Organization's Departments. The collection is performed by interviews, meetings, etc.. and the people involved are connected and relationships are created.

Figure 5. The strategic direction

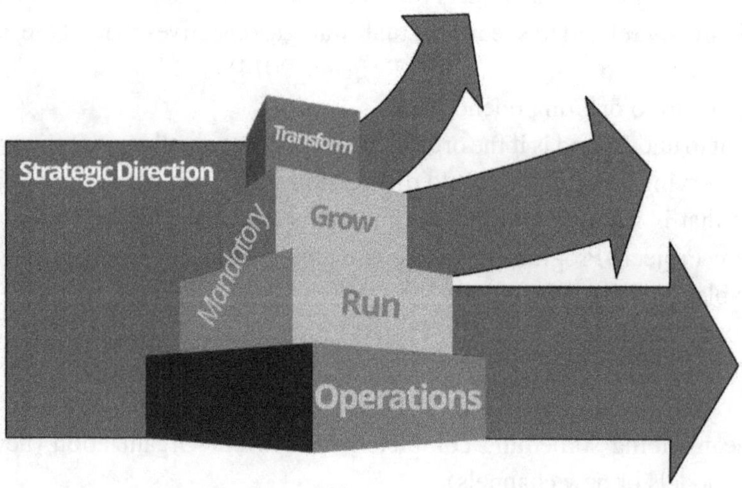

This connection crafted during the portfolio collection could be interrupted for most part of the year if not well managed and capitalized. Organizations should then maintain alive this relationship managing stakeholders expectations at a Portfolio level continuously engaging a communication between Demand and Business with a sort of continuous Demand Management attitude.

A second opportunity is that a *Continuous Demand Management* approach can simplify the portfolio collection, prioritization and selection.

A Demand management that proactively and constantly (during the whole lifecycle of the portfolio) collects, prioritizes and pre-selects new initiatives will minimize exclusions and simplify the selection process. When comes the time of a new collection, prioritization and selection, a proactive approach would have probably already excluded many new initiatives (for example, not aligned with the strategy or for example without the right expected performance). The best Demand Management possible is a Demand that would produce a set of initiatives already aligned with the strategy bringing exclusions close to zero. Organizations should then use Demand to simplify and minimize the prioritization and selection activities that without this preparation are very complex, time-consuming and often not fully successful. This concept of continuous Demand Management could be paired with the scheduling system called Kanban (Ohno, 1988). This pairing must be further investigated, but the concept of a continuous connection between the production where the materials are consumed and the repository where materials are stored is similar to a Demand Management system where projects produce outputs (and benefits) and the Organization updates the requests (as a consequence of the achievement of the Strategic Objectives or their change). Kanban maintains inventory levels, a signal is sent to produce and deliver a new shipment as material is consumed in a lean manufacturing system. Demand Management being constantly connected with the business could support a lean flow in the portfolio management process.

Continuous Demand management and the connection established with the business could also be a supporting opportunity for the *Portfolio Governance*. Once the portfolio is approved, components implementation will start. During the implementation there will be: changes, status reporting, performance metrics, reviews, benefits analysis and so on. Some components will be completed, some will be stopped and maybe the portfolio will have new components to be inserted. Having a strong relationship with the stakeholders (and with the business) the DM can strongly support the organization in managing Portfolio changes.

When in the prioritization and selection of portfolios are utilized baskets with an assigned budget, Demand management could help the *Decisions regarding the right financing level of these baskets.*

What usually happen is that on the base of a set of selection rules initiatives are assigned to categorized baskets and within these baskets they will be ranked to select the best set of initiatives feasible for the budget assigned (at the specific basket) at the level of risk accepted.

The decision about the amount of money to assign to baskets (that is usually a top-down strategic decision) could be helped using the bottom-up information gathered from the Demand. Having the full view of the whole set of initiatives can help the financing activities. Decide the amount of resources available for any basket is always a strategic decision but this decision has to consider what has been shown by the demand management activities. Often baskets are containers of projects broken down to the fact that they are kind of "transform", "grow", "run" or "mandatory" projects. If there is an evidence of a strong request of initiatives in the "run" area this must be taken into consideration assigning the entire budget available.

Figure 6. Relationship between demand and project management

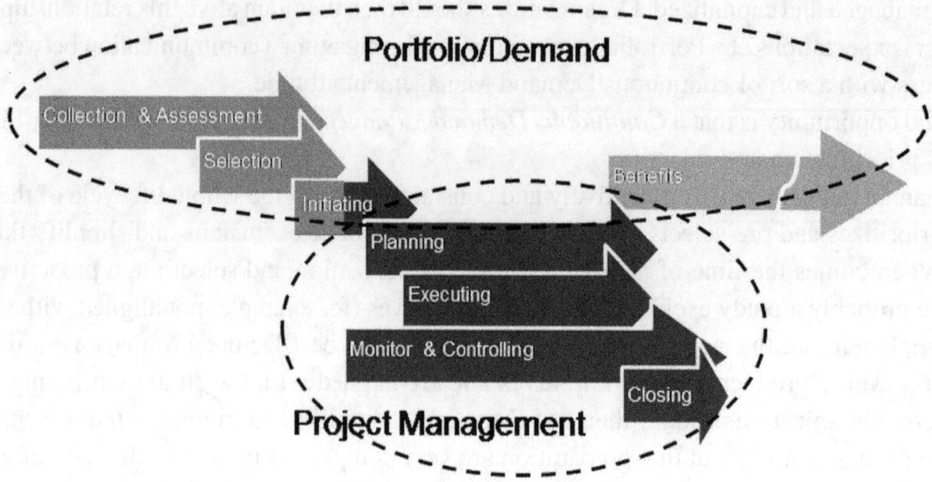

Portfolio/Demand, and Project management have to work together during the project lifecycle. Project life-cycle (PMI, 2013) shows many connections between them (Figure 6). Portfolio/Demand will be responsible for the collection, assessment and selection and when the projects are selected the implementation phase will begin. The first point of contact is during the Initiating and Planning phases where the project manager (PM) is supposed to do a detailed planning (called in this Chapter post-selection). Demand management can give a strong support to PMs transferring all that information gathered during the collection and the assessment. Once the project is planned and started the project manager will be focused on "doing things right" producing deliverables and the Demand would be able to support him/her (for example) to clarify some requirements or assess some deliverables. PM and Demand can have another point of contact in benefits managements activities. Benefits could arise during the project lifecycle, at the end of the project lifecycle or five months or years far from the closing of the project. In the idea of the authors, Demand manager could play an important role in doing a sort of projects follow-up, assessing and evaluating the benefits produced by the projects (when for example are not part of Programs), managing original stakeholders expectations initially collected.

Demand Management Implementation

Most of the Demand Management activities are concentrated in the timescale before the prioritization and selection. This means that without a continuous demand management approach at the end of these tasks few more effort is requested on this kind of duties. In this situation Demand management could be managed by a temporary team within the Portfolio Management structure even if some specialization (Demand managers can be focused on a specific set of requestors or strategic objectives) would help. The authors have also observed the creation of a separate Demand Management Function within the Organizational structure supervised by a responsible. In this second situation the continuous DM was applied and the relationship with the business and/or requestors was more stable. In the case of the creation of a separate Demand Management function has been observed that other responsibilities were assigned to this structure (process management or else).

Based on the inconstant level of effort requested by Demand Management activities authors think that the best organizational position of a Demand Management structure is within the Project Portfolio Management Function (including also the Project Management Office – PMO) but with a specialized team applying continuous demand management.

FUTURE RESEARCH DIRECTIONS

Demand management within project portfolio management is an emerging discipline that can gather experience from other fields where demand is more structured (IT, production, ..). An improvement of the methodology supported by real applications is desirable. Also the definition of a maturity model in its implementation is an area of further research.

Finally, the pairing of Continuous Demand Management and Lean Management is an interesting argument for a future research.

CONCLUSION

For Demand Management to be a real opportunity in Portfolio Management:

1. Should be organized and planned respecting the interpretation of the matter and the maturity that the Organization has. Decisions about "Full competition" between Old, Ongoing and New initiatives, budget assignment and baskets of budget, initiatives classification and assessment, should be taken in advance as they will influence the way this activity will be performed.
2. Should be treated as a specific matter to manage within the Portfolio Management and assigned as a clear responsibility to a specific team. This activity that is mainly executed during the portfolio definition continues during the portfolio life-cycle as somehow Demand Management Structure could represent the operative sponsorship of the initiatives selected. During Portfolio review the results from DM and several indicators measured (internal customer satisfaction, portfolio/budget composition, Projects rejected/stand-by, etc..) could support future decisions.
3. Strategic planning when properly defined will simplify Demand and Selection. If the Organization has a defined Strategic direction with more than one year of visibility and this direction is broken down into key strategic streams (Programs) the selection within those streams will be assigned to the responsible and the initiatives will compete inside the specific defined stream/direction. In this scenario what will be yearly reviewed is the opportunity to proceed in that direction and not the single "steps" to perform.
4. The duration of the phase of New initiatives assessment before the prioritization and selection is an issue that often produces delays in the approval and authorization of the Portfolio. Doing some New initiatives collection sessions during the year to anticipate the final phase will gives more time to assess new ideas.
5. The final aim of a good DM activity is to maximize the strategic alignment of the portfolio minimizing the number of the requests rejected or delayed to also maximize the internal customer satisfaction.

6. Demand is also an opportunity for Project Managers as the roles can collaborate during the project lifecycle. If the initial assessment and the selection will be managed within the Portfolio Management activities, once projects are selected, the Initiating phase and operative Planning of projects could be done together to properly transfer the objectives to the implementation. Moreover, Demand could support PMs in the continuous connection with the business during the implementation, somehow giving them more time to deliver. Demand could also perform benefits management during project lifecycle and after the closing, when benefits are measurable months or years after the delivery of the final output (as in Figure 6).

REFERENCES

Bell, S. C. (2012). *Run Grow Transform: Integrating Business and Lean IT*. New York: CRC Press. doi:10.1201/b12718

Cannon, D. (2011). *ITIL Service Strategy 2011 Edition*. London, UK: The Stationary Office.

Croxton, K. L., Lambert, D. M., García-Dastugue, S. J., & Rogers, D. S. (2008). The Demand Management Process. In D. Lambert (Ed.), *Supply Chain Management: Processes, Partnerships, Performance*. Supply Chain Management Institute.

Gentle, M. (2007). *IT Success: Towards a New Model for Information Technology*. Hoboken, NJ: John Wiley & Sons.

Goldratt, E. M. (1997). *Critical Chain*. Great Barrington, MA: North River Press.

Kaplan, R. S., & Norton, D. P. (1996). *The Balanced Scorecard – translating strategy into action*. Harvard Business School Press.

Mentzer, J. T., & Moon, M. A. (2005). *Sales forecasting management: a demand management approach*. Thousand Oaks, CA: Sage.

Ohno, T. (1988). Toyota Production System: Beyond Large-Scale Production (English translation ed.). Portland, OR: Productivity Press.

Piot, J., & Baschab, J. (2007). *The Executive's Guide to Information Technology* (2nd ed.). Hoboken, NJ: John Wiley & Sons.

Project Management Institute (PMI). (2013). A guide to the project management body of knowledge (PMBOK® guide) (5th ed.). Newtown Square, PA: PMI.

Romano, L. (2013). *Rise and Fall of Project Portfolio Management: Triumph and Collapse: A Case Study*. Paper presented at the 2013 PMI Global Congress, Istanbul, Turkey.

Romano, L. (2014). *Corporate Strategy for PMs. Why strategic alignment and awareness is so important*. Paper presented at the 2014 PMI Global Congress, Dubai, UAE.

Romano, L., Grimaldi, R., & Colasuonno, F. S. (2016). *Demand management as a critical success factor in Portfolio Management*. Paper presented at the 2016 PMI Global Congress, Barcelona, Spain.

Symons, C. (2006). *How IT Must Shape And Manage Demand*. Cambridge, MA: Forrester Research.

Vollmann, T. E., Berry, W. L., Whybark, D. C., & Jacobs, F. R. (2004). *Manufacturing Planning and Control for Supply Chain Management*. Boston, MA: McGraw-Hill.

KEY TERMS AND DEFINITIONS

Component: A project, a program or an operation managed as a group within a Portfolio.

Demand Management: Demand represents the set of activities of Collection and Assessment necessary to start the overall portfolio budgeting, prioritization and selection. Collection is the process an organization puts in place to collect ideas, projects, needs, etc. This collection will support the portfolio definition, as it will produce a list of programs/projects/actions to assess, prioritize, and select. Collection is focused on Old Initiatives not previously selected, Ongoing Components and New Initiatives. Assessment creates what is usually called the business case (BC). The BC contains at least information about needs, objectives, deadlines, budget, requirements and expected benefits.

Initiative: Proposed projects, programs or operations to be prioritized and selected to become Portfolio Components.

Initiatives Collection: Is the activity performed in Demand Management to gather all the initiatives within an organization that could contribute to the composition of the approved Portfolio.

Initiatives Prioritization: Is the activity to create a ranking among the initiatives based on some parameters.

Project Management: Project management is the application of knowledge, skills and techniques to execute projects effectively and efficiently. It's a strategic competency for organizations, enabling them to tie project results to business goals — and thus, better compete in their markets.

Project Portfolio Management: Centralized management of processes, methods, and technologies used by project managers and project management offices (PMOs) to analyze and collectively manage current or proposed projects based on numerous key characteristics.

Project: A temporary systems or work systems that are constituted by teams within or across organizations to accomplish particular tasks under time constraints.

Projects Selection: Project Selection usually refers to choosing the best choice from various proposals based on some key indicators.

Strategy: Is a high level plan to achieve one or more goals under conditions of uncertainty.

Chapter 9
Project Portfolio Selection Using a D.E.A. Approach

António M. Amaral
Polytechnic Institute of Viana do Castelo, Portugal

Madalena Araújo
University of Minho, Portugal

ABSTRACT

The project management area uses several techniques and tools to identify, select, monitor and manage the projects portfolio of the organizations. However, these techniques still present problems and difficulties which, sometimes, inhibit their use. Project Portfolio Management (PPM) is considered a problem of considerable difficulty and complexity, which requires its constant monitoring by the organization, according to the strategic guidelines chosen. Thus, this paper presents an innovative approach for selecting the portfolio of projects by using DEA, and the development of a set of generic indicators, to support the decision makers in considering multiple projects. Each decision maker can use all or some of the indicators proposed, thus each one's knowledge, sensitivity and intuition are taken into account, namely for indicators such as risk perception, level of innovation, market clock speed, project's complexity.

INTRODUCTION

Project management has been, over time, an area with tremendous growth and prominence within organizations. However, it presents problems and difficulties that require a careful analysis to tackle the complexities and peculiarities that commonly are associated with it (Yeo, 1993; Shou & Huang, 2010). Organizations continue to face considerable difficulties in meeting schedule and cost estimates. According to the 10th edition of the CHAOS report of Standish Group, almost 51% of all projects inquired in the survey fail in attaining the cost and schedule estimates and functionality requirements (Henry, McCray, Purvis, & Roberts, 2007). Furthermore, Mankins & Steele (2005) indicate that companies only perform 63% of their strategies potential value and Johnson (2008) reported that 66% of the organizational strategies are never implemented. It is evident that, somehow, the development of techniques and

DOI: 10.4018/978-1-5225-2151-8.ch009

their applications are far from converging, and the large corporations face numerous problems with this hiatus (Fernandes, 2004).

Today's business environment is extremely complex and dynamic which requires making faster decisions, better allocation of the organizational scarce resources, and a clearer strategic focus (Elonen & Artto, 2003). Despite all the differences on markets, cultural environment, and organizational objectives, some changes are modifying the way business occurs, turning competitive advantages difficult to accomplish. In a global marketplace scenario, changes are constant and with variable amplitude. Organizations need to be alert to all movements to counter-answer and re-align themselves with the new market conditions (Amaral & Araújo, 2009).

Cooke Davies, T. (2002) and Pheng & Chuan (2006) pointed that despite of several past studies carried out to assess the key factors that contribute to project success, those factors are not sufficient to foresee it, to the extent that projects are developed in a dynamic environment and can be positively and/or negatively influenced by a multiple nature of factors, which might limit their overall performance. As an example, the project manager leadership style (Turner & Müller, 2005; Van der Voet, 2014; Kissi, Dainty, & Tuuli, 2013), the relationship with the project team members (Mota, Almeida, & Alencar, 2009; Aga, Noorderhaven, & Vallejo, 2016) the managerial practices used (Chen & Lee, 2007; Eik-Andresen, Johansen, Landmark, & Sørensen, 2016), and the top management involvement (Hermano & Martín-Cruz, 2016) seem to be directly related to the project performance.

Müller, Martinsuo, & Blomquist (2008) demonstrated the existence of a positive relationship between associating the organizational strategy and the projects portfolio selection with the performance achieved. Other studies point to the projects prioritization as being a determining factor and key of success of the projects portfolio (Cooper, Edgett, & Kleinschmidt, 2001; Elonen & Artto, 2003). Others state that there is a positive influence between the projects portfolio performance and the organizational results obtained (Cooper, Edgett, & Kleinschmidt, 2004a,b; Killen, Hunt, & Kleinschmidt, 2008).

According to Archer & Ghasemzadeh (1999) the project portfolio is defined as a group of projects that compete for scarce resources and are conducted under the sponsorship or management of a particular organization towards the achievement of their strategic objectives. At the same time, Cooper, Edgett, & Kleinschmidt (2001) point out that the Project Portfolio Management (PPM) is a dynamic decision process, which requires continuous updating and information review to be able to select the best solution every time. Englund and Graham (1999) emphasize the importance of assessing, prioritizing and selecting projects to the portfolio based on the strategic direction of the organization. Thus, managers, face an utmost challenge of selecting the proper projects to the portfolio, pondering which projects have the greatest potential to create value to the organization (Menke, 1991; Chu, Hsu, & Fehling, 1996). Part of this challenge is divided in tackling the "right projects" and the other in ''doing projects right''.

Elonen and Artto (2003) and Cooper, Edgett, & Kleinschmidt (1998, 2000) have identified, and pointed out, the common problems in project selection and portfolio management, faced by companies. So the following reasons can be related with the difficulties on managing, and on selecting, the proper projects to the portfolio:

1. **No Link Between Strategy and Project Selection:** Projects tend not to be fully related with the organization's strategic objectives, which affects the organization overall performance;
2. **Poor Quality Portfolios:** The organizations, normally, do not have judicious criteria for selecting viable projects from half-baked ideas;

3. **Reluctance to Kill Projects:** There is, commonly, an umbilical relationship between the organization (team members) and the project itself, which sometimes constitutes a major organizational failure for continuing investing scarce resources in an unviable project;
4. **Scarce Resources:** A lack of focus and management capability, to balance properly the resources, often creates additional pressure to multitask, contributing to produce unexpected errors and not assimilating the important lessons from the project development;
5. **Selection of Short-Term and Easy Projects:** Companies tend to implement easy and cheap projects, which consequently reduces their potential to prosper and to achieve competitive advantages;
6. **Information Overflow and Lacking Quality of Information:** Regardless of the quality and sophistication of the portfolio selection and decision tools, it is fundamental to obtain the proper information to make accurate decisions;
7. **Decision Making Based in Power:** Usually the decision is an exercise of power, which means that there may be situations where decisions tend not to reflect the organizational future success, by being deprived of the sphere of influence and power of the top management.

Project Portfolio Management (PPM) seeks to improve organizational performance and efficiency (Ireland, 1997; Patanakul, 2015), to coordinate interrelated projects and diminish project time cycle (PMI, 2008; 2013), as well as acquire and develop learning mechanisms to outperform the competition. The PPM processes must include the project alignment with the business strategy, the selection of the proper projects, the allocation and balancing of the organizational resources and the periodical reassessment of the mix of projects, to check whether the selection is still aligned with the main business goals (Kremmel, Kubalík, & Biffl, 2011; Reyck *et al.*, 2005; Amaral, Araújo, & Pereira, 2010; Kaiser, El Arbi, & Ahlemann, 2015).

The main research objective here reported is focused on the important challenge above described –the selection of the "right projects" for the portfolio creation. The research contribution approach uses a specific selection technique – Data Envelopment Analysis. Expectedly, the projects selected for the organizational portfolio will enhance the organizational value and potentiate its overall performance. Hence, the suggested approach intends to tackle some of the common problems of PPS previously presented. In the Background section these points will be fully described and analyzed.

This chapter is organized as follows. Firstly, it describes the research methodology selected and the literature review supporting the theme. Subsequently, it is described the DEA approach for the Project Portfolio Selection (PPS) with a theoretical example. Finally, the main results and conclusions are pointed out, as well as, the future research directions.

RESEARCH METHODOLOGY

There is a considerable time lag and utility between the formal investigation procedure and the real-world practice. This happens because the combination of the scientific rigor expected for the validation process and the relevance/usability for organizations is in most traditional approaches completely disjointed (Platts, 1993; Saunders, Lewis & Thornhill, 2012). Thus, according to Susman & Evered (1978), the increased level of sophistication of the methods and techniques developed over time, stumbles with the conditioned usefulness of these in solving common problems in organizations. The vision that supports the adoption of a single paradigm, in which the mathematical logic governs, by principle, and all the planning and justification of adopted options and the results obtained are being gradually replaced, especially in highly complex and dynamic areas (Bjork & Ottosson, 2007). The process development is an extremely complex task and, somehow, unique for each organization, meaning that it is particularly difficult, if not impossible, to formulate standard solutions that might work in any context, scenario or situation (Ottosson, 2003).

This process of acting is based on periods of observation and understanding of the realities, supported by in-depth study of solutions found in the literature. The proposed methodology is composed of four main steps. It began with an extensive literature review in the PPM research area. In the second step, we selected what we consider the best tool and approach towards solving the alignment problem and the selection of the right projects to the portfolio. The DEA technique was the approach selected. The selection of Indicators, and adequate metrics, to characterize projects, was done based on the literature reviewed. The following topics were considered: strategic alignment, economic and financial analysis, project activities network analysis (pondering the synergies and precedence between projects), discrimination of the number or resources, whether human, technical or financial over the lifetime of the project, per a defined unit of time. However, we decided to make an exploratory study to obtain the project managers professional's opinion about the consistency of the metrics, and about the variance that each metric (KPI) could have, based in their experience. We used the LinkedIn forum and some interviews with project managers for assisting us in this matter. With their feedback, we randomly generated scores for being tested in a small example of the DEA approach.

BACKGROUND

Project Portfolio Management: A Thematic Perspective

According to Martinsuo & Lehtonen (2007, p.57), "Efficiency of project portfolio management, therefore, could be determined by estimating the degree to which the portfolio fulfils its objectives: strategic alignment, balance across projects, and value maximization". In this sense, the projects selection and balancing, the establishment of organizational goals, the resource management and the analysis of the organizational constraints is an extremely important and demanding task (Islei, Lockett, Cox, & Stratford, 1991; Coulon, Ernst, Lichtenthaler & Vollmoeller, 2009; Killen, Hunt, & Kleinschmidt, 2008; Martinsuo & Lehtonen, 2007). The PPM aims to enhance performance and the organizational efficiency (Ireland, 1997), to coordinate interrelated projects and to reduce project life cycle (PMI, 2008; 2013), as well as to acquire and develop learning mechanisms to overcome competition. The PPM processes must include the portfolio alignment within the organization's strategy, the selection of the projects plus adjusted, the allocation and balancing of the organizational resources (Chao, Kavadias, & Gaimon, 2009) and the periodic revaluation of the project mix, to see if the selection is still aligned with key business goals (Kremmel, Kubalík & Biffl, 2011; Reyck, et al, 2005).

Presently, there are several methodologies and models for PPM (Deng, Wang, & Xia, 2000; Ghasemzadeh & Archer, 2000). However, there is no standard structure universally accepted that permits the selection, implementation, monitoring and control of the projects portfolio (Dong, Du, Wang, Chen, & Deng, 2004). The various techniques developed allow us to estimate, evaluate and select the projects portfolio (Cooper, Edgett & Kleinschmidt, 2001). Nevertheless, most of these are not widely used by its complexity and because they require large amounts of input data, which makes them almost inaccessible to understand and use by the majority of the decision agents (Cooper, 1993). Among the techniques available, the optimization approaches are the most common in the quantitative methods (Jackson, 1983) and those which address the most relevant issues. However, in large scale, they failed to capture and to gain acceptability among the users (Mathieu & Gibson, 1993), perhaps by the increase of sophistication and complexity of the models developed without the corresponding practical impact (Hess, 1993). One of the important causes for not adopting these techniques is because they, normally, prescribe solutions for PPS without allowing the proper incorporation of judgment, experience and knowledge of the decision makers.

Project Portfolio Alignment with Organizational Strategy

Projects and project management serve as primary capabilities of an organization to respond to change and thereby maintain a competitive edge (Turner, 1999). Projects may be considered as building blocks in the design and execution of future strategies of the organization (Cleland, 1999). Several authors have emphasized the importance of linking projects and their management to strategy and proposed different models describing how the management processes at a project level or a multi-project levels can be integrated with the organizational strategy management process (Cooper, Edgett, & Kleinschmidt, 1998; Bridges, 1999; Spradlin & Kutolowski, 1999; Englund & Graham, 1999).

The strategic alignment is a key concept in the models of strategy formulation. The incessant search for strategic fit has been traditionally associated with improvements in the organizational performance (Miles & Snow, 1994; Zajac, Kraatz & Bresser, 2000). Xu, Cavusgil & White (2006) studied whether the interrelationships between strategy, organizational structure and processes could influence organizational performance. They concluded that all those dimensions were positively related to the increasing of performance. However, the way to measure performance and efficiency in an organization oriented to projects, should be seen far beyond a mere compliance with time or of budget constraints (Shenhar, Dvir, O. Levy & Maltz, 2001). The criteria that underpin the success of a project should consider its contribution to the organization's strategy. Thus, to measure the success of the organizational projects is essential to evaluate its strategic alignment, particularly in an organizational context with multiple projects.

However, the existing literature about strategic alignment in project management is slightly vague. Some studies point out the relationship between business strategy and project selection as being part of the natural alignment process (Cooper, Edgett & Kleinschmidt, 1998; Englund and Graham, 1999; Hartman, 2000). Others point the dynamic decision process by which an organization updates and reviews its ongoing projects, as a key element for achieving the strategic alignment (Turner and Simister, 2000; Cooper, Edgett and Kleinschmidt, 1998). Other authors such as Henderson & Venkatraman (1999) and Sabherwal, Hirschheim, & Goles (2001) suggest that strategic alignment is an ongoing process with no start date or end. This argument is reinforced by Jarvenpaa & Ives (1993) and Chen, Sun, Helms, & Jih (2008), which consider that the strategic alignment is achieved only in short periods of time and it needs to be continually set for realignment. In an allegorical way, they expose the process of organizational alignment as a "target" in continuous movement, and that only briefly this alignment is achieved and maintained. Nevertheless, it is necessary to understand what does the concept of alignment and if it has repercussions on the functioning of the organization. This concept cannot be analyzed from a purely theoretical or abstract perspective. Necessarily should be translated into concrete and specific organizational mechanisms that support and promote the coveted strategic alignment.

The strategic alignment is an ongoing and dynamic process in which a wide range of internal and external events affect its definition. The monitoring mechanisms are essential for ensure that the strategic alignment can become a reality. However, due to the market dynamics, organizational processes and structure the strategic alignment ambition can become often tortuous and extremely demanding. Therefore, a clear definition of communication channels between top management and middle management, and preferably extends to the whole organization, it is essential to develop a common understanding on the strategic definition of the organization is known for everyone, and everyone feels involved in their definition and implementation. While the literature suggests that the alignment is a deliberate and rational process, there is empirical evidence reported by Rondinelli, Rosen, & Dori (2001) that in practice the alignment process is chaotic, complex and often imperfect. According to the authors, the introduction of lessons learned reinforces the mechanisms of learning, which fosters agility and speed of decisions and promotes the strategic alignment of the organization.

Project Portfolio Selection (PPS)

Shenhar, Dvir, O. Levy, & Maltz (2001) point out that the project portfolios can be transformed into powerful strategic weapons, therefore it can be considered the central blocks of the implementation of the idealized strategy (Dietrich & Lehtonen, 2005; Grundy, 2000). The main areas of influence of organizational strategy are reflected on the future positioning of the organization (organizational objectives), management of organizational resources and in the design of new ideas, or in identifying new market opportunities that may be materialize in the development new organizational designs.

One of the problems often pointed by organizations is the lack of available resources and the strategic 'myopia'. Although the organization may possess the necessary resources, often they do not contribute to achieving the planned performance. This situation will lead us to the problem of resource allocation in the organization. However, an important question is raised by Wheelwright & Clark (1992), in theirs' analogy of the "canary cage" as a parallel to project portfolio management. They make an interesting association between the various canaries and project portfolio, highlighting the impact of the behavior of the new canaries (projects) when put it in the cage without assessing their effect on pre-existing canaries in the cage, and vice versa. The project portfolio management teams are often worried and burdened with issues such as projects' prioritization, the redeployment of staff, decision processes, strategic alignment, among many other routine issues of management (Artto & Dietrich, 2004; Patanakul & Milosevic 2009), which consume completely the project team and limit time available to consider and study the changing and multiple effects of the projects in the portfolio. Wheelwright & Clark (1992) and Engwall & Jerbrant (2003) argue that the redistribution of organizational resources generally produces negative effects in the most unexpected places of the portfolio. So, to overcome this, there is a necessity for these to be considered into the strategic definition process and priority function of the projects within the portfolio.

Among the first scholars who focused on PPM, the research emphasis was on choosing the right number of projects (Blichfeldt & Eskerod, 2008). Thus, the researchers suggested several approaches, which consider various aspects of the PPM problem, namely, the strategic intent of the project, factors for project selection, and several qualitative and quantitative project selection models have been thoroughly discussed by Meredith & Mantle (2000). The Portfolio selection involves a comparison of projects, which compete between each other. There are numerous portfolio selection techniques that can be used to carry out the desired portfolio selection. Some of them will be briefly mentioned: a) Ad hoc approaches; b) Comparative approaches including Q-Sort (Souder, 1984), pair wise comparison (Martino,

1995), the Analytic Hierarchy Procedure (AHP) (Saaty *et al.*, 1980; Dey & Gupta, 2001); c) Scoring models (Martino, 1995); d) Portfolio matrices (Hax & Majluf, 1996) generally used as strategic decision making tools, and also to allocate resources among competing projects; e) and Optimization models (Abdelaziz, Aouni, & Fayedh, 2007; Doerner, Gutjahr, Hartl, Strauss, & Stummer, 2006; Kavadias & Loch, 2003), fuzzy and artificial intelligence algorithms (Lin & Hsieh, 2004; Costantino, Di Gravio, & Nonino, 2015) which are generally based on some form of mathematical programming, to support the optimization process and to include project interactions such as resource dependencies and constraints.

The literature reviewed covers several different knowledge areas which contribute to the decision-making process of project portfolio selection, addressing different approaches, applications tools, and methodologies. Mehrez & Sinuany-Stern (1983) used utility function and Dey, Tabucanon, & Ogunlana (1996) applied the goal programming. Coffin & Taylor (1996) used fuzzy theory for the project selection process. Ghasemzadeh & Archer (2000) presented a 0–1 integer linear programming model for selecting and scheduling an optimal project portfolio. AHP has been used by Dey & Gupta (2001) to resolve decision-making issues in project selection. Matheson & Matheson (1998), for example, described the importance of developing an organizational strategy previous to the selection of the R&D Portfolio. Kendall & Rollins (2003) highlighted the importance of the top management support in the resolution of the resources distribution and reprioritization problem. Jeffrey & Leliveld (2003) noticed some basic team skills to build a proper business case, like understanding the assumptions behind those calculations, analyzing the sensitivity of these results and evaluating the risks that might impact project returns.

Several techniques were developed towards properly assessing the financial value of projects (Benaroch, 2002: McGrath & MacMillan, 2000). Most importantly, however, one should choose a valuation methodology, be it return on investment (ROI), internal rate of return (IRR), net present value (NPV) or economic value added (EVA), or a mixture of them, and consistently apply it/them. Thorp (1999) identified the following types of interdependencies: sequential dependencies, overlapping outcomes, competition for scarce resources, and change bottlenecks. Goldman (1999) highlighted the typical constraints that should be managed in the portfolio alignment process: scarce human resources, staff capabilities, budgets and infrastructure. Projects are unique in nature. Hence, each model has its own pros and cons for various applications. Datz (2003) points out the main benefits organizations should expect from adopting PPM approaches. These include: (1) maximizing the value of IT investments while minimizing risk, (2) improving communication and alignment between IT and business leaders, and (3) encouraging business leaders to act as team players, allowing planners to allocate resources more efficiently and to terminate projects.

Since the original DEA study presented by Charnes, Cooper and Rhodes (1978), there has been a rapid dissemination of this technique in several research fields. Over then 3,000 publications were produced in the last 40 years. DEA is a very flexible method of comparing the efficiency performance of various decision-making units (DMUs). The definition of the DMU is quite flexible, although it is common to be associated to individuals, organizations, and in our case the DMUS will be projects. DEA is concerned with measuring the relative efficiency of the various DMUs as they convert their inputs into outputs. As a non-parametric method, DEA does not require or assume any functional relationship between the inputs and outputs. Instead, a weighting scheme is used.

Among the multitude of problems related to project portfolio selection, this work is focused on the projects analysis towards constituting the portfolio. Cooper, Seiford, Thanassoulis, & Zanakis (2004) presented several examples of applications of the DEA in multiple situations and different activity sectors like: banking, hospitals, universities, police, telecommunications, army, etc. The DEA capabilities, in our opinion, can turn it into a powerful technique to rank the portfolio' candidate projects, assessing different Key Performance Indicators (KPIs).

DATA ENVELOPMENT ANALYSIS (D.E.A.) APPROACH

Data Envelopment Analysis (DEA), a non-parametric linear programming method, was used to assess the projects indicators and choose the proper ones to the portfolio based on their performance. DEA was introduced by Charnes, Cooper, & Rhodes (1978) and it is a fractional programming model that estimates the relative efficiencies of a homogeneous set of units by considering multiple sets of inputs and outputs. According to Charnes, Cooper, & Rhodes (1978), DEA has the following advantages in assessing project productivity: a) it does not require functional relationships between inputs and outputs; b) multiple inputs and outputs can be considered concurrently; c) it has the ability to identify inefficient projects; and d) using DEA sensitivity analysis, the sources and amounts of inefficiency for each inefficient project can be found.

A conventional single performance criterion, whether it measures profitability, strategic focus, project value added, is clearly insufficient to determine the excellence of an enterprise. Consequently, several studies suggested that a multi-factor performance measurement model should be used to characterize it (Chin, Pun, & Lau, 2003). DEA uses a mathematical programming model to estimate best-practice frontiers without a priori underlying functional form assumption through computing multi-input/multi-output values (Guan & Ma, 2003). The major advantage of the DEA approach is not to require any assumptions about the function form. That means that DEA does not need any prior information on the underlying functional forms and weights among various input and output factors. Thus, DEA is particularly suitable for analyzing multiple inputs and multiple outputs production systems (Charnes, Cooper, Golany, Seiford, & Stutz, 1985; Zhu, 2000, 2002).

The method introduced by Charnes, Cooper & Rhodes (1978) was subsequently applied to measure the efficiency of many organizations in the public and private sectors. The DEA method has been extensively used by researchers to evaluate the efficiency of both non-profit organizations such as schools, hospitals and military operations, as in organizations with lucrative purposes, such as banks, restaurants, etc. Mathematically, the DEA model equates to the resolution of the corresponding linear programming problem where the relative efficiency value is obtained by the ratio of the weighted sum of outputs to the weighted sum of inputs, as well as the sensitivity analysis of the solution. The modelling provides to the decision-maker the possibility to create scenarios and simulating situations in search of the greatest possible efficiency of its organizational unit, comparing it with the results obtained by the competition.

In addition to, it is possible to highlight the organizational units more efficient, known as Units-Reference, whose efficiency serves as basis for comparison to other units (peer group). The DEA allows the performance evaluation of an Organizational Unit among a number of organizational units that have the same inputs and outputs. In this sense, there is the notion of relative efficiency, meaning an Organizational Unit reaches a certain degree of efficiency, as compared to an efficient Organizational-Unit, with the same set of inputs and outputs. Thus, the improvements that this unit must pursue to become efficient can be identified.

As being a technique for assessing relative efficiency of comparable units, with a view to improve their performances, the DEA requires that the units are part of a homogeneous whole, where comparisons of Organizational Units make sense. A group of units can be uniform to meet the objectives of the DEA when: 1) the units into account perform the same tasks with the same goals; 2) the variables (inputs and outputs) which characterize the performance of all the group's units are equal, except for differences in intensity or magnitude. Thus, by analogy, it is assumed that the organizational units are the projects in the evaluation and selection process for the portfolio.

As mentioned above, the efficiency measure (h_0) is obtained as follows (Equations 1 e 2):

$$Efficiency = \frac{Weighted\ Sum\ of\ Outputs}{Weighted\ Sum\ of\ Inputs} \quad (1)$$

The objective function of the CCR (Charnes, Cooper and Rhodes) model:

$$\max h_0 = \frac{\sum_{r=1}^{t} U_r Y_{rj_0}}{\sum_{i=1}^{m} V_i X_{ij_0}} \quad (2)$$

Subject to

$$\begin{aligned} &\frac{\sum_r U_r Y_{rj}}{\sum_i V_i X_{ij}} \leq 1, for\ each\ project\ j \\ &U_r, V_i \geq \in \\ &j = 1,\ldots,n; r = 1,\ldots,t; i = 1,\ldots,m \end{aligned} \quad (3)$$

where

$U_r = weight\ attributed\ to\ output\ r$
$Y_{rj} = value\ of\ output\ r\ in\ Project\ j$
$V_i = weight\ attributed\ to\ input\ i$
$X_{ij} = value\ of\ input\ i\ in\ Project\ j$
$\in = small\ positive\ amount$

According to the results obtained through Equation (3):

For h_0 equals to 1 – the respective Target Unit is efficient relative to other Organizational Units;
For h_0 less than 1 – the respective Target Unit is not efficient relative to other Organizational Units.

Thus, to obtain the efficiency value of h_0 for a target unit it must be adapted to the objective function, so that the weights chosen for the multiple inputs and outputs are the ones that best characterize the Organizational Unit. As can be seen, the CCR model is not linear (fractional programming). The technique used for its linearization is linear programming. Thus, the DEA model becomes a linear programming model (Cooper, Seiford, & Tone, 2007; Joro, Korhonen, & Wallenius, 1998; Aoki, Sato, & Tsuji, 2006; Charnes, Cooper & Rhodes, 1978).

Normally to simplify the process of obtaining the solution, it is preferred to use the DUAL model of this problem, for two distinct reasons. Firstly, because the computational effort to solve the linear programming model (PRIMAL) grows in proportion to the power of the number of restrictions.

Typically, the number of DMUs, in this case projects, is considered greater than the sum of inputs and outputs, which requires more time and memory for obtaining a solution. Secondly, the PRIMAL resolution cannot determine the maximum solution of the slacks (Cooper, Seiford, & Tone, 2007). In the example presented, the number of projects under consideration is 7, which is clearly lower than the sum of the inputs and outputs (5 + 5 = 10). The application of DEA requires the definition of a set of project performance indicators, which were thought to be generic and diversified. The proposed indicators come from different elements whose combination produces essential information to the project alignment, the economic evaluation, the financial and operational conditions and, therefore, enables a rather complete and appropriate selection of the projects towards the portfolio constitution.

To apply the DEA, we began by defining a group of indicators. The indicators proposed were developed based on the literature review performed, complemented with the authors' sensibility on the subject and supported by the project managers' professional opinion about the consistency of the metrics, based in their experience. The combination of these elements produces information considered critical to guarantee the project alignment, the economic, financial and operational assessment of the project towards selecting the proper portfolio. The indicators are divided in inputs and outputs, and their description/characterization can be seen below.

D.E.A: Inputs

X1 = $\dfrac{Project\ Schedule}{Market\ Clock\ speed}$: This indicator trics to assess the gap between the project lifetime and the market dynamics. Thus, the selection of projects must be aligned with the market's clock speed. For example, it makes no sense to develop projects during two years when the market changes every six months, i.e. the ratio should be less than 1.

X2 = $\dfrac{Nr.\ Critical\ Resources}{Total\ Nr.\ of\ Resources}$: This indicator measures the concentration of important organizational resources per project. The organizational resources are scarce, and the concentration must be properly determined towards increasing the profitability of the resources.

X3 = Cost/Benefit Ratio: The cost benefit analysis lists project revenues with the expenses in terms of ratio. It is a crude indicator, it does not take into account the time when the expenses or revenues occur, but it is usually appreciated by companies. A project is considered profitable when the cost/benefit ratio <1, i.e. when the benefits outweighs the costs. An investment project is all the more interesting the lower the cost/benefit ratio.

X4 = Risk Perception: The risk perception is quantified by the decision agents and varies between 0 and 5, being 0 the absence of risk and 5 corresponding to the most complex and sensitive environments in which the degree of volatility is very high;

X5 = Critical Path Method (CPM): It is a technique widely used for determining the optimum duration and sequence of the network activities of a project which includes a list of all activities required to complete the project, the time (duration) that each activity will take to completion, and the dependencies between the activities

D.E.A: Outputs

Y1 = ROI: This indicator reflects the return on investment (ROI). Despite of the literature indication that the selection of projects should not only rely on economic and financial indicators, it is of common and mandatory use. Projects must have this type of information available. This indicator is usually presented in monetary values or percentage.

Y2 = Net Present Value (NPV): This indicator determines the present value of the project's cash flows at a given interest rate.

Y3 = Internal Return Rate (IRR): This indicator represents the maximum return rate of the project. It means that it is the discounted rate that, for the whole project's lifetime, turns the NPV equal to zero.

Y4 = Gross Value Added (GVA): A productivity metric that measures the difference between output and intermediate consumption. Gross value added provides a quantity of money for the amount of goods and services that have been produced, less the cost of all inputs and raw materials that are directly attributable to that production.

Y5 = Degree of Innovation Expected: The degree of innovation expected varies between 0 and 5, and quantifies the level of impact that each project may have on the technological structure, and its level of attractiveness in emerging markets that can enhance organizational performance.

D.E.A.: Theoretical Example

The evaluation and selection phase of projects portfolio, according to the DEA method, was accomplished using the software package DEA-Warwick, developed at the University of Warwick (Thanassoulis, 2001). This has an interface with two windows: a data table (input file - Input), and a file "log" as a text output. The input text file has a specific format and presents one of the software window in tabular form. Subsequently, the list of inputs and outputs, select and refer them to the appropriate indicators lists. (See Figure 3) The menu "Execute" provides for the use of priorities for variables such as: 1) efficiencies, which sets the limits, lower and upper; 2) peer groups; 3) "targets"; and 4) weights. (See Figure 4).

Figure 1 identifies 7 projects under review with the 10 indicators presented above for the evaluation and selection process.

Figure 2 presents the options menu for the model selection and of the objective function type, among other elements. In this case, it is intended to maximize the outputs and minimize the inputs, so both options have been selected. After selecting the model and the type of objective function it is necessary to create a list of inputs and outputs (Figure 3), and establish the difference between them. In the case of inputs, no project is efficient if it is possible to reduce one of the inputs, increase other or reduce the value of any output. For outputs, no project will be considered effective if to increase an output it is required the reduction of other output or the increasing of an input value.

Figure 1. DEA's input data: projects indicators values

	KPI1	KPI2	KPI3	KPI4	KPI5	KPI6	KPI7	KPI8	KPI9	KPI10
PROJECTO1	69.00	30.00	67.00	22605.00	65.70	28.50	33790.00	50.00	6.87	70.00
PROJECTO2	20.00	13.00	25.00	1449.00	20.20	9.00	3440.00	85.00	2.00	20.00
PROJECTO3	17.00	25.00	10.00	-269.00	-4.40	63.20	1750.00	40.00	1.70	30.00
PROJECTO4	27.00	13.00	55.00	1120.00	16.50	35.10	3092.00	50.00	2.73	50.00
PROJECTO5	17.00	40.00	-5.00	-1115.00	-33.30	187.90	705.00	20.00	1.70	45.00
PROJECTO6	60.00	45.00	-10.00	-3769.10	-23.20	283.10	1050.00	40.00	6.00	30.00
PROJECTO7	34.00	40.00	-20.00	-3088.60	-42.30	326.90	800.00	50.00	2.43	40.00

Figure 2. Model selection and objective function type

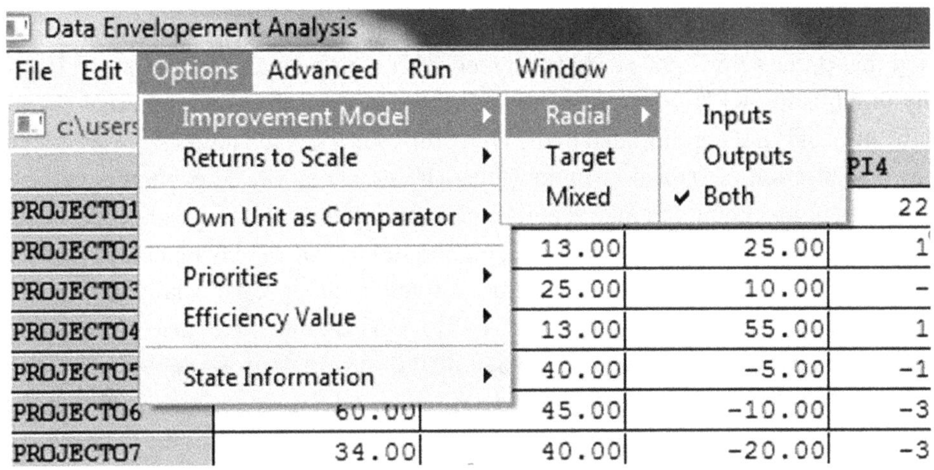

Figure 3. Inputs and outputs selection

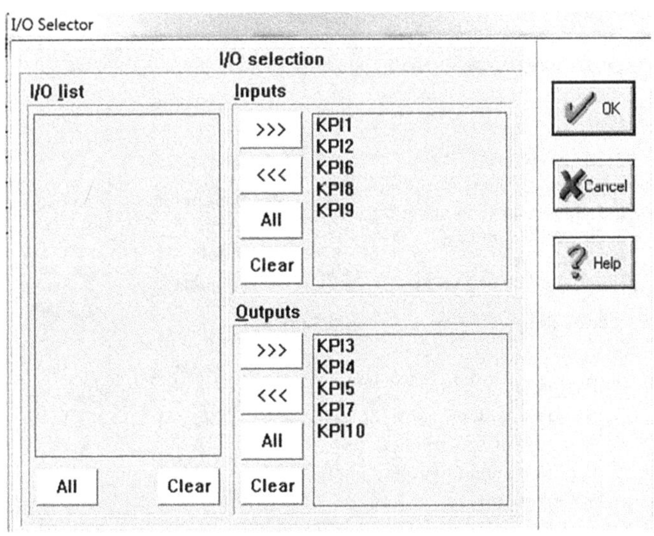

Figure 4 shows the parameterizations menu, wherein it is assumed that the model is radial with constant returns to scale and which seeks to optimize both elements (inputs and outputs). The final DEA output lists the efficiencies, and shows the number of efficient projects obtained. Additionally, it provides key information for sensitivity analysis in order to assess the inefficient projects and to address the right actions towards becoming equally efficient.

Figure 5 shows the list of efficient projects, which take the value 100. So, as we can see the projects that should be selected for the portfolio are: P_1, P_2, P_4 and P_5. The projects P_6, P_7 and P_3 were not able to attain the efficiency curve. The output allows us to know, for each of the inefficient projects, which are their peer projects and what should be done to reverse the situation, either through the reduction of inputs or by increasing outputs. Therefore, through a detail analysis of project P6 and its KPIs' behavior, it can be mentioned that project P6 is not properly aligned with the organizational strategy. In particular, by the necessity of adjusting KPI1 which is related with the project schedule vs. market clock speed. The duration of the project is not appropriated to the type of market in which it will be inserted. Furthermore, it presents a concentration of critical resources for its implementation. This point is very sensitive and creates difficulties in managing the interdependencies among the portfolio and therefore the risk associated with the implementation of this project is higher and it also can be supported by the value of its CPM (KPI9). In the same way, the outputs are not attractive enough, especially, those outputs related to the economic-financial behavior (KPI3, KPI4, KPI5, KPI7) and to the degree of innovation expected (KPI10). Thus, the P6 project can take advantage of the information available by its peer's projects (P1 and P5) to test the sensitivity and analyze what it needs to change towards attaining the efficiency curve. Any of the scenarios presented by its peer projects is valid and ensures the maximum score (100), hence the possibility of being selected to the portfolio. Some of the adjustments are feasible and easier to perform, other are extremely demanding and might clash with the idiosyncrasies and vicissitudes inherent to the project. In Figure 6, the DEA output data is presented in the form of percentage changes

Figure 4. Menu execute: parameters selection

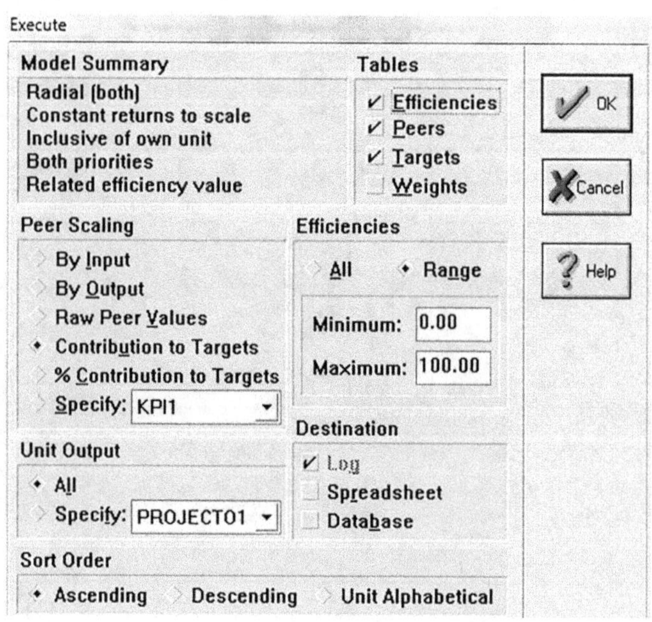

Figure 5. Final DEA output data: table of efficiencies and peers

```
Input/output radial model will be used
Table of efficiencies (radial)

 43.64 PROJECTO6   70.35 PROJECTO7   88.54 PROJECTO3
100.00 PROJECTO1  100.00 PROJECTO2  100.00 PROJECTO4
100.00 PROJECTO5

Table of peer units
Peers for Unit PROJECTO6 efficiency    43.64% radial
 PROJECTO6                 PROJECTO1  PROJECTO5
    ACTUAL       LAMBDA        0.304      0.456
      60.0 -KPI1                21.0        7.7
      45.0 -KPI2                 9.1       18.2
     283.1 -KPI6                 8.7       85.6
      40.0 -KPI8                15.2        9.1
       6.0 -KPI9                 2.1        0.8
     -10.0 +KPI3                20.4       -2.3
   -3769.1 +KPI4              6867.3     -508.1
     -23.2 +KPI5                20.0      -15.2
    1050.0 +KPI7             10265.3      321.3
      30.0 +KPI10               21.3       20.5

Peers for Unit PROJECTO7 efficiency    70.35% radial
 PROJECTO7                 PROJECTO4  PROJECTO5
    ACTUAL       LAMBDA        0.277      0.736
      34.0 -KPI1                 7.5       12.5
      40.0 -KPI2                 3.6       29.4
     326.9 -KPI6                 9.7      138.3
      50.0 -KPI8                13.8       14.7
       2.4 -KPI9                 0.8        1.3
     -20.0 +KPI3                15.2       -3.7
   -3088.6 +KPI4               310.1     -820.6
     -42.3 +KPI5                 4.6      -24.5
     800.0 +KPI7               856.2      518.8
      40.0 +KPI10               13.8       33.1

Peers for Unit PROJECTO3 efficiency    88.54% radial
 PROJECTO3                 PROJECTO1  PROJECTO4  PROJECTO5
    ACTUAL       LAMBDA        0.013      0.404      0.239
      17.0 -KPI1                 0.9       10.9        4.1
      25.0 -KPI2                 0.4        5.2        9.5
      63.2 -KPI6                 0.4       14.2       44.8
      40.0 -KPI8                 0.7       20.2        4.8
       1.7 -KPI9                 0.1        1.1        0.4
      10.0 +KPI3                 0.9       22.2       -1.2
    -269.0 +KPI4               294.7      451.9     -266.0
      -4.4 +KPI5                 0.9        6.7       -7.9
    1750.0 +KPI7               440.5     1247.7      168.2
      30.0 +KPI10                0.9       20.2       10.7
```

that will be needed to ensure that inefficient projects might be converted into equally efficient projects. Thus, the DEA output data identifies the "target" projects and inefficient projects, further indicating the percentage that must be improved so that the scenario could be reversed.

The output data provided by the software package DEA-Warwick allows to obtain a relative ranking of the organizational units, in this case projects. The DEA output data allows knowing the "target" value that each project should achieve, assessing the robustness of the solutions and enhancing the sensitivity testing. Under these circumstances, it is possible to correct strategies and redefine news orientations to the inefficient projects towards attaining the efficiency level. The Projects that achieved 1 are the ones who reached the maximum level of efficiency. Those are the ones that should be considered for the project portfolio selection. Projects which are not efficient can be adjusted based on assessing the data provided by the DEA output pointing which indicators must be improved to reach the efficiency level. Therefore, it shows the potential for future reassessment – where projects can be improved.

Figure 6. Final DEA output data: table of efficiencies and targets

Table of target values

Targets for Unit PROJECT06 efficiency 43.64% radial

VARIABLE	ACTUAL	TARGET	TO GAIN	ACHIEVED
-KPI1	60.0	28.7	52.2%	47.8%
-KPI2	45.0	27.3	39.2%	60.8%
-KPI6	283.1	94.3	66.7%	33.3%
-KPI8	40.0	24.3	39.2%	60.8%
-KPI9	6.0	2.9	52.3%	47.7%
+KPI3	-10.0	18.1		-55.3%
+KPI4	-3769.1	6359.2		-59.3%
+KPI5	-23.2	4.8		-484.9%
+KPI7	1050.0	10586.6	908.2%	9.9%
+KPI10	30.0	41.8	39.2%	71.8%

Targets for Unit PROJECT07 efficiency 70.35% radial

VARIABLE	ACTUAL	TARGET	TO GAIN	ACHIEVED
-KPI1	34.0	20.0	41.2%	58.8%
-KPI2	40.0	33.0	17.4%	82.6%
-KPI6	326.9	148.0	54.7%	45.3%
-KPI8	50.0	28.6	42.9%	57.1%
-KPI9	2.4	2.0	17.4%	82.6%
+KPI3	-20.0	11.5		-173.2%
+KPI4	-3088.6	-510.5		
+KPI5	-42.3	-19.9		
+KPI7	800.0	1375.0	71.9%	58.2%
+KPI10	40.0	47.0	17.4%	85.2%

Targets for Unit PROJECT03 efficiency 88.54% radial

VARIABLE	ACTUAL	TARGET	TO GAIN	ACHIEVED
-KPI1	17.0	15.8	6.8%	93.2%
-KPI2	25.0	15.2	39.3%	60.7%
-KPI6	63.2	59.4	6.1%	93.9%
-KPI8	40.0	25.6	36.0%	64.0%
-KPI9	1.7	1.6	6.1%	93.9%
+KPI3	10.0	21.9	118.7%	45.7%
+KPI4	-269.0	480.6		-56.0%
+KPI5	-4.4	-0.4		
+KPI7	1750.0	1856.3	6.1%	94.3%
+KPI10	30.0	31.8	6.1%	94.3%

With the utilization of this technique it is advised to perform a close monitoring to the different phases commonly considered in the project portfolio management, especially with the project strategic alignment, as well as the monitoring and control phase. It is also extremely important to involve the top management of the company as well as the leading project managers from the project management office (PMO). This is clearly an utmost factor towards guaranteeing the organizational learning process through the compilation of lessons learned.

FUTURE RESEARCH DIRECTIONS

As future developments, there is an ambition to apply this approach to some business sectors and companies of different sizes and complexities, as well as to compile and identify a set of metrics adjusted to any business area and to a special context of an organization. The aim is also providing a significant number of different tools and techniques, so that depending on the organization's level of maturity in project management, complexity and size, technology and skills, the most suitable and efficient approach will be suggested.

Other future work we intend to undertake, is to model in detail all the following phases of the project portfolio selection and management, in one or more organizations with a strong tradition in managing portfolios, and with an extensive history data to analyze and compare the decisions taken and the techniques used with the new approaches developed. The following phases previously mentioned will be treated, namely adapting or developing a technique or model for assigning and balancing the organizational scarce resources, and, finally, introducing a way to monitor and control the whole system where all the different phases take part.

This broad and integrative approach is mandatory to produce an awakening call into the organization. PPM goes beyond the adoption of one or other technique or even of a particular software. If that was the case, all the organizations were extremely efficient which is not the reality. Therefore, if the organizations have the intention to be different from competition and aspire to the development of sustainable competitive advantages, which are difficult to replicate, they must take into account several aspects, namely (PMI & Deloitte, 2015): a) connect project execution with the organization' strategic roadmap; b) seek simplicity in the adoption and selection of tools and techniques; c) create a portfolio-oriented culture, focused in the capacitation of the workers with the purpose of developing strong competencies. Organizations that encourage this type of environment will definitely gain higher analytical power, which will contribute to making better and faster decisions, more awareness to the lessons learned during the portfolio management and therefore greater organizational maturity.

Finally, as mentioned by Roth & Kleiner (1998, p.58), "Good intentions are not enough to guarantee improvements – commitment, support and skill are all essential. Furthermore, a clear and shared understanding of the organization's objectives is important if organization's are to learn collectively and thereby reap the significant benefits associated with collaborative reflection".

CONCLUSION

The organizational urge for using and applying new tools, methods and techniques for increasing their competitiveness is tremendous. The market competitive pressing, the reduction of error margins and the need to do things perfectly at the first shot are creating an increasing demand for solutions that can resolve those problems, achieving the best performance possible with the minimum risk and cost. There is no consensus about the type of method or technique that automatically improves any organization, despite of their own problems or status, restrictions and competitive advantages, strengths and weaknesses. Nevertheless, project management tries to see the organization as a whole, and systematically challenge the difficulties encountered with new re-thinking processes in order to increase the organizational performance.

The project management literature is rich in presenting several techniques and methods for the selection of projects portfolio. However, despite of numerous examples found, these do not solve the problems of simultaneously treating strategic alignment of projects and weighting of generic metrics, in order to improve the projects portfolio selection process. So it is very important to develop a flexible decision support system that takes into account all the more appropriate selection criteria for projects under review, involving the decision makers in this process and giving users a quick analysis tool that helps them assess the impacts and consequences of changes produced in the projects portfolio (Andersen & Jessen, 2003).

Thus, this paper presents an innovative approach for selecting the portfolio of projects by using DEA, and the development of a group of generic indicators, to support the decision makers in considering multiple projects. Each decision maker can use all or some of the indicators proposed, thus each one's participation, knowledge, sensitivity and intuition are considered, namely for indicators such as risk perception, level of innovation, market clock speed, project's complexity. This is also considered a critical factor for successful implementation of a technique, which is, achieving the involvement of top management. It is easier when they fully understand the method and actively participate in the decision process. The development of the indicators proposed is not a closed process. According to the business area and the projects' unique characteristics it might be necessary to introduce new metrics. However, we believe that the indicators presented are a good starting point and generic enough to be able to be applied in any business area.

The utility gained with the application of DEA for selecting the right projects to the portfolio is unquestionable. Despite of not having perform any comparison between the different methods described in the literature. It is possible to claim that the DEA adoption for the PPS predicts the pre-screening of projects for ensuring the portfolio' alignment, allows the maintenance of projects that might be able to became efficient and throughout the sensitivity analysis it is possible to 'kill projects' which is one of the hardest tasks that is needed to perform during the PPM.

REFERENCES

Abdelaziz, F. B., Aouni, B., & Fayedh, R. E. (2007). Multi-objective stochastic programming for portfolio selection. *European Journal of Operational Research, 177*(3), 1811–1823. doi:10.1016/j.ejor.2005.10.021

Aga, D. A., Noorderhaven, N., & Vallejo, B. (2016). Transformational leadership and project success: The mediating role of team-building. *International Journal of Project Management, 34*(5), 806–818. doi:10.1016/j.ijproman.2016.02.012

Amaral, A., & Araújo, M. (2009). Market attractiveness index: a decision analysis technique for market assessment. In *International Conference on Industrial Engineering and Systems Management* (pp. 1080–1093). IESM.

Amaral, A., Araújo, M., & Pereira, G. (2010). A Multi-Criteria Decision Model for Dynamically Managing the Projects Portfolio. In *VI European-Latin-American Workshop on Engineering Systems* (pp. 270–277). SELASI.

Andersen, E. S., & Jessen, S. A. (2003). Project maturity in organisations. *International Journal of Project Management, 21*(6), 457–461. doi:10.1016/S0263-7863(02)00088-1

Aoki, S., Sato, Y., & Tsuji, H. (2006). *DEA as Strategy Decision Tool for Performance Improvement. IEEE International Conference on Systems, Man and Cybernetics.* https://doi.org/10.1109/ICSMC.2006.384681

Archer, N. P., & Ghasemzadeh, F. (1999). An integrated framework for project portfolio selection. *International Journal of Project Management, 17*(4), 207–216. doi:10.1016/S0263-7863(98)00032-5

Artto, K., & Dietrich, P. (2004). Strategic business management through multiple projects. In P. Morris & J. K. Pinto (Eds.), *The Wiley guide to managing projects* (pp. 144–176). London: John Wiley & Sons.

Benaroch, M. (2002). Managing Information Technology Investment Risk: A Real Options Perspective. *Journal of Management Information Systems, 19*(2), 43–84.

Björk, E., & Ottosson, S. (2007). Aspects of consideration in product development research. *Journal of Engineering Design*, *18*(3), 195–207. doi:10.1080/09544820600675966

Blichfeldt, B. S., & Eskerod, P. (2008). Project portfolio management – Theres more to it than what management enacts. *International Journal of Project Management*, *26*(4), 357–365. doi:10.1016/j.ijproman.2007.06.004

Bridges, D. (1999). Project portfolio management: ideas and practices. In L. Dye & J. Pennypacker (Eds.), *Project portfolio management – selecting and prioritizing projects for competitive advantage* (pp. 45–54). West Chester, PA: Center for Business Practices.

Chao, R. O., Kavadias, S., & Gaimon, C. (2009). Revenue Driven Resource Allocation: Funding Authority, Incentives, and New Product Development Portfolio Management. *Management Science*, *55*(9), 1556–1569. doi:10.1287/mnsc.1090.1046

Charnes, A., Cooper, W. W., Golany, B., Seiford, L., & Stutz, J. (1985). Foundations of data envelopment analysis for Pareto-Koopmans efficient empirical production functions. *Journal of Econometrics*, *30*(1), 91–107. doi:10.1016/0304-4076(85)90133-2

Charnes, A., Cooper, W. W., & Rhodes, E. (1978). Measuring the efficiency of decision making units. *European Journal of Operational Research*, *2*(6), 429–444. doi:10.1016/0377-2217(78)90138-8

Chen, R.-S., Sun, C.-M., & Helms, M. M. (2008). Aligning information technology and business strategy with a dynamic capabilities perspective: A longitudinal study of a Taiwanese Semiconductor Company. *International Journal of Information Management, 28*(5), 366–378. https://doi.org/10.1016/j.ijinfomgt.2008.01.015

Chen, S. H., & Lee, H. T. (2007). Performance evaluation model for project managers using managerial practices. *International Journal of Project Management*, *25*(6), 543–551. doi:10.1016/j.ijproman.2007.03.004

Chin, K.-S., Pun, K.-F., & Lau, H. (2003). Development of a knowledge-based self-assessment system for measuring organisational performance. *Expert Systems with Applications*, *24*(4), 443–455. doi:10.1016/S0957-4174(02)00192-6

Chu, P.-Y. V., Hsu, Y.-L., & Fehling, M. (1996). A decision support system for project portfolio selection. *Computers in Industry*, *32*(2), 141–149. doi:10.1016/S0166-3615(96)00067-X

Cleland, D. I. (1999). The strategic context of projects. In L. Dye & J. Pennypacker (Eds.), *Project portfolio management – selecting and prioritizing projects for competitive advantage* (pp. 3–22). West Chester, PA: Center for Business Practices.

Coffin, M. A., & Taylor, B. W. III. (1996). Multiple criteria R&D project selection and scheduling using fuzzy logic. *Computers & Operations Research*, *23*(3), 207–220. doi:10.1016/0305-0548(96)81768-0

Cooke-Davies, T. (2002). The real success factors on projects. *International Journal of Project Management*, *20*(3), 185–190. doi:10.1016/S0263-7863(01)00067-9

Cooper, R., Edgett, S., & Kleinschmidt, E. (2001). Portfolio management for new product development: Results of an industry practices study. *R & D Management*, *31*(4), 361–380. doi:10.1111/1467-9310.00225

Cooper, R. G. (1993). *Winning at New Products: Accelerating the Process from Idea to Launch.* Cambridge, MA: Perseus Publishing.

Cooper, R. G., Edgett, S. J., & Kleinschmidt, E. J. (1998). Best Practices for Managing R&D Portfolios. *Research-Technology Management, 41*(4), 20–33. https://doi.org/10.1080/08956308.1998.11671219

Cooper, R. G., Edgett, S. J., & Kleinschmidt, E. J. (2000). New Problems, New Solutions: Making Portfolio Management More Effective. *Research-Technology Management, 43*(2), 18–33. https://doi.org/10.1080/08956308.2000.11671338

Cooper, R. G., Edgett, S. J., & Kleinschmidt, E. J. (2004a). Benchmarking Best NPD Practices—I. *Research-Technology Management, 47*(1), 31–43. https://doi.org/10.1080/08956308.2004.11671606

Cooper, R. G., Edgett, S. J., & Kleinschmidt, E. J. (2004b). Benchmarking Best NPD Practices—II. *Research-Technology Management, 47*(3), 50–59. https://doi.org/10.1080/08956308.2004.11671630

Cooper, W. W., Seiford, L. M., Thanassoulis, E., & Zanakis, S. H. (2004). DEA and its uses in different countries. *European Journal of Operational Research, 154*(2), 337–344. doi:10.1016/S0377-2217(03)00173-5

Cooper, W. W., Seiford, L. M., & Tone, K. (2007). *Data Envelopment Analysis: A Comprehensive Text with Models, Applications, References and DEA-Solver Software* (2nd ed.). New York: Springer.

Costantino, F., Di Gravio, G., & Nonino, F. (2015). Project selection in project portfolio management: An artificial neural network model based on critical success factors. *International Journal of Project Management, 33*(8), 1744–1754. doi:10.1016/j.ijproman.2015.07.003

Coulon, M., Ernst, H., Lichtenthaler, U., & Vollmoeller, J. (2009). An overview of tools for managing the corporate innovation portfolio. *International Journal of Technology Intelligence and Planning, 5*(2), 221–239. doi:10.1504/IJTIP.2009.024191

Datz, T. (2003). Portfolio management – how to do it right. *CIO Magazine,* (2).

Deng, X., Wang, S., & Xia, Y. (2000). Criteria, Models and Strategies in Portfolio Selection. *Advanced Modeling and Optimization, 2*(2), 79–104.

Dey, P. K., & Gupta, S. S. (2001). Feasibility analysis of crosscountry pipeline projects: A quantitative approach. *Project Management Journal, 32*(4), 50–58.

Dey, P. K., Tabucanon, M. T., & Ogunlana, S. O. (1996). Hierarchical approach to project planning. *Hierarchical Approach to Project Planning. Applied Mathematical Modelling, 20*(9), 683–698. doi:10.1016/0307-904X(96)00049-2

Dietrich, P., & Lehtonen, P. (2005). Successful management of strategic intentions through multiple projects – Reflections from empirical study. *International Journal of Project Management, 23*(5), 386–391. doi:10.1016/j.ijproman.2005.03.002

Doerner, K. F., Gutjahr, W. J., Hartl, R. F., Strauss, C., & Stummer, C. (2006). Pareto ant colony optimization with ILP preprocessing in multiobjective project portfolio selection. *European Journal of Operational Research, 171*(3), 830–841. doi:10.1016/j.ejor.2004.09.009

Dong, J., Du, H. S., Wang, S., Chen, K., & Deng, X. (2004). A framework of Web-based Decision Support Systems for portfolio selection with OLAP and PVM. *Decision Support Systems*, *37*(3), 367–376. doi:10.1016/S0167-9236(03)00034-4

Eik-Andresen, P., Johansen, A., Landmark, A. D., & Sørensen, A. Ø. (2016). Controlling a Multibillion Project Portfolio - Milestones as Key Performance Indicator for Project Portfolio Management. *Procedia: Social and Behavioral Sciences*, *226*, 294–301. doi:10.1016/j.sbspro.2016.06.191

Elonen, S., & Artto, K. A. (2003). Problems in managing internal development projects in multi-project environments. *International Journal of Project Management*, *21*(6), 395–402. doi:10.1016/S0263-7863(02)00097-2

Englund, R. L., & Graham, R. J. (1999). From Experience: Linking Projects to Strategy. *Journal of Product Innovation Management*, *16*(1), 52–64. doi:10.1016/S0737-6782(98)00046-0

Engwall, M., & Jerbrant, A. (2003). The resource allocation syndrome: The prime challenge of multi-project management? *International Journal of Project Management*, *21*(6), 403–409. doi:10.1016/S0263-7863(02)00113-8

Fernandes, G. (2004). *Desenvolvimento de Metodologias para Avaliação de Projectos de Investimento Multisectorial*. Guimarães, Portugal: Universidade do Minho.

Ghasemzadeh, F., & Archer, N. P. (2000). Project portfolio selection through decision support. *Decision Support Systems*, *29*(1), 73–88. doi:10.1016/S0167-9236(00)00065-8

Goldman, C. (1999). Align Drive – Expert Advice. *CIO Magazine, 5*.

Grundy, T. (2000). Strategic project management and strategic behaviour. *International Journal of Project Management*, *18*(2), 93–103. doi:10.1016/S0263-7863(98)00076-3

Guan, J., & Ma, N. (2003). Innovative capability and export performance of Chinese firms. *Technovation*, *23*(9), 737–747. doi:10.1016/S0166-4972(02)00013-5

Hartman, F. (2000). *Don't park your brain outside: A practical guide to improving shareholder value with SMART management*. Newtown Square, PA: Project Management Institute.

Hax, A., & Majluf, N. S. (1996). *The Strategy Concept and Process: A Pragmatic Approach* (2nd ed.). Upper Saddle River, NJ: Prentice-Hall.

Henderson, J. C., & Venkatraman, H. (1999). Strategic alignment: Leveraging information technology for transforming organizations. *IBM Systems Journal, 38*(2.3), 472–484. https://doi.org/10.1147/SJ.1999.5387096

Henry, R. M., McCray, G. E., Purvis, R. L., & Roberts, T. L. (2007). Exploiting organizational knowledge in developing IS project cost and schedule estimates: An empirical study. *Information & Management*, *44*(6), 598–612. doi:10.1016/j.im.2007.06.002

Hermano, V., & Martín-Cruz, N. (2016). The role of top management involvement in firms performing projects: A dynamic capabilities approach. *Journal of Business Research*, *69*(9), 3447–3458. doi:10.1016/j.jbusres.2016.01.041

Hess, S. W. (1993). Swinging on the Branch of a Tree: Project Selection Applications. *Interfaces*, *23*(6), 5–12. doi:10.1287/inte.23.6.5

Ireland, L. R. (1997). Managing multiple projects. In Managing multiple project in the twenty-first century (pp. 21–34). New York: Marcel Dekker Inc.

Islei, G., Lockett, G., Cox, B., & Stratford, M. (1991). A decision support system using judgmental modeling: A case of R&D in the pharmaceutical industry. *IEEE Transactions on Engineering Management*, *38*(3), 202–209. doi:10.1109/17.83753

Jackson, B. (1983). Decision methods for selecting a portfolio of R&D projects. *Research Management*, *26*(5), 21–26.

Jarvenpaa, S. L., & Ives, B. (1993). Organizing for Global Competition. *Decision Sciences*, *24*(3), 547–580. doi:10.1111/j.1540-5915.1993.tb01293.x

Jeffrey, M., & Leliveld, I. (2003). Best Practices in IT Portfolio Management. *MIT Sloan Management Review*, *45*(3), 41–49.

Joro, T., Korhonen, P., & Wallenius, J. (1998). Structural Comparison of Data Envelopment Analysis and Multiple Objective Linear Programming. *Management Science*, *44*(7), 962–970. doi:10.1287/mnsc.44.7.962

Kaiser, M. G., El Arbi, F., & Ahlemann, F. (2015). Successful project portfolio management beyond project selection techniques: Understanding the role of structural alignment. *International Journal of Project Management*, *33*(1), 126–139. doi:10.1016/j.ijproman.2014.03.002

Kavadias, S., & Loch, C. H. (2003). Optimal Project Sequencing with Recourse at a Scarce Resource. *Production and Operations Management*, *12*(4), 433–444. doi:10.1111/j.1937-5956.2003.tb00213.x

Kendall, G., & Rollins, S. (2003). *Advanced Project Portfolio Management and the PMO: multiplying ROI at warp speed.* J. Ross Publishing. Retrieved from http://www.jrosspub.com/advanced-project-portfolio-management-and-the-pmo.html

Killen, C. P., Hunt, R. A., & Kleinschmidt, E. J. (2008). Project portfolio management for product innovation. *International Journal of Quality & Reliability Management*, *25*(1), 24–38. doi:10.1108/02656710810843559

Kissi, J., Dainty, A., & Tuuli, M. (2013). Examining the role of transformational leadership of portfolio managers in project performance. *International Journal of Project Management*, *31*(4), 485–497. doi:10.1016/j.ijproman.2012.09.004

Kremmel, T., Kubalík, J., & Biffl, S. (2011). Software project portfolio optimization with advanced multiobjective evolutionary algorithms. *Applied Soft Computing*, *11*(1), 1416–1426. doi:10.1016/j.asoc.2010.04.013

Lin, C., & Hsieh, P.-J. (2004). A fuzzy decision support system for strategic portfolio management. *Decision Support Systems*, *38*(3), 383–398. doi:10.1016/S0167-9236(03)00118-0

Mankins, M. C., & Steele, R. (2005, July 1). *Turning Great Strategy into Great Performance*. Retrieved August 11, 2016, from https://hbr.org/2005/07/turning-great-strategy-into-great-performance

Martino, J. P. (1995). *R&D Project Selection*. New York: Wiley.

Martinsuo, M., & Lehtonen, P. (2007). Role of single-project management in achieving portfolio management efficiency. *International Journal of Project Management*, *25*(1), 56–65. doi:10.1016/j.ijproman.2006.04.002

Matheson, D., & Matheson, J. (1998). *The smart organization*. Boston, MA: Harvard Business School Press.

Mathieu, R. G., & Gibson, J. E. (1993). A methodology for large-scale R&D planning based on cluster analysis. *IEEE Transactions on Engineering Management*, *40*(3), 283–292. doi:10.1109/17.233190

McGrath, R. G., & MacMillan, I. C. (2000). Assessing Technology Projects Using Real Options Reasoning. *Research-Technology Management*, *43*(4), 35–49. https://doi.org/10.1080/08956308.2000.11671367

Mehrez, A., & Sinuany-Stern, Z. (1983). An Interactive Approach for Project Selection. *The Journal of the Operational Research Society*, *34*(7), 621–626. doi:10.1057/jors.1983.143

Menke, M. M. (1991). Tools for improving the quality of R&D management. In *Technology Management: The New International Language* (pp. 162–165). https://doi.org/10.1109/PICMET.1991.183602

Meredith, J. R., & Mantle, S. J. (2000). *Project Management: A Managerial Approach* (4th ed.). New York: Wiley.

Miles, R., & Snow, C. (1994). *Fit, Failure and the Hall of Fame: How Companies Succeed or Fail*. New York, NY: Free Press.

Mota, C. M. de M., de Almeida, A. T., & Alencar, L. H. (2009). A multiple criteria decision model for assigning priorities to activities in project management. *International Journal of Project Management*, *27*(2), 175–181. doi:10.1016/j.ijproman.2008.08.005

Müller, R., Martinsuo, M., & Blomquist, T. (2008). Project portfolio control and portfolio management performance in different contexts. *Project Management Journal*, *39*(3), 28–42. doi:10.1002/pmj.20053

Ottosson, S. (2003). Participation action research-: A key to improved knowledge of management. *Technovation*, *23*(2), 87–94. doi:10.1016/S0166-4972(01)00097-9

Patanakul, P. (2015). Key attributes of effectiveness in managing project portfolio. *International Journal of Project Management*, *33*(5), 1084–1097. doi:10.1016/j.ijproman.2015.01.004

Patanakul, P., & Milosevic, D. (2009). The effectiveness in managing a group of multiple projects: Factors of influence and measurement criteria. *International Journal of Project Management*, *27*(3), 216–233. doi:10.1016/j.ijproman.2008.03.001

Pheng, L. S., & Chuan, Q. T. (2006). Environmental factors and work performance of project managers in the construction industry. *International Journal of Project Management*, *24*(1), 24–37. doi:10.1016/j.ijproman.2005.06.001

Platts, K. W. (1993). A Process Approach to Researching Manufacturing Strategy. *International Journal of Operations & Production Management*, *13*(8), 4–17. doi:10.1108/01443579310039533

PMI. (2008). *A Guide to the Project Management Body of Knowledge* (4th ed.). Newtown Square, PA: PMI.

PMI. (2013). *A Guide to the Project Management Body of Knowledge* (5th ed.). Newtown Square, PA: PMI.

PMI, & Deloitte. (2015). *Delivering on Strategy The Power of Project Portfolio Management* (Thought Leadership Series). Newtown Square, PA: PMI.

Reyck, B. D., Grushka-Cockayne, Y., Lockett, M., Calderini, S. R., Moura, M., & Sloper, A. (2005). The impact of project portfolio management on information technology projects. *International Journal of Project Management*, *23*(7), 524–537. doi:10.1016/j.ijproman.2005.02.003

Rondinelli, D., Rosen, B., & Drori, I. (2001). The struggle for strategic alignment in multinational corporations: Managing readjustment during global expansion. *European Management Journal*, *19*(4), 404–416. doi:10.1016/S0263-2373(01)00043-3

Roth, G., & Kleiner, A. (1998). Developing organizational memory through learning histories. *Organizational Dynamics*, *27*(2), 43–60. doi:10.1016/S0090-2616(98)90023-7

Saaty, T. L., Rogers, P. C., & Pell, R. (1980). Portfolio selection through hierarchies. *Journal of Portfolio Management*, *6*(3), 16–21. doi:10.3905/jpm.1980.408749

Sabherwal, R., Hirschheim, R., & Goles, T. (2001). The Dynamics of Alignment: Insights from a Punctuated Equilibrium Model. *Organization Science*, *12*(2), 179–197. doi:10.1287/orsc.12.2.179.10113

Saunders, M. N. K., Lewis, P., & Thornhill, A. (2012). *Research Methods for Business Students* (6th ed.). Harlow, UK: Financial Times/ Prentice Hall.

Shenhar, A. J., Dvir, D., Levy, O., & Maltz, A. C. (2001). Project Success: A Multidimensional Strategic Concept. *Long Range Planning*, *34*(6), 699–725. doi:10.1016/S0024-6301(01)00097-8

Shou, Y., & Huang, Y. (2010). Combinatorial auction algorithm for project portfolio selection and scheduling to maximize the net present value. *Journal of Zhejiang University SCIENCE C*, *11*(7), 562–574. doi:10.1631/jzus.C0910479

Souder, W. E. (1984). *Project Selection and Economic Appraisal*. New York: Van Nostrand Reinhold.

Spradlin, C. T., & Kutoloski, D. M. (1999). Action-Oriented Portfolio Management. *Research-Technology Management*, *42*(2), 26–32. https://doi.org/10.1080/08956308.1999.11671270

Susman, G. I., & Evered, R. D. (1978). An Assessment of the Scientific Merits of Action Research. *Administrative Science Quarterly*, *23*(4), 582–603. doi:10.2307/2392581

Thanassoulis, E. (2001). Introduction to the Theory and Application of Data Envelopment Analysis: A foundation text with integrated software. Boston: Kluwer Academic Publishers. doi:10.1007/978-1-4615-1407-7

Thorp, J. (1999). *The information paradox – realizing the business benefits of IT*. Toronto: McGraw-Hill.

Turner, J., & Simister, S. (2000). *The Gower handbook of project management* (3rd ed.). Aldershot, UK: Gower.

Turner, J. R., & Müller, R. (2005). The project manager's leadership style as a success factor on projects: A literature review. *Project Management Journal, 36*(1), 49–61.

Turner, R. J. (1999). *The handbook of project based management* (2nd ed.). London: McGraw-Hill.

Update, H. M. (2008, February 27). *Execute Your Strategy—Without Killing It.* Retrieved August 11, 2016, from https://hbr.org/2008/02/execute-your-strategy-without-1

van der Voet, J. (2014). The effectiveness and specificity of change management in a public organization: Transformational leadership and a bureaucratic organizational structure. *European Management Journal, 32*(3), 373–382. doi:10.1016/j.emj.2013.10.001

Wheelwright, S. C., & Clark, K. B. (2011). *Revolutionizing Product Development: Quantum Leaps in Speed, Efficiency and Quality.* New York: Free Press.

Xu, S., Cavusgil, S. T., & White, J. C. (2006). The Impact of Strategic Fit among Strategy, Structure, and Processes on Multinational Corporation Performance: A Multimethod Assessment. *Journal of International Marketing, 14*(2), 1–31. doi:10.1509/jimk.14.2.1

Yeo, K. T. (1993). Systems thinking and project management — time to reunite. *International Journal of Project Management, 11*(2), 111–117. doi:10.1016/0263-7863(93)90019-J

Zajac, E. J., Kraatz, M. S., & Bresser, R. K. F. (2000). Modeling the dynamics of strategic fit: A normative approach to strategic change. *Strategic Management Journal, 21*(4), 429–453. doi:10.1002/(SICI)1097-0266(200004)21:4<429::AID-SMJ81>3.0.CO;2-#

Zhu, J. (2000). Multi-factor performance measure model with an application to Fortune 500 companies. *European Journal of Operational Research, 123*(1), 105–124. doi:10.1016/S0377-2217(99)00096-X

Zhu, J. (2002). *Quantitative Models for Performance Evaluation and Benchmarking: Data Envelopment Analysis with Spreadsheets and DEA Excel Solver.* Boston, MA: Kluwer Academic Publishers.

KEY TERMS AND DEFINITIONS

DEA: Data Envelopment Analysis is a non-parametric linear programming method, introduced by Charnes, Cooper & Rhodes (1978) and it is a fractional programming model that estimates the relative efficiencies of a homogeneous set of units by considering multiple sets of inputs and outputs.

Key Performance Indicators (KPIs): Variables that are being considered as assessment criteria for the projects evaluation. The KPIs considered in this chapter, based on an extensive literature review and experts' perception, were a combination of the information considered critical to guarantee the project alignment, the economic, financial and operational assessment of the project towards selecting the proper portfolio. The indicators were divided according to their being inputs and outputs.

Market Clock Speed: The concept of market clock-speed captures the rate of market change driven by endogenous factors (i.e. technological; competitive; consumption). This concept will be extremely important for the organizational awareness of the rhythm of change and therefore to devise the actions needed towards attaining sustainable competitive advantages.

Peer Projects: Based on the DEA output data, the projects considered inefficient have a 'peer project' which is an efficient project; that helps the decision agent performing sensitivity analysis towards defining what should be done, in order to position itself on the efficiency curve.

Project Portfolio Management Cycle: The PPM cycle considers the alignment, selection, scheduling and monitoring/control phases of the entire set of projects in the organizational portfolio. Hence, it allows the creation of an excellent base of information that, with some extension and analysis may be transformed into organizational knowledge, facilitating the *post-mortem* analysis of the decisions taken and of the market conditions in a specific period of time. This ability can enhance the organizational learning, gathering valuable lessons in order to avoid the repetition of past errors.

Risk Perception: It is a metric based on a mix of personal experience, thematic sensibility and technical expertise of the decision agents towards the consideration of the risks involved in selecting some projects into the portfolio.

Strategic Alignment: The definition of a group of portfolio metrics to provide regular if not continuous feedback of the portfolio performance. The provision of detailed information to the project management team would allow them to decide, in each moment, the best projects portfolio favoring, as well, the strategic alignment with the organizational objectives.

Target KPIS: Based on the DEA output data, the projects considered inefficient have a 'Target KPIs' which could be inputs or outputs, and that helps the decision agent to perform sensitivity analysis towards defining what inputs or outputs should be worked on and in which amount in order to achieve the efficiency curve.

Chapter 10
Project Selection Frameworks and Methodologies for Reducing Risks in Project Portfolio Management

Fabio Nonino
Sapienza University of Rome, Italy

ABSTRACT

Extracting and consolidating knowledge from past projects can help managers in selecting projects with the correct level of riskiness, while market analysis gives directions for reaching the objective of a balanced project portfolio. To this extent, the chapter discusses strategic importance of project selection and the role of risks and uncertainties in project portfolio management and presents some fundamental and innovative frameworks and project selection methodologies for balancing risks. Finally, the chapter proposes a model containing an innovative methodology, based on artificial neural networks, to help managers in balancing project portfolio and assessing projects during the selection phase on the basis of risks, uncertainties and critical success factors.

INTRODUCTION

Project portfolio management (PPM) extends the objective of realizing successful projects to the alignment with strategic business objectives, but expected project success still remains the main determinant for projects selection. But management knows it and so do project managers: selection of new projects cannot be based only on quasi-guaranteed short-term revenues as the year-to-year viability of a company depends on its ability to innovate, the uncertain long-term returns on the company's total innovation investment.

The contemporary competitive environment, with its widespread lack of information, misleading signs and difficulties in forecasting future scenarios, makes the investments in the acquisition and management of projects always riskier. Consequently, one of the objectives of manager is the assessment of risk

DOI: 10.4018/978-1-5225-2151-8.ch010

across project portfolio. Companies must learn to manage innovation strategically to achieve a competitive advantage through a well-balanced portfolio. *But what does it mean to balance a project portfolio?*

As regard new markets and innovative products, firms should construct a portfolio selecting projects that balance riskiness of long-term return of investment for projects that will become the engines of blockbuster growth with guaranteed short-term revenues. Therefore, companies should align project portfolio with their strategic business objectives, achieving maximal project portfolio value by combining performances of projects in order to maximize the shareholders' value while balancing resource allocation and risks (Costantino *et al.*, 2015).

Achieving maximal project portfolio value for the resources used is often complicated by multiple selection criteria, subjective and imprecise assessments and project interdependencies. Project critical success factors (PCSFs) can serve as manageable criteria to prevent possible causes of failures with an effective project selection process, taking into account company strategic objectives, project manager's experience and the competitive environment.

The first section discusses strategic importance of project selection and the role of risks and uncertainties in project portfolio management. The subsequent section examines some fundamental and innovative frameworks and project selection methodologies for balancing project portfolio risks. The last part of the chapter proposes a framework an innovative methodology to help managers in assessing projects during the selection phase. An artificial neural network (ANN), scalable to any set of PCSFs, classifies the level of project's riskiness by extracting the experience of project managers from a set of past successful and unsuccessful projects taking into account risks and uncertainties.

BACKGROUND

The main objectives of the project portfolio management are the identification, the ranking, the prioritization, the selection and the authorization of projects or programs. Project selection is a strategic process aimed at evaluating individual projects or groups of projects and then choosing which implement so that the objectives of the parent organization are achieved (Meredith *et al.*, 2015). However, too often it fails (Ghapanchi *et al.*, 2012) due to complexity caused by many factors, exogenous and endogenous, such as uncertainty, interrelationships among projects, changes over time and stakeholders behaviour.

Project portfolio selection is the result of multiple and conflicting objectives. The first challenge in managing project portfolio is translate qualitative objectives in measurable and manageable quantitative goals. The second is to identify the interdependence of projects driven by common objectives and often scarce resources. The third is managing risk and uncertainties while balancing revenues and investments, reaching the so-called ambidexterity, i.e. exploitation of consolidated products/services and standardized processes vs. exploration of new business opportunities.

Risks and Uncertainties in Project Portfolio Selection

The process of protection from *risks* and *uncertainties* represents a fundamental component of the project portfolio and project management activities and needs of models, frameworks and methodologies translated in systematic procedures. Managers can reach a proper control of the projects' portfolio, balancing the overall exposure to risks, only with a clear perception of the expected results on every single project; in this context, risk analysis can help project managers to handle a portfolio of projects with different characteristics (Costantino *et al.*, 2015).

Project Risk Management supports managerial and organizational control (Söderlund, 2004) to minimize criticalities by identifying potential risks and correct responses to avoid project failure due to shifts and gaps from the target values. Nevertheless, leveling up the complexity grows. For instance, at project portfolio level risk management should takes into account interdependencies regarding resources, knowledge, and strategy (Sanchez *et al.*, 2008). Furthermore, in cases where resource limitations are at fault for failing projects, a project selection model that incorporated the *risk of resource limitations* could have aided the decision maker in avoiding such mistakes (Schniederjans & Santhanam, 1993).

Which Are Risks in Project Portfolio Management?

Project portfolio risk management is essential in any industry. As asserted by Abbasianjahromi and Rajaie (2012), portfolio management of construction project requires taking into account the risks, which are inherent in the industry. Especially in the project selection phase is inevitable. Also BPR projects, due to their nature, require a careful management of risks which can be categorized in three general groups of "business", "financial" and "organization" in which organizational risk – consisting of four dimensions of structure, culture, technology and human resource – plays a critical role in the associated risk of BPR (Remenyi and Heafield, 1996). As regards R&D portfolio management, the research by Floricel and Ibanescu (2008) shows that high-velocity environments favor structured as well as integrated portfolio management approaches, while high-growth environments favor approaches that are structured, but commit significant resources to each project as well.

Risk management at the project level is more important for R&D-dominated project portfolios, whereas the integration of risk information is more important with high levels of turbulence and portfolio dynamics (Teller et al., 2014).

As a matter of fact, risks are dynamics because of the environmental changes. Consequently, companies should face these changes by adapting portfolio management processes to competitive context that change more or less rapidly. Floricel and Ibanescu (2008) suggest that the level of dynamism of risks depends on the following patterns of environmental dynamics:

- **Velocity:** Advances in the frontier of functionality, performance and cost brought about by technological innovation.
- **Turbulence:** The extent of perceived discontinuity in environmental change with respect to past trends and anticipated directions.
- **Growth:** The perception of increasing resource inflows.
- **Instability:** The perception of a steady and diverse array of competitive moves by other strategic actors, such as product imitation and promotional wars, and from competitors entering with cheap or substitute products.

Risks or Uncertainties?

As well-known by project managers and team members, risk is a combination of the probability of an event (with a desirable and undesirable occurrence) and the consequences associated with that event.

Project risk management requires the identification and the estimation of probability of occurrence and impacts of risks associated to the project activities. Information used in estimating risk can be derived from expert opinion, technical data, or previous experience with similar projects (Archer and Ghasemzadeh, 1999).

The most advanced companies estimate overall risks in the project portfolio using models which combine the risks of each activity, including interdependent events and resources. Models used in analyzing risk include Monte Carlo simulation, decision theory and Bayesian statistical theory. However, these techniques are not widely used because they are too complex and require too much input data, they provide an inadequate treatment of risk and uncertainty, they fail to recognize interrelationships and interrelated criteria, they may just be too difficult to understand and use, or they may not be used in the form of an organized process (Cooper, 1993). As project managers know, in the majority of projects a significant level of complexity affects project life cycle and different sources of risk influence its success (Cagno *et al.*, 2007):

- Indeterminateness, ambiguity or poor definition and sharing of targets.
- Lack or low measurability of targets and a consequent low capability of evaluating and recognize performances.
- Inadequate resource allocation, i.e. right resources but wrongly managed or insufficient resources due to a wrong estimation.
- Incorrect and not detailed identification of all the customer's and company's requirements.
- Fast evolving markets and industries with a continuous need of targets re-alignment and re-planning.
- Inaccurate planning or errors in implementation of project management processes.

Nevertheless, in current competitive context *uncertainty* is increasing day by day and managers take strategic decisions on project portfolio (like a tender's participation or a project authorization) under non-deterministic conditions which are source of risks. Uncertainty is the unknown, whereas risk is what can go wrong (Shenhar and Dvir, 2007). Some scholars and practitioners have encouraged the use of the broader concept of uncertainty management instead of risk management (Petit, 2012). Uncertainty management implies exploring and understanding the sources of project risks. The focus is on the *inputs* (external and internal resources, market and organizational dynamics, evolution of financial markets…) that could affect projects rather than on the project activities. From PPM perspective, this means to discover and to proactively manage factors and resources with create high variability in organizational activities outside individual project contexts that have impacts on a number of projects. This perspective highlights the need to put in place different approaches and techniques to address some aspects of project related uncertainty.

Generally, project uncertainty comes from technical, market, organization or financial factors. Operationalization of uncertainty concept and its use in PPM is a practice still in its infancy. Some authors (e.g. Huang, 2010; Huang, 2011; Huang, 2012; Huang and Qiao, 2012 and Huang and Ying, 2013) introduced uncertainty theory to portfolio selection using experts' estimation rather than historical data, an uncertain risk curve and an uncertain risk index. Petit (2012) showed how to map certainties and uncertainties using five dimension: technical, market, organizational, financial and norms and regulations. Table 1 reports sources of uncertainty in four portfolio studied by the author.

Table 1. Mapping of the sources of uncertainty. Source: Petit, 2012.

	Soft1	Soft2	Fin1	Fin2
Technical	3rd party product	3rd party product		
	Technology	Technology		
Market	Match product with customers' needs	Match product with customer needs	Match product with customer needs	Match product with customer needs
	Competitor's offering	Competitor's offering		
	New customers			
	New market			
	New applications			
Organizational			Availability of resources	Availability of resources
Financial		Funding structure		
Norms and regulations			Content of Basel agreement	Content of new accounting regulations
			Interpretation of Basel agreement	interpretation of new accounting regulations

MAIN FOCUS: BALANCING RISKS ACROSS PROJECT PORTFOLIO

Balancing the portfolio in terms of risk and time to complete because companies does not want too much investment in high risk or long term projects (Ghasemzadeh and Archer, 2000) because an over-commitment to high risk projects may jeopardize the future of the organization (Cooper, 1993).

Cooper *et al.* (1997, 2001) recognized that balancing the diversification of the projects in the portfolio in terms of various tradeoffs, such as high risk versus sure profits or make or buy, should be an objective of PPM as much as the alignment of the mix of projects in the portfolio with the strategic goals of the organization or the value of the portfolio in terms of long-term profitability, return-on-investment and likelihood of success.

Even if the Standard for Portfolio Management published by PMI addresses portfolio risk management and provides guidelines for integrating risk management into project portfolio management, only a few frameworks and methodologies have been developed that integrate risk management into project portfolio management (Teller *et al.*, 2014.). Below some of the most important frameworks and methodologies are described.

Frameworks for Balancing Risk across Project Portfolio

The classic strengths, weaknesses, opportunities, and threats (SWOT) analysis can be a fruitful method for identifying potential projects. A first advantage of this framework is that forces company's leaders to explicitly consider risks (Kloppenborg and Laning, 2012). Moreover, having a clear identification of threats and opportunities that can arise, and evaluating any possible alternative in terms of project sustainability (Ghosh and Jintanapakanont, 2004), allows companies containing the level of uncertainty and setting up the risk identification.

An interesting framework in which risk is considered as a balancing between new projects' exploration and products' exploitation, is the Innovation Ambition Matrix (Nagji and Tuff, 2012), a refinement of the classic Ansoff's matrix. It is a useful PPM tool for suggesting how selecting projects among growth initiatives in line with company's strategy. The matrix (Figure 1) replaces Ansoff's binary choices of product and market (old versus new) with a range of values: novelty degree of a company's offerings (on the x axis) and novelty degree of its customer markets (on the y axis).

Nagji and Tuff suggest that firms that excel at total innovation management simultaneously invest at three levels of ambition:

- In the band of activity at the lower left of the matrix are core innovation initiatives which correspond to incremental changes to existing products and incremental inroads into new markets;
- In the band of activity at the upper right are transformational initiatives, which correspond to disruptive products designed to create new offers and to serve new markets and customer needs;
- In the middle are adjacent innovations, which can share characteristics with core and transformational innovations, which correspond to leverage existing capabilities but necessitate putting those capabilities to new products.

The research of Nagji and Tuff shows that companies that allocated about 70% of their innovation activity to core initiatives, 20% to adjacent ones, and 10% to transformational ones outperformed their peers. Of course some contextual factors change the proportion of investments on the three initiatives: typology of industry, company's competitive position and company's stage of development.

The analysis of industry impact could be conducted using the classic industry attractiveness - business strength matrix (Figure 2).

Figure 1. Innovation ambition matrix
Source: Nagji & Tuff, 2012.

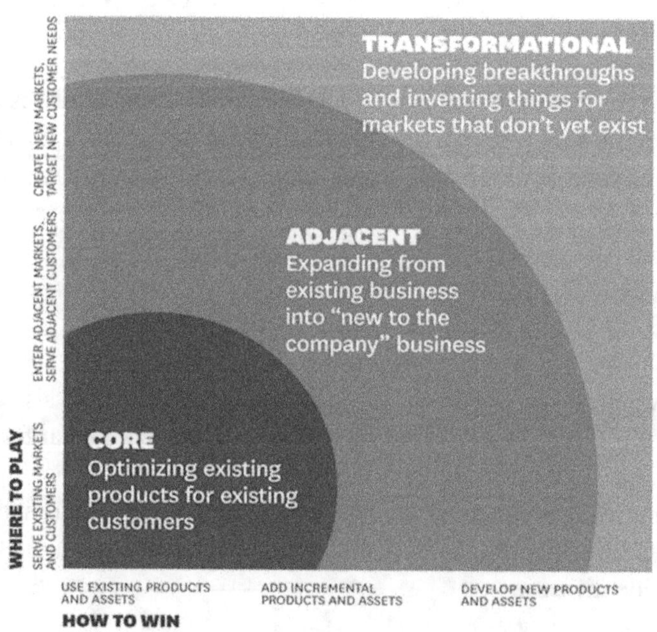

Figure 2. Industry attractiveness: business strength matrix
Source: Proposed by Lin & Hsieh, 2004 from Hax & Majluf, 1983

Business strenght \ Industry attractiveness	High	Medium	Low
High	Investment and growth	Selective growth	Selectivity
Medium	Selective growth	Selectivity	Harvest/Divest
Low	Selectivity	Harvest/Divest	Harvest/Divest

As suggested by Lin and Hsieh (2004), the classic GE Multifactor Portfolio Matrix, firstly developed by Hax and Majluf in 1983, could be used to help managers to better understand the competitive position of strategic business units (SBUs) based primarily on industry attractiveness, driven by external and uncontrollable factors, and business strength, based on the critical success factors, which is largely controllable by the firm.

Day (2007) proposes a modified version of the classic risk matrix (Figure 3). Each project is placed on the matrix by determining its score on two dimensions: the familiarity of the company to the intended market (x axis) and to the product or technology (y axis).

Riskier projects, i.e. with high probability of failure, are in the upper right. The probability of failure should be estimated by analyzing the market and industry through a representative number of interviews. Portfolio managers should posit companies' projects on the risk matrix on the basis of project characteristics. The projects can be represented with a circle and the length of diameter could be proportional to the project's estimated revenue, the estimated investment or absorption of scarce resources.

Another framework, born in the context of project portfolio management is risk-reward bubble diagram. In basic and most popular diagram (Figure 4), the probability of technical success of projects is assigned to the vertical axis while net present values are assigned to the horizontal axis (Moustafaev, 2010). Circles represent projects, their area is proportional to the project size while the color of each circle could denote the program or the product typology. Projects belonging to the four quadrants have different names: oysters, pearls, white elephants and bread and butter.

As already discussed before, companies should select and initiate, on average, pearl projects, the core initiatives, for about 70% of their resources, and a 10% of oyster projects, the transformational ones, considering an absorption of the 10% of capabilities. Adjacent projects are between pearl and oyster projects.

Figure 3. Risk matrix
Source: Day, 2007.

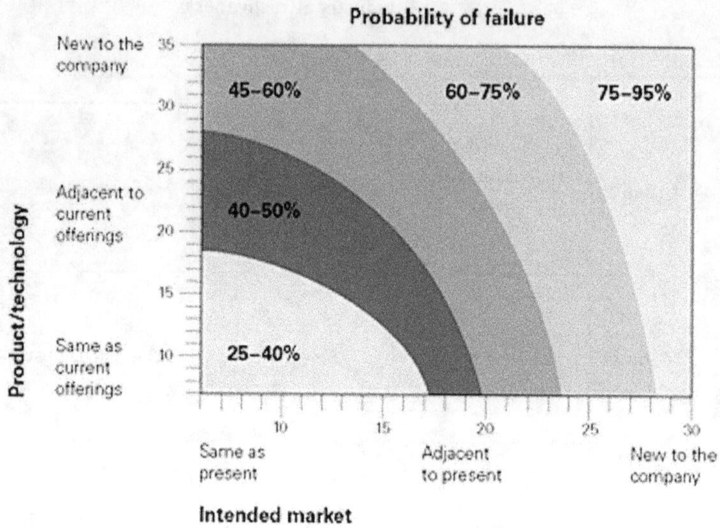

Figure 4. Risk-reward bubble diagram
Source: Moustafaev, 2010.

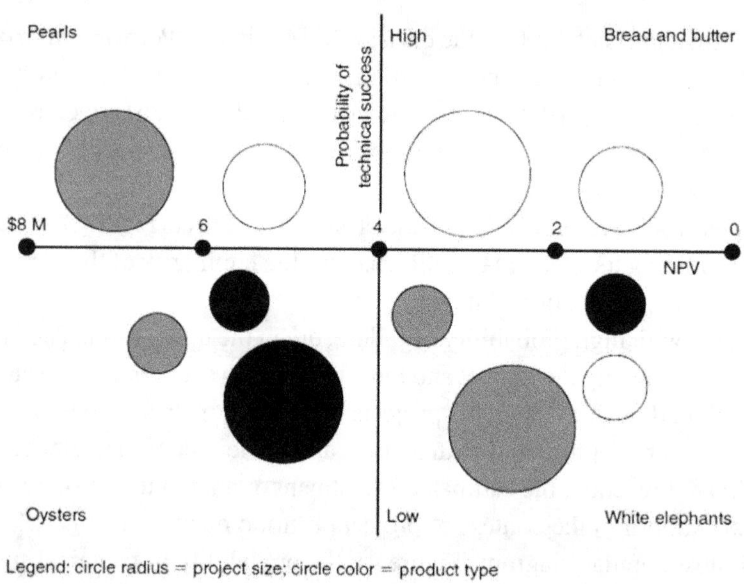

As reported by Cooper *et al.* (2002) fifteen years ago, the most popular bubble diagram among companies was Risk vs. Reward chart, where risk was considered a measure of probability of success. Nevertheless, companies considered also other bubble diagrams as reported in Table 2.

Bubble diagram in Figure 5, used by 3M and reported by Cooper et al. (2002), aims to deal with environmental uncertainties by considering probability of development and scale up success vs. NPV with optimistic and pessimistic estimates. The size and shape of the bubble measure the uncertainty of

Table 2. Popular bubble diagrams plot: rank ordered by popularity

Rank	Type of Chart	First Dimension Plotted		Second Dimension Plotted
1	Risk vs. Reward	Reward: NPV, IRR, benefits after years of launch, market value	by	Probability of success (technical, commercial, overall)
2	Newness	Technical newness	by	Market newness
3	Ease vs. Attractiveness	Technical feasibility	by	Market attractiveness (growth, potential, consumer appeal, life cycle)
4	Strength vs. Attractiveness	Competitive position (strengths)	by	Attractiveness (market growth, technical maturity, years to implementation)
5	Cost vs. Timing	Cost to implement	by	Time to implement
6	Strategic vs. Benefit	Strategic focus or fit	by	Business intent, NPV, financial fit, attractiveness
7	Cost vs. Benefit	Cumulative reward	by	Cumulative development costs

Source Cooper et al., 2002.

Figure 5. 3M's risk-reward bubble diagram showing uncertainties
Source: Cooper et al., 2002.

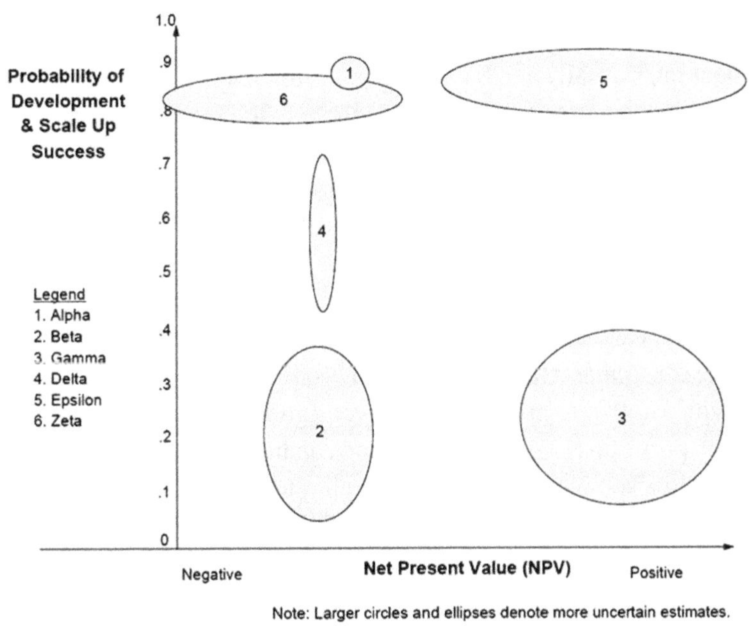

projects: large bubbles reveal projects with high uncertainty in both dimensions, small bubbles reveal projects with low uncertainty.

As will be reported in the next paragraph, the most advanced project selection methodologies use multi-criteria scoring involving particular optimization algorithms. Managerial frameworks for the project prioritization on the basis of multiple selection criteria taking into account risks and resource constraints, are the so-called Project/Program evaluation matrices. For instance, a format for the project evaluation matrix is shown in the simplified example proposed by Kloppenborg and Laning (2012) in Table 3. In this example companies utilize three information to determine the "value/risk efficiency frontier" with regard to available capital:

- The forecast capital needs of the project in the budget year.
- The weighted strategic value of each project.
- The weighted strategic risk of deferring each project.

SOLUTIONS AND RECOMMENDATIONS

Risk-Based Project Selection Methodologies

In the project portfolio management, the gathering of possible projects, their prioritization and selection usually involve particular optimization algorithms or management techniques that make use of specific project selection criteria (Kaiser *et al.*, 2015). Project selection approaches can be distinguished between financial and non-financial models while project selection methodologies range from single criteria cost-benefit analysis to multi-criteria scoring and ranking methods, or subjective evaluation methods.

As regards financial models, researchers proposed also selection model for investment decisions based on risks where discount rates usually act as a risk measurement indicator (e.g. WACC) and profitability indicators (e.g. NPV, IRR, benefits after years of launch, market value) act as objectives. Jafarizadeh and Ramazani Khorshid-Doust (2008) considered as principal selection criteria the semi-deviation of return, i.e. the measure of risk of projects that is more consistent with the definition of risk as the probability of unwanted outcomes.

A relevant instrument for valuing information technology (IT) investments and prioritizing a portfolio of projects is the real options analysis (Bardhan *et al.*, 2004). Real options can start from real data on expected project benefits and costs in different scenarios to calculate the option value of all projects considering also budget constraints. Bardhan *et al.* (2010) developed a prioritization approach to integrate real option analysis with a software project portfolio optimization model; their approach is focused on information technology portfolio risk management and can helps managers to make effective decisions, such as for investments in a service-oriented architecture, to enable flexible IT capabilities and shows the importance of balancing project-specific risks with the potential value derived across a multi-period horizon.

A multi-criteria qualitative method for the risk assessment of a project could be based on the NTCP diamond-shaped model proposed by Shenhar and Dvir (2007) and designed for analysing expected benefits and risks of a project. The four dimension of the model are:

- **Novelty:** How new is the project's product to customers and users: derivative, platform, breakthrough.
- **Technology:** How much new technology is required: low-tech, medium-tech, high-tech, super high-tech.

Table 3. Simplified value/risk project portfolio optimization model

Project Description	Planning Year Project Cost ($Millions)	Project Value					Weighted Value Score	Project Deferral Risk					Weighted Value Score	Combine Weighted Value Risk Score
		Strategy Areas and Weighting						Strategy Areas and Weighting						
		Financial Impact	Reliability Impact	Customer Impact	Regulatory Impact	System Performance		Financial Impact	Reliability Impact	Customer Impact	Regulatory Impact	System Performance		
		40%	20%	20%	10%	10%		40%	20%	20%	10%	10%		
Project A	$5.50	7	7	7	2	4	6.20	7	7	7	9	4	6.90	13.10
Project B	$10.00	4	8	3	8	8	5.40	9	8	3	8	8	7.40	12.80
Project C	$16.40	8	1	3	5	5	5.00	5	4	3	5	5	4.40	9.40
Project D	$3.00	2	4	5	8	5	3.90	8	4	6	4	5	6.10	10.00
Project E	$16.90	9	1	5	5	5	5.80	5	3	6	5	6	4.90	10.70
Project F	$9.00	2	6	9	9	9	5.60	7	7	10	9	9	8.00	13.60
Planning year budget limit	$25.00													
Selected project spend forecast	$24.50													

Source: Kloppenborg & Laning, 2012.

- **Complexity:** How complex is the product, the task and the project organization: assembly, system, array.
- **Pace:** How critical is the time frame: regular, fast/competitive, time-critical, blitz.

As shown in Figure 6, projects can be classified using the four dimensions and level of risks associated creates four areas of risk: low, medium, high and super-high. Authors suggest to quantify risk levels assigning a scale of 1 to 4 and to use a weights for each dimension (a, b, c, d) basing on the specific competitive context to determine a combined risk value. The formula for the risk assessment is the following:

$$R = a*N + b*T + c*C + d*P$$

The combined risk of a fast/competitive platform project based on high-tech technology with a system level of complexity in a context characterized by weights 0.2, 0.2, 0.4, 0.2 is:

$$R = 0.2*2 + 0.2*2 + 0.4*2 + 0.2*2 = 2$$

The literature presents a number of studies addressing project selection using multi-criteria scoring adopting different methodologies: fuzzy decision support system, genetic algorithm-based multi-criteria, multi-objective particle swarm optimization for project selection problem, Data Envelopment Analysis and analytic network process. Moreover, also simplified simulation model are proposed.

Figure 6. Risk assessment using Diamond model
Source: Shenhar & Dvir, 2007.

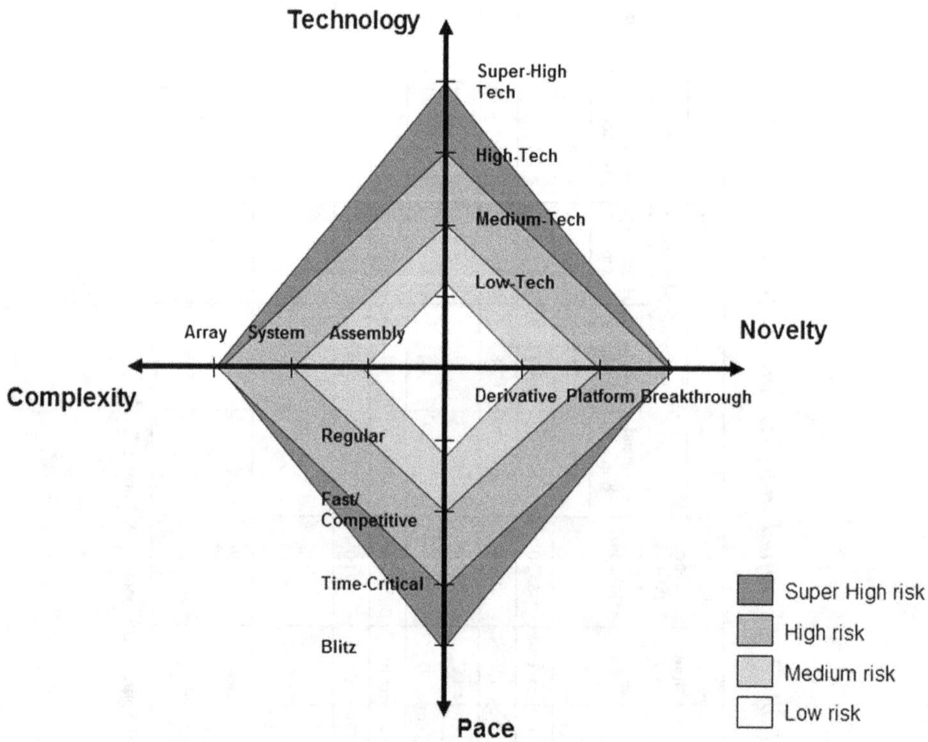

Abbasianjahromi and Rajaie (2012) proposed a model which attempts to optimize project selection based on the endurable risk level of a company with regard to the existing portfolio applying the fuzzy multi criteria decision-making approaches. Hall *et al.* (2015) considered a project selection problem where each project has an uncertain return with partially characterized probability distribution; to model and evaluate this risk, they proposed and justify a general performance measure, the underperformance riskiness index (URI) and defined a special case of the URI, the entropic underperformance riskiness index (EURI), for the project selection problem. Eilat *et al.* (2006) proposed a DEA based methodology for constructing and valuating balanced portfolios of R&D projects using three indices, risk, efficiency and balance: (1) the risk index for a project is the product of the projects overall budget and the probability that the project will not succeed. (2) the efficiency index for a project is the efficiency score computed by the CCR model and (3) the balance index for a project is computed as a ratio of the DEA – BSC score and the CCR score of that project.

Also Artificial Neural Networks (ANNs) can be used to create a project selection model able to "learn" the knowledge from historical project selection. Artificial neural network model is a non-parametric method, therefore it is superior in the ranking and the selection of projects compared to regression analysis, that is a parametric method (Olanrewaju *et al.*, 2011). In the following paragraph a framework for balancing risks based an artificial neural network model is proposed.

A Framework for Balancing Project Portfolio Risks Based on An Artificial Neural Network Model

Project critical success factors (PCSFs) are those governable factors that increase the ability of organizations to carry a project through its full implementation and which allows managers to set the operative priorities and determine the actions that can drive towards success. Consequently, organization must drive factors to reduce the risk of project failure.

A useful knowledge base is the project implementation profile (PIP), developed Slevin and Pinto in 1986 and tested in different PM context (Pinto, 1990), contains ten critical factors crucial for the implementation of a successful project (see Table 4).

Among the several studies which verified and discusses the PIP, the research of Cooke-Davies (2002) analyzed 136 projects (by 23 organizations) obtaining 12 CSFs partially overlapping PIP and explicitly considering four CSFs related to risk management: company-wide education on risk management, organization's processes for assigning ownership of risks, risk register, up-to-date risk management plan.

The model for early assessment of project success is based on critical success factors of project implementation using Artificial Neural Network (ANN) and it is the result of a research conducted by Costantino *et al.* (2015) and tested on data coming from 150 project of a leader Italian EPC contractor. The three main advantages of artificial neural networks in project selection are:

1. Ease of use because ANN extracts implicit knowledge from past experience without involving managers in complex and fallible judgements.
2. Applicability to any industry, project types, and company because customizable to any critical success factors framework.
3. Dynamic learning capacity of ANN models which can allow a review of project evaluation during the project lifecycle.

Table 4. The ten key factors of the project implementation profile

Factors	Definition
Project mission	Initial clearly defined goals and general directions.
Top management support	Willingness of the top management to provide the necessary resources and authority/power for project success.
Project schedule/plan	A detailed specification of the individual actions steps for project implementation.
Client consultation	Communication, consultation, and active listening to all impacted parties.
Personnel	Recruitment, selection, and training of the necessary personnel for the project team.
Technical tasks	Availability of the required technology and expertise to accomplish the specific technical action steps.
Client acceptance	The act of "selling" the final project to its ultimate intended users.
Monitoring and feedback	Timely provision of the comprehensive control information at each stage in the implementation process.
Communication	The provision of an appropriate network and necessary data to all key actors in the project implementation.
Troubleshooting	Ability to handle unexpected crises and deviations from plan.

Source: Slevin & Pinto, 1986.

Figure 7 shows how a company can use the ANN assessment model in the project selection and the two "learning processes" of the model. The enterprise environmental factors and knowledge gained in previous projects, the organizational process assets, are crucial for identifying and preparing accurate and viable tenders starting from the project statement of work (SOW) and, subsequently, the business case.

In the model, risks are considered inside project portfolio selection process and inside the individual project analysis. Companies start from risk balance analysis using one of the strategic framework proposed in the previous paragraph. This requires a strategic definition of certain portfolio dimensions, such as novelty degree of project vs novelty degree of its customer for the Innovation Ambition Matrix or probability of technical success of projects vs net present value for the Risk-reward Bubble Diagram. These information are fundamental for both selecting project and both updating critical success factors. The model requires also a statement of project critical success factors. However, managers can use the previous experience to define or to re-define project PCFSs.

In this first learning process, portfolio managers can express their judgment for a new project on a PCSFs' questionnaire (see for instance the PIP model reported in the first section) to provide the vector of inputs while the neural network gives as output an estimated degree of success, based on previous knowledge stored in its nodes and on the information coming from the business case. If the response is adequate, project fits the company's project portfolio strategy in terms of relevance and of a "standard" level of risk. If the response is not adequate (low degree of success), managers can modify the project characteristics related to the PCSFs or accept and higher level of risk. The model supports the simulation of interventions, testing one or more PCSFs, in both positive and negative way, to evaluate different project scenarios and the impact of improvements before their implementation.

If the company's management approves the project and it advances to initiating phase, the project sponsor and/or the project manager will prepare the project charter, which serve as the basis for project evaluation. Key performance indicators, basing on the same project CSFs, will evaluate project performances, according to the project portfolio strategy. The final version of business case containing the

Figure 7. Framework for balancing project and portfolio risks using an ANN model
Source: adapted from Costantino, Di Gravio, & Nonino, 2015.

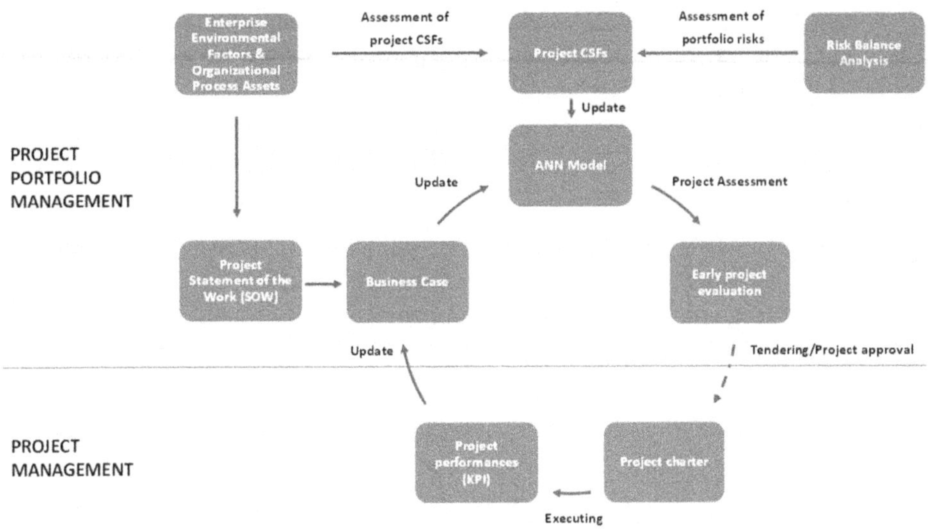

project assessment, traditionally used to increase company's project knowledge base, will allow the model update (second learning process). Increasing the number of projects in assessment and the feedbacks on the performances enables the re-engineering of the model. Modifying the architecture or replicating the learning process on a bigger amount of data, the capability of classification improves, reducing the number of errors and increasing the level of accuracy.

The ANN assessment model allows the reduction of projects' risk failure by identifying their degree of success according to an early evaluation of PCSFs.

FUTURE RESEARCH DIRECTIONS

This chapter highlights the strategic importance of project selection and the role of risks and uncertainties in project portfolio management. Recently, Teller *et al.* (2014) analyzed a sample of 177 project portfolios finding that formal risk management at the project level and integration of risk information at the portfolio level together with simultaneous risk management at both levels are positively associated with overall project portfolio success. But what does it mean simultaneous risk management at both levels?

Frameworks and project selection methodologies for balancing project portfolio risks, proposed in literature and adopted by companies, consider the two levels in a separate way. Researches on usable methodologies which integrate of project risk management at project and portfolio levels are still far from effective solutions.

Most advanced techniques for project selection using multi-criteria scores are not widely used because too complex as they require too much data and very specific expertise. Moreover, they fail to recognize strategic interrelationships and interrelated resources and objectives among projects.

Finally, majority of project selection models don't provide an adequate treatment of uncertainties. Uncertainty management is closer to the concept of strategy as it regards the management of variability of the inputs to project portfolio activities, but risk management does not cover the complete spectrum addressed by this perspective.

CONCLUSION

An early evaluation of the expected success of projects is a very tough process so organizations should set up tools and methods that could help managers to forecast performances. Risk of projects' failure is different from risk of project management failure. Companies' managers should be aware about the difference between *project success*, that measures the achievement of the overall objectives, and *project management success*, that measures the performance of the management process. Project success is next to the idea of effectiveness (achieved vs. targeted objectives) while project management success is next to the idea of efficiency (consumed resources vs. achieved targets). Project management is only one of the many factors that can influence the success or the failure of a project like, for example, organizational structure, size of the project, industrial sector, different perspectives of the stakeholders, different stages of the life cycle (Turner and Müller, 2005).

Project and portfolio management need innovative flexible, adaptive and evolutive managerial models able to respond to a wider concept of success, a concept based on the value of projects based on business results and on expectations emerging from different perspectives. The uncertain competitive environment is becoming increasingly unpredictable due to the sources of uncertainty, those technical, market, organization or financial factors triggered and nurtured by stakeholders' expectations. So innovative project selection frameworks and methodologies for reducing risks in project portfolio management should start from those expectations and use the risk of not meet expectations as fundamental criteria for selecting projects and evaluating their success.

The framework proposed in the chapter uses an artificial neural network scalable to any set of project critical success factors, classifies the level of project's riskiness by extracting the experience of project managers from a set of past successful and unsuccessful projects taking into account risks and uncertainties. The model is one of few attempts of balancing project portfolio by integrating project and portfolio levels during the selection phase on the basis of the analysis of both risks and uncertainties; but there is still much work to do to overcome managers' reluctance in adopting complex portfolio frameworks demonstrating their real effectiveness.

The next challenge of project management discipline is to design simple, flexible and effective models able to embrace and navigate the complexity of projects' landscape characterized by uncertainties and challenging stakeholders' expectations and able to drive managers and companies towards higher levels of projects' success.

REFERENCES

Abbasianjahromi, H., & Rajaie, H. (2012). Developing a project portfolio selection model for contractor firms considering the risk factor. *Journal of Civil Engineering & Management*, *18*(6), 879–889. doi:10.3846/13923730.2012.734856

Archer, N. P., & Ghasemzadeh, F. (1999). An integrated framework for project portfolio selection. *International Journal of Project Management*, *17*(4), 207–216. doi:10.1016/S0263-7863(98)00032-5

Bardhan, I., Bagchi, S., & Sougstad, R. (2004). Prioritizing a portfolio of information technology investment projects. *Journal of Management Information Systems*, *21*(2), 33–60.

Bardhan, I.R., Kauffman, R.J., & Naranpanawe, S. (2010). IT project portfolio optimization: A risk management approach to software development governance. *IBM Journal of Research and Development, 54*(2), paper 2.

Cagno, E., Caron, F., & Mancini, M. (2007). A Multi-Dimensional Analysis of Major Risks in Complex Projects. *Risk Management, 9*(1), 1–18. doi:10.1057/palgrave.rm.8250014

Cooper, R. G. (1993). *Winning At New Products.* Addison-Wesley.

Cooper, R. G., Edgett, S. J., & Kleinschmidt, E. J. (2001). Portfolio management for new product development: Results of an industry practices study. *R & D Management, 31*(4), 361–380. doi:10.1111/1467-9310.00225

Cooper, R.G., Edgett, S.J., & Kleinschmidt, E.J. (2002). Portfolio management: fundamental to new product success. *The PDMA ToolBook 1 for New Product Development, 9*, 331-364.

Cooper, R. G., Edgett, S. J., & Kleinshmidt, E. J. (1997). *Portfolio Management for New Products.* Hamilton, ON: McMaster University.

Costantino, F., Di Gravio, G., & Nonino, F. (2015). Project selection in project portfolio management: An artificial neural network model based on critical success factors. *International Journal of Project Management, 33*(8), 1744–1754. doi:10.1016/j.ijproman.2015.07.003

Day, G. S. (2007, December). Is it real? Can we win? Is it worth doing? *Harvard Business Review*, 110–120. PMID:18283921

Eilat, H., Golany, B., & Shtub, A. (2006). Constructing and valuating Balanced Portfolios of R&D Projects with Interactions: A DEA Based Methodology. *European Journal of Operational Research, 172*(3), 1018–1039. doi:10.1016/j.ejor.2004.12.001

Floricel, S., & Ibanescu, M. (2008). Using R&D portfolio management to deal with dynamic risk. *R & D Management, 38*(5), 452–467. doi:10.1111/j.1467-9310.2008.00535.x

Ghapanchi, A. H., Tavana, M., Khakbaz, M. H., & Low, G. (2012). A methodology for selecting portfolios of projects with interactions and under uncertainty. *International Journal of Project Management, 30*(7), 791–803. doi:10.1016/j.ijproman.2012.01.012

Ghasemzadeh, F., & Archer, N. P. (2000). Project portfolio selection through decision support. *Decision Support Systems, 29*(1), 73–88. doi:10.1016/S0167-9236(00)00065-8

Ghosh, S., & Jintanapakanont, J. (2004). Identifying and assessing the critical risk factors in an underground rail project in Thailand: A factor analysis approach. *International Journal of Project Management, 22*(8), 633–643. doi:10.1016/j.ijproman.2004.05.004

Hall, N. G., Long, D. Z., Qi, J., & Sim, M. (2015). Managing Underperformance Risk in Project Portfolio Selection. *Operations Research, 63*(3), 660–675. doi:10.1287/opre.2015.1382

Hax, A. C., & Majluf, N. S. (1983). The use of the industry attractiveness - business strength matrix in strategic planning. *Interfaces, 13*(2), 54–71. doi:10.1287/inte.13.2.54

Huang, X. (2008). Mean-variance model for fuzzy capital budgeting. *Computers & Industrial Engineering, 55*(1), 34–47. doi:10.1016/j.cie.2007.11.015

Huang, X. (2010). *Portfolio Analysis: From Probabilistic to Credibilistic and Uncertain Approaches*. Berlin: Springer-Verlag. doi:10.1007/978-3-642-11214-0

Huang, X. (2011). Mean-risk model for uncertain portfolio selection. *Fuzzy Optimization and Decision Making, 10*(1), 71–89. doi:10.1007/s10700-010-9094-x

Huang, X. (2012). A risk index model for portfolio selection with returns subject to experts estimations. *Fuzzy Optimization and Decision Making, 11*(4), 451–463. doi:10.1007/s10700-012-9125-x

Huang, X., & Qiao, L. (2012). A risk index model for multi-period uncertain portfolio selection. *Information Sciences, 217*, 108–116. doi:10.1016/j.ins.2012.06.017

Huang, X., & Ying, H. (2013). Risk index based models for portfolio adjusting problem with returns subject to experts evaluations. *Economic Modelling, 30*, 61–66. doi:10.1016/j.econmod.2012.09.032

Jafarizadeh, B., & Ramazani Khorshid-Doust, R. (2008). A method of project selection based on capital asset pricing theories in a framework of mean–semideviation behavior. *International Journal of Project Management, 26*(6), 612–619. doi:10.1016/j.ijproman.2007.09.004

Kaiser, M. G., El Arbi, F., & Ahlemann, F. (2015). Successful project portfolio management beyond project selection techniques: Understanding the role of structural alignment. *International Journal of Project Management, 33*(1), 126–139. doi:10.1016/j.ijproman.2014.03.002

Kloppenborg, T. J., & Laning, L. J. (2012). *Strategic Leadership of Portfolio and Project Management*. New York: Business Expert Press. doi:10.4128/9781606492956

Lin, C., & Hsieh, P.-J. (2004). A fuzzy decision support system for strategic portfolio management. *Decision Support Systems, 38*(3), 383–398. doi:10.1016/S0167-9236(03)00118-0

Meredith, J. R., Mantel, S. J., & Shafer, S. M. (2015). *Project Management: A Managerial Approach* (9th ed.). Hoboken, NJ: John Wiley & Sons.

Moustafaev, J. (2010). *Delivering exceptional project results: A practical guide to project selection, scoping, estimation and management. J.* Ross Publishing.

Nagji, B., & Tuff, G. (2012). Managing Your Innovation Portfolio. *Harvard Business Review, 3*(4), 1–5.

Olanrewaju, O. A., Jimoh, A. A., & Kholopane, P. A. (2011). Comparison between regression analysis and artificial neural network in project selection. In *IEEE International Conference on Industrial Engineering and Engineering Management* (pp. 738-741). doi:10.1109/IEEM.2011.6118014

Petit, Y. (2012). Project portfolios in dynamic environments: Organizing for uncertainty. *International Journal of Project Management, 30*(5), 539–553. doi:10.1016/j.ijproman.2011.11.007

Pinto, J. K. (1988). Variations in Critical Success Factors Over the Stages in the Project Life Cycle. *Journal of Management, 14*(1), 5–18. doi:10.1177/014920638801400102

Pinto, J. K. (1990). Project Implementation Profile: A tool to aid project tracking and control. *International Journal of Project Management, 8*(3), 173–182. doi:10.1016/0263-7863(90)90020-C

Remenyi, D., & Heafield, A. (1996). Business process re-engineering: Some aspects of how to evaluate and manage the risk exposure. *International Journal of Project Management, 14*(6), 349–357. doi:10.1016/0263-7863(96)00013-0

Sanchez, H., Robert, B., & Pellerin, R. (2008). A project portfolio risk-opportunity identification framework. *Project Management Journal, 39*(3), 97–109. doi:10.1002/pmj.20072

Schniederjans, M., & Santhanam, R. (1993). A multi-objective constrained resource information system project selection method. *European Journal of Operational Research, 70*(2), 244–253. doi:10.1016/0377-2217(93)90042-L

Shenhar, A. J., & Dvir, D. (2007). *Reinventing Project Management. The Diamond approach to successful growth and innovation*. Boston, MA: Harvard Business School Publishing.

Slevin, D. P., & Pinto, J. K. (1986). The Project Implementation Profile: New tool for project managers. *Project Management Journal, 18*(4), 57–71.

Söderlund, J. (2004). Building theories of project management: Past research, questions for the future. *International Journal of Project Management, 22*(3), 183–191. doi:10.1016/S0263-7863(03)00070-X

Teller, J., Kock, A., & Gemünden, H. G. (2014). Risk Management in Project Portfolios Is More Than Managing Project Risks: A Contingency Perspective on Risk Management. *Project Management Journal, 45*(4), 67–80. doi:10.1002/pmj.21431

Turner, J. R., & Müller, R. (2005). The project manager's leadership style as a success factor on projects: A literature review. *Project Management Journal, 36*, 49–61.

Chapter 11
Project Portfolio Management Growth and Operation:
Portfolio Management Structure, Operations, Risk, and Growth

Frank R. Parth
Project Auditors LLC, USA

ABSTRACT

Developing a portfolio management system that can effectively and efficiently select and prioritize the projects that best support strategic goals, this is only the start of portfolio management. To ensure that the enterprise portfolio management system (EPMS) can continue to operate and grow as the organizational environment changes and the strategic goals change, the EPMS must be implemented within the organizational structure that ensures it will remain relevant in the future. We discuss two architectures to the administrative housing of the EPMS, within a PMO or as a separate stand-alone organization. Both have their advantages and disadvantages. In either case, once the EPMS is implemented it must be controlled and managed as any other group within the larger organization. This requires a structure, roles and responsibilities, personnel and IT resources, an annual budget, and all the other administrative functions required to manage a department. As the maturity level of the EPMS evolves the growth must be managed to continue to support the organization.

INTRODUCTION

There are two aspects to understand regarding the development of an enterprise portfolio management system (EPMS). The first is that it does not exist in isolation within the larger organization, it must fit within the organizational structure and culture of that organization.

The second is that it must evolve and change as the larger organization evolves and changes. Strategic plans no longer look 10 years into the future. The external economic, cultural, competitive, and technological environment is changing much more rapidly, and strategic plans must adapt and change at the same pace. The EPMS must be able to deal with more frequent changes in strategic goals.

DOI: 10.4018/978-1-5225-2151-8.ch011

It has been pointed out many times that the projects within the portfolio should be prioritized according to the strategic goals of the organization. But what happens when those goals change? While employees tend of think of strategic goals as those lofty 5 or 10 year plans that everyone is working towards, the executives realize that in this fast-paced, internationally competitive environment that companies work in they need to re-examine the strategic goals much more often than that. According to Cabanis-Brewin (Cabanis-Brewin 2000), approximately 70 - 90% of strategic goals are never achieved.

BACKGROUND

It is important to distinguish between project/program management and portfolio management. At a project level the project manager tracks which activities are ahead of schedule, on schedule, or behind schedule. Similarly the project manager tracks cost expenditures compared to the budget and monitors project risks.

At a portfolio level, the system should track which projects and programs are on/ahead of/or behind schedule. Which projects/programs have overspent their budget or are under budget. The EPMS is less concerned with individual project progress than it is with the overall progress of the entire portfolio. Consider an example. The EPMS has shown that a major internal project is 6 months behind schedule and $500,000 over budget. The earned value metrics show that at the current rate of progress the project will be a year late in delivering any revenue to the company.

From a project management perspective the team is in a damage control effort, working overtime to make up for the late schedule. However, the EPMS gives us options at a portfolio level. We can look at the schedule delay and perhaps re-allocate resources from another project to help the schedule delays. Or we may look at the revenue shortfall and see if the revenue can be made up from another project, or even whether the project should be killed altogether and the resources re-allocated to other projects. At the portfolio level we have more options than worrying about a single project.

A further consideration is that the goal of an EPMS is to select and prioritize those projects which best satisfy the organization's strategic goals. As multiple authors have pointed out (see, for example, Anyosa 2010), most project managers in the organization are not aware of the strategic goals, and the executives who select the strategic goals are not aware of their own internal capabilities and limitations in successfully completing those projects.

ORGANIZATIONAL STRUCTURE

Effectively operating an EPMS requires a strong organizational structure. There are two basic options for developing an EPMS within the context of the overall organization. It could be a stand-alone organization or it could be within the overall structure of a Program or Portfolio Management Office (PMO).

Creating a portfolio organization is no different than creating any other brand new group within an organization, and no simpler, either. It can be extremely challenging from both a structural standpoint and from a political one to create a new group. Especially since this new group can significantly change the decision-making power within the organization and remove the ability of many managers to select their own projects.

Roles and job descriptions will need to be identified within the framework of the organization. Typical roles at this level include the Portfolio Executive, the Portfolio Manager, an administrator, and a higher-level Steering Committee. Responsibilities are generally as follows:

Portfolio Executive

The portfolio executive is a senior level individual responsible for the line of business in which the portfolio has been created and they act as the EPMS sponsor. If the EPMS supports multiple lines of businesses, this role may performed by the Portfolio Steering Committee.

Portfolio Manager

The portfolio manager is the individual who is responsible for managing the portfolio on a day-by-day basis, ensuring that overall status of the portfolio is understood and that the portfolio executive has the necessary information to make informed decisions. It is responsible for managing the portfolio but does not own it or have decision-making authority.

Portfolio Administrator

The portfolio administrator is focused on supporting the portfolio manager with the administrative aspects of the portfolio, ensuring that:

- Status reports have been received.
- Documentation updates are being made.
- Communications are consistent and the information needed to understand the health of different aspects of the portfolio is in place and available for analysis.

Portfolio Steering Committee

The portfolio steering committee supports the project sponsor in overseeing the portfolio. The portfolio steering committee acts in an advisory role or in a decision making role depending on the organization. It is normally comprised of senior management from the primary business units that are involved with or impacted by the portfolio.

EPMS Within A PMO

Many, perhaps most, portfolio management is done within the organizational structure of a PMO. The PMO has a variety of services it offers depending on the specific PMO of the overall organization. The most effective PMOs are customized to the organization's needs and culture and there is little consistency in structure or function across different industry sectors.

Attempts have been made by multiple consulting groups to bring some consistent structure to the PMO, categorizing the services offerings into just a few major areas. According to PMI's Pulse of the Profession (PMI 2013) there are five primary categories for a PMO:

1. **Organizational Unit PMO/Business Unit PMO/Divisional PMO/ Departmental PMO:** Provides project-related services to support a business unit or division within an organization including, but not limited to, portfolio management, governance, operational project support and human resources utilization.
2. **Project-Specific PMO/Project Office/Program Office:** Provides project-related services as a temporary entity established to support a specific project or program. May include supporting data management, coordination of governance and reporting, and administrative activities to support the project or program team.
3. **Project Support/Services/Controls Office or PMO:** Provides enabling processes to continuously support management of project, program or portfolio work throughout the organization. Uses the governance, processes, practices, and tools established by the organization and provides administrative support for delivery of the project, program or portfolio work within its domain.
4. **Enterprise/Organization-Wide/Strategic/Corporate/Portfolio/Global PMO:** The highest-level PMO in organizations having one, this PMO is often responsible for alignment of project and program work to corporate strategy, establishing and ensuring appropriate enterprise governance, and performing portfolio management functions to ensure strategy alignment and benefits realization.
5. **Center of Excellence/Center of Competency:** Supports project work by equipping the organization with methodologies, standards and tools to enable project managers to better deliver projects. Increases the capability of the organization through good practices and a central point of contact for project managers.

Of these five categories, only the first and the fourth are involved with portfolio management. The Organizational/BU/Divisional/Departmental PMO is involved with project selection and reporting at a lower level of the organization. The Enterprise/Organization-wide/Strategic/ Corporate/Portfolio/Global PMO is involved with true portfolio management at the top levels of the organization.

Research done by multiple organizations consistently reports that the PMO should report as high in the organization as necessary for it to accomplish its work. For an enterprise-level PMO, the PMO should report to an executive vice-president or a senior vice-president. For example, a Forrester Consulting report (Forrester, 2013) commissioned by PMI is shown in Figure 1.

This gives the PMO the broad authority it needs to identify and to prioritize projects that can affect the entire organization.

Forrester's study yielded four key findings about successful PMOs:

- They have a seat at the executive table. Strategic results require strategic positioning. PMOs that are highly effective in driving business growth report to varying levels of executive management, ranging from senior vice president to the C-level, and are regarded as members of executive management. Champions are strategically positioned, too. The majority of the leaders interviewed have highly visible sponsorship at the C-level.
- They are a vital part of the strategic planning team. Since portfolio management is a core competency, PMOs actively participate in strategic planning and help shape strategy by providing feedback to executives about performance, labor costs, and customer feedback.
- They embrace core competencies. Excellence in project management remains a critical capability for PMOs. The most successful organizations recognize the specific role of the project manager and build significant learning and development programs to mature project management skills.

Figure 1. PMO reporting relationships

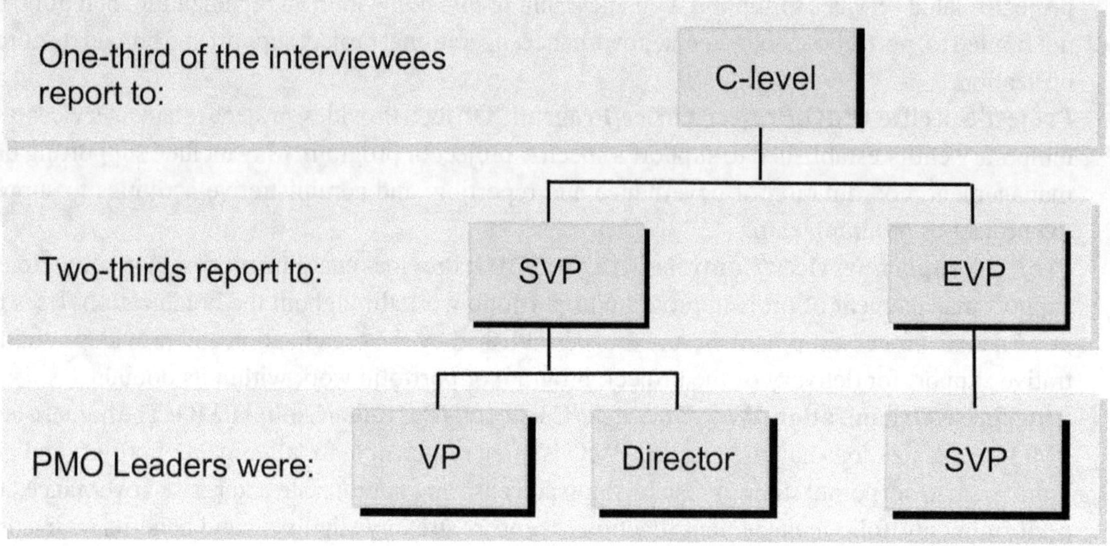

- They use consistent objectives across industry and regions. Customer-facing or business-facing, strategic PMOs share the same objectives: Drive success through alignment with business stakeholders and operational excellence. Meeting these objectives is differentiated by such factors as orientation, region, and culture.

Building the EPMS within a PMO structure makes the most sense from an organizational efficiency standpoint. The PMO is often charged with setting up best practices for project management, standardizing project approaches and documents, setting up metrics, and so on. Managing the portfolio becomes more efficient when it is closely tied to the project management office.

Case Study of a Successful EPMS Implementation

Let's look at one success story in Portfolio Management – Chevron Oil Company. This material is based on a presentation given on 4 March, 2009, by Janinne Franke of Chevron's IT department and is used with permission. They developed advanced capabilities in IT portfolio management by having a thorough understanding of how it can benefit the business and centralizing portfolio management in a Portfolio Management Office for each business unit. Following a process of continuous improvement, this is an on-going effort with changes within the EPMS to adapt to a changing environment.

In 2009 Chevron was the 6th largest company in the world by revenues with over 65,000 employees worldwide. Their IT group had over 6,900 people located in 64 locations around the world. Before they began a transformation of IT, the department was focused on their customer's, their business unit's, immediate needs. While this is normal for IT departments, it is a very tactical approach, not a strategic one. The end result is generally a patchwork of non-integrated systems, numerous applications and no long term planning. Chevron's goal was to transform the IT organization to focus on the best way to achieve long-term business strategies.

IT had five key focus areas:

1. Run and support Chevron's IT assets securely, safely, reliably and efficiently.
2. Improve reliability, the transparency of IT spend, and our overall project planning, prioritization and execution capabilities.
3. Deliver the critical few IT Investment Strategy initiatives with excellence.
4. Sustain the value of these investments through effective support and an improved ability to extract the intended value.
5. Shape the 10-year vision and strategy, and set priorities for Information Technology at Chevron.

The emphasis of the PMO was on the second focus area – improve reliability, the transparency of IT spend, and the overall project planning, prioritization and execution capabilities. Although in addition the third focus area involves identifying the critical few IT investment strategy initiatives is also a valid goal of portfolio management.

How were they going to achieve this? Their stated objective was to develop processes, tools and analytics to enable, measure, and advise in the following areas:

- **Balanced Portfolio:** Balance projects according to the organization's strategy and other parameters in order to achieve a desired return. Maximize the value of the Portfolio via key metrics while keeping an acceptable level of risk.
- **Optimized Resources:** Allocate resources to the highest value projects and ensure that resources are being appropriately utilized. Manage the 'peaks and valleys' of resource use.
- **High Value Work:** Ensure that the Project Portfolio reflects the business strategy and that the breakdown of spending aligns with business priorities.

In order to achieve their ultimate goal of being a great business partner, beginning in 2005 the Portoflio Management Office created processes for becoming first a great service provider, then a good business partner, then a great business partner. Each of these goals had a series of lower-level goals to accomplish. One the way to becoming a great service provider, their steps include understanding the business needs first, then achieving operational excellence, then managing their IT costs.

On their way to becoming a good business partner, the steps involved first understanding the business strategies, translating those strategies to clear credibility gaps, then finally aligning IT strategy, portfolio, and the enterprise architecture. It was in these steps shown in Figure 2 that the portfolio management process was created and implemented.

Once this was achieved, they used their portfolio management process to develop an IT strategy that was integrated with and supports the business strategy. (This process puts the ownership of IT strategy on the business, where it properly belongs. It's the business who should be driving IT's strategy and let IT determine how best to achieve that strategy.)

A normal project selection process under a portfolio management system selects the projects that are most beneficial (usually using financial criteria) at an acceptable level of risk. For Chevron, their system includes financial calculations and risk assessments, but in addition they filter projects for strategic fit:

- **Enterprise Strategic Fit:** Support of strategy with emphasis on an enterprise-level view.
- **Business Unit Strategic Fit:** Support to specific Business Unit level strategies.

Figure 2. Chevron's portfolio management process growth

Because the oil/gas industry sector is highly-regulated, Chevron's first filtering criteria was related to whether this is a compliance project or not. (Any regulated industry must use this filter as a first one before any other filters are utilized).There is no progress without measurement. Management must know where they are to understand whether actual improvement has been made or not. Chevron developed a 5-tier maturity model similar to that developed by the Software Engineering Institute's Capability Maturity Model (CMM). They defined four areas of competency (Strategy, Process, Tools/Technology, and Organizational Capability) and measure these across five levels of maturity listed below and as shown in Figure 3:

Level 1: Informal.
Level 2: Defined.
Level 3: Managed.
Level 4: Measured.
Level 5: Optimized.

Not all of Chevron's business units aspired to be at level five on all competency levels. Some were happy to stop at level three which would be the minimum rating of an impactful Portfolio Management Office. Any level lower than that would move the Portfolio Management Office to a project management office.

The end result of an effective PMO is enhancing business values in:

1. **Planning:**
   a. Enhanced partnership between Business and IT enables business strategy.
   b. Objective project selection and prioritization based on business drivers.
   c. Balanced Project Portfolio mix to maximize return.

Figure 3. Chevron's maturity model

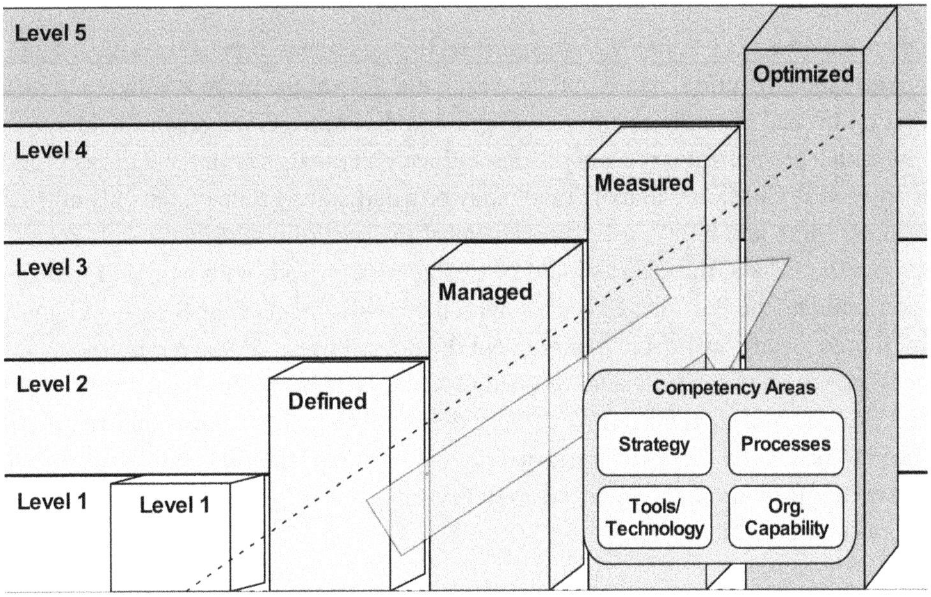

   d. Comprehensive data enables improved decision making around resource allocation and portfolio investment.
   e. Relationship visibility between all projects, programs and portfolios and alignment to business strategy.
   f. Reduction of disparate Portfolio Management tools.
   g. Reduce number of projects by understanding cross-functional synergies / overlaps / redundancies.

2. **Execution:**
   a. Greater agility to respond to changes in business conditions decreases time-to-market.
   b. Improved On Time On Budget performance through enhanced project planning capability.
   c. Reduced cycle times through improved and standardized Portfolio Management processes.
   d. Productivity gains through increased automation and process refinement.
   e. Cost avoidance and reduction of project delays by more proactive resource planning and optimization.
   f. Maximize the efficient use of resources and assets with an emphasis on safety and reliability.
3. **Realization:**
   a. Centralized Project and Program data enables improved decision quality through portfolio analytics.
   b. Ability to monitor progress through measured attributes and KPIs (Key Performance Indicators) against business objectives.
   c. Application of industry performance benchmarks.
   d. More control for continuous improvement.

While other approaches are possible, the one Chevron used is very well thought out and well planned.

EPMS as a Stand-Alone Organization

If your organization does not have a PMO, the portfolio management organization must stand on its own. The more broadly the portfolio selection process is charged with, the more it is likely to be an independent organization instead of nestled within a PMO. For a division's IT organization there is more likely a PMO within which the portfolio process resides and which manages both local projects and programs. For an enterprise-wide EPMS it will more than likely be a dedicated group which only engages in project selection, prioritization, and high-level management of the portfolio metrics.

In developing the EPMS, the effort should be treated as a project, with a project manager, a project sponsor (who should be the Portfolio Executive with the involvement of the Steering Committee), and a project team. It is especially critical in planning out the project to gather the requirements for the EPMS to determine whether the system can be developed in-house with no commercial products or to purchase a commercial product and then customize it. In either case the expectations and requirements of the executives need to be clearly identified, prioritized, and built into the final solution.

As a project, the primary steps involved in developing the EPMS are only slightly different than planning out most other projects. They are:

- **Identify the Business Drivers:** Why are we doing this?
- **What are the goals of the EPMS**: What do we want to accomplish.
- **Define the Boundaries:** Is the EPMS limited to a single group such as IT or marketing? Does it extend to other parts of the organization? Does it cover the entire enterprise?
- **Inventory the Existing Projects:** Which will be included in the portfolio? Will the portfolio only include new, not-yet-started-projects or will existing projects be incorporated?
- **Define the stakeholders:** Who needs to be involved and what is their decision-level authority.
- **Gather and Analyze the Requirements:** Interview stakeholders to determine their expectations, analyze existing business processes, review documents, and use other requirements-gathering techniques as needed.
- **Define the Level of Formality of the EPMS:** This is a delicate area and will require full concurrence and strong support of the Steering Committee.
    - Does the EPMS provide guidance to the Steering Committee who will make all the decisions?
    - Does it have formal authority to decide which projects to do and which not to do?
    - Will it only provide monitoring for projects the Steering Committee selects without other input?
    - Can it move money and personnel resources around from one project to another or only make recommendations?
- **Design and Implement the EPMS Solution:** Will a pathfinder implementation be done first in a small group to validate the approach or will the nuclear option, rolling it out across the entire organization, be the implementation approach.
    - The design should identify the organizational structure, roles and responsibilities, staffing, and operating budget in addition to the actual physical/software/process solution.
- **Define the EPMS Success Criteria:** How will we know the system actually works as expected?
- **Validate the Outputs of the EPMS:** Is it selecting and prioritizing the projects that the executives would have?

- **Ensure Future Expansion Capabilities:** As the EPMS matures and the organization grows and changes the EPMS can grow and adapt.

Both project management and an Enterprise Portfolio Management System are what systems engineers call socio-technical systems. They are combinations of people using processes and technology to accomplish goals. When everything comes together just right, the end result is far more effective and efficient than if the different parts of the end system are done independent of each other and without consideration for the other parts, see Figure 4.

If one area of this triad is ineffective, the results are poor and the other areas must compensate for it. If the people in the portfolio management area don't have the right tools or processes, the entire EPMS will be inefficient and not deliver the results expected. If the people themselves are inexperienced or untrained in project and portfolio management the results will be the same – the EPMS will not deliver what was expected or needed.

In order to ensure that everything comes together just right, the EPMS must be designed for the right combination of people, processes, and technology, and then thoroughly planned out just as any other project would be.

There are two basic approaches to developing an EPMS. The first is to design the system and the processes, the second is to buy a commercial package that does most of what you need and the customize it. The software portions of the EPMS can be hosted on your internal IT infrastructure or in "the cloud". This gives you the greatest flexibility, the greatest privacy, and the most control over your portfolio. Hosting it internally generally provides greater security.

For a commercial EPMS package you can buy it and host it internally, or host it as a SaaS (Software as a Service) product and have the software vendor host your system. In this approach you can implement

Figure 4. Overlap of people, process, and technology

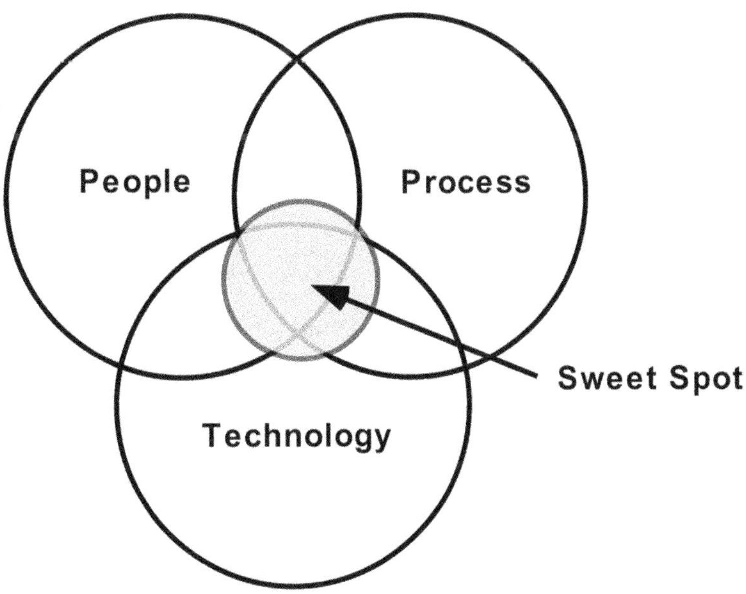

much more quickly because the configuration has already been done by the vendor. You're basically just leasing the software from them. Why would you not use this approach?

- You can't configure the system in a way that's best for your organization.
- There are on-going maintenance costs that continue as long as the vendor hosts the system.
- You're giving your internal and proprietary information to an outside party for hosting on their IT system.

Since most portfolio management vendors that offer SaaS charge by the seat, the costs can easily run into the tens of thousands of dollars per year whereas rolling your own EPMS is a one-time expense (plus on-going internal software maintenance costs).

The EPMS should be compatible with the organization's existing project planning/reporting application. This way project managers and team members only have to input data once and it can be propagated upwards into the EPMS. This means, of course, that the systems have to be able to access the same data and pull up reports at various levels. It also means that all project managers must be using the same, or data-compatible, project management tools which are configured to the same metrics.

When we develop a project plan for the EPMS implementation, it's just like a project plan for any other project we lead. Typical parts of the plan may include:

- Management plan.
- Requirements.
- Schedule.
- Budget.
- Quality.
- HR plan.
- Communications plan.
- Risk.
- Procurement (if any).
- Ancillary Areas.
  - Change Management.
  - Metrics.
  - Organizational Change Management.
  - Configuration Management.
  - Data Management.
  - etc.

Does a project manager need to do all of these in detail for every project? Absolutely not. The project manager must decide what to do, and to what extent, to make this project as successful as possible.

For these areas, it is expected by upper management that the project management plans will be written to ensure that the PM has thought through exactly how she or he will manage the project. For a project the size and effort of an EPMS implementation it should be adequate to write a single project management document that covers all of these areas rather than specific management plans for each part of the project (unless internal guidelines require it).

There are multiple consultants that have come up with CSF's (Critical Success Factors) for successful EPM implementations. They all say pretty much the same things. Gartner (Gartner 2004) found six CSFs for a portfolio management system that are common to many such recommendations:

- Making a portfolio management process work requires strong governance and holding participants accountable.
- Portfolio management is such a major undertaking that it needs to be treated as a project itself to succeed.
- It needs a process owner and a qualified support team.
- Having a disciplined process means that all proposals go through the same screening. The process is ongoing and approved initiatives are reviewed when conditions change.
- The objective prioritization framework should include investment categories and risk-adjusted evaluation criteria.
- Communication and education programs are needed to develop stakeholder buy-in and support for the project portfolio management process.
- To facilitate the use of PPM, provide tools that make compliance easier. Tools ensure consistency and support group decision making.

All of these should be taken into account when planning out the implementation process.

ONGOING OPERATIONS OF THE PORTFOLIO

There are multiple aspects to managing the operations of the EPMS. Just like any other group or department in the organization, there are governance and oversight requirements, there are personnel resource management needs, there are budgetary reporting and management requirements, and so on. There are also those aspects unique to portfolio management – tracking portfolio performance, balancing benefits and risk among multiple projects, reporting portfolio status. A substantial part of the design effort for the EPMS is to identify its operational requirements:

- What do the daily operations look like? What parts of the project selection and monitoring process are automated and what parts are performed manually.
- What parts of the larger organization are included in the portfolio management process?
- What are the roles and responsibilities? While much of the portfolio decision-making will be programmed into the software tools, there is still a need to identify the organization chart, roles and responsibilities, and all the normal aspects of a group within a larger organization.
- What type of portfolio configuration management will be required?
- What are the regulatory requirements, if any, that apply to portfolio management. Are health-care-related projects included? Are financial projects included? Are there unique management and reporting requirements for different types of projects?
- How often is the portfolio updated?
  - When a new project request comes in?
  - Weekly?
  - Monthly?

    - Quarterly
    - During annual strategic planning?
- How frequently is the portfolio re-balanced?
- What is the level of authority for decision-making? How expensive does a project have to be before a decision is elevated to a higher level of management?
- At what stage can a project be cancelled and the resources released for other projects?
- When a higher priority project is approved such as projects mandated by regulatory agencies, are existing projects cancelled or put on hold to free up the resources?

Whether the EPMS is within a PMO or exists as a stand-alone organization, it must operate within the constraints of the larger organization. If the EPMS is enterprise-wide, then it will be designed to operate at multiple levels, each level concentrating on the projects within that particular level as shown in Figure 5 (for convenience, we show the reporting relationships for a PMO, there are equivalent hierarchies for a sole EPMS):

Then within each level there might be more dedicated systems, such as an EPMS that supports only the IT department within a business unit.

Portfolio Risk Management

Part of the portfolio selection process must include estimating the probability of a project being successful as well as estimating both project risk and the overall portfolio risk level.

Project risk analysis begins when the project is first being considered for approval. If the project is approved, a more detailed risk analysis is done by the project manager and is revisited regularly during the execution phase of the project. We don't have enough accurate detailed information to calculate project benefits with great assurance. The same applies to assessing the projects risks – we can't predict them perfectly. But we can do it well enough to determine if this is a risky project or not.

Figure 5. Reporting relationships

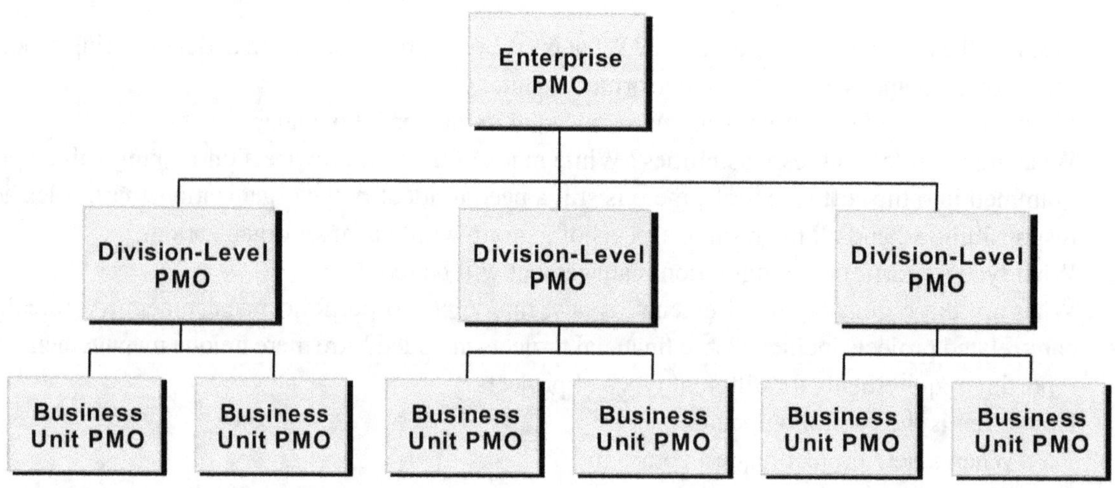

Even without knowing the detailed risks of the proposed projects we can assess at a high level which projects are risky by looking at the typical risks for the *type* of project and our own organizational history in doing those projects. A company that has a strong background in developing manufacturing facilities has a good history of what the risks are in doing a new plant. A company that does a lot of software programming understands those risks pretty well. A pharmaceutical company has a thorough understanding of the risks in developing a new drug compound. A construction company that decides to develop its own project management software is creating a high-risk project, because they just don't have the background or experience to do it. This level of risk understanding is adequate for comparing new projects against each other.

Portfolio-level risk has four aspects to it:

- Developing the wrong products.
- Delivering products too late or too much over budget.
- Wasting resources working on low-priority projects.
- Wasting resources by working on duplicate projects.

Developing the wrong product is obviously a waste of the organization's time and money. This is something that a portfolio management system cannot prevent if the management wants to try it. But the EPMS system can point out the dangers in doing so by allocating it a high risk.

Delivering the final product too late or too much over budget will have a negative impact on the financial justifications done for the business case. If the product is completed very late there is lost opportunity for the planned benefits. If it is significantly over budget the return on investment will not be as good as it was initially calculated to be. This is where our pre-project risk assessment can help. If we don't have experience with this type of project the risk analysis will point this out as a high-risk project.

The portfolio risk is the average of the individual risks of all the projects in the portfolio. We risk-score each project individually, add up all the risk scores, and divide by the number of projects. This part is simple. What is not simple is determining how much risk the Steering Committee is willing to take in exchange for benefits. As we mentioned earlier, the more risky the project the greater the benefits, but the higher the risk of failure. The projects that are low risk generally provide low benefits also. A survey performed by eQuest Consulting (2005) of project portfolios in Australia and New Zealand companies found that, on average, most projects were divided between low risk and medium risk as shown in Figure 6.

The portfolio risk is determined primarily by the risks of the individual projects that are included in the portfolio, but it is also influenced by outside factors. Any resources, such as staff, that any one project shares with other projects increases the portfolio risk. If our portfolio is a collection of public works construction projects, the risk of the whole portfolio is increased when the price of steel doubles (as it did in 2007-2008). This new level of risk is now the baseline for judging new projects. If our portfolio is the collection of all IT projects in the organization, then the risk is multiplied by the fact that one group of IT developers is working on all projects. A good EPMS will allow for input to common project risk factors independent of any one project. This allows for continually updating the risk level of the portfolio due to factors outside the individual projects. If a project is cancelled or successfully completed, the portfolio should rebalance the overall risk by taking out the risk of that particular project.

In portfolio risk management, there are risks that can multiply under the right circumstances. If multiple projects within the portfolio utilize the same resources, then care must be taken to ensure that those resources are available to all projects as needed. If one project in the portfolio runs behind the expected

Figure 6. Risk allocation among projects within a portfolio

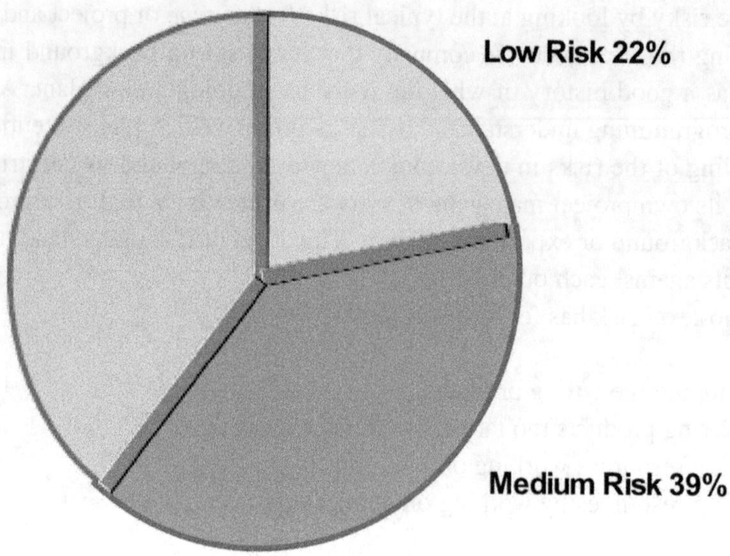

schedule and ties up critical resources, that has a ripple effect on the other projects in the portfolio that need that resource. Portfolio management tools can help identify those risks that impact multiple projects so that they can be avoided. A scarce resource is a danger point in projects, whether that scarce resource is a person with particular skills, a piece of equipment that many projects need, or a shortage of materials. If there is only one construction crane available for three projects, then the schedules must be built around its availability and it should be identified as a risk

PORTFOLIO MATURITY

The most effective approach to designing the organization charged with portfolio management is to make it part of a Program Management Office (PMO). The PMO already has much of the structure required to manage projects and programs and so incorporating portfolio management within itself is a more efficient approach. If the organization does not have a PMO, or the PMO is structured so that it is a center of best practices rather than a management office, the EPMS should be designed as a stand-alone organization.

If the PMO/EPMS is designed, put into operations, and then left static, it will suffer the same fate as other abandoned children, it will wither and die as the world around it keeps evolving. The system must be designed to also evolve and change to remain relevant to the organization. A static organization is a like a piece of sand that falls into a river, it will quickly be washed away.

There have been multiple articles in the literature about various maturity models for portfolio management, many of them following the original 5-level Capability Maturity Model developed by the Software Engineering Institute.

Dochtermann (Dochtermann, et al 2011) illustrate such a simple system. The five (5) levels of this PPM Maturity Model cover the spectrum of how organizations and the PM community can view EPM and outline a roadmap for how they can progress from simple ad-hoc task management, to complete end-to-end Portfolio Management, Knowledge Management, and eventually Strategic Execution.

1. **Low PPM Maturity:** No organization consciously chooses to be at a basic level of maturity. Managing projects and initiatives is usually an organic process that begins with 'what works' and quickly becomes inadequate as the organization begins to grow beyond its original parameters. As organizations gain in their understanding of how to get things done, an effective set of processes, tools, and technologies are implemented, usually resulting in improved organizational efficiency.
2. **Growth of PPM Project Management:** At this level the introduction of PM tools and methodology provide a better means of managing projects by assisting users in the management of work, analyzing the added information regarding the time and resources allocated to the tasks, allocating costs and budgets, and creating schedules to aid the team with the planning of deliverables for their projects.
3. **Progressing Level of PPM Program Management:** As the complexity of business interactions increase, the need for a higher level of consolidation (creation of programs) also occurs. The integration of business intelligence metadata needs to be threaded within the PM structure. Stand-alone tools make it difficult to consolidate or "roll-up" data to support the needs of Demand Management, Capacity Planning, Prioritization of Work, and Business Value Planning.
4. **Progressing Level of PPM Portfolio Management:** Portfolios of projects or programs, and other work that are grouped together, can now be initiated to facilitate effective management of that work to meet the strategic business objectives of the business. Additionally, Business Intelligence and Reporting provide senior executives portfolio, program, and project data, presenting current and accurate information to assist in making informed executive and managerial decisions. PPM is now enabling organizations to begin taking advantage of visibility of bottom up analysis (a rolling up of task work/efforts/results) as well as top down analysis (ensuring the alignment of project initiatives to strategic business goals).
5. **High Level of PPM Strategic Execution:** At this level of PPM maturity it becomes clear how Portfolio Strategy is influenced by the vision and long-range intentions of an organization. Moving along the Strategy and Vision segment of the model, we can also see how Business Goals and Priorities, which are established and overseen at the Executive Level, can incorporate key metrics to help direct and measure the delivery of work by program and project teams.

Similarly, a Portfolio Maturity Model might have the common five level tier structure shown in Figure 7 (adapted from Gartner 2010). These levels range from least mature, Level 1, to fully mature, Level 5. The levels can be applied to any business process, but the dimensions that make up the model are unique to a role or a process.

Level 1: Reactive: No organization consciously chooses to be at a Level 1 maturity. Generally, some external event, like rapid growth, change in market conditions or a merger/acquisition, causes the organization to lumber out of its previous state (which is generally unconscious competence) like a bear awakening from hibernation.

Level 2: Emerging Discipline: Level 2 is defined as "emerging discipline" because this is the point where the organization decides that the plate spinning and ball juggling of Level 1 simply can't go on anymore, and that slowing down just long enough to get organized is a make-or-break situation. Depending on how long an organization stayed at Level 1 and depending on its culture, Level 2 can be a massive swing of the pendulum from an "anything goes, just get it done" environment to

Figure 7. Adapted from Gartner's project portfolio management maturity model

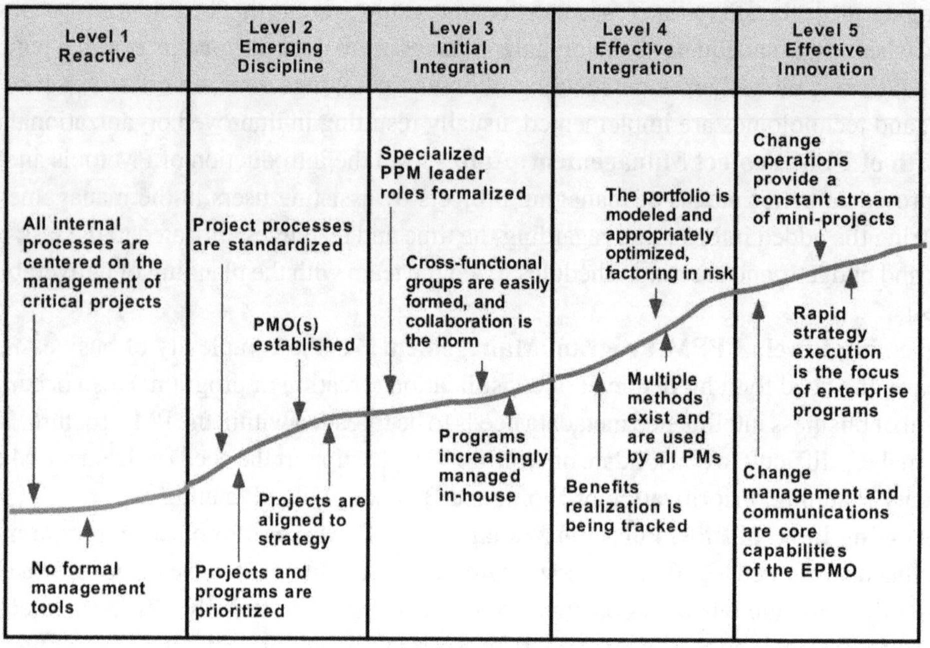

a process-driven, moribund organization where rules get followed, and nothing gets done at the most extreme level.

Level 3: Initial Integration: The most useful competency for a PPM function at Level 3 is the ability to think holistically, focusing on the whole and not the parts. This entails being able to understand how a change in one area will affect others, how changes should be made and in what order to achieve maximum results. Level 3 concentrates on just enough of everything to get things working. It's not perfection, but it is the beginning of a state of conscious competence.

Level 4: Effective Integration: Hard work and more process will not get an organization to Level 4. The process maturity approach of other models has led to the belief that process is the sole measure of excellence and maturity, and when it comes to PPM, we can say definitively that it isn't true. Level 4 is defined as effective integration and is once again a return to the state of unconscious competence that preceded Level 1. At Level 4, the enterprise begins to focus on being project-capable, not because there is some mistaken belief that project management processes are a "silver bullet" for all organizational problems, but because there is a realization that the fastest, least expensive way to accomplish anything new and different is through the mechanism of setting up a project or program.

Level 5: Effective Innovation: Level 5 has a touch of Camelot attached to it. It is a dream and a goal that occasionally becomes a reality. The hallmarks of Level 5 from a PPM perspective have to do with a complete change in how organizations function. Innovation is no longer an afterthought. Innovation becomes a continuous process everywhere in the organization. To accomplish this, the organization begins to split into two conjoined halves. Like the brain, the operational side of the organization begins to embrace fully the concept of "change operations," while the development side of the organization turns to more exploratory and classically innovative initiatives.

DEALING WITH STRATEGIC CHANGES

Organizations live in a dynamic environment. Fitzroy and Hulbert (Fitzroy and Hulbert 2004) classified the environment into three levels:

- **The World Environment:** The broad social/technical/economic worldwide environment in which the organization competes. These influences affect virtually all organizations simultaneously. While some changes can happen rapidly, the more common influences are the rise of the Orient in manufacturing, population growth, and the aging of the population in the more developed countries.
- **The Industry Environment:** The factors that impact a specific industry such as the construction industry or the aerospace industry. These influences can include the lack of skilled resources specific to the industry, market conditions, entry barriers, etc.
- **The Specific Competitive Environment:** This is the environment created by the relationships the organization has with its competitors, its collaborators (consultants and supply chain), and finally the organization's customers.

Boston Consulting Group (BCG) emphasized this rapidly changing role as follows: *In this environment, if companies are to remain competitive, they must simultaneously optimize both how they run the business and how they change the business, the latter typically through the development and implementation of programs of new strategic initiatives.* (BCG 2013).

Organizations that live in a highly dynamic environment, such as almost any software, or technology-driven environment (think how fast smart phones have changed!) face a lot of uncertainty. Taking two years to develop a new product when the environment can change within six months is highly risky and requirements a strong forecasting capability. You want your product to come out at the front end of the technology when it's released, not a year after your competitors have released their own versions.

The uncertainty about what the future is, what technologies will be available, what your competitors are doing, and even what your strategic goals will be in two years creates an environment that must constantly be reviewed and changes made to adapt.

Regular review of the portfolio by the Steering or Governance Committee is crucial to continued success. The committee should add, kill, or reprioritize the projects in the project registry. According to McDonough and Spital (McDonough and Spital 2003), portfolios reviewed quarterly do better than those reviewed semi-annually, although this might depend on the type of projects under review.

So how should the portfolio react when the goals change? Your design of the EPM system has to take this possibility into account and be sufficiently flexible enough to support it. There are basically three major answers to this question, and which one is correct depends on how upper management decides they want to handle it.

When the strategic goals change the portfolio should be re-examined for its congruence with the new goals. Projects that no longer support the new goals after being reassessed need to be identified and a decision made as to how to disposition them.

1. First option, if a project no longer supports the new strategic goals, is to determine if you need to create a replacement project or if you even need to do a replacement project. If a higher priority

project is facing cost over-runs the Steering Committee could use the resources from the cancelled project to support the overrun.

2. Second option is to simply pick the next higher priority project from the existing list of proposed projects. This has the benefit of already having gone through the assessment and prioritization process.
3. Third option is allow the division that "owns" the cancelled project to propose another project that is important to them. This communicates that a group whose project is cancelled will not be punished for cancelling a project. That type of decision-making freedom is beneficial to the organization. The downside to this option is that it lends itself to political manipulation in which a group can get a project done that would not have scored highly if it went through the normal assessment process.

While not a primary consideration, a cancelled project also frees up resources. Sometimes this is a consideration that should be taken into account.

If the strategic goals change, we have to reweight the new goals. Upper management must tell us (not us them) what the importance of each goal is and how much weight it has in the overall calculation. When we have each project fill out the detailed question sheet that determines its costs and benefits, we have to weight each answer so that we apply higher weights to the more important goals.

As a thought experiment, let us consider a fictional company, MegaNews International. MegaNews International (MNI) is a multi-national conglomerate with over 50,000 employees worldwide. 2008 revenues were over $25 billion US dollars, operating income was $3.9 B, cash and cash equivalents were $6 B, and they had $34 B in assets worldwide. Net income from all operations was $2.8 B. This was a 6% growth over 2014. Its world-wide holdings include ownership or has significant interest in 10 movie studios, 50 television stations, 25 cable channels, 5satellite TV channels, 100 newspapers, 10 magazines, one publishing company, and various other associated enterprises such as real estate development and holding companies.

MegaNews International has spent the past 6 months determining what its strategic goals are for the next 3 years. Following the structure of the Balanced Scorecard (Kaplan & Norton 1992), its primary goals are the following:

1. **Financial:**
    a. Increase net revenue by increasing profit margins by 5% per year.
    b. Increase sales by 10% per year.
2. **Customer Relationship:**
    a. Develop stronger customer relationships.
    b. Become a full service news provider.
3. **Internal Process:**
    a. Achieve operational excellence through a strong emphasis on process improvement and process ownership.
    b. Achieve project management excellence.
    c. Improve our internal customer relationship processes.
4. **Employees:**
    a. Build a high performance corporate culture and values.
    b. Recognize and accept change as a necessary part of the industry.

In addition to its strategic goals, MegaNews is required to abide by the local and national laws and regulations in every country in which they deliver the news. The Corporate CIO has just returned to the US headquarters in Los Angles from the annual strategic planning session held at corporate HQ in Australia and finds the current list of projects on his desk shown in Table 1.

The project portfolio process has selected these projects through financial calculations and risk analysis as the projects best supporting strategic goals. The results are as follows in Table 2.

What happens if management decides to change the strategic goals to adapt to the new financial environment? Compare the old strategic goals with the new ones in Table 3.

There is a new emphasis on increasing revenues and profit margins and a new emphasis on Internet-based revenue. We now have a new goal of increasing internal productivity by 10% to save costs, among other new goals. To support the new goals, since we created the initial project list, two new projects have been proposed:

Table 1. MegaNews International projects list

1. New privacy laws that will take effect in 12 months in Europe require us to strengthen our web site registration database. a. This is a regulatory-driven, mandatory project.
2. A new law in California requires us to change our web site so that viewers must "opt-in" to receive our e-mail newsletters rather than "opt-out" from receiving it. This must be completed within three months. a. This is a regulatory-driven, mandatory project.
3. Corporate finance wants to install a data warehouse to manage all of the financial information. No given timeframe. a. Estimated cost: $2.5 million, b. Estimated benefit: $50,000 per year in improved productivity by corporate finance. c. Resources required: 10 people for 6 months.
4. We want to have a new web site to compile news from other sources and allow viewers to buy it from us. a. Estimated cost: $4 million. b. Estimated benefit: $1.5 million/year. c. Resources required: 10 people for 6 months.
5. We are opening new US headquarters in Los Angeles and need to tie their LAN into the corporate network. The construction schedule says it will be ready for IT within 4 months. a. Estimated cost: $0.5 million. b. Estimated benefit: $100,000 per year. c. Resources required: 5 people for 3 months.
6. United Press International, a major news feed for us, is upgrading their news distribution network within the next six months and we need to modify our IT infrastructure to tie into it. a. While not a regulatory-driven project, this project is considered mandatory because it will significantly impact our ability to deliver our product – news.
7. We need a new service to allow us to deliver user-customized financial news via apps for smart phones, tablets, and PDAs with wireless connections. a. Estimated cost: $5 million. b. Estimated benefit: $2 million/year from advertising. c. Resources required: 25 people for 6 months.
8. We are going to put news screens into each Starbucks Coffee Shop in the US showing news headlines from around the world. This will be done over the next three years. a. Estimated cost: $20 million. b. Estimated benefit: $10 million/year from advertising. c. Resources required: 6 people for 36 months.
9. Our web site is currently written in English, we intend to internationalize it by creating versions in multiple languages. a. Estimated cost: $6 million. b. Estimated benefit: $2 million/year from advertising. c. Resources required: 25 people for 6 months.

Table 2. Financial calculations for MegaNews projects

Proj.	Project	Cost Estimate	Annual Benefits	Payback Period	NPV	ROI	Benefit/ Cost
A	New European privacy laws that take effect in 6 months require us to strengthen our website registration.	$ 1 M	N/A	N/A	N/A	N/A	N/A
B	A new US law requires us to change our website so that viewers "opt-in" to receive our e-mail newsletters rather than "opt-out". Due 3 mo.	$ 0.5 M	N/A	N/A	N/A	N/A	N/A
C	Corporate finance wants to install a data warehouse to manage all financial data.	$ 2.5 M	$50,000	50 years	- $2.13M	-0.9	-0.01
D	We want to have a new website to compile news from other sources and allow viewers to buy it from us.	$ 4 M	$1.5 M	2.67	$1.84M	-0.875	-1.88
E	We are opening new US headquarters in Los Angeles and need to tie their LAN into the corporate network.	$ 0.5 M	$100,000	5.00	- $93k	1	1
F	UPI is upgrading their news network. We need to modify our system to tie into it.	$ 3.5 M	N/A	N/A	N/A	N/A	N/A
G	We need a new service to allow us to deliver user-specific news via smart phones and tablets. Revenue will come from ads.	$ 5 M	$2 M	2.50	$2.76M	1	2
H	We are going to put news screens into US Starbucks, showing news headlines from around the world. The revenue will come from ads.	$ 20 M	$10 M	2.00	$18.45M	1.5	2.5
I	We will internationalize our website it by creating versions in multiple languages. Revenue will come from ads.	$ 6 M	$ M	3.00	$1.8M	0.667	1.67

Table 3. Changes in strategic goals

Old Strategic Goals	New Strategic Goals
1. Financial: a. Increase net revenue by increasing profit margins by 5% per year. b. Increase sales by 10% per year. **2. Customer Relationship:** a. Develop stronger customer relationships. b. .2. Become a full service news provider. **3. Internal Process:** a. Achieve operational excellence through a strong emphasis on process improvement and process ownership. b. Achieve project management excellence. c. Improve our internal customer relationship processes. **4. Employees:** a. Build a high performance corporate culture and values. b. Recognize and accept change as a necessary part of the industry.	**1. Financial:** a. Increase overall revenue by increasing profit margins by 10% per year. b. Increase revenue from Internet operations by 20% per year. **2. Customer Relationship:** a. Become the #1 provider of world-wide news on the Internet. b. Become a full service news provider through Internet, electronic media (radio and TV), and print outlets. **3. Internal Process:** a. Achieve project management excellence. b. Improve our internal productivity by 10%. **4. Employees:** a. Treat our employees as highly skilled assets. b. Recognize and accept change as a necessary part of the industry.

- Improve our internal business processes by consolidating existing processes and eliminating unneeded ones. This will cost $150M and will improve productivity by 5%.
- We can significantly expand our own Internet News Portal into an e-commerce site for a cost of about $2M. This could be rolled out in phases over a period of 18 months and provide $1M in annual revenues.

Doing the financial calculations for these two projects (Note: for the first project, assuming 20,000 people with an average salary of $80,000, a 1% increase in productivity is the same as saving the work of 200 employees. 200 employees make $16M per year) we see that in Table 4.

Project K, while promising to improve our internal business processes, does not look promising in the calculations. Project L, which provides a revenue stream, looks much better and would be prioritized at the same level as existing Project G.

The portfolio should be rebalanced approximately every 6 months. Too often and the project work is disrupted too often and teams get discouraged when their projects are cancelled because something more financially sexy was approved. Not often enough and too much time is wasted on projects that are not as beneficial as ones waiting in the queue. Regulatory projects are very disruptive because they can interrupt projects in work to meet unexpected regulatory changes, often with tight deadlines.

SOLUTIONS AND RECOMMENDATIONS

While it is not possible to significantly change the environment the organization operates in, a basic principle of systems engineering says the organization must be as flexible as the environment itself. If the environment changes rapidly, the organization must be highly adaptive. If the environment changes very slowly, the organization itself can be structured for slower and more deliberate changes.

In order for the EPMS to remain effective as the larger organization evolves and changes, the EPMS must itself evolve from a localized group providing only project selection to a larger, more inclusive role including overall portfolio metrics, risk analysis, and rebalancing of the portfolio as the environment changes. More mature portfolio management offices have a broader scope of work and more responsibility than newly implemented offices.

In order to operate efficiently, the EPMS should be built into the PMO rather than be designed as a stand-alone organization.. There is a significant amount of overlap in the data that both organizations require as well as in roles and responsibilities of personnel and the more intimately they work together the more efficient the operations become.

Table 4. Projected benefits of new projects to support new goals

Proj.	Project	Cost Estimates	Annual Benefits	Payback Period	NPV	ROI	Benefit/ Cost
K	Improve internal business processes	$ 150 M	$16 M	9.38 yrs	-$79.7M	-0.467	0.53
L	expand our own Internet News Portal into an e-commerce site	$ 2 M	$1 M	2	$1.85	0.15	1.00

In order to be most effective, the PMO/EPMS should report as high up in the organization as is feasible. In some international organizations the head of the PMO sits at the executive table along with the heads of the other major departments. Involvement in the strategic planning process allows strategic plans to be built taking into account existing work and resource limitations.

When implementing the EPMS, it should be done first in a localized part of the organization as a path-finder project. As lessons are learned and the organization understands better what the EPMS can provide the system can be expanded into larger parts of the organization until it becomes enterprise-wide. When the author designed the PMO for the Saline Water Conversion Corporation in Riyadh, Saudi Arabia, the first implementation was designed to minimize any disruptions to the existing organization. Over a period of 3-5 years the PMO would expand and evolve, gaining personnel and processes to cover all projects within the organization (Parth 2015).

AREAS FOR FUTURE RESEARCH

Must of the literature on portfolio management focuses on the design of the process and on the filtering metrics that a portfolio management system uses to identify and prioritize projects. There is a significant amount of research that still needs to be done in how to most efficiently operate and grow the EPMS. There is also more research required in how to rebalance the portfolio once the organization's strategic goals change.

CONCLUSION

This chapter touches on more of the operational aspects of a portfolio management system rather than on its design or on the financial filtering criteria required to select and to prioritize projects. We discussed the differences between creating the EPMS within a PMO or as a stand-alone organization. We briefly discussed different types of PMOs and how some are appropriate for portfolio management but some are not. We provided an example of a highly successful EPMS implementation within the structure of a corporate-level IT PMO for an international organization.

Once the EPMS is implemented, it must be managed as any other department within the organization, including personnel and budgetary management. Because the larger organization is not static, the EPMS itself must grow and mature in order to remain relevant and provide a strong portfolio of projects even though the strategic goals of the organization keep changing.

REFERENCES

Anyosa, V. (2010). *Linking Portfolio, Program and Projects to Business Strategy*. Paper presented at the 2010 PMI Asia Pacific Congress, Melbourne, Australia.

BCG. (2013). *Strategic Initiative Management – the PMO Imperative*. Joint publication of Boston Consulting Group and PMI.

Cabanis-Brewin, J. (2000). Interview with Richard Russell of the Balanced Scorecard Collaborative. *Project Management Best Practices Report*, *2*(9), 1.

Forrester Consulting. (2013). *Strategic PMOs Play A Vital Role In Driving Business Outcomes*. Author.

Dochtermann, D., Jesus-Olhausen, A. L., & Cermak, T. (2011). *Introduction to a Project Portfolio Management Maturity Model*. Paper presented at the 2011 PMI North American Congress. Retrieved from http://www.equestconsulting.com.au/EQuest_Consulting_EPM_Survey_2005.pdf

Fitzroy, P., & Hulbert, J. M. (2004). *Strategic management: Creating value in a turbulent world.* New York, NY. Wiley.

Gartner Group. (2004). *Gartner Shines the Light on PPM.* Retrieved from http://www.gantthead.com/article.cfm?ID=219526

Gartner Group. (2010). *White paper published 2010*. Retrieved March 2011 from www.gartner.com/DisplayTimument?Tim_cd=205800&ref=g_rss

Kaplan, R. S., & Norton, D. P. (1992, January-February). The Balanced Scorecard – Measures That Drive Performance. *Harvard Business Review*, 71–79. PMID:10119714

McDonough, E. F., & Spital, F. C. (2003). Managing project portfolios. *Research-Technology Management*, *46*(3), 40–46.

Parth, F. R. (2015). *Project Control Through an Effective PMO - A Case Study*. Paper presented to the UAE chapter of AACE, Abu Dhabi, UAE..

PMI. (2013). *Pulse of the Profession - PMO Frameworks*. PMI.

KEY TERMS AND DEFINITIONS

EPMS: Enterprise Portfolio Management System: (EPMS). The organization-wide portfolio management system including tools, processes, and resources. Distinguished from a lower-level portfolio management system.

PMO: Portfolio Management Office or Program Management Office. When a PMO is used to manage a program it is the Program Management Office. When a PMO is used to manage the portfolio of projects it is the Portfolio Management Office.

Portfolio: The collection of all projects within an organization. They may be managed individually or managed collectively.

Program: A group of related projects managed as a single group in order to obtain control not available by managing the projects in isolation.

Project: A project consists of a unique set of processes consisting of coordinated and controlled activities with start and end dates, performed to achieve project objectives. (ISO 21500).

Steering Committee: The high-level group of executives that has overall responsibility and oversight of the portfolio.

Chapter 12
Project Portfolio Management and Organization:
An Integrated and Circular Model

Lucia Aiello
Sapienza University of Rome, Italy

Mauro Gatti
Sapienza University of Rome, Italy

ABSTRACT

The chapter is an overview on organizational models for project management, identifying the characteristics of a possible reference model that joins to the necessity of portfolio management. The approach to portfolio management requires attention to the integrated management of projects; this is why the organizational structure matrix "differentiated" could be a useful reference point. This chapter proposes, therefore, a reworking of the organizational structure design criteria considering both the Value Chain of Porter is the matrix structure "differentiated". Ultimately, the contribution configures the characteristics of the organizational model for portfolio in relation to the type of project - internal/process, external/product mix - in order to improve the performance of internal projects whose objectives are not always explicit. The basic idea of this work is to apply the concept of Porter's value chain not only functions but also the portfolio of projects that the company has.

INTRODUCTION

Various proposals have been advanced over time in literature to describe models for project management, but rarer is the case of such analysis for portfolio management. The analysis of the main literature on project management, portfolio management and their connections with the organizational design, particularly in relation to the organizational structure, highlights a different approach from the one shown in this chapter, which is instead an "integrated and circular model for portfolio".

Studies in project management have identified a plurality of organizational structures differentiated according to the hierarchical importance of the project on technical and specialized areas (functions).

DOI: 10.4018/978-1-5225-2151-8.ch012

Some authors (i.e. Tonchia and Nonino, 2007) propose different types of organizational structure for project or multi-project management: 1. weak matrix structure; 2. balanced matrix structure; 3. strong matrix structure; 4. pure projects organization; 5. "separate property" organizational matrix. Of equal importance is the approach known as value chain (Porter, 1986), which is applicable in case of coordination of multiple projects simultaneously.

The best way to be aligned with the new needs of organizational structure for Portfolio would be a new approach of structure. Thus the authors will pragmatically develop a systematic approach to active management, assuming that this is a worthwhile goal.

The first necessary ingredient for success in dynamic organizations is recognition of the challenge, which requires a new approach of organizational structure.

Johnson, Scholes, and Whittington (2008) consider that the strategy can be defined as *the direction and scope of an organization over the long term: which achieves advantage for the organization through its configuration of resources within a challenging environment, to meet the needs of markets and to fulfill stakeholder expectations*. Romano (2015) affirms that *strategy is the direction and scope of an organization over the long-term: which appears to be able to produce an advantage for the organization*. In line with this concept it is that the competitive advantage would be the key factor for new organizational strategy in portfolio management and thus in project management.

Romano (2015) considers that an organization needs a strategic vision to describe the future that this organization wants to create; organizational structure – in this context – is crucial to portfolio development. The strategic vision should be a key factor for the organization. Based on this vision in mid- and short-term organizations, Romano stated that *there is a need to define a mission that can be broken down into several objectives. Objectives are more manageable than a "vision," as they are conceptually smaller and more measurable, and are used to transfer the vision into results. Strategic objectives must be, at the very least, quantifiable, measurable, and timed. The executive performance of an organization can be measured by the level of achievement of the strategic objectives.*

Project management literature indicates as the first element to start a project the definition of the organizational structure, from which derives the identification of the human resources required and the communication that they are involved into project.

The second element is to define and map the project phases, thus:

1. Start-up.
2. Pianification.
3. Supply.
4. Implementation and monitoring.
5. Closing the project.

The last element is represented by the management of project that is synthetized into individuation/ mapping of nine knowledge areas from PMI (Tonchia e Nonino, 2007: 3), attributable to:

1. **Management of the Project Integration (PIM, Project Integration Management):** This area guarantees the efficacy and efficiency of the coordination of different projects.
2. **Management of Objectives and Scope Of Project (PSM, Project Scope Management):** This area ensures that the objectives of project are consistent with the project planning, through a clearly definition of the process.

3. **Project Human Resource Management (PHRM):** This area is dedicated to the mapping and assignment of tasks, responsibilities and optimal job placement of human resource to realize the project. These aspects could be defined consistently with the goals to achieve.
4. **Project Quality Management (PQM):** This area defines the quality assurance process.
5. **Project Time Management (PTM):** This area ensures compliance with the timetable for objectives' achievement.
6. **Project Cost Management (PCM):** This area is tasked with planning, estimating, cost allocation and monitoring to ensure the project is completed within the approved budget.
7. **Project Risk Management (PRM):** This area plans, identifies, analyzes and responds to risk, monitoring and controlling them during the project.
8. **Project Communication Management (PCM):** This area takes the role of generation, collection, distribution, storage, retrieval, and ultimate disposition of project information.
9. **Project Procurement Management (PPM):** This area organizes the acquisition processes of product or services by entities outside the project team (other groups or individuals that refer to functions; individuals or other companies).

The exposure of this work requires dissemination of project management base concepts.

A project is a set of complex and interrelated activities, whose finality is a well-defined objective, accessible through synergistic and coordinated efforts. This area is responsible to carry out its duties within a predetermined time and with a precise amount of human and financial resources available.

Sometimes, Project Management (PM) is associated - wrongly - only to companies that work on the base of job orders. Differently, PM, both historically and in the reality of today's competitive environments, has always been part of human life, and the great works have always followed a project approach. Archibald (2003), one of the main researcher in project management, shows this aspect in his contributes.

Among the basic principles of project management, there is also the characterization of the global uniqueness of the elements of the project, namely:

1. The objective.
2. The time, economic-financial, human resources (or other) limits.
3. The specificity compared to other floors.
4. The specific organization of the project.

The portfolio concept starts from the definition of program(s): when projects under the same management are more than one, it is possible to consider it a program. In this situation, the coherence of all projects with the purpose of the program is important.

The variables of project management can be defined on the basis of the management concept. The distinction between "core" and "extra-core" business activities is mandatory, as specified in the following lines:

1. **Operation:** Typical activities of the sector, such as manufacturing, engineering, research and development. All assets that are owned by the logistics process and product/service innovation process.
2. **Extra-Operative:** Activities not directly related with the sector in which the company operates, such as administration and control.

The first characteristic that PM must consider is the case of interconnected activities among different projects, avoiding overlapping in the period of time in which the projects coexist.

Management variables can be summarized as follows:

1. Define the distinctive features of the project.
2. Manage the quality – level and goal – of the project.
3. Manage the time of realization of the project.

The core business is fully involved in the project, so it is essential to consider how the activities performed by the project are involved in the business processes, this is related to logistics and innovation.

The logistics process covers the activities ranging from purchasing to distribution (in the chain of the primary assets); the innovation process, the ones ranging from infrastructure to management of suppliers (in the chain of secondary assets). Project Management competence is tightly linked to the innovation process.

It is important to distinguish, at this point, project management by operation management. Operation Management is responsible for the conformity of the product/service quality, the standard time management & delivery and the standard cost management. Project Management is concerned with the quality of the defined level against objectives, duration of the project (time-to-market) and the spending budget.

Project management can identify five areas of application:

1. Design and development of product.
2. Design of service.
3. Management of orders of construction/product/service.
4. Engineering-To-Order.
5. Planning and management of business performance improvement.
6. Public research and international cooperation.

These application areas depend from two fundamental elements:

1. Customers' requirements.
2. Perspective.

Customer requirements can be "not specified a priori" or "a priori known"; the prospect can be "internal" or "external".

In particular:

1. The scope of public research and international cooperation has an inside perspective and a target customer.
2. The scope of the improvement of internal processes has a principal customer and an internal perspective.
3. The scope of the design and development of product and services shows a market perspective and a target customer.
4. The scope of the order management is characterized by a customer client and from a market perspective.

Design and Development of Product

The design and the development of a product is related to:

1. Technology development.
2. Development of product.

Design a product line that is oriented to the market starts from the definition of the differences between the products and the identity of the line. Product innovation may relate to the improvement or the change of the core concept of the product.

Innovation can be:

- Radical, new concept and product architecture.
- Incremental, improvement of the product.
- Modular, new concept.
- Architecture, new architecture.

The innovation, therefore, depends on two variables, the core concept of the product and the link between concept and components (product architecture).

Design of Service

Service design may relate to three areas: the first one is the service offered to the customer by industrial and commercial companies to integrate their products; the second one is the service of the tertiary sector; the last one is that of non-profit organizations and public administrations.

Service is a set of tangible and intangible benefits, explicit and implicit (Normann, 1992). The management of a service requires the recognition and application of psychological and behavioral skills related to customer perception and to service complexity.

The Management of Contracts

Order management is an area where the client is a society that requires to others the fulfillment of a work or a service, through an order.

Companies operating on commission can receive specificities of realization of the service running, or develop their own part of the design and/or engineering from the client.

The Design of the Business Improvement

To address the issue of the design of improvement in the company there's the need to start from the concept of strategic change.

Strategic change: redefinition of the objectives and the means to achieve greater competitive advantage.

The strategic change requires strategic flexibility, a concept that involves four aspects:

1. Rapid change of the competitive priorities within the business
2. Width and positioning of the strategic options, at time "t", within the business.
3. Speed of moving from a business to another.
4. Extent of the potential accessible business.

Public and Private Research, and International Cooperation

The application field of research and cooperation relates to research projects and mainly involves public institutions, private non-profit institutions and enterprises.

Based on these introductory reflections and analysis, the work aims to present an overview on organizational model for project management, offering the ideal one for the portfolio management.

The analysis compares the main references in literature about organizational models for project, first comparing the strengths and weaknesses of each one and then comparing them with the needs of portfolio management.

In literature emerge different proposals for models for the project but not for portfolio. This work, therefore, proposes an integrated, circular organizational model for portfolio, defined as "integrated and circular model for portfolio". The analysis of the main literature on project management, portfolio management and the connections with the organizational design, in particular with reference to the organizational structure, detects a different approach.

In project management we have been proposed various organizational structures in relation to the hierarchical importance of the project on the functions. As already written Tonchia and Nonino (2007) propose five types of organizational structures for the management of projects or multi-project:

1. Weak matrix structure for the project;
2. Structure for project balanced matrix;
3. Project structure with a strong matrix;
4. Organization for pure projects;
5. Matrix Organizational Structure "Differentiated".

The approach to portfolio requires an attention to the integrated management of the projects, therefore, it is necessary to start from the differentiated matrix organizational structure.

Another important insight detected by Tonchia and Nonino (2007) – when there is the coordination of multiple projects simultaneously – is the approach to the value chain (Porter, 1991).

The work, therefore, will go to proposing a recasting of the organizational structure considering both the Value Chain (Porter's value chain) and the "differentiated" matrix structure.

In the second analysis, the contribution attempts to map the characteristics of the organizational model for Portfolio in relation to the type of portfolio – internal/process, external/product, mix – in order to improve the performance of internal projects, whose objectives are not always considered.

The basic idea is to apply the chain of Porter's value not to the functions but at the project portfolio.

The research design is represented in Figure 1.

The analysis puts in comparison the principle literature on organizational model of enterprises which work for project. We are going to compare the main strengths and weaknesses of the models, and then we will compare this with the needs of portfolio management.

Figure 1. Research design

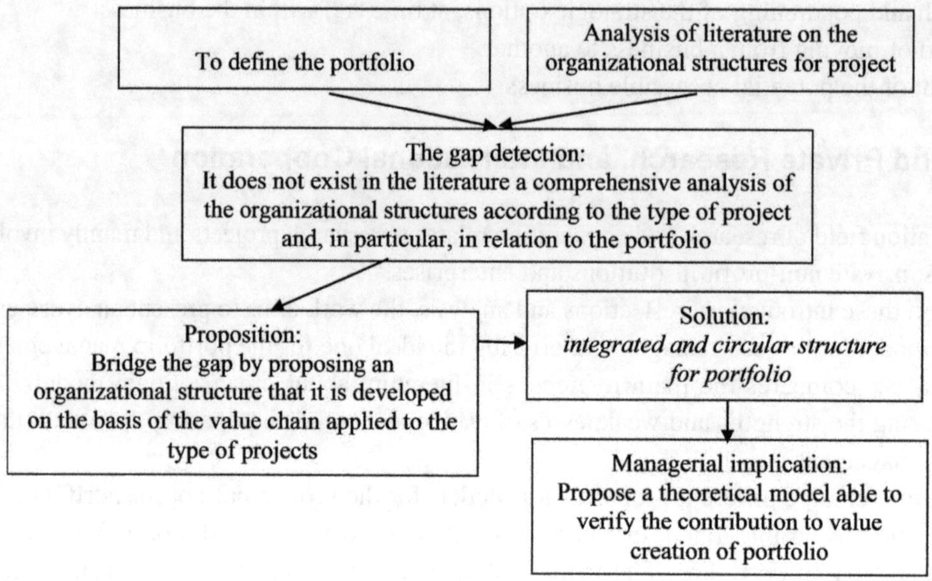

The aim of this contribution is to explain how designing an organizational structure based on the project's ability to create value, it is possible to define the best priority and hierarchical connection between the functions in relation to the need of create value, rather than the arbitrary choices direction.

BACKGROUND AND MAIN FOCUS AREAS IN PROJECT PORTFOLIO MANAGEMENT AND ORGANIZATION

Organizational Structures

The analysis starts from a basic concept: the overcoming of functional and hierarchical trumpeting in the organizational structure for the project and the interconnection of projects regardless of type but compared to their contribution to the value chain.

The organizations, regardless of the type of projects - "inner", "outer", "mixed" - must overcome the functional and hierarchical barriers, therefore, must be flexible. There are two dimensions to be involved: **line**, which belongs to the functions; project, which is part of the project. In this case there are two management levels, the function manager and the project manager respectively.

Traditionally the managers of function must ensure compliance with the standards of efficiency and effectiveness characterizing the functions, as well as the management, maintenance and growth of resources and similar skills, their allocation to the various projects. The project manager is responsible to make the best use of resources allocated to the project. Two figures of the same level but operating on the vertical (line managers) and horizontal line (project manager) of the organizational structure.

In relation to the hierarchical force of the two managers there have been developed, in literature, three types of organizational structures:

1. A weak matrix, in which the hierarchical force is of the line manager.
2. A balanced matrix, in which every manager has authority on the competence line.
3. A strong matrix, in which the hierarchical force is the project manager.

In Figure 2 the link between the different levels that operate into an organization is represented, particularly, the hierarchical level. In the figure is possible to see that into this structure the vertical line is stronger than that horizontal; in this case the allocation of resources and priorities is determined with respect to the priority choices of the function. In the figure, thus, the bold lines indicate the priority of the hierarchical level over the level indicated by dashed line. This model has an important limitation i.e. the waste of energy and resources along the hierarchical line to the intersection with the project. Moreover, in this model, it is not possible to identify priorities among the individual projects and thus to their contribution to organizational strategy.

Figure 3 shows the structure in which the chain of command has equal strength both horizontally and vertically; in this case the allocation of resources and priorities is determined equitably with respect to the function and priority choices of the project. The model seems to have a limit, that is, the difficulty of defining the right balance between the hierarchy of the function and the project. In this model, however, it is difficult to identify the contribution of individual projects to the definition of the value.

Figure 4 shows the model in which the hierarchical structure is stronger horizontally than vertically. In this case, the allocation of resources and priorities is determined with respect to the priorities of the project. The limitation of the model is, as for the weak matrix model, the dispersion of energy and resources along the project line; also in this model it is not possible to identify priorities among the individual projects and thus their contribution to organizational strategy.

Based on the limitations presented by the traditional organizational structures, other variables and characteristics of project management were analyzed, bringing the work to consider the role of multi-project management.

Figure 2. Structure for project to weal matrix
Source: Elaboration on Tonchia, Nonino, 2007.

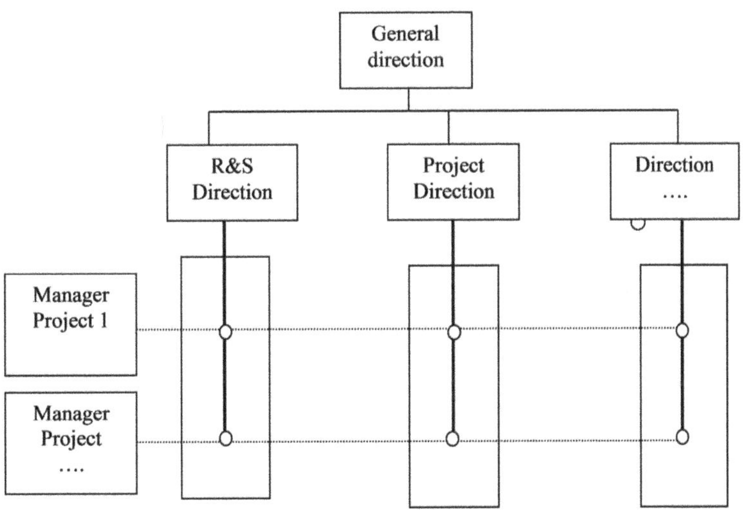

Figure 3. Structure for project to balanced matrix
Source: Elaboration on Tonchia, Nonino, 2007.

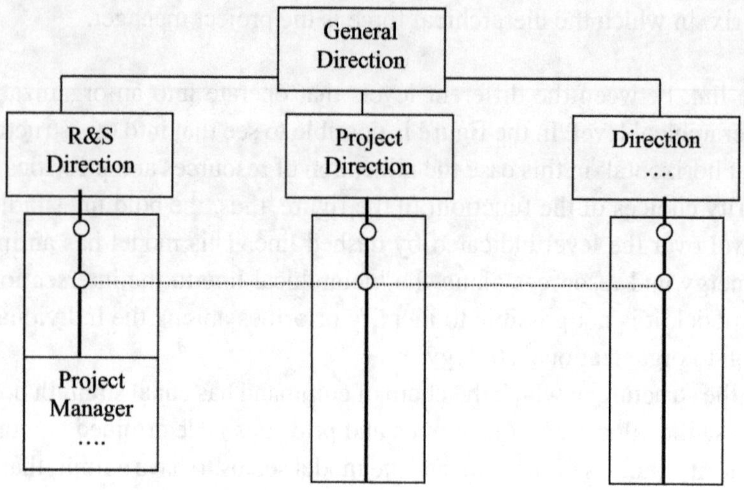

Figure 4. Structure for project to strong matrix
Source: Elaboration on Tonchia, Nonino, 2007.

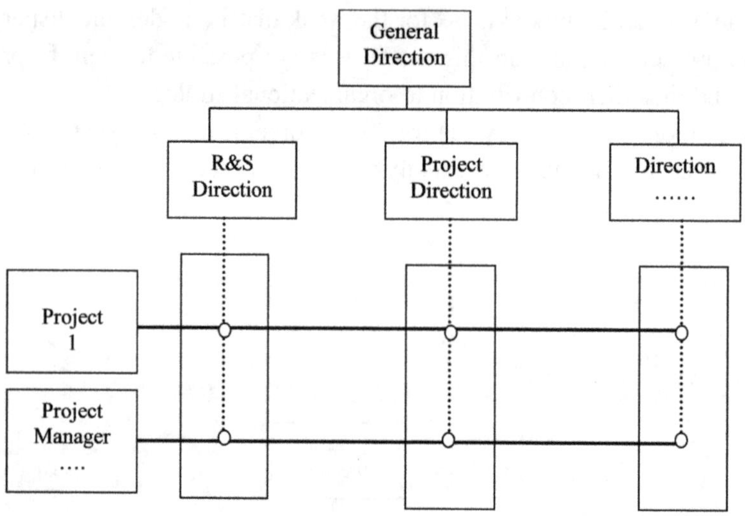

Multi-Project Management (MPM) determines important organizational consequences. There are four steps in the evolution of the organizational strategies that lead to a modern organization for the project, which, however, can coexist in time:

1. Separated functional department and sequential development phases.
2. Functions and development phases integrated and overlapped, with the coordination of a "light" project manager, that may become also the hierarchical boss, if needed ("heavy" project manager).
3. Functions and various integrated projects and, in parallel, the coordination of multi-project managers, with a possible role of the hierarchical leaders.

4. Designed intra-company and inter-company team (joint project management, contract design and manufacturing for Original Equipment Manufacturers-OEMs).

This results in different organizational methods classified on inter-project based learning (linked to the transfer of knowledge between projects) and project focus (on individual components or system and its connections).

However, there are organizational matrices called "differentiated" (Nobeoka, 1993), which allow to complete simultaneously "intersections" between functional managers and project managers (Figure 5).

Based on the kind of intersections with the functions – that can be "heavy" or "light" – it will be possible to support more projects with a different level of intensity variously distributed.

In organizing multi-project it becomes even more crucial the concept of coordination, which can include five typologies:

1. Mutual informal control by peers among the various project managers (informal peer control).
2. A so-called "dual matrix", in which the project managers are formally placed within a planning office (constitutes a column of classical matrix organization).
3. A control "charismatic" by a "leader".
4. A hierarchical control by a multi-project manager.
5. Coordination carried out by one of the functions or departments.

The key aspect of the structure for projects in differentiated matrix is the definition of priorities among the differentiated projects. This is a fundamental aspect in considering the relevance of the strategic objectives and those of the projects.

The model is not able to define and specify the organization's structure and role of portfolio management. The model does not show the contribution of the project, therefore, the portfolio's ability to create value.

Figure 5. Priority of project and responsible management
Source: Elaboration on Nobeoka, 1993, Structure for project to differentiated matrix.

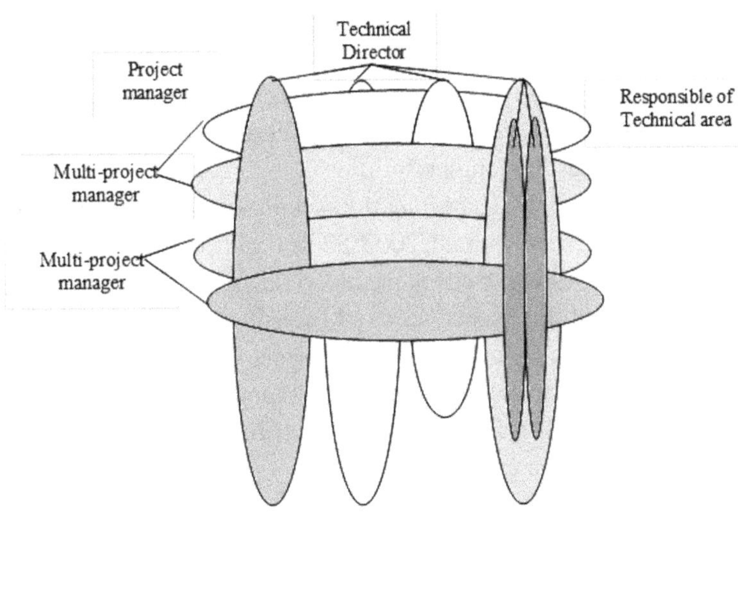

But are such organizational structures adequate to ensure the fulfillment of the underlying concept that inspired this research? Would it be possible to break down the functional and hierarchical structure of the organization considering the projects contribution to the value chain? In this perspective there's the need to link the organizational structure of the portfolio and then consider the entire portfolio as a whole to contribute to value creation.

Starting from the organizational structure proposed by Nobeoka (1993), the work aims to propose a new organizational structure defined *integrated and circular structure for portfolio*, through the analysis of the value chain and its application to the portfolio. This study is one of the first explorations of the effectiveness and efficiency of organizational structure for portfolio development over time. Conceptual frameworks and findings for organizational structure and management will contribute to the understanding of project development management and strategy by both researchers and practitioners.

Based on the background no defined organizational structure is able to consider the project's ability to contribute to value creation, nowadays. No organizational structure considers the design of the hierarchical levels in relation to value creation.

Project Portfolio Management

Quoting Archibald (2003)*projects exist in every type of human enterprise (...). Projects have starting and ending points in time and progress through a number of life cycle phases.*

For the authors, the important aspects of this discipline are planning, control, project management and portfolio activities.

PMI (2013) has defined the standard for Portfolio Management, among which *it includes interrelated organizational processes by which an organization evaluates, selects, prioritizes, and allocates its limited internal resources to best accomplish organizational strategies consistent with its vision, mission, and values*. Portfolio also includes aspects such as the assessment, selection and prioritization through which organizations will allocate internal resources to the different activities.

This indicates, as proposed in the model presented by the authors, that the portfolio has a decisive role in the ability of projects to contribute to value creation.

For The Standard for Portfolio Management (PMI, 2013b) Portfolio management is *the coordinated management of one or more portfolios to achieve organizational strategies and objectives*. It allows to focus on the right projects, investing time and money on what is aligned with objectives, in line with the strategy. The strategy is *the direction and scope of an organization over the long-term: which achieves advantage for the organization through its configuration of resources within a challenging environment, to meet the needs of markets and to fulfill stakeholder expectations* (Johnson, Scholes, and Ehittington, 2008: 13). Thus, the strategies must be long period.

In the organizational perspective it is important the *assignment of integrative responsibilities related to each project and project portfolio* (Archibald, 2003: 82-106 and 201-225). For each organizational area to which the unit refer the matrix, allows to check the individual resources and therefore, their allocation.

Before going into the details of this aspect we should consider the characteristics of the project portfolio management. As earlier stated, the model authors propose in this work aims precisely to overcome, among other things, issues related to the distinction of responsibility for design and function, better clarifying them in relation not to the hierarchy but to the contribution of the project area to value creation.

The characteristics of the portfolio are:

1. **Purpose:** Project selection and prioritization.
2. **Focus:** Strategic.
3. **Planning Emphasis:** Medium-term.

For Archibald (2003)*a project portfolio consists of the programs and projects supporting a given higher-level strategy (…) to define more than one portfolio on a strategic basis in large organizations to reflect product line, geographic or technological divisions of the organization, industry or market.*

We can consider three types of project portfolios (Combe and Githens, 1999):

1. **Value-Creating:** Strategic or enterprise projects.
2. **Operational:** Projects that make the organization more efficient and satisfy some fundamental functional work.
3. **Compliance:** "Must-do" projects required to maintain regulatory compliance.

The quality of the project portfolio management is increasingly at the attention of scholars and practionaries. Which are, then, the characteristic features of the project portfolio management? To define them, we propose a work of Dye and Pennipacker (2000) in which the authors depict a high-level comparison of Project Portfolio Management and Multiple Project Management (Table 1).

The authors (Dye et al., 2000) consider that the portfolio management develops on these points:

1. The objective is project selection and prioritization;
2. The focus is strategic; the planning emphasis is the long and mid-term; the responsibility is of top managers.

The peculiarity of the project portfolio management is to act on a strategic level in the medium to long term, so we believe that, in the proposition of a structure for the portfolio, we must consider the contribution to the creation of the value of the project in its single vision and overall (the portfolio).

In this sense it is useful to consider the strategic objective and how the portfolio helps to achieve this objective (Figure 6).

Table 1. Main differences between portfolio and multiple project management

	Project Portfolio Management	Multiple Project Management
Purpose	Project Selection and Prioritization	Resource allocation
Focus	Strategic	Tactical
Planning Emphasis	Long & Medium-Term (annual/quarterly)	Short-Term (day-to-day)
Responsibility	Executive/Senior Management	Project/Resource Managers

Source: Dye and Pennipacker, 2000.

Figure 6. Project portfolio
Source: Archibald, 2003, p. 13.

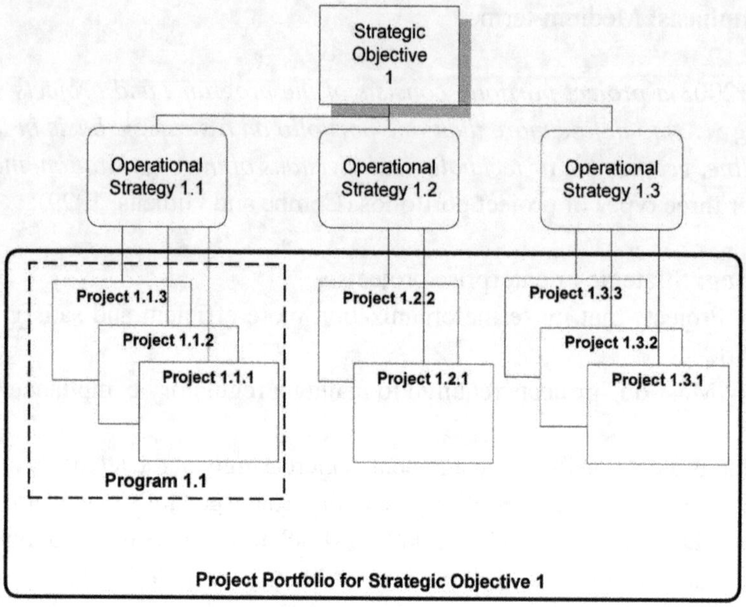

INTO ARCHIBALD'S PERSPECTIVE (2003), A TYPICAL PROJECT PORTFOLIO MANAGEMENT PROCESS

1. Define the project portfolios required.
2. Define the project categories within each portfolio based on uniform criteria.
3. Identify and group all current and proposed projects within appropriate categories and programs.
4. Validate all projects with the organization's strategic objectives.
5. Prioritize projects within programs and portfolios.
6. Develop the project portfolio master schedule.
7. Establish and maintain a key resources data bank.
8. Allocate available resources to programs and projects within portfolios.
9. Compare financial needs (primarily cash flow) with availability.
10. Decide how to respond to shortfalls in money or other key resources and approve list of funded projects and their priorities.
11. Plan, authorize, and manage each program and project using the organization's PM process and supporting systems and tools for each project category. This step comprises the entire practice of what has traditionally been thought of as "project management".
12. Periodically reprioritize, reallocate resources to, and reschedule all programs and projects as requires within each portfolio (Archibald, 2003: 87, 177-179).

Project portfolio requires a corporate perspective (Shenhar, 2004), where an integration between the organization's strategic objectives and the operational management is crucial (Levine, 2005).

The objective of Portfolio must be that of "transform strategy into reality" (Souza, Carneiro and de-Mello, 2015:119).

The portfolio should be consistent with the organization's strategy and integrated to it; we remember that, under the managerial perspective, the organization's strategy considers the definition of strategic objectives related to the effectiveness, efficiency and equity into point of view of organizational survival, development and growth of the organization. In this process it is necessary to analyze the contribution of each activity - and related function - to create value for the organization's stakeholders. Consistent with the reflections conducted so far we proposed a circular and integrated structure for the portfolio based on the Porter's value chain model. The proposed model will be built on the basis of the organizational structure of Nobeoka (2003).

In theoretical perspective *it is important to understand the antecedents that would lead to portfolio management as well as to understand the consequences of portfolio management, e.g., on a firm's performance and attainment of its strategic objectives, on employee satisfaction etc.* (Souza, Carneiro, Bandeira-de-Mello, 2015: 120).

Project Portfolio Management discipline states that there is the need of an integrated vision of the set of projects that an organization puts in place. According to the writers an integrated analysis in key value creation should be performed. This combines two key areas of "survival" and "growth" for an organization: sustainability analysis and organizational design.

AN INTEGRATED AND CIRCULAR STRUCTURE FOR PORTFOLIO MANAGEMENT

In the previous paragraph we have identified the strategic importance of the Portfolio, but we must also reflect on the fact that Bible and Bivis stated that: *project portfolio management does not guarantee success in achieving strategic goals and objectives, (…) projects that best accomplish organizational objectives and contribute to achieving the organization's vision* (2012: 10).

Nobeoka affirms that *since the management of new product development has become a central issue in global competition, numerous academic researchers in recent years have undertaken studies of how effective and efficient projects have been in various industries* (1993: 2). Most of the empirical research has focused on the innovation process and on managerial or organizational approaches as well as on performance measures for individual projects. Streams of studies have explored factors that led individual projects to success in the marketplace (Maidique, 1984; Rothwell, Freeman, Horlsey, Jervis, Robertson and Townsend., 1974; Zirger and Maidique, 1990).

Some authors (Meskendahl, 2010; Shenhar, 2004) consider that the Portfolio management is not an end in itself, but rather a means to attain of organizational objectives.

The project is seen as a sort of "start-up" whose fundamental aspect is to consider its life cycle and its contribution to the creation of value in terms of cost benefit for the organization and all the stakeholders at the same time. Is in this context that we should think in terms of project portfolio, i.e. *the projects must be managed on a portfolio basis* (Archibald, 2003). In this overview, portfolio management must involve efficiency and effectiveness, thus there is difference between success of portfolio management and success of the portfolio (Souza et al., 2015: 121).

Starting from the reflections conducted so far, it is believed that is possible to bridge the gap found in the literature through the analysis of value creation and the project's contribution to it. The representations proposals in the following figures have the role to soften the gap detected.

In Figure 7 authors propose the integrated and circular structure for the Portfolio in which the portfolio manager is responsible for overseeing the entire value chain and for analyzing the value of the contribution of the projects. In the situation described, the organization has both internal and external projects/on order. The internal projects (outside the Value Contribution Area) affect, indirectly, the area of the value contribution and are administered under the supervision of the multi-project manager. For example, the goal could be to make more efficient work processes through increased computerization, or develop smart working to create more dynamic and flexible work environments.

The on order-external projects (inside the Value Contribution Area) are those that contribute directly to the value of the contribution. Some examples are the production of an aircraft or a component of a plane or even the design of an innovative line of car.

The priority of a project over another is indicated by the overlapping of projects, the most prevalent is superimposed on the secondary; in this case the allocation of resources is a priority for the overlay project (Figure 7). This project, generally, contributes most.

In fact, usually, the projects overlay to others if they are more strategic for value creation.

In the model they show two key concepts: 1. The integration; 2. The circularity.

1. **Integration:** Represented by the connection between Portfolio and project/s and the chain of value represented from the value of the contribution.

Figure 7. Integrated and circular structure for portfolio

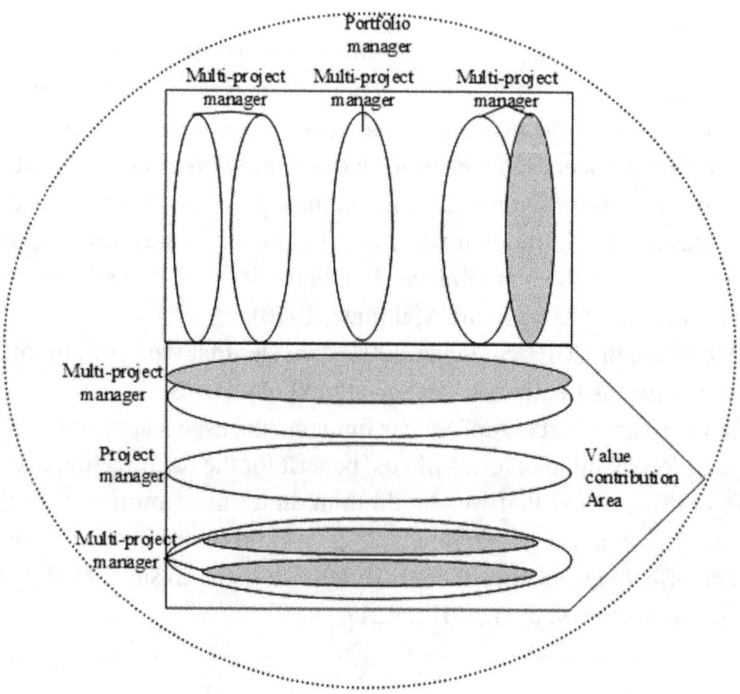

2. **Circularity:** Represented by the dashed circle whose area is the space within which the project manager moves, taking control on the entire integrated process.

The decision to integrate the structure for the project at the value chain depends on the fact that one of the priorities, often underestimated, is that the organization must check how individual projects create value for the different stakeholders; clearly, for external orders it is intuitive because the project is sold and there is an economic return. For internal projects, instead, it is underestimated how they can contribute to the value, considering them often, only a cost, without checking the resulting benefits.

In addition, the integration can reduce conflicts between the department manager and project manager because the organizational structure is not hierarchical but based on projects priority based on the contribution to the value.

The organizational structure should be designed considering prior the project's ability to create value and, based on this, the hierarchical connections should be defined. The value of the contribution is more important than the fact that projects are internal or external.

According to Souza, Carneiro and Bandeira-de-Mello (2015) the portfolio management combines an individual project view to improve the effectiveness of each project with an organization-wide focus to select the appropriate set of projects according to the set of strategic objectives, collectively running them in an integrated and harmonic fashion.

The Portfolio Manager Oversees All Considering Projects, Specifically Their Contribution to Value Creation

The Multi-project or project manager is responsible for the group or individual project or projects; in case of more complex projects we will have a project manager that is interested in each project.

What is the difference between the projects represented in the vertical direction and those in the horizontal? The first ones are internal projects that are part of the functions and/or internal processes, the second ones are part of the external orders.

Often, within a project, other projects develop and branch out; in this case it is more complex to identify and separate the contribution of the value of each project and sub-project.

The model changes in relation to the presence or absence of the projects on order and internal (Figures 8 and 9).

The interesting aspect is that the model doesn't think anymore by activities or functions but by projects; projects are well distinguished and then analyzed based on their indirect contribution - internal projects - or direct - for external projects or on order.

Lacking the element of hierarchical priorities, we assume that the cost and waste of resources and energies to develop and implement hierarchical priorities are canceled or dimensioned for the benefit of coordination.

Speaking about coordination refer to the matrix in Table 2, which summarizes the different types of coordination requirements depending on cross-functional interdependency and inter-project interdependency in a specific component design. When inter-project interdependency is not a critical issue, cross-functional coordination may be more important in component design, and only project coordination may be greatly needed.

Table 2. Coordination typologies of project. Source: elaboration on Nobeoka, 1993, coordination and project management

Interdependency Typology	Coordination Needs
Intra-project interdependency Low & Inter-project interdependency Low	Conventional "Matrix Organization
Intra-project interdependency Low & Inter-project interdependency High	Functional (Inter-project) Coordination
Intra-project interdependency High & Inter-project interdependency Low	Project (Cross-functional) Coordination
Intra-project interdependency High & Inter-project interdependency High	Both Project and Functional coordination (System-level Coordination)

Specifically, Nobeoka (1993: 34-35) considers the essential matrix: *when multiple projects share a technology or design, there is interdependency between these projects. When a component is not cross-functionally interdependent, the component design can be coordinated between multiple projects within each function. However, because most components are still interdependent with other components, both project and functional coordination may be needed to manage inter-project interactions.*

The coordination matrix allows you to check the type of coordination with respect to the intersection between the levels - high or low - of interdependence intra-project and inter-project. The matrix shows the vital role of coordination mechanisms - even better identifiable through the organizational structure models proposed.

The following figures present the model applied to organizations in which the projects are only internal (Figure 8) and in which the projects are only external or on order (Figure 9).

Figure 8. Integrated and circular structure for portfolio: internal projects

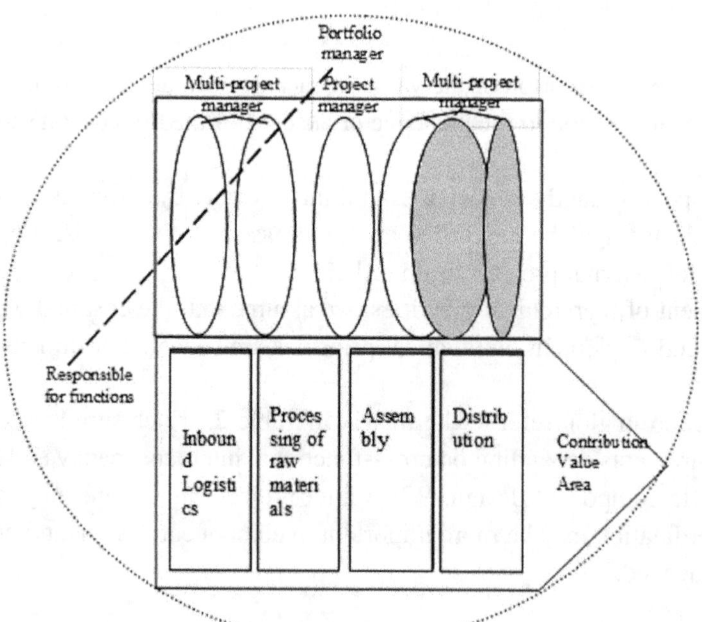

Figure 9. Integrated and circular structure for portfolio: projects on order

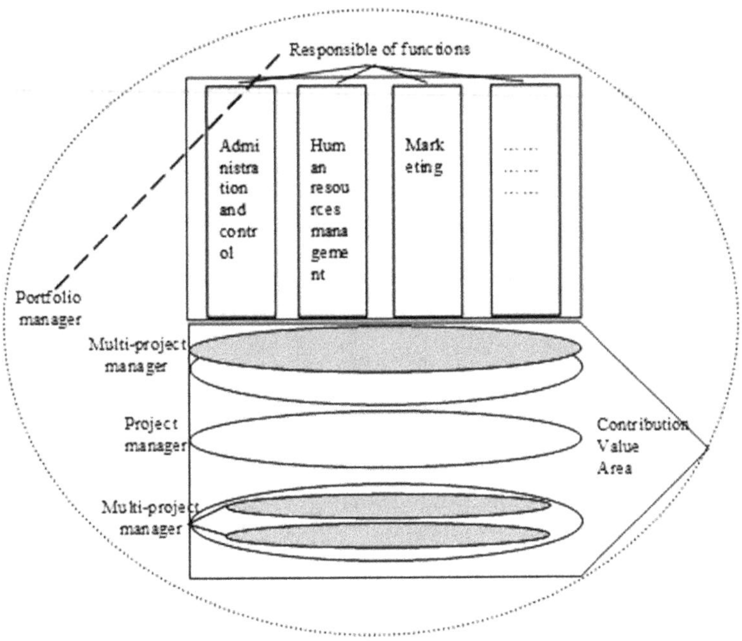

The first type relates to those companies in which the process of transformation of raw materials into finished products is for traditional functions – from inbound logistics up to the output – and the consumer and users are recipients of a product (good or service). In the second case, the company has only external projects or on order, so the characteristic activities are organized by project, conversely the secondary activities are organized by functions. Into current competitive environment the second type is becoming less widespread, as it is difficult that organizations operating on commission have not even one internal projects; for completeness we also offer the model in which the projects are only external or on order.

In the model for internal projects, the contribution to the creation of the value is only indirect so the portfolio manager takes care of the whole process of the value chain but he/she has to interface with managers or department heads, working mainly to the definition of project evaluation and, in cooperation with the functions manager, of the entire value chain.

In the model for external projects, the contribution to the creation of the value of the projects is just direct, thus, the portfolio manager takes care of the whole process of the value chain but he has to interface with managers / heads of secondary functions collaborating mainly in the definition of the evaluation projects and, in collaboration with the functions manager, of the entire value chain.

CONCLUSION

The work already proposed - mainly focused on how to maximize performance in one project at a time – has noticed some needs, particularly, a fundamental gap: it does not exist in the detailed literature a punctual analysis of the organizational structures in relation to the type of project and, most of all, in relation to the portfolio.

The first theoretical analysis results showed that the portfolio management within the organizational structure must be connected to strategy and objectives.

The characteristics of the portfolio, in fact, have shown that there is a close connection between portfolio, strategy and objectives of the organization and then between portfolio and organization's ability to implement the strategy and achieve goals.

Strategically, the organization's ability to meet the needs of its stakeholders - internal and external - and to create value also depends on its organizational structure.

The literature review found that, basically, the different organizational structures for project may vary with the hierarchical priority between the project manager and the department manager, meaning that the design of the structure depends on the hierarchy, and it is a priori defined.

The framework we propose is basically an attempt to organize and develop the organizational structure for portfolio.

The study showed that, in fact, every project in a portfolio view, contributes - directly or indirectly - to the value of the contribution. This means that as already stated *the organizational structure should be designed considering prior the project's ability to create value and, based on this, the hierarchical connections should be defined. The value of the contribution is more important than the fact that projects are internal or external.*

It matches considerations which are important to verify the priority of project based on value creation area, since the value creation is fundamental into hierarchical choices. We propose the value chain approach in planning of organizational structure. This approach is usually considered in the evaluation of the analysis of the contribution to the value creation of the company's activities and to check which are vital and essential for the organization.

The organizational structure of the proposed model – based on the value chain and applied to the type of projects – is defined *integrated circular structure* for portfolio. It can verify the contribution to value creation in the portfolio and, in accordance to that, design the organizational unit within interior of the structure and the hierarchy about the priorities for the contribution to the area of value. In this case the organizational structure may be more efficient because the hierarchy and the allocation of resources takes place on the basis of real priority and importance of the project for the organization whose primary objective is to create value. The framework we propose is basically an attempt to simplify and organize the organizational structure. It matches considerations which are important to decision makers who need to make organizational programme decisions. Since value creation should be directly involved with the structure development, the integrated and circular model will be essential to implement each technique used, leaving the choice of specific techniques up to the decision makers. This approach also allows each technique chosen to be integrated into a value creation system which provides far better and more acceptable organizational structure than those generated by previously structure, as we have discussed. In this approach, the portfolio can be managed and organized by the Portfolio Manager in the best way, especially without wasting resources and energy in the allocation of resources to the different projects; so it can be better defined the value of the single project, and then, the portfolio.

FUTURE RESEARCH AND DIRECTIONS

Specifically, this paper examined the question of organizational structure for portfolio management. The work conducted has been purely theoretical, and this is not only the search limit but also the basis for addressing the future directions.

In accordance with this reflection, the future analysis will lead to empirically determine whether the new model proposition may have the suitable characteristics to satisfy the needs of companies working for projects - internal, external and mixed - in order to allow the organization to design an organizational structure adequate to the needs of the portfolio.

It would be crucial to apply the model to a sample of companies with sound characteristics, in order to verify its adequacy. At first level, it would be necessary to verify the needs of companies involved with respect to the design of their organizational structure. The next level concerns the requirements the new organizational structures can satisfy.

Based on the results we have obtained, an extensive development effort is under way to implement the suggested frame work as an integrated decision support system, and to test it in real organizational structure.

This structure will include a capacity to generate optimal solution for Portfolio Management. In future research we will develop three phases of work: 1. theorized model tests; 2. definition of the sample to apply the model.

From the frame work we have established, it is also clear that future research is needed into generic requirements for decision support in project portfolio organization, including: 1. determine which organizational structures are preferred by portfolio management efficiency and efficacy; 2. find in which situations a value to the Portfolio can be provided by the way the Organization is structured; 3. examine the scope of strategic decisions which are made outside the purview of the organizational structure for portfolio.

In a next work, authors will develop an initial testing phase to evaluate the usability and usefulness of the organizational structure for portfolio. A second phase will show the system to users in real application environments, to get feedback on the system's modeling capabilities. A third phase will be to implement the system in several corporate environments in order to determine which adjustment are needed to tailor it to company use. This phase will also include the evaluation of the system in a group decision environment. From the framework we have established, it is also clear that further research is needed into the generic requirements for decision support in organizational structure for portfolio, including: (a) determining which modeling techniques are preferred by decision makers and how to simplify them, (b) examining the scope of strategic decisions which are made outside the purview of the integrated and circular structure for portfolio, to ease the process to connect the portfolio to value creation.

REFERENCES

Archibald, R. D. (2003). *Managing High-Technology Programs and Projects*. New York: Johon Wiley & Sons.

Combe, M. W., & Gregory, D. G. (1999). Managing Popcorn Priorities: How Portfolios and Programs Align Projects With Strategies.*Proceedings of the PMI 1999 Seminars and Symposium*.

Johnson, G., Scholes, K., & Wittington, R. (2008). *Exploring Corporate Strategy*. Pearson Education.

Levine, H. (2005). *Project Portfolio management: a practical guide to selecting projects, managing portfolios and maximizing benefits*. New York: John Wiley & Sons, Inc.

Maidique, M. A., & Zirger, B. J. (1984). A Study of Success and Failure in Product Innovation: The Case of the U.S. Electronics Industry. *IEEE Transactions on Engineering Management, EM-31*(4), 4, 192–203. doi:10.1109/TEM.1984.6447537

Meskendahl, S. (2010). The influence of business strategy on project portfolio management and its success: A conceptual framework. *International Journal of Project Management, 28*(8), 807–817. doi:10.1016/j.ijproman.2010.06.007

Nobeoka, K. (1993). *Multi-project management: strategy and organization in automobile product development* (Doctoral dissertation). Massachusetts Institute of Technology, Sloan School of Management.

PMI. (2013a). The standard for portfolio management (3rd ed.). Newton Square, PA: Project Management Institute, Inc.

Porter, M. E. (1991). Towards a dynamic theory of strategy. *Strategic Management Journal, 12*(S2), 95–117. doi:10.1002/smj.4250121008

Project Management Institute. (2013b). A guide to the project management body knowledge (PMBOK) (5th ed.). Newton Square, PA: Project Management Institute Project Management Institute.

Romano, L. (2015). *Vision-Strategy-Objectives-Projects-Outputs & return. Do we need an ultimate management model?* Paper presented at the 2015 PMI Global Congress, Orlando, FL.

Shenhar, A. (2004). Strategic project leadership: Toward a strategic approach to project management. *R & D Management, 34*(5), 569–578. doi:10.1111/j.1467-9310.2004.00363.x

Young, M., & Young, R. (2012). The rise and fall of project management: are we observing the birth of a new discipline? *Journal of Project, Program & Portfolio Management, 3*(1).

Zirger, B. J., & Maidique, M. (1990). A Model of New Product Development: An Empirical Test. *Management Science, 36*(7), 867–883. doi:10.1287/mnsc.36.7.867

KEY TERMS AND DEFINITIONS

Circularity: Represented by the dashed circle whose area is the space within which the project manager moves, taking control of the entire integrated process.

Integrated Circular Model: Organizational structure based on the value chain and its integration with Portfolio and project/s. Tris model representes the space within which the project manager moves taking control of the entire integrated process.

Integration: It is represented by the connection between Portfolio and project/s and the chain of value that is represented from the value of the contribution.

Organizational Structure: The organizational structure is the tactical organization structure; everything is constructed on its foundations and can take different forms, more or less desirable depending on the type of business and of its primary success factors.

Portfolio: The coordinated management of one or more portfolios to achieve organizational strategies and objectives. A project portfolio consists of the programs and projects supporting a given higher-level strategy. In large organizations more than one portfolio can be defined on a strategic basis to reflect product line, geographic or technological divisions of the organization, industry or market.

Project Management: Organization of the project; in literature, the first element from which start it is the definition of the organization, from which derive the organizational structure, the definition of the project and human resources and communications to be allocated to it. Management integration of project management (PIM, project integration management); this guarantees the effective and efficient coordination of the various projects. The PM is responsible for the management of the objectives and scope of the project (PSM, project management scope); this ensures that the project objectives are set consistently with the plan of the project, through a clear definition of the necessary processes. In addition, it allocates the human resources of the project (PHRM, project human resource management); this area is delegated to the mapping and assignment of roles, responsibilities and optimal integration of human resources to implement the project in relation to the need for integration and project goals. The PM is responsible for the quality of the project (PQM, project quality management); this defines the quality assurance process of the project. Another important area is the management of the project time (PTM, project time management); this ensures the respect of the time frame for the achievement of the project objectives. The PM is also decisive for the allocation of project costs (PCM, project cost management); this area is entrusted with planning, estimating, cost allocation and monitoring to ensure the project is completed within the approved budget. Another area of the PM is the project risk management (PRM, project risk management); this area is responsible for planning, identify, analyze and respond to the risks and their monitoring and control during the project. PCM (project communication management) performs the task of the generation, collection, distribution, storage, retrieval, and ultimate disposition of project information. Finally, the PM defines the project supplies (PPM, project procurement management); this area is organizing the processes of acquisition of external entities products or services to the project group (other groups or individuals that are owned by functions; individuals or other companies).

Chapter 13
Program and Portfolio Management Relationship and Support

Ginger Levin
SKEMA University, USA & University of Wisconsin – Platteville, USA

Nicole Pitotti
Nexen Spa, Italy

ABSTRACT

Ideally, the portfolio is at the highest level of an organization as it shows the organization's truest intent, direction, and priorities. But, portfolios can exist at various levels such as business units, departments, divisions, and even at the program level. At the program level, the program manager can be considered a mini portfolio manager. The objective is at any time to ensure the portfolio represents a view of its selected components and reflects the organizational strategy and objectives regardless if the programs or projects have interdependencies, as the portfolio represents all the work under way in the organization. This means portfolio management includes all the activities to identify and align organizational priorities, determine governance and performance frameworks, measure the value/benefit of what is being done, make investment decisions, foster communication, and manage resource allocation. This chapter illustrates the various interrelations between program and portfolio management to show how programs can support portfolio in delivering business value.

INTRODUCTION

Once upon a time in Egypt, pharaohs expected to become Gods in their afterlife. To prepare for the next world they built temples to the Gods and massive pyramid tombs for themselves. The Giza Pyramids complex was built following this main purpose. Pharaoh Khufu began the first Giza pyramid project, the largest of the complex, circa 2550 B.C. His son, Pharaoh Khafre, built the second pyramid at Giza together with the Sphinx, a sort of sentinel for the pharaoh's tomb. The third of the Giza Pyramids was built by Pharaoh Menkaure circa 2490 B.C. Each of the pyramids is but a part of the larger complex,

DOI: 10.4018/978-1-5225-2151-8.ch013

which includes a palace, temples, and other features. They are an excellent way to explain the differences in a project, a program, and a portfolio.

The portfolio represents the organization's truest intent so, in relating it to the Pyramids, assume someone in ancient Egypt determined that the large complex of the Pyramids would be one of many initiatives to be pursued – the portfolio consists of all the work under way including projects, programs, and sub-portfolios.

The Pyramids then are a program, with projects and operational work, and represent a group of projects that when managed together as a program will have more benefits than if the projects were undertaken in a standalone way. The projects are the individual pyramids – a temporary and unique undertaking to provide a product, as in this example, a service, or a result. While projects provide benefits, a single pyramid would not have the lasting sustainable benefits provided by the program of all the pyramids.

The purpose of this chapter is to highlight the interrelations between portfolio management and program management and to explain how programs can support effective portfolio management.

BACKGROUND

The literature on project management is quite rich and increases over time around the landmark of the Project Management Institute (PMI's) *A Guide to the Project Management Body of Knowledge (PMBOK)* published for the first time in 1982, and now at its Fifth Edition in 2013. No doubt that it has come to a certain degree of consensus in giving definitions of the basic concept of "project", which definitely is building block for any other theory in the field of project, program and portfolio management. Thus, as most everyone working in the field of project management knows, projects are widely recognized as time—limited, discrete endeavors undertaken to create a unique product, service or result.

When two or more projects are managed as one, the basis for a program may be in place. In 2006, PMI fulfilled the need for a standard in this filed with the publication of *The Standard for Program Management*, now at its Third Edition (2013), in which a program is defined as "a group of related projects, subprograms, and program activities that are managed in a coordinated way to obtain benefits and control not available from managing them individually." (PMI, 2013a, p.4).

Programs mostly include individual projects. In some cases, large programs may also have sub-programs in them. They also may include some operational work, such as ongoing operations or program activities with training or maintenance as examples. Some programs have non-project components, such as the infrastructure needed to manage the program or having a core team or a Program Management Office (PMO) to support the program.

The key point is that programs are established to deliver more benefits than if the sub-programs, projects, and operational work were managed as standalone activities. The purpose of benefits is to generate business value, enhance current capabilities, facilitate business change, maintain an asset base, offer new products and services to the market, or develop new capabilities for the company, to list a few. Benefits are the key rather than deliverables as with a focus on benefits, there is an emphasis on sustaining the business value a program can bring to its end users, customers, suppliers, and operational and support groups. As an example programs provide a consulting company with the ability to deliver benefits to the stakeholders/customers, while at the same time delivering business value to the sponsoring organization.

Programs then are a means to execute corporate strategies and achieve business or organizational goals and objectives. Some programs deliver benefits incrementally, while others deliver them at the end. For example, a business modernization program may include a project to standardize and consolidate financial management across multiple sites, a project to improve personnel hiring and performance appraisals, and a project to streamline logistics. Each project can be on different schedules and deliver incremental benefits, but the modernization effort is not complete until all the projects are done for business improvement. For programs that deliver at the end, such as a space program, it is not complete with all benefits delivered until it is operational. With a program, one is establishing it as it consists of projects, sub-programs, and operational work that have interdependencies between them. A program structure is not used if the projects within them are all for the same client, or all use comparable technology. The key in establishing a program then is the interdependencies between its components, and by setting up a program structure, one is better able to deliver more benefits than if the components were managed in a standalone fashion.

Program management, therefore, oversees the interdependencies between the various components of the program, and the program manager manages and controls them within the typical drivers of project management of time, cost, effort, and customer satisfaction. The purpose is to meet the defined requirements but also to achieve benefits available only through a coordinated managing approach.

Many other leading authors in this field gave definitions of what a program is.

Thiry (2015, p.19) in the second edition of his book "Program Management" defines program as *a collection of change actions purposely grouped together to realize value for a number of stakeholders*, explaining that grouping actions within a program must be purposeful, identifying interdependencies and synergies between stakeholders. He says programs comprise projects and transition and integration activities to be managed together to create sustainable change, either strategic or operational, to realize targeted benefits, either strategic or tactical.

Shimzu (2012, p.7), in his book "Fundamentals of Project Management" explains how program management constitutes the foundation of superior business management and growth by defining a program as *an undertaking that coordinates multiple projects in order to achieve significant organizational objectives.*

According to the Office of Government Commerce (OGC), also responsible for Projects IN Controlled Environments (PRINCE2), a program is *a temporary, flexible organization created to coordinate, direct and oversee the implementation of a set of related projects and activities in order to deliver outcomes related to the organization's strategic objectives* (OGC, 2007, p.5).

This definition is particularly interesting because it clearly states that a program requires an organization, and it is aimed at achieving strategic outcomes, which brings the discussion about the program management definition much closer to portfolio management.

The first appearance of the concept of portfolio dates back to 1952, when Henry Markowitz wrote an article titled "Portfolio Selection", pointing out the idea of analyzing investments not by their single individual merit but rather by looking at how different investments perform relative to each other within the entire economic market. Given that his approach was primarily directed to the financial investment community, the philosophy behind it actually provided other researchers with the right basis to expand this concept over time. In the PMI's "Standard for Portfolio Management" now at its Third Edition (2013) a portfolio is defined as *a component collection of programs, projects, or operations managed as a group to achieve strategic objectives. The components may not necessarily be independent or have related objectives. The portfolio components are quantifiable, that is, they can be measured, ranked, and prioritized* (PMI, 2013b, p. 3).

Generally speaking, the portfolio is ideally at the highest level of an organization as it shows the organization's truest intent, direction and priorities.

McFarlan and Benko, contend that if you want to find out where your company is going to be three to five years from now, you do not have to look at your stated strategy but at your project portfolio. It is where investments are made, and it is those investments that determine your firm's direction (Benko & McFarlan, 2003).

Projects deserve to be deeply analyzed and integrated together to avoid the risk of just managing multiple projects, which is rather different from managing a program or a portfolio. Selection and prioritization prove to be critical phases.

As a result, portfolio management consists of managing the entire set of projects, programs, sub-portfolios, and operational work to accomplish organizational strategies consistent with the organization's vision, mission, and values.

Looking at these definitions, projects and programs prove to be different along many dimensions. The time bound nature that is one of the major characteristic of a projects is not always valid for programs, since many do not necessarily have a stated end date, and some programs may never end. On the other hand, inspired by the purpose of gaining organizational or even strategic objectives, programs are made up of a number of projects but can also include operational activities, which are, by definition, excluded from the concept of a project. In both cases, these differences contribute to enlarge the distance between projects and programs moving program management toward the world of portfolio management. How they get in touch and cope with each other is what this chapter is going to explore.

PROGRAM AND PORTFOLIO MANAGEMENT: A DETAILED COMPARISON

Managing Programs

Managing related projects as a program allows the cost, schedule, effort, and benefits to be integrated and optimized across the projects and ensures project outcomes are continuously aligned with program goals in support of the organization's goals. There are three recognized types of programs according to PMI.

The first is *strategic* - i.e. programs born within the company's strategic planning process as they are the means through which the company realizes its vision and mission. Many of these strategic programs then are usually managed through portfolio management processes and procedures in order to ensure that they support strategic goals and objectives. Examples are a new product or service launch or an organizational redesign.

The second is *compliance* - i.e. programs derived from legislations, regulations or contractual obligations, such as international banking regulations, fuel emission standards, or data privacy and security. Since they are a sort of "must do" activity, their contribution to the company's strategic vision is somehow meaningless, and they may lack a tangible return on investment. The program management activities may not be as detailed as those for the strategic programs.

The third is *emergent* - i.e. programs resulting from related initiatives as they turn out to have a common outcome, capabilities, and strategic objective to pursue. They are grouped together if the organizational leaders decide they could add more benefits as a whole than if managed separately, rather than deciding to start a program and then determining the projects that would comprise it. They may be under way for some time before a decision is made to set up a program. Often, the emergent program is recognized later in the life cycle, so the initial program management activities have been done. These initial activities, though, when the decision is made to manage these projects as a program, should not be forgotten and may need to be completed again to ensure all the benefits have been identified and can be realized effectively.

Leaving behind the second type, which appears to have minor strategic value, it is possible to assume that programs can be either the result of a top-down approach (strategic programs) or of a bottom up one (emergent). In both cases, they are used as a managerial tool, a framework, to group a number of projects.

But, managing a program is not simply managing a group of projects. Program and multi-project management are not synonyms. Typically, the primary concern of multi-project managers is common resource management across a number of projects. More often than not, together with capital, they share human resources, which have to be allocated taking into account multiple plans from different projects, in order to finish the work(s) as the magic triangle of project management dictates, i.e. on time, in line with the budget and satisfying the quality requested. Therefore, the objective of multi-project management still is the deliverable, even if there is more than one at the same time. Programs instead, as will be deeply discussed later on in this chapter, encompass much more than common resource management: they have a strategic more than tactic nature. Figure 1 reflects the differences in project, multi-project and program management in relation to the project activity put in place (the input side) and the expected result in terms of business objectives or benefits (the output side).

As is it common practice in project management, in order to ensure control throughout the entire life cycle of a project, also in program management the work is broken up into discrete stages or phases. As a consequence of the different nature of a project and a program, the purpose of life cycle management differs in the two different cases: the project life cycle is used to produce a deliverable, while the program life cycle serves to manage outcomes and benefits derived from the coordinated management of several projects.

Figure 1. Differences among project, multi-projects and programs

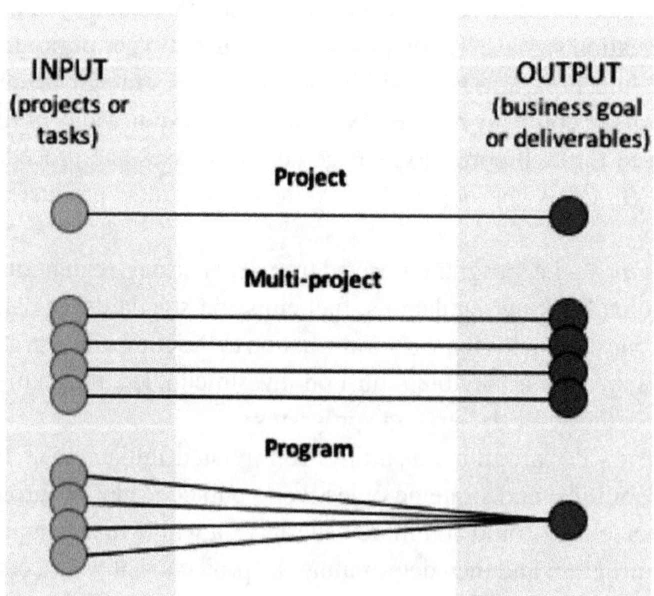

The phases outlined in the three dominant standards [PMI, OGC, and Program and Project Management for Enterprise Innovation (P2M)], although different in the name, seem to be relatively consistent, as they agree on a formulation/definition stage, meant to identify the needs and expectations, understand the program's basic objectives, and prepare the business case for the program. This stage is completely distinct from the deployment/execution stage. The standards also agree that there will be phase-gates between each of the stages (Thiry, 2015).

1. **Definition:** Definition of the strategic objectives and expected program outcomes, making the business case and obtaining the authorization to proceed. The scope of the program and benefits realization strategy are initiated and refined during the program definition stage and then reviewed and updated as necessary at each program life cycle (Thiry, 2015).
2. **Benefits Delivery:** Where the actual work of the program through its subprograms, projects, and operational work is done, i.e. component planning and authorization, oversight and integration, and transition to closure.
3. **Closure:** The work is complete, and the benefits are transitioned to an operations or support group to maintain, to customers, and end users. Hopefully its benefits will be sustained for years to come.

Traditionally, throughout the entire program life cycle, program managers have the traditional five process groups described by PMI, which are valid for programs as well as for projects.

- **Initiating:** I.E. all the tasks, processes and skills needed to start the work, including the definition of the program and its constituent projects and activities, and the agreement from stakeholders, which is crucial because it proves that the program is aligned with strategy and most of all, because it can literally make or break the program. Key outputs of this process groups are the program charter and a preliminary program scope statement.
- **Planning:** Which sets the stage for all the activity within the program, from defining the program's total scope to developing a high-level schedule, cost and resources for all constituent projects and activities in order to undertake the best roadmap to deliver the program's planned benefits. Here is also where interrelations among the different constituents are deeply analyzed and integrated, and where risks at program level are identified, as the different constituents are now thought of as a whole. The major output of the planning process group is the program management plan, in which all the elements needed to carry out the program are set forth (the program work breakdown structure [PWBS], organization, budget, milestones, metrics, communication plan, etc.), providing the track to follow in executing the program.

The planning process is something that normally follows the program initiation, but actually it is performed and updated as required whenever there are major changes and also as recommended by its Governance Board or Steering Committee during phase gate or performance reviews. Further, since programs last longer than projects, their funding is provided typically at the beginning of a fiscal year, and the program is reviewed to ensure its objectives are in line with the organization's strategic objectives such that re-planning may be required at this time as well.

- **Executing:** I. E. performing work necessary to achieve the program's objectives as established in the plans and deliver the program's benefits, integrating all program's components and resources. Compared against the program management plan, this process group provides the information needed to elaborate each project's status report to program reports.
- **Monitoring and Controlling:** Which is not linear but hovers over the whole program and so happens throughout the entire program life cycle. It consists in monitoring and reporting progress against the benefit delivery expectations, updating program plans as required, identifying areas in which changes may be required, and managing them accordingly together with a Governance Board or Steering Committee set to oversee the program and its strategic value.

This implies that, unlike standalone single projects, which are undertaken to deliver a specific outcome and possibly stay there until they have fulfilled this goal, programs can be renewed to confirm they are addressing still valid business requirements and whether or not they are doing so as they are currently conceived. Later on in this chapter the authors will examine what this means at a portfolio level.

- **Closing:** Consisting in formally finalizing all program activities, including all constituent projects, executing a transition and a sustainment plan, archiving, obtaining final approvals, and preparing a final report.

Given that process groups seem to be quite similar between project and program management, there is no doubt that the strategic nature is much more evident in programs than in projects. If this is valid, then it turns out to be a necessity that the strategic fit of a program is constantly maintained. To ensure the program and its components remain in alignment with the organization's strategic objectives, it may be necessary to add a project, change a project, terminate a project, or even terminate the whole program if it no longer is in alignment – of course, once costs are sunk into projects or programs, it is difficult to make the decision to terminate them. If it is necessary to terminate a project in the program, its interdependencies with other projects should be considered; the same is the case if a new project is added. At this level, programs prove to have interactions with the portfolio domain, which will be analyzed in the following section.

Managing Portfolios

Similar to projects and program, and maybe even more, setting up a portfolio is not something that gets done in a day. Stages and phases break down the complex work that an organization should do to be sure of having the right strategy executed by the right programs and projects. Unlike a program or project life cycle, though, which is named a "cycle" but actually has a starting and end point, the portfolio life cycle is a real cycle. It is performed continuously and repeatedly throughout the organization and is never ending unless the organization ceases to exist. The portfolio also is established such that its leaders can constantly react to any kind of change, both coming from the internal and from the external environment. A portfolio management life cycle can be summarized as follows (Weidman, 2007):

1. **Prepare:** Portfolio set up, defining the terms, scope and definition of the portfolio, and gaining agreement on the basic portfolio model to use.
2. **Plan:** Prioritization of the components of the portfolio, based on decision-making activities for progression, suspension or rejection of work requests, balancing, and optimization.
3. **Execute:** Schedule and resource assignment for the entire portfolio, supported by detailed planning.
4. **Harvest:** Ensure successful program and project delivery, with ongoing program and project tracking and reporting. Tracking guarantees portfolio realignment. In the long term, the result will assess the effectiveness of the portfolio process and propose changes to improve the whole cycle in the future.

According to the PMI (2013b) Standard, portfolio management in a formalized way is divided, again, into three process groups – Defining, Aligning, and Authorizing and Controlling. These groups prove to be interrelated among each other in a complex flow that goes from organizational strategy/objectives and the organizational process context to program and project management processes. As these interrelations are complex and iterative, it is important to recognize that process groups do not depict the portfolio life cycle nor the portfolio management phases. This is particularly evident in analyzing the relationship between the Defining process groups, the Aligning process group, and the Authorizing and Controlling process groups. The Defining process group will be discussed more in detail, as it comprehends the processes that set the stage for portfolio management.

- **Defining:** It is all about planning.

Basically, it is where organizational strategy and objectives will be implemented in the portfolio as it is established. It encompasses the development of all the plans used as baselines.

At a strategic level, it is where the high-level organization strategy investment decisions are evaluated by the decision makers to define the strategic goals, which must be reflected by the portfolio. The *portfolio strategic plan*, as one of the two key deliverables of this group, describes how the portfolio is structured and its roadmap, including the portfolio's vision and objectives, benefits, results and expected value; the set of components selected through a stated prioritization model; the type and quantity of resources needed; funds allocation; organizational structure; and organization and areas. At least at its first definition, to develop the plan, the organizational leaders need to review the existing inventory of work under way. The problem, though, is that most organizations lack the inventory, and it is a challenge for them to determine what is being done, who is responsible, and the goals and objectives of the work in progress. Then, the inventory needs to be maintained each time a new component is added, finishes, is modified, is deferred, or is terminated. The *portfolio* is the other key output. It is all the work that is adopted and grouped together to facilitate effective management of the work to meet organizational objectives, which is why it is not static.

At a governance level, as governance is essential for portfolio management, the Defining process group comprehends the portfolio governance model definition. The portfolio management plan is the main output of the Develop Portfolio Management process in the PMI's (2013b) Portfolio Governance Management Knowledge Area. It defines the focus and intent of managers in identifying, approving, procuring, prioritizing, balancing, managing, and reporting the portfolio of components to meet the organization's strategic objectives. To ensure portfolio governance, some type of oversight group is needed, the Portfolio Review Board, for example, and it should consist of the highest-level executives who can make decisions at the level of the portfolio. They approve portfolio components, and this approval it is done by a thorough review of the proposed component's business case to ensure it contributes to the organization's strategy and objectives. Then the Board prioritizes the components to determine which ones are of the highest priority to the organization especially if resources are limited. Periodically, it may also conduct specific reviews of the various components to ensure they are realizing their benefits as planned. The members of this Board also have to be prepared to make decisions to terminate components if they are not contributing to the strategic goals and objectives even though there are sunk costs to consider. Considering the organization's vision, implementation strategy, resource capacity, and short- and long-term organizational plans, it establishes and tailors the decision-making rights and authorities; responsibilities; rules; and protocols needed to manage progress based on portfolio risks toward the achievement of strategic goals and objectives.

At a performance level, the Defining process group serves to establish how the portfolio is analyzed and measured in terms of scope, time, cost, schedule, and resources, in order to see if changes are needed to the component mix. Portfolio metrics are set at the component level and then are rolled up to the portfolio level. The aim is to oversee benefits realization, defining the expected benefits for the stakeholders, how they are measured, and who is responsible. All of this information is generally provided as stated within the Portfolio Performance Management Plan, as its purpose is to explain how portfolio value is defined and how resources are allocated to components.

- **Aligning:** When the portfolio is up and running.

Logically active after the Defining, it is what is done when the portfolio is in place. The objective here is to manage and optimize the portfolio so the organization's goals and objectives are always met. In order to do so, each of the components, being a program, a project, or an operational activity such as information technology, human resource management, or accounting, to list a few, is categorized, evaluated, selected, or modified to ensure it is aligned with the organization's strategy, and most of all, that it *stays* aligned. Indeed, that is why some components are terminated: to avoid programs, projects or operational activities that are pursued if they are not worth the investment and will not contribute to the organization's business value. To manage strategic change is essential. Any time the strategic plan is reviewed, pre-existing portfolios or inventories of work should be validated against organizational strategy updates to ensure consistency with the existing vision, mission, goals, and objectives. Then, by comparing new and existing components with one another, it may be necessary to add, modify, or divest some components to ensure alignment with the strategic plan.

- **Authorizing and Controlling:** At any stage.

It consists of two processes to authorize and provide portfolio oversight. These processes are an ongoing part of the portfolio and are usually an ongoing function of the Portfolio Review Board. Authorizing is not mere authorization to start, but it is active whenever strategic changes take place. It comprehends the Review Board approval to add any new components or to terminate existing ones. Provide portfolio oversight includes making sure that the management practices agreed upon are correctly followed, in order to guarantee each component provides appropriate guidance and reporting to the portfolio manager and, as a consequence, to the stakeholders.

Clearly, these processes are not done once and for all, as continuous alignment to strategy is the basic principle of a portfolio. They are active whenever strategic goals and objectives change, at the time of the budget cycle, and whenever there is a significant change such as a merger or acquisition or a leadership change.

The Interrelations between Portfolio and Program Management

Going back to the Pyramid example, it is now more evident how projects and programs are linked with the portfolio. Actually, they are entities *within* the portfolio. At the same time, though, a program consists of a "portfolio" of projects (Ribbers and Schoo, 2015).

Figure 2 shows these interactions. The portfolio level provides information on overall organizational strategies and priorities. It is the top of the hierarchy, the whole Giza pyramid complex. There may be sub-portfolios in place at various business units and/or departments and divisions.

Project management is the lower level, with the single effort undertaken to produce the desired deliverable, such as the single pyramid construction, or the Sphynx.

In between of these two levels there are programs, as collection of related projects and non-project work managed together. If the three Great Pyramids would have been built together, they would have been a program.

The portfolio is at the highest level of an organization as it represents the organization's path to achieving its strategic goals. As noted, it consists of programs, sub-programs, projects, and operational work. A project or an operational activity may be reporting individually to the portfolio and considered each time there is a meeting of the Portfolio Review Board. Programs do the same, but they consist of sub-programs, projects, and operational work grouped together. Regardless, the portfolio level provides guidance to programs, projects, and operational work each time it meets, and these activities may be reprioritized. The programs, projects, and operational work provide status updates to the portfolio so its

Figure 2. Portfolio, program, and project management interactions

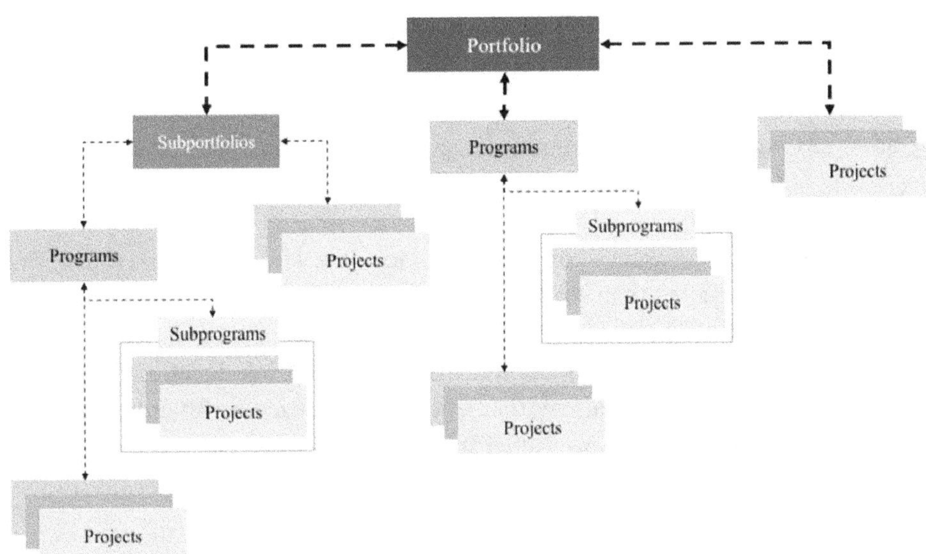

members can ensure they continue to support the strategic goals or need change to do so. Further if they are not contributing as the strategic goals may have changed, a program may be able to add a project or terminate another to ensure it does change, and the program manager can provide this information in the report to the Portfolio Review Board. This approach in program management shows it must ensure its components support organizational objectives meaning the program manager becomes a portfolio manager overseeing the program's components and with the support of the Governance Board makes comparable decisions to those at the Portfolio Review Board level.

Interestingly, the portfolio level also provides information on the disposition of requested changes. As program managers strive to take a broader view of change and embrace and exploit it, at the portfolio level, there is continual monitoring of the internal and external environment for changes. It is important to program, sub-program, and project managers as if there is a change in strategic direction or a new regulatory initiative since, for example, this change may affect the priority of work being done in the organization as resources may be needed elsewhere.

From a practical point of view, portfolio management processes and program management processes prove to be interconnected alongside most of the process groups previously defined. Of course, the level of these interconnection, their type and frequency may vary.

Generally speaking, because of the parent - child relationship between the portfolio and a program, it is easy to consider that the program initiating and planning process groups will be more affected by the portfolio domain than during executing, monitoring and controlling or closing. The reason for this tendency is that the portfolio provides inputs to the program and project "below" in the form of strategic goals and benefits but also in terms of resource allocation, requirements and constraints, which the program manager will use to build the program's scope, schedule, and budget. In this case, the information and control direction goes from the portfolio to the program domain. On the other way around, the information and controlling direction flows from a program to the portfolio as far as executing, monitoring and controlling and closing process groups are concerned as they relate to status information reporting, budget and schedule metrics, and most of all, change requests and approvals.

If there is a strategic change in direction, such as new leadership changing the overall strategy, a merger, or an acquisition leading to a change in strategic goals and objectives, typically this is portfolio-level information. That information is provided to the program manager to see the effect on his or her program. The program manager then provides performance and status reports back to the portfolio level along with any change requests that may affect work elsewhere.

Table 1 is useful to show the differences in managers' work at the project, program, or portfolio level.

Focusing on some of the items in the program and portfolio column, there are some interesting points to note:

- Program managers must be aware of the possibility to come across changes from both outside and inside of the program. Rather than striving to minimize change, the program manager still wants an integrated change control process use but emphasizes embracing and exploiting change to the program's advantage. So does the portfolio manager at a portfolio level, i.e. monitoring changes in the broader internal and external environment. This approach is difficult as it is easy to resist change, but each change in an organizational strategic goal should be viewed as a way for the program and for the portfolio to somehow benefit and provide greater business value to the organization, and if not, simply to adapt to it.

Table 1. Detailed comparison between project, program, and portfolio

	Projects	Programs	Portfolios
Scope	Set, limited scope with clearly defined deliverables.	Broad scope with flexible boundaries to meet medium-term expected business benefits.	Organizational scope adapted to corporate goals.
Change	Change should be avoided; baseline is key.	Change is first seen as an opportunity.	Monitor environmental changes that affect the corporate strategy.
Success	Measured through respect of cost, time, quality preset parameters: the PM triangle.	Measured in financial terms, value creation and benefits delivery.	Measured in terms of overall portfolio performance: maximum results, minimal resources.
Leadership	Transactional leadership. Authority-based directive style, management of alternatives, conflict resolution. Rational decision making.	Facilitation style, management of powerful stakeholders, conflict resolution. Intuitive decision making.	Administrative style, focused on adding value, power results from allocation of resources. Rational decision making.
Role	Task and parameters management; product (project output) delivery.	Pacing and interfacing of projects; business benefits delivery.	Resources management across the portfolio; deliver value to corporate stakeholders.
Responsibility	Project output delivery to parameters; reporting, performance-based focus.	Strategic decision implementation, develop opportunistic emergent strategies.	Align portfolio with corporate strategy, adjust portfolio in regard to changes in the organizational environment.
Main tasks	Negotiate scope, define the work breakdown structure [WBS], minimize adverse risks, manage delivery of the product of the project. Maintain project team stamina and motivation, monitor and control external team.	Coordinate project resources and key deliverables, market the program and build the business case on a regular basis; develop and maintain project managers' team spirit and contribution to the program.	Allocate resources to portfolio components; reassess portfolio on an ongoing basis; collect and use program and project data to make decisions.
Control	Monitor and control tasks and project parameters retrospectively against baseline; report to project sponsor.	Appraise project deliverables and resources usage prospectively against expected benefits; report to business stakeholders.	Measure aggregate value of portfolio retrospectively against preset corporate performance indicators; report to corporate stakeholders.

Source: Thiry, 2008 in Gower Management Handbook 4th Edition, Chapter 3 and 4.

- Success is measured through realized and sustained benefits rather than an emphasis solely on deliverables. Last but not least the goal of a program manager is to ensure benefits, as well as the goals, schedules, and budgets, of each component are met.
- The portfolio is focused in on strategy, with the main purpose being in managing change, from wherever it comes (internal organizational context or external environment).

Therefore, portfolio management and program have many similarities and also differences. The portfolio focuses on ensuring that projects and programs are aligned to the organizational strategy, and resource allocation is made accordingly to a certain degree of priority, which is consistent with the organization's strategic vision or its 'to-be' or end state. Programs are focused on achieving organizational objectives as they result from the coordinated management of benefits. Nevertheless, they both have their main purpose in ensuring that what the organization is doing is something that is worth doing. To remain aligned to strategy, the portfolio as well as programs need continuous oversight. Any changes in the composition of portfolios or programs should be carefully evaluated. If this it the case, the practice the portfolio and the program managers have to follow is the same, as it will be highlighted in the following section.

The Role of Managers

To pursue the objective of this chapter to point out how program and portfolio managers' roles turn out to be closer than they appear, it is useful to go back to Table 1 and focus on the management lines.

By comparing the project, program and portfolio columns as far as management is concerned, it is not difficult to underline that the main difference is between the project and the program column, while the portfolio and programs are closer because of the strategic focus they have.

Obviously, managers have many roles and responsibilities, which are critical to achieve success, both in program and in portfolio management. The different context and nature of the two determines a different position of these two roles in the organizational hierarchy. Managers with portfolio management roles are found at medium or higher levels, typically as a director, a vice president, or a Chief Portfolio Officer, while program management roles are typically found at a medium level of management, such as department manager or director (Blomquist and Müller, 2006).

Program managers basically coordinate effort of the various project managers involved in the program, but they do not practically manage the individual project. Nevertheless, their "to do list" is not shorter, as they:

- Identify and oversee interdependencies between projects and operational work.
- Provide a framework to manage related efforts considering factors such as strategic benefits, coordinated planning, interdependencies, deliverable integration, resource pools, and optimized pacing.
- Coordinate common program activities. such as information technology, finance, and procurement, resolving resource conflicts across components.
- Respond to risks and issues across the program
- Ensure the program's efforts are aligned with organizational strategic goals.
- Resolve scope/schedule/cost/quality issues within a shared governance cycle and tailor program management activities to address unique cultural, socio-economic, political and environmental differences.

Interactions between the two levels - project and program management - are iterative and continually performed. The program manager works with project managers following project management practices but also focuses at a higher level with key stakeholders to show each project's relevance to organizational objectives as well as that of the program. Information flows from the program to its projects especially in the planning phase and then from projects back to the program especially in the executing and closing phases. It is done through the program manager's decision-making capability along with engaging stakeholders and is overseen by a governance structure, similar to that of a Portfolio Review Board in portfolio domain.

An example of information flowing from the projects to the program in addition to overall status information is from an emergent program. As the program's schedule is developed, it uses the existing project schedules as a starting point.

Often, a person managing one of the projects in the program is appointed as the program manager for the emergent program until it is complete, and unless someone is appointed temporarily to replace this person as the project manager, it adds duties to duties. Such approach is not recommended, as it diverts the program manager's time from the overall program and loses its focus on interdependencies and strategic alignment.

The role of the *portfolio manager* is focused on strategy, with success based on the investment, performance, and benefit realization relative to the entire portfolio. As the ultimate goal is to have a balanced executable plan that constantly guarantees the link between portfolio and strategy, there are six key areas in which portfolio managers operate:

- Maintaining portfolio alignment.
- Allocating financial resources.
- Allocating human resources.
- Allocating material or equipment resources.
- Measuring component performance.
- Managing risks.

The emphasis is on coordinating management activities at a higher level than those associated with individual projects. It is worth noting that managing issues and risks at the program or portfolio level is definitely different than managing them at a project level, as they may affect more than just one component and may affect other programs and projects under way. An issue at the program level also is more than just a risk that has occurred and represents concerns about the program. Addressing issues also means optimizing resources during the course of the program, evaluating the total cost of ownership, and configuration management across the program components. This means that program and portfolio managers need resource management competencies.

Precisely defining the needed skills for an effective program/portfolio manager is inherently difficult. Surely, because of the differences earlier discussed, being an excellent project manager does not necessarily mean being an excellent program/portfolio manager. The required competencies differ based on the uncertainty and complexity of the work to be done. In case of programs and sub-portfolios, the skills may also differ even in the same organizational unit as they face different challenges. Nevertheless, there are some general characteristics to consider:

- **Communication:** As a matter of fact, research done in the 1980s has shown that project managers spend about 90% of their time communicating, and this number continues to be the trend today; it increases on programs and even more in portfolios because there are more interested stakeholders involved (team members, sponsors, customers, vendors, and senior managers to list a few) that have to interact seamlessly and collaboratively with the team and the stakeholders, enhancing stakeholders and Board members collaboration.
- **Stakeholder Management:** Management means stakeholder identification, expectations and engagement. Stakeholder relationships need to be maintained to ensure the work achieves its desired benefits, and it is not a one-time activity, but it is continuous. Program managers prepare stakeholder engagement plans to help support stakeholders to align their expectations and improve overall acceptance of the program benefits. The program's communications plan focuses

on addressing stakeholder needs and expectations and providing messages in a timely way and in desired formats.

- **Leadership:** Is critical to establish the work's direction, both identifying interdependencies, tracking progress, and making decisions. It is embedded in the program and portfolio managers' job and occurs throughout the course of his or her work.
- **Conflict Resolution and Experience in Managing Issues:** Addressing them systematically and effectively as they occur at different levels of the program and the portfolio. Conflict resolution is using the five modes of conflict as appropriately hoping a collaborative method can be employed to merge the diverse perspectives of the different people involved. It also recognizes that conflicts can be both positive or negative but will occur on programs and at the portfolio level.
- **Strategic Visioning and Planning:** Are needed to align Boards and benefits with long-term organizational goals. Once these goals and benefits have been defined, structured plans can be prepared to execute the components. For program management, a benefit realization plan is a best practice to follow and it is a baseline document for the program. It includes the identified benefits, how they will be measured, a description of the benefit, key stakeholders involved, assumptions and constraints, a schedule to realize the benefit, and methods to report on the benefit's status at frequent intervals.
- **Appropriate Knowledge:** This is primarily true for program managers as it related to the program's area of focus. This does not mean being a technical expert, but it does mean having the knowledge to manage the diverse set of projects and other work that is in the program and learning the knowledge area of the program to be able to speak intelligently about it to the rest of the team. It also means recognizing the program manager is an expert at program management and delivering the expected benefits and the strategic value from the program. He or she will have technical subject matter experts (SMEs) to help with the technical issues that will arise. However, it is incumbent on the program manager to facilitate an atmosphere of knowledge sharing within the program team, rather than a knowledge is power approach, and to set up a repository that is easy to access, which contains policies, procedures, and processes to follow but also the lessons learned and knowledge assets that have been contributed throughout the program.
- **Adaptation:** The program manager must be able to easily adapt to the uncertainties involved with his or her program quickly as well as with the unpredictable nature of the environment, making agile adjustments in the approach if needed. Given the influences of environment and context on the portfolio, this is key for portfolio managers as well. The constant rate of change requires a focus on organizational agility and subsequent program agility to best respond to it.

According to Levin and Ward (2011), following a similar approach to that in PMI's "Competency Development Framework for Project Managers", Second Edition (2007), it is possible to separate competencies into performance and personal. The performance ones relate to program/portfolio life cycle management and the activities to be pursued, while the personal ones are needed throughout the life cycle phases to make sure the program/portfolio is a success .

Performance Competencies

- Defining the program.
- Initiating the program.

- Planning the program.
- Executing the program.
- Monitoring and controlling the program.
- Closing the program.
- Defining the portfolio.
- Aligning the portfolio.
- Authorizing and Controlling the portfolio.

Personal Competencies

- Communicating.
- Leading.
- Building relationships.
- Negotiating.
- Thinking critically.
- Facilitating.
- Mentoring.
- Embracing change.
- Thinking strategically

The personal competencies above listed prove to be valid for programs but also for portfolio managers. In both cases, the optimum is to have a blend of control-oriented leadership and management with goal-centric adaptive skills.

Therefore, if the program manager needs a broad view as to what is under way throughout the organization to convey the program's importance, the portfolio manager takes an even more broader view with a continual focus on both internal and external changes or potential changes. Ideally, they have a close relationship and work together as much as possible, which can occur more easily if the program is part of an organizational unit with a sub-portfolio than if the organization lacks sub-portfolios.

SOLUTIONS AND RECCOMENDATIONS: IMPLEMENTING EFFECTIVE PORTFOLIO MANAGEMENT THROUGH PROGRAMS

The main driver for a company to decide to implement portfolio management is to move from a tactical approach, in which the same, routine work is pursued as desired by clients, to a strategic view in which the company's programs, projects, and operational work is the portfolio, and all work then is prioritized for greater effectiveness. Nevertheless, as professionals in the field can confirm, portfolio does this breakthrough, but this does not mean it is flawless. If the main reasons that drive companies to set up a portfolio are to forge the link between component selection and business strategy and to yield the right balance of project and investments, it is evident that these are the fields in which organizations expect the major added value in terms of portfolio effectiveness; yet these seems to be also the areas of most critical portfolio "sore point" that have to be properly addressed in order to achieve portfolio management greater benefits. In relation to this, in the following lines some key statement in implementing ef-

Table 2. Reasons why to use program in PPM implementation

"Must Do" in Implementing Successful Portfolio Management	Reasons for Using Programs
1. Make the Business Case for Portfolio Management	Resource Allocation
2. Establish the Portfolio Management Process	Avoid Too Many Projects
3. Agree on Portfolio Criteria to Ensure Strategy Implementation	Strategic Fit Is Granted
4. Regularly Hold Portfolio Review Meetings	Make Go/Kill/Hold Decision
5. Enable Managers to Deliver Success	Delegate

fective portfolio management in the organizations are suggested as recommended, "must do" activities. Related to each one of them, the authors have tried to enlighten the "reasons why" the use of programs within the portfolio could be of help. Table 2 summarizes what will be discussed more in detail below.

Must Do #1: Make the Business Case for Portfolio Management

Each proposed component of the portfolio, being a single project, a program or an operational activity, requires a business case that the portfolio sponsors take to the Portfolio Review meeting. Actually, implementing portfolio management (or even enhancing what exists) is a project. As such, it should follow the same processes as any other new initiatives, meaning that a business case should be done for the portfolio as a whole, as it produces benefits but also demands for costs, and they both should be clearly stated. Benefits include, among others, making better decisions avoiding late, over budget, and runaway programs and projects; and avoiding programs and projects that do not satisfy business objectives. Doing so can reduce costs as it avoids "wasting" money. Typically, the business case should include the purpose statement, the strategic objectives identified, and the relative benefits expected as well as the resources required to achieve those benefits. Once the inventory is set up, then a process is needed to maintain it each time a new component is added, another one finishes, or is terminated as it does not support goals and objectives, and its resources are better allocated elsewhere.

Reason Why #1: Resource Allocation

Lack of resources is often the most frequent complaint in every business: too many projects and not enough resources to implement them. In a moment where it seems as though resources are more constrained than ever before, and it does not seem to improve, one of the key reasons for portfolio management is to ensure that the existing work is necessary. Non effective resource allocation could be even more dangerous than lack of resources itself. Gone are the days where one could pursue a 'pet' project even if he or she felt it was a breakthrough initiative. Continual monitoring of supply and demand is critical to portfolio success. Supply refers to resource capacity, which is more than just people and includes funding, materials, and equipment. Resource demand, as used in portfolio management, is the resource requirements from the components. The goal is to ensure the resource capacity is optimally allocated against resource requirements or demand based on known organizational priorities and potential values.

By using programs, "buckets" of resources are allocated to a "basket" of projects. The responsibility of resource allocation to the program component is up to the program manager, who is accountable for the distribution of the agreed-upon budget allocated to the whole program to the single component. In this way, projects in the program compete for resources only within the boundaries of the program itself and not against any other projects in the portfolio. Programs close off portions of portfolio resources that are managed throughout the portfolio management process as if they were "in isolation". Re-allocation or moving resources from a project to another, maybe more critical, is thus easier and more burdensome even once budget and funds have been assigned to individual projects. Because they all serve the same purpose or objective, the strategic nature of programs ensure that resources are allocated reflecting the organization's business strategy. Money is where strategy is.

Must Do #2: Establish the Portfolio Management Process

The portfolio management process is an iterative process. What is more, it is a cultural change, that moves the common "habit" from fishing and selecting what one wants to work on to a structured view in which there is a process to follow.

Figure 3 shows the continuous nature of portfolio management. Once the initial prioritization criteria are agreed upon and programs and projects have defined business cases, there is continuous monitoring.

Monitoring is necessary to ensure the benefits in the business case are being realized as planned and to ensure the program or project continues to support the organization's strategic objectives. There is continual prioritization since strategic goals do change, and resources are constrained. Prioritization and rebalancing occur as new programs and projects are added to the portfolio, others end, or are terminated. As the balancing continues, communication messages as to the priority level of programs and projects are needed – some organizations arrange it and let people know the importance level of their program or project by number; others provide a list of the top 10 or top 25. The goal is to have a continuous flow of programs and projects at all times.

Figure 3. The continuous nature of portfolio management
Source: Adapted from Levin & Rad, 2005.

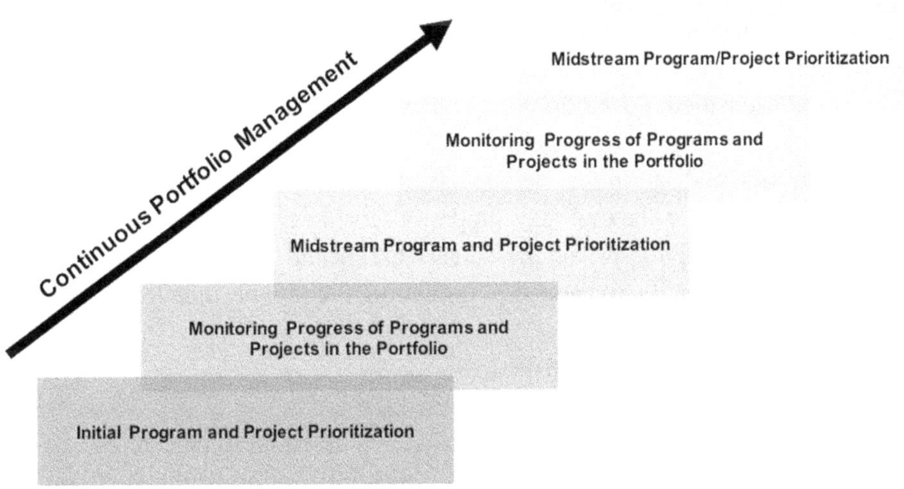

Reason Why #2: Avoid Too Many Projects

Surely the portfolio management process is complex, and even if it varies from organization to organization, it is time consuming, always. As a result, the goal is to make the process as less burdensome as possible. Interdependencies among portfolio components, the rate of potential changes that may occur, and the quality of the information available are practical aspects to take into account. Therefore, if on one hand there is the tendency to favor small, well defined and fast projects as they realize the desired benefits quickly and are more easily in control; on the other there is the evidence that a myriad of projects inevitably makes the portfolio management process heavier.

The use of programs prevents the portfolio from being too fragmented and as a consequence too complex to manage. What is more, the general concern over the long-term and is not well identified and unforeseeable-ending projects is overcome by programs: just because they are a mini-portfolio within the large portfolio, their objectives are clear and fixed to the organizational strategy, while the projects beneath them may "come and go" to best adhere to the environmental changes and market challenges. Tactics should not take over strategy.

Must Do #3: Agree on Portfolio Criteria to Ensure Strategy Implementation

As the organization formulates officially its vision or 'to be' state, and mission or why it is important, some key questions to consider are: What are our priorities for the short and long term? What deliverables and benefits do we need to meet our goals? How does each program and project meet our business priorities? What resources do we need to complete the deliverables? But most of all, are we supporting the programs and projects that in turn support our strategic goals?

Determining the prioritization criteria is one of the most difficult tasks in portfolio management and is a subject on which there are pages and pages in the literature. For this chapter, it is important to note that organizations should select the evaluation criteria that best support the achievement of organizational strategy and objectives and use them throughout the entire portfolio life cycle to reassess strategic fit. Each component is aligned to one or more strategic objectives, and any new proposal must show how it supports attainment of organizational objectives. The priority of each component guides financial allocation decisions. Similarly, the priority of each portfolio component guides resource planning, hiring, scheduling, and capability allocations, including long-range talent management. Material, equipment, or space allocations also are affected by the component's priority including long-range capital investments and planning. Measuring portfolio component performance, the portfolio's support to organizational goals' implementation is ensured. Each component is evaluated for positive and negative risks, either internal or external, and how these risks may impact the strategic plan and objectives.

Numerous prioritization and scoring models are available in the market place, but adopting one of them is not the first thing to do as the tool may support a scoring system that is not the one the leaders and the portfolio manager want to follow. Set the criteria up first and gain agreement – a difficult process – then select the tool. Remember the old adage of not letting the tool become the fool!

Reason Why #3: Strategic Fit Is Granted

If portfolio management is about doing the right things, it is essential to be sure of being on the right track and more importantly to stay there. To do this, the prioritization of the portfolio component is something that is not done once and for all, as it may be affected by changes, coming both from outside and the inside of the company. Assessing the value of a project is inherently difficult. Establishing its value in comparison to the whole number of portfolio component is even more complex and time consuming in the portfolio review process.

By having programs as portfolio components, because of their strategic nature, the alignment to the organizational objectives are somehow taken for granted; this is especially true for strategic programs as they really are a "piece" of strategy deployed through projects. They accomplish on their own part of the strategic plan the organization put in place at a portfolio level. The time required to see the results of the work is definitely much longer than the frequency of the portfolio review within the year. Therefore, at least for the mid-course portfolio review, reassessing their strategic fit may be meaningless. They can be put aside, making the process simpler and shorter for the portfolio manager.

Must Do #4: Regularly Hold Portfolio Review Meetings

Portfolio oversight is vital. To ensure the prioritization and balancing process is not a one-off activity, but rather is an ongoing, regularly performed one, a physical governance structure should be in place.

The portfolio review process enables planning for optimizing and authorizing the portfolio. It then involves approving proposed components based on their business case and reviewing, analyzing, and changing the portfolio components to create an optimal balance to achieve the organization's strategy and objectives. The Portfolio Review Board is part of the governance model as described in the Portfolio Management Plan. Without regular meetings by such a Board, and communicating its decisions through a decision log after each meeting, people in the organization will not take portfolio management seriously and will feel as if it is the 'fad' of the day. The Board members should continually monitor the portfolio to ensure there is alignment with strategy and objectives and make governance decisions in response to portfolio performance, component changes, and issues and risks to ensure the portfolio mix is the best for the organization.

How much governance is enough? The answer is it depends, but typically when portfolio management is being introduced, the Board should meet bi-weekly and then monthly; it should not meet quarterly until it is fully implemented, and at any time, ad hoc meetings should be called. Further, at least an annual review helps to identify opportunities or needs for improvement. Typically, this frequency is also driven by the budget cycle, when the work for the fiscal year is proposed and funding is determined. As a general rule, the frequency should be in line with the nature of portfolio: in order to appreciate progress, the frequency cannot be too short otherwise the review would it be a mere exercise with no added value. Project management techniques used also should be taken into account in setting the review frequency: in the short run, progresses are more evident in an agile approach.

Reason Why #4: Make Go/Kill/Hold Decisions

Managers seem to be unwilling to stop projects once they have sunk costs. Moreover, the same difficulty seems to appear when there is the need to touch "pet" projects. In both cases, the result is an inefficient project selection process. This may happen early in the life of the portfolio, when the project proposals are evaluated and ranked, or during the Portfolio Review stage, when the strategic value of the component is reassessed. Therefore, it involves all the process groups above defined and it is valid throughout the entire portfolio management process.

The use of programs allows the making of go/kill/hold decision to be kept at a program rather than at a portfolio level. The advantage is that the program manager typically has a more specific and detailed technical knowledge of the program elements than the portfolio manager has of all the portfolio components. As a result, go/kill/hold decisions are performed in a more appropriate manner and with utmost care on the basis of single project tracking progresses, reporting, performance measure and results.

Must Do #5: Enable Managers to Deliver Success

Competencies in project, program and portfolio management is a *conditio sine qua non* for portfolio success. But, frameworks, processes and planning are just tools that help people. It is people that do the work.

In order to be successful, strategy should be translated into specific deliverables by people who feel empowered to do so (Thiry, 2015). In many organizations, though, the traditional control-based approach is used, in which one party delegates the work to another one and exercise control over it. This is a transactional style of leadership with explicit knowledge as the focus as shown on the left hand side of Figure 4. In this approach program managers are considered *super project managers*. Their responsibility is just to deliver the program as functional or line managers who practically "own" the projects. It is comparable in a way to McGregor's Theory X approach, assuming people dislike working and want to avoid it.

More progressive organizational leaders, instead, favor an innovative "power-based approach" that empower program managers with some guidelines but enables them to make decisions even when there is uncertainty. It is more of a stewardship approach in which a person is motivated by higher-order needs as they identify with the organization and with its strategies and are committed to them. It is similar to McGregor's Theory Y approach. Program managers develop the program objectives from that of the organization's strategy, identify benefits after consulting with key stakeholders, and initiate projects that will form the program, being capable of making decisions under uncertainty and with a changing

Figure 4. Leadership vs. role
Source: Thiry, 2015, p.126.

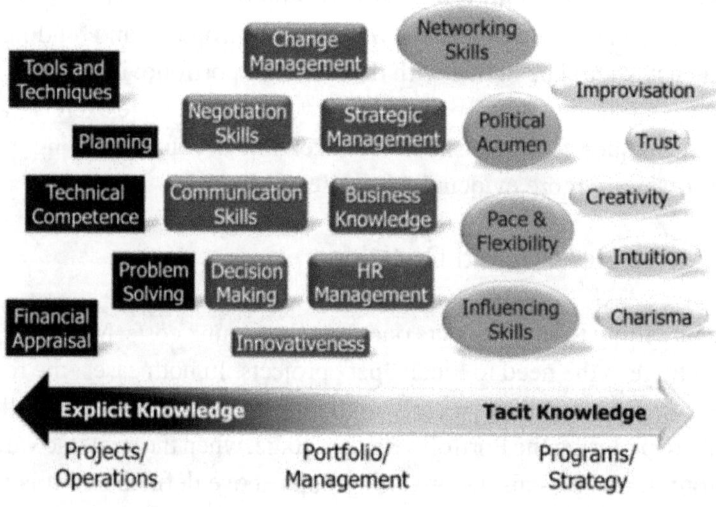

context. It is a transformational leadership approach based on tacit knowledge as shown in the right side of Figure 2. Portfolio management relies on such a power-based methodology.

Reason Why #5. Delegate

As broadly discussed in this chapter, if programs are mini-portfolio, then program managers are mini-portfolio managers. By using programs, the portfolio is divided in autonomous units that should be managed in relation but somehow independently from the portfolio as a whole. The responsibility is assigned to managers who are in charge of managing all aspects of this microcosm that is the program (resource, deliverables, time, program components composition), coherently with their level of seniority. Program managers indeed are always chosen from the medium level in the organizational hierarchy which guarantees the appropriate maturity and professional experience. Plus, more often than not, they are experts in the field, which allows them the appropriate knowledge in decision making on go/kill/hold.

Delegation is a win-win strategy in multi-project environment as it empowers people to do their best through a power based approach; at the same time, it allows portfolio manager to "get rid" of part of his or her difficult job. Collaboration is the key.

FUTURE RESEARCH DIRECTIONS

Programs and portfolios inter-relate in many ways. As noted in this chapter, a program manager is really a 'mini portfolio manager' as he or she is making decisions based on business cases as to the sub-programs, projects and operational work to be in the program, the distribution of resources, the extent of empowerment of the project and operations managers, the frequency of it its Governance Board meetings, and other oversight initiatives. Also as noted in this chapter, portfolio management, while introduced in 1952 in the financial arena, and from the authors' personal experience was used in some companies beginning in the 1960s, it was not until the various Associations issued standards and launched certifications in both fields that they assumed a greater level of interest. Research in leading Journals and presentations at Conferences and other Forums, along with doctoral level dissertations and thesis, have contributed greatly to the interest in the field since the 1980s.

The next steps are to ingrain these functions in organizations that now may be focused on being project based or enhance their significance if the organization has program and portfolio management as core areas. How to do so will differ by the type of organization and its unique products and services. To us, the evidence is clear. The limited resources and the dismal trend of projects that are completed on time and within budget make a compelling case to change the culture from 'fishing' to a defined portfolio management. To do so, hopefully executive leaders recognize the need for such change, and it is a top-down driven approach they support with a Portfolio Management Office, a Chief Portfolio Manager, and a Portfolio Review Board at the highest level.

However, if not, it is up to us, as the project professionals, to make the business case from 'fishing' to 'structured'. To do so, we can present a business case to a sponsor or manager, or we can take the step of recognizing the best way to start is to suggest using a program to manage interrelated projects and ongoing work and then to manage this program as one would manage a portfolio at the highest level – with a charter; plans; a Governance Board; and the ability to add, defer, or terminate a project that is not contributing to strategic objectives or realizing benefits. As the program manager, we focus on the business case to show our program is linked to strategic objectives, and we are providing reports to our managers and stakeholders at all levels showing the benefits a program can bring. Managers then realize the greater use of programs can further assist in managing interdependencies and resource allocation. While programs have been in existence for centuries, they are now recognized as a desired strategy.

The goal leads to more programs and receptive stakeholders such that the obvious next step is to move to managing one's department or division through structured portfolio management showing results, then to a business unit level, and then to the organizational level.

To paraphrase from the former US President, Ronald Reagan, 'the future is not for the faint hearted' – therefore, be prepared to exploit and embrace this change in your organization and demonstrate why it is essential to do so.

CONCLUSION

From the management point of view, program and portfolio have more similarities than imagined. Of course, since the portfolio is made of programs, operational work, and single projects, is it important to recognize when multiple projects should be managed as a program when there is a justification in terms of added value gained to introduce a layer of management between corporate portfolio management and portfolio management (BIS, 2010). From the strategic management point of view, the main driver for the management of multiple project in different forms - as a program - is the change in business environment of an organization. Changes in the environment imply systemic or organizational changes. In these changes, program management provides a framework for the management of complexity and risk with the general intent of implementing business strategy (Morris & Pinto, 2010).

A portfolio comprised of programs in addition to projects proves to be more effective in addressing some critical aspects of portfolio management, namely the allocation of resources and the portfolio review process activities. The base concept is that program management supports portfolio management not only in terms of strategy implementation but also in practice, unburdening the whole process and making it easier to manage for the portfolio manager.

Portfolio management is a culture change, but without it, an organization can lose market share, lose customers, focus on programs and projects that lack value, and the list can only continue. The objective is to become a mature portfolio management organization using sophisticated techniques. However, implementing it throughout the organization takes time for everyone to buy into the change.

REFERENCES

Benko, C., & McFarlan, F. W. (2003). *Connecting the dots*. Boston: Harvard Business School Press.

Blomquist, T., & Müller, R. (2006). *Middle managers in program and project portfolio management: Practices, roles and responsibilities.*Newtown Square, PA: Project Management Institute.

Department of Business Innovation and Skills (BIS). (2010). *Guidance for managing programmes: understanding programmes and programme management*. Retrieved from https://www.gov.uk/government/uploads/system/uploads/attachment_data/file/31978/10-1256-guidelines-for-programme-management.pdf

Levin, G., & Rad, P. (2005). *Metrics for project management: Formalized approaches*. Vienna: Management Concepts.

Levin, G., & Ward, J. L. (2011). *Program complexity A competency model*. Boca Raton, FL: CRC Press.

Morris, P., & Pinto, J. K. (2010). *The Wiley guide to project, program, and portfolio management*. Hoboken, NJ: Wiley & Sons.

Office of Government Commerce. (2007). *Managing successful programmes*. Norwich, UK: The Stationery Office.

Project Management Institute. (2013). *The standard for program management* (3rd ed.). Newtown Square, Pennsylvania: Project Management Instiute.

Ribbers, P. M. A., & Schoo, K. C. (2002). Program management and complexity of ERP implementations. *Engineering Management Journal*, *14*(2), 45–52. doi:10.1080/10429247.2002.11415162

Shimizu, M. (2012). *Fundamentals of Program Management*. Newtown Square, PA: Project Management Institute.

Thiry, M. (2008). *The Gower Handbook of Project Management* (4th ed.). Farnham, UK: Gower.

Thiry, M. (2015). *Program Management*. Farnham, UK: Gower.

Wideman, M. R. (2007). *Ten steps to comprehensive project Portfolio management - Part 2 The project portfolio management life cycle*. Retrieved from http://www.maxwideman.com

KEY TERMS AND DEFINITIONS

Delegate: Assign part of work to other people, relying on their competency and professionality to carry on the work in behalf of the designed owner.

Power-Based Approach: Modus operandi that enhance the ability of managers to make their own decision based on personal self-confidence and commitment to the company.

Program: Sub-programs, projects, and operational work grouped together to attain more benefits for its customers and end users than if they were managed separately.

Support: Provide help and collaboration in order to achieve success.

Strategic Fit: Level of alignment between portfolio components and organizational overall objectives.

Chapter 14
Managing Change:
Strategies and Tactics to Review the Portfolio

Joy Gumz
Project Auditors LLC, USA

ABSTRACT

The falling price of crude oil has caused the price of diesel and gasoline to drop, workers to be laid off, and competitors to consider merging. It has also provided a real-world view of companies applying project portfolio management as projects have been delayed, put on hold indefinitely, or closed down completely. Energy companies have shelved $400bn of spending on new oil and gas projects since the price collapse, delaying millions of barrels a day in future output from the Gulf of Mexico, Africa, Kazakhstan, and other areas (Adams, 2016). The price of crude oil, which traded above $100 since 2011 has dropped over 50% since September 2014 due to a lack of global demand plus continued production by Saudi Arabia and others. This chapter will look at strategies and tactics used by companies including Chevron, Royal Dutch Shell, and Total SA in reviewing and rebalancing their project portfolios. These approaches have application to other industry sectors.

INTRODUCTION

What is the value of a portfolio review? And how important is it to portfolio management? According to Robert G. Cooper, portfolio reviews are one of ten "best practices" in portfolio management. Based on studies conducted by Cooper with Scott Edgett, they found ten best practices (Cooper & Edgett, 2006):

1. Focus on data integrity [early in the project]; front-end load the project.
2. Install a systematic project management process with stage-gates that work.
3. Adopt an incremental commitment or "options" approach.
4. Know when to walk away from a project.
5. Categorize projects into buckets and use different criteria for different buckets.
6. Since there is no one best way to pick projects, triangulate by using two to four methods.

DOI: 10.4018/978-1-5225-2151-8.ch014

7. Try scorecards, one of the top-rated but overlooked methods, for stage-gate decisions.
8. Use success criteria for stage-gate decisions.
9. Use financial measures other than NPV when appropriate.
10. Build in periodic portfolio reviews to force rank your projects.

So portfolio reviews are important. But what can be learned from E&P companies (exploration and production companies whose mission is the discovery and development of oil & gas fields) about portfolio reviews? Are these companies really experts at this process – or in the realm of portfolio management?

Let's take a closer look at the ten best practices above. Examining Chevron as an example, they would easily score an 8 or 9 on the best practices above, and perhaps even a 10. Since 1996, Chevron has used a well-defined five phase project methodology with stage-gates called CPDEP (pronounced chip-dip) which stands for Chevron Project Development and Execution Process. Phase 1 involves framing the business goal to be pursued and ensuring that it aligns with the business objectives. Phase 2 involves the search for and identification of the best alternative that meets the criteria developed in Phase 1. Phase 3 involves the development of the alternative selected in Phase 2. The first three phases are referred to as "Front End Loading." Research in oil & gas has shown that a majority of a project's value is identified in these three phases. Comparing these practices with our list of ten, we can check Practices 1 and 2 are done.

What else does Chevron do that would be considered best practice according to Robert Cooper? Projects are funded incrementally to explore different development options with gates enforced through decision review boards. The largest investment called Final Investment Decision is not made until at least three gates have been successfully passed. Chevron uses indexes during the early phases to gauge how well the project is defined, including PDRI, the Project Definition Rating Index. It uses Net Present Value (NPV) as well as other criteria for financial measures. Chevron benchmarks projects and designates some as pacemakers, meaning they should be in the top 10% performers for their project category. They categorize projects into different types to balance the portfolio. We will look more at different dimensions use for portfolio balancing later in this chapter. Looking back to our list of practices, we can check off Practices 3, 5, 8, and 9.

And they know when to shut down a project if the risks become too high. In 2002, Chevron settled with the State of Florida for Destin Dome Unit leases rather than fight with environmental groups and the state about drilling. Shutting down a project is not always easy but it's essential to the overall portfolio management process. There is no point in performing portfolio reviews if the review results are simply filed on a shelf. That's a checkbox for Practices 4.

We'll look at practices 6 and 7 in more depth in this chapter as well how Chevron and Royal Dutch Shell perform portfolio reviews. Many of these practices are applicable across a wide variety of industries, especially for capital-intensive sectors. Some leading practices, such as Decision Analysis which is used by Chevron, are applicable to all sectors.

Recognizing that their project portfolio is critical to the stock value of the company and of high interest to its web site visitors which includes shareholders, employees, regulators and potential investors, in March 2016, Chevron placed additional emphasis by adding a specific menu option entitled "project portfolio" on its web site's main page. The link gives the ability to select one of the top 8 to 10 capital projects for more detail. The financial results of Chevron have held up surprisingly well, when one considers the 50% plus price drop in their main product. Well-run E&P companies know robust portfolio management including regular periodic portfolio reviews are the only way to stay solvent. The last market upheaval was just a few years ago during the Great Recession (2008-2009) when 62 U.S.

companies focused on only E&P activities (excludes oil companies with activities other than E&P such as pipelines and refineries) filed for bankruptcy protection.

To accomplish financial stability during such turbulence, these companies have not been sitting still. Portfolio reviews have led to selecting certain assets for disposal, prompt valuation of those assets, and subsequent sale. It also means continually seeking improved operational efficiency. Strategic Decision Review Boards have delayed Final Investment Decision for multiple large projects; others have been placed projects on hold. In the stage-gate decision process, projects have been 'recycled' to improve the business case, with the goal of lowering costs through a variety of methods.

The objectives of this chapter are to present challenges that organizations have in optimizing their project portfolios and practical approaches for portfolio reviews. Many of the examples will be from upstream project portfolio management, but we will also include examples from pharmaceutical and construction industries.

In this chapter, we will look at practices that we consider "good" and others we consider "leading". We'll consider tools that provide visualization and the use of Excel. We'll discuss processes that are used to update project portfolios when roles and responsibilities are split among several groups and individuals and there is probably no 'PMO'. In all cases, organizations must consider their environment and culture to determine what will work best for them, and use organizational change management to introduce changes. In essence, good portfolio review process comes down the six elements shown in Figure 1 (Project Auditors LLC, 2016).

1. Integrated processes of project management with portfolio management.
2. Motivated personnel who understand their roles & responsibilities.
3. Training and education of those personnel.
4. Tools & templates that support the processes and personnel.

Figure 1. A solid portfolio review process requires all six elements
Source: © 2016, Project Auditors LLC. Used with permission.

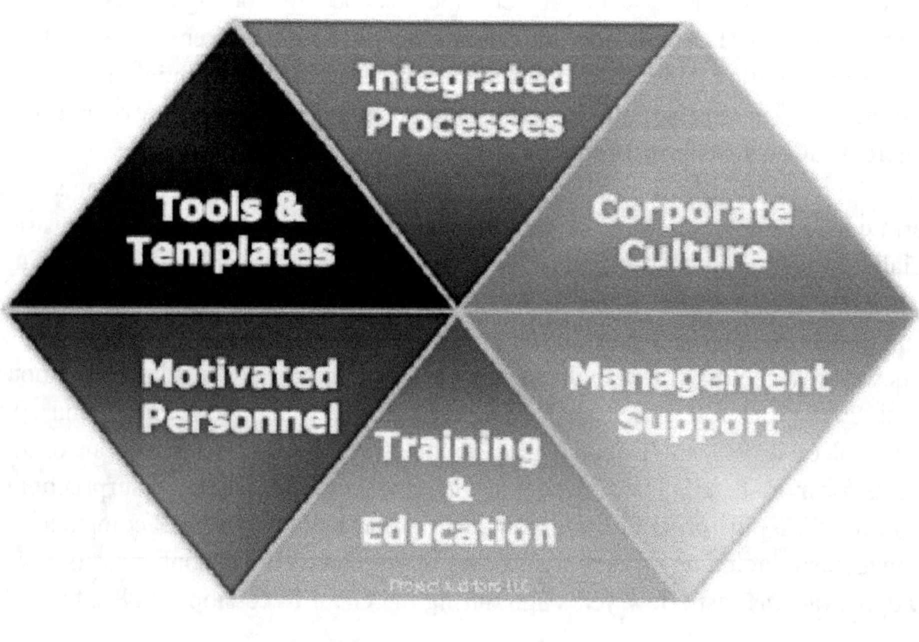

5. Corporate culture, and
6. Management support.

BACKGROUND

Optimizing a projects portfolio is hardly a phrase that will generate excitement at a cocktail party. And unlike many good business ideas, it certainly can't be explained on a single cocktail napkin. Yet as economic volatility and global complexity increase, updating a projects portfolio to account for changes in an orderly, timely manner is essential.

The companies that are most advanced in portfolio management are not the banks – as can be seen from the global financial crisis of 2008; it is the large international oil companies who have been dealing with high risk, high reward nature of their project portfolios for many decades, especially in their E&P business. Oil companies typically segment their business into E&P or upstream, midstream and downstream. Upstream includes license acquisition, exploratory drilling, appraisal and field development. Downstream encompasses refineries and storage. Midstream covers pipelines and transportation. Upstream projects are higher risk because the days of 'easy oil' are past. There are a few places in the world where drilling for oil remains low cost, such as Kuwait, where the production cost per barrel was less than $1.50 in 2011. Of course, that does not include the cost of the defense of the country of Kuwait, or it would be much higher.

Portfolio analysis and optimization has over the last 20 years progressed as tools and techniques have improved. Using multiple methods for analysis and project selection is regarded as a best practice, especially if projects have higher complexity and/or higher risk. Allocation of scarce resources is a fundamental goal, whether human resources or monetary capital are the more scarce of the two. Selection tools include the following methods.

Rank and Cut: This is the project selection approach taught in fundamental project management classes. Using Net Present Value (NPV) and/or other financial measurements such as Internal Rate of Return (IRR), projects are ranked and capital and other resources allocated. It is a simplistic and deterministic approach.

Sensitivity Analysis Tools: Sensitivity analysis helps identify the variables that are most critical to the project decision. Tornado diagrams, decision trees, and radar charts are common tools, very often created in Excel. The Guide to the Project Management Body of Knowledge includes both tornado diagrams in and decision trees in its section on Quantitative Risk Analysis and Modeling Techniques.

A radar chart, sometimes known as a spider or star chart, is an effective tool for presenting complicated data and plotting significance. They can be useful when comparing competing projects and examining related attributes. Chevron uses them as part of its project management methodology to quantitatively assess the quality of its decisions and determine what areas require further examination.

Stochastic models: These models incorporate a certain degree of randomness, or unpredictability producing a range of outcomes with different probabilities. Software programs to do Monte Carlo simulation such as @Risk and Crystal Ball have been available since 1987.

Scenario planning: Performing what-if analysis has always been desirable, and technology advances have provided software tools with scenario planning capabilities. Various options, choices, and outcomes can be explored which then allow for advance planning and negotiations ultimately providing better results.

Efficient Frontier: Harry Markowitz wrote his ground-breaking book on investment portfolio management for which he (and two others) received the Nobel Prize in 1990. By plotting expected return and the return variance, he defined a curve called the "efficient frontier": a portfolio on this curve has the smallest variance for a given expected return (Markowitz, 1952). Software is now available that can plot the efficient frontier enabling visualization of the portfolio.

MANAGING CHANGE IN PORTFOLIO

Issues, Controversies, Problems

What are the challenges that prevent organizations from having a strong portfolio management process? *Five problems* were summarized by Cooper (Cooper, Edgett, & Kleinschmidt, 1997):

1. The resulting portfolio did not reflect the organization's strategy.
2. The portfolio was poor quality.
3. The stage-gate process for project management were ineffective and that affected the portfolio.
4. Too many projects were approved for the limited resources available.
5. The portfolio management process resulted in short-term lower risk projects being selected over riskier but potential break-through projects.

In the author's experience, some organizations have even more basic problems: obtaining accurate project data. By nature, the data describing that status of a project is outdated within a short period of time. Yet portfolio review requires a reasonably updated status of the project as well as its outlook, which is based on estimates. Who will collect that data and ensure it is updated periodically, along with the other information needed for a review? Will the same data be obtained for all projects allowing a comparison? Does the process contain all the necessary steps?

Poor selection and/or review processes often result in an unbalanced portfolio. To remain viable, organizations must distribute their portfolio among various types of projects, especially those in highly regulated industries. Projects might be maintenance, upgrades, regulatory/compliance, new production, etc. The exact categories will depend on the industry, but every company is likely to have some projects that are required due to regulation; however, not all these projects have the same urgency. In 2012, a major international bank discovered it was spending 70% of its project money on compliance projects and only 2% on new products. Clearly, its project portfolio was unbalanced as shown in Figure 2.

An executive director warned that if no action were taken, "We will be a very compliant bank with no customers." (Gumz, 2015).

A second problem is that organizations have too many projects in the mix. This can be the result of underestimating the effort required, underestimating productivity, or lack of good data regarding resource availability and in particular how resources are being used (operations vs. projects vs. administrative).

Specific Challenges in E&P Project Portfolio Management

There are also specific challenges with E&P project portfolio management. Experts in oil and gas agree: easy oil is gone. E&P projects are now more complex. This complexity can come from different

Figure 2. The unbalanced portfolio problem

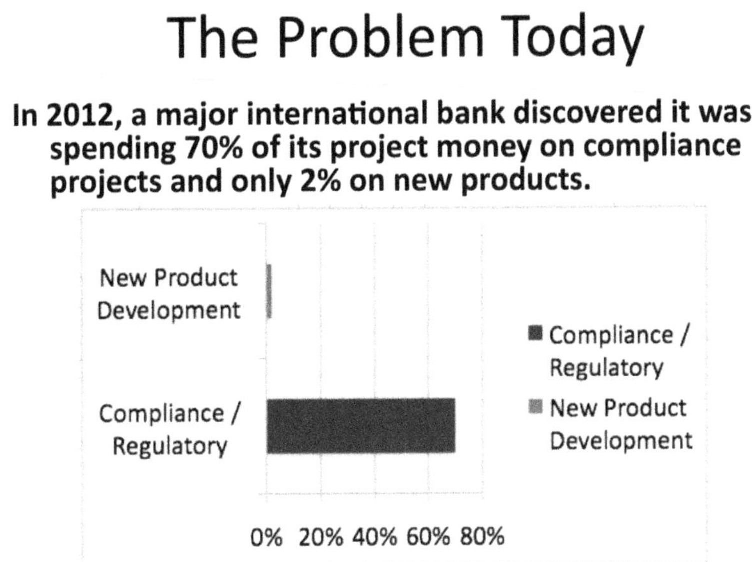

factors, such as the technical nature of the project or its geography. Deepwater wells are more complex than wells in shallower water. The geographical location of a well can be more challenging because of distance from other facilities and lack of infrastructure. There is an increased need to keep costs in line with original estimates through innovation and efficiency. Projects that experience a cost blowout can result in a higher breakeven point $/BoE (barrel of oil equivalent).

The uncertain nature of oil prices is a challenge to accurate estimation of project revenues. A change energy companies have recently faced is the drop in the price of oil, as shown by a benchmark price for Brent crude oil in Figure 3 (Trading Economics, 2016). E&P companies have long recognized the potential and actual volatility of oil and gas prices; they calculate metrics on the breakeven point on projects and even individual wells. ExxonMobil and Royal Dutch Shell use risk-based quantitative metrics e.g. project value at P90 (90% probability) and P10 (10% probability), to prioritize projects and in Shell's case, make investment decisions.

The goal of long term growth requires a balanced project portfolio. For E&P, balance includes geographical diversification to mitigate political risk, different resource types and different well types (on-shore, shallow water, deepwater). Different resource types and well types require specific expertise and know-how. Resource types may be divided into two broad groups, conventional and unconventional, and then subdivided further into the specific hydrocarbon: oil, gas, LNG, tight gas, tight oil, etc. Unconventional resources that are lower in value than conventional crude oils because they are difficult and costly to produce and refine. They include extra-heavy oil, oil sands, tight / shale gas, and oil shale. Unconventional resources account for the majority of the world's existing hydrocarbon resources. A report on oil and gas megaprojects published by the consulting firm EY in 2014 found that some companies did not have a balanced portfolio for a surprising reason; their project portfolio was "overly diverse and poorly aligned" which resulted in unnecessarily stretching resources, increasing risk in the portfolio and diluting the potential value of inter-project linkages. (EYGM Limited, 2016).

Figure 3. Price of Brent crude oil 1970 to 2016
Source: © 2016, Trading Economics. Used with permission.

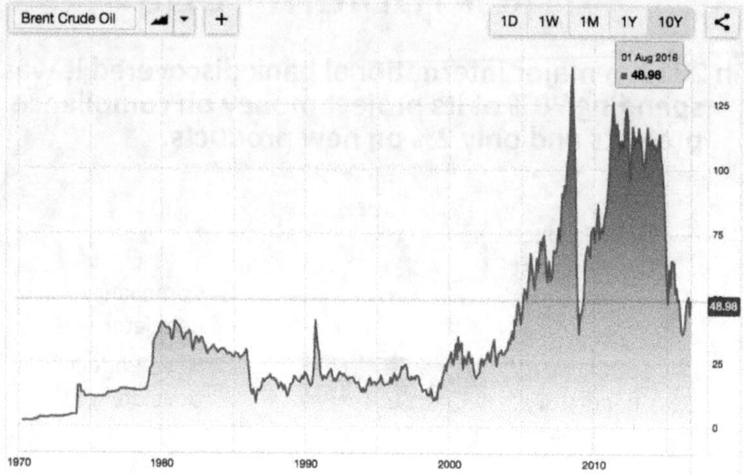

Companies need a pipeline of projects at different stages while managing their reserves by either keeping them stable or ideally increasing them; fields in production must be balanced with new discoveries. The potential for oil price volatility and the stochastic and evolving estimates of reserve levels to means that portfolio management requires careful scenario analysis and stress-testing the portfolio.

Eventually the question arises as to which E&P projects or assets are 'non-core' and may be up for disposal. Recognizing synergies among projects helps in pinpointing the right projects for disposal. Awareness of synergies in the portfolio is important as well as recognizing potential synergies with other business units within the company or external organizations in the region. Synergies may arise from different aspects, including company capabilities, staff know-how, geography and local infrastructure/facilities. Both Chevron and ExxonMobil have recently put more emphasis on the fact that they are integrated energy companies, and are making an effort to use product from their upstream activities as feedstock for downstream activities. This integration is not always simple as refinery feedstock requirements may not match the product the upstream business unit is producing. For example, a refinery may need heavy crude feedstock while their E&P unit has an excess production of light sweet oil from shale production. If the refinery adjusts to take the different feedstock, it would require a multi-year capital project. It can take two to three years to retrofit a refinery to process the volume of light crude oil to make such a project worthwhile. And what changes will happen in those two or three years?

Synergies can also be gained by using know-how and skills that the company already has or leveraging relationships and knowledge from working in a particular country. Being able to sell a product locally, e.g. gas utilization by a local power or industrial plant can dictate whether a project is successful, as the additional cost for transportation and distribution may make the product noncompetitive.

Company philosophy on the size and objectives of its projects can also have an effect on its resulting portfolio. Large companies as Chevron, Royal Dutch Shell and ExxonMobil want a mix of larger, medium and small projects. In 2010, Statoil, the oil company of Norway, stated, "We see a structural shift in our non-sanctioned project portfolio from a few large, complex projects to a high number of mainly smaller projects or sub-sea tie-backs. This requires a high level of standardized technical concepts as well as simplified development processes." (Statoil, 2010) This type of decision is philosophical and effects the nature of the portfolio and how it should be balanced.

In summary, E&P companies can have the challenges Cooper has pointed out and more. More complex projects mean expense estimates may have wider estimate ranges which affects input data on which the portfolio management process depends. Revenue of projects depends on the commodity price of oil which is an open competitive market. Multiple aspects must be considered to balance the portfolio but not make it too diverse. A pipeline of projects at different phases must be maintained all the while managing reserves. To add the most value, synergies among projects in the portfolio must be recognized.

MANAGING CHANGE STRATEGIES AND TACTICS: SOLUTIONS AND RECOMMENDATIONS

A recommendation for improved portfolio optimization is to improve the portfolio review process and to take advantage of improved tools and techniques. To do this, we have looked at the existing practice of companies who expect market volatility: the E&P segment of international oil companies. Although an environmentalist may have their own point of view, it takes skill to navigate price drops of 50%, political unrest leading to asset confiscation/loss, and technological risk and not only remain in business but attract shareholders. We have also reviewed papers from experts such as Robert G. Cooper, as well as existing standards from professional associations as PMI.

In this chapter, we will review strategies and tactics from firms who:

1. Have been doing portfolio management for decades.
2. Use a decentralized decision-making process, and
3. Do portfolio management as a core business process because of the risk including market risk and political risk.

The history of Chevron starts in 1879, with the founding of Pacific Coast Oil Company in the San Joaquin Valley of California. Through growth and mergers, it became part of Standard Oil. When Standard Oil was split up in 1911, it became Standard Oil of California. After it merged with Gulf Oil in 1984, it legally changed its corporate name to Chevron, which it had long-used as a brand name for gasoline Today it is an integrated energy company with over 75 exploration and production (E&P) projects in progress with Chevron's share worth over $250M; thirty-one of these are classified as major capital projects (Chevron, 2016b). Its downstream business also owns refineries and service stations. We will be examining the E&P portfolio (upstream) rather than downstream.

Chevron operates with decentralized business units that are accountable to a central headquarters organization which allocates capital and provides support and functional expertise. Certain processes are standard across business units, such as CPDEP, its project management methodology, and CSOC, its Capital Stewardship Ownership Capability approach.

Project management has always been a fundamental in oil & gas. Accounting rules for the oil & gas industry are one of the reasons. There are two basic methods of financial accounting and reporting:

- The full cost method, and
- The successful efforts method.

Exploration activities center around specific projects undertaken to locate geologic structures with likely accumulation of oil and/or gas. Tracking the costs of each project is essential for management to know its profitability. Regulatory agencies impose specific reporting requirements. Detailed project historical cost records are kept because of contracts or other legal requirements such as a joint venture.

Robust portfolio management is also a necessity. Projects take large amounts of capital expenditures (CAPEX) and years (sometimes decades) to develop. Oil companies must continually make investment decisions about and allocate CAPEX to new projects that fit the portfolio within the company's constraints to develop their project pipeline. These new projects eventually replace projects that are at the end of their life cycle and when they move to production status, generating new cash to sustain the company's future cash flow. The strategy for growth must also balance short-term shareholder returns and project investment opportunities for long-term corporate growth. This requires not only a solid strategy but also effective implementation of the strategy to achieve the planned objectives. Companies with E&P business units such as Chevron, ExxonMobil, Royal Dutch Shell, and Total S.A. all stress the need for capital discipline and the trade-off against the potential for future growth in their annual reports (Chevron, 2016a), (ExxonMobil, 2016), (Royal Dutch Shell, 2016), (Total S.A., 2016). Chevron defines Portfolio Management as, "the continuous process of identifying, selecting, and managing the optimum set of portfolio investments to realize maximum business value." (Franke, 2008). The same definition can be used for its capital investments in E&P projects or its IT PMO.

Expertise in portfolio management is a necessity in the industry at least in part due to accounting rules. Oil & gas reserves, both proved and unproved, must be reported as well as financial results. Unlike some companies that do not even know how many projects they have or their cost, E&P companies must include their reserve information and it is externally audited annually as part of the financial statement audit. Calculation of proved reserves is complex. Some companies are conservative in their proved reserves measurements, choosing not to assign any proved reserves until the project has advanced to the stage where the field development plan has received all relevant formal approvals. At that point, the reserves can be declared proved, even if the project is subsequently placed on hold later.

In 2004, Royal Dutch Shell was fined $120M by the US Securities and Exchange Commission and £17M by the British Financial Services Authority for overstating its reserves by 23%. And unlike the banking scandals of 2008/2009, heads rolled. RDS's chairman, Philip Watts, its head of oil and gas, Walter van de Vijver, and the chief financial officer, Judy Boynton all resigned. Its borrowing costs also became more expensive since it lost its credit rating of AAA.

So how do companies such as Chevron do their portfolio reviews? As explained earlier, Chevron and other integrated energy companies use a stage-gate project management methodology; Chevron's methodology is named CPDEP. In these companies, capital investment decision making is a gated process. Project phases begin with a business assessment, move on to alternatives selection, scope definition, execute (detailed engineering & construction), start-up/evaluate/operate, and finally end with abandonment. At each stage-gate between the phases, a decision is made with to proceed, put the project on hold, discontinue the project, or rework/refine the phase to meet the gate criteria. Up to the scope definition decision gate, all decisions are made in the context of the portfolio of opportunities. At a high level, the Project Management Methodologies of integrated energy companies are quite similar. Different companies may name their phases slightly differently, but the objectives of each phase are the same. The number of phases can vary. At Chevron, the business assessment of identifying and assessing opportunities is seen as one phase; Royal Dutch Shell divides the business assessment into two phases, Identify and Assess. Some companies view abandonment as the last phase. A solid stage-gate approach improves decision quality and ensures projects are re-examined to determine they still fit in the overall portfolio.

To advance to the next stage, approval by a project-level Decision Review Board is required. Let's take a look at typical roles and responsibilities, as shown in Table 1. The Decision Executive is chair of the DRB and selects its members. For the state-gate reviews, a Decision Support Package is prepared by Strategy/Decision Support. The DRB will generally receive a pre-read in advance of the meeting and then meet to discuss whether to advance the project, hold, stop or recycle. To recycle means the project must fix / redo / refine its work and then resubmit. Information on project status at each stage-gate and the decisions taken has to communicated to the Strategy/Decision Support in each Business Unit for each region. The status and forecast project capital needs are included when the Business Unit makes a request for capital allocation as part of the annual budgeting cycle. There is some back and forth between headquarters and the Business Unit on the amount of money the BU can expect for the year, divided into usually three tranches.

One of the key roles at Chevron is the "endorser". This role is often but not always under the CFO. Along with creating the business strategy, they allocate CAPEX to the project, actively confirm projects are still a strategic fit, and ensure standardized processes are used.

ROLES AND RESPONSIBILITIES

When evaluating portfolio management, one question every organization should ask: how well are roles and responsibilities defined? Does information for portfolio review flow smoothly so it is available when needed – or does it continually have to be pulled out? And how accurate is the data?

Once the information has flowed to the Business Unit's Strategy / Decision Support group, they periodically prepare a decision support package for the portfolio review. This allows projects to be ranked against other projects and to be viewed within the capital constraints for that Business Unit's allocated amount. Portfolio reviews are typically held four times a year; some companies do portfolio reviews biannually or only once a year during the annual budgeting cycle. The goal is to ensure BU has the correct set of approved or "Go" projects, the pipeline is relatively even across the planning time horizon, there is diversity among project types, the right mix and balance of projects is present, projects have been assigned the right priorities, and sufficient resources are available to undertake the "Go" projects.

During the review, all E&P projects in that region initially are in the mix. CAPEX, which has been allocated by headquarters, is divided into three buckets: exploration for long-term value, base business for near-term value, and major capital projects for long term value. The bucket allocations used by Chevron for its 2015-2016 E&P budget were ~10% exploration, ~60% major capital projects, and ~30% base business (includes maintenance and compliance).

Economic models of Net Present Value and after-tax cash flow for major projects are essential in E&P so the most updated estimates for this data is part of the Decision Support Package and presentation.

Some companies evaluate their projects on various factors using a score-card approach. "Must do" projects are highlighted—projects that are almost completed and are still good ones or are deemed to be strategically essential. These "must do" projects are removed from the mix, they are designated as top priority, the CAPEX they require is subtracted from the BU allocation to reserve it, and their resources are protected.

The remaining projects are prioritized within each bucket. Comparisons are made on various attributes among the projects, using visualization tools. Projects are ranked and capital allocated until there is no CAPEX remaining for that bucket.

Table 1. Typical roles and responsibilities

Role	Perspective	Typical Responsibilities
Decision Review Board (DRB)*	Project Level	• Gate keeper for decision to proceed with a project to the next phase. • Endorses Project Control Plan and Project Roadmap. • Gives the mandate (charter) to the project team. • Secures functional resources and alignment. • Engages in technical and business review. • Reviews Decision Support Package for gate-review, Project Execution Plans, Risk Management Plan, and other key documents. • Monitors progress on peer reviews / audit actions follow-up and closure. • Ensures all stakeholders are aware of key issues and project progress. • Provides a forum for the Project Manager to seek help in resolving issues. • Contributes lessons learned from their area of expertise. After FID (Final Investment Decision): • Confirms the mandate (charter) of the project team. • Owns the high level risks and appropriate risk response. • Provides resources to ensure the project is sufficiently staffed. • Verifies compliance with and approves deviations from the Project Control Plan. • Participates and contributes to retrospective / look back sessions.
Project Manager	Project Level	• Provides leadership for project team. • Establishes framework for making and implementing quality decisions. • Ensures process for quality decisions is followed. • Ensures timely and quality completion of all deliverables. • Makes multiple day-to-day project decisions. • Performs a project look back and solicits input from the project team.
Decision Executive	Project Level	• Determines where Stage 1 work concept selection) takes place in organization. • Endorses categorization project which determines amount of process to be applied. • Chair of DRB prior to FID. • Selects and engages DRB. • Engages other executives. • Establishes and communicates expectations. • Endorses key deliverables e.g. Risk Register and Risk Management Plan. • Ultimately accountable for project and business outcomes. • Ultimately arbitrates project decisions. • With PM, identifies project look back participants and schedules project look-back.
Strategic DRB	Portfolio Level	• Authorizes funding of FID. • Sets timing of next review if funding is withheld.
Endorser	Portfolio Level	• Creates business strategy. • Allocates capital among sub-organizations. • Approves funding to advance project. • Actively confirms strategic fit of project. • Drives and ensures use of processes.
Strategy / Decision Support**	Portfolio Level	• Appraise and evaluate new business opportunities. • Analyze the portfolio against different criteria to understand and mitigate the risk for delivery and develop future opportunities for success. • Deliver annual Venture Plan with clearly defined options for accelerated portfolio growth and performance improvement. • Provide continuous program optimization through dynamic global opportunity portfolio management. • Deliver analysis and advice to senior executives. • If a support team is in place, provides leadership for team of analysts.

* DRB composition depends on project planned CAPEX and the category level is endorsed by the DE. Composition of DRB often changes upon FID when different board members are appointed. Different companies use different terms are for the DRB oversight group; Investment Management Committee is another name.

**Strategy / Decision Support may be a small team led by a manager

Finally a check for balance is done. Diversification among different countries, technical risk, and product is checked. Oil, gas and LNG (liquefied natural gas) prices are not linked, so diversification is a way to reduce risk. Figure 4 shows an example (Chevron, 2014).

One of the challenges in project portfolio management is economics: allocation of scarce resources. For some industries, this is capital; for others it is human resources. Some strategies and tactics for portfolio management can be applied regardless of the primary constraint. In industries where human resources are primary constraint rather than capital, a comparison could be done of the resources going to projects across relevant dimensions, such as the split by market, by project type, by business area, or by risk level. Below is a recap of some of the strategies and tactics used.

Strategies

1. **Organizational Placement:**
    a. Placement within the organization is often under the CFO, as the budget is driven from the CFO and capital allocation process is linked with budgeting.
    b. An alternative placement is under marketing.

Figure 4. Capital and exploration allocation for Chevron 2014-2016

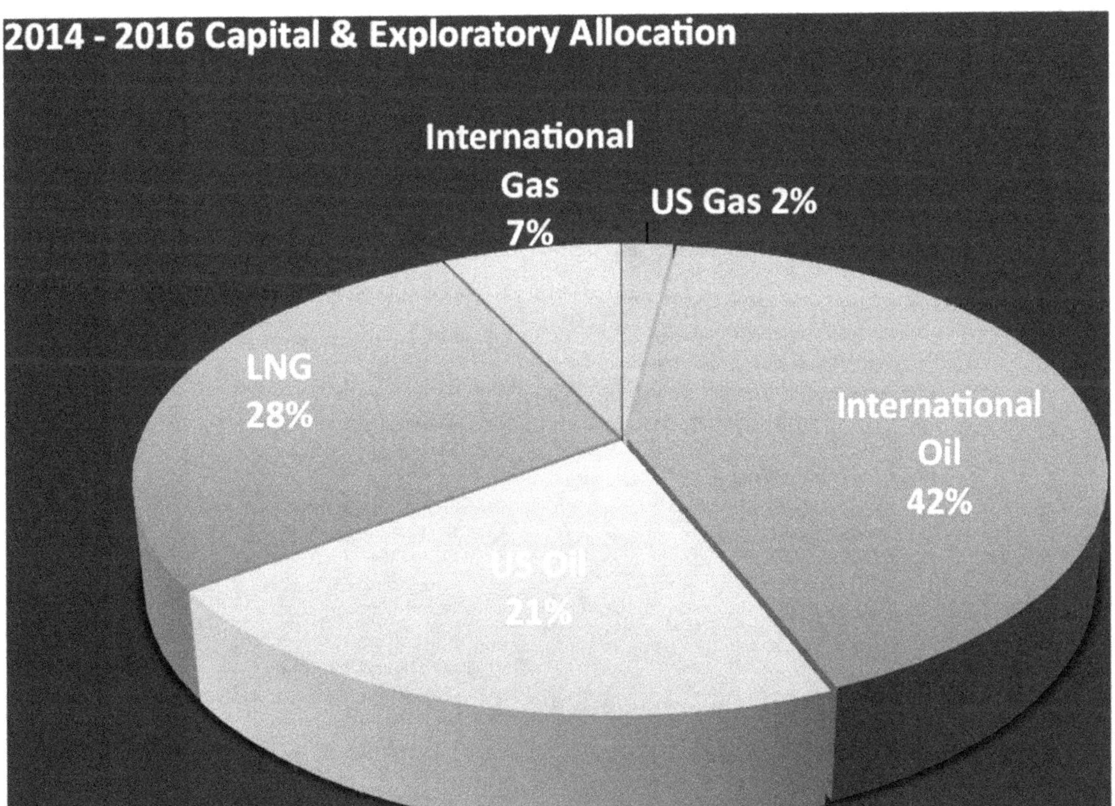

2. **Strategic Decision Review Board:** Outputs include: Portfolio update including health indicators, risks, schedule, cost and general status, priority changes, funds re-allocated, resource discussion, and high risks to be addressed.
3. **Agreement on Definitions:**
   a. **Definition of 'Must Do":** The definition of what constitutes a "must do" project versus a "discretionary" project must be clearly understood and applied consistently.
   b. **Definition of Portfolio Segments:** Chevron uses three segments: exploration for long-term value, base business for near-term value, and major capital projects for long term value. Royal Dutch Shell also uses three: current cash-flow generation, growth (future cash engines), and future potential. It uses different strategies for each of them, with tailored technology approaches, distinctive markets and financial targets.
4. **Proactive Portfolio Updates:** Process is to frequently update the portfolio to reflect emerging situations to allow situations to be proactively addressed.
5. **Strategic Index:** A Strategic Index is sometimes used in the ranking of projects. Figure 5 lists the scorecard factors recommended by Cooper for NPD (Cooper & Edgett, 2006). E&P companies usually consider these factors as strategically related and compile metrics but necessarily as part of a scorecard:
   a. Maturity of the Opportunity.
   b. Final Investment Decision (FID) date.
   c. Potential Volumes.
   d. Expected Production.
   e. Strategic partnership e.g. joint venture.
   f. Competitive advantage (differentiation).
   g. Country Risk.

Figure 5. Scorecard factors including strategic fit
Source: © 2006 Dr. Robert G. Cooper and Dr. Scott J. Edgett. Used with permission. Adapted from Cooper, R., & Edgett, S. (2006). Ten ways to make better portfolio and project selection decisions. PDMA Visions Magazine, XXX, 3, June 2006, 11-15. www.stage-gate.com.

Factor 1: Strategic Fit & Importance
- Alignment of project with organization's strategy
- Importance of project to the strategy
- Impact of project on organization

Factor 2: Product & Competitive Advantage
- Compelling value proposition
- Unique benefits
- Differentiator

Factor 3: Market Attractiveness
- Market size
- Market potential
- Margins
- Presence or lack of competition

ECV=Expected Commercial Value
IRR=Internal Rate of Return
NPV=Net Present Value

Factor 4: Core Competency Leverage
- Technology
- Operations
- Distribution
- Marketing

Factor 5: Technical Feasibility
- Technical complexity
- Size/number of technical gaps
- Track record with technology
- Results of proof of concept phase

Factor 6: Financial Rewards
- Financial return (NPV, IRR, ECV)
- Size of financial opportunity
- Productivity Index (PI)
- Certainty of financial estimates
- Level of risk & ability to manage risk

Financial reward is usually the dominant factor and accuracy of economic models critical to portfolio success.

6. **Economic Models:** Substantial analysis is performed to produce an economic model for the project and simulate various conditions, and perform what-if analysis. Financial Calculations include
   a. Value (NPV).
   b. Value Investment Ratio (VIR).
   c. Capital Outlay (CAPEX / OPEX / EXPEX: Expenses for Exploring).
   d. Payback time.
   e. Break-even price.
   f. Competitive advantage (differentiation).
   g. Country Risk.
   h. Unit Technical Cost.
   i. Upside/downside at high / low oil price range.
7. **Decision Quality:** To improve decision-making capabilities, Chevron has implement Decision Quality across the organization.
8. **Choices in Managing the Portfolio:**
   a. Accelerate investment (strategic growth drivers).
   b. Protect.
   c. Recycle / Fix or Divest underperformers.
9. **Risk:**
   a. **Chevron:** Directing a higher proportion of CAPEX to projects with better returns and higher probability of returns and shorter duration. Projects that are enhancements to existing assets, known as "brownfield" opportunities, are more likely to be selected than greenfield or mega-projects that have more risk, require more CAPEX, and have longer project cycles.
   b. In 2010, Statoil of Norway moved to reduce risk and control CAPEX. They made a structural shift in their non-sanctioned project portfolio (projects prior to FID) from a few large, complex projects to a high number of mainly smaller projects or sub-sea tie-backs. The smaller projects require a high level of standardized technical concepts and use simplified development processes.

Decision Analysis (DA) and Decision Quality (DQ)

Chevron is one of the few companies that has implemented a comprehensive framework for decision making throughout the organization. This is relatively rare; almost three-quarters of companies have no formal corporate-wide approach to making major, complex decisions. (Neal & Spetzler, 2015). And Chevron has this in place for some time; in 2000, then-CEO & Chairman David O'Reilly insisted that DQ become mandatory on all capital expenditures over $50 million. Decision Executives were required to become certified in the fundamentals of the approach by taking in-house courses. Decision analysts were embedded in the organization around the world and became part of the Chevron capital stewardship process, CSOC. The author of this chapter was able to observe Decision Analysis and Decision Quality while a consultant at Chevron in 2001.

The six elements of Decision Quality that characterize high-quality decisions are (Neal & Spetzler, 2015):

1. An appropriate frame, including a clear understanding of the problem and what needs to be achieved.
2. Creative, feasible alternatives from which to choose the one with a high probability of success as it is defined.
3. Meaningful information that is reliable, unbiased, and reflects all relevant uncertainties and intangibles.
4. Clarity about desired outcomes, including acceptable tradeoffs.
5. Solid reasoning and sound logic that includes considerations of uncertainty and insight at the appropriate level of complexity.
6. Commitment by all stakeholders necessary to achieve effective action.

As part of its decision-making process, Chevron uses a spider chart tool to graphically display the six elements. Individuals perform a self-assessment which can then be compared to gain consensus for the group. Figure 6 shows four team member individual ratings (dashed lines) on the six elements. The average is shown as a solid line.

In 2014, Chevron received the first Raiffa-Howard Award for Organizational Decision Quality. The award is named for Professor Howard Raiffa of Harvard University and Professor Ronald A. Howard of Stanford University who first developed the concepts, and is awarded by the Society of Decision Professionals. In judging finalists, the award panel considered these questions:

1. Is DQ part of the organizational culture?
2. Do decision makers have the knowledge and abilities to use DQ constructively and are they in the proper roles?
3. Are decision boards frequently used for major decisions?
4. Do decision processes engage the right people and have the rigor to achieve DQ?

Figure 6. Decision quality chart

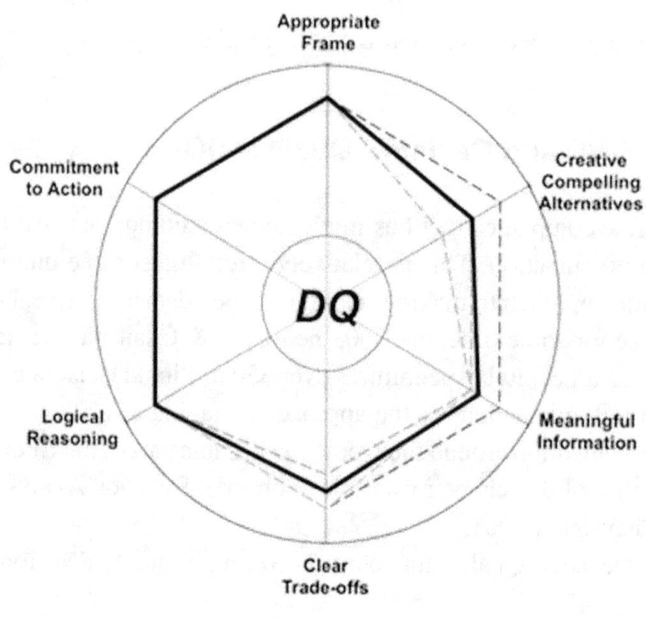

5. Are tools used theoretically sound and adequately address the needs during different decisions?
6. Do decision support staff have respect, capabilities and trust?
7. Are benefits from organizational decision quality apparent and clearly recognized?

Larry Neal, former manager of Decision Analysis at Chevron Corporation and now retired, has observed the following benefits of using a decision making framework. With an organization-wide approach to decision-making, the probability of circumventing individual decision-maker's inherent bias can be reduced and perhaps circumvented. Another benefit is the organization-wide common language that is introduced; using terms and definitions in the same way can speed up the making and reviewing of decisions. Instead of merely "good enough" decisions, the end result of more high quality decisions can, according to Mr. Neal, "add up to billions of dollars in additional value." (Neal & Spetzler, 2015).

SDP has cited 8 common frustrations with decision-making at organizations (Society of Decision Professionals, 2016):

- A range of compelling alternatives is not offered. The options presented sometimes address symptoms rather than the real problem.
- Too much time is spent analyzing decisions with little impact while too little time is devoted to the big, difficult decisions.
- The wrong people make the decision. Too many have veto power; too few the power to make things happen.
- The decisions are complex to analyze; the result is analysis paralysis.
- Everybody has different objectives and no one can agree on the trade-offs.
- There is so much uncertainty that, in the end, uncertainty is ignored.
- The decisions are ok, but the execution is unsatisfactory.
- The organization has a culture of gut-feel macho decision-making.

If any of these situations apply to your organization, DA may be an approach to consider.

Who has implemented a decision-making framework? Pharma companies are one sector. They have expensive R&D portfolios of multi-year drug projects. Companies include Pfizer, who has a Portfolio and Decision Analysis group. The group manages the R&D and drug portfolios, and is responsible for the analysis of complex business decisions. Pfizer received the Raiffa Howard Award in 2015.

In examining project portfolios, pharmaceutical R&D and E&P organizations share some common characteristics. Many of their projects are high-risk, high potential reward with long cycles and high cost. Phased decision-making and stage-gates are used to manage risk. But what company would not benefit from a more systematic decision analysis approach? DA could also decision-makers recognize if organizational culture is a potential barrier to decision quality. Organizations that are seeking to improve their project portfolio management practices are likely to benefit from efforts to reduce bias and improve the quality of their decision-making.

Tactics

1. **Process:**
   a. Front load the project as this provides solid information that is critical to both PM and PfM (portfolio management). Part of this process is ensuring information needs are defined for

each of the Go/Kill stage-gates. The stage-gate process results feed into the portfolio review process and both must be working for them to be effective. Sometimes project teams are unclear as to what deliverables are needed for a stage-gate review for the executives to make Go/Kill decisions. If a Decision Review Board needs to know "expected production" to plus-or-minus 10 percent, it needs to be a then make that requirement very clear to project teams. Chevron does this through its CPDEP (Chevron Project Development and Execution Process) stage-gate project management methodology and decision support package that is prepared for each gate. Front-end loading is moving more of the work effort forward, in essence changing the shape of the S-curve, at least in part. The objective is to do the front-end homework of key engineering and analysis activities before a project moves into the development phase.

b. Recognition that the budgeting cycle and PM stage-gate process both must be integrated with the PfM processes.

c. Recognition that portfolio must be balanced in terms of compliance/revenue producing and maintenance projects.

2. **Tools:**

a. Use of Decision Support Systems that include efficient frontier, real options analysis, genetic algorithms and advanced capabilities

b. Use of visualization tools to build on excel and/or database. Visualization tools can make a complex portfolio easier to understand. Filters can be set allowing layering to be done. Must do projects (base portfolio), and then view discrete scenarios where different projects are selected. It can also simplify understanding the timing of funding which is often done in blocks or tranches. Different attributes to be compared on the x and y axes including NPV vs. probability of success, concept attractiveness vs. ease of implementation, histograms showing the upcoming years CAPEX and production, markets, and product lines (oil/gas/LNG). Figure 7 compares the probability of success by using a proxy of ownership percentage against the NPV for the project. The size of the circle indicates relative CAPEX, and the color indicates the extraction method / technical approach. The projects are from Royal Dutch Shell's past portfolio, with data compiled by the author in a spreadsheet (Figure 8).

Nestlé S.A. has found value in using a visualization tool for its portfolio management. Nestlé identified portfolio optimization as one of three areas where it could focus to improve return-on-investment. An internal tool, code named ATLAS, was used to assess 100% of the portfolio, generating a graph comparing project investments, allowing decision-makers to determine whether to accelerate the project, protect the current investment, or fix it. (Nestlé S.A., 2015). The format is simple and uses a design similar to the graph created by the Boston Consulting Group in the early 1970s to show how organizations with multiple business units should categorize the units to allocate resources. Business units were placed in one of four quadrants: cash cows, Dogs, stars, or question marks, based on market growth rate (y-axis) vs. market share relative to competitors (x-axis). In a quarterly earnings call in 2013, Wan Ling Martello, Chief Financial Officer said the tool provides a common language and framework so the business can see more clearly the financial side and not become too emotional. Business executives now admit to her, "Look, we were going to ask for investment in x, y, and z, but we've run this exercise and we know it's actually not really value accretive [adding value]." (Nestlé S.A., 2013).

Figure 7. Probability of success vs. NPV
Source: © 2016 TIBCO Software Inc. Used with permission. All rights reserved.

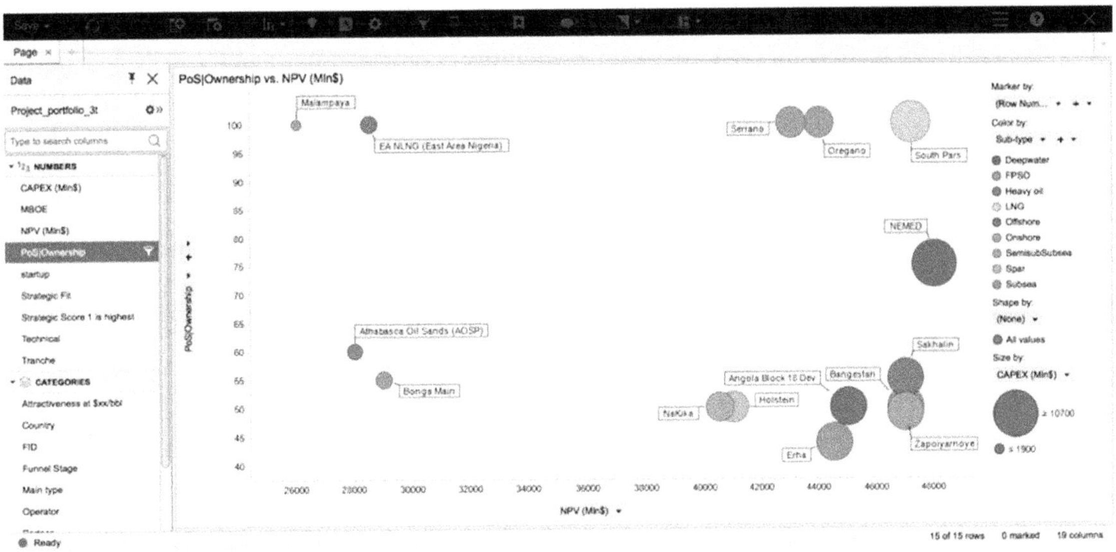

Figure 8. Spreadsheet data used to generate bubble diagram

Project Name	Main type	Sub-type	NPV (Mln$)	CAPEX (Mln$)	FID	Country	Operator	Partner	PoS / Ownership
Malampaya	Gas	Subsea	26000	1900	Post	Philippines	Shell		100.00
Athabasca Oil Sands (AOSP)	Oil	Heavy oil	28000	2900	Post	Canada	Shell	Chevron	60.00
EA NLNG (East Area Nigeria)	Gas	Offshore	28500	3300	Post	Nigeria	Shell		100.00
Bonga Main	Oil	FPSO	29000	3600	Post	Nigeria	Shell	Nigeria	55.00
NaKika	Oil	SemisubSubsea	40500	6600	2001	US	Shell	BP	50.00
Holstein	Oil	Spar	41000	6800	2001	US	BP	Chevron	50.00
Serrano	Oil	Subsea	43000	6900	2001	US	Shell		100.00
Oregano	Oil	Subsea	44000	7100	2001	US	Shell		100.00
Erha	Oil	FPSO	44500	8500	2002	Nigeria	ExxonMobil	Shell	43.75
Angola Block 18 Dev	Oil	Deepwater	45000	8600	2004	Angola	BP	Shell	50.00
Bangestan	Oil	Onshore	47000	8650	TBD	Iran	Shell		49.00
Sakhalin	Oil	Offshore	47000	8700	TBD	Russia	ExxonMobil	Shell	55.00
Zapoiyarnoye	Gas	Onshore	47000	8800	TBD	Russia	Gazprom	Shell	50.00
South Pars	Gas	LNG	47200	9400	TBD	Iran	Shell		100.00
NEMED	Gas	Deepwater	48000	10700	TBD	Egypt	Shell	ExxonMobil	75.00

3. **Techniques:**
    a. Diversification.
    b. Use of economic models to model the expenses (CAPEX, OPEX, taxes) and revenues of project to determine cash flow over time rather than just NPV, and using simulation to analyze these models under different assumptions.
    c. Cost control: Rigorously analyzing costs of projects. Delaying projects so they can be analyzed for improvements prior to execution. Renegotiation with government on licensing and royalties and contractors.

   d. Careful selection of project attributes and categories (see example spreadsheet Figure 8) used to create bubble diagrams and other visualization charts (cash flow over project life cycle). Bubble charts, radar / spider charts, tornado diagrams are used to visualize the complex data. Sensitivity analysis of NPV to oil price volatility, a project delay and CAPEX overrun.
   e. Selling project assets that are non-core based on strategic index (SI) and key attributes. Competitor analysis may be useful in determining potential buyers.
4. **Metrics:**
   a. Strategic Index.
   b. Using metrics other than benefit realization to measure portfolio management effectiveness. Capital intensive industries use ROCE (Risk on Capital Employed) and/or ROACE (Risk on Adjusted Capital Employed). Risk adjusted return on capital is sometimes used by companies who have implemented enterprise risk management.
   c. Profitability Index.
   d. Pace of execution – A simple metric to demonstrate how well the work is proceeding and provide an early warning sign if things are going wrong is the number of missed/met milestones. Note: For organizations using an Agile methodology, planned/actual points delivered per sprint can be used.
   e. Profitability versus competitors, e.g. well drilling cost.
   f. In comparison, for New Product Development (NPD) portfolios, metrics include NPD profitability versus funds spent; NPD profitability versus competitors; percentage of NPD projects meeting sales and profit targets; and on-time performance) (Cooper & Edgett, 2006).
   g. Metrics for Royal Dutch Shell include strategic (i - vi) and financial/economic (vii – xi), partial list (Stegink, 2011):
      i. Competitive Advantage.
      ii. Strategic Partnering.
      iii. Planned Production.
      iv. Timing of Final Investment Decision.
      v. Potential Volumes.
      vi. Country Risk.
      vii. NPV (after tax).
      viii. Value Investment Ratio (NPV / Investment).
      ix. CAPEX.
      x. Break-even price.
      xi. Payback time.

For IT project portfolios, at a minimum management wants information on resource utilization tracking and other data for capacity planning. Human resources are the scarce resource in IT, requiring allocation. Yet many IT organizations do not gather accurate time tracking data. Lack of accurate data makes capacity and capability analysis more of an estimating process than a technique in optimizing the portfolio (process 5.3 in the Standard for Portfolio Management). (Project Management Institute, 2013).

IT project metrics that are computed may include:

- % On Time Completed.
- % Completed Within Budget.

- % Completed with Scope Met.
- % Placed on hold.
- % Cancelled.
- Budget Variance Trends, and
- Customer Satisfaction.

Customer satisfaction is often used as a proxy for answering a key question: did the project deliver the promised benefits? This does not have to be complex; a simple three question survey that is administered to the project sponsor /Decision Executive after the project is finished can suffice.

Organizations that want quantification must build in the steps as part of the project. At the beginning of the project measure the baseline and set a goal. Baseline measurements of error rates or re-work may be easier to measure than hours or effort. Then measure the results at the end of the project. The results must be consistently applied and tracked by project and across the portfolio to provide reliable quantification. Determining when to measure at the end of the project can be difficult, as changes may not be fully adopted and efficient just because the project has ended.

5. **Balance:** Organizations that recognize the need to balance their portfolios may evaluate multiple dimensions: risk versus return, maintenance and regulatory versus growth or project types: e.g., new products, product improvements, cost reductions, compliance, maintenance and fixes, and fundamental research, short-term versus long-term new product projects, across various markets, across technologies, different product categories. Cooper uses these buckets when considering balance for NPD: New products,

Platforms and technology developments, Improvements, modifications, and extensions, and Customer requests. (Cooper & Edgett, 2006).

6. **Evaluation Criteria:** Different types of projects should use different criteria for evaluation. For example, quantitative financial criteria such as cash flow may be suitable for relatively predictable projects, such as improvements and modifications; but for innovation projects, using qualitative criteria and/or a scorecard may be necessary as the financial numbers may be difficult to estimate with any accuracy.

Note: One of the problems many organizations face is trying to execute too many projects concurrently. E&P companies are not immune to this. However, the better companies avoid this tendency and their portfolio review process uses forced ranking to prioritize projects.

The trade-off between future potential and disciplined capital spending is one of several dimensions E&P companies consider when evaluating their portfolio. The portfolio is also balanced by region/location, by energy source (gas, oil, LNG, tight gas) and by time to first production.

Implementing a portfolio review process requires:

- **Organizational Change:** An understanding of the level of acceptance of change within the organization is critical.
- **Executive Support:** Senior management and key stakeholders must be on-board and supportive of both the process and change required to implement it.
- **Leveraging Existing Processes and Data:** Building and integrating with existing processes and using existing data is more effective than starting from scratch. Integrating the portfolio review process with the budgeting process and capital allocation is key.
- **Balancing Complexity and Precision While Avoiding Data Overload:** Realize many of the numbers are estimates, and use retrospective look backs to improve estimates. Use visualization tools if possible – but do not go overboard on the data and graphics. Too much does not add clarity.
- **Setting Clear Objectives:** Ensure the portfolio review objectives are clear from the start.

Retrospectives or look backs are useful to see if the portfolio is delivering as expected. Advanced E&P companies, such as Chevron and Royal Dutch Shell examine their portfolio results periodically to determine what adjustments need to be made. Typical problems with E&P are not the process but the devilish details. Royal Dutch Shell found that its major projects had been under delivering the production they had promised leading to lower than expected revenue, and that later follow-on phases had under-delivered as well. They also found most project schedules had aggressive schedules compared to reality. In essence, they over-promised and under-delivered. Recommendations included country diversification with potential investments in Brazil, Kazakhstan or Angola as growth was too dependent on Nigeria and ensuring realism in project schedules and forecasts.

CONCLUSION

Andy Brogan, a consultant in EY's London office, says, "Going forward to the next decade it's probably going to be a lot more volatile, more uncertain and a lot more ambiguous than the last one. So getting the project right won't be enough by itself. In order for companies to really thrive they're also going to be able to adapt their portfolios as they respond to or anticipate events." (Brogan, 2016) Companies may have to adapt to change through proactive project portfolio management with regular portfolio reviews where decisions are made to invest, divest or retain are a first step in a larger process.

The need for optimizing a project portfolio is frequently stated. However, the management practices for reviewing a project portfolio have not been extensively discussed. In this chapter, we have described the organizational placement, strategy and tactics, and the tools and techniques used by companies in their portfolio reviews. Because E&P companies operate in a volatile, high-risk environment, many of the examples cited have come from leaders in this industry, including Chevron and ExxonMobil. Some concepts such as Decision Analysis can be implemented regardless of industry to improve the quality of their portfolio management decisions. The best organizations strive to continually improve. Portfolio management reviews are an area where relatively small improvements in process can have tremendous benefits.

REFERENCES

Adams, C. (2016, January 14). *Delayed oil projects total nears $400bn.* Retrieved January 14, 2016, from http://www.ft.com/intl/cms/s/0/50bbaec2-ba0e-11e5-bf7e-8a339b6f2164.html

Brogan, A. (2016). *EY - Portfolio Management in Oil and Gas – EY - Global.* Retrieved August 21, 2016, from http://www.ey.com/GL/en/Industries/Oil---Gas/EY-portfolio-management-in-oil-and-gas

Chevron. (2014). Chevron Corporation's 2014 Security Analyst Meeting. *Upstream.* Retrieved April 22, 2016 from http://phx.corporate-ir.net/External.File?item=UGFyZW50SUQ9MjI0MjU2fENoaWxkSUQ9LTF8VHlwZT0z&t=1

Chevron. (2016). *2015 Annual report.* Retrieved April 22, 2016, from https://www.chevron.com/-/media/chevron/annual-report/2015/2015-Annual-Report.pdf

Chevron. (2016). *Upstream Oil and Gas Appendix.* Retrieved April 22, 2016, from http://library.corporate-ir.net/library/13/130/130102/items/327910/901D806B- 1FF6-4C26-8FBE-B656CC890DF0_7-Upstream_&_Gas_Projects_--_Appendix.pdf

Cooper, R., & Edgett, S. (2006). Ten ways to make better portfolio and project selection decisions. *PDMA Visions, 3*(June), 11–15.

Cooper, R., Edgett, S., & Kleinschmidt, E. (1997). *Portfolio Management in New Product Development: Lessons from Leading Firms.* Academic Press.

ExxonMobil. (2016). *Annual report 2015.* Retrieved April 22, 2016, from http://cdn.exxonmobil.com/~/media/global/files/summary-annual-report/2015_Summary_Annual_Report.pdf

EYGM Limited. (2016). *Spotlight on oil and gas megaprojects.* Retrieved July 2, 2016, from http://www.ey.com/Publication/vwLUAssets/EY-spotlight-on-oil-and-gas-megaprojects/$FILE/EY-spotlight-on-oil-and-gas-megaprojects.pdf

Franke, J. (2008). *Strategy.* Planning & Organizational Capability Corporate Department & Services, Chevron.

Gumz, J. (2015). *Keynote Speech.* Paper presented at PMO and Portfolio: Synergies to face a changing future, Milan, Italy.

Markowitz, H. M. (1952). *Portfolio Selection*. The American Finance Association.

Neal, L., & Spetzler, C. (2015). *An Organization-wide Approach to Good Decision Making.* Retrieved April 22, 2016, from https://hbr.org/2015/05/an-organization-wide-approach-to-good-decision-making

Nestlé, S. A. (2013). *2013 Half Year Results Conference Call Transcript.* Retrieved May 15, 2016 from http://www.nestle.com/asset-library/Documents/Investors/Transcripts/H1%20Results%20Transcript-2013.pdf

Nestlé, S. A. (2015). *Strategic Decisions Conference.* Nestlé Capital Efficiency and Portfolio Management. Retrieved May 15, 2016, from http://www.nestle.com/asset-library/Documents/Library/Presentations/Investors_Events/Sanford-Bernstein-Strategic-Decisions-Conf-FXR-Sept2015.pdf

Project Auditors LLC. (2016). *Hexagon Model.* Retrieved July 20, 2016, from http://www.projectauditors.com/Consulting/ConsultingHome.php

Project Management Institute. (2013). *Standard for portfolio management* (3rd ed.). Newtown Square, PA: Project Management Institute, Inc.

Royal Dutch Shell. (2016). *Annual Report and Form 20-F 2015.* Retrieved April 22, 2016, from http://reports.shell.com/annual-report/2015/

Society of Decision Professionals. (2016). *Frustrations.* Retrieved Aug 21, 2016, from http://decision-quality.org/frustrations/

Statoil. (2010). *A strategy for value creation and growth.* Retrieved August 21, 2016, from http://www.statoil.com/annualreport2010/en/strategy/pages/astrategyforvaluecreationandgrowth.aspx

Stegink, D. (2011). Upstream International Portfolio Management.*SPE International Conference*, Amsterdam, The Netherlands.

Total, S. A. (2016). *2015 Edition: Registration document.* Retrieved May 20, 2016, from http://www.total.com/sites/default/files/atoms/files/registration_document_2015.pdf

Trading Economics. (2016). *Brent crude oil 1970 to 2016.* Retrieved August 20, 2016, from http://www.tradingeconomics.com/commodity/brent-crude-oil

KEY TERMS AND DEFINITIONS

BOE: Barrels of Oil Equivalent.

Capital Expenditure (CAPEX): Expenditures creating future benefits. Investments in property, plant and equipment that have a useful life greater than one year and are depreciable assets, which has important tax effects, and ultimately project profitability implications.

Capital Allocation: Determining which projects to fund and, if ownership is less than 100%, the percentage level of equity invested, because there are more projects than investment capacity. Projects compete with each other for the finite amount of CAPEX.

Decision Analysis: The discipline for achieving clarity in complex and uncertain decision situations.

Downstream: A component of the production chain that refers to the refining, processing, and purifying of petroleum crude oil and/or natural gas, as well as the marketing and distribution.

Exploration and Production (E&P): The discovery and development of oil and gas fields.

High Grading: A mining term for extracting the highest grades in an ore deposit. The grades across a deposit vary in quality and extraction plus processing cost. To earn the highest profit per ton, only the highest grades in the deposit would be mined. In E&P, the term is used when the projects with better reward/risk profiles (efficient frontier) under conservative assumptions (price) are selected for the portfolio. Benefits are that CAPEX will be controlled as certain project assets that do not meet the profile are targeted for disposal.

Non-Core Assets: Assets that are determined to be not essential to an organization's strategy; these assets are generally slated for sale or disposal.

Unconventional Resource: Hydrocarbon resource that requires the application of external stimulation to flow to the wellbore, in comparison with a conventional resource that will flow on its own. Unconventional resources are lower in value than conventional crude oils because they are difficult and costly to produce and refine. Examples are extra-heavy oil, oil sands, tight / shale gas, and oil shale.

Upstream: A component of the production chain that refers to the exploration and production activities associated with finding and extracting underground or underwater crude oil and/or natural gas.

Value Investment Ratio (VIR): A useful metric for ranking projects because it allows quantifying the amount of value created per unit of investment, it is defined as Net Present Value divided by the Total Investment amount, or $VIR = \frac{NPV}{Total\ Investment}$. Another name for Value Investment Ratio is Profitability Index.

Compilation of References

Abbasianjahromi, H., & Rajaie, H. (2012). Developing a project portfolio selection model for contractor firms considering the risk factor. *Journal of Civil Engineering & Management*, *18*(6), 879–889. doi:10.3846/13923730.2012.734856

Abdelaziz, F. B., Aouni, B., & Fayedh, R. E. (2007). Multi-objective stochastic programming for portfolio selection. *European Journal of Operational Research*, *177*(3), 1811–1823. doi:10.1016/j.ejor.2005.10.021

Abdollahyan, F. (2012). *Management of Value as PPM Strategy*. Paper presented at the 2012 PMI EMEA Congress, Marseille, France.

Adams, C. (2016, January 14). *Delayed oil projects total nears $400bn*. Retrieved January 14, 2016, from http://www.ft.com/intl/cms/s/0/50bbaec2-ba0e-11e5-bf7e-8a339b6f2164.html

Aga, D. A., Noorderhaven, N., & Vallejo, B. (2016). Transformational leadership and project success: The mediating role of team-building. *International Journal of Project Management*, *34*(5), 806–818. doi:10.1016/j.ijproman.2016.02.012

Amaral, A., Araújo, M., & Pereira, G. (2010). A Multi-Criteria Decision Model for Dynamically Managing the Projects Portfolio. In *VI European-Latin-American Workshop on Engineering Systems* (pp. 270–277). SELASI.

Amaral, A., & Araújo, M. (2009). Market attractiveness index: a decision analysis technique for market assessment. In *International Conference on Industrial Engineering and Systems Management* (pp. 1080–1093). IESM.

Andersen, E. S., & Jessen, S. A. (2003). Project maturity in organisations. *International Journal of Project Management*, *21*(6), 457–461. doi:10.1016/S0263-7863(02)00088-1

Anyosa, V. (2010). *Linking Portfolio, Program and Projects to Business Strategy*. Paper presented at the 2010 PMI Asia Pacific Congress, Melbourne, Australia.

Aoki, S., Sato, Y., & Tsuji, H. (2006). *DEA as Strategy Decision Tool for Performance Improvement. IEEE International Conference on Systems, Man and Cybernetics*. https://doi.org/10.1109/ICSMC.2006.384681

Archer & Ghasemzadeh. (2004). *Project Portfolio Selection and Management*. San Francisco, CA: Wiley & Sons.

Archer, N. P., & Ghasemzadeh, F. (1999). An integrated framework for project portfolio selection. *International Journal of Project Management*, *17*(4), 207–216. doi:10.1016/S0263-7863(98)00032-5

Archer, N., & Ghasemzadeh, F. (2007). Project portfolio selection and management. In P. W. G. Morris & J. K. Pinto (Eds.), *The Wiley Guide to Project Program & Portfolio Management* (pp. 94–112). Hoboken, NJ: John Wiley & Sons. doi:10.1002/9780470172391.ch11

Archibald, R. D. (2003). Managing High-Technology Programs and Projects (3rd ed.). Hoboken, NJ: John Wiley & Sons. Retrieved from www.russarchibald.com

Archibald, R. D. (2008). *The Interfaces Between Strategic Management of an Enterprise and Project Portfolio Management Within the Enterprise.* 22nd IPMA World Congress, Milan, Italy. Retrieved from http://russarchibald.com/recent-papers-presentations/strategic-enterprise/

Archibald, R. D. (2013). *A Global System for Categorizing Projects.* The International Project Management Association/ IPMA's Project Perspectives 2013. Retrieved from http://www.ipma.world/assets/re-perspectives_2013.pdf

Archibald, R. D. (2013). *Leading and Managing Innovation.* Paper presented at the 2013 PMI Frankfurt Project Zone Germany Congress. Retrieved from http://russarchibald.com/recent-papers-presentations/innovation-projec-manage/innovation-pmifc/

Archibald, R., Di Filippo, I., & Di Filippo, D. (2012). The Six Phase Comprehensive Project Life Cycle Model Includes the Project Incubation-Feasibility Phase and the Post-Project Evaluation Phase. *PM World Journal, 1*(5). Available at http://pmworldjournal.net/?article=the-six-phase-comprehensive-project-life-cycle-model-including-the-project-incubationfeasibility-phase-and-the-post-project-evaluation-phase-2

Archibald, R. D. (2003). *Managing High-Technology Programs and Projects.* New York: Johon Wiley & Sons.

Archibald, R. D., & Archibald, S. C. (2015). *Leading and Managing Innovation - What Every Executive Team Must Know about Project, Program, and Portfolio Management.* Boca Raton, FL: CRC Press, Taylor & Francis Group. Retrieved fromhttp://leadingandmanaginginnovation.com/

Artto, K., & Dietrich, P. (2004). Strategic business management through multiple projects. In P. Morris & J. K. Pinto (Eds.), *The Wiley guide to managing projects* (pp. 144–176). London: John Wiley & Sons.

Aurik, J. C., Fabel, M., & Jonk, G. J. (2015). *The future of strategy: A transformative approach to strategy for a world that won't stand still.* New York: McGraw-Hill Education.

Badewi, A. (2015). The impact of project management (PM) and benefits management (BM) practices on project success: Towards developing a project benefits governance framework. *International Journal of Project Management.* doi:.10.1016/j.iproman.2015.05.005

Bain & Company. (2015). *Strategic Planning.* Retrieved 17 August, 2016, from http://www.bain.com/publications/articles/management-tools-strategic-planning.aspx

Baker, N. R., & Freeland, J. (1975). Recent advances in R&D benefit measurement and project selection methods. *Management Science, 21*(10), 1164–1175. doi:10.1287/mnsc.21.10.1164

Baker, N. R., & Pound, W. H. (1964). R and D project selection: Where we stand. *IEEE Transactions on Engineering Management, Volume, EM-11*(4), 124–134. doi:10.1109/TEM.1964.6446420

Bannister, F., & Remenyi, D. (2009). Multitasking: The Uncertain Impact of Technology on Knowledge Workers and Managers. *The Electronic Journal Information Systems Evaluation, 12*(1), 1–12.

Bardhan, I.R., Kauffman, R.J., & Naranpanawe, S. (2010). IT project portfolio optimization: A risk management approach to software development governance. *IBM Journal of Research and Development, 54*(2), paper 2.

Bardhan, I., Bagchi, S., & Sougstad, R. (2004). Prioritizing a portfolio of information technology investment projects. *Journal of Management Information Systems, 21*(2), 33–60.

BCG. (2008). Retrieved 17 August, 2016, fromhttp://tutor2u.net/business/strategy/bcg_box.htm

BCG. (2013). *Strategic Initiative Management – the PMO Imperative.* Joint publication of Boston Consulting Group and PMI.

Bell, C. R., & Harari, O. (2001). *Beep Beep! Competing in the Age of the Road Runner*. New York, NY: Warner Books, Inc.

Bell, S. C. (2012). *Run Grow Transform: Integrating Business and Lean IT*. New York: CRC Press. doi:10.1201/b12718

Benaroch, M. (2002). Managing Information Technology Investment Risk: A Real Options Perspective. *Journal of Management Information Systems*, *19*(2), 43–84.

Benko, C., & McFarlan, F. W. (2003). *Connecting the dots*. Boston: Harvard Business School Press.

Björk, E., & Ottosson, S. (2007). Aspects of consideration in product development research. *Journal of Engineering Design*, *18*(3), 195–207. doi:10.1080/09544820600675966

Blichfeldt, B. S., & Eskerod, P. (2008). Project portfolio management – Theres more to it than what management enacts. *International Journal of Project Management*, *26*(4), 357–365. doi:10.1016/j.ijproman.2007.06.004

Blomquist, T., & Müller, R. (2006). *Middle managers in program and project portfolio management: Practices, roles and responsibilities*. Newtown Square, PA: Project Management Institute

Box, S., & Platts, K. (2005). Business process management: Establishing and maintaining project alignment. *Business Process Management Journal*, *11*(4), 370–387. doi:10.1108/14637150510609408

Bracker, J. (1980). The Historical Development of the Strategic Management Concept. *Academy of Management Review*, *5*(2), 219–224.

Brandenburger, A. M., & Malebuff, B. J. (1996). *Co.opetition*. Doubleday.

Bridges, D. (1999). Project portfolio management: ideas and practices. In L. Dye & J. Pennypacker (Eds.), *Project portfolio management – selecting and prioritizing projects for competitive advantage* (pp. 45–54). West Chester, PA: Center for Business Practices.

Brogan, A. (2016). *EY - Portfolio Management in Oil and Gas – EY - Global*. Retrieved August 21, 2016, from http://www.ey.com/GL/en/Industries/Oil---Gas/EY-portfolio-management-in-oil-and-gas

Buffett, M., & Clark, D. (2006). *The Tao of Warren Buffett*. New York: Scriber.

Cabanis-Brewin, J. (2000). Interview with Richard Russell of the Balanced Scorecard Collaborative. *Project Management Best Practices Report*, *2*(9), 1.

Cagno, E., Caron, F., & Mancini, M. (2007). A Multi-Dimensional Analysis of Major Risks in Complex Projects. *Risk Management*, *9*(1), 1–18. doi:10.1057/palgrave.rm.8250014

Cannon, D. (2011). *ITIL Service Strategy 2011 Edition*. London, UK: The Stationary Office.

Carroll, L., & Tenniel, J. (1965). 6. In *Alice's adventures in Wonderland*. London: Macmillan.

Chandler, A. D. Jr. (1962). *Strategy and Structure: Chapters in the History of the Industrial Enterprise*. Cambridge, MA: The MIT Press.

Chao, R. O., Kavadias, S., & Gaimon, C. (2009). Revenue Driven Resource Allocation: Funding Authority, Incentives, and New Product Development Portfolio Management. *Management Science*, *55*(9), 1556–1569. doi:10.1287/mnsc.1090.1046

Charnes, A., Cooper, W. W., Golany, B., Seiford, L., & Stutz, J. (1985). Foundations of data envelopment analysis for Pareto-Koopmans efficient empirical production functions. *Journal of Econometrics*, *30*(1), 91–107. doi:10.1016/0304-4076(85)90133-2

Charnes, A., Cooper, W. W., & Rhodes, E. (1978). Measuring the efficiency of decision making units. *European Journal of Operational Research*, *2*(6), 429–444. doi:10.1016/0377-2217(78)90138-8

Chen, R.-S., Sun, C.-M., & Helms, M. M. (2008). Aligning information technology and business strategy with a dynamic capabilities perspective: A longitudinal study of a Taiwanese Semiconductor Company. *International Journal of Information Management, 28*(5), 366–378. https://doi.org/10.1016/j.ijinfomgt.2008.01.015

Chen, S. H., & Lee, H. T. (2007). Performance evaluation model for project managers using managerial practices. *International Journal of Project Management*, *25*(6), 543–551. doi:10.1016/j.ijproman.2007.03.004

Chevron. (2014). Chevron Corporation's 2014 Security Analyst Meeting. *Upstream*. Retrieved April 22, 2016 from http://phx.corporate-ir.net/External.File?item=UGFyZW50SUQ9MjI0MjU2fENoaWxkSUQ9LTF8VHlwZT0z&t=1

Chevron. (2016). *2015 Annual report*. Retrieved April 22, 2016, from https://www.chevron.com/-/media/chevron/annual-report/2015/2015-Annual-Report.pdf

Chevron. (2016). *Upstream Oil and Gas Appendix*. Retrieved April 22, 2016, from http://library.corporate-ir.net/library/13/130/130102/items/327910/901D806B- 1FF6-4C26-8FBE-B656CC890DF0_7-Upstream_&_Gas_Projects_--_Appendix.pdf

Chin, K.-S., Pun, K.-F., & Lau, H. (2003). Development of a knowledge-based self-assessment system for measuring organisational performance. *Expert Systems with Applications*, *24*(4), 443–455. doi:10.1016/S0957-4174(02)00192-6

Christensen, C. M. (2012, November 3). A Capitalist's Dilemma, Whoever Wins on Tuesday. *The New York Times*.

Chu, P.-Y. V., Hsu, Y.-L., & Fehling, M. (1996). A decision support system for project portfolio selection. *Computers in Industry*, *32*(2), 141–149. doi:10.1016/S0166-3615(96)00067-X

Cleland, D. I. (1999). The strategic context of projects. In L. Dye & J. Pennypacker (Eds.), *Project portfolio management – selecting and prioritizing projects for competitive advantage* (pp. 3–22). West Chester, PA: Center for Business Practices.

Cleland, D. I. (1999). The Strategic Context Of Projects. In *Project Portfolio Management: Selecting ad Prioritizing Projects for Competitive Advantage*. Centre for Business Practices.

Coffin, M. A., & Taylor, B. W. III. (1996). Multiple criteria R&D project selection and scheduling using fuzzy logic. *Computers & Operations Research*, *23*(3), 207–220. doi:10.1016/0305-0548(96)81768-0

Collins, J. (2001). *Good to Great*. HarperCollins Publishers Inc.

Combe, M. W., & Githens, G. D. (1999). Managing Popcorn Priorities: How Portfolios and Programs Align Projects with Strategies. *Proceedings of the PMI 1999 Seminars & Symposium.*Newtown, CT: Project Management Institute.

Combe, M. W., & Gregory, D. G. (1999). Managing Popcorn Priorities: How Portfolios and Programs Align Projects With Strategies.*Proceedings of the PMI 1999 Seminars and Symposium.*

Cook, D. (2007). *The 5 Reasons Organizations choose the Wrong Projects*. Paper presented at the 2007 Project Management – Setting the Standard conference by the Australian Institute of Project Management National Conference, Hobart, Tasmania.

Cooke-Davies, T. (2002). The real success factors on projects. *International Journal of Project Management*, *20*(3), 185–190. doi:10.1016/S0263-7863(01)00067-9

Cooper, R. G., Edgett, S. J., & Kleinschmidt, E. J. (1998). Best Practices for Managing R&D Portfolios. *Research-Technology Management, 41*(4), 20–33. https://doi.org/10.1080/08956308.1998.11671219

Cooper, R. G., Edgett, S. J., & Kleinschmidt, E. J. (2000). New Problems, New Solutions: Making Portfolio Management More Effective. *Research-Technology Management, 43*(2), 18–33. https://doi.org/10.1080/08956308.2000.11671338

Cooper, R. G., Edgett, S. J., & Kleinschmidt, E. J. (2003). *Best Practices in Product Innovation: What Distinguishes Top Performers*. Product Development Institute. Retrieved from www.prod-dev.com

Cooper, R. G., Edgett, S. J., & Kleinschmidt, E. J. (2004a). Benchmarking Best NPD Practices—I. *Research-Technology Management, 47*(1), 31–43. https://doi.org/10.1080/08956308.2004.11671606

Cooper, R. G., Edgett, S. J., & Kleinschmidt, E. J. (2004b). Benchmarking Best NPD Practices—II. *Research-Technology Management, 47*(3), 50–59. https://doi.org/10.1080/08956308.2004.11671630

Cooper, R., Edgett, S., & Kleinschmidt, E. (1997). *Portfolio Management in New Product Development: Lessons from Leading Firms.* Academic Press.

Cooper, R.G., Edgett, S.J., & Kleinschmidt, E.J. (2001). New Product Development: Results of an Industry Practices Study. *R&D Management Magazine, 31*(4).

Cooper, R.G., Edgett, S.J., & Kleinschmidt, E.J. (2002). Portfolio management: fundamental to new product success. *The PDMA ToolBook 1 for New Product Development, 9*, 331-364.

Cooper, . (1999). Multilevel design of performance measurement systems: Enhancing strategic dialogue throughout the organization. *Management Accounting Research, 10*(3), 233–261. doi:10.1006/mare.1998.0098

Cooper, R. G. (1993). *Winning At New Products.* Addison-Wesley.

Cooper, R. G. (1993). *Winning at New Products: Accelerating the Process from Idea to Launch.* Cambridge, MA: Perseus Publishing.

Cooper, R. G., Edgett, S. J., & Kleinschmidt, E. J. (2002). Portfolio management: fundamental to new product success. In P. Belliveau, A. Griffin, & S. Somermeyer (Eds.), *The PDMA Toolbook for new product development*. Hoboken, NJ: John Wiley & Sons.

Cooper, R. G., Edgett, S. J., & Kleinschmidt, E. J. (2005). Benchmarking Best NPD Practices. *Research-Technology Management*, *47*(1), 31–43.

Cooper, R. G., Edgett, S. J., & Kleinshmidt, E. J. (1997). *Portfolio Management for New Products*. Hamilton, ON: McMaster University.

Cooper, R., & Edgett, S. (2006). Ten ways to make better portfolio and project selection decisions. *PDMA Visions, 3*(June), 11–15.

Cooper, R., Edgett, S., & Kleinschmidt, E. (2001). Portfolio management for new product development: Results of an industry practices study. *R & D Management, 31*(4), 361–380. doi:10.1111/1467-9310.00225

Cooper, W. W., Seiford, L. M., Thanassoulis, E., & Zanakis, S. H. (2004). DEA and its uses in different countries. *European Journal of Operational Research, 154*(2), 337–344. doi:10.1016/S0377-2217(03)00173-5

Cooper, W. W., Seiford, L. M., & Tone, K. (2007). *Data Envelopment Analysis: A Comprehensive Text with Models, Applications, References and DEA-Solver Software* (2nd ed.). New York: Springer.

Costantino, F., Di Gravio, G., & Nonino, F. (2015). Project selection in project portfolio management: An artificial neural network model based on critical success factors. *International Journal of Project Management, 33*(8), 1744–1754. doi:10.1016/j.ijproman.2015.07.003

Coulon, M., Ernst, H., Lichtenthaler, U., & Vollmoeller, J. (2009). An overview of tools for managing the corporate innovation portfolio. *International Journal of Technology Intelligence and Planning*, *5*(2), 221–239. doi:10.1504/IJTIP.2009.024191

Croxton, K. L., Lambert, D. M., García-Dastugue, S. J., & Rogers, D. S. (2008). The Demand Management Process. In D. Lambert (Ed.), *Supply Chain Management: Processes, Partnerships, Performance*. Supply Chain Management Institute.

Dale E. (1973). *Management: Theory and Practice*. McGraw-Hill.

Datz, T. (2003). Portfolio management – how to do it right. *CIO Magazine*, (2).

David, F. R. (2011). *Strategic management: Concept & cases* (13th ed.). Upper Saddle River, NJ: Prentice Hall.

Davis, K. (2014). Different stakeholder groups and their perceptions of project success. *International Journal of Project Management*, *32*(2), 189–201. doi:10.1016/j.ijproman.2013.02.006

Davis, K. (2016). A method to measure success dimensions relating to individual stakeholder groups. *International Journal of Project Management*, *34*(3), 480–493. doi:10.1016/j.ijproman.2015.12.009

Day, G. S. (2007, December). Is it real? Can we win? Is it worth doing? *Harvard Business Review*, 110–120. PMID:18283921

deCarvalho, M. M., Patah, L. A., & Bido, D. (2015). Project management and its effects on project success: Cross-country and cross-industry comparisons. *International Journal of Project Management*, *33*(7), 1509–1522. doi:10.1016/j.ijproman.2015.04.004

Delvin, J. (2005). Using the analytic hierarchy process to improve enterprise project portfolio management. In H. A. Lavine (Ed.), *Project portfolio management: A practical guide to selecting projects, managing portfolios, and maximizing benefits*. San Francisco, CA: Jossey-Bass.

Deng, X., Wang, S., & Xia, Y. (2000). Criteria, Models and Strategies in Portfolio Selection. *Advanced Modeling and Optimization*, *2*(2), 79–104.

Department of Business Innovation and Skills (BIS). (2010). *Guidance for managing programmes: understanding programmes and programme management*. Retrieved from https://www.gov.uk/government/uploads/system/uploads/attachment_data/file/31978/10-1256-guidelines-for-programme-management.pdf

Dey, P. K., & Gupta, S. S. (2001). Feasibility analysis of crosscountry pipeline projects: A quantitative approach. *Project Management Journal*, *32*(4), 50–58.

Dey, P. K., Tabucanon, M. T., & Ogunlana, S. O. (1996). Hierarchical approach to project planning. *Hierarchical Approach to Project Planning. Applied Mathematical Modelling*, *20*(9), 683–698. doi:10.1016/0307-904X(96)00049-2

Diedrich, P., & Lehtonen, P. (2005). Successful management of strategic intentions through multiple projects – reflections from empirical study. *IJPM*, *23*(5), 386–391.

Dietrich, P., & Lehtonen, P. (2005). Successful management of strategic intentions through multiple projects – Reflections from empirical study. *International Journal of Project Management*, *23*(5), 386–391. doi:10.1016/j.ijproman.2005.03.002

Dochtermann, D., Jesus-Olhausen, A. L., & Cermak, T. (2011). *Introduction to a Project Portfolio Management Maturity Model*. Paper presented at the 2011 PMI North American Congress.

Dochtermann, D., Jesus-Olhausen, A. L., & Cermak, T. (2011). *Introduction to a Project Portfolio Management Maturity Model*. Paper presented at the 2011 PMI North American Congress. Retrieved from http://www.equestconsulting.com.au/EQuest_Consulting_EPM_Survey_2005.pdf

Doerner, K., Gutjahr, W., Hartl, R., Strauss, C., & Stummer, C. (2006). Pareto ant colony optimization with ILP preprocessing in multiobjective project portfolio selection. *European Journal of Operational Research, 171*(3), 830–841. doi:10.1016/j.ejor.2004.09.009

Dong, J., Du, H. S., Wang, S., Chen, K., & Deng, X. (2004). A framework of Web-based Decision Support Systems for portfolio selection with OLAP and PVM. *Decision Support Systems, 37*(3), 367–376. doi:10.1016/S0167-9236(03)00034-4

Doz, Y. L., & Kosonen, M. (2008). *Fast strategy: How strategic agility will help you stay ahead of the game*. Harlow, UK: Pearson/Longman.

Dye, L. D., & Pennypacker, J. (2000). Project Portfolio and Managing Multiple Projects: Two Sides of the same Coin? *Proceedings. of the 2000 PMI Seminars & Symposium.*

Dye, L. D., & Pennypacker, J. S. (1999). *Project Portfolio Management: Selecting ad Prioritizing Projects for Competitive Advantage*. Centre for Business Practices.

Dye, L. D., & Pennypacker, J. S. (Eds.). (1999). *Project Portfolio Management – Selecting and Prioritizing Projects for Competitive Advantage*. West Chester, PA: PM Solutions' Center for Business Practices.

Eik-Andresen, P., Johansen, A., Landmark, A. D., & Sørensen, A. Ø. (2016). Controlling a Multibillion Project Portfolio - Milestones as Key Performance Indicator for Project Portfolio Management. *Procedia: Social and Behavioral Sciences, 226*, 294–301. doi:10.1016/j.sbspro.2016.06.191

Eilat, H., Golany, B., & Shtub, A. (2006). Constructing and valuating Balanced Portfolios of R&D Projects with Interactions: A DEA Based Methodology. *European Journal of Operational Research, 172*(3), 1018–1039. doi:10.1016/j.ejor.2004.12.001

Elonen, S., & Artto, K. A. (2003). Problems in managing internal development projects in multi-project environments. *International Journal of Project Management, 21*(6), 395–402. doi:10.1016/S0263-7863(02)00097-2

Englund, R. L., & Graham, R. J. (1999). From Experience: Linking Projects to Strategy. *Journal of Product Innovation Management, 16*(1), 52–64. doi:10.1016/S0737-6782(98)00046-0

Englund, R., Randall, L., & Bucero, A. (2012). *The complete project manager: Integrating people, organizational, and technical skills*. New York: Management Concepts Inc.

Engwall, M., & Jerbrant, A. (2003). The resource allocation syndrome: The prime challenge of multi-project management? *International Journal of Project Management, 21*(6), 403–409. doi:10.1016/S0263-7863(02)00113-8

ExxonMobil. (2016). *Annual report 2015*. Retrieved April 22, 2016, from http://cdn.exxonmobil.com/~/media/global/files/summary-annual-report/2015_Summary_Annual_Report.pdf

EYGM Limited. (2016). *Spotlight on oil and gas megaprojects*. Retrieved July 2, 2016, from http://www.ey.com/Publication/vwLUAssets/EY-spotlight-on-oil-and-gas-megaprojects/$FILE/EY-spotlight-on-oil-and-gas-megaprojects.pdf

Fernandes, G. (2004). *Desenvolvimento de Metodologias para Avaliação de Projectos de Investimento Multisectorial*. Guimarães, Portugal: Universidade do Minho.

Fitzroy, P., & Hulbert, J. M. (2004). *Strategic management: Creating value in a turbulent world.* New York, NY. Wiley.

Floricel, S., & Ibanescu, M. (2008). Using R&D portfolio management to deal with dynamic risk. *R & D Management, 38*(5), 452–467. doi:10.1111/j.1467-9310.2008.00535.x

Flyvbjerg, B. (2009). Survival of the Unfittest. *Oxford Review of Economic Policy, 25*(3), 344–367. doi:10.1093/oxrep/grp024

Forrester Consulting. (2013). *Strategic PMOs Play A Vital Role In Driving Business Outcomes*. Author.

Franke, J. (2008). *Strategy*. Planning & Organizational Capability Corporate Department & Services, Chevron.

Gartner Group. (2004). *Gartner Shines the Light on PPM*. Retrieved from http://www.gantthead.com/article.cfm?ID=219526

Gartner Group. (2010). *White paper published 2010*. Retrieved March 2011 from www.gartner.com/DisplayTimument?Tim_cd=205800&ref=g_rss

Gentle, M. (2007). *IT Success: Towards a New Model for Information Technology*. Hoboken, NJ: John Wiley & Sons.

Ghapanchi, A. H., Tavana, M., Khakbaz, M. H., & Low, G. (2012). A methodology for selecting portfolios of projects with interactions and under uncertainty. *International Journal of Project Management*, *30*(7), 791–803. doi:10.1016/j.ijproman.2012.01.012

Ghasemzadeh, F., & Archer, N. P. (2000). Project portfolio selection through decision support. *Decision Support Systems*, *29*(1), 73–88. doi:10.1016/S0167-9236(00)00065-8

Ghosh, S., & Jintanapakanont, J. (2004). Identifying and assessing the critical risk factors in an underground rail project in Thailand: A factor analysis approach. *International Journal of Project Management*, *22*(8), 633–643. doi:10.1016/j.ijproman.2004.05.004

GMC, Inc. (2012). *The Growth Management Process for Strategic Management*. Truckee, CA: Growth Management Center, Inc. Retrieved from http://www.agendas.net/

Goldman, C. (1999). Align Drive – Expert Advice. *CIO Magazine, 5*.

Goldratt, E. M. (1997). *Critical Chain*. Great Barrington, MA: North River Press.

Graham, M., & Englund, R. (1999). Creating an Environment for Project Success. San Francisco, CA: Jossey Bass Editors.

Grant, R. M., & Jordan, J. (2015). *Foundations of strategy* (2nd ed.). Hoboken, NJ: Wiley and Sons.

Grundy, T. (1998, February). Strategy implementation and project management. *International Journal of Project Management*, *16*(1), 43–50. doi:10.1016/S0263-7863(97)00016-1

Grundy, T. (2000). Strategic project management and strategic behaviour. *International Journal of Project Management*, *18*(2), 93–103. doi:10.1016/S0263-7863(98)00076-3

Guan, J., & Ma, N. (2003). Innovative capability and export performance of Chinese firms. *Technovation*, *23*(9), 737–747. doi:10.1016/S0166-4972(02)00013-5

Gumz, J. (2015). *Keynote Speech*. Paper presented at PMO and Portfolio: Synergies to face a changing future, Milan, Italy.

Hall, N. G., Long, D. Z., Qi, J., & Sim, M. (2015). Managing Underperformance Risk in Project Portfolio Selection. *Operations Research*, *63*(3), 660–675. doi:10.1287/opre.2015.1382

Hammer, M., & Champy, J. (1998). *Re-engineering the Corporation*. New York: HarperCollins.

Hartman, F. (2000). *Don't park your brain outside: A practical guide to improving shareholder value with SMART management*. Newtown Square, PA: Project Management Institute.

Harvard Business School On-line Forum. (n.d.). *Why Don't Managers Think Deeply?* Accessed March 02, 2016 from http://hbswk.hbs.edu/item/5952.html

Harvard. (2014). *Organigraphs: Drawing How Companies Really Work*. Retrieved January 29, 2016, from https://hbr.org/1999/09/organigraphs-drawing-how-companies-really-work

Hax, A. C., & Majluf, N. S. (1983). The use of the industry attractiveness - business strength matrix in strategic planning. *Interfaces*, *13*(2), 54–71. doi:10.1287/inte.13.2.54

Hax, A., & Majluf, N. S. (1996). *The Strategy Concept and Process: A Pragmatic Approach* (2nd ed.). Upper Saddle River, NJ: Prentice-Hall.

Henderson, J. C., & Venkatraman, H. (1999). Strategic alignment: Leveraging information technology for transforming organizations. *IBM Systems Journal, 38*(2.3), 472–484. https://doi.org/10.1147/SJ.1999.5387096

Henry, R. M., McCray, G. E., Purvis, R. L., & Roberts, T. L. (2007). Exploiting organizational knowledge in developing IS project cost and schedule estimates: An empirical study. *Information & Management*, *44*(6), 598–612. doi:10.1016/j.im.2007.06.002

Hermano, V., & Martín-Cruz, N. (2016). The role of top management involvement in firms performing projects: A dynamic capabilities approach. *Journal of Business Research*, *69*(9), 3447–3458. doi:10.1016/j.jbusres.2016.01.041

Hess, S. W. (1993). Swinging on the Branch of a Tree: Project Selection Applications. *Interfaces*, *23*(6), 5–12. doi:10.1287/inte.23.6.5

Hiner, J. (2012). *Look beyond the dollar signs to validate your projects*. Retrieved Nov, 2012 from http://blogs.techrepublic.com.com/hiner/?p=2773&tag=nl.e053

Hrebiniak, L G. (2013). *Making Strategy Work: Leading Effective Execution and Change*. Upper Saddle River, NJ: FT Press.

Hrebiniak, L. G. (2006). Obstacles to effective strategy implementation. *Organizational Dynamics*, *35*(1), 12–31. doi:10.1016/j.orgdyn.2005.12.001

Huang, X. (2008). Mean-variance model for fuzzy capital budgeting. *Computers & Industrial Engineering*, *55*(1), 34–47. doi:10.1016/j.cie.2007.11.015

Huang, X. (2010). *Portfolio Analysis: From Probabilistic to Credibilistic and Uncertain Approaches*. Berlin: Springer-Verlag. doi:10.1007/978-3-642-11214-0

Huang, X. (2011). Mean-risk model for uncertain portfolio selection. *Fuzzy Optimization and Decision Making*, *10*(1), 71–89. doi:10.1007/s10700-010-9094-x

Huang, X. (2012). A risk index model for portfolio selection with returns subject to experts estimations. *Fuzzy Optimization and Decision Making*, *11*(4), 451–463. doi:10.1007/s10700-012-9125-x

Huang, X., & Qiao, L. (2012). A risk index model for multi-period uncertain portfolio selection. *Information Sciences*, *217*, 108–116. doi:10.1016/j.ins.2012.06.017

Huang, X., & Ying, H. (2013). Risk index based models for portfolio adjusting problem with returns subject to experts evaluations. *Economic Modelling*, *30*, 61–66. doi:10.1016/j.econmod.2012.09.032

IPMA Individual Competence Baseline 4th Version (ICB4). (2015). Retrieved from http://products.ipma.world/product/icb/

Ireland, L. R. (1997). Managing multiple projects. In Managing multiple project in the twenty-first century (pp. 21–34). New York: Marcel Dekker Inc.

Irwin, R. D., Terry, G.R., & Rue, L.W. (1982). Principles of Management. Dow Jones-Irwin.

Islei, G., Lockett, G., Cox, B., & Stratford, M. (1991). A decision support system using judgmental modeling: A case of R&D in the pharmaceutical industry. *IEEE Transactions on Engineering Management*, *38*(3), 202–209. doi:10.1109/17.83753

Jackson, B. (1983). Decision methods for selecting a portfolio of R&D projects. *Research Management*, *26*(5), 21–26.

Jackson, S. E., Joshi, A., & Erhardt, N. L. (2003). Recent research on team and organizational diversity: SWOT analysis and implications. *Journal of Management*, *29*(6), 801–830. doi:10.1016/S0149-2063(03)00080-1

Jafarizadeh, B., & Ramazani Khorshid-Doust, R. (2008). A method of project selection based on capital asset pricing theories in a framework of mean–semideviation behavior. *International Journal of Project Management*, *26*(6), 612–619. doi:10.1016/j.ijproman.2007.09.004

Jarvenpaa, S. L., & Ives, B. (1993). Organizing for Global Competition. *Decision Sciences*, *24*(3), 547–580. doi:10.1111/j.1540-5915.1993.tb01293.x

Jeffrey, M., & Leliveld, I. (2003). Best Practices in IT Portfolio Management. *MIT Sloan Management Review*, *45*(3), 41–49.

Johnson, G., Scholes, K., & Wittington, R. (2008). *Exploring Corporate Strategy*. Pearson Education.

Johnson, T. W., & Stinson, J. E. (1978). *Management Today and Tomorrow*. Addison-Wesley Educational Publishers Inc.

Joro, T., Korhonen, P., & Wallenius, J. (1998). Structural Comparison of Data Envelopment Analysis and Multiple Objective Linear Programming. *Management Science*, *44*(7), 962–970. doi:10.1287/mnsc.44.7.962

Jugdev, K., & Müller, R. (2005). A retrospective look at our evolving understanding of project success. *Project Management Journal*, *36*(4), 19–31.

Kahneman, D. (2012). *Thinking, Fast and Slow*. New York: Farrar, Straus and Giroux.

Kaiser, M. G., El Arbi, F., & Ahlemann, F. (2015). Successful project portfolio management beyond project selection techniques: Understanding the role of structural alignment. *International Journal of Project Management*, *33*(1), 126–139. doi:10.1016/j.ijproman.2014.03.002

Kaplan, R. S., & Norton, D. P. (1992, January-February). The Balanced Scorecard – Measures That Drive Performance. *Harvard Business Review*, 71–79. PMID:10119714

Kaplan, R. S., & Norton, D. P. (1996). *The Balanced Scorecard – translating strategy into action*. Harvard Business School Press.

Kavadias, S., & Loch, C. H. (2003). Optimal Project Sequencing with Recourse at a Scarce Resource. *Production and Operations Management*, *12*(4), 433–444. doi:10.1111/j.1937-5956.2003.tb00213.x

Kendall, G., & Rollins, S. (2003). *Advanced Project Portfolio Management and the PMO: multiplying ROI at warp speed*. J. Ross Publishing. Retrieved from http://www.jrosspub.com/advanced-project-portfolio-management-and-the-pmo.html

Killen, C. P., Hunt, R. A., & Kleinschmidt, E. J. (2008). Project portfolio management for product innovation. *International Journal of Quality & Reliability Management*, *25*(1), 24–38. doi:10.1108/02656710810843559

Kissi, J., Dainty, A., & Tuuli, M. (2013). Examining the role of transformational leadership of portfolio managers in project performance. *International Journal of Project Management*, *31*(4), 485–497. doi:10.1016/j.ijproman.2012.09.004

Kloppenborg, T. J., & Laning, L. J. (2012). *Strategic Leadership of Portfolio and Project Management*. New York: Business Expert Press. doi:10.4128/9781606492956

Kloppenborg, T. J., Manolic, C., & Tesch, D. (2009). Successful sponsor behaviors during project initiation: An empirical investigation. *Journal of Managerial Issues*, *20*(1), 140–159.

Kloppenborg, T. J., Tesch, D., & Manolis, C. (2014). Project success and executive sponsor behaviors: Empirical life cycle stage investigations. *Project Management Journal*, *45*(1), 9–20. doi:10.1002/pmj.21396

Koontz, H., O'Donnell, C., & Weihrich, H. (1990). *Essentials of Management. McGraw-Hill Education.*

Kremmel, T., Kubalík, J., & Biffl, S. (2011). Software project portfolio optimization with advanced multiobjective evolutionary algorithms. *Applied Soft Computing*, *11*(1), 1416–1426. doi:10.1016/j.asoc.2010.04.013

Krumm, F. V., & Rolle, C. F. (1992). Management and application of decision and risk analysis in Du Pont. *Interfaces*, *22*(6), 84–93. doi:10.1287/inte.22.6.84

Kumar, R., Ajjan, H., & Niu, Y. (2008). Information technology portfolio management: Literature review, framework, and research issues. *Information Resources Management Journal*, *21*(3), 64–87. doi:10.4018/irmj.2008070104

Kvint, V. (2005). *Business and Strategic Management*. St. Petersburg, Russia: St. Petersburg University of Humanities and Social Sciences' Publishing House.

Lagace, M. (2003). *Putting the Project Puzzle Together*. Harvard Business School Working Knowledge. Available at http://hbswk.hbs.edu/item/3389.htm

Lancaster, H. (1995, January 17). Reengineering Authors Reconsider Reengineering: An interview with Michael Hammer and James Champy. *Wall Street Journal*.

Lassa, T. (2009, March). GM's Survival Strategy: Divisions, Nameplates to Disappear. *Motor Trend Magazine*.

Leliveld, I., & Jeffery, M. (2003). *IT portfolio management challenges and best practices*. Kellogg School of Management.

Levine, H. (2005). *Project Portfolio management: a practical guide to selecting projects, managing portfolios and maximizing benefits*. New York: John Wiley & Sons, Inc.

Levine, H. (2005). *Project Portfolio Management: A Practical Guide to Selecting Projects, Managing Portfolios, and Maximizing Benefits*. Jossey Bass.

Levine, H. A. (2005). *Project Portfolio Management*. San Francisco, CA: Jossey-Bass.

Levine, H. A. (2005). *Project portfolio management: A practical guide to selecting projects, managing portfolios, and maximizing benefits*. San Francisco, CA: Jossey-Bass.

Levin, G., & Rad, P. (2005). *Metrics for project management: Formalized approaches*. Vienna: Management Concepts.

Levin, G., & Ward, J. L. (2011). *Program complexity A competency model*. Boca Raton, FL: CRC Press.

Lin, C., & Hsieh, P.-J. (2004). A fuzzy decision support system for strategic portfolio management. *Decision Support Systems*, *38*(3), 383–398. doi:10.1016/S0167-9236(03)00118-0

Lorenzana, C. C. (1993). *Management Theory and Practice*. Manila, Philippines: RexBook Store.

Lycett, M., Rassau, A., & Danson, J. (2004). Programme management: A critical review. *International Journal of Project Management*, *22*(4), 289–299. doi:10.1016/j.ijproman.2003.06.001

Maidique, M. A., & Zirger, B. J. (1984). A Study of Success and Failure in Product Innovation: The Case of the U.S. Electronics Industry. *IEEE Transactions on Engineering Management*, *EM-31*(4), 4, 192–203. doi:10.1109/TEM.1984.6447537

Malach-Pines, A., Dvir, D., & Sadeh, A. (2009). Project Manager-project (PM-P) fit and project success. *International Journal of Operations & Production Management*, *29*(3), 268–291. doi:10.1108/01443570910938998

Maniak, R., Midler, C., Lenfle, S., & Le Pellec-Dairon, M. (2014). Value Management for Exploration Projects. *Project Management Journal*, *45*(Sept/Oct), 55–66. doi:10.1002/pmj.21436

Mankins, M. C., & Steele, R. (2005, July 1). *Turning Great Strategy into Great Performance*. Retrieved August 11, 2016, from https://hbr.org/2005/07/turning-great-strategy-into-great-performance

Mankins, M. C., & Steele, R. (2005). Turning great strategy into great performance. *Harvard Business Review*, *83*(7), 65–72. PMID:16028817

Markowitz, H. M. (1952). *Portfolio Selection*. The American Finance Association.

Markowitz, H. M. (1992, March). Portfolio Selection. *The Journal of Finance*, *7*(1), 77–91.

Martino, J. P. (1995). *R&D Project Selection*. New York: Wiley.

Martinsuo, M., & Killen, C. P. (2014). Value management in project portfolios: Identifying and assessing strategic value. *Project Management Journal*, *45*(2), 56–70. doi:10.1002/pmj.21452

Martinsuo, M., & Lehtonen, P. (2007). Role of single-project management in achieving portfolio management efficiency. *IJPM*, *25*(1), 56–64.

Martinsuo, M., & Lehtonen, P. (2007). Role of single-project management in achieving portfolio management efficiency. *International Journal of Project Management*, *25*(1), 56–65. doi:10.1016/j.ijproman.2006.04.002

Matheson, D., & Matheson, J. (1998). *The smart organization*. Boston, MA: Harvard Business School Press.

Mathieu, R. G., & Gibson, J. E. (1993). A methodology for large-scale R&D planning based on cluster analysis. *IEEE Transactions on Engineering Management*, *40*(3), 283–292. doi:10.1109/17.233190

McDonough, E. F., & Spital, F. C. (2003). Managing project portfolios. *Research-Technology Management*, *46*(3), 40–46.

McFarland, W. (2012). *This is Your Brain on Organizational Change*. Retrieved April, 2016 from https://hbr.org/2012/10/this-is-your-brain-on-organizational-change

McFarlan, F. W. (1981). Portfolio Approach to Information Systems. Boston. *Harvard Business Review*, *59*(5), 142–150.

McGrath, R. G., & MacMillan, I. C. (2000). Assessing Technology Projects Using Real Options Reasoning. *Research-Technology Management, 43*(4), 35–49. https://doi.org/10.1080/08956308.2000.11671367

McGrath, G. R., & Macmillan, I. C. (2000). Assessing technology projects using real options reasoning. *Research-Technology Management*, *43*(4), 35–49.

Mehrez, A., & Sinuany-Stern, Z. (1983). An Interactive Approach for Project Selection. *The Journal of the Operational Research Society*, *34*(7), 621–626. doi:10.1057/jors.1983.143

Menke, M. M. (1991). Tools for improving the quality of R&D management. In *Technology Management: The New International Language* (pp. 162–165). https://doi.org/10.1109/PICMET.1991.183602

Mentzer, J. T., & Moon, M. A. (2005). *Sales forecasting management: a demand management approach*. Thousand Oaks, CA: Sage.

Meredith, J. R., & Mantle, S. J. (2000). *Project Management: A Managerial Approach* (4th ed.). New York: Wiley.

Meredith, J. R., & Suresh, N. C. (1986). Justification Techniques for Advanced Manufacturing Technologies. *International Journal of Production Research, 24*(5), 1043–1057. doi:10.1080/00207548608919787

Meskendahl, S. (2010). The influence of business strategy on project portfolio management and its success. A conceptual framework. *International Journal of Project Management, 28*(8), 807–817. doi:10.1016/j.ijproman.2010.06.007

Miles, R., & Snow, C. (1994). *Fit, Failure and the Hall of Fame: How Companies Succeed or Fail.* New York, NY: Free Press.

Milrood, B. (2011). Why Should Anyone Be Led by a Project Manager. Garter special briefing for ENI University. *Project Manager 2014.* Retrieved from http://www.slideshare.net/msproject/garter-project-manager-2014

Mintzberg, H. (1978, May). Patterns in Strategy Formation. *Management Science. INFORMS, 24*(9), 934–948.

Mintzber, H., & Van der Heyden, L. (1999, September-October). Organigraphs: Drawing How Companies Really Work. *Harvard Business Review.*

Morris, P., & Jamieson, A. (2005). Moving from corporate strategy to project strategy. *Project Management Journal, 36*(4), 5–18.

Morris, P., & Pinto, J. K. (2007). *The Wiley guide to project, program, and portfolio management.* Hoboken, NJ: Wiley & Sons.

Mota, C. M. de M., de Almeida, A. T., & Alencar, L. H. (2009). A multiple criteria decision model for assigning priorities to activities in project management. *International Journal of Project Management, 27*(2), 175–181. doi:10.1016/j.ijproman.2008.08.005

Moustafaev, J. (2010). *Delivering exceptional project results: A practical guide to project selection, scoping, estimation and management. J.* Ross Publishing.

Müller, R., Martinsuo, M., & Blomquist, T. (2008). Project portfolio control and portfolio management performance in different contexts. *Project Management Journal, 39*(3), 28–42. doi:10.1002/pmj.20053

Müller, R., & Turner, R. (2007). The influence of Project Managers on project success criteria and project success by type of project. *European Management Journal, 24*(4), 1346–1357.

Nagji, B., & Tuff, G. (2012). Managing Your Innovation Portfolio. *Harvard Business Review, 3*(4), 1–5.

Neal, L., & Spetzler, C. (2015). *An Organization-wide Approach to Good Decision Making.* Retrieved April 22, 2016, from https://hbr.org/2015/05/an-organization-wide-approach-to-good-decision-making

Nestlé, S. A. (2013). *2013 Half Year Results Conference Call Transcript.* Retrieved May 15, 2016 from http://www.nestle.com/asset-library/Documents/Investors/Transcripts/H1%20Results%20Transcript-2013.pdf

Nestlé, S. A. (2015). *Strategic Decisions Conference.* Nestlé Capital Efficiency and Portfolio Management. Retrieved May 15, 2016, from http://www.nestle.com/asset-library/Documents/Library/Presentations/Investors_Events/Sanford-Bernstein-Strategic-Decisions-Conf-FXR-Sept2015.pdf

Nobeoka, K. (1993). *Multi-project management: strategy and organization in automobile product development* (Doctoral dissertation). Massachusetts Institute of Technology, Sloan School of Management.

Office of Government Commerce. (2007). *Managing successful programmes.* Norwich, UK: The Stationery Office.

Ohno, T. (1988). Toyota Production System: Beyond Large-Scale Production (English translation ed.). Portland, OR: Productivity Press.

Olanrewaju, O. A., Jimoh, A. A., & Kholopane, P. A. (2011). Comparison between regression analysis and artificial neural network in project selection. In *IEEE International Conference on Industrial Engineering and Engineering Management* (pp. 738-741). doi:10.1109/IEEM.2011.6118014

Online Etymology Dictionary. (n.d.). Retrieved June 29, 2016, from http://www.etymonline.com/

Ottosson, S. (2003). Participation action research-: A key to improved knowledge of management. *Technovation*, *23*(2), 87–94. doi:10.1016/S0166-4972(01)00097-9

Parth, F. R. (2002). *PMO Development at Toyota Financial Services*. Paper presented at ProMac 2002 International Conference on Project Management, Singapore.

Parth, F. R. (2015). *Project Control Through an Effective PMO - A Case Study*. Paper presented to the UAE chapter of AACE, Abu Dhabi, UAE.

Parth, F. R. (2015). *Project Control Through an Effective PMO - A Case Study*. Paper presented to the UAE chapter of AACE, Abu Dhabi, UAE..

Patanakul, P., & Milosevic, D. (2009). The effectiveness in managing a group of multiple projects: Factors of influence and measurement criteria. *International Journal of Project Management*, *27*(3), 216–233. doi:10.1016/j.ijproman.2008.03.001

Patankul, P. (2015). Key attributes of effectiveness in managing project portfolio. *International Journal of Project Management*, *33*(5), 1084–1097. doi:10.1016/j.ijproman.2015.01.004

Patterson, R. W., & Conner, D. (Eds.). (1982, April). Building Commitment to Organizational Change. *Training and Development Journal*, 18-30.

Payne, H. (1995). Management of multiple simultaneous projects: A state-of-the-art review. *International Journal of Project Management*, *13*(3), 163–168. doi:10.1016/0263-7863(94)00019-9

Pellegrinelli, S. (1997). Programme management: Organising project based change. *International Journal of Project Management*, *15*(3), 141–149. doi:10.1016/S0263-7863(96)00063-4

Perry, R., & Hatcher, E. (2008). *How Project and Portfolio Management Solutions Are Delivering Value to Organizations*. White paper published by IDC Sept. 2008.

Petit, Y. (2012). Project portfolios in dynamic environments: Organizing for uncertainty. *International Journal of Project Management*, *30*(5), 539–553. doi:10.1016/j.ijproman.2011.11.007

Petit, Y., & Hobbs, B. (2012). *Project Portfolios in Dynamic Environments*. Newtown Square, PA: Project Management Institute Publications.

Petro, Y., & Gardiner, P. (2015). An investigation of the influence of organizational design on project portfolio success, effectiveness and business efficiency for project-based organizations. *International Journal of Project Management*, *33*(8), 1717–1729. doi:10.1016/j.ijproman.2015.08.004

Pfeiffer, P. (2004, October). Environmental Project Management in Brazilian Municipalities. Experiences of a Brazil-Germany Technical Cooperation Project. *PMI GovSig Magazine*, 10.

Pheng, L. S., & Chuan, Q. T. (2006). Environmental factors and work performance of project managers in the construction industry. *International Journal of Project Management*, *24*(1), 24–37. doi:10.1016/j.ijproman.2005.06.001

Pietersen, W. (2016). *Von Clausewitz on War: Six Lessons for the Modern Strategist*. Retrieved October 16, 2016 from http://www.gsb.columbia.edu

Pinto, J. K. (1988). Variations in Critical Success Factors Over the Stages in the Project Life Cycle. *Journal of Management, 14*(1), 5–18. doi:10.1177/014920638801400102

Pinto, J. K. (1990). Project Implementation Profile: A tool to aid project tracking and control. *International Journal of Project Management, 8*(3), 173–182. doi:10.1016/0263-7863(90)90020-C

Pinto, J. K. (2004). The elements of project success. In D. I. Cleland (Ed.), *Field guide to project management* (pp. 14–27). Hoboken, NJ: Wiley & Sons. doi:10.1002/9780470172346.ch2

Pinto, J. K. (2007). *Project management: Achieving competitive advantage* (3rd ed.). Upper Saddle River, NJ: Prentice Hall.

Piot, J., & Baschab, J. (2007). *The Executive's Guide to Information Technology* (2nd ed.). Hoboken, NJ: John Wiley & Sons.

Platts, K. W. (1993). A Process Approach to Researching Manufacturing Strategy. *International Journal of Operations & Production Management, 13*(8), 4–17. doi:10.1108/01443579310039533

PMI, & Deloitte. (2015). *Delivering on Strategy The Power of Project Portfolio Management* (Thought Leadership Series). Newtown Square, PA: PMI.

PMI. (2008). *A Guide to the Project Management Body of Knowledge* (4th ed.). Newtown Square, PA: PMI.

PMI. (2012). *2012 Pulse of the Profession – Project Portfolio Management: Driving Success from the Top Down.* Project Management Institute.

PMI. (2013). *Pulse of the Profession - PMO Frameworks.* PMI.

PMI. (2013a). The standard for portfolio management (3rd ed.). Newton Square, PA: Project Management Institute, Inc.

Porter, M. (2008). Retrieved 17 August, 2016, from http://en.wikipedia.org/wiki/Michael_Porter

Porter, M. E. (1991). Towards a dynamic theory of strategy. *Strategic Management Journal, 12*(S2), 95–117. doi:10.1002/smj.4250121008

Prieto, B. (2011). Systemic Innovation and the Role of Program Management as an Enabler in the Engineering & Construction Industry. *PM World Today, 13*(8).

Project Auditors LLC. (2016). *Hexagon Model.* Retrieved July 20, 2016, from http://www.projectauditors.com/Consulting/ConsultingHome.php

Project Management Institute (PMI). (2013). A guide to the project management body of knowledge (PMBOK® guide) (5th ed.). Newtown Square, PA: PMI.

Project Management Institute (PMI). (2013). *The standard for portfolio management* (3rd ed.). Newtown Square, PA.

Project Management Institute (PMI). (2013a). A guide to the project management body of knowledge (PMBOK® guide) (5th ed.). Newtown Square, PA.

Project Management Institute (PMI). (2014). Navigating complexity. A practical guide. Newtown Square, PA: PMI.

Project Management Institute. (2013). *Standard for portfolio management* (3rd ed.). Newtown Square, PA: Project Management Institute, Inc.

Project Management Institute. (2013). *The standard for program management* (3rd ed.). Newtown Square, Pennsylvania: Project Management Instiute.

Project Management Institute. (2013a). *A guide to the project management body of knowledge* (5th ed.). Newtown Square, PA: Author.

Project Management Institute. (2013a). A guide to the project management body of knowledge (PMBOK® guide) (5th ed.). Newtown Square, PA: Author.

Project Management Institute. (2013b). A guide to the project management body knowledge (PMBOK) (5th ed.). Newton Square, PA: Project Management Institute Project Management Institute.

Project Management Institute. (2013b). *PMI's pulse of the profession: PMO frameworks*. Retrieved from http://www.pmi.org/~/media/PDF/Publications/PMI_Pulse_PMO-Frameworks.ashx

Project Management Institute. (2013b). The standard for portfolio management (3rd ed.). Newtown Square, PA: Author.

Rad, P., & Levin, G. (2008). What is project portfolio management? *AACE International Transactions*, TC31-TC34.

Rankins, G. J. (2006) Aligning Projects to Strategy using Balanced Scorecards and Benefits Models.*Proceedings 3rd International Conference on Project Management.*

Ray, M., & Myers, R. (1989). *Creativity in Business*. Broadway Books.

Remenyi, D., & Heafield, A. (1996). Business process re-engineering: Some aspects of how to evaluate and manage the risk exposure. *International Journal of Project Management*, *14*(6), 349–357. doi:10.1016/0263-7863(96)00013-0

Reyck, B. D., Grushka-Cockayne, Y., Lockett, M., Calderini, S. R., Moura, M., & Sloper, A. (2005). The impact of project portfolio management on information technology projects. *International Journal of Project Management*, *23*(7), 524–537. doi:10.1016/j.ijproman.2005.02.003

Ribbers, P. M. A., & Schoo, K. C. (2002). Program management and complexity of ERP implementations. *Engineering Management Journal*, *14*(2), 45–52. doi:10.1080/10429247.2002.11415162

Risk. (n.d.). Retrieved May 29, 2016, from https://en.wikipedia.org/wiki/Risk

Rizzuto, J. (2005). *Trading Places*. Retrieved March 15, 2015 from http://www.projectsatwork.com/article.cfm?ID=226042

Robin, M. (2000, March). Learning By Doing. *Knowledge Management.*

Romano L. (2016). Corporate Strategy from the Bottom: Project Portfolio Management Can Help Clarify Your Strategy. *International Journal of Information Communication Technologies and Human Development*, *8*(4), 34-50.

Romano, L. (2013). *Rise and Fall of Project Portfolio Management: Triumph and Collapse: A Case Study*. Paper presented at the 2013 PMI Global Congress, Istanbul, Turkey.

Romano, L. (2013a). *Rise and Fall of Project Portfolio Management: Triumph and Collapse: A Case Study.* Paper presented at the 2013 PMI Global Congress, Istanbul. Turkey.

Romano, L. (2013b). *How to evolve a Project Portfolio using Balanced Scorecards: a case study*. Paper presented at the 2013 PMI Global Congress, New Orleans, LA.

Romano, L. (2014). *Corporate Strategy for PMs. Why strategic alignment and awareness is so important*. Paper presented at the 2014 PMI Global Congress, Dubai, UAE.

Romano, L. (2014). *Corporate Strategy for PMs. Why strategic alignment and awareness is so important.* Paper presented at the 2014 PMI Global Congress, Dubai. UAE.

Romano, L. (2015). *Vision-Strategy-Objectives-Projects-Outputs & return. Do we need an ultimate management model?* Paper presented at the 2015 PMI Global Congress, Orlando, FL.

Romano, L., Grimaldi, R., & Colasuonno, F. S. (2016). *Demand management as a critical success factor in Portfolio Management.* Paper presented at the 2016 PMI Global Congress, Barcelona, Spain.

Romano, L., Grimaldi, R., & Colasuonno, F. S. (2016). *Demand management as a critical success factor in Portfolio Management.* Paper presented at the 2016 PMI Global Congress, Barcelona. Spain.

Romano, L., Grimaldi, R., & Colasuonno, F. S. (2016, May). *Demand management as a critical success factor in Portfolio Management.* Paper presented at the 2016 PMI Global Congress, Barcelona, Spain.

Rondinelli, D., Rosen, B., & Drori, I. (2001). The struggle for strategic alignment in multinational corporations: Managing readjustment during global expansion. *European Management Journal, 19*(4), 404–416. doi:10.1016/S0263-2373(01)00043-3

Roth, G., & Kleiner, A. (1998). Developing organizational memory through learning histories. *Organizational Dynamics, 27*(2), 43–60. doi:10.1016/S0090-2616(98)90023-7

Royal Dutch Shell. (2016). *Annual Report and Form 20-F 2015.* Retrieved April 22, 2016, from http://reports.shell.com/annual-report/2015/

Saaty, T. L. (1980). *The Analytic Hierarchy Process.* New York: McGraw-Hill.

Saaty, T. L. (1999). *Decision Making for Leaders: The Analytic Hierarchy Process for Decisions in a Complex World.* Pittsburgh, PA: RWS Publications.

Saaty, T. L., Rogers, P. C., & Pell, R. (1980). Portfolio selection through hierarchies. *Journal of Portfolio Management, 6*(3), 16–21. doi:10.3905/jpm.1980.408749

Sabherwal, R., Hirschheim, R., & Goles, T. (2001). The Dynamics of Alignment: Insights from a Punctuated Equilibrium Model. *Organization Science, 12*(2), 179–197. doi:10.1287/orsc.12.2.179.10113

Sanchez, H., Robert, B., & Pellerin, R. (2008). A project portfolio risk-opportunity identification framework. *Project Management Journal, 39*(3), 97–109. doi:10.1002/pmj.20072

Santosus, M. (2003, September 15). Why More is Less. *CIO Magazine.*

Saunders, M. N. K., Lewis, P., & Thornhill, A. (2012). *Research Methods for Business Students* (6th ed.). Harlow, UK: Financial Times/ Prentice Hall.

Schiemann, W. (1992, April). Why Change Fails. *Across the Board.*

Schniederjans, M., & Santhanam, R. (1993). A multi-objective constrained resource information system project selection method. *European Journal of Operational Research, 70*(2), 244–253. doi:10.1016/0377-2217(93)90042-L

Schwartz, P. (1991). *The Art of the Long View.* Doubleday.

Serra, C. M., & Kunc, M. (2015). Benefits realization management and its influence on project success and the execution of business strategies. *International Journal of Project Management, 33*(1), 53–66. doi:10.1016/j.ijproman.2014.03.011

Sheetz-Runkle, B. (2014). *The Art of War for Small Business: Defeat the Competition and Dominate the Market with the Masterful Strategies of Sun Tzu.* New York: AMACOM, American Management Association.

Shenhar, A. (2004). Strategic project leadership: Toward a strategic approach to project management. *R & D Management, 34*(5), 569–578. doi:10.1111/j.1467-9310.2004.00363.x

Shenhar, A. J., & Dvir, D. (2007). *Reinventing Project Management. The Diamond approach to successful growth and innovation.* Boston, MA: Harvard Business School Publishing.

Shenhar, A. J., Dvir, D., Levy, O., & Maltz, A. C. (2001). Project Success: A Multidimensional Strategic Concept. *Long Range Planning, 34*(6), 699–725. doi:10.1016/S0024-6301(01)00097-8

Shenhar, A., & Dvir, D. (2007). *Reinventing project management.* Boston, MA: Harvard Business School Press.

Shenhar, A., & Levy, O. (1997). Mapping the dimensions of project success. *Project Management Journal, 28*(2), 5.

Shimizu, M. (2012). *Fundamentals of Program Management.* Newtown Square, PA: Project Management Institute.

Shou, Y., & Huang, Y. (2010). Combinatorial auction algorithm for project portfolio selection and scheduling to maximize the net present value. *Journal of Zhejiang University SCIENCE C, 11*(7), 562–574. doi:10.1631/jzus.C0910479

Simon and Garfunkel. (1964). *Sounds of silence* [CD]. Nashville, TN: CBS.

Slevin, D. P., & Pinto, J. K. (1986). The Project Implementation Profile: New tool for project managers. *Project Management Journal, 18*(4), 57–71.

Society of Decision Professionals. (2016). *Frustrations.* Retrieved Aug 21, 2016, from http://decisionquality.org/frustrations/

Söderlund, J. (2004). Building theories of project management: Past research, questions for the future. *International Journal of Project Management, 22*(3), 183–191. doi:10.1016/S0263-7863(03)00070-X

Souder, W. E. (1984). *Project Selection and Economic Appraisal.* New York: Van Nostrand Reinhold.

Spradlin, C. T., & Kutoloski, D. M. (1999). Action-Oriented Portfolio Management. *Research-Technology Management, 42*(2), 26–32. https://doi.org/10.1080/08956308.1999.11671270

Statoil. (2010). *A strategy for value creation and growth.* Retrieved August 21, 2016, from http://www.statoil.com/annualreport2010/en/strategy/pages/astrategyforvaluecreationandgrowth.aspx

Stegink, D. (2011). Upstream International Portfolio Management.*SPE International Conference*, Amsterdam, The Netherlands.

Stephans, J. (n.d.). *Market Realist.* Retrieved February 9, 2016, from http://marketrealist.com/

Stoner, J. A. F. (1982). *Management.* Madison, WI: Prentice-Hall.

Strategic Management. (2008). Retrieved from http://en.wikipedia.org/wiki/Strategic_management

Strategy. (n.d.). Retrieved August 29, 2016, from https://en.wikipedia.org/wiki/Strategy

Susman, G. I., & Evered, R. D. (1978). An Assessment of the Scientific Merits of Action Research. *Administrative Science Quarterly, 23*(4), 582–603. doi:10.2307/2392581

SWOT Analysis. (n.d.). Retrieved April 29, 2016, from https://en.wikipedia.org/wiki/SWOT_analysis

Symons, C. (2006). *How IT Must Shape And Manage Demand.* Cambridge, MA: Forrester Research.

Teller, J., Kock, A., & Gemünden, H. G. (2014). Risk Management in Project Portfolios Is More Than Managing Project Risks: A Contingency Perspective on Risk Management. *Project Management Journal, 45*(4), 67–80. doi:10.1002/pmj.21431

Thanassoulis, E. (2001). Introduction to the Theory and Application of Data Envelopment Analysis: A foundation text with integrated software. Boston: Kluwer Academic Publishers. doi:10.1007/978-1-4615-1407-7

Thiry, M. (2008). *The Gower Handbook of Project Management* (4th ed.). Farnham, UK: Gower.

Thiry, M. (2010). *Program Management*. Farnham, UK: Gower.

Thompson, A. (2015). *Ford Motor Company's Vision Statement, Mission Statement - Panmore Institute*. Retrieved February 29, 2016, from http://panmore.com/ford-motor-company-vision-statement-mission-statement

Thompson, A. A., Strickland, A. J., & Gamble, J. E. (2009). *Strategia Aziendale*. Milano: McGraw-Hill.

Thompson, A. A., & Strickland, A. J. III. (2003). *Strategic Management: Concepts and Cases*. McGraw-Hill.

Thorp, J. (1999). *The information paradox – realizing the business benefits of IT*. Toronto: McGraw-Hill.

Tikkanen, H., Kujala, J., & Artto, K. (2007). The marketing strategy of a project-based firm: The Four Portfolios Framework. *Industrial Marketing Management*, *36*(2), 194–205. doi:10.1016/j.indmarman.2006.03.006

Total, S. A. (2016). *2015 Edition: Registration document*. Retrieved May 20, 2016, from http://www.total.com/sites/default/files/atoms/files/registration_document_2015.pdf

Trading Economics. (2016). *Brent crude oil 1970 to 2016*. Retrieved August 20, 2016, from http://www.tradingeconomics.com/commodity/brent-crude-oil

Turner, J. R., & Müller, R. (2005). The project manager's leadership style as a success factor on projects: A literature review. *Project Management Journal*, *36*(1), 49–61.

Turner, J., & Simister, S. (2000). *The Gower handbook of project management* (3rd ed.). Aldershot, UK: Gower.

Turner, R. J. (1999). *The handbook of project based management* (2nd ed.). London: McGraw-Hill.

United Kingdom Government. (n.d.). *Best Management Portfolio*. Available at: http://webarchive.nationalarchives.gov.uk/20110822131357/http:/www.cabinetoffice.gov.uk/resource-library/best-management-practice-bmp-portfolio

Update, H. M. (2008, February 27). *Execute Your Strategy—Without Killing It*. Retrieved August 11, 2016, from https://hbr.org/2008/02/execute-your-strategy-without-1

Urusov, D. (2005). *IT Portfolio Management Model*. White paper published June 2005. Retrieved January 2006 from www.projectperfect.com.au

van der Voet, J. (2014). The effectiveness and specificity of change management in a public organization: Transformational leadership and a bureaucratic organizational structure. *European Management Journal*, *32*(3), 373–382. doi:10.1016/j.emj.2013.10.001

Vector Consulting Services. (n.d.). Retrieved June 29, 2016, from https://consulting.vector.com/

Vergara, A. J., & Boyer, L. T. (1977). Portfolio theory: Applications in construction. *Journal of the Construction Division*, *103*(1), 23–38.

Vincenti, L. (1985). *La Vita Di Napoleone Bonaparte*. Milano: Alberto Peruzzo Editore.

Vollmann, T. E., Berry, W. L., Whybark, D. C., & Jacobs, F. R. (2004). *Manufacturing Planning and Control for Supply Chain Management*. Boston, MA: McGraw-Hill.

Ward, J., & Daniel, E. (2006). *Benefits management: Delivering value from IS & IT investments*. England: Wiley.

Wheelwright, S. C., & Clark, K. B. (1992). Creating project plans to focus product development. *Harvard Business Review*, *70*(2), 70–82. PMID:10117370

Wheelwright, S. C., & Clark, K. B. (2011). *Revolutionizing Product Development: Quantum Leaps in Speed, Efficiency and Quality*. New York: Free Press.

Wideman, M. R. (2007). *Ten steps to comprehensive project Portfolio management - Part 2 The project portfolio management life cycle*. Retrieved from http://www.maxwideman.com

Wikipedia. (2016). *Definition of Adaptation*. Retrieved 27 July, 2016, from https://en.wikipedia.org/wiki/Adaptation

Witten, J., & Bentley, L. (2006). *Systems analysis and design methods* (7th ed.). Boston, MA: McGraw Hill.

Xu, S., Cavusgil, S. T., & White, J. C. (2006). The Impact of Strategic Fit among Strategy, Structure, and Processes on Multinational Corporation Performance: A Multimethod Assessment. *Journal of International Marketing*, *14*(2), 1–31. doi:10.1509/jimk.14.2.1

Yeo, K. T. (1993). Systems thinking and project management — time to reunite. *International Journal of Project Management*, *11*(2), 111–117. doi:10.1016/0263-7863(93)90019-J

Young, M., & Young, R. (2012). The rise and fall of project management: are we observing the birth of a new discipline? *Journal of Project, Program & Portfolio Management, 3*(1).

Yu, A. G., Flett, P. D., & Bowers, J. A. (2005). Developing a value-centered proposal for assessing project success. *International Journal of Project Management*, *23*(6), 428–436. doi:10.1016/j.ijproman.2005.01.008

Zajac, E. J., Kraatz, M. S., & Bresser, R. K. F. (2000). Modeling the dynamics of strategic fit: A normative approach to strategic change. *Strategic Management Journal*, *21*(4), 429–453. doi:10.1002/(SICI)1097-0266(200004)21:4<429::AID-SMJ81>3.0.CO;2-#

Zhu, J. (2000). Multi-factor performance measure model with an application to Fortune 500 companies. *European Journal of Operational Research*, *123*(1), 105–124. doi:10.1016/S0377-2217(99)00096-X

Zhu, J. (2002). *Quantitative Models for Performance Evaluation and Benchmarking: Data Envelopment Analysis with Spreadsheets and DEA Excel Solver*. Boston, MA: Kluwer Academic Publishers.

Zirger, B. J., & Maidique, M. (1990). A Model of New Product Development: An Empirical Test. *Management Science*, *36*(7), 867–883. doi:10.1287/mnsc.36.7.867

Zwikael, O., & Smyrk, J. (2012). A general framework for gauging performance of initiative to enhance organizational value. *British Journal of Management*, *23*(1), S6–S22. doi:10.1111/j.1467-8551.2012.00823.x

About the Contributors

Luca Romano is an executive manager, author and professor with international consulting experience in Project, Program, Portfolio management, Organization and Training. In these fields he has more than 20 years of experience as Practice Manager and Project Director managing consulting projects for international consulting firms in several sectors. He is Professor and Lecturer in many EU Universities and Business Schools, teaching Project/Program/Portfolio Management, Operations Management and Strategic Planning. Since 2012 is a Project Management Institute (PMI) International Congress Speaker presenting numerous researches and case studies on Project Portfolio Management. He is also author of several articles on Strategic Management, Portfolio and Project Management. Since 2016 he is Director of Professional Development at PMI Central Italy Chapter.

***

Lucia Aiello is a Professor to contract in Management and Organization, Sapienza, University of Rome. Her research interests are: HRM. Digital Content Technology and its Applications. Business Innovation for SMEs and Project Mnagement. She is member of journals and scientific association. She holds a degree in Tourism Management, University of Naples, and a Ph.D. in Marketing and Communication, University of Salerno. She is reviewer of international journals and conference, as IGIGlobal; JDTA; JANC; EURAM. She has been Assistant to CPC, (2012-2014), B.S.Laboratory International Symposium, Universitas Mercatorum, January, 23-24, 2014. She has published in international books, journals and conference proceedings. The main publications are Management of Cultural Products: E-Relationship Marketing and Accessibility Perspective, USA: IGIGlobal, 2014. Cultural Relationship Management, Business Systems Review, 2(3). The Relationship Tourist and e-Retailer. Conceptual Models: "E-agility' Matrix" & "Circle of e-Relationship, in IJNCAIM, 2(2), 2012. Internet management for communication-distribution interaction as a means to maximize customer consumption experience: the Volagratis Case, in Pantano et all., ATMR, USA: IGIGlobal, 2011.

António Amaral is an Industrial Engineer (2005) from University of Minho and holds a Ph.D. in Industrial and Systems Engineering also from University of Minho. Worked as an Operations Engineer in Sociedade de Transportes Coletivos do Porto – STCP, SA. Worked as an Invited Assistant Professor in the Production and Systems Department at University of Minho and as an Assistant Professor in the Faculty of Business Economics and Social Sciences at Lusófona University of Porto. Member of the technical commission – CT175, ONS APOGEP, for working groups GT4 – Portfolio Management and GT5 – Governance. Presently, works as an Invited Adjunct Professor at the Business School of the Polytechnic Institute of Viana do Castelo, in the disciplinary group of Organisation, Logistics and Marketing. He is also a researcher of the ALGORITMI Research Centre in the Industrial Engineering and Management Line. His research interests are on Engineering Economics, mainly on Project Evaluation and Management, Risk Analysis, Portfolio Management, Organizational Knowledge and Learning, Organizational Maturity and Sustainability.

Andrea Aparo, Italian and Swiss citizenship. Founding partner of Goto10 Ltd., CEO of ProTer Ltd., Industry Expert for The European House-Ambrosetti. Until December 2014, Senior Advisor to the CEO of Ansaldo Energia S.p.A. From 2003 to 2011, head of the Technology Intelligence of Finmeccanica SpA, Rome. Since 1973 experimental physicist: researcher, Visiting Scientist at the MIT Laboratory for Computer Science, Assistant to the President of the Italian governmental agency ENEA, member of Italian government, and EEC committees. From 1987 to 1998 he worked for the Fiat Group in executive positions. From June 1998 to February 1999, Executive Coordinator of the Trustees 21 project at the World Economic Forum in Geneva, Switzerland. Entrepreneur and consultant; University professor: teaches Corporate Strategy at the University of Rome "Sapienza"; Adjunct Professor from 2000 to September 2014 at the Politecnico di Milano; has been Assistant Director of MiNE, Master in the New Economy, MBA dedicated to the new economy, at the Catholic University of Piacenza. Scientific journalist, writer, and blogger. Has contributed or written hundreds of articles and several books. Regularly hosted in radio and TV broadcasts as expert of technology and strategy. He has a long experience as public speaker in USA, Europe, Australia, Japan. Two marriages, two divorces, two wonderful sons.

Madalena Araújo is a Chemical Engineer (1977) from University of Coimbra (Portugal) and holds a M.Sc. in Industrial Management (1983) and a Ph.D. in Production Engineering (1986), both from Birmingham University (U.K.). She is Faculty member of Minho University (Portugal) since 1981, in the Production and Systems Department (DPS), School of Engineering. In October 2005 qualified with Habilitation and since June 2009 is a Full Professor on Industrial and Technology Management of DPS. She is a researcher of the ALGORITMI Research Centre and leader of the Industrial Engineering and Management Line. Her research interests are on Engineering Economics, mainly on Decision and Utility Modelling, Project Evaluation and Management, Risk Analysis, Multicriteria Modelling, and their applications in manufacturing and technology management, as well as specialized applications in the Energy and Environment fields. She is author and coauthor of around one hundred papers and supervised a few dozens of M.Sc. dissertations and Ph.D. theses. More information on: http://pessoais.dps.uminho.pt/madalenaraujo.

Russell D. Archibald, PhD (Hon), MScME, BSME, PMP, PMI Fellow and founding member, and Honorary Fellow APM/IPMA (member of the Board of IPMA/INTERNET 1974-83). He has held engineering and executive positions in the U.S Air Force (Senior Pilot and aircraft design engineer), aerospace, petroleum, telecommunications, and automotive industries in the USA, France, Mexico and Venezuela. Since 1982 he has consulted to companies, agencies and development banks in 16 countries on 4 continents, and has taught project management principles and practices to thousands of managers and specialists around the world. He is co-author with Shane Archibald of Leading and Managing Innovation, 2013, author of Managing High-Technology Programs and Projects, 3rd ed. 2003, also published in Russian, Italian, and Chinese, and has co-authored 15 other books (in English, Italian, Japanese, Portuguese, and Hungarian) and presented many papers on project management. Web site: www.russarchibald.com.

Alfonso Bucero, MSc, CPS, PMP, PMI-RMP, PfMP, PMI Fellow, is the founder and Managing Partner of BUCERO PM Consulting. He managed IIL Spain for almost two years, and he was a Senior Project Manager at Hewlett-Packard Spain (Madrid Office) for thirteen years. Alfonso is a PMI member, and a member of ALI (Asociación de Licenciados, Ingenieros y Doctores en Informática). Alfonso was the founder, Sponsor and President of PMI Barcelona, Spain Chapter until April 2005, and he is an IPMA Assessor. He was a member of the CoPAT (Congress Project Action Team) of PMI EMEA 2005 Congress in Edinburgh, 2006 PMI EMEA Congress in Madrid, and PMI EMEA Congress in Budapest. He was graduated in The "Leadership Institute Master Class 2007" on October 2007 in Atlanta (PMI Global Congress). He has been the last the President of PMI Madrid Spain Chapter. He was a PMI Component Mentor for Region 8 South for three years, and he was a PMIEF Engagement Committee Member. He received the PMI Distinguished Contribution Award on October 9th, 2010. He also received the PMI Fellow Award on October 22nd, 2011. Alfonso has a Computer Science Engineering degree by "Universidad Politécnica (Madrid)", and now he is finishing his PhD. in "Project Management" at the University of Zaragoza in Spain. He has 27 years of practical experience and twenty two of them in project management worldwide. He has managed and consulted projects in different countries along Europe. Since 1994, he is a frequent speaker at International PM Congresses and Symposiums. Alfonso has delivered PM training and consulting services in Spain, Mexico, UK, Belgium, Germany, France, Denmark, Costa Rica, Brazil, USA, and Singapore. As Project Management believer, he defends that Passion, Persistence and Patience as keys for project success. He authored the book "Dirección de Proyectos, una nueva vision" published by "LITO GRAPO Editors) in IIL Mexico on June 2003. And he is a contributor of Chapter 7 of the book "Creating the Project Office". Published on February 2003 by Jossey-Bass Editors (San Francisco/California), authored by Robert J. Graham., Paul Dinsmore and Randall L. Englund. Alfonso co-authored with Randall L. Englund the book "Project Sponsorship" published by Josse- Bass Editors by May 2006. He has authored the book "Today is a Good Day" – Attitudes for achieving project success, published by Multimedia Publishing in Canada on last February 2010. He has also contributed to some professional magazines in Russia (SOVNET), India (ICFAI), Argentina and Spain. Alfonso co-authored with Randall L. Englund the book "The Complete Project Manager" and "The Complete Project Manager Toolkit" that was published by Management Concepts last March 2012. Alfonso got published a new book: "The Influential Project Manager" on the first quarter of 2014 by CRC Editors in the US. Alfonso coauthored with Randall L. Englund the second Edition of the book "Project Sponsorship" published by PMI on October 2015. Alfonso has published several articles at national and international PM magazines. He was a Contributing editor of PM Network (Crossing Borders) for six years, published by the "Project Management Institute".

Francesco Colasuonno is the director of the demand and digital processes at INAIL (the Italian government agency for the insurance against work-related injuries). He previously was the director of the application department, INPS Technical Secretary Department. He has extensive experience managing government IT projects.

Roberta Grimaldi, PMP, has a degree in economics and 20 years' professional experience in IT governance. She is responsible for the IT planning and control department in I.N.A.I.L (the Italian government agency for the insurance against work-related injuries) and is responsible for these processes: vendor management, budgeting, portfolio management, project planning and control.

Joy Gumz, CPA, CISA, PMP, has consulted with numerous Global 2000 organizations, including Chevron, Lockheed Martin, SAP AG, and Siemens. She has taught project management and auditing courses at KPMG UK, the Majid Al Futtaim Group, the Department of Homeland Security, Parker-Hannifin, the University of Sharjah, California State University and the University of California as well as to other global organizations. She has also reviewed the IT project management practices at several privately held entrepreneurial firms and Global 2000 companies. Financial companies she has worked with include Credit Suisse, Susquehanna Bancshares, Keybank, and Oriental Financial Group. Her work in project management, audit, controls, and assurance has given her unique insights into working with C-level executives and board members. She has also worked with several organizations to improve their project and program portfolio management (PPPM) practices. While with Ernst & Young in Chicago, she worked in their audit and management consulting practices in Chicago. After leaving Ernst & Young, she began a consulting career that has spanned numerous industries: financial services, high tech, hospitality/resort, construction, health care, wholesale, retail, consumer products, oil & gas, and others. Her expertise in ERP and cost systems has allowed her to consult in Germany, Switzerland, Italy, the U.K., and the Middle East. She led a project in Europe that successfully implemented Peoplesoft at a global pharmaceutical company in record time, and has performed risk assessments and project audits for organizations worldwide. In addition to consulting and teaching, she has developed the curriculum and content for several courses in project management and auditing. Ms. Gumz has published numerous papers in project management and is an international speaker. She gave the keynote speech at a conference on project portfolio management held by the PMI Northern Italy Chapter at Milan in 2015. She has presented on PCI DSS standards at a national ISACA conference. In 2013, she presented on the merger of United and Continental Airlines at the PMI EMEA Global Congress in Istanbul. She was a founding member of PMI's Technology Member Advisory Group, a 10 member global board that advises PMI on IT.

Ginger Levin, PMP, PgMP, Author, Consultant and Educator, specializes in portfolio and program management, the PMO, KM, metrics, and organizational capability assessments. She presents and gives seminars at PMI events; won PMI's Eric Jenett Award in 2014; is an active PMI volunteer; is the editor, author, or co-author of 20 books; and manages(d) PMOs, programs, and projects for 50 years. She is an Adjunct Professor at SKEMA University and the University of Wisconsin-Platteville. Dr. Levin received her doctorate from The George Washington University and won the Outstanding Dissertation Award from its School of Government and Business Administration. linkedin.com/in/gingerlevin

Fabio Nonino is Associate Professor of Project Management at Sapienza University of Rome (Department of Computer, Control, and Management Engineering). He is professor of Project Management at the Master of Science Course in Management Engineering and professor of business management at the at the Bachelor Course in Management Engineering. He authored and coauthored over 80 scientific papers on topics of Innovation Management, Project Management, Knowledge Management, Operations and Supply Chain Management and he is the author of the book "The Guide to Project Management" edited by Il Sole 24 Ore. His main publications appeared in International Journal of Project Management, Supply Chain Management: An international Journal, Production Planning & Control, Omega – The Journal of Management Science, International Journal of Production Research and Technological Forecasting and Social Change. He is member of the editorial board of Kybernetes - The international journal of cybernetics, systems and management sciences and the International Journal of Information Systems and Supply Chain Management.

Brandon Olson, PhD, PMP, is the Chair of the Computer Information Systems department at the College of St. Scholastica and director of the Master of Arts in Information Technology Leadership and the Master of Science in Project Management degree programs. Dr. Olson holds a PhD in Information Technology with a specialization in Project Management and a master's degree in Computer Information Resource Management. His research interests include project management, knowledge management, and IT strategy. Prior to entering academia, Dr. Olson worked for 15 years in the pharmaceutical, healthcare, and business services industries. Dr. Olson is also the Co-chair of Community and Outreach programs for the Minnesota chapter of the Project Management Institute.

Frank Parth, MS, MSSM, MBA, PMP is the CEO of Project Auditors LLC, a past member of PMI's Board of Directors, and is currently on the Board of Directors of the PMI Educational Foundation. Mr. Parth brings 35 years experience in project management to his teaching and consulting work. He had his first career in the aerospace industry, ending as the assistant technical director in the Integration Offices of a $12B satellite program. In 1993 Mr. Parth began consulting in program management and systems engineering while teaching in the Graduate School of the University of Southern California. He headed up systems engineering at TRW Information Systems during a major infrastructure upgrade and has created Program Management Offices (PMOs) for several Fortune 1000 companies. He supported the Majid al Futaim Group (UAE) in managing and auditing construction projects in the Arabian Gulf region. He led the full risk analysis for the $10B Aramco's SATORP oil refinery in the Jubail Industrial District and worked with Saudi Arabian Airlines (Saudi) during their privatization efforts. Other engagements have included auditing both construction and IT projects, setting up effective project management practices, and managing projects. He has consulted to clients in multiple industry sectors, including telecom, construction, high tech, chemical processing, utilities, government, aerospace, healthcare, mining, the consulting industry, financial services, and aerospace. He is currently developing a PMO and significantly improving the project management processes for the Saline Water Conversion Corporation (SWCC) in Riyadh, KSA to more effectively manage projects. Mr. Parth teaches project management courses throughout the world. He is a guest lecturer at USC's Marshall School of Business and at the American University of Sharjah (AUS) in the UAE and is an accomplished international speaker. He has taught project management and systems engineering at the University of California, Irvine since 1994 and was core to the creation of UCI's Project Management Certificate Program and in developing the Business Analyst and the Systems Analyst Certificate Programs. In 2003, UCI recognized him with an Outstanding Service Award. In 2006 PMI recognized him for his contribution and service to the North American Congress Project Action Team, and in 2009 he received PMI's Distinguished Contribution Award. Mr. Parth has undergraduate and graduate degrees in physics, a Masters in Systems Management from USC, and an MBA from the Peter F. Drucker and Masatoshi Ito Graduate School. He has co-authored or contributed to multiple books in project management and has published numerous papers in project management and systems engineering. He is actively involved with PMI, serving on local and national committees, was PMI's Project Manager for the Standard for Program Management, 2nd edition published in 2008 and was on the core team for the PMBOK 6th edition.

Nicole Pitotti is a consultant and PMO since 2012. Master degree in International Business Management, she focused on Project and Portfolio Management working in the field of business consulting both in private industries and in the Italian public sector. Her Master degree thesis entitled "Project Portfolio Management: Projects Selection Phase" was awarded the prize for Most Notheworthy Dissertation by European School of Economics among all the students' works worldwide.

Index

N

O

P

R

S

T

U

V

W

www.ingramcontent.com/pod-product-compliance
Lightning Source LLC
LaVergne TN
LVHW060404300926
849162LV00006B/1341